LITERATURE REVIEWS
IN SPORT PSYCHOLOGY

LITERATURE REVIEWS IN SPORT PSYCHOLOGY

SHELDON HANTON
AND
STEPHEN D. MELLALIEU
EDITORS

Nova Science Publishers, Inc.
New York

LIBRARY OF CONGRESS CATALOGING-IN-PUBLICATION DATA
Literature reviews in sport psychology : Sheldon Hanton and Stephen Mellalieu, editors.
    p. cm.
Includes index.
ISBN 1-59454-904-4
1. Sports--Psychological aspects. 2. Sports literature. I. Hanton, Sheldon. II. Mellalieu, Stephen.
GV706.4.L575   2006
796.01--dc22   2005034744

Published by Nova Science Publishers, Inc. ✦ New York

CONTENTS

INTRODUCTION

Sheldon Hanton*
University of Wales Institute, Cardiff, United Kingdom
Stephen D. Mellalieu
Swansea University, United Kingdom

Sport Psychology research has developed and expanded considerably over the last decade or two. Its accelerating volume of research output embraces a wide variety of topics having both academic and practical impact, and relating to other areas of Sports Science and also the broader overall discipline of "mainstream" psychology. In this busy and developing arena, the healthy and productive evolution of a research topic requires the periodic summarization, reflection, and feedback that is the domain of the literature review. A review acts as the primary catalyst for a topic's emerging organization, reorganization and structure, and generates perspectives and pointers for further study directions; it establishes reference points and foundations for continued progress. By its very nature it tends to be a larger publication than a typical focused research paper.

The pathways to publication of Sport Psychology research are often severely congested. For example, in 2004, four of the main refereed outlets for original research in Sport Psychology: *The Sport Psychologist*, the *Journal of Applied Sport Psychology*, the *Journal of Sport and Exercise Psychology,* and the *Psychology of Sport and Exercise* received over 400 submissions (private communications). Inevitably the space that established journals can afford to grant to review articles is limited, both in terms of the article size and the frequency with which topics can be visited. Although reviews that appear in books usually enjoy a larger and more appropriate space allocation, they typically have not carried the hallmark of external independent peer review that journal publication provides.

Our ambitious intention is that *Literature Reviews in Sport Psychology* addresses these issues by providing an 'essential library' for sport psychologists who embrace the theory-to-practice philosophy. This collection presents a number of contemporary reviews of significant and popular topics from some prominent researchers within each area. An important and distinctive feature of this volume is that all the chapters have been subjected to peer-review

---

* Correspondence concerning this introduction should be addressed to Sheldon Hanton, Cardiff School of Sport, University of Wales Institute, Cardiff, (UWIC), Cyncoed, Cardiff CF23 6XD, United Kingdom. Telephone: +44 (0)29-2041-6952. Fax: +44 (0)29-2041-6768. E-mail: SHanton@uwic.ac.uk

by expert referees, a process usually reserved solely for journal publications. This book offers up-to-date literature reviews with a distinctive conceptual, theoretical, and practical focus. We hope that the reviews contained within this edited text will promote a more systematic approach to advancing knowledge in the discipline and assist in the development of theoretical frameworks for future research.

This book is primarily intended to catalyze and facilitate continued research and development and should appeal as a comprehensive, thought-provoking resource for graduates, doctoral students, academics, and professionals working in sport psychology related fields. Through our policy of allowing independence to the contributors of this book, every chapter was envisaged to be a discrete contribution, each with its own implications and recommendations for future study. It was not our intention as editors to attempt to coordinate a synthesis of these subject areas into one comprehensive theory of sport psychology, but to provide researchers and practitioners the opportunity of exploring a range of sub-disciplines to guide their activities. Although this book is aimed primarily at active researchers, nevertheless, each of the authors has disseminated the body of research work into practical implications for professional practice and, therefore, each chapter should be valuable to practitioners as well as researchers.

The format of each chapter has been standardized as much as possible to resemble works published in academic journals. For example, the narrative is generally divided into several parts: An abstract summarizing the central tenets of the review; an introduction to the chapter and the conceptual area; a subsection clarifying and defining the key terms adopted; an up-to-date and comprehensive exposition, discussion, and critical analysis of both qualitative and quantitative research; the implications of this work for professional practice are presented as are future research directions to conclude.

This book contains 10 chapters. In the *first*, Stephen Mellalieu, Sheldon Hanton, and David Fletcher review the literature that focuses on the positive aspects and consequences of competitive anxiety. Drawing on contemporary research, their chapter explores the mechanisms by which anxiety can have a positive effect on athletes' psychological states and sport performance. The key implications of their discussion are used to make recommendations for professional practice and future research.

In the *second* chapter, Sharleen Hoar, Kent Kowalski, Patrick Gaudreau, and Peter Crocker review the sport coping literature. Their contribution addresses the diverse body of literature and focuses on key issues including: how coping is conceptualized in sport, coping measurement issues, key antecedents and outcomes of the coping process in sport, and coping within applied professional practice. The area of coping presents sport researchers with many exciting challenges. The utilization of existing conceptual frameworks and the corresponding methodologies with the research developments in the associated fields of health, development, and social psychology will advance sport scientists' understanding of the coping process.

In chapter *three*, Scott Cresswell and Robert Eklund review literature on athlete burnout in order to stimulate additional research. Within their discussion the authors highlight inconsistencies in approaches to the study of athlete burnout and propose guidelines for possible future research. In addition they elaborate on current theoretical explanations and comment upon the potential utility of stress based approaches, commitment theory, and self-determination theory, as frameworks for guiding future studies in the area.

Chapter *four*, written by Claudio Robazza, presents an overview of the emotion-performance relationship mainly through the perspective of the Individual Zones of Optimal Functioning (IZOF) model as recently applied to emotions and psychobiosocial states. The theoretical underpinnings of the IZOF model are provided together with indications for professionals involved in helping athletes attain control over their states and achieve best conditions to perform.

In the *fifth* chapter in this volume Kieran Kingston, Chris Harwood, and Chris Spray provide a review of three contemporary motivation theories that are currently at the forefront of research in sport. In addition to presenting a theoretical overview, their contribution considers recent research developments, and proposes guidelines for possible future study both within and across the theories.

Nick Holt and Sharleen Hoar, in chapter *six*, then proceed to review the construct of social support. In order to summarize the literature and provide a framework for their chapter, they present a model of the social support process in sport. This model reflects structural, functional, and perceptual dimensions of social support, along with mechanisms, moderators, and outcomes of social support in sport. Important theoretical issues and potential areas of future research are highlighted.

Chapter *seven* is entitled "A Review of Team Roles in Sport". Here Mark Eys, Mark Beauchamp, and Steven Bray review literature pertaining to role involvement in a sport environment. Their chapter directs attention to conceptual and practical issues and suggests future directions pertaining to multiple elements of role involvement. These include role ambiguity, efficacy, conflict, acceptance, and satisfaction as well as the development and successful performance of individual roles on a sport team.

Chapter *eight* written by Todd Loughead and James Hardy examines the literature on team cohesion. Their chapter addresses the theoretical, conceptual, and measurement issues influencing cohesion research. They also review the research conducted to date and offer guidelines on how sport psychologists and coaches can foster group cohesion using team building protocols.

Penultimately in chapter *nine*, Lynne Evans, Ian Mitchell, and Stuart Jones provide an updated review of the research into athletes' psychological responses to injury and adherence to rehabilitation programs. The review examines current conceptual models of injury rehabilitation, developments in intervention research, and some of the methodological issues that have been inherent within the research to date. Finally, for practitioners and researchers alike they explore the applied implications.

In the *tenth* and final chapter, David Fletcher, Sheldon Hanton, and Stephen Mellalieu review literature on organizational stress from the fields of mainstream and sport psychology in order to reflect on what this work can tell us about stress in sport organizations. Their chapter helps to focus attention on the important conceptual and theoretical issues relating to organizational stress in competitive sport, how such issues effect performers, and the role psychologists can play in better understanding the nature of this phenomenon.

In: Literature Reviews in Sport Psychology
Editors: S. Hanton and S. D. Mellalieu, pp. 1-45

ISBN 1-59454-904-4
© 2006 Nova Science Publishers, Inc.

Chapter 1

A COMPETITIVE ANXIETY REVIEW: RECENT DIRECTIONS IN SPORT PSYCHOLOGY RESEARCH

Stephen D. Mellalieu,[*]
Swansea University, United Kingdom
Sheldon Hanton and David Fletcher
University of Wales Institute, Cardiff, United Kingdom

ABSTRACT

This chapter provides a review and discussion of the recent move towards the positive aspects and consequences of competitive anxiety. Following a description of competitive stress-related terminologies, conceptual and psychometric developments are considered including the notion of directional anxiety interpretations. The commentary then focuses on the theories and models that outline the potential positive aspects of anxiety in relation to athletic performance. Applied implications and future research directions are also discussed together with a number of explicatory statements regarding the nature of the precompetitive stress experience in sport.

Keywords: Competitive stress response, sporting performance, positive consequences, direction

INTRODUCTION

The topic of competitive anxiety has enjoyed a large prominence in the sport psychology literature, and is often cited as one of the most studied areas in the discipline (Biddle, 1997; Jones, 1995a; Tenenbaum and Bar-Eli, 1995; Woodman and Hardy, 2001). A number of

---

[*] Correspondence concerning this chapter should be addressed to Stephen D. Mellalieu, Department of Sports Science, Swansea University, Swansea, SA2 8PP, United Kingdom. Tel: 44-1792-513-101, Fax: 44-1792-513-171 E-mail: s.d.mellalieu@swan.ac.uk

reviews have been published that have periodically provided both a comprehensive and contemporary review of the literature (e.g., Burton, 1998; Gould, Greenleaf, and Krane, 2002; Hardy, Jones, and Gould, 1996; Jones, 1995a, 1995b; Smith, Smoll, and Wiechman, 1998; Woodman and Hardy, 2001). Collectively, these offer an interesting and informative insight into the relationship between competitive anxiety and performance, while separately each emphasizes different aspects of the association. For example: Jones (1995a) commented on measurement and design advances; Burton (1998) outlined the development of measures of the state response; Smith et al. (1998) discussed the re-conceptualization of trait anxiety in sport; Woodman and Hardy (2001) reviewed the cognitive aspects of the anxiety-performance relationship; and Gould et al. (2002) presented an integrated perspective of the measurement of arousal, activation, anxiety, and performance.

Since anxiety is a negative emotion, researchers have historically tended to focus on the potentially negative effects on performance. However, a theme that emerges from some of the reviews (e.g., Jones, 1995a; Woodman and Hardy, 2001) is that, under some circumstances, anxiety can have positive consequences in performance environments. Jones (1995a) remarked that:

> The experience of competitive anxiety has, particularly in the North American sport psychology literature, been viewed as negative and to have debilitative consequences for performance. This view is, however, at odds with a body of literature which has emanated from other areas of psychology which suggests that anxiety can sometimes have positive consequences. (p. 462)

Despite acknowledging the importance of the benefits of anxiety in sport, no single body of work has focused upon this area to any great extent. Consequently, in this chapter we explore in greater detail the mechanisms by which such a negative emotional response might have a positive effect on a performer's psychological state and subsequent athletic performance. To the best of our knowledge this review is the first to focus specifically on this area and discuss recent directions in sport psychology research which examine this phenomenon.

This chapter comprises five sections. The opening section summarizes the conceptual distinctions in the terminology adopted in the study of competitive stress and provides a brief overview of the extant literature examining competitive stressors in sport. The remainder of this chapter focuses on the study of the competitive anxiety response itself. First, the major historical, conceptual and psychometric developments are identified, such as state-trait and multidimensional (i.e., cognitive and somatic) conceptualizations and the various instruments developed to measure the construct. Next, we discuss recent advances in competitive anxiety research, including frequency of symptoms experienced and performers' directional interpretations of symptoms associated with the response. Here, we describe the origins of direction, the mechanisms underlying the concept, and its context in the competitive stress process. The wealth of literature that has investigated potential moderators of the direction response is then discussed together with some key issues that have recently arisen relating to positive consequences of symptom interpretation for performance. The next section then describes the models and theories that consider these potentially positive aspects of anxiety upon performance. Finally, the remainder of this chapter presents applied practice implications and outlines future areas for research, including a series of explicatory statements regarding the competitive stress experience in sport.

DEFINITION OF TERMS

The study of competitive stress and anxiety in sport has been hindered by a lack of consistency in the use of key terms (Burton, 1998; Gould et al., 2002; Hardy et al., 1996; Jones, 1995a; Jones and Hardy, 1990; Woodman and Hardy, 2001). For example, stress has often been used interchangeably to describe a stimulus or a response of a person-environment interaction. This is despite there being a clear conceptual distinction between the terms 'stressor' and 'strain' (Beehr, 1998; Beehr and Franz, 1987; Fletcher, Hanton, and Mellalieu, this volume). 'Stressors' refer to events, situations or conditions, while 'strain' describes an individual's negative response to stressors. In the sporting arena, performers encounter a variety of competitive demands and react in different ways.

Contemporary conceptualizations view 'stress' not as a factor that resides in either an individual or the environment but rather as a relationship between the two (Lazarus, 1981). Researchers have argued that a transactional, rather than an interactional perspective, should be adopted to emphasize the relational meaning construed by an individual operating in a particular environment (cf. Fletcher et al., this volume; Lazarus, 1999). Here, transaction refers to the dynamic relationship that occurs between the environmental demands and a person's resources, while relational meaning describes the meaning a person construes from his or her relationship with the environment. Stress has, therefore, been defined as:

> An ongoing process that involves individuals transacting with their environments, making appraisals of the situations they find themselves in, and endeavoring to cope with any issues that may arise. (Fletcher et al., this volume)

In line with the conceptual standpoint adopted by Fletcher et al. (this volume), the following definitions of competitive stress related terms are presented:

- *Competitive stress*: an ongoing transaction between an individual and the environmental demands associated primarily and directly with competitive performance.
- *Competitive stressors*: the environmental demands (i.e., stimuli) associated primarily and directly with competitive performance.
- *Competitive strain*: an individual's negative psychological, physical and behavioral responses to competitive stressors.
- *Competitive anxiety*: a specific negative emotional response to competitive stressors.

For the purposes of clarification, the potential effects of competitive stressors on individuals are not inherently negative. Indeed, the competitive stress process can result in positive psychological and performance consequences. Traditionally, however, researchers have tended to combine athletes' perceived 'sources of stress' with their emotional responses, rather than focusing on the relationship between aspects of the stress process (Fletcher et al., this volume; see also Hanton, Fletcher, and Coughlan, 2005). Arguably, this has led to an assumption that all competitive stressors and responses are associated with negative connotations.

COMPETITIVE STRESSORS

Investigations of competitive stressors have tended to focus on two main lines of inquiry, namely the preperformance stressors encountered by athletes and the antecedents of the competitive anxiety response. The study of competitive stressors largely emanates from a body of literature that has used qualitative interviews to study elite athletes general experiences or 'sources of stress' (e.g., Gould, Jackson, and Finch 1993a, 1993b; Hanton, Fletcher, et al., 2005; Holt and Hogg, 2002; James and Collins, 1997; Noblet and Gifford, 2002; Scanlan, Ravizza, and Stein, 1989; Scanlan, Stein, and Ravizza, 1991). A range of stressors have been identified including: the physical preparation of the athlete; the level of opposition; pressures and expectations to perform; team atmosphere; relationship issues with significant others; the nature of the event; and issues regarding self-presentation and social evaluation. These potential sources of strain illustrate the highly demanding environment of the competitive sport arena.

In a related line of inquiry, researchers have also examined the specific antecedents of competitive anxiety (e.g., Anshel and Wells, 2000; Hammermeister and Burton, 1995, 2001; Hanton and Jones, 1995, 1997; Jones, Swain, and Cale, 1990, 1991; Krane, Williams, and Feltz, 1992; Lane, Terry, and Karageorghis, 1995). These include: perceptions of readiness for peak performance (Hanton and Jones, 1995; Jones et al., 1990; Lane et al., 1995); the performers' attitude toward previous performances (Jones et al., 1990); and perceptions of environmental conditions and position goal (Hanton and Jones, 1995, 1997; Jones et al., 1990). Research also suggests that differences exist as a function of both personal and situation characteristics, such as gender (Jones et al., 1991), skill level (Hanton and Jones, 1997), and the nature of the sport (Krane et al., 1992). For example, females' cognitive anxiety responses have been shown to be predicted by readiness to perform and the importance of doing well, while males' cognitive anxiety responses have been predicted by their opponents' ability in relation to themselves and their perceived likelihood of winning (Jones et al., 1991).

COMPETITIVE ANXIETY

This section provides an overview of significant advances in the conceptualization and measurement of competitive anxiety. It is not our intention here to comprehensively cover these developments; more detailed descriptions can be found in other reviews such as Burton (1998), Jones (1995a) and Smith et al. (1990). A major advance occurred when researchers identified anxiety as a response to specific situations rather than solely a unitary phenomenon across all contexts. Situation-specific measures were subsequently developed in areas such as test anxiety (Mandler and Sarason, 1952), audience anxiety (Pavio and Lambert, 1959), and fear of negative evaluation, social avoidance and distress (Watson and Friend, 1969), and found to be better predictors of behavior than general anxiety scales. In sport psychology, a number of sport-specific instruments such as the Sports Competition Anxiety Test (SCAT; Martens, 1977) and Competitive State Anxiety Inventory (CSAI; Martens, Burton, Rivkin, and Simon, 1980) were also found to be better predictors of competitive anxiety than existing general measures such as the STAI (see Burton, 1998; Martens, Vealey, and Burton, 1990).

Spielberger (1966) then developed a state-trait theory of anxiety in response to criticisms that existing measures such as the Manifest Anxiety Scale (MAS; Taylor, 1953) and IPAT scale (Cattell, 1957) assessed dispositional traits, and failed to consider fluctuations in transitory or immediate emotional states (Smith et al., 1998). Spielberger (1966) described state anxiety as varying from moment-to-moment and fluctuating proportionately to the perceived threat in a situation. Trait anxiety refers to a predisposition to appraise situations as threatening resulting in state anxiety. The State Trait Anxiety Inventory (STAI; Spielberger, Gorsuch, and Luschane, 1970) was subsequently developed to assess both state and trait components and has been adopted by researchers to assess responses across a range of domains including sport (cf. Smith et al., 1998).

Another conceptual advance was the separation of anxiety into the components of cognitive and somatic anxiety (Borkovec, 1976; Davidson, 1978; Davidson and Schwartz, 1976; Liebert and Morris, 1967; Schwartz, Davidson, and Goleman, 1978; Wine, 1971). Morris, Davis, and Hutchings (1981) defined cognitive anxiety as 'the cognitive elements of anxiety, such negative expectations and cognitive concerns about oneself, the situation at hand and potential consequences' (p. 541); and somatic anxiety as 'one's perception of the physiological-affective elements of the anxiety experience, that is, indications of autonomic arousal and unpleasant feeling states such as nervousness and tension' (p. 541). Following the introduction into sport psychology of this multidimensional conceptualization of anxiety, Martens and colleagues (Martens, Vealey, Burton, Bump, and Smith, 1990) developed the Competitive State Anxiety Inventory-2 (CSAI-2) to measure the intensity of performers' cognitive and somatic responses, and also self-confidence. Subsequent research employing the CSAI-2 has provided evidence to support the separation of cognitive and somatic components as a function of antecedents (Gould, Petlichkoff, and Weinberg, 1984; Jones, Swain, and Cale, 1990; 1991), temporal characteristics (Gould et al., 1984; Jones et al., 1991; Martens et al., 1990), performance outcomes (Burton, 1988; Gould, Petlichkoff, Simons, and Vevera, 1987; Jones and Cale, 1989; Parfitt and Hardy, 1987, 1993), goal attainment expectancies (Krane et al., 1992) and in response to interventions (Burton, 1990; Maynard and Cotton, 1993). A trait version of the CSAI-2, the Competitive Trait Anxiety Inventory-2 (CTAI-2), and the Sports Anxiety Scale (SAS; Smith, Smoll, and Schutz, 1990) have also been developed to assess multidimensional competitive trait anxiety (e.g., Albrecht and Feltz, 1987; Eubank, Collins, and Smith, 2002; Jones and Swain, 1995; Smith, Smoll, and Barnett, 1995; White and Zellner, 1996).

Up to this point researchers in competitive anxiety had solely focused on the assessment of the 'intensity' of the response. Intensity refers to the amount or level of the symptoms experienced by an athlete. Recent developments suggest, however, that a greater understanding of the anxiety response may be gleaned by considering additional dimensions of the response. Such an approach has also helped to explain the potential positive aspects of the response to competitive stress. The next two sections consider research that has examined the frequency with which anxiety symptoms are experienced and performers' directional interpretations of these symptoms with regard to performance.

Frequency of Cognitive Intrusions

Frequency of cognitive intrusions refers to the amount of time (expressed as a percentage) that thoughts and feelings about the competition occupy a performer's mind (Swain and Jones, 1993). The conceptual rationale for the study of this dimension derives from the temporal nature of the transaction process that views the competitive stress response as a product over time (e.g., Lazarus and Folkman, 1984). Consequently, it is important that psychologists consider the dynamics of the ongoing process in order to establish how stressful events are managed (cf. Folkman and Lazarus, 1985). Interestingly, research also suggests that individuals are able to more accurately recall the frequency over the intensity of their responses (Diener, Sandevik, and Pavot, 1991; Kardum, 1999; Thomas and Diener, 1990). Intensity information is suggested to be difficult to encode because there is no natural system by which emotional intensity can be defined by the individual. Conversely, it is hypothesized that humans are biologically more prepared to store and review frequency based information (Diener et al., 1991).

Traditionally, the time to event paradigm has been adopted to examine the temporal nature of performers' anxiety responses at intervals prior to competition (i.e., 7 days, 48 hours, 24 hours and 1 hour). A wealth of research has examined how the intensity of an athlete's precompetitive response differs in the lead up to competition (for a review, see Cerin, Szabo, Hunt, and Williams, 2000). Generated from Martens, Vealey et al.'s (1990) work on Multidimensional Anxiety Theory (MAT), several predictions were proffered regarding temporal changes in the intensity of symptoms. Somatic anxiety was hypothesized to increase to a peak prior to competition and then subside, while cognitive anxiety and self-confidence would remain relatively stable during the precompetition period as long as expectations regarding performance remained unchanged. Findings from subsequent studies broadly supported these predictions (e.g., Caruso, Dzewaltowski, Gill, and McElroy, 1990; Gould et al., 1984; Krane and Williams, 1987; Martens, Burton, et al., 1990; Swain and Jones, 1991, 1993; Wiggins, 1998) with several variables observed to moderate changes in anxiety levels over time. These included: sex and gender role endorsement (Jones and Cale, 1989; Jones et al., 1991; Swain and Jones, 1991, 1993; Wiggins, 1998); skill level (Perkins and Williams, 1994); sport type (Krane and Williams, 1987); level of competition (Davids and Gill, 1995); competitiveness (Jones and Swain, 1992); success and failure (Caruso et al., 1990; Jones et al., 1991); and perceived ability (Hall, Kerr, and Matthews, 1998).

In addition to the MAT predictions, Swain and Jones (1993) suggested that the intensity of state anxiety one week when compared to one hour before performance did not equate to a complete reflection of an athlete's emotional state. In other words, a similar intensity of symptoms does not necessarily mean that the overall affective state is identical. Based upon their preliminary investigation in 1991, Swain and Jones (1993) added a frequency scale to each item of the CSAI-2 asking the participant to respond to "How frequently do you experience this thought or this feeling at this stage?" on a continuum ranging from 1 ("*never*") to 7 ("*all of the time*"). Change-over-time comparisons (2 days, 1 day, 2 hours, 30 minutes prior to competition) revealed that while the intensity of cognitive anxiety remained stable across the data collection points the frequency of such symptoms significantly increased as the event approached. Temporal patterning for somatic anxiety intensity and frequency was found to be congruent, with both dimensions showing progressive increases as the event neared. For self-confidence both the intensity and frequency of responses remaining unchanged over the 2 day pre-event period.

The implication from these findings is that researchers need to consider not only the intensity of the competitive anxiety response but also the frequency with which symptoms are experienced. An additional dimension that has received increasing attention -- and also alludes to positive performance consequences -- is the notion of directional interpretations of anxiety symptoms.

Directional Interpretation of Symptoms

> The responsibility as England's kicker does scare me. I worry all the time about it, but the important thing is that I know I can worry about it. It's not a bad thing, or a detrimental thing, to worry. As long as when I go to take the kick, my routine is there, and my visualization, I can be as fearful as I like and think: 'I'm really, really concerned about this'. But as long as everything is in place, the ball will go where you want it to. (Wilkinson, 2003, p. 47)

This quote from Johnny Wilkinson, the England Rugby Union team's goal-kicker, illustrates the notion that anxieties associated with sport performance do not necessarily have negative connotations with regard to performance. The first sport psychology investigation to allude to the potential positive consequences of anxiety on performance was conducted by Mahoney and Avener (1977). They compared the psychological skills used by United States gymnasts who were either successful or unsuccessful in qualifying for the 1976 Olympic Games, with qualifiers reporting that they used their anxiety as a stimulant to better performance. This theme was resurrected in the early 1990's following a series of investigations that questioned the traditional view that increases in competitive anxiety were negative to performance (cf. Martens, Burton, et al., 1990), instead suggesting that performance can be enhanced by increases in intensity levels (e.g., Jones and Cale, 1989; Jones, Cale, and Kerwin, 1988; Parfitt and Hardy, 1987). Consequently, Parfitt, Jones, and Hardy (1990) and Burton (1990) suggested that anxiety-related symptoms could be perceived by some athletes as facilitating mental preparation and performance.

Based on these suggestions Jones (Jones, 1991; Jones and Swain, 1992) introduced the notion of 'direction' into the competitive anxiety literature. Directional interpretations refers to the extent with which the intensity of the cognitive and perceived physiological symptoms are labeled as either positive or negative to performance on a facilitative-debilitative continuum. To examine the efficacy of directional interpretations within competitive anxiety, Jones and Swain (1992) modified the original CSAI-2 by adding a debilitative-facilitative scale to each item that rated whether the intensity of symptoms experienced were interpreted as facilitative or debilitative towards future performance.

Support for the notion of direction can be found in other areas of psychology (cf. Jones, 1995a). For example, in the test anxiety literature Alpert and Haber (1960) distinguished between debilitating and facilitating anxiety and constructed a scale that measured both dimensions of the response (i.e., the Achievement Anxiety Test; AAT; Alpert and Haber, 1960) and provided a stronger predictor of academic performance than conventional anxiety scales. Other studies have also demonstrated the value of distinguishing between debilitative and facilitative anxiety states (e.g., Carrier, Higson, Klimoski, and Peterson, 1984; Couch, Garber, and Turner, 1983; Gaeddert and Dolphin, 1981).

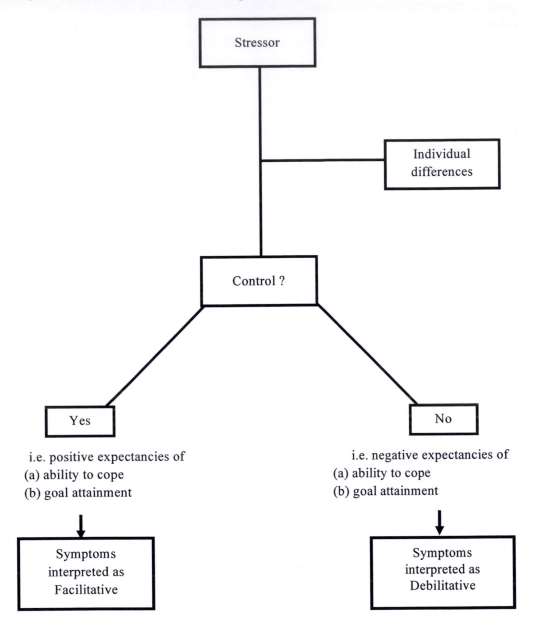

Figure 1: A model of debilitative and facilitative competitive state anxiety (reproduced with permission from Jones, 1995).

Initial attempts to explain the notion of direction came from Jones's (1995a) control model of facilitative and debilitative anxiety (see figure 1). Drawing on the work of Carver and Scheier (1986, 1988), the model hypothesized that a combination of individual difference variables and the performers' ability to control a stressor determined how athletes' interpret anxiety associated symptoms (as debilitative or facilitative to performance). Control, conceptualized as the cognitive appraisal of the degree of influence the performer was able to exert over both the environment and the self, was viewed as the central mediating factor. Individuals who appraised that they possessed a degree of control over the situation, were able to cope with their anxiety, and achieve their goals (i.e., coping or positive expectancy of goal achievement) were predicted to interpret symptoms as facilitative to performance. In comparison, performers who appraised that they were not in control, could not cope with the situation at hand, and possessed negative expectancies regarding goal attainment were predicted to interpret such symptoms as debilitative (Jones, 1995a). Jones (1995a) suggested that direction essentially represented an additional level of cognitive appraisal during which a performer interpreted the meaningfulness of symptoms following an initial or earlier appraisal.

Control Processes

Until recently, theorists have failed to explain in any detail the cognitive processes that underlie the control element that leads to symptoms interpreted in a facilitative or debilitative manner. A notable exception can be found in the recent work of Fletcher and Fletcher (2005) and their meta-model of stress, emotion, and performance (see Fletcher et al., this volume). The model divides the stress process into three stages: (1) the person-environment (P-E) fit; (2) the emotion-performance (E-P) fit; and (3) the subsequent coping and overall outcome (COO). The negative consequence of any incongruence in the first stage represents the competitive anxiety response (i.e., psychological strain associated with a negative primary and secondary appraisal of a competitive stressor). It is the second stage of the model, during which tertiary and quaternary appraisal processes occur, that is purported to be analogous with the notion of direction. This stage focuses on the E-P fit which represents an individual's ability to deal with his or her cognitive and somatic reactions to stressors (e.g., the level of competitive anxiety intensity experienced).

Tertiary and Quaternary Appraisal

The second stage of the model is essentially a further aspect of an individual-environment transaction and comprises tertiary (an evaluation whether the emotion experienced is relevant to performance) and quaternary (evaluation of coping options) appraisal processes. These processes contribute to a performer's emotional orientation and whether stress responses are interpreted as facilitative or debilitative to performance. Specifically, in the context of this chapter, how an individual labels anxiety and its associated cognitive and somatic symptoms will subsequently determine the overall nature of his or her preperformance feeling state. According to this conceptualization, a negative emotion such as competitive anxiety may, therefore, precede a positive emotional 'orientation' towards performance.

Similar to the perspective adopted by Jones (1995a) in his model of control, whereby individual differences were hypothesized to influence symptom interpretation, the meta-model (Fletcher and Fletcher, 2005; Fletcher et al., this volume) also predicts that the competitive stress process is moderated by various personal and situational characteristics. The next section reviews the extant research that has investigated the influence of individual difference variables upon performers' interpretations of their anxiety and associated symptoms.

Individual Differences

Since the introduction of Jones's (1995a) model of control the majority of direction studies have focused on examining the individual difference element. A range of personal and situational moderators have been identified and the following section views the relevance of these variables in the interpretation of symptoms associated with competitive anxiety. For convenience, we group the personal factors under the following subsections of trait anxiety, cognitive bias, positive and negative affect, self-confidence, neuroticism and extraversion, hardiness, coping strategies, psychological skills, achievement motivation, competitiveness, and gender. The situational variables are under the subsections of skill level, competitive experience, sport type, cohesion, locus of control, and performance level.

Trait Anxiety

The first personality factor to be considered is competitive trait anxiety. While several studies have examined the potential moderators of the intensity and direction of the competitive trait anxiety response (e.g., Hanton, O'Brien, and Mellalieu, 2003; Jones and Swain, 1995; Perry and Williams, 1998) only one study has considered how competitive trait anxiety may affect subsequent interpretations of state symptoms. Hanton, Mellalieu, and Hall's (2002) comparison of high and low trait anxiety in soccer players found that the high trait group responded with significantly greater state intensity than the low trait group. With regard to direction, however, no differences were found in the interpretation of cognitive and somatic symptoms between high and low trait anxiety groups. The preliminary findings regarding symptom intensity support Martens, Burton et al.'s (1990) premise that highly trait anxious performers will generally respond to stressful situations by demonstrating high levels of state anxiety. However, more research is needed to examine the role of trait anxiety and symptom interpretation.

Cognitive Bias

One explanation for the moderating effects of trait anxiety upon symptom interpretation is through the cognitive bias of an individual. This notion is based upon Beck's (1976) theoretical account of emotional vulnerability that suggests individuals who are vulnerable to anxiety exhibit a cognitive processing bias for the threatening interpretation of ambiguous information. In a series of investigations Eubank and colleagues (Eubank, Collins, and Smith, 2000, 2002) found that anxiety debilitators showed a processing bias for threatening information, while anxiety facilitators were biased toward emotionally positive stimuli. Eubank et al. explained these findings by suggesting that although facilitators of anxiety symptoms are sensitive to positive interpretations of ambiguous stimuli they may be able to keep negative affect under control by an effortful avoidance of threat, which could be viewed as an effective strategy for coping with stress.

In a related study Jones, Smith, and Holmes (2004) investigated the bias in the processing of anxiety related stimuli and differences in symptom interpretation due to the cognitive defense mechanism characteristic of different personality types (high-anxious, low-anxious, repressor and defensive high-anxious) which served to either magnify or minimize the threat experienced (cf. Eysenck, 1997). Jones et al. (2004) hypothesized that the tendency to report symptoms as facilitative to performance would be characteristic of repressors (i.e., individuals who report low anxiety levels as they genuinely believe they are not experiencing negative affect) rather than high-anxious and low-anxious individuals. While repressors and low-anxious individuals reported lower levels of anxiety intensity than the high-anxious group the repressors also reported their symptoms experienced as more facilitative to performance than the high-anxious individuals. Jones et al.'s findings suggest, therefore, that the cognitive biases of repressors may serve to reduce the intensity of anxiety experienced rather than influence the directional interpretation of symptoms.

Positive and Negative Affect

Positive and negative affect are two relatively independent personality variables that have been identified in social psychological studies of affective structure and have been described as an individual's tendency to display adaptive or aversive mood states (e.g., Watson and Clark, 1984; Watson and Tellegen, 1985). Positive affect reflects the extent to which a person feels enthusiastic, active or alert, with high positive affect characterized by moods associated with full concentration, eagerness and pleasurable engagement. Negative affect is viewed as a general dimension of subjective distress, with high negative affect reflected by unpleasant mood states, including anger, contempt, fear and nervousness. Jones et al. (1994) suggested that a performer's affective state may influence, or in someway be related to his or her interpretation of anxiety symptoms. Subsequently, Jones, Swain, and Harwood (1996) found that negative affect was related to the intensity of cognitive and somatic anxiety responses while positive affect had a greater significant correlation than negative affect in the interpretation of both cognitive and somatic anxiety symptoms. Similar findings were also noted by Cerin (2004) with positive affect significantly predicting cognitive and somatic anxiety direction. Finally, in a follow-up to Jones et al.'s (1996) study, Hanton and Mellalieu (in press) compared facilitators and debilitators of symptoms associated with competitive anxiety with positive affect and negative affect respectively, and found that debilitators experienced lower positive affect and greater negative affect than their facilitating counterparts.

Collectively, these findings suggest that performers' symptoms interpretation may be predicted by positive and negative affect (Jones et al., 1994). Specifically, high negative affect individuals appear to consistently perceive symptoms as debilitative, while performers high on positive affect tend to interpret their symptoms as more facilitative. Negative affect therefore reflects a relatively stable disposition to experience negative emotional states, or a 'vulnerability factor', while high positive affect may be viewed as a 'resiliency factor' characterized by high levels of self-esteem and self-confidence. Interestingly, in Hanton and Mellalieu's (in press) study, facilitators of symptoms associated with competitive anxiety also experienced greater levels of self-confidence than debilitators, a finding that appears to be consistent across other direction studies (e.g., Jones et al., 1994; Jones and Swain, 1995; Perry and Williams, 1998).

Self-confidence

One of the most robust findings to emerge from the direction literature is that facilitators of symptoms associated with competitive anxiety report greater levels of self-confidence than their debilitating counterparts (e.g., Hanton and Jones, 1997; Hanton, Jones, and Mullen, 2000; Jones et al., 1994; Jones and Swain, 1995; Perry and Williams, 1998). High correlations have also been reported between the self-confidence and the direction subscales of the CSAI-2 (Jones et al., 1993, 1996). Self-confidence has subsequently been suggested in some way to act as a resiliency factor and protect against the debilitating effects of anxiety (Hardy et al., 1996; Mellalieu, Neil, and Hanton, in press). In order to explore the nature of this relationship Hanton, Mellalieu, and Hall (2004) conducted interviews with elite performers regarding their experiences of precompetitive symptoms. Increases in cognitive symptoms accompanied by low self-confidence were perceived as outside of the performers' control and debilitating to performance, while the presence of high self-confidence and cognitive symptoms led to positive perceptions of control and facilitating interpretations.

Although Hanton, Mellalieu et al.'s (2004) findings suggest self-confidence influences symptom interpretation, the qualitative nature of their design prevented any inferences being made regarding specific mediating or moderating effects. It is apparent, however, that above all other individual difference variables self-confidence may be the most significant factor in discriminating how athletes manage and interpret stressful situations (Hardy et al., 1996).

Neuroticism and Extraversion

Neuroticism is a personality trait that is characterized by the tendency to experience negative affect, while extraversion is associated with the predisposition to experience positive affect. Cerin (2004) has recently considered the influence of neuroticism and extraversion upon anxiety intensity and symptom interpretation. Significant interactions were identified for neuroticism and negative affect upon cognitive anxiety direction, and neuroticism and somatic anxiety intensity upon somatic anxiety direction. For extraversion, a positive relationship was identified with cognitive anxiety direction and a negative one with cognitive anxiety intensity. In addition, individuals who were higher in extraversion interpreted their symptoms as more facilitative to performance than the lower extraversion individuals. Cerin noted that as neurotics tend to be more negativistic and ruminative than non-neurotics it is possible that the accentuated self-awareness may make them more distractible and vulnerable to fluctuations in body sensations and negative cognitions. Subsequently, this negativistic attitude may contribute to a more negative appraisal of the influence of symptoms upon performance. For extraverts, their higher levels of optimum stimulation, sensation seeking, assertiveness, and tendency to experience positive emotions may lead to them reacting to events in a more positive manner than that of non-extraverts. They may also perceive the same symptoms as more facilitative to performance than non-extroverts because of their tendency to be optimistic and behave proactively when confronted with problematic or threatening situations (cf. Cerin, 2004).

Hardiness

Hardiness refers to an individuals' ability to remain healthy in the face of stressful life events and comprises the three elements of commitment, control, and challenge (Kobasa, 1979). Although the positive effects of a 'hardy' personality (such as reduced life stress) have been demonstrated in clinical psychology only Hanton, Evans, and Neil (2003) have studied the relationship with competitive anxiety symptoms. In an examination of the effects of skill level and hardiness upon trait anxiety responses, elite athletes high in hardiness reported lower competitive anxiety levels, more facilitative interpretations of these symptoms and higher self-confidence levels when compared to their nonelite counterparts. These findings suggest that a hardy personality moderates how competitive anxiety is interpreted by performers. A possible mechanism for this influence may be the hardy performer's ability to transform the appraisal of a stressor in a more positive fashion (cf. Hanton, Evans, et al., 2003).

Coping Strategies

Studies investigating the relationship between coping and competitive anxiety direction have examined the specific strategies employed by performers with either facilitating or debilitating interpretations of symptoms (Eubank and Collins, 2000; Jerome and Williams, 2000; Ntoumanis and Biddle, 2000). For example, Ntoumanis and Biddle (2000) found that facilitating interpretations of competitive anxiety symptoms were related to increased effort, suppression of competing activities, and problem-focused coping including positive emotional and motivational outcomes. Debilitating perceptions of symptoms were associated with behavioral disengagement and an inability to regulate emotions. Jerome and Williams (2000), and Eubank and Collins (2000), have also found that facilitators used more problem- and emotion-focused coping strategies in response to stress; whereas, debilitators were limited in their use of coping constructs. These findings support Jones's (1995a) proposal that coping is a key construct in the control individuals have over themselves and their environment. Moreover, facilitating interpretations of symptoms appears to be a representation that effective coping is taking place (Eubank and Collins, 2000).

Psychological Skills

A number of studies have investigated the relationship between psychological skills and competitive anxiety. For example, Fletcher and Hanton (2001) examined the intensity and direction of competitive state anxiety as a function of 'high' and 'low' psychological skill usage in nonelite swimmers. Findings showed that performers who reported greater use of relaxation strategies experienced lower levels of anxiety and interpreted symptoms as more facilitative to performance than their low usage counterparts. Similar results were found by Maynard and colleagues who employed an intervention approach with nonelite soccer players (Maynard, Hemmings, and Warwick-Evans, 1995; Maynard, Smith, and Warwick-Evans, 1995). The relaxation strategy adopted was found to reduce the intensity of anxiety symptoms and increase facilitative interpretations of symptoms and levels of self-confidence. Other investigations that have adopted the use of psychological skill-based interventions, such as mental imagery, have also reported increases in facilitative interpretations of symptoms (e.g., Hale and Whitehouse, 1998; Page, Sime, and Nordell, 1999).

A final line of inquiry has been to examine the effects of multimodal psychological skill packages upon symptom interpretation. Hanton and Jones's (1999b) multiple baseline design used a combined goal setting, imagery, and self-talk package with elite swimmers who were debilitated by cognitive and somatic symptoms. No changes were reported in the intensity of symptoms but increases occurred in facilitative interpretations, self-confidence and performance. Using a similar mental skill package combination to Hanton and Jones, Mamassis and Doganis (2004) also showed increases in facilitating interpretations of symptoms, self-confidence and performance in an experimental versus control group of junior tennis players.

Taken together the studies that have considered the influence of psychological skills upon symptom interpretation suggest that nonelite athletes use primarily relaxation strategies to reduce and interpret anxiety intensity levels as facilitative, relying minimally on other psychological skills. In contrast, elite athletes appear to maintain their intensity levels and use a combination of psychological skills, including goal setting, imagery, and self-talk strategies to restructure the interpretation of their symptoms as facilitative (Hanton and Jones, 1999a).

Achievement Motivation

Despite the wealth of investigations that have examined the relationships between motivational constructs, such as achievement goal orientation, and the subsequent affective responses (see Kingston, Spray, and Harwood, this volume) only Ntoumanis and Biddle (1998) have considered the relationship with anxiety symptom interpretation. In their study, Ntoumanis and Biddle examined achievement goal orientations, perceived motivational climate, and perceptions of the intensity and direction of competitive state anxiety. While no significant relationships were found between task orientation and direction, the effect of ego orientation on the intensity and direction of cognitive and somatic anxiety was reported to be exerted through self-confidence. In addition, no significant relationships were found between motivational climates and competitive anxiety intensity and direction. These findings suggest that motivational climates may have an indirect impact on affective responses through the different goal orientations, while self-confidence again appears to be a powerful construct in helping performers cope with the debilitating effects of stress.

Competitiveness

A further motivational construct that has been examined in relation to anxiety interpretation is the competitive orientation or competitiveness of the performer. Here competitiveness refers to the desire to enter and strive for success in sporting competition (Gill and Deeter, 1988). In the first empirical study of direction, Jones and Swain (1992) compared intramural athletes with high and low competitive orientations. No differences in the intensity of the cognitive and somatic symptoms were reported, or in the somatic symptom interpretation. However, the higher competitive group rated cognitive anxiety symptoms as more facilitative to performance than the less competitive group.

Gender

Investigations that have examined the effects of gender upon the intensity of the competitive anxiety response have generally found that females report higher levels of competitive state and trait anxiety than males (e.g., Jones and Cale, 1989; Martens, Burton, et al., 1990). However, only Perry and Williams (1998) have directly examined gender differences in symptom interpretation. In their comparison of advanced, intermediate and novice male and female tennis players the authors reported no differences in cognitive or somatic anxiety intensity. Overall, though, males did report more facilitative interpretations of their cognitive and somatic responses when compared to their female counterparts. Perry and Williams's findings suggest that male athletes may vary in their use of cognitive processes for dealing with their respective precompetitive experiences. One explanation for these differences could be due to the fact males also reported greater levels of self-confidence than females which may in some way have helped them to protect against debilitating symptom interpretations (cf. Hardy et al., 1996). Alternatively, it has been suggested that females possess more willingness to report their feelings than males, particularly those of an unpleasant nature (cf. Jones, 1990). Females may therefore be more likely to present a more accurate reflection of their symptoms as they feel a greater social acceptability of reporting anxiety.

Skill Level

Skill level is one of the original and most frequently studied situation variables and considers how elite and nonelite individuals may differ in their symptom interpretation (Eubank, Collins, and Smethhurst, 1995; Jones et al., 1994; Jones and Swain, 1995). One of the first studies conducted was by Jones et al. (1994) who reported no differences in the intensity of cognitive and somatic state anxiety of elite and nonelite swimmers, but found that the elite swimmers interpreted their symptoms as more facilitative to performance than their nonelite counterparts. Similar findings have also been observed by Jones and Swain (1995) and Eubank et al. (1995) in the sports of cricket and badminton respectively. A further degree of skill level evaluation was adopted by Perry and Williams (1998) who compared the intensity and direction of competitive trait anxiety responses of advanced, intermediate and novice tennis players. While no differences were observed between groups for somatic anxiety intensity the novice group reported lower cognitive anxiety intensity. For direction, only advanced players reported more facilitative interpretations of cognitive and somatic symptoms than their novice and intermediate counterparts, providing partial support for the previous studies.

These and other recent findings regarding skill level (e.g., Hanton, Evans, et al., 2003; Hanton and Connaughton, 2002) suggest that elite performers do not differ from their nonelite counterparts in terms of the intensity of precompetitive anxiety responses experienced. It does appear, however, that elite individuals typically have a more positive interpretation of these symptoms in terms of their consequences for performance.

Competitive Experience

Whereas skill can be viewed as an objective individual ability and performance (Martens, Vealey, et al., 1990) at a particular sporting level (e.g., national, international), the concept of competitive experience is associated with the familiarity of the competitive environment (Cerin et al., 2000). In their qualitative investigation of elite swimmers' preparation for competition, Hanton and Jones (1999a) noted that the acquisition of mental skills was a gradual progression over the athletes' careers with initial experiences of cognitive and somatic symptoms associated with competitive anxiety viewed invariably as debilitating to performance. Later, however, the development of cognitive skills and strategies underlying the facilitative interpretation of symptoms were reported to be acquired via natural learning experiences and various educational methods. Mellalieu et al. (2004) also considered the notion of competitive experience while investigating the intensity and direction of symptoms associated with anxiety as a function of the activities of a gross explosive (rugby) and fine motor-skilled (golf) nature. In both sports the experienced performers reported lower intensity and more facilitative interpretations of symptoms than their less experienced counterparts.

The observations of Hanton and Jones (1999a) and Mellalieu et al. (2004) suggest that the level of competitive experience might be a more sensitive indicator of psychological skill development than solely the achievement of elite status (i.e., skill level). In addition, although higher skilled performers are generally assumed to possess greater competitive experience it may be possible for an athlete to be categorized as highly skilled yet be very low in experience due to a sudden rise in performance level. From a psychological development perspective, such an increase in performance may be premature for the athlete if important competitive experiences are absent.

Sport Type

A further situation variable that has been suggested to moderate anxiety direction is the nature of the sport (Jones, 1995a; Jones et al., 1994). Differences in interpretation have been compared as a function of activities that vary in terms of fine and gross motor skill requirements (e.g., Hanton, Jones, and Mullen, 2000; Mellalieu et al., 2004). Collectively, the findings suggest that while no differences exist in the intensity of competitive anxiety symptoms, athletes who participate in relatively explosive motor skilled sports (e.g., rugby union) report their competitive anxiety states as more facilitative to performance than participants from sports of finely controlled skills such as pistol shooting and golf. These findings clearly highlight the necessity to consider each sport separately when evaluating the appropriate psychological preparation required for competition.

Cohesion

As well as the study of individual variables, the impact of group moderators upon anxiety symptom interpretation has also been examined. Specifically, Eys, Hardy, Carron, and Beauchamp (2003) compared the relationship between task cohesion and the intensity and direction of competitive anxiety symptoms. Athletes who perceived their cognitive anxiety symptoms as facilitative reported greater perceptions of task-related attraction to the group (ATG-T) and task group-integration (GI-T) than athletes who perceived their cognitive anxiety symptoms as debilitative. In addition, athletes who perceived their somatic anxiety symptoms as facilitative also reported higher perceptions of GI-T. Although preliminary in nature, these findings suggest that highly cohesive teams are likely to experience competitive state anxiety differently than members of less cohesive teams. Furthermore, perceptions of task cohesion appear to be related to individuals' symptom interpretation. This highlights that improvements or changes in the dynamics of the team may therefore enhance the psychological state of the individual.

Control

The ability to control a stressor is pivotal in determining how athletes' interpret anxiety symptoms as debilitative or facilitative to performance (Jones, 1995a). Support has been found in several studies that have measured control both indirectly, by using performers' goal attainment expectations (e.g., Hanton, O'Brien, et al., 2003; Jones and Hanton, 1996; O'Brien, Hanton, and Mellalieu, 2005), and directly (Ntoumanis and Jones, 1998) through measures such as the Internal-External Locus of Control Scale (I-E scale; Rotter, 1966). For example, Jones and Hanton (1996) and Hanton, O'Brien et al. (2003) found that individuals with positive expectancies of goal attainment reported their symptoms as more facilitative to performance than those with negative expectations, who were debilitative. Ntoumanis and Jones's (1998) comparison of symptom interpretation in internal and external locus of control groups found that those athletes with an internal locus of control perceived the intensity of their trait anxiety symptoms as more facilitative to performance than those who viewed themselves as having an external locus of control.

While these studies provide some support for Jones's (1995a) model the cross-sectional nature of the designs employed means that no firm conclusion can be drawn about the moderating or mediating effects of perceptions of control. Interestingly, several recent qualitative investigations of the precompetitive stress experience have provided some descriptive explication regarding this issue and the mechanisms underlying directional interpretations. Specifically, anxiety responses perceived to be under the performers' control have been reported as having facilitative consequences for performance while symptoms outside of control have been viewed as debilitative (Hanton and Connaughton, 2002, Hanton, Mellalieu, et al., 2004).

Performance Level

Despite the apparent significance of the relationship between precompetitive symptom interpretation and subsequent performance only a few studies have directly investigated this association. One of the first was Jones, Swain, and Hardy's (1993) comparison of club-level gymnasts who were divided into good and poor performance groups based on their beam competition scores. While no significant differences emerged in the intensity of responses, the more successful gymnasts were found to experience greater facilitative interpretations of their cognitive and somatic anxiety symptoms than their less successful counterparts.

Other studies have attempted to explain the relationship between symptom interpretation and performance by assessing the amount of performance variance accounted for by the direction subscale of the CSAI-2 (Edwards and Hardy, 1996; Jerome and Williams, 2000; Swain and Jones, 1996) For example, Swain and Jones (1996) indicated that the direction dimensions predicted more variance in basketball performance than the intensity dimension alone, while the addition of the direction scales increased the amount of performance variance explained on top of that predicted by the intensity scales (Swain and Jones, 1996). In contrast, Edwards and Hardy (1996) reported that both direction subscales failed to explain any variance in netball performance, while Jerome and Williams's (2000) investigation of recreational and semi-professional bowlers revealed that the only significant predictor of performance was somatic anxiety direction.

One reason for the equivocal findings may be that previous studies have only assessed anxiety symptoms preperformance rather than during competition. In an attempt to compare pre and in-event measures, Butt, Weinberg, and Horn (2003) found that cognitive and somatic anxiety direction and self-confidence intensity and direction predicted a significant amount of performance variance for the 1st and 2nd halves of field hockey matches respectively. Further, the results also indicated that the anxiety and self-confidence measurements obtained during competition were more strongly related to performance than the pre-game measures.

Collectively, the studies investigating Jones's (1995a) control model suggest consistent trends between groups of individuals in relation to anxiety interpretation. Specifically, a broad range of personal and situation variables moderate performers' symptom interpretations. Findings also support the value of distinguishing between the intensity and the direction of symptoms experienced in competitive situations. Further, direction may actually be a more sensitive variable in distinguishing between group differences when compared solely with the intensity of the response (Hanton, Cropley, Mellalieu, Neil, and Miles, in press; Jones and Hanton, 2001; Mellalieu, Hanton, and Jones, 2003; Swain and Jones, 1996).

Temporal Patterning

In addition to the consideration of other dimensions of the competitive anxiety response, such as frequency and direction, researchers have highlighted the importance of adopting a process orientated approach that emphasizes the study of stress longitudinally over time (Cerin et al., 2000; Cerin, Szabo, and Williams, 2001; Hanton, Thomas, and Maynard, 2004; Lazarus, 1999). As discussed earlier in the frequency of cognitive intrusions section, a wealth of literature exists examining the intensity of the competitive anxiety responses in the lead up to competition. Using a time to event paradigm general support has been found for Martens, Vealey et al.'s (1990) predictions that cognitive anxiety and self-confidence remain unchanged in the lead up to competition while somatic anxiety increases and peaks directly prior to performance. The temporal nature of the intensity of the response has also been shown to be moderated by several situation and individual difference factors (see Cerin et al., 2000). Until recently limited attention had been given to assessing how the different dimensions of anxiety unfold over time. This section therefore considers how researchers have taken the study of the temporal nature of competitive stress over time further by exploring the complexities of all three anxiety dimensions.

The first study to combine the assessment of more than one dimension using the time to event paradigm was Wiggins's (1998) examination of the intensity and direction of the anxiety response in the period 24 hours prior to competition. Significant increases over time were reported for somatic anxiety intensity, decreases for self-confidence, and no changes for cognitive anxiety intensity or anxiety interpretation. This latter finding led Wiggins to conclude that once athletes had interpreted their symptoms associated with competitive anxiety as either facilitative or debilitative towards performance this interpretation did not change. Similar findings were reported by Butt et al. (2003) in their examination of the fluctuations in intensity and direction throughout competition (directly prior to competition, first half, second half, directly postcompetition) using retrospective recall measures. Butt et al. found that the only significant changes from pre to postcompetition occurred in cognitive anxiety intensity and self-confidence, while during performance, self-confidence and the intensity and direction of cognitive and somatic anxiety were reported to remain relatively stable.

Recent research by Hanton and colleagues has combined the study of the intensity, frequency and direction dimensions of the anxiety response (e.g., Hanton et al., 2002; Hanton, Thomas, et al., 2004; Thomas, Maynard, and Hanton, 2004). The first of these was Hanton et al.'s (2002) qualitative investigation of elite performers' retrospective perceptions and causal beliefs regarding temporal experiences of competitive anxiety and related symptoms in the lead up to competition. While theoretical predictions were supported for the intensity and frequency of the temporal patterning of anxiety, in contrast to Wiggins (1998) and Butt et al. (2003), interpretations of symptoms were reported to change as the competition approached. Specifically, cognitive and somatic symptoms were interpreted as facilitative during the preparation phase for competition, but debilitative directly before performance. Hanton et al. suggested this finding was potentially due to the athletes experiencing forms of both preparatory and performance anxiety (cf. Burton, 1998; Mellalieu et al., 2003).

The next investigation of all three anxiety dimensions was an empirical study by Hanton, Thomas et al. (2004) who examined the temporal patterns of symptoms in a 7 day precompetition phase (7 days, 48 hours, 24 hours, 2 hours, 30 minutes) as a function of skill level (elite versus nonelite). Differences were found only in the direction dimension with elite performers' more facilitative in their interpretation of cognitive and somatic symptoms through the week preceding competition. For both groups, greater temporal changes were noted in the frequency of responses in the time leading up to the event. In an attempt to further discriminate changes in symptoms as a function of anxiety interpretation Thomas et al. (2004) examined competitive state anxiety responses in the lead up to competition across the three dimensions in performers with varying symptom interpretations (i.e., 'facilitators', 'debilitators' and 'mixed interpreters'). Facilitators displayed increased intensities of self-confidence, more positive interpretations of cognitive and somatic symptoms, increased frequency of self-confidence symptoms and decreased frequency of cognitive anxiety symptoms than debilitators and mixed interpreters throughout the precompetition period. Time-to-competition effects also indicated that directional interpretations of cognitive and somatic responses became less positive close to competition and the frequency of cognitive and somatic symptoms increased towards the event. Taken collectively, Thomas et al.'s results appear to suggest therefore that debilitators differ in their symptom responses when compared to facilitators (i.e., intensity and frequency). Not only do debilitators view anxiety symptoms as negative towards performance, they also think about these symptoms more often preceding competition. In addition, they experience lower levels of self-confidence and think about these symptoms less often as competition moves closer.

To accompany the study of the temporal patterning of anxiety symptoms experienced across the competition period researchers have developed abbreviated scales that allow faster assessment of responses. These include the Mental Readiness Form (MRF; Murphy, Greenspan, Jowdy, and Tammen, 1989), the Anxiety Rating Scale-Cognitive (ARS-C) and Somatic (ARS-S) instruments (Cox, Russell, and Robb, 1998, 1999), and Immediate Anxiety Measurement Scale (IAMS; Thomas, Hanton, and Jones, 2002). While some investigators have questioned the psychometric properties of short form scales (e.g., Edwards and Hardy, 1995; Hardy, 1996) there appears to be consistent support for the adoption of abbreviated scales where time may be limited and preclude the use of full length instruments (e.g., Butt et al., 2003; Cox et al., 1999; Krane, 1994; Krane, Joyce, and Rafeld, 1994; Thomas et al., 2002).

Key Issues

The recent emphasis towards the study of the positive effects of the anxiety response, and in particular the notion of facilitating interpretations of symptoms associated with anxiety, has stimulated considerable discussion among sport psychology researchers (e.g., Burton, 1998; Burton and Naylor, 1997; Hardy, 1997, 1998; Jones, 1995a; Jones and Hanton, 2001; Mellalieu et al., 2003). Within the discourse three main themes have emerged that relate to measurement, rhetorical and theoretical issues.

Measurement

The first measurement issue relates to the utility of the modified CSAI-2 to accurately assess direction (Burton, 1998; Burton and Naylor, 1997). Burton suggested that the modified CSAI-2 creates a measurement confound because individuals rate the facilitative or debilitative nature of their perceived anxiety symptoms in a constant fashion despite experiencing variable levels of anxiety intensity. Specifically, different individuals may experience a wide range of intensity levels yet may rate these levels to be equally facilitating or debilitating to forthcoming performance. Similarly, one performer may experience a small number of symptoms at an intense level while another may experience a large number of symptoms at a lesser level of intensity, both which may be perceived as equally facilitating or debilitating to performance. Clearly such cases represent different cognitive and somatic symptoms experienced yet both will have similar scores as assessed by the modified CSAI-2.

The next measurement issue lies in the ambiguous wording of several items of the CSAI-2 (Burton, 1998; Lane, Sewell, Terry, Bartram, and Nesti, 1999; Woodman and Hardy, 2001). Woodman and Hardy (2001) noted that the use of the term "concern" in the item wording of the cognitive anxiety scale is not necessarily a reflection of worry or cognitive anxiety, but rather a perception of the importance of the upcoming event. This point is emphasized by Cerin (2003), who suggested that the cognitive subscale of the CSAI-2 may be confounding threat and challenge related appraisals (e.g., fear and worry versus excitement, interest or eagerness). Further support for the concerns regarding the ambiguous wording of items has come from studies examining of the factor structure of the CSAI-2 intensity subscales (e.g., Cox, Martens, and Russell, 2003; Iosifidou and Doganis, 2001; Tsorbatzoudis, Barkoukis, Sideridis, and Grouios, 1998), the comparison of the CSAI-2 with other affective measures (Cerin, 2003, 2004) and the completion of the scale in response to excited and anxious scenarios (Jones and Uphill, 2004).

Woodman and Hardy (2001) also pointed out that some of the items originally selected for the CSAI-2 might not reflect the most salient aspects of precompetitive anxiety for some athletes. Indeed, the CSAI-2 and self-report measures in general can only assess the perceived cognitive and somatic symptoms that are *commonly associated* with the competitive anxiety response by certain but not all individuals. Consequently, while one athlete may view items such as "my heart is racing" as reflecting somatic symptoms of anxiety, another may view "I feel jittery" as irrelevant. Despite these measurement issues Woodman and Hardy (2001, p. 302) noted "…the CSAI-2 has been, and continues to be, the choice of predilection for most researchers with an interest in competitive state anxiety."

Rhetorical

One issue that has received little attention within this area relates to the rhetoric used by researchers. Historically, there has been inconsistency with the use of terms (cf. Burton, 1998; Burton and Naylor, 1997; Hardy, 1998; Jones, 1995a). Burton (1990), for example, noted that anxiety states could be 'positive' and helpful in facilitating mental preparation and performance, while Parfitt et al. (1990) suggested that positive performance effects could be associated with cognitive and somatic anxiety. Parfitt et al. also discussed the notion that some performers may 'perceive' or label symptoms as facilitating to performance. Later, Jones (1995a) used the term 'facilitative anxiety states' to refer to how performers labeled their cognitive and physiological symptoms in a positive manner in relation to performance. He also noted, however, that a state in which symptoms were perceived as facilitating to performance was unlikely to represent a state of anxiety.

Hardy (1997) also highlighted that athletes may interpret their symptoms as facilitative to performance and that anxiety could, under certain circumstances, enhance performance. In response, Burton and Naylor (1997) argued against Hardy's assertion that anxiety can be facilitative to performance. In a subsequent rebuttal, Hardy (1998) called for a reconceptualization of the competitive anxiety construct, but also maintained his position that anxiety may result in improvements in performance.

These issues emphasize the importance of rhetoric in the competitive anxiety literature and highlight three main areas: 1) the notion of 'positive anxiety' or 'facilitative anxiety', 2) facilitative interpretations of competitive anxiety, and 3) the positive effects of anxiety on performance. It is important, therefore, to clarify the rhetoric in order that researchers can examine the different relationships that explain the positive consequences of anxiety states upon performance. We suggest that the terms 'positive anxiety' and 'facilitative anxiety' are oxymorons best avoided as they suggest anxiety is a positive emotion. We recommend that 'facilitative interpretations of symptoms associated with competitive anxiety' is more appropriate and, importantly, accurate. This term refers to a specific negative emotion and associated symptoms which are appraised by the individual as having a beneficial influence on performance (Jones, 1995a). It is also important to distinguish this term from anxiety as a negative emotion actually having a positive effect upon performance or the positive effect of anxiety on performance. This refers to a specific negative emotion which has been deemed to have a beneficial influence on performance – regardless of whether the individual appraises the emotion as facilitative or debilitative (Hardy, 1997, 1998; Parfitt et al., 1990).

Theoretical

Following on from the rhetorical issues, three main theoretical issues emerge. First, regarding the oxymoron of positive or facilitative anxiety, Burton (Burton and Naylor, 1997; Burton, 1998) suggested that the direction approach confounded the labeling of anxiety with other more positive emotions which had simply been mislabeled as facilitative anxiety. However, Jones (1995a) discussed the notion of facilitative anxiety 'states', rather than that of facilitative anxiety *per se*, whereby the overall affective state experienced was deemed as facilitating to performance rather than anxiety itself being a positive emotion.

From this theoretical issue emerged the importance of considering the labeling of thoughts and feelings in understanding performers' positive and negative precompetitive states. Consequently, the second theoretical issue regards the contention that the positive effects of anxiety occur through performers' facilitative interpretations of competitive anxiety and its associated symptoms (Jones and Hanton, 2001). Evidence to explain this view can be found in a series of recent studies conducted to compare the type and content of the precompetitive affective response experienced (i.e., positive or negative) of facilitators and debilitators of symptoms associated with competitive anxiety (Hanton and Mellalieu, in press; Jones and Hanton, 2001; Mellalieu et al., 2003). Performers who identified symptoms on the CSAI-2 as facilitative to performance reported greater positive and lower negative affective responses. Conversely, debilitators of symptoms associated with competitive anxiety indicated significantly higher scores on negative and lower scores on positive affective responses. Facilitators also reported greater perceptions of mental readiness, self-confidence and positive perceptions of physical state, while content analysis of the responses experienced by performers revealed that 90% of the feelings experience were perceived as positive for performance by facilitators, compared with a mere 30% of labels for debilitators (Mellalieu et al., 2003).

These findings suggest that the way performers interpret competitive anxiety will influence the 'orientation' (Fletcher and Fletcher, 2005) of their overall affective state. This perspective differs subtlety from Burton's (Burton, 1998; Burton and Naylor, 1997) and

Jones's (1995a) views because it indicates that rather than anxiety being confounded with positive emotions, performers can experience competitive anxiety symptoms while experiencing positive feeling states. One explanation for this notion can be found in Fletcher and Fletcher's (2005, Fletcher et al., this volume) meta-model of stress, emotions and performance. Performers may experience competitive anxiety as an initial consequence of primary and secondary appraisal of a stressor. However, following further tertiary and quaternary appraisal, this response may be interpreted as necessary and/or facilitative to performance, leading to the generation of a positive feeling state (e.g., excitement). This cognitive process accounts for findings that have shown performers can experience ambivalent affect in the precompetitive period (Cerin, 2004; Hanton and Mellalieu, in press, Jones and Hanton, 2001; Mellalieu et al., 2003). It also appears to explain how traditional anxiety inventories, such as the CSAI-2, can easily confound a negative emotion with positive feeling states (cf. Burton and Naylor, 1997; Burton, 1998).

The final theoretical contention addresses whether anxiety can actually have a positive effect (i.e., outcome) on performance. In citing Lazarus' (1991) model of emotion, Burton (Burton and Naylor, 1997; Burton, 1998) suggested that negative emotions would always have a negative affect on performance and positive emotions a beneficial effect (cf. Martens, Burton, et al., 1990). In response, researchers have argued that negative emotions, such as anxiety, can have a positive effect upon performance (Hardy, 1997, 1998; Woodman and Hardy, 2001). Hardy (1997, 1998) has explained these direct effects through various anxiety-performance approaches including processing efficiency theory (Eysenck and Calvo, 1992) and catastrophe models (Hardy, 1990). In processing efficiency theory the presence of anxiety symptoms signals to the performer the importance of the upcoming event, and the need to muster all available resources in order to perform the necessary actions on the field (Hardy, 1997). In catastrophe models, under low levels of physiological arousal, rises in the intensity of cognitive anxiety symptoms may lead to enhanced performance (Hardy and Parfitt, 1991). The descriptions of such positive consequences of anxiety will be discussed in greater detail in the next section that considers the various explanations for the anxiety-performance relationship.

THE ANXIETY-PERFORMANCE RELATIONSHIP

A key issue pervading the literature that is of central concern to sport psychology researchers and practitioners alike is the relationship between anxiety and performance. This section discusses some of the theories and models that allude to the potential positive consequences of this relationship. These include arousal-based explanations, the zone of optimal functioning hypotheses, multidimensional anxiety theory, catastrophe models and processing efficiency theory. Further detailed description of these and additional anxiety-performance approaches can be found in other reviews of the topic (e.g., Burton, 1998; Gill, 1994; Jones, 1995a; Raglin, 1992; Woodman and Hardy, 2001).

Arousal-based Approaches

Initial inquiries attempted to determine the anxiety-performance relationship through arousal-based explanations. For example, drive theory (Spence and Spence, 1966) purported that an increase in drive or arousal was associated with a linear increase in performance providing that the learned dominant response was one of a correct skill execution. This approach was superceded in sport psychology by the inverted-U hypothesis (Oxendine, 1970) that described the relationship between arousal and performance through an inverted-U (see Anshel, 1990; Landers and Arent, 2001). Increases in arousal up to an 'optimal' level were suggested to result in positive performance gains, beyond which performance decrements occurred. Optimal levels of arousal were also suggested to be dependent on the type of task, with more complex tasks requiring lower arousal levels for optimal performance (cf. Landers and Arent, 2001). Despite their intuitive appeal, however, drive theory and the inverted-U hypothesis have been criticized for their simplistic nature and a failure to explain how arousal affects performance (Gill, 1994; Hardy, 1990; Hardy et al., 1996; Krane, 1992; Neiss, 1988).

A recent approach that accounts for the positive aspects of the arousal-performance relationship is that of reversal theory (Kerr, 1993). Based upon the work of Apter (1982, 1984), the theory suggests that motivation is influenced by changes or reversals between four paired alternate meta-motivational states. In a telic state, high physiological arousal will be interpreted as anxiety; whereas in a paratelic state, high physiological arousal will be experienced as excitement. Equilibrium in the desired meta-motivational state is achieved when minimal differences arise between an individual's preferred and actual arousal state. In addition, contingent upon the perceived pleasure or hedonic tone of the individual, performers can also suddenly reverse from the experience of high arousal as excitement to one of anxiety (Kerr, 1997). Unlike the inverted-U hypothesis, high levels of physiological or felt arousal may not automatically lead to detrimental performance consequences and may actually be beneficial.

Although some support exists for the tenets of reversal theory (see Kerr, 1997), and the fact that it attempts to explain the more positive aspects of the individual's competitive affective experience, the approach has been suggested as offering little in terms of explaining *how* and *why* anxiety (through changes in arousal states) might affect motor performance (cf. Woodman and Hardy, 2001).

Zones of Optimal Functioning (ZOF)

To overcome the limitations of the nomothetic approach to the study of the anxiety–performance relationship, Hanin (1980, 1986) introduced an intraindividual idiographic method to explain how a given level of anxiety could lead to optimal performance. This approach was initially developed as a practical tool for helping athletes 'get in the zone' and determine their optimal levels of unidimensional anxiety within certain limits or bands known as 'zones of optimal functioning' (ZOF) to maximize performance (Hanin, 1980, 1986, 1989). Hanin proposed that every athlete possesses an optimal preperformance anxiety zone within which performance levels were greatest. Anxiety levels below or above these bands were proposed to be consistent with inhibited performance (see Robazza, this volume, for a full description). Dependent upon athlete preferences, therefore, high levels of competitive anxiety could lead to optimal performance. A number of investigations have partially supported the ZOF hypothesis (e.g., Annesi, 1998; Gould, Tuffey, Hardy, and Lochbaum, 1993; Krane, 1993; Randle and Weinberg, 1997; Thelwell and Maynard, 1998; Turner and Raglin, 1991; Woodman, Albinson, and Hardy, 1997). The theory itself is also intuitively appealing as it helps to identify an optimal zone for anxiety by employing the individual as a unit of analysis (due to the great variability amongst athletes) and has practical significance for applied sport psychologists in that peak performance can be identified relatively easily (Hardy et al., 1996).

Although ZOF has received criticizm (see Gould and Tuffey, 1996; Hardy et al., 1996; Hardy and Parfitt, 1991; Woodman and Hardy, 2001) the approach has received considerable success in its application to the investigation of a broader range of emotions rather than anxiety alone (cf. Gould and Udry, 1994). A theoretical and methodological framework has subsequently been developed to conceptualize, describe and assess zones of optimal functioning of individuals' emotional states (see Robazza, this volume).

Multidimensional Anxiety Theory (MAT)

In contrast to Hanin's approach that suggests an appropriate emotional zone exists for optimal performance (e.g., high levels of anxiety can have positive performance effects), multidimensional anxiety theory (MAT; Martens, Burton, et al., 1990) describes the relationship between the specific components of the competitive state anxiety response and performance. While self-confidence is predicted to exhibit a positive linear association with performance and somatic anxiety a quadratic or inverted-U relationship (i.e., performance increases up to a given level of symptom intensity), cognitive anxiety is suggested to exhibit a negative linear relationship with performance. Burton's (1998) review of the relationship between the separate components of anxiety and performance indicated that of the sixteen studies examined, only two strongly supported the theoretical predictions (i.e., Burton, 1988; Taylor, 1987); six provided moderate or partial support (i.e., Barnes, Sime, Dienstbeir, and Plake, 1986; Gould et al., 1987; Jones and Cale, 1989; Krane, Williams, and Feltz, 1992; Maynard and Cotton, 1993; Williams and Krane, 1993); and eight provided weak support that was unable to demonstrate any anxiety-performance relationship (i.e., Caruso et al., 1990; Gould et al., 1984; Hammermeister and Burton, 1995; Karteroliotos and Gill, 1987; Martin and Gill, 1991; Maynard and Howe, 1987; Maynard, Smith, et al., 1995; McAuley, 1985).

Although MAT provides some indication of the positive influence that somatic anxiety (up to moderate levels) and self-confidence can have upon performance, it hypothesizes that elevated levels of cognitive anxiety will invariably be negative and detrimental, with no positive consequences. In addition, the findings from recent meta-analyses suggest weak to moderate relationships between the subcomponents of multidimensional anxiety and performance (e.g., Craft et al., 2003; Woodman and Hardy, 2003) and emphasize both conceptual and methodological shortcomings (see also Burton, 1988, 1998; Jones, 1995a, 1995b; Raglin, 1992; Woodman and Hardy, 2001). One particular criticism is that MAT attempts to explain the additive as opposed to interactive effects of the competitive anxiety subcomponents upon performance (see Hardy, 1990; Woodman and Hardy 2001).

Catastrophe Models

Hardy and colleagues' cusp catastrophe model describes the interactive effects of cognitive anxiety and physiological arousal on performance (Hardy, 1990; Hardy, 1996; Hardy and Parfitt, 1991). Specifically, in contrast to MAT, elevations in cognitive anxiety can have positive performance consequences contingent upon physiological arousal levels. When cognitive anxiety levels are low, variations in physiological arousal invoke relatively small performance effects characterized by a mild inverted-U type reaction. However, under conditions of high cognitive anxiety, increasing levels of physiological arousal, up to a certain point, will lead to positive effects on performance. Continued increases in physiological arousal may, however, eventually result in dramatic performance decrements characterized by a 'catastrophic' drop in performance levels.

Although a growing body of research has examined the predictions of the catastrophe model the findings are equivocal (e.g., Edwards and Hardy, 1996; Edwards, Kingston, Hardy, and Gould, 2002; Hardy, 1996; Hardy and Parfitt, 1991; Hardy et al., 1994; Krane, Joyce, and Rafeld, 1994; Woodman et al., 1997). This has been suggested to be due in part to methodological issues (see Cohen, Pargman, and Tenenbaum, 2003) and the fact that the catastrophe approach is a model and not a theory and cannot therefore explain the mechanisms through which the anxiety components may interact to effect performance (Hardy, 1996; Woodman and Hardy, 2001).

In their reexamination of the cusp catastrophe model, Cohen et al. (2003) failed to find any empirical and theoretical support for the model's predictions. They also highlighted the need to consider more sophisticated multidimensional approaches and account for potential mediating variables such as self-confidence, effort, coping and other self-regulatory mechanisms. The five-dimensional butterfly model (Hardy and Parfitt, 1991), incorporating self-confidence and task complexity, would appear to be such a model to assist in understanding how high cognitive anxiety levels may lead to positive performance effects. While no direct test of the butterfly model has as yet been conducted Hardy, Woodman, and Carrington's (2004) preliminary investigation has found some support for the role of self-confidence in such a catastrophe framework.

Processing Efficiency Theory

A further theoretical approach to explain the notion that high anxious individuals may sometimes perform better than their low anxious counterparts is processing efficiency theory (PET; Eysenck and Calvo, 1992). Based upon Eysenck's (1986) work in the field of cognitive psychology, the experience of high anxiety symptoms is suggested to lead to positive performance consequences (cf. Hardy 1997). Eysenck (1992) purported that cognitive anxiety served two principal functions. Firstly, it consumed some of an individual's attentional capacity for the task, effectively reducing working memory capacity due to task irrelevant cognitive activity or worry, thereby impairing processing efficiency. Secondly, cognitive anxiety or worry also signals the importance of the task to the individual and may lead to an increased investment in the task if a below par performance is perceived. This reduction in effective capacity can be countered by an increased effort (Eysenck, 1986) and while processing efficiency is impaired, performance effectiveness may therefore be maintained or even enhanced under conditions of high anxiety but at the expense of utilizing a greater proportion of the available resources. Preliminary research has supported the application of PET in sport psychology (see Murray and Janelle, 2003; Williams, Vickers, and Rodrigues, 2002), particularly in those sports that tax working memory (cf. Woodman and Hardy, 2001).

PRACTICAL IMPLICATIONS

This section will focus upon the practical implications that emanate from the literature that has examined the positive aspects of competitive anxiety and in particular, the recent emphasis upon directional interpretations associated with the symptom response. Traditionally, stress management strategies have adopted the matching hypothesis (Davidson and Schwartz, 1976) to align individual treatments to specific problems (i.e., cognitive, somatic) via mental skill packages aimed at symptom reduction (e.g., Burton, 1989; Maynard and Cotton, 1993; Prapavessis, Grove, McNair, and Cable, 1992). However, the recent investigation of other anxiety dimensions, such as frequency and direction, has altered how applied sport psychologists practice their profession. Here we discuss two significant practical aspects relating to the type (i.e., approaches to help the performer appraise symptoms in a positive way) and timing (i.e., when these symptoms occur) of stress management interventions.

Type of Stress Management Intervention

When tailoring interventions to deal with the effects of competitive stress, practitioners should consider the numerous personal and situational variables that have been identified to moderate the competitive anxiety response. For example, while support has been found for the efficacy of psychological strategies (e.g., relaxation techniques) in reducing competitive anxiety intensity and debilitating interpretations of associated symptoms (e.g., Hale and Whitehouse, 1998; Maynard, Hemmings, et al., 1995; Maynard, Smith, et al., 1995) such methods may not be appropriate for the activation and arousal demands of certain sports. In particular, the reduction of anxiety intensity may decrease the performer's activation state, and subsequent mental and physical readiness for competition. Indeed, it may not be possible, or even desirable, to reduce such symptoms via stress management techniques due to the relative high levels of activation states required for task performance (Hanton and Jones, 1999a, 1999b; Hanton et al., 2000; Hanton, Wadey, and Connaughton, 2005; Mellalieu et al., 2004). In these circumstances practitioners should attempt to initiate a cognitive strategy that restructures negative interpretations of competitive state anxiety, rather than reducing symptom intensity *per se*. Performers may need to reduce symptom intensity, restructure cognitions, and then reactivate to appropriate levels, particularly if individuals possess insufficient confidence to protect against negative interpretations of symptoms. Such a strategy may be relevant for nonelite athletes who consistently report lower self-confidence levels and debilitating symptom interpretations when compared to their elite counterparts (Fletcher and Hanton, 2001; Hanton and Jones, 1999b; Jones et al., 1994). Elite performers who are debilitators may however be better advised to implement some cognitive restructuring techniques using psychological skills and strategies to interpret their anxiety as facilitative to performance including a combination of goal setting, self-talk, and imagery (Hale and Whitehouse, 1998; Hanton and Jones, 1999a, 1999b; Hanton, Wadey, et al., 2005; Jones and Hanton, 1996).

A final practical implication regarding the type of strategy utilized arises from the consistent finding in the individual difference literature that facilitators of symptoms associated with the anxiety response report greater levels of self-confidence than debilitators (cf. Hanton, Mellalieu, et al., 2004). Above all other individual difference variables self-confidence may therefore be the most significant factor in discriminating how athletes manage and interpret stressful situations (Hardy et al., 1996). Indeed, recent meta-analyses by Hardy and Woodman (2003) and Craft et al. (2003) have reported that self-confidence displays the strongest and most consistent relationship with performance over and above the intensity of competitive anxiety symptoms experienced.

The nature by which athletes use self-confidence to manage stress was identified in Hanton, Mellalieu et al.'s (2004) qualitative investigation of the relationship between self-confidence and competitive anxiety intensity and symptom interpretation. In this study, elite performers reported using cognitive confidence management strategies including mental rehearsal, thought stopping, and positive self-talk to protect against debilitating interpretations of competitive anxiety. The performers also highlighted that the specific antecedents of self-efficacy, in particular, images of enactive mastery, were utilized when employing cognitive confidence enhancement strategies. Hanton, Mellalieu et al.'s (2004) findings suggest that practitioners should focus upon developing confidence protection strategies that build robust perceptions of the athlete's enactive mastery or performance accomplishments, as they appear to have the most salient influence upon self-confidence symptoms and protection against anxiety debilitation. In conjunction with the use of mental imagery, individual-specific mental skill packages should therefore be developed that incorporate other forms of efficacy enhancement. These may include forms of verbal persuasion such as positive self-talk or external encouragement from the coach or significant others.

Timing of Stress Management Intervention

When considering suitable stress management interventions practitioners also need to account for the temporal nature of the stress response from both a macro and micro perspective. At a macro level we can consider the temporal nature of how performers' responses change across their career, while at a micro level we can explore the temporal patterning of the precompetitive response in the build up to a specific event or competition.

One example of the study of temporal responses at a macro level is Hanton and Jones's (1999a) investigation of the cognitive skills and strategies underlying elite swimmers' interpretations of prerace thoughts and feelings, from early experiences through to their current status. In their study the authors identified that the development of positive perceptions of prerace symptoms occurred via natural experiences and various educational methods. Specifically, the swimmers reported that at an early age they were told prerace nerves could be positive and subsequently, with experience, they began to interpret their symptoms in a facilitating manner towards performance. The implications of these findings are that at an early stage in their careers athletes need to be educated that emotions and thoughts and feelings experienced in the precompetition period as unpleasant or discomforting may not necessarily be debilitative or harmful to competition. Consequently they should be taught the key psychological skills, such as the use of goal setting, self-talk, and imagery, as part of the mental preparation element of their prerace routine to enable effective stress management (Hanton and Jones, 1999a).

At a micro-level, several studies have identified that the patterns of change in the cognitive labeling of affective states in the precompetition period may be as significant as the type and intensity of feeling reported by an athlete (e.g., Hanton, Thomas, et al., 2004; Mellalieu et al., 2003; Thomas et al., 2004). For the practitioner these findings suggest that a detailed assessment of an athlete's precompetitive temporal patterning state is required. This will allow the implementation of a series of carefully designed cognitive intervention strategies to manage not only the intensity but also the frequency and direction of the performers' thoughts and feelings across a temporal range beyond that of the traditional hour before competition. One such approach was adopted by Hanton and Jones (1999b) whose multi-modal intervention with competitive swimmers consisted of teaching the psychological skills of goal setting, imagery and self-talk in order to change interpretations of symptoms associated with anxiety from debilitative to facilitative in the pre-race phase over the course of a competitive season.

FUTURE DIRECTIONS

In light of the recent the body of literature that has investigated the positive consequence of the anxiety response upon performance and the study of the cognitive and motivational processes underpinning this relationship several areas are apparent for further study. These include the conceptualization and measurement of competitive stress, the study of existing and additional moderators of symptom interpretation, and the integration of theoretical approaches to explain the anxiety-performance relationship.

Conceptualization and Measurement

The conceptual issues outlined briefly in this chapter and discussed in detail by Fletcher et al. (this volume) reveal a number of important implications for future research. First, the competitive stress process should be viewed as a dynamic rather than a static event (Lazarus, 1999). Methods and instruments need to be designed to assess the overall phenomenon and incorporate the competitive stressor, affective response, coping strategy, and subsequent behavior (Cerin et al., 2000). These may include full and single item psychometric measures, interviews, experience sampling methods (ESM), and possible behavioral assessment techniques. Although such procedures are common in the applied and professional practice literature, comparison of one method to the other or several methods collectively, have not specifically been examined. Recent advancements have been made towards the use of such measures through the adoption of short form and in-event assessment (Cerin et al., 2001; Eubank and Collins, 2000; Thomas et al., 2002), and retrospective recall (Tenenbaum, Lloyd, Petty, and Hanin, 2002; Wilson, Raglin, and Harger, 2000).

Recent research examining the competitive stress process also suggests that anxiety alone accounts for little variance in performance when compared to the 'recipe of emotions' that constitute the broader affective precompetitive response (Cerin, 2003; Gould and Udry, 1994; Robazza, this volume). Performers not only appear to differ in the type of affective state experienced but also in the labeling of that response towards performance (Fletcher et al., this volume; Hanton and Mellalieu, in press; Jones and Hanton, 2001; Mellalieu et al., 2004). Rather than focusing exclusively on the anxiety component of the stress process future studies should consider designs that incorporate the idiosyncratic nature of mental states (Hanin, 1997, 2000) and the range of cognitive, affective, and behavioral experiences that have been identified in the lead up to competition. One example is Cerin's (2004) recent multilevel mixed idiographic/nomothetic interactional study of the intensity and direction of competition anxiety and affect in the week leading up to competition in Tae Kwon Do practitioners. Cerin considered the interaction of both personal (positive and negative affect) and situational factors (temporal proximity) in moderating the relationship with anxiety direction, affective responses and proximity to competition. The adoption of such designs in future will allow researchers to identify and explain both the intra- and inter-individual differences that may occur in the competitive stress process.

Individual Differences

A further line of research into the study of competitive anxiety is to continue to examine the individual difference factors that predict debilitated and facilitated symptom interpretations in performers. In our earlier section we summarized the findings and key implications from these individual differences and in this section we highlight three potential lines of enquiry emphasized by several of these authors in relation to the study of perceived control, psychological skills usage, and the development of competitive experience respectively. We then draw attention to some additional situation and personal variables that are also considered worthy of future investigation.

Although the notion of control is central to Jones's (1995a) model of debilitative and facilitative anxiety and while behavioral, affective, and physiological consequences are suggested to be influenced as a function of locus of control beliefs, little empirical evidence exists regarding the direct relationship between control perceptions and athletic performance (Ntoumanis and Jones, 1998). Several qualitative and empirical investigations have provided indirect support for the model (e.g., Hanton and Connaughton, 2002; Hanton, Mellalieu, et al., 2004; Hanton, O'Brien, et al., 2003) but few studies have assessed its relationship with the stress response directly and with contemporary measurement procedures (cf. Fink, Johnson, and Porter, 2001; Ntoumanis and Jones, 1998). The underlying mechanism for this process, particularly how symptoms are appraised in a positive manner towards performance, presents an area worthy of further consideration. Ntoumanis and Jones (1998) also recommended exploring the individual difference factors which can mediate the adoption of a particular locus of control.

Another area worthy of attention is the psychological skills used by performers to maintain a degree of control over the competitive stressor. Fletcher and Hanton (2001) suggested that future research in this area should examine the effectiveness of different interventions in eliciting positive symptom interpretations and performance improvements, particularly the efficacy of one strategy versus another, or the effects of combining different strategies to form a psychological skills package. They also highlighted the need to identify which psychological skill, or their combination, most contributes to the affective response in conditions of competitive stress.

A further important avenue to pursue is how performers learn to develop the necessary psychological skills in order view their precompetitive symptoms experienced in a positive manner towards performance. Hanton and Jones's (1999a) qualitative investigation of elite swimmers suggested that psychological skills were developed via a combination of natural learning experiences and various educational methods. The authors recommended that future investigation was needed to corroborate and detail these learning experiences across other sport type samples and classifications. One such study by Mellalieu et al. (2004), for example, has found that differences existed in symptom interpretation in several sports as function of the level of experience. Hanton and Jones (1999a) have also highlighted the need to identify the time scale and amount of competitive experience required in order for a performer to develop the necessary psychological skills to interpret cognitive and somatic symptoms as facilitative even in the most stressful of environments.

In addition to the investigation of existing moderators of the competitive stress response the study of other potential factors is also worthy of attention. With regard to situational factors, the wider effects of psychosocial factors upon the competitive stress response would seem to be a fruitful area of inquiry. While there has been considerable development in the understanding of the constructs that contribute to the development of positive dynamics in teams such as cohesion (see Loughead and Hardy, this volume) and collective efficacy (cf. Feltz and Lirgg, 1998; Spink, 1990), there has been little or no study of the potential negative effects of competitive stress. For example, Hanin (1986) has discussed the notion of inter-group anxiety among teams and groups, while negative relationships have been observed between perceptions of group dynamics and intra-individual competitive anxiety responses (Beauchamp, Bray, Eys, and Carron, 2003; Eys et al., 2003).

As well as the examination of situational factors, there is also a need to consider the specific effects of personal moderators upon the competitive stress response. Preliminary investigations of resilience traits such as self-confidence, hardiness, extraversion, and positive affectivity would appear to suggest differences in coping behaviors and stress responses (e.g., Cerin, 2004; Hanton, Evans, et al., 2003; Hanton and Mellalieu, in press). The study of these and other traits such as determination, optimism and enthusiasm (cf. Carver and Scheier, 1999) that represent some form of psychological resilience or mental toughness may allow researchers greater comprehension of athletes' psyche. Evidence from the personality literature in a variety of organizational and social environments also suggests powerful predictive potential of general theories of personality, such as the big five (McCrae and Costa, 1996). Given these recent advancements in the assessment of dispositional traits (cf. McCrae and Costa, 1997) clear potential exists for a re-examination of the role of personality in sport. There is also a need to consider the effects of individuals with repressive coping styles on the accuracy of self-report anxiety questionnaires (cf. Jerome and Williams, 2000; Jones et al., 1994). Indeed, a failure to account for individuals who deny having elevated levels of symptom intensity may result in cases of individuals being denoted as low-anxious on self-report items when in fact they are actually repressors.

Theoretical Integration

While this chapter has alluded to several theories and models that purport to explain the positive effects of anxiety in relation to competition, such as ZOF, MAT, catastrophe models, and PET, there is a need to incorporate these existing conceptual approaches to provide an integrated explanation for the anxiety-performance relationship. Davis and Cox (2002) for example, combined the assessment of ZOF and anxiety direction in their investigation of anxiety-performance relationships in competitive swimmers, while other researchers (e.g., Edwards et al., 2002; Woodman and Hardy, 2001) have highlighted the potential shared variability in catastrophe models and PET and between specific theories such as the conscious processing hypothesis (Masters, 1992) and the theory of ironic processes of mental control (cf. Wegner, 1997) to explain the potential positive consequences of anxiety-upon performance.

Further progress must also be made in relation to the mechanisms by which anxiety and related symptoms (see Robazza, this volume) actually influence performance (cf. Janelle, 2002; Jones, 2004; Mellalieu, 2003). For example, in acknowledging existing stress-performance theories Janelle (2002) pointed out that there is little empirical evidence to document the mechanisms that underlie the proposed performance changes. Existing theories merely purport attentional mechanisms to be responsible for how fluctuations in emotional, cognitive and physiological states might manifest themselves in performance variability. Janelle (2002) has provided some progress to overcome these and other limitations in order to account for the variation in athletic performance through his description of the relationship between anxiety, arousal and visual attention.

In attempting to explain anxiety effects on performance, there is also a need to examine the influence upon each of the individual components of performance (Parfitt et al., 1995; Parfitt and Hardy, 1993). Parfitt and Pates's (1999) adoption of a broadband approach to the investigation of the anxiety performance relationship (i.e., the effect of one stressor on several sub-components of performance) has identified that different competitive state responses (cognitive and somatic anxiety, self-confidence) exert differential effects upon aspects of actual performance (anaerobic power, working memory). The adoption of an interdisciplinary approach may be particularly useful here, for example, Collins and colleagues (Collins, Jones, Fairweather, Doolan, and Preistly, 2001) have used movement kinematics to evaluate changes in movement patterns associated with concurrent changes in anxiety levels. Among their findings support was found for the notion that one of the mechanisms via which anxiety influences performance was through the interaction of task constraints and individual movement control parameters, which lead to consequent changes in action. Combining these and other interdisciplinary methods provides an interesting avenue and challenge for researchers to assess the apparent complex explanations for the mechanisms by which the competitive stress response influences performance.

CONCLUDING REMARKS

This review is the first to consider in detail the beneficial side to competitive anxiety in sport, and the positive consequences associated with the competitive stress response as opposed to the traditional focus on the potentially negative effects on performance. Specifically, we explored the mechanisms by which such a negative emotional response might have a positive effect on a performer's psychological state and subsequent athletic performance. Based on the literature reviewed here, and the predictions of the meta-model of stress, emotions and performance (Fletcher and Fletcher, 2005; Fletcher et al., this volume), we outline five statements that summarize our current position regarding competitive anxiety and sport performance:

1. Competitive stressors are not inherently positive or negative.
2. Performers' appraise these stressors resulting in positive and/or negative responses.
3. Competitive anxiety is an example of a specific negative emotional response.
4. Cognitive and somatic symptoms of competitive anxiety (together with other competitive stress-related emotions) are further appraised as facilitative or debilitative to performance, resulting in positive or negative feeling states.
5. These feeling states can have a positive or negative effect on performance.

We hope these statements serve to provide a clear basis for future conceptualization of the competitive stress process, and the relationship between anxiety and athletic performance.

ACKNOWLEDGEMENTS

This review is part of an ongoing program of work currently being undertaken by the authors addressing conceptual and measurement issues within the context of stress and anxiety in sport. We would like to thank the reviewers for their excellent contributions to this chapter.

REFERENCES

Albrecht, R. R., and Feltz, D. L. (1987). Generality and specificity of attention related to competitive anxiety and sport performance. *Journal of Sport Psychology, 9,* 231-248.

Alpert, R., and Haber, N. N. (1960). Anxiety in academic achievement situations. *Journal of Abnormal Social Psychology, 61,* 207-215.

Annesi, J. J. (1998). Applications of the individual zones of optimal functioning model for the multimodal treatment of precompetitive anxiety. *The Sport Psychologist, 12,* 300-316.

Anshel, M. H. (1990). Toward a validation of a model for coping with acute stress in sport. *International Journal of Sport Psychology, 21,* 58-83.

Anshel, M. H., and Wells, B. (2000). Personal and situational variables that describe coping with acute stress in competitive sport. *Journal of Social Psychology, 140,* 434-450.

Apter, M. J. (1982). *The experience of motivation: The theory of psychological reversals.* New York: Academic Press.

Apter, M. J. (1989). *Reversal theory: Motivation, emotion and personality.* London: Routledge.

Bandura, A. (1977). Self-efficacy: Towards a unifying theory of behavioral change. *Psychological Review, 84*, 191-215.

Barnes, M. W., Sime, W., Dienstbier, R., and Plake, B. (1986). A test construct of the CSAI-2 questionnaire on male elite college swimmers. *International Journal of Sport Psychology, 17*, 364-374.

Beauchamp, M. R., Bray, S. R., Eys, M. A., and Carron, A. V. (2003). The effect of role ambiguity on competitive state anxiety. *Journal of Sport and Exercise Psychology, 25,* 77-92.

Beck, A. T. (1976). *Cognitive therapy and the emotional disorders.* Madison, CT: International Universities Press.

Beehr, T. A. (1998). An organizational psychology meta-model of occupational stress. In C. Cooper (Ed.), *Theories of organizational stress* (pp. 6-27). New York: Oxford University Press.

Beehr, T. A., and Franz, T. M. (1987). The current debate about the meaning of job stress. In J. M. Ivancevich and D. C. Ganster (Eds.), *Job stress: From theory to suggestion* (pp. 5-18). New York: Haworth Press.

Biddle, S. J. H. (1997). Current tends in sport and exercise psychology research. *The Psychologist, 46*, 63-69.

Borkovec, T. D. (1976). Physiological and cognitive processes in the regulation of anxiety. In G. E. Schwartz and D. Shapiro (Eds.), *Consciousness and self-regulation: Advances in research* (Vol. 1, pp. 261-312). New York: Plenum.

Burton, D. (1988). Do anxious swimmers swim slower? Re-examining the elusive anxiety performance relationship. *Journal of Sport and Exercise Psychology, 10,* 45-61.

Burton, D. (1989). Winning isn't everything: Examining the impact of performance goals on collegiate swimmers' cognitions and performance. *The Sport Psychologist, 3,* 105-132.

Burton, D. (1990). Multimodal stress management in sport: Current status and future directions. In G. Jones and L. Hardy (Eds.), *Stress and performance in sport* (pp. 171-201). Chichester, UK: Wiley.

Burton, D. (1998). Measuring competitive state anxiety. In J. L. Duda (Ed.), *Advances in sport and exercise psychology measurement* (pp. 129-148). Morgantown, WV: Fitness Information Technology Inc.

Burton, D., and Naylor, S. (1997). Is anxiety really facilitative? Reaction to the myth that cognitive anxiety always impairs performance. *Journal of Applied Sport Psychology, 9,* 295-302.

Butt, J., Weinberg, R., and Horn, T. (2003). The intensity and directional interpretation of anxiety: Fluctuations throughout competition and relationship to performance. *The Sport Psychologist, 17,* 35-54.

Caruso, C. M., Dzewaltowski, D. A., Gill, D. L., and McElroy, M. A. (1990). Psychological and physiological changes in competitive state anxiety during non-competition and competitive success and failure. *Journal of Exercise Physiology, 12,* 6-20.

Carver, C. S., and Scheier, M. F. (1986). Functional and dysfunctional approaches to anxiety: The interaction between expectancies and self-focused attention. In R. Schwarzer (Ed.), *Self-related cognitions in anxiety and motivation* (pp. 111-146). Hillsdale, New Jersey: Erlbaum.

Carver, C. S., and Scheier, M. F. (1988). A control-process perspective on anxiety. *Anxiety Research, 1,* 17-22.

Carver, C. S., and Scheier, M. F. (1998). *On the self-regulation of behavior*. New York: Cambridge University Press.

Carver, C. S., and Scheier, M. F. (1999). Stress, coping, and self-regulatory processes. In L. A. Pervin and O. P. John (Eds.), *Handbook of personality: Theory and research* (2nd Ed., pp. 553-575). New York: Guilford Press.

Carver, C. S., Scheier, M. F., and Weintraub, J. K. (1989). Assessing coping strategies: A theoretically based approach. *Journal of Personality and Social Psychology, 56,* 267-283.

Cattell, R. B. (1957). *The IPAT Anxiety Scale*. Champaign, IL: Institute for Personality and Ability Testing.

Cerin, E. (2003). Anxiety versus fundamental emotions as predictors of perceived functionality of precompetitive emotional states, threat, and challenge in individual sports. *Journal of Applied Sport Psychology, 15,* 223-238.

Cerin, E. (2004). Predictors of competitive anxiety direction in male Tae Kwon Do practitioners: A multilevel mixed idiographic/nomothetic interactional approach. *Psychology of Sport and Exercise, 5,* 497-516.

Cerin, E., Szabo, A., Hunt, N., and Williams, C. (2000). Temporal patterning of competitive emotions: A critical review. *Journal of Sports Sciences, 18,* 605-626.

Cerin, E., Szabo, A., and Williams, C. (2001). Is the experience sampling method (ESM) appropriate for pre-competitive emotions? *Psychology of Sport and Exercise, 2,* 27-45.

Cohen, A., Pargman, D., and Tenenbaum, G. (2003). Critical elaboration and empirical investigation of the Cusp catastrophe model. *Journal of Applied Sport Psychology, 15,* 144-159.

Collins, D., Jones, B., Fairweather, M., Doolan, S., and Preistley, N. (2001). Examining anxiety associated changes in movement patterns. *International Journal of Sport Psychology, 31,* 223-242.

Cox, R. H., Martens, M. P., and Russell, W. D. (2003). Measuring anxiety in athletics: the revised Competitive State Anxiety Inventory-2. *Journal of Sport and Exercise Psychology, 25,* 519-533.

Cox, R. H, Russell, W. D., and Robb, M. (1998). Development of a CSAI-2 short form for assessing competitive state anxiety during and immediately prior to competition. *Journal of Sport Behavior, 21,* 30-40.

Cox, R. H, Russell, W. D., and Robb, M. (1999). Comparative concurrent validity of the MRF-L and ARS competitive state anxiety rating scales for volleyball and basketball. *Journal of Sport Behavior, 22,* 310-320.

Craft, L. L., Magyar, M., Becker, B. J., and Feltz, D. L. (2003). The relationship between competitive state anxiety inventory-2 and sport performance: A meta-analysis. *Journal of Sport and Exercise Psychology, 25,* 44-65.

Davids, K., and Gill, A. (1995). Multidimensional state anxiety prior to different levels of sport competition: Some problems with simulation tasks. *International Journal of Sport Psychology, 26,* 359-382.

Davidson, R. J. (1978). Specificity and patterning in biobehavioral systems. *American Psychologist, 33,* 430-436.

Davidson, R. J., and Schwartz, G. E. (1976). The psychobiology of relaxation and related stress: A multiprocess theory. In D. I. Mostofsky (Ed.), *Behavioral control and modification of physiological activity* (pp. 399-442). Englewood Cliffs, NJ: Prentice Hall.

Davis, J. E., and Cox, R. H. (2002). Interpreting direction of anxiety within Hanin's Individual Zone of Optimal Functioning. *Journal of Applied Sport Psychology, 14*, 43-52.

Diener, E., Sandvik, E., and Pavot, W. G. (1991). Happiness is the frequency, not the intensity, of positive vs. negative affect. In F. Strack., M. Argyle, and N. Schwarz (Eds.), *Subjective well being: An interdisciplinary perspective* (pp. 119-139). Oxford: Pergamon Press.

Edwards, T. C., and Hardy, L. (1995). Interactive affects of facilitators and debilitators of cognitive and somatic anxiety, self-confidence and performance. *Journal of Sports Sciences, 13*, 28-36.

Edwards, T., Kingston, K., Hardy, L., and Gould, D. (2002). A qualitative analysis of catastrophic performances and associated thoughts, feelings, and emotions. *The Sport Psychologist, 16*, 1-19.

Eubank, M., and Collins, D. (2000). Coping with pre- and in-event fluctuations in competitive state anxiety: A longitudinal approach. *Journal of Sports Sciences, 18,* 121-131.

Eubank, M., Collins, D., and Smith, N. (2002). Anxiety and ambiguity: It's all open to interpretation. *Journal of Sport and Exercise Psychology, 24,* 239-253.

Eubank, M. R., Smith, N. C., and Smethhurst, C. J. (1995). Intensity and direction of multidimensional competitive state anxiety: Relationships to performance in racket sports. *Journal of Sports Sciences, 13*, 30-35.

Eys, M. A., Carron, A. V., Beauchamp, M. R., and Bray, S. R. (2003). Role ambiguity in sport teams. *Journal of Sport and Exercise Psychology, 25,* 534-550.

Eys, M. A., Hardy, J., Carron, A. V., and Beauchamp, M. R. (2003). The relationship between task cohesion and competitive state anxiety. *Journal of Sport and Exercise Psychology, 25,* 66-76.

Eysenck, M. W. (1992). *Anxiety: The cognitive perspective.* London: Lawrence Erlbaum.

Eysenck, M. W. (1997). *Anxiety and cognitions: A unified theory.* Hove, UK: Psychology Press.

Eysenck, M. W., and Calvo, M. G. (1992). Anxiety and performance: The processing efficiency theory. *Cognition and Emotion, 6*, 409-434.

Feltz, D. L., and Lirgg, C. D. (1998). Perceived team and player efficacy in hockey. *Journal of Applied Psychology, 83*, 557-564.

Fink, D., Johnson, M. L., Kennedy, C., and Porter, C (2001). Correlation between state anxiety and locus of control. *Research Quarterly for Exercise and Sport, 72*, A-87.

Fletcher, D., and Fletcher, J. (2005). A meta-model of stress, emotions and performance: Conceptual foundations, theoretical framework, and research directions [Abstract]. *Journal of Sports Sciences, 23,* 157-158.

Fletcher, D., and Hanton, S. (2001). The relationship between psychological skills usage and competitive anxiety responses. *Psychology of Sport and Exercise, 2*, 89-101.

Fletcher, D., Hanton, S., and Mellalieu, S. D. (this volume). An organizational stress review: Conceptual and theoretical issues in competitive sport. In S. Hanton and S. D. Mellalieu (Eds.), *Literature reviews in sport psychology.* Hauppauge, NY: Nova Science.

Folkman, S., and Lazarus, R. S. (1980). An analysis of coping in middle-aged community sample. *Journal of Health and Social Behavior, 21,* 219-239.

Gill, D. L. (1994). A sport and exercise psychology perspective on stress. *Quest, 46*, 20-27.

Gould, D., Greenleaf, C., and Krane, V. (2002). Arousal-anxiety and sport behavior. In T. Horn (Ed.), *Advances in sport psychology* (pp. 207-241). Champaign, IL: Human Kinetics.

Gould, D., Jackson, S. A., and Finch, L. M. (1993a). Sources of stress in national champion figure skaters. *Journal of Sport and Exercise Psychology, 15*, 134-159.

Gould, D., Jackson, S. A., and Finch, L. M (1993b). Life at the top. The experiences of US national champion figure skaters. *The Sport Psychologist, 7, 354-374.*

Gould, D., Petlichkoff, L., Simons, J., and Vevera, M. (1987). Relationships between Competitive State Anxiety Inventory-2 sub-scales scores and pistol shooting performance. *Journal of Sport Psychology, 9*, 33-42.

Gould, D., Petlichoff, L., and Weinberg, R. S. (1984). Antecedents of temporal changes in and relationships between CSAI-2 subcomponents. *Journal of Sport Psychology, 6, 289-304.*

Gould, D., and Tuffey, S. (1996). Zones of optimal functioning: A review and critique. *Anxiety, Stress and Coping, 9*, 53-68.

Gould, D., Tuffey, S., Hardy, L., and Lochbaum, M. (1993). Multidimensional state anxiety and middle distance running performance: An exploratory examination of Hanin's (1980) zone of optimal functioning hypothesis. *Journal of Applied Sport Psychology, 5*, 85-94.

Gould, D., and Udry, E. (1994). Psychological skills for enhancing performance: Arousal regulation strategies. *Medicine and Science in Sports and Exercise, 26*, 478-485.

Hale, B. D., and Whitehouse, A. (1998). The effects of imagery-manipulated appraisal on intensity and direction of competitive anxiety. *The Sport Psychologist, 12*, 40-51.

Hall, H. K., Kerr, A. W., and Matthews, J. (1998). Precompetitive anxiety in sport: The contribution of achievement goals and perfectionism. *Journal of Sport and Exercise Psychology, 20*, 194-217.

Hammermeister, J., and Burton, D. (1995). Anxiety and the Ironman: Investigating the antecedents and consequences of endurance athletes' state anxiety. *The Sport Psychologist, 9*, 29-40.

Hammermeister, J., and Burton, D. (2001). Stress, appraisal, and coping revisited: Examining the antecedents of competitive state anxiety with endurance athletes. *The Sport Psychologist, 15*, 66-90.

Hanin, Y. L. (1980). A cognitive model of anxiety in sports. In W.F. Straub (Ed.), *Sport psychology: An analysis of athlete behavior* (pp. 236-249). Ithica. NY: Movement Publications.

Hanin, Y. L. (1986). State-trait anxiety research on sports in the USSR. In C. D. Spielberger and R. Diaz-Guerrero (Eds.), *Cross cultural anxiety* (Vol. 3, pp. 45-64). Washington, DC: Hemisphere.

Hanin, Y. L. (1989). Interpersonal and intragroup anxiety in sports. In D. Hackfort and C. D. Spielberger (Eds.), *Anxiety in sports: An international perspective* (pp. 19-28). Washington, DC: Hemisphere.

Hanton, S., and Connaughton, D. (2002). Perceived control of anxiety and its relationship with self-confidence and performance: A qualitative explanation. *Research Quarterly for Exercise and Sport, 73,* 87-97.

Hanton, S., Cropley, B., Mellalieu, S. D., Neil, R., & Miles, A. (in press). Experience in sport and its relationship with competitive anxiety. *International Journal of Sport and Exercise Psychology.*

Hanton, S., Evans, L., and Neil, R. (2003). Hardiness and the competitive trait anxiety response. *Anxiety, Stress, and Coping, 16,* 167-184.

Hanton, S., Fletcher, D., and Coughlan, G. (2005). Stress in elite sport performers: A comparative study of competitive and organizational stressors. *Journal of Sports Sciences, 10,* 1129-1141.

Hanton, S., and Jones, G. (1995). Antecedents of multidimensional state anxiety in elite competitive swimmers. *International Journal of Sport Psychology, 26,* 512-523.

Hanton, S., and Jones, G. (1997). Antecedents of competitive state anxiety as a function of skill level. *Psychological Reports, 81,* 1139-1147.

Hanton, S., and Jones, G. (1999a). The acquisition and development of cognitive skills and strategies. I: Making the butterflies fly in formation. *The Sport Psychologist, 13,* 1-21.

Hanton, S., and Jones, G. (1999b). The effects of a multimodal intervention program on performers. II: Training the butterflies fly in formation. *The Sport Psychologist, 13,* 22-41.

Hanton, S., Jones, G., and Mullen, R. (2000). Intensity and direction of competitive anxiety as interpreted by rugby players and rifle shooters. *Perceptual and Motor Skills, 90,* 513-521.

Hanton, S., and Mellalieu, S. D. (in press). Facilitative anxiety: Myth or mislabeled? In. F. Columbus (Ed.), *Advances in Psychology Research.* Hauppauge, NY: Nova Science.

Hanton, S., Mellalieu, S. D., and Hall, R. (2002). Re-examining the competitive anxiety trait-state relationship. *Personality and Individual Differences, 33,* 1125-1136.

Hanton, S., Mellalieu, S. D., and Hall, R. (2004). Self-confidence and anxiety interpretation: A qualitative investigation. *Psychology of Sport and Exercise, 5,* 379-521.

Hanton, S., Mellalieu, S. D., and Young, S. (2002). A qualitative investigation into temporal patterning of the precompetitive anxiety response and its effects on performance. *Journal of Sports Sciences, 20,* 911-928.

Hanton, S., O'Brien, M., and Mellalieu, S. D. (2003). Individual differences, perceived control and competitive trait anxiety. *Journal of Sport Behavior, 26,* 39-55.

Hanton, S., Thomas, O., and Maynard, I. (2004). Competitive anxiety responses in the week leading up to competition: the role of intensity, direction and frequency dimensions. *Psychology of Sport and Exercise, 15,* 169-181.

Hanton, S., Wadey, R., & Connaughton, D. (2005). Debilitative interpretations of competitive anxiety: A qualitative examination of elite performers. *European Journal of Sport Science, 5,* 123-136.

Hardy, L. (1990). A catastrophe model of anxiety and performance. In J. G. Jones and L. Hardy (Eds.), *Stress and performance in sport* (pp. 81-106). Chichester, UK: Wiley.

Hardy, L. (1996). Testing the predictions of the cusp catastrophe model of anxiety and performance. *The Sport Psychologist, 10,* 140-156.

Hardy, L. (1997). The Coleman Roberts Griffiths address: Three myths about applied consultancy work. *Journal of Applied Sport Psychology, 9,* 277-294.

Hardy, L. (1998). Responses to the reactants on three myths in applied consultancy work. *Journal of Applied Sport Psychology, 10,* 212-219.

Hardy, L., Jones, G., and Gould, D. (1996). *Understanding psychological preparation for sport: Theory and practice of elite performers.* Chichester, England: Wiley.

Hardy, L., and Parfitt, G. (1991). A catastrophe model of anxiety and performance. *British Journal of Psychology, 82,* 163-178.

Hardy, L., Parfitt, G., and Pates, J. (1994). Performance catastrophes in sport: A test of the hysteresis hypothesis. *Journal of Sports Sciences, 12,* 327-334.

Hardy, L., Woodman, T., and Carrington, S. (2004). Is self-confidence a bias factor in higher-order catastrophe models? An exploratory analysis. *Journal of Sport and Exercise Psychology, 26,* 359-368.

Holt, N. L., and Hogg, J. M. (2002). Perceptions of stress and coping during preparations for the 1999 women's soccer World Cup finals. *The Sport Psychologist, 16,* 251-271.

Iosifidou, P., and Doganis, G. (2001). Confirmatory factor analysis of the Greek version of the Competitive State Anxiety Inventory-2. *International Journal of Sport Psychology, 32,* 400-405.

James, B., and Collins, D. (1997). Self-presentational sources of competitive stress during performance. *Journal of Sport and Exercise Psychology, 19,* 17-35.

Janelle, C. M. (2002). Anxiety, arousal and visual attention: A mechanistic account of performance variability. *Journal of Sports Sciences, 20,* 237-251

Jones, G. (1990). A cognitive perspective on the processes underlying the relationship between stress and performance in sport. In J. G. Jones and L. Hardy (Eds.), *Stress and performance in sport* (pp. 171-201). Chichester, England: Wiley.

Jones, G. (1991). Recent issues in competitive state anxiety research. *The Psychologist, 4,* 152-155.

Jones, G. (1995a). More than just a game: Research developments and issues in competitive state anxiety in sport. *British Journal of Psychology, 86,* 449-478.

Jones, G. (1995b). Competitive anxiety in sport. In S. J. H Biddle (Ed.), *European perspectives on exercise and sport psychology* (pp. 128-153). Champaign, IL, Human Kinetics.

Jones, G., and Cale, A. (1989). Relationships between multidimensional competitive state anxiety and motor subcomponents of performance. *Journal of Sports Sciences, 7,* 129-140.

Jones, G., Hanton, S., and Connaughton, D. (2002). What is this thing called Mental Toughness? An investigation with elite performers. *Journal of Applied Sport Psychology, 14,* 211-224.

Jones, G., and Hanton, S. (1996). Interpretation of anxiety symptoms and goal attainment expectations. *Journal of Sport and Exercise Psychology, 18,* 144-158.

Jones, G., and Hanton, S. (2001). Pre-competition feeling states and directional anxiety interpretations. *Journal of Sports Sciences, 19,* 385-395.

Jones, G., and Hardy, L. (1990). *Stress and performance in sport.* Chichester, England: Wiley.

Jones, G., Hanton, S., and Swain, A. B. J. (1994). Intensity and interpretation of anxiety symptoms in elite and non-elite sports performers. *Personality and Individual Differences, 17,* 657-663.

Jones, G., and Swain, A. B. J. (1992). Intensity and direction dimensions of competitive state anxiety and relationships with competitiveness. *Perceptual and Motor Skills, 74,* 467-472.

Jones, G., and Swain, A. B. J. (1995). Predispositions to experience facilitating and debilitating anxiety in elite and non-elite performers. *The Sport Psychologist, 9,* 201-211.

Jones, G., Swain, A. B. J., and Cale, A. (1990). Antecedents of multidimensional competitive state anxiety and self-confidence in elite intercollegiate middle distance runners. *The Sport Psychologist, 4*, 107-118.

Jones, G., Swain, A. B. J., and Cale, A. (1991). Gender differences in precompetition temporal patterning and antecedents of anxiety and self-confidence. *Journal of Sport and Exercise Psychology, 13*, 1-15.

Jones, G., Swain, A. B. J., and Hardy, L. (1993). Intensity and direction dimensions of competitive state anxiety and relationships with performance. *Journal of Sports Sciences, 11*, 533-542.

Jones, G., Swain, A. B. J., and Harwood, C. (1996). Positive and negative affect as predictors of competitive anxiety. *Personality and Individual Differences, 20*, 109-114.

Jones, K. A., Smith, N. C., and Holmes, P. S. (2004). Anxiety symptom interpretation and performance predictions in high-anxious, low-anxious and repressor sport performers. *Anxiety, Stress and Coping, 17*, 187-199.

Jones, M. V. (2003). Controlling emotions in sport. *The Sport Psychologist, 17*, 471-486.

Jones, M. V., and Uphill, M. (2004). Responses to the Competitive State Anxiety Inventory-2(d) by athletes in anxious and excited scenarios. *Psychology of Sport and Exercise, 5*, 201-212.

Kardum, I. (1999). Affect intensity and frequency: Their relation to mean level and variability of positive and negative affect and Eysenck's personality traits. *Personality and Individual Differences, 26*, 33-47.

Kerr, J. H. (1993). An eclectic approach to psychological interventions in sport: Reversal theory. *The Sport Psychologist, 7*, 400-418.

Kerr, J. H. (1997). *Motivation and emotion in sport: Reversal theory*. Methuen: Psychology Press.

Kingston, K. M, Spray, C. M., and Harwood, C. G. (this volume). Motivation in sport: A goal directed intention approach. In S. Hanton and S. D. Mellalieu (Eds.), *Literature reviews in sport psychology*. Hauppauge, NJ: Nova Science.

Kobasa, S. C. (1979). Stressful life events, personality and health: An inquiry into hardiness. *Journal of Personality and Social Psychology, 42*, 707-717.

Krane, V. (1992). Conceptual and methodological considerations in sport anxiety research from the inverted-U hypothesis to catastrophe theory. *Quest, 44*, 72-87.

Krane, V. (1993). A practical application of the anxiety-athletic performance relationship: Zone of optimal functioning hypothesis. *The Sport Psychologist, 7*, 113-126.

Krane, V. (1994). The mental readiness form as a measure of competitive state anxiety. *The Sport Psychologist, 8*, 189-203.

Krane, V., Joyce, D., and Rafeld, J. (1994). Competitive anxiety, situation criticality and softball performance. *The Sport Psychologist, 8*, 58-72.

Krane, V., and Williams, J. M. (1987). Performance and somatic anxiety, cognitive anxiety and confidence changes prior to competition. *Journal of Sport Behavior, 10*, 47-56.

Krane, V., Williams, J. M., and Feltz, D. (1992). Path analysis examining relationships among cognitive anxiety, somatic anxiety, state confidence, performance expectations, and golf performance. *Journal of Sport Behavior, 15*, 279-295.

Landers, D. M., and Arent, S. M. (2001). Arousal-performance relationships. In J. M. Williams (Ed.), *Applied sport psychology: Personal growth to peak performance* (pp. 206-228). Palo Alto, CA: Mayfield.

Lane, A. M., Sewell, D. F., Terry, P. C., Bartram, D., and Nesti, M. S. (1999). Confirmatory factor analysis of the competitive state anxiety inventory-2. *Journal of Sports Sciences*, *17*, 505-512.

Lane, A. M., Terry, P. C., and Karageorghis, C. (1995). Antecedents of multidimensional competitive state anxiety and self-confidence in duathletes. *Perceptual and Motor Skills*, *80*, 911-919.

Lazarus, R. S. (1981). The stress and coping paradigm. In C. Eisdorfer, D. Cohen, A. Kleinman, and P. Maxim (Eds.), *Models for clinical psychopathology* (pp. 177-214). New York: Spectrum.

Lazarus, R. (1991). *Emotion and adaptation.* New York: Oxford University Press.

Lazarus, R. S. (1999). *Stress and emotion: A new synthesis.* London: Free Association Books.

Lazarus, R. S., and Folkman, S. (1984). *Stress, appraisal and coping.* New York: Erlbaum.

Liebert, R. M., and Morris, L. W. (1967). Cognitive and emotional components of test anxiety: A distinction and some initial data. *Psychological Reports*, *20*, 975-978.

Loughead, T. M., and Hardy, J. (this volume). Team cohesion: From theory to research to team building. In S. Hanton and S. D. Mellalieu, (Eds.), *Literature eviews in sport psychology.* Hauppauge, NJ: Nova Science.

Mahoney, M. J. and Avener, M. (1977). Psychology of the elite athlete: An exploratory study. *Cognitive Therapy and Research*, *1*, 135-141.

Mamassis G., and and Doganis, G. (2004). The effects of a mental training program on juniors pre-competitive anxiety, self-confidence, and tennis performance. *Journal of Applied Sport Psychology, 16*, 118-137.

Mandler, G., and Sarason, S. B. (1952). A study of anxiety and learning. *Journal of Abnormal and Social Psychology*, *47*, 166-173.

Martens, R. (1977). *Sport competition anxiety test.* Champaign, IL: Human Kinetics.

Martens, R., Burton, D., Rivkin, F., and Simon, J. (1980). Reliability and validity of the Competitive State Anxiety Inventory (CSAI). In C. H. Nadeau, W. C. Halliwell, K. M. Newell and G. C. Roberts (Eds.), *Psychology of motor behavior and sport-1979* (pp. 91-99). Champaign, IL: Human Kinetics.

Martens, R., Burton, D., Vealey, R. S., Bump, L., and Smith, D. E. (1990). Development and validation of the Competitive State Anxiety Inventory-2 (CSAI-2). In R. Martens, R. S. Vealey, and D. Burton (Eds.), *Competitive anxiety in sport* (pp. 117-213). Champaign, IL: Human Kinetics.

Martens, R., Vealey, R. S., and Burton, D. (1990). *Competitive anxiety in sport.* Champaign, IL: Human Kinetics.

Martin, J. J., and Gill, D. L. (1991). The relationships among competitive orientation, sport-confidence, self-efficacy, anxiety, and performance. *Journal of Sport and Exercise Psychology*, *13*, 149-159.

Masters, R. S. W. (1992). Knowledge, knerves, and know-how: The role of explicit versus implicit knowledge in the breakdown of a complex motor skill under pressure. *British Journal of Psychology, 83,* 343-358.

Maynard, I. W., and Cotton, P. C. J. (1993). An investigation of two stress management techniques in a field setting. *The Sport Psychologist*, *7*, 375-387.

Maynard, I. W., Hemmings, B., and Warwick-Evans, L. (1995). The effects of a somatic intervention strategy on competitive state anxiety and performance in semi-professional soccer players. *The Sport Psychologist*, *9*, 51-64.

Maynard, I. W., and Howe, B. L. (1987). Interrelations of trait and state anxiety with game performance of rugby players. *Perceptual and Motor Skills, 64,* 599-602.

Maynard, I. W., Smith, M. J., and Warwick-Evans, L. (1995). The effects of a cognitive intervention strategy on competitive state anxiety and performance in semi-professional soccer players. *Journal of Sport and Exercise Psychology, 17,* 428-446.

McAuley, E. (1985). Modeling and self-efficacy: A test of Bandura's model. *Journal of Sport Psychology, 7,* 283-295.

McCrae, R. R., and Costa, P. T., Jr. (1996). Toward a new generation of personality theories: Theoretical contexts for the five factor model. In J. S. Wiggins (Ed.), *The five factor model of personality: Theoretical perspectives* (pp. 51-87). New York: Guilford Press.

McCrae, R. R., and Costa, P. T., Jr. (1997). Personality trait structure as a human universal. *American Psychologist, 52,* 509-516.

Mellalieu, S. D. (2003). Mood matters: But how much? A comment on Lane and Terry (2000). *Journal of Applied Sport Psychology, 15,* 99-114.

Mellalieu, S. D., Hanton, S., and Jones, G. (2003). Emotional labeling and competitive anxiety in preparation and competition. *The Sport Psychologist, 17,* 157-174.

Mellalieu, S. D., Hanton, S., and O'Brien, M. (2004). Intensity and direction dimensions of competitive anxiety as a function of sport type and experience. *Scandinavian Journal of Science and Medicine in Sport, 14,* 326-334.

Mellalieu, S. D., Neil, R., & Hanton, S. (in press). An investigation of the mediating effects of self-confidence between anxiety intensity and direction. *Research Quarterly for Sport and Exercise.*

Morris, L. W., Davis, M. A., and Hutchings, C. H. (1981). Cognitive and emotional components of anxiety: Literature review and a revised worry-emotionality scale. *Journal of Educational Psychology, 73,* 541-555.

Murphy, S. M., Greenspan, M., Jowdy, D., and Tammen, V. (1989, October). *Development of a brief rating instrument of competitive anxiety: Comparison with the CSAI-2.* Paper presented at the meeting of the Association for the Advancement of Applied Sport Psychology, Seattle, WA.

Murray, N. P., and Janelle, C. M. (2003). Anxiety and performance: A visual search examination of the processing efficiency theory. *Journal of Sport and Exercise Psychology, 25,* 171-187.

Neiss, R. (1988). Reconceptualizing arousal: Psychobiological states in motor performance. *Psychological Bulletin, 103,* 345-366.

Noblet, A. J., and Gifford, S. M. (2002). The sources of stress experienced by professional Australian footballers. *Journal of Applied Sport Psychology, 14,* 1-13.

Ntoumanis, N., and Biddle S. J. H. (1998). The relationship between competitive anxiety, achievement goals, and motivational climates. *Research Quarterly for Exercise and Sport, 69,* 176-187.

Ntoumanis, N., and Biddle, S. J. H. (2000). Relationship of intensity and direction of competitive anxiety with coping strategies. *The Sport Psychologist, 14,* 360-371.

Ntoumanis, N., and Jones, G. (1998). Interpretation of competitive trait anxiety symptoms as a function of locus of control beliefs. *International Journal of Sport Psychology, 29,* 99-114.

O'Brien, M., Hanton, S., & Mellalieu, S. D. (2005). Intensity and direction of competitive state anxiety as a function of perceived control and athlete input into the generation of competition goals. *Australian Journal for Science and Medicine in Sport, 8,* 418-427.

Oxendine, J. P. (1970). Emotional arousal and motor performance. *Quest, 13,* 23-32.

Page, S. J., Sime, W., and Nordell, K. (1999). The effects of imagery on female college swimmers' perceptions of anxiety. *The Sport Psychologist, 13,* 458-469.

Paivio, A., and Lambert, W. E. (1959). Measures and correlates of audience anxiety. *Journal of Personality, 27,* 1-17.

Parfitt, C. G., and Hardy, L. (1987). Further evidence for the differential effect of competitive anxiety on a number of cognitive and motor sub-systems. *Journal of Sports Sciences, 5,* 517-524.

Parfitt, C. G., and Hardy, L. (1993). The effects of competitive anxiety on the memory span and rebound shooting tasks in basketball players. *Journal of Sports Sciences, 11,* 517-524.

Parfitt, C. G., Hardy, L., and Pates, J. (1995). Somatic anxiety and physiological arousal: Their effects upon a high anaerobic, low memory demand task. *International Journal of Sport Psychology, 26,* 196-213.

Parfitt, C. G., Jones, G., and Hardy, L. (1990). Multidimensional anxiety and performance. In G. Jones and L. Hardy (Eds.), *Stress and performance in sport* (pp. 43-80). Chichester, UK: Wiley.

Parfitt, C. G., and Pates, J. (1999). The effects of cognitive and somatic anxiety and self-confidence on components of performance during competition. *Journal of Sports Sciences, 17,* 351-356.

Perkins, T. G., and Williams, A. M. (1994). Self-report and psychophysiological measures of anxiety in novice and experienced abseilers. *Journal of Sports Sciences, 12,* 206-207.

Perry, J. D., and Williams, J. M. (1998). Relationship of intensity and direction of competitive trait anxiety to skill level and gender in tennis. *The Sport Psychologist, 12,* 169-179.

Prapavessis, H., Grove, J. R., McNair, P. J., and Cable, N. T. (1992). Self-regulation training, state anxiety, and sport performance: A psychophysiological case study. *The Sport Psychologist, 6,* 213-229.

Raglin, J. (1992). Anxiety and sport performance. *Exercise and Sport Sciences Reviews, 20,* 243-274.

Randle, S., and Weinberg, R. (1997). Multidimensional anxiety and performance: An exploratory examination of the zone of optimal functioning hypothesis. *The Sport Psychologist, 11,* 160-174.

Robazza, C. (this volume). An emotion review. In S. Hanton and S. D. Mellalieu, (Eds.), *Literature reviews in sport psychology.* Hauppauge, NJ: Nova Science.

Rotter, J. B. (1966). Generalized expectancies for internal versus external control of reinforcement. *Psychological Monographs, 80* (Whole No 609).

Scanlan, T. K., Rivazza, K., and Stein, G. L. (1989). An in-depth study of former elite figure skaters: I. Introduction to the project. *Journal of Sport and Exercise Psychology, 11,* 54-64.

Scanlan, T. K., Stein, G. L., and Ravizza, K. (1991). An in-depth study of former elite figure skaters: III. Sources of stress. *Journal of Sport and Exercise Psychology, 13,* 102-120.

Schwartz, G. E., Davidson, R. J., and Goleman, D. J. (1978). Patterning of cognitive and somatic processes in self-regulation of anxiety: Effects of meditation versus exercise. *Psychosomatic Medicine, 40*, 321-328.

Smith, R. E., Smoll, F. L., and Barnett, N. P. (1995). Reduction of children's sport performance anxiety through social support and stress-reduction training for coaches. *Journal of Applied Developmental Psychology, 16*, 125-142.

Smith, R. E., Smoll, F. L., and Schutz, R. W. (1990). Measurement correlates of sport-specific cognitive and somatic trait anxiety: The Sport Anxiety Scale. *Anxiety Research, 2,* 263-280.

Smith, R. E., Smoll, F. L., and Weichman, S. A. (1998). Measurement of trait anxiety in sport. In J. Duda. (Ed.), *Advances in sport and exercise psychology measurement.* (pp. 129-148). West Virginia: Fitness Information Technology.

Spence J T., and Spence, K. W. (1966). The motivational components of manifest anxiety: Drive and drive stimuli. In C. D. Spielberger (Ed.), *Anxiety and behavior* (pp. 291-326). New York: Academic Press.

Spielberger, C. D. (1966). Theory and research on anxiety. In C. D. Spielberger (Ed.), *Anxiety and behavior* (pp. 3-20). New York: Academic Press.

Spielberger, C. D., Gorsuch, R. L., and Lushene, R. L. (1970). *Manual for the state-trait anxiety inventory.* Palo Alto, CA: Consulting Psychologists.

Spink, K. S. (1990). Group cohesion and collective efficacy of volleyball teams. *Journal of Sport and Exercise Psychology, 12*, 301-311

Swain, A. B. J., and Jones, G. (1991). Gender role endorsement and competitive anxiety. *International Journal of Sport Psychology, 22*, 50-65.

Swain, A. B. J., and Jones, G. (1992). Relationships between sport achievement orientation and competitive state anxiety. *The Sport Psychologist, 6*, 42-54.

Swain, A. B. J., and Jones, G. (1993). Intensity and frequency dimensions of competitive state anxiety. *Journal of Sports Sciences, 11*, 533-542.

Swain, A. B. J., and Jones, G. (1996). Explaining performance variance: The relative contributions of intensity and direction dimensions of competitive state anxiety. *Anxiety, Stress and Coping, 9*, 1-18.

Taylor, J. A. (1953). A personality scale of manifest anxiety. *Journal of Abnormal and Social Psychology, 48*, 285-290.

Taylor, J. (1987). Predicting athletic performance with self-confidence and somatic and cognitive anxiety as a function of motor and physiological requirements in six sports. *Journal of Personality, 55,* 139-153.

Tenenbaum, G., and Bar-Eli, M. (1995). Contemporary issues in exercise and sport psychology research. In S. J. H. Biddle (Ed.), *European perspectives in sport and exercise psychology* (pp. 290-323). Chichester, UK: Wiley.

Tenenbaum, G., Lloyd, M., Pretty, G., and Hanin, Y. (2002). Congruence of actual and retrospective reports of pre-competition emotions in equestrians. *Journal of Sport and Exercise Psychology, 24,* 271-288.

Thelwell, R. C., and Maynard, I. W. (1998). Anxiety-performance relationships in cricketers: Testing the zone of optimal functioning hypothesis. *Perceptual and Motor Skills, 87,* 675-689.

Thomas D. L., and Diener, E. (1990). Memory accuracy in the recall of emotions. *Journal of Personality and Social-Psychology, 59*, 291-297.

Thomas, O., Hanton, S., and Jones, G. (2002). An alternative approach to short-form self-report assessment of competitive anxiety. *International Journal of Sport Psychology, 33,* 325-336.

Thomas, O., Maynard, I., and Hanton, S. (2004). Temporal aspects of competitive anxiety and self-confidence as a function of anxiety perceptions. *The Sport Psychologist, 18,* 172-188.

Tsorbatzoudis, H., Barkoukis, V., Sideridis, G., and Grouios, G. (2002). Confirmatory factor analysis of the Greek version of the Competitive State Anxiety Inventory-2 (CSAI-2). *International Journal of Sport Psychology, 33,* 182-194.

Turner, P. E., and Raglin, J. S. (1991). Anxiety and performance in track and field athletes: A comparison of ZOF and inverted-U theories. *Medicine and Science in Sport and Exercise, 23,* S119.

Watson, D., and Clark, L. A. (1984). Negative affectivity: The disposition to experience aversive emotional states. *Psychological Bulletin, 96,* 219-235.

Watson, D., and Friend, R. (1969). Measurement of social evaluative anxiety. *Journal of Consulting and Clinical Psychology, 33,* 448-457.

Watson, D., and Tellegen, A. (1985). Toward a consensual structure of mood. *Psychological Bulletin, 98,* 219-235.

Wegner, D. M. (1997). Why the mind wanders. In J. D. Cohen and J. W. Schooler (Eds.), *Scientific approaches to consciousness* (pp. 295-315). Hillsdale, NJ: Earlbaum.

White, S. A., and Zellner, S. R. (1996). The relationship between goal orientation, beliefs about the cause of sport success, and trait anxiety among high school, intercollegiate, and recreational sport participants. *The Sport Psychologist, 10,* 58-72.

Wiggins, M. S. (1998). Anxiety intensity and direction: Preperformance temporal patterns and expectations in athletes. *Journal of Applied Sport Psychology, 10,* 201-211.

Wilkinson, J. (2003, October). How to be the best kicker in the world. *The Observer Sport Monthly,* p. 47.

Williams, A. M., Vickers, J., and Rodrigues, S. (2002).The effects of anxiety on visual search, movement kinematics, and performance in table tennis: A test of Eysenck and Calvo's processing efficiency theory. *Journal of Sport and Exercise Psychology, 24,* 438-455.

Williams, J. M., and Krane, V. (1992). The psychological characteristics of peak performance. In J. M. Williams (Ed.), *Applied sport psychology: Personal growth to peak performance* (pp. 137-147). Mountain View, CA: Mayfield.

Wilson, G. S., Raglin, J. S., and Harger, G. J. (2000). A comparison of the STAI and CSAI-2 in five-day recalls of precompetition anxiety in collegiate track and field athletes. *Scandinavian Journal of Medicine and Science in Sports, 10,* 51-54.

Wine, J. D. (1971). Test anxiety and direction of attention. *Psychological Bulletin, 76,* 92-104.

Woodman, T., Albinson, J. G., and Hardy, L. (1997). An investigation of the zones of optimal functioning hypothesis within a multidimensional framework. *Journal of Sport and Exercise Psychology, 19,* 131-141.

Woodman, T., and Hardy, L. (2001). Stress and anxiety. In R. Singer, H. A. Hausenblas, and C. M. Janelle (Eds.), *Handbook of research on sport psychology* (pp. 290-318). New York: Wiley.

Woodman, T., and Hardy, L. (2003). The relative impact of cognitive anxiety and self-confidence upon sport performance: A meta-analysis. *Journal of Sports Sciences, 21,* 443-457.

In: Literature Reviews in Sport Psychology   ISBN 1-59454-904-4
Editors: S. Hanton and S. D. Mellalieu, pp. 47-90   © 2006 Nova Science Publishers, Inc.

Chapter 2

A REVIEW OF COPING IN SPORT

Sharleen D. Hoar[*]
The University of Lethbridge, Canada
Kent C. Kowalski
University of Saskatchewan, Canada
Patrick Gaudreau
McGill University, Canada
Peter R. E. Crocker
The University of British Columbia, Canada

ABSTRACT

The purpose of this chapter is to provide a review of the coping construct and the associated research within sport psychology. Over the past two decades, a burgeoning amount of attention and research has emerged attesting to the recognition of the central importance of coping in the emotion process of sport. Since a comprehensive review of this literature would require a complete volume onto itself, this review includes what we believe to be important issues in the sport coping literature. To this end, we (1) discuss how coping is conceptualized in sport research, (2) highlight key coping measurement issues, (3) identify key antecedents and outcomes of the coping process, (4) discuss implications for professional practice, and (5) address future directions for sport coping research.

Key words: emotion, coping, stress, review, sport

[*] Correspondence concerning this article should be addressed to Sharleen D. Hoar, Department of Kinesiology and Physical Education, The University of Lethbridge, Canada, Tel: 403-329-2591, Fax: 403-380-1839, Email: sharleen.hoar@uleth.ca

INTRODUCTION

Stress in sport can be associated with a number of negative events including violence, illness and injury, performance difficulties, burnout, and others. This has led many researchers and practitioners to focus on grasping the complexity of the stress process and its consequences on performance and well-being. Although there are multiple components to the stress process, coping has been identified as a critical component. Therefore, it is not surprising that research attention and knowledge about stress and coping has increased tremendously over the last 25 years. This literature reveals an enormous range of topics related to coping in sport including coping skills training programs (Anshel, 1990; Crocker, Alderman, and Smith, 1988; Smith, 1980), descriptive studies about how athletes cope with competitive stress (Crocker, 1992; Gould, Eklund, and Jackson, 1993), measurement development (Gaudreau and Blondin, 2002; Kowalski and Crocker, 2001; Smith, Schutz, Smoll, and Ptacek, 1995), and studies that have linked coping to theoretically meaningful variables such as social support, appraisal of threat, goals, emotions, gender, performance, and injury (e.g., Campen and Roberts, 2001; Crocker and Graham, 1995; Dugdale, Eklund, and Gordon, 2002; Gaudreau, Lapierre, and Blondin, 2001; Gould, Udry, Bridges, and Beck, 1997a; Ntoumanis, and Biddle, 1998, 2000; Prapavessis and Grove, 1995; Smith and Christensen, 1995).

Clearly, one of the biggest challenges we face is attempting to integrate the vast literature on coping and sport. Although fascinating by its very complexity, a comprehensive review of all the issues and topics related to coping in sport would require a separate book. Thus, the purpose of this chapter is to provide a review of what, we believe, are the important issues in the sport coping literature. To accomplish this goal we will (1) clarify what is coping and how it can be differentiated from related concepts, (2) discuss coping measurement issues, (3) identify key antecedents and outcomes of the coping process, (4) discuss implications for professional practice, and (5) address future directions for sport coping research.

CONCEPTUAL ISSUES: WHAT IS COPING?

Coping is part of a long research tradition investigating self-regulation and adaptation (Matthews, Schwean, Campbell, Saklofske, and Mohamed, 2000; Parker and Endler, 1996). Considerable empirical attention has been devoted to the behavioral and cognitive skills associated with sport-related performance outcomes. Multidimensional constructs such as basic psychological skills (e.g., Murphy and Tammen, 1998), mood regulation strategies (e.g., Stevens and Lane, 2001), defense mechanisms (e.g., Seheult, 1997), and coping (e.g., Hardy, Jones, and Gould, 1996) have been proposed as fundamental mechanisms in understanding athletic performance and psychological adaptation. Each of these is important in helping people strive towards psychological adaptation; nevertheless, they can be distinguished conceptually, functionally, and theoretically. In this section, the conceptual boundaries of the coping construct are delineated, and we will address important questions such as:

- To what extent does the coping construct depart from other self-regulation processes?

- Is there a hierarchical conceptual framework for coping?
- Should coping be conceptualized as trait-like behavioral tendencies, state-like responses to specific life encounters, or both?

Coping and Other Adaptation Mechanisms

Scholars have conceived self-regulation as an organizational construct within which specific adaptation mechanisms are nested (e.g., Cramer, 1998; Matthews et al., 2000). In operational terms, self-regulation represents the "cognitive, affective, motivational, and behavioral components that provide the individual with the capacity to adjust his or her actions and goals to achieve desired results in light of changing environmental conditions" (Zeidner, Boekaerts, and Pintrich, 2000, p. 751). From an adaptation perspective, constructs such as coping, defense mechanisms, basic psychological skills, and mood regulation fall within the tenets of self-regulation. Despite their commonality, each of these mechanisms plays a slightly different, yet complementary, role in the psychological adaptation process. Table 1 presents a definition for each of these adaptation mechanisms and proposes three ontological dimensions upon which they can be classified and distinguished (for a more extensive discussion, see Cramer, 1998).

According to Lazarus and Folkman (1984), *coping* represents the constantly changing cognitive and behavioral efforts to manage the specific external and internal demands of a stressful situation. From a functional perspective, coping encompasses actions that are used to change and/or avoid a situation and one's emotions. *Defense mechanisms,* on the other hand, are used unconsciously to protect oneself from the negative emotional consequences of a threatening situation. These mechanisms purportedly allow the individual to distort reality to protect against distressing emotions and to avoid ego-threatening stimuli or situations. Albeit serving the functions of emotional management and avoidance, defense mechanisms are of limited use to alter the objective situational demands. *Mood regulation* represents the thoughts and behaviors used deliberately and intentionally to eliminate, increase, maintain, or change one's moods or emotions. Similar to coping, mood regulation includes direct and indirect efforts (i.e., avoidance) to manage emotional states. Like defense mechanisms, however, mood regulation tends to overlook actions directed toward the external demands of a situation. Finally, *basic psychological skills* are oriented toward the self-regulation of behavioral, emotional, and cognitive states underlying successful performances. Individuals use psychological skills to master the objective requirements of a situation and to manage their internal states, but unlike coping and defense mechanisms, avoidance is typically not featured as a key self-regulatory function. In general, given its multidimensional and multifunctional properties, coping covers a larger conceptual domain compared to the other mechanisms.

Table 1. Conceptual analysis of coping and related constructs.

Construct	Definition	Adaptive	Types of efforts			Functional role			Intentionality	
			Behavioral	Cognitive	Unconscious	Manage the situation	Manage the emotions	Avoid situation and emotion	Deliberate and conscious (volition)	Non-intentional and unconscious
Coping	Constantly changing cognitive and behavioral efforts to manage the specific external and/or internal demands of a stressful situation (Lazarus and Folkman, 1984).	X	X	X		X	X	X	X	
Defense mechanisms	Unconscious mechanisms used to protect oneself from the negative emotional consequences of a threatening situation (Cramer, 1998).	X			X		X	X		X
Mood regulation	Thought and behaviors used deliberately and intentionally to eliminate, increase, maintain, or change one's moods or emotions (Parkinson and Totterdell, 1999; Rusting and Nolen-Hoeksema, 1998).	X	X	X			X	X	X	
Basic psychological methods	Specific actions directed toward the self-regulation of behavioral, emotional, and cognitive states underlying successful athletic performance (Murphy and Tammen, 1998; Thomas, Murphy and Hardy, 1999).	X	X	X		X	X		X	

Conceptual Organization of the Coping Construct

Two broad approaches have typically been used to operationalize coping (Krohne, 1996). A micro-analytical approach focuses on organizing similar coping actions into a series of conceptually distinct and mutually exclusive coping strategies (e.g., Carver, Scheier, and Weintraub, 1989; Folkman and Lazarus, 1985). A macro-analytical approach operates at a higher level of analysis by aggregating coping actions into a limited number of factors (e.g., Amirkhan, 1990; Endler and Parker, 1994), which correspond to the multiple functions that coping actions play within the psychological adaptation process.

Researchers have proposed several conceptual models that combine micro- and macro-analytical approaches of coping (e.g., Ayers, Sandler, West, and Roosa, 1996; Connor-Smith, Compas, Wadsworth, Thomsen, and Saltzman, 2000; Walker, Smith, Garber, and Van Slyke, 1997). In a comprehensive review, Skinner, Edge, Altman, and Sherwood (2003) proposed a hierarchical framework that integrated three levels of coping (i.e., instances, strategies, and families). The lower level of the hierarchy is represented by coping instances, which correspond to the myriad of behavioral and cognitive actions that individuals use to manage a stressful situation. At an intermediate level, coping instances are categorized into a variety of well-defined, homogeneous, and mutually exclusive coping strategies (i.e., ways of coping). Finally, families of coping can also be construed by organizing coping strategies into a limited number of higher-order dimensions of coping.

Most conceptual models of coping feature at least two higher-order coping dimensions (Compas and Epping, 1993; Lazarus, 1991, 2000). *Problem-focused coping* (viz., task-oriented, primary engagement, active) refers to the actions through which individuals try to manage the situational demands and to reduce the discrepancy between a current situation and a desirable outcome. It includes coping strategies like active coping, planning, and effort expenditure. *Emotion-focused coping* (viz., emotion-oriented, secondary engagement, accommodative, passive) represents actions to manage emotions and includes coping strategies like seeking emotional support, acceptance, and positive reappraisal. A third higher-order dimension often proposed is *avoidance coping* (viz., disengagement, withdrawal), which represents actions whereby individuals disengage themselves from a situation and from the process of striving actively toward the achievement of desirable outcomes (Amirkhan, 1990; Endler and Parker, 1994; Seiffge-Krenke, 1995). Coping theorists debate about the inclusion of avoidance as a functional coping category (Endler and Parker, 1990, 1994; Lazarus, 1999). Endler and Parker (1990, 1994) asserted that the coping goals of avoidance (i.e., social and mental diversion and delay of confrontation with a stressor) are important for adaptation and represent a conceptually distinct functional dimension. Other theorists, however, argue that avoidance coping may represent complementary (i.e., emotion-focused coping) rather than orthogonal aspects of the coping process (Aldwin, 2000; Lazarus, 1999). In addition, there may be other higher-order dimensions of coping as well, such as *distraction-oriented coping*, which corresponds to actions through which individuals focus momentarily on external stimuli and cognitive activities unrelated to the stressful situation (Ayers et al., 1996; Endler and Parker, 1994; Gaudreau and Blondin, 2004a). Other coping models in sport, although conceptually similar, emphasize approach and avoidance coping as two broad higher-order dimensions, each consisting of cognitive and behavioral sub-dimensions (e.g., Anshel, 2001).

Trait-like versus State-like Conceptualizations of Coping

A third and related conceptual issue is whether coping should be observed as trait-like behavioral tendencies or as state-like responses to specific life encounters (Schwartz, Neale, Marco, Shiffman, and Stone, 1999; Schwarzer and Schwarzer, 1996). This controversy has bearing for theory, measurement, and research methodology. A dispositional approach contends that individuals are using coping actions in a relatively stable manner across time and that their coping responses remain consistent across situations. Advocates of this position have developed generic instruments applicable across a variety of life domains (e.g., Carver et al., 1989; Endler and Parker, 1994). The trait-like approach contrasts with the state-like (situational) approach, which emphasizes that coping actions change across life domains as well as across different situations within a given life domain (e.g., Lazarus and Folkman, 1984; Somerfeld, 1997).

A growing body of research is emerging within the sport domain investigating temporal stability and situational consistency of coping (e.g., Anshel and Andersen, 2002; Bouffard and Crocker, 1992; Crocker and Isaak, 1997; Gaudreau et al., 2001; Haney and Long, 1995; Masters and Lambert, 1989; Pensgaard and Ursin, 1998; Quinn and Fallon, 1999; Udry, 1997). Results of these studies are mixed, although in general they provide weak to moderate evidence of variability in sport participants' coping. Lazarus (1991) and other coping theorists (e.g., Aldwin, 2000; Carver et al., 1989; Coyne and Gottlieb, 1996; Folkman, 1991) that advocate a state view of coping claim that person by situation interactions exist that are exerted upon coping strategy choices, which may be reflected in *preferred* ways of coping across situations that are appraised in similar ways. That is, an athlete may choose to use a particular coping strategy or set of strategies across events because the adaptive significance and requirements of the threatening situations are judged to be similar in nature. This suggests that weak to moderate stability in coping should be expected. However, our understanding of the state-like or trait-like nature of coping in sport has often been limited by measurement and design. Many sport studies were conducted with small samples, and failure to find significant changes in coping across situations might be attributed to low statistical power rather than to the trait-like nature of coping. Additionally, it has been suggested that measurement problems might be involved in the failure to find strong evidence of stability or flexibility in sport participants' coping (e.g., Crocker and Isaak, 1997; Gaudreau et al., 2001; Udry, 1997). Additionally, researchers have yet to examine the factorial invariance of measurement instruments across different types of situations experienced in the sport domain (for a discussion of these issues, see Schutz, 1998).

MEASUREMENT OF COPING IN SPORT

Conceptual and measurement issues are intimately linked. The development of coping measures can be a deductive (theoretically driven) or inductive (empirical driven) process. As Schwarzer and Schwarzer (1996) stated, both approaches should operate "reciprocally in a spiral-shaped process" (p. 129). Theory is often used to determine the instruments considered most appropriate for a given research topic; however, the use of those instruments subsequently help us to define and revise theory and provide many of the building blocks of "knowledge" in a particular field. Although there have been a number of qualitative studies in sport coping research (see Crocker, Kowalski, and Graham, 1998, for an overview), the vast majority of research in coping in sport has used quantitative based instruments. As a result, a review of coping instruments used in sport research is important to provide a contextual understanding of sport coping knowledge base.

There are a number of challenges presented when choosing which coping measures to review. First, coping measures are often developed for specific studies (e.g., Anshel, 1996; Meyers, Bourgeois, Stewart, and LeUnes, 1992; Thomas et al., 1999) or are embedded as dimensions within other scales (e.g., Masters, Ogles, and Jolton, 1993). Second, measures that assess constructs conceptually similar to coping within the sport literature are often couched within and defined by concepts other than "coping" (e.g., Stevens and Lane, 2001; Ninedek and Kolt, 2000). Third, there are unique approaches taken in unpublished manuscripts and thesis dissertations that have the potential to benefit the field but are more difficult to access. For example Hoar (2003), modifying a technique used by Compas (1998) in mainstream psychology looked at interpersonal sport stress in young adolescents through the use of open-ended responses to questionnaire items in combination with ratings of the function of each strategy. To review every measure that has been used in sport coping research would be beyond the scope of this chapter. Instead, we will review quantitative instruments previously identified within the sport coping literature (i.e., Crocker et al., 1998) in addition to a number of recent sport-related measures that have been developed to address concerns of earlier research.

Sport Modifications of Ways of Coping

The original Ways of Coping questionnaire (Folkman and Lazarus, 1985; Folkman, Lazarus, Dunkel-Schetter, Delongis, and Gruen, 1986) consisted of 50 items comprising eight coping factors: confrontive coping, distancing, self-controlling, seeking social support, accepting responsibility, escape-avoidance, planful problem-solving, and positive reappraisal. Each scale was designed to fall within the general problem-focused and emotion-focused coping dimensions. Using a 4-point scale, participants indicate the extent to which each coping action is used to manage a self-recalled situation. Although a number of conceptual issues concerning the Ways of Coping have subsequently been raised by various authors (e.g., Carver et al., 1989; Schwartzer and Schwartzer, 1996; Stone, Kennedy-Moore, Newman, Greenberg, and Neale, 1992), the Ways of Coping Questionnaire has been used extensively in coping research and has provided a framework for many of the measures currently used in sport coping research.

Ways of Coping Checklist for Sport
The Ways of Coping Checklist for Sport (WOCS), developed by Madden and colleagues (Madden, Kirkby, and McDonald, 1989; Madden, Summers, and Brown 1990), consists of 54 items assessing eight coping dimensions: problem-focused coping, seeking social support, general emotionality, increased effort and resolve, detachment, denial, wishful thinking, and emphasizing the positive. There is limited support for the reliability and validity of the WOCS in the context of middle distance running slumps and competitive basketball stress (Madden et al., 1989, 1990). Madden and colleagues reported the internal consistency values for the full 54-item scale as alpha = .91 (but did not report reliability values for specific scales) and provided preliminary validity evidence.

Recent evidence questions the measurement properties of the WOCS. Grove, Eklund, and Heard (1997), using confirmatory factor analysis procedures, showed that the factor structure suggested by Madden et al. (1989, 1990) was not supported for athletes reporting coping with performance slumps. Although they suggested that a four- or five-factor WOCS model provided a stronger fit to the data, concerns over factor instability on the WOCS raised by Crocker et al. (1998) remain relevant. Grove et al. (1997) recommended against using the WOCS exclusively to assess slump-related coping.

Modified Ways of Coping Checklist

Crocker (1992) developed the Modified Ways of Coping Checklist (modified-WCC) to assess coping with a recent stressful situation. Sport specific modifications made to the original Ways of Coping were based on athletes' written responses and interviews as well as on a factor analysis of the resultant scale. The final modified-WCC consisted of 38 items and eight coping dimensions: active coping, problem-focused, social support, positive reappraisal, wishful thinking, self-control, detachment, and self-blame.

In assessing the reliability and validity of the modified-WCC, Crocker recommended *against* using the modified-WCC as a coping measure in sport. A number of internal consistency values on the coping dimensions were below .70 (and none were above .80) suggesting potential reliability concerns with the instrument. In addition, although the involvement of athletes in the development of the modified-WCC suggests increased content validity, the unstable factor structure of the measure is a weakness seen consistently across various sport modifications of the original Ways of Coping measure (Crocker et al., 1998).

Higher Order Ways of Coping

Haney and Long (1995) modified the Ways of Coping to assess broad (higher order) dimensions of coping. They developed an 18-item measure from a series of confirmatory factor analysis procedures to assess engagement (11 items) and disengagement coping (7 items). Mixed support for the reliability and validity of the higher order Ways of Coping measure were reported (Haney and Long, 1995). Internal consistency values of the scales were acceptable (engagement, alpha = .82; disengagement, alpha = .75); however, the fit-indexes for the measurement model were weak. Although there was some support for construct validity of the measure by showing engagement coping as positively related to sport performance (basketball free-throws and field hockey/soccer penalty shots) and disengagement coping as negatively related to performance, concerns over the relevance of items to sport and the level of coping assessed have been voiced (Crocker et al., 1998). As a result of these limitations, we recommend against its use.

Modified COPE

The modified COPE (MCOPE; Crocker and Graham, 1995) consists of items from Carver et al.'s (1989) original COPE, which have been modified to increase their relevance to sport. As well, additional scales deemed appropriate to sport were added. The MCOPE asks participants to indicate how much they use particular coping actions during a stressful performance situation. It consists of 48 items comprising 12 coping dimensions: active coping, seeking social support for instrumental reasons, planning, seeking social support for emotional reasons, denial, humor, behavioral disengagement, venting of emotion, suppression of competing activities, self-blame, wishful thinking, and increasing effort. Similar to the original COPE, both state and dispositional versions of the MCOPE have been used (e.g., Giacobbi and Weinberg, 2000). As well, it has subsequently been translated into French (Gaudreau et al., 2001). There is relatively extensive evidence regarding the reliability of the MCOPE scales (Bouffard and Crocker, 1992; Crocker and Graham, 1995; Crocker and Isaak, 1997; Eklund, Grove, and Heard, 1998; Gaudreau and Blondin, 2002; Giacobbi and Weinberg, 2000; Ntoumanis and Biddle, 1998). Internal consistency values on the MCOPE are generally above .70, although across various studies MCOPE subscale values tend to be lowest (and often below .70) for denial, suppression of competing activities, wishful thinking, and self-blame.

Although validity evidence for the MCOPE has been primarily indirect (see Crocker et al., 1998), Eklund and colleagues (1998) conducted a direct test of the factorial validity of the MCOPE comparing various MCOPE measurement models. Six hundred and twenty-one athletes responded on the MCOPE to how they coped with performance slumps. Using confirmatory factor analyses, Eklund et al. concluded that the strongest MCOPE measurement model was a 10-factor model that combined the two seeking social support scales and the active coping and planning scales (Ntoumanis and Biddle, 1998, similarly combined the two seeking social support scales based on an exploratory factor analysis). Despite some desirable psychometric properties, such as the intercorrelations among scales and acceptable internal consistency values, the fit indexes for the 10-factor COPE model were modest at best, suggesting improvements to the measurement model can be made. However, despite their limitations, the COPE and MCOPE are among the most commonly used measures in sport coping research.

Athletic Coping Skills Inventory–28

The Athletic Coping Skills Inventory-28 (ACSI-28; Smith et al., 1995) was developed to assess sport-specific psychological skills thought to be instrumental to sport performance. The ACSI-28 has 28 items consisting of seven psychological skills dimensions (coping with adversity, peaking under pressure, goal setting/mental preparation, concentration, freedom from worry, confidence and achievement motivation, and coachability), which can be combined into a composite personal resources score. The ACSI-28 is unique compared to other measures discussed to this point in that (1) its original development was based on athletes' responses (the measures discussed above were originally designed with non-sport populations and then modified for sport) and (2) it assesses basic psychological skills as opposed to actual coping behavior.

Smith et al. (1995) provided extensive reliability and validity evidence regarding the ACSI-28 in their original paper describing its development. One-week test-retest values were shown to range from .47 to .87 with 97 college athletes, and internal consistency values ranged from .62 to .86 with 1027 varsity high school athletes. In addition, convergent and construct validity were supported by correlations between ACSI-28 scales and various measures of cognitive-behavioral coping skills, coping, sport anxiety, self-efficacy, self-esteem, and performance (Smith et al., 1995; Smith and Christensen, 1995). There is also preliminary reliability and validity support for a Greek-translated version of the ACSI-28 (Goudas, Theodorakis, and Karamousalidis, 1998). Despite its strengths, the ACSI-28 is probably best considered as a measure of psychological skills than actual coping (Crocker et al., 1998) and as a result will be of limited use to those wanting to access actual coping responses in sport.

Coping Function Questionnaire

To address the need for a measure assessing the functional goals of specific coping strategies, Kowalski and Crocker (2001) developed the Coping Function Questionnaire (CFQ). It consists of 18 items, which assess problem-focused, emotion-focused, and avoidance coping function. Participants are asked to recall the most stressful situation experienced in sport in the past year and then to respond to items assessing each of the three coping function dimensions. The CFQ was designed for use in conjunction with other measures of specific coping strategies in order to gain insight into the function(s) of specific coping strategies (rather than assuming the function of those strategies). Kowalski and Crocker provided reliability and validity evidence for the measure in their original development paper. With a sample of 683 adolescent sport participants, internal consistency values ranged from .80 to .92, and correlations with other coping measures supported the convergent validity of the three functional dimensions. The factorial validity of the scale was tested using confirmatory factor analyses, which demonstrated an acceptable model fit and preliminary evidence of gender invariance in the three-factor measurement model.

An important strength of the CFQ is that it was designed specifically for, and with, adolescent sport participants. However, because it assesses coping function, the measure will only give a partial portrait about the overall coping process. Therefore, it might best be used concurrently with alternative measures (such as the MCOPE) that assess coping at the strategy level. As well, the CFQ measurement model can likely be improved through scale modifications, and a reduction of the number items seems warranted due to conceptual overlap among the wording of items within each coping function dimension.

Coping Inventory for Competitive Sport

Gaudreau and Blondin (2002) developed the Coping Inventory for Competitive Sport (CICS) to assess coping during various phases of a competitive event. It consists of 39 items measuring 10 coping strategies (thought control, mental imagery, relaxation, effort expenditure, logical analysis, seeking support, venting of unpleasant emotion, mental distraction, disengagement/resignation, and social withdrawal), which are nested within three second order dimensions of coping (task-oriented coping, distraction-oriented coping, and disengagement-oriented coping). In addition to the English CICS, there is both French (Inventaire des Stratégies de Coping en Compétition Sportive) and Spanish versions (S. Marquez, personal communication, January 30, 2004). Gaudreau and Blondin (2002) provided initial support for the reliability and validity of the French version of the CICS with a sample 316 athletes. Eight of the 10 scales had internal consistency values above .80 (logical analysis and disengagement/resignation had alpha values of .67 and .68 respectively). Convergent validity of the CICS was supported by correlations with other measures of coping (WCQ and MCOPE), cognitive appraisal, and affect. Various fit indexes also supported the 10-factor measurement model. Results of a recent validation study replicated successfully the

10-factor measurement model and provided initial support for the hypothesized 3-factor hierarchical model (Gaudreau and Blondin, 2004a). A multiple-group analysis suggested that both models were mainly invariant across samples of athletes participating in individual and team sports. Furthermore, a series of studies (Amiot, Gaudreau, and Blanchard, 2004; Gaudreau and Blondin, 2004) have shown that each second order dimension of coping correlated uniquely with a series of antecedent and outcome variables.

Strengths of the CICS are that it was developed from a strong theoretical foundation, that it was developed through a multistage process of factor analysis, and that the principal dimensions remained consistent throughout the multistage process. However, because the CICS was created to assess coping across various stages of sport competition, future validation work needs to examine the longitudinal factorial invariance of the CICS first- and second-order measurement models.

Coping Scale for Korean Athletes

Yoo (2000) developed the culturally-specific coping scale for Korean Athletes (CSKA). The CSKA was designed to capture both specific coping styles and higher order coping dimensions. The CSKA has 32 items to assess four coping styles (problem-focused, emotion-focused, avoidance, and transcendent coping) and two higher order coping dimensions (direct and indirect coping). Yoo reported internal consistency values for all scales as greater than .80, moderate correlations among scales, and preliminary factorial validity support for the higher order and first order models. The CSKA is important in that it recognizes that cultural differences, such as the wording of items and relevant scale dimensions, should be considered in coping assessment. For example, the transcendental coping dimension on the CSKA seems to have emerged from the unique cultural context.

Supporting Yoo's (2000) cultural approach to the assessment of coping in sport, others have also recognized the need for culturally specific/relevant coping measures (Anshel, Jamieson, and Raviv, 2001). A challenge with these approaches is that coping actions differ in relevance (and possibly function) to a specific culture, thereby creating difficulty in comparison across studies from different cultures. Such a challenge might be necessary, however, in order to understand more adequately the coping behavior of individuals from various cultural backgrounds. Just as using non-sport specific measures in the sport context is problematic, the use of culturally non-sensitive measures (both in terms of wording and conceptual dimensions) should also be of concern for sport coping researchers. Overall, the recent development of measures such as the CFQ, CICS, and CSKA reflects sport coping researchers' recognition that coping varies not only situationally and temporally, but also across groups of sport participants.

ANTECEDENTS OF COPING

Sport researchers have spent considerable energy in identifying *characteristic* coping responses to better understand the stress process and predict the ways in which sport participants manage difficult situations. In addition, this line of inquiry is important for advocating intervention programs that effectively assist athletes in improving coping skills (e.g., Smith, 1999). Although, most research has been atheoretical in nature, sport scientists have been successful in identifying relevant person and socio-environment factors that are potentially related to coping responses in sport.

What appears to be particularly relevant to understanding individual differences in coping responses is the relation between person and socio-environment antecedents (Crocker, Kowalski, Hoar, and McDonough, 2004; Lazarus, 1991). This type of study is rarely done because of the complex nature of the potential person-environment interaction (Lazarus, 1999). A common approach has been to isolate possible clusters of coping antecedents and to examine independent mediator or moderator effects on coping (e.g., Krohne, 1996). This approach has been advanced as a parsimonious method to facilitate an understanding about the development of coping, although theorists acknowledge that rarely (if ever) are person and environmental antecedents independent from each other (Aldwin, 2000). In keeping in line with this approach, we differentiate between a variety of person and environmental antecedents that influence coping in sport.

Readers should be aware that considerable conceptual confusion exists in the description of mediating and moderating effects of coping antecedents within the literature. This has direct relevance to the empirical testing and conclusions drawn about the relationships that exist between factors (Baron and Kenny, 1986). To clarify, a mediator variable represents the *generative mechanism* (i.e., causal agent) through which a focal independent variable (e.g., specific person or environmental factor) exerts its influence on a coping encounter. For instance, a model assuming mediation would suggest that the positive feedback provided by a coach influences coping responses of athletes indirectly, through its effects on perception of control and sport-related confidence. In contrast, a moderator variable *affects* the nature of the causal relation (e.g., direction and strength) between a specific person or socio-environmental variable and the choice of a coping action (see Baron and Kenny, 1986, for a thorough discussion on mediator and moderator variables). For example, it may be that perceived control is a significant predictor of coping in challenging situations (i.e., competition, rehabilitation), while being of lesser importance in situations exerting lower levels of stress (i.e., training).

Social and Environment Antecedents

Sport researchers interested in the contextual antecedents of coping assume that there are environmental elements or features that 'pull for' different types of solutions and coping responses (Aldwin, 2000). Specifically, differences in sport environments are theorized to influence (1) the choice of coping actions applied in a given situational context and (2) the effectiveness of coping (Aldwin, 2000; Folkman, 1991; Lazarus, 1999).

Lazarus (1991) suggested that there are four primary social and environmental antecedents that influence coping responses: Demands, constraints, opportunities, and culture. The interaction between these variables results in a set of cues through which an individual evaluates (1) the social resources that are available to the individual during the interaction (i.e., social support), and (2) the personal resources (i.e., coping) that are required to manage the situation. Empirical research (Aldwin, 2000) demonstrates that individuals conceptualize socio-environmental cues according to (1) content type, (2) the accentuated social roles, and

(3) the appraised impact for well-being (i.e., appraisals of loss, threat, and challenge). The first two categories are viewed to have a more global or stable influence on coping, while situation appraisals are viewed to be flexible in nature, as they change across situations and over time.

Content Type

Coping has been studied in a variety of sport contexts such as competition (e.g., Anshel and Wells, 2000; Hammermeister and Burton, 2001; Ntoumanis, Biddle, and Haddock, 1999), athletic injury (e.g., Gould et al., 1997a; Johnson, 1996; Manual et al., 2002), practice/training (e.g., Madden et al., 1989; Prapavessis, Grove, Maddison, and Zillmann, 2003), and retirement from sport (e.g., Grove, Lavallee, and Gordon, 1997; Ungerleider, 1997). Sport researchers have also examined different situations within the same context (Anshel and Kaissidis, 1997; Anshel et al., 2001; Gould, Finch, and Jackson, 1993; Gould, Udry, Bridges, and Beck, 1997b). For example, Anshel and his colleagues have examined coping responses of sport participants to stressors within competition including bad referee calls, cheating opponents, errors in play, weather conditions, losing in game/match or success of opponent, spectator pressure, pressure from coaches, and pressure from teammates. Finally, as we highlighted earlier in this chapter, sport researchers have also examined coping in relation to different time periods within a situation, including during phases of competition, phases of injury recovery, and repeated competitive attempts.

Two important issues limit our ability to make conclusions about the influence of different situations on the selection of coping responses. First, much of the sport coping research has studied coping within a single environmental setting (be it a 'general' sport context or a specific situation). To understand the influence of social and environmental factors in the choice and efficacy of sport participant's coping requires that the actual coping responses must be *concurrently and simultaneously* measured across contexts, situations, and at different points along that situation (Gaudreau et al., 2001; Lazarus and Folkman, 1984). This has been rarely done in sport. A scarcity of sport studies exist that compare coping efforts across a variety of social environmental settings. Moreover, it is assumed that features or elements (i.e., demands, constraints, and opportunities) are in some manner qualitatively different across sport environments. For example, the practice context is viewed differently from that of the competitive context (Crocker and Isaak, 1997). Sport researchers rarely delineate the objective element(s) that characterize the experience of a particular context, situation, or time period.

Social Roles

Individuals assume a number of social roles (Pearlin, 1989), which can be family-related (e.g., parent, child, sister, brother), formal (e.g., gender, ethnic, socioeconomic status), informal (e.g., friend), and work-related (e.g., student, employee, athlete, coach, sport administrator). Accompanying these roles are expected patterns of behaviors that are defined, in part, by cultural beliefs and are socially learned (Aldwin, 2000; Lazarus, 1999). Thus, the coping choices that sport participants make can be largely understood in terms of the social roles they embody. Social roles that have received attention in the sport literature include (1) sport roles, (2) ethnic roles, and (3) gender roles.

Sport Roles

Social roles assumed within sport are 'athlete', 'teammate', 'coach', 'official', and/or 'administrator'. Associated with the sport social role are specific belief systems, accepted social norms for standards of behavior, and the provision of specific social resources; all of which influence athletes coping choices (Gill, 2003; Grove, Lavallee, Gordon, and Harvey, 1998; Hardy and Crace, 1991). Poczwardowski and Conroy (2002) reported that elite athletes and high performing artists utilize qualitatively different coping strategies serving the coping functions of appraisal coping, emotion-focused coping, problem-focused coping, avoidance coping, and coping failure in the management of performance success and failure. Furthermore, ballet dancers scores on the Sports Inventory for Pain (SIP; Meyers et al., 1992) revealed that the dancers used less direct coping (e.g., 'ignore pain', 'accept the pain', and 'tough it out'), less cognitive (e.g., 'mental strategies'), and more catastrophizing (e.g., 'despair when injured', 'dwell on pain', and 'feel it is unbearable') compared to recreational runners, high school and collegiate intramural runners, elite equestrians, and elite and high school rodeo performers (Encarnacion; Meyers, Ryan, and Pease, 2000). Collectively, these studies provide indirect evidence that the 'athlete' social role contributes to individual differences in coping efforts among individuals.

Ethnic Roles

Sport scientists have examined individual differences in coping among athletes from Australia, Greece, Hong Kong, Israel, and Korea. Results from this research have revealed some differences in athletes' coping. Using qualitative interview methodology, Park (2000) found that Korean national team athletes differed from U.S. national team figure skaters (as reported by Gould, Finch, et al., 1993) in the use of hobbies and prayer to manage competitive demands. Hobbies (e.g., music, movies, videos, and books) and prayer, respectively, emerged as 33% and 22% of Korean coping efforts. Other research (e.g., Yoo, 2000, 2001) has confirmed the importance of prayer for Korean athletes. Comparing Australian and American athletes, Anshel, Williams, and Williams (2000) reported that Australian athletes used approach-emotion coping efforts to a greater extent across a variety of stressors experienced during competition. Similarly, Anshel et al. (2001) found that male and female Israeli athletes used a high amount of avoidance-task and avoidance-emotion strategies in managing difficult competitive situations; a finding that was associated with cultural beliefs about control. They explained that emotional control (i.e., focus of self and away from the task) was understood by Israeli people to be a more effective coping strategy in situations of low controllability because it moderates emotional arousal and improves adaptation to the stress.

Within any particular country, there are likely to be many different cultural beliefs that could impact on coping in sport. A general weakness of this body of sport research is that the beliefs of a culture are assumed and not studied directly. Transactional theorists advocate that culture should not be treated as a monolithic construct (Aldwin, 2000). "Cultures are not a single unified force that shapes behaviors; instead, they consist of multiple mazes that create different pathways for different subcultural groups such as males and females, ethnic groups, and maybe even across different sports" (Crocker, Kowalski, et al., 2004; p. 347). Consequently, researches should ensure that confounding variables remain equivalent across subcultural groups before any valid inference can be drawn from cross-cultural studies on coping.

Gender Roles

Gender differences in coping have been a topic of great interest among sport researchers (e.g., Anshel and Delany, 2001; Anshel et al., 2001; Anshel and Kaissidis, 1997; Anshel, Williams, and Hodge, 1997; Crocker and Graham, 1995; Goyen and Anshel, 1998; Gaudreau and Blondin, 2002; Kolt, Kirkby, and Linder, 1995; Kowalski and Crocker, 2001; Maniar, Curry, Sommers-Flannigan, and Walsh, 2001; Manuel et al., 2002; Park, 2000; Pensgaard and Roberts, 2003; Yoo, 2001). One of the most robust findings in sport literature is that males and females generally cope differently. Female sport participants report higher use of social support (e.g., Crocker and Graham, 1995; Kowalski and Crocker, 2001), help-seeking (e.g., Maniar et al., 2001), and increased effort (e.g., Gaudreau and Blondin, 2002) than males to manage difficult situations in sport. Additionally, females report directing coping efforts more intensely towards emotion coping functions compared to males (Goyen and Anshel, 1998; Kowalski and Crocker, 2001; Yoo, 2001). Males, on the other hand, report higher scores on active coping and venting emotions compared to females (e.g., Anshel et al., 2001; Gaudreau and Blondin, 2002). Some research demonstrates that during specific situations, such as during competitive events and interpersonal conflicts, males use more problem-focused coping than females (Anshel and Kaissidis, 1997; Anshel et al., 1997; Goyen and Anshel, 1998; Yoo, 2001). Also, it has been reported that male athletes are less responsive to pain compared to female athletes (Meyers, Bourgeois, and LeUnes, 2001; Roderick, Waddington, and Parker, 2000). In a recent meta-analysis of sex differences in coping of 50 studies (four of which had sport-specific samples), Tamres, Janicki, and Helgeson (2002) showed that women were more likely than men to engage in most types of coping, but that the nature of the stressor was an important moderator of gender differences. However, when they examined *relative* coping (how much one strategy is used compared to other strategies) separately with an independent sample, men favored more active coping and avoidance strategies.

Explanations for gender differences in coping include socialization and the adoption of traditional gender-roles (Aldwin, 2000; Boekaerts, 1996; Frydenberg, 1997; Rudolph, 2002; Tamres et al., 2002). The gender socialization hypothesis argues that girls are encouraged to express emotion and turn to others for emotional support during times of stress whereas boys are discouraged from displaying emotions and asking for help because it signifies weakness (Tamres et al., 2002). Boys are more likely to cope with stress by denying a problem or avoiding it because they are socialized to conceal their emotions.

The actual coping efforts of individuals are not solely guided by a single social role. In sport, some authors have argued that the attitudes and values embodied within the 'sport' role (i.e., competitiveness, autonomy, and achievement) may interact with gender roles to intensify traditional masculine gender-role and are incompatible with the traditional feminine gender-role (Gill, 2003; Messner, 1992; Miller and Levy, 1996). In boys, a strong masculine identity has been associated with a greater tendency to ignore and conceal pain and injury in sport compared to other contexts (Nixon, 1993; Roderick et al., 2000). In contrast to boys whose masculine gender-role attitudes and behaviors are encouraged within sport, girls who participate in sport may experience a gender-role conflict. That is, female athletes may experience conflict between the values and proscribed behaviors associated with sport and the societal expectations of femininity (Czisma, Wittig, and Schurr, 1988; Miller and Levy, 1996). Consequently, girls' coping efforts may be less representative of traditional gender-role in the sport context. Generally, no support for the gender-role conflict has been demonstrated in the sport literature (Allison, 1991; Miller and Levy, 1996). Nevertheless, sport researchers should be aware of how social roles potentially interact to affect coping efforts within the sport context.

Situational Appraisals

People can choose coping responses based on information from the objective demands, constraints, and social resources of the social environment and the potential impact to one's well-being (Aldwin, 2000). Situations vary greatly in the objective and subjective cues of loss, threat, and/or challenge (Lazarus, 1999). For example, elite competitive experiences (e.g., Olympic Games) are assumed to be intensely demanding with limited access to social resources compared to that of training sessions that are conducted in one's community.

Sport researchers have exclusively examined coping in relation to the *subjective* evaluation (as opposed to objective indices) of a situation in terms of threat and challenge. For example, Ntoumanis and Biddle (2000) examined the relationship between debilitative/facilitative interpretations of competitive anxiety and coping use with a sample of 356 British University athletes. Their study revealed that interpretations of cognitive and somatic competitive anxiety as facilitative (i.e., positive and challenging) was significantly related to increasing effort and suppression of competing activities. In contrast, athletes who viewed their anxiety as debilitative (i.e., negative and threatening) used behavioral disengagement and venting of emotions. Consistent across studies, sport participants who view situations negatively tend to report using avoidance strategies to manage the associated stress whereas approach or instrumental coping is associated more with positive perceptions of the situation (Anshel and Delany, 2001; Anshel and Kaissidis, 1997; Madden et al., 1990; Ntoumanis and Biddle, 2000). This finding has been demonstrated in the management of competitive demands, injury, and performance slumps.

The understanding of social-environmental cues in terms of loss, threat, and challenge is, therefore, influenced by both objective features of the situation and by person factors. Lazarus (1999) asserts that key moderators of the relationship between appraisals and coping are (1) point-in-time (i.e., the imminence, timing, and duration of the demands of the situation) and (2) perceived controllability. Threat appraisals are proposed to be more strongly associated with point-in-time factors (Lazarus, 1999). The assessment for the potential of harm during a situation is related to the temporal features of the situation. Alternatively, situations are more likely to be viewed as challenging when there is strong familiarity with the situation, predictability, and clarity in demands that are to be met (Lazarus, 1999).

Temporal Situational Features and Situational Appraisals

Sport research that has examined shifts in coping across points-in-time has primarily studied changes across a competitive event (e.g., Anshel and Andersen, 2002; Crocker and Isaak, 1997; Gaudreau, Blondin, and Lapierre, 2002; Gaudreau et al., 2001; Haney and Long, 1995; Masters and Lambert, 1989) and across phases of injury recovery (Quinn and Fallon,

1999; Udry, 1997). In general, these studies revealed that the utilization of coping efforts changes across stages/phases of a competitive event and/or injury rehabilitation program. For example, Crocker and Isaak (1997) reported that youth swimmer's utilization of planning, suppression of competing activities, positive reappraisal, venting of emotions, humor, and self-blame varied substantially across the competitive encounters. Similarly, Gaudreau et al. (2001) found that strategies such as active coping, increased effort, suppression of competing activities, seeking social support, positive reappraisal, and wishful thinking were used more frequently during the days before a golf tournament compared to the competition per se.

As theorized by Lazarus (1991, 1999), the variance in coping utilization observed across situations is associated, in part, with the appraisal of threat which changes over the course of a situation. During periods of low threat, individuals experience an increased capacity to apply coping resources. In contrast, periods of high threat impose a debilitating effect on coping utilization (Lazarus, 1991). Sport scientists, however, have not tested this proposition as it relates to changes in coping observed at different points in time. Athletes appraisals of a competitive event a day prior to its occurrence reflect lower levels of threat compared to assessments made just prior to or during the event (Mahoney and Avener, 1977). This, in turn, is likely to contribute at least in part to the results that have been obtained in the sport coping literature. Future study is required to confirm this prediction.

Perceptions of Control and Situational Appraisals

It is well established that coping behaviors are related to perceptions of control (Aldwin, 2000; Lazarus, 1991; Skinner, 1995). Sport research is consistent with empirical studies in the non-sport coping literature and demonstrates that problem-focused coping is strongly associated with high perception of control and that emotion-focused coping is strongly associated with low perception of control (Anshel and Kaissidis, 1997; Daly, Brewer, Van Raalte, Petitpas, and Sklar, 1995; Gaudreau and Blondin, 2002; Haney and Long, 1995; Johnson, 1996; Kaissidis-Rodafinos, Anshel, and Porter, 1997; Taylor and May, 1996). Skinner (1995) stated that perception of control can change over time, which is reflected in structural developmental changes (e.g., cognitive and social functioning; see development section) and the extent to which well-learned coping responses are effectively executed in relation to environmental demands. Thus, an athlete who successfully meets his/her goal within a demanding sport situation is likely to develop strong control and/or efficacy beliefs about future actions in similar situations. In return, increasing control about is likely to lead to more adaptive form of coping responses in future situations involving similar demands and constraints.

Person-related Antecedents

In addition to social and environmental antecedents, the choice of coping strategies used during a stressful event is also influenced by important person variables (Aldwin, 2000; Folkman, 1991; Krohne, 1996; Lazarus, 1999). Lazarus (1999) argued that the ways in which an individual perceives information about the self and their environment, applies meaning to the informational cues, and coordinates action (i.e., coping) is influenced by three person-related antecedents including (1) goals and goal hierarchies (i.e., motivation), (2) beliefs about self and the world, and (3) personal resources. Some of these factors are conceptualized as personality attributes that mature slowly across life-span (e.g., optimism, achievement orientations, trait anxiety), while others change are known to change rapidly and constantly across situations and settings (e.g., self-esteem, achievement goals, self-efficacy).

Personality Antecedents

Motivation Antecedents

A key antecedent determining individual differences in coping responses is discerning 'with what' the sport participant is attempting to manage. Transactional theorists (e.g., Aldwin, 2000; Boekearts, 1996; Lazarus, 1991) argue that the thwarting of important and meaningful goals is a necessary condition of coping. Goals vary in content (e.g., social, task, social-comparison) and the degree to which they are valued by an individual. This, in turn, leads to individual differences in coping (Gaudreau et al., 2002; Lazarus, 1991). Sport scientists have a limited understanding about the influence of motivation on individual differences in coping. Nevertheless some studies have emerged in the literature that have investigated the relation between coping and (a) risk-taking motivation, (b) attributional styles, and (c) goal-orientations.

Sensation-seeking and Risk-taking Motivation

Zuckermann (1979, 1983) proposed that sensation-seeking is a biologically based personality disposition that reflects individual differences in the optimum levels of arousal. Smith, Ptacek, and Smoll (1992) examined sensation-seeking motivation in the context of injury vulnerability among varsity athletes. They found no evidence that high sensation-seeking would influence injury vulnerability by increasing risk-taking behaviors. Sensation-seeking was found to be positively related to several coping subscales of the ACSI-28. Coping, however, was not found to moderate the relationship between sensation seeking and injury susceptibility.

Attributions

According to Weiner (1985), emotional states are the result of both the achievement outcome and the reasons people attribute to the cause of the outcome. Attributions are proposed to differ according to perceptions of (a) the locus of causality (i.e., internal or external to the person), (b) stability of the environmental event over time, and (c) controllability of the event. Specific emotional states, in turn, give rise to a host of specific psychological (e.g., self-esteem, pride, hopelessness, relaxation, and affect) and behaviors responses (e.g., helping, achievement, strivings, and effort; Weiner, 1986). An equivocal pattern of findings has emerged among the few studies that exist within the sport literature. In the context of competitive stress, Sellers and Peterson (1993) reported that global based internal and stable attributions significantly related to emotion-focused coping responses among a sample of collegiate football players. In the context of impression-management, Prapavessis et al. (2003) reported that athletes with strong handicapping tendencies (i.e., actions during performance situations that facilitate external reasons for failure and internal reasons for success) used more denial/avoidance, wishful thinking, and emotion-focused coping than low self-handicappers.

Goal Orientations

Another motivation disposition identified as an antecedent of coping behavior is goal orientations. Goal orientations are dispositional tendencies to perceive competence in achievement settings either in reference to self (i.e., task orientation) or to normative other (i.e., ego-orientation; Ntoumanis et al., 1999). Only a few studies directly linked goal orientations with individual differences in coping. Based on sport-related literature on motivation and on the cognitive-motivational-relational model of stress and emotion (Lazarus, 1991), Ntoumanis and Biddle (1998) predicted that (a) ego-oriented athletes would be more likely to display a lack of effort and persistence, devalue activities, and select inappropriate tasks and strategies when managing competitive stress, whereas (b) task-oriented individuals would display behaviors that reflect challenge seeking, use of effective coping strategies, and high effort when managing competitive stress. Path analysis confirmed the researchers' predictions. With a sample of 356 British varsity athletes, it was demonstrated that a high task-orientation was significantly related to suppression of competing activities, while a high ego-orientation was related to venting of emotions. A similar pattern of results has been demonstrated with elite Norwegian athletes (Pensgaard and Roberts, 2003).

Beliefs about Self and the World

Beliefs a person has about himself and the world influence cognitive appraisal and consequently the choices of coping responses (Lazarus, 1991). In the sport literature, two preliminary lines of research have emerged investigating the role of athletic identity (e.g. Grove et al., 1997) and self-esteem (e.g., Bourgeois, Loss, Meyers, and LeUnes, 2003; Lane, Jones, and Stevens, 2002; Smith et al., 1995) on sport participants' coping.

Athletic Identity

A strong athletic identity has been suggested to be a problem for athletes who are retiring from sport (Baillie, 1993). Specifically, athletes with a strong athletic identity are less likely to prepare for the transition, develop an adequate social network, and are more likely to experience high levels of distress upon retirement (Baillie, 1993; Grove et al., 1997). Grove et al. studied the relationship between athletic identity and the coping strategies used during retirement from sport in 51 retired New Zealand national team members. Results revealed that retired athletes with a strong athletic identity used more venting of emotions, mental disengagement, behavioral disengagement, reliance on denial, seeking out emotional and instrumental support, and suppression of competing activities compared to retired athletes with weaker athletic identities.

Self-esteem

Self-esteem, or the overall subjective evaluation about the self, is an important attribute influencing sport participants' goal directed behavior (Fox, 1997). It has been reported that sport participants with high self-esteem increase efforts, seek out difficult goals, and persist in the face of failure to a greater extent than individuals with low levels of self esteem (Fox, 1997). Lane and colleagues (2002) revealed that junior table tennis players with low self-esteem endorsed behavioral disengagement and self-blame coping strategies during competitive stress to a greater extent than their high self-esteem counterparts.

Personal Resources

A third category of personality antecedents in sport participants' coping is personal resources. These consist of attributes such as health and energy, attractiveness, money, social skills, education, supportive family and friends, and dispositions to view situations in a positive way (i.e., optimism). These resources are proposed to influence what an individual is able to do (and not do) when attempting to manage difficult situations (Lazarus, 1999). In the sport coping literature, individual differences in coping have been associated with the personal resources of (1) coping styles (e.g., Anshel, 1996, Jerome and Williams, 2000), (2) trait anxiety (e.g., Eubank and Collins, 2000; Giacobbi and Weinberg, 2000), (3) trait-confidence (e.g., Grove and Heard, 1997), and (4) dispositional optimism (e.g., Grove and Heard, 1997).

Coping Styles

Coping styles have received the most attention as a personal resource influencing sport participant's choices of coping strategies. Debate exists in the literature regarding the conceptual nature of coping styles. Several sport researchers who advocate the existence of coping styles (e.g., Anshel, 1996; Anshel and Anderson, 2002; Anshel and Weinberg, 1996, 1999; Giacobbi and Weinberg, 2000; Kaissidis-Rodanfinos and Anshel, 2000) have demonstrated empirical support for habitual patterns of coping that are consistent across situations and over time. Defined in this way, coping styles are conceptually equivalent to coping traits. That is, both are defined *empirically* as actions characteristic to the individual (Lazarus, 1999).

In contrast to the atheoretical approach to determining coping styles, other sport researchers have applied theoretical coping-style propositions to the sport context, differentiating between coping traits and styles. This perspective assumes that underlying person attributes, traits, or dispositions (i.e., goal orientation, beliefs) interact in such a way as to create a stable coping structure (i.e., coping style) that influences how environmental information is perceived and interpreted in terms of both personal meaning and coping choices (Krohne, 1996; Lazarus, 1999). Krohne and Hindel (1988) examined the influence of a vigilant and cognitive-avoidant coping style on 36 elite table tennis players' perceptions of stress during practice and competitive events. Athletes who tended to focus attention on threat relevant information and intensified their attempts to reduce uncertainty in the environmental demands were classified as having a 'vigilant' coping style. Conversely, athletes who used a 'cognitive avoidance' coping style were described to avoid threat-relevant information and deny attempts at reducing emotional arousal. The authors confirmed predictions that coping styles are associated with specific cognitive appraisals. Athletes who used a vigilant and/or a low cognitive-avoidance coping style were more likely to experience competitive state anxiety during competition.

Work completed by Jean Williams and her colleagues (e.g., Jerome and Williams, 2000; Ryska, 1993; Williams and Krane, 1992) has applied a multivariate model of coping-style that is based on the personal attributes of trait-anxiety and social desirability (Krohne and Rogner, 1982). Specifically the interaction of these attributes give rise to four independent coping styles (Krohne, 1996; Williams and Krane, 1992) including: (1) low anxious (low trait anxiety, low social desirability), (2) repressive (low trait anxiety, high social desirability), (3) high-anxious or sensitive (high trait anxiety, low social desirability), and (4) defensive high-anxious (high trait anxious, high social desirability). Research using this model hypothesizes that individuals differ in subjective and objective stress reactions (Krohne, 1996). Jerome and Williams (2000) and Williams and Krane (1992) reported significant differences in athletes with a repressive style favoring lower levels of state anxiety and higher levels of self-confidence during a competitive event. Ryska (1993), however, did not demonstrate differences among the four groups in reported levels of competitive state anxiety. This pattern of findings is consistent with what has been reported in the general coping literature. Lazarus (1999) concluded that the inconsistency in the coping style research makes it hard to argue that coping styles have much to do with the way people cope with specific threats in particular situations. Further, he stated that:

> "My complaint is not with the style concept itself, but the kind of measurement that has become fashionable for it, and the failure to relate these styles to what people do from a process standpoint...Motivational traits and situational intentions seem to provide a good organizational framework..." (Lazarus, 1999, p. 110).

Trait-anxiety

Sport researchers who study competitive trait anxiety as an antecedent of coping assume that high trait anxious individuals have a characteristic perceptual style or a tendency to disengage from goals that render them to become preoccupied with distressful emotions (Giacobbi and Weinberg, 2000). Empirical research supports these propositions (Bresler and Pieper, 1992; Eubank and Collins, 2000; Giacobbi and Weinberg, 2000). Athletes who report high competitive trait anxiety respond to competitive stress applying (a) greater efforts of denial, behavioral disengagement, self-blame, and wishful thinking, and (b) less efforts of planning, positive reinterpretation, social support, and problem-solving compared to their low competitive trait anxiety counterparts.

Trait Self-confidence and Optimism

Contrary to trait anxiety, positive ways of thinking such as trait self-confidence and dispositional optimism are purported to produce challenge-based appraisals of stressful situations, which in turn, facilitate effective coping (Hardy et al., 1996). Dispositional optimism is defined as a trait-like expectancy for successful outcomes, while trait self-confidence represents a generalized expectancy for successful outcomes in sport situations (Grove and Heard, 1997). Optimism has been linked to coping efforts in the non-sport literature (e.g., Iwanaga, Yokoyama, and Seiwa, 2004; Scheier and Carver, 1992). In a study with 213 collegiate athletes, Grove and Heard (1997) reported that in the context of coping with performance slumps, trait self-confidence and optimism related positively to problem-focused coping and negatively with emotion-focused coping.

Developmental Antecedents

While personality factors describe individual differences that are primarily invariant across the lifespan; developmental factors, on the other hand, are person-based variables that give rise to systematic differences among individuals over time (Skinner, 1995). For example, cognitive capacities, motivation orientations, and social skills are important person attributes that are developmental in nature and have been suggested to impact the stress and coping process in sport and other contexts (Crocker, Hoar, Kowalski, McDonough, and Neifer, 2004; Crocker, Kowalski, et al., 2004).

Knowledge about developmental coping antecedents in the sport context is lacking. To date two lines of research exist that seek to describe developmental individual differences. One line has examined *age* differences in coping responses (e.g., Bäckman and Molander, 1986a, 1986b, 1991; Goyen and Anshel, 1996; Madden et al., 1989). This research provides descriptive evidence regarding the changing nature of coping over the lifespan; however, chronological research alone does not advance our understanding of the underlying coping mechanisms. Development processes are age-related but not age-dependent (Brustad, 1998). A second line of developmental research within the sport coping literature describes *expertise* differences in coping (e.g., Cleary and Zimmerman, 2003). This line improves upon the limitations of age-related research. A change in expertise in sport is likely to be more predictive of qualitative shifts in coping because achievement of expertise requires maturation of physical, psychological, and social developmental-based variables (Weiss and Williams, 2004).

Age-related Changes

Based on the non-sport literature (e.g., Aldwin, Sutton, Chiara, and Spiro, 1996; Fields and Prinz, 1997), we would expect that children, adolescents, and adults have differential application of coping in sport. In one of the only coping studies to apply a developmental approach, Hoar (2003) described the coping responses of 626 early adolescent athletes between the ages of 11 and 15 years to an interpersonal stressor in sport. From the total sample, 51 athletes did not report experiencing stress in their interactions with others in sport. Those who did experience stress were more likely to be males under the age of twelve. Results revealed that the most common sources of interpersonal stress included disagreements with coach and teammates, offences committed by opponents, and problems with referees. On average, athletes reported, through an open-ended measure (that did not assume specific coping strategies), the application of two or three coping strategies to manage their stress. Higher order classification of the coping strategies revealed that athletes used active coping, mental disengagement, and seeking social support most frequently. Coping strategies were found to serve multiple coping functions, which was moderated by gender. That is, a single coping strategy (e.g., active coping) could be used for problem-focused, emotion-focused, and/or avoidance coping functions. Early adolescent females applied greater emotion-focused coping than males; which, in turn, applied more avoidance coping efforts than their female counterparts.

Among those studies that have compared sport participants coping during the adolescent and early adulthood years, it has been found that coping is situation specific but that across demanding competitive situations adolescents generally utilize a mixture of problem-solving and emotion-focused coping efforts, whereas adults primarily use problem-focused coping (Goyen and Anshel, 2001; Madden et al., 1989). These findings generally support what has been reported in the developmental and aging coping literature (Aldwin, 2000; Fields and Prinz, 1997; Frydenberg, 1997; Seiffge-Krenke, 1995). A major assumption of developmental coping research is that *adaptive* self-regulation is guided by the personal and social resources that are available to an individual at a specific point in the lifespan (Aldwin, 2000; Compas, 1998; Compas, Connor-Smith, Saltzman, Thomsen, and Wadsworth, 2001; Skinner and Edge, 1998). Very little evidence, however, exists to confirm this assumption (particularly in the sport context). One promising line of research to understand how sport participants' coping develops over time is the study of expertise in sport.

Sport Expertise

Scant research has examined individual differences in coping associated with levels of sport expertise (e.g., Cleary and Zimmerman, 2003; McLeod, Kirkby, and Madden, 1994). As one example, Cleary and Zimmerman (2003) studied differences in self-regulatory forethought (i.e., goals, strategy choice, and self-efficacy) and self-reflection processes (e.g., attributions, and feelings of satisfaction) associated with expertise in basketball. Results demonstrated significant differences in elite participants self-regulatory forethought and self-reflection processes compared to the non-elite and novice participants. Elite participants reported more technique based coping strategies, attributed success and failure to problems of strategy execution (i.e., internal and unstable attributions), and displayed higher self-efficacy for the task compared to the non-experts and the novices. This study suggests that individual differences among sport participants' coping are due, in part, to differences associated with expertise.

Antecedents of Coping Summary

In summary, sport research has identified a number of person and social-environmental antecedents that contribute to individual differences in sport participants' coping. For example, sport participants who hold a task goal orientation, attributions that are internal and unstable, low levels of competitive trait anxiety, and high levels of self-esteem, trait self-confidence and dispositional optimism tend to utilize active problem-solving efforts to manage difficult situations in sport. Alternatively, sport participants who hold an ego goal orientation, attributions that are stable, repressive coping styles, high levels of competitive trait anxiety, and low levels of self-esteem, state self-confidence and dispositional optimism have a tendency to utilize coping efforts that are more emotion-focused and avoidant in nature. Sport researchers, however, should interpret these findings cautiously. A number of challenges and limitations are inherent to the study of coping among different groups of sport participants. First, many of the existent studies reported weak effect sizes, poor methodological design, and have not been replicated in the sport literature. Second, conceptually, isolation of antecedent factors does not truly represent the transactional nature of coping (Aldwin, 2000; Lazarus 1991, 1999). As such, future research should examine whether person and socio-environmental interactions could improve our understanding of the selection of coping responses across various sport settings. Researchers should also examine whether person-related variables mediate the relationship between socio-environmental variables and the use of coping strategies.

OUTCOMES OF COPING

There are a number of challenges associated with identifying outcomes of coping responses. First, in many cases relationships between coping and hypothesized outcomes are likely bi-directional. Coping is not a static process. As a result of re-appraisal of outcomes, subsequent coping behavior is likewise influenced. Second, in order to determine outcomes of coping efforts, data needs to be collected at more than one time period, which increases both the time and cost of research. Third, just as there are challenges to the conceptualization and assessment of coping, there are similar challenges associated with many proposed outcomes of coping. However, despite these challenges, a number of studies have examined various potential functional, emotional, and psychosomatic outcomes of coping.

Functional Outcomes

Absolute Indices of Sport Performance

Whereas performance is a core focus of sport science research, there is limited empirical research on how coping influences absolute indices of athletic performance. In general, the literature suggests a weak relationship between coping and performance. For example, Haney and Long (1995) found weak relationships between coping and performance in simulated basketball free throw and soccer/field hockey penalty shot competitions. Engagement-oriented coping correlated positively with both performance and performance satisfaction whereas disengagement-oriented coping was associated negatively with both outcomes. Using a prospective design, Smith et al. (1995) found that pre-season psychological skills of high-school athletes did not predict coaches' rating of ability and performance at the end of the season. In a similar study with professional baseball players, Smith and Christensen (1995) investigated the associations of self-report and coaches rating of psychological skills with end-of-season statistical data (i.e., batting average of field players and earned run average of the pitchers). Their findings indicated that psychological skills predicted an additional 20 to 38% of performance variance over and above overall evaluation of physical ability, although these results suggest more about psychological skills than actual coping.

Goal Attainment and Discrepancy Indices

A major part of inter-individual differences in absolute sport performance is determined by physical, biomechanical, technical, and tactical factors that cannot be overcome by adaptation processes such as coping strategies. As a result, only a small amount of variance in absolute performance will likely be attributed to coping. Nevertheless, it has been suggested that coping can contribute to an understanding of why some athletes attain their goals whereas others fail to perform to the best of their capacities (Cerin, Szabo, Hunt, and Williams, 2000; Gaudreau Blondin, Lapierre, 2002). A number of studies have shown task-oriented coping strategies (i.e., thought control, mental imagery, effort expenditure, logical analysis, and seeking support) to be associated with greater perceived goal attainment whereas disengagement-oriented coping strategies (i.e., disengagement/resignation and venting of unpleasant emotions) related to lower levels of goal attainment (Gaudreau and Blondin, 2002).

A second line of inquiry has relied on a series of discrepancy indices to assess the influence of coping on self-referenced criteria of performance. Smith et al. (1995) created a talent-performance discrepancy index to classify athletes as overachievers, normal achievers, and underachievers. Athletes whose performance ratings exceeded their physical ability ratings scored significantly higher than other athletes on three pre-season psychological skills (i.e., coping with adversity, concentration, and coachability) and on the total score of the ASCI-28. Using a more direct assessment of coping (as opposed to psychological skills), Gaudreau et al. (2002) demonstrated that coping strategies used during a competitive round of golf correlated with a performance-goal discrepancy index. Results indicated that lower levels of performance-goal discrepancy were negatively related to task-oriented coping strategies (i.e., active coping, planning, increased effort, positive reappraisal, suppression of competing activities) and positively related to disengagement-oriented coping strategies (i.e., behavioral disengagement and venting of emotions). These findings were replicated and expanded in a recent study conducted with a sample of golfers participating in a provincial level golf championship (Gaudreau and Blondin, 2004b). Results revealed that when golf handicap (i.e., an objective index of athletic ability) was partialed out (i.e., holding a variable constant and thereby removing its effect on two variables; Meehl, 1970), the relationships between coping and performance-goal discrepancy remained significant.

Longevity and Desire to Continue in Sport

The capacity to adapt successfully to stressful experiences across multiple domains may have an impact on career longevity and desire to subsequently participate in competitive sports. Smith and Christensen (1995) examined whether psychological skills could predict survival in professional baseball over a three-year period. Consistent with expectations, the three-year survivors had significantly higher psychological skills ratings on all but two subscales of the ASCI-28 (i.e., confidence and freedom from worry). Interestingly, ratings of psychological skills provided by coaches were better predictors of survival than the athletes' self-reports. More recently, Kim and Duda (2003) examined the relationships between coping and desire to continue in sport with samples of Korean and American athletes. Active problem-focused coping correlated positively with desire to continue in sport, whereas avoidance-withdrawal coping was associated with lower intention to continue playing the next year.

Emotional Outcomes

Competitive State Anxiety

Despite the widespread sport-related literature on multidimensional state anxiety, little empirical attention has been devoted to the potential influence of coping strategies on cognitive and somatic state anxiety. Although limited, research suggests that task-oriented coping strategies are mainly unrelated to competitive state anxiety. To some extent, however, there are consistent significant associations between disengagement-oriented strategies (i.e., venting of emotions and behavioral disengagement) and higher levels of cognitive and somatic state anxiety (Gaudreau and Blondin, 2002; Ntoumanis and Biddle, 2000). The existent literature on the coping-anxiety relationships is based on cross-sectional designs, making it difficult to ascertain whether coping or anxiety comes first. Also, the failure to account for the facilitative or debilitative effect of anxiety may explain the equivocal findings reported in the coping literature. For instance, Ntoumanis and Biddle (2000) showed that task-oriented coping strategies (i.e., increased effort and suppression of competing activities) related favourably to facilitative anxiety whereas disengagement-oriented coping strategies (i.e., behavioral disengagement and venting of emotions) were associated to debilitative anxiety. These results suggest that perceiving the anxiety as facilitative or debilitative could moderate the relationships between coping strategies and the intensity of somatic state anxiety.

Affective States

Coping has been theorized to be a critical aspect of the emotion process (Lazarus, 1991) and coping should therefore have an influence on affective outcomes. Generally, sport research is consistent with the hypothesis that task-oriented coping strategies should correlate positively with positive affect whereas emotion- and disengagement-oriented coping should correlate positively with negative affect (Crocker and Graham, 1995; Gaudreau et al., 2002; Ntoumanis et al., 1999). For example, Gaudreau and Blondin (2002) reported that task-oriented coping strategies shared an average of 18% of variance with positive affect whereas disengagement-oriented coping strategies shared an average of 15% of variance with negative affect. Results of a recent study by Kim and Duda (2003) indicated that active problem-focused coping was associated with higher levels of sport-related satisfaction and enjoyment in both Korean and American samples. They also demonstrated that avoidance-withdrawal coping correlated negatively with these affective outcomes in the Korean sample of athletes. Similarly, psychological skills have been found to be positively correlated with various dimensions of multidimensional flow state (Jackson, Thomas, Marsh, and Smethurst, 2001).

Despite the appealing nature of these results, Crocker and Graham (1995) suggested that coping and affective states should be examined more thoroughly to determine whether their relationships could be explained by other variables. A recent meta-analytical review of the literature illustrated that progress toward goal attainment leads to more positive emotional outcomes (Koestner, Lekes, Powers, and Chicoine, 2002). Consistent with this literature, Gaudreau et al. (2002) tested the mediating role of performance-goal discrepancy in the relationships between coping strategies and affective states during and 24 hours after a competition. They showed that performance-goal discrepancy partially mediated the coping-affect relationships. These results have been replicated in a recent path analytical study in which various indices of goal attainment (i.e., performance-goal discrepancy, performance-norm discrepancy, and perceived goal attainment) partially mediated the coping-affect relationships (Gaudreau and Blondin, 2004b). Using affective data collected prior to and following a sport competition, Amiot et al. (2004) demonstrated that coping contributed significantly to perceived goal attainment which, in turn, predicted increases in positive emotion and decreases in negative emotion across stages of a competition.

Psychosomatic Outcomes

Athletic Injuries

Athletic injuries can cause negative outcomes such as psychological distress, frustration, interpersonal conflicts with partners and friends, and substantial decrease in life-satisfaction. Understanding how athletes manage the multiple demands associated with an athletic injury is of particular concern for rehabilitation theory and practice. Udry (1997) examined a small sample of athletes ($n = 25$) who underwent knee surgery by following them across five points within the first 12 weeks of the rehabilitation process (Udry, 1997). Coping strategies used to manage health problems associated with the injury explained between 12% (three week post-surgery) and 44% (nine week post-surgery) of the behavioral adherence to the rehabilitation program. Specifically, instrumental coping was the strongest predictor of adherence at each wave of the study. In addition, palliative coping was also strongly associated to adherence at each wave of the rehabilitation process. These findings suggest that coping could contribute, at least to some extent, to a more rapid return to the competition as well as to lower likelihood of repeated injuries. However, it is likely that *both* problem-focused and emotion-focused coping strategies are important for athletes to use in order to effectively manage injury (Cornelius, 2002).

Despite coping being featured as a key process in psychological based models of athletic injury (e.g., Andersen and Williams, 1988) and the recognition by at least some sport trainers and athletic therapists that coping plays a roll in effective injury rehabilitation (e.g., Ford and Gordon, 1998), the relationship between coping and vulnerability to injury has received limited empirical attention. In a study with high-school varsity athletes, psychological skills were not related to time loss due to injuries during the upcoming season (Smith, Smoll, and Ptacek, 1990). They did find, however, that psychological skills moderated the relationship between negative life-events and time loss due to injuries. Negative life events led to a greater likelihood of subsequent injuries when athletes reported low levels of pre-season psychological skills. It seems that high levels of psychological skills might buffer the effect of negative life-events on the likelihood of having subsequent injuries. However, other factors such as optimism, hardiness, or global self-esteem might also be important in the coping process (Ford, Eklund, and Gordon, 2000).

Burnout

According to Smith (1986), burnout represents a psycho-physiological state that is experienced as a result of failure to effectively manage the excessive demands associated with training and competition. Using a small sample of national level junior tennis players, Gould, Udry, Tuffey, and Loehr (1996) showed that burned out players were less likely to use planning strategies and were lower on positive reinterpretation and growth compared to their non-burned out counterparts. They recommended that the context of the specific stressful situation encountered be considered to better understand differences in coping between burned out and non-burned out athletes. Furthermore, in addition to sport demands, athletes must manage a variety of demands emanating across other domains of their life. Thus, the capacity to cope effectively with these demands and to resolve potential conflicts across life domains should be taken into account to provide a comprehensive portrait of the psychological factors leading to and sustaining burnout in sport. All people involved in sport might experience burnout, such as athletic directors (Martin, Kelley, and Eklund, 1999) and coaches (Kelly, Eklund, and Ritter, 1999), suggesting that it is important to study the coping process across different sport roles.

IMPLICATIONS FOR PROFESSIONAL PRACTICE

The body of literature on coping in sport has great potential to inform professionals in the field. Individual studies are useful in providing insight into various components (i.e., appraisal, coping resources, coping strategies, effectiveness of coping) of emotion-based theoretical models that feature coping as a key process, such as Lazarus's cognitive-motivational-relational theory (see Crocker, Kowalski, and Graham, 2002). Also, studies reporting cultural and gender differences in coping, as well as those demonstrating differences in perceived effectiveness of various strategies, demonstrate the need to consider many factors when designing intervention programs. This emerging knowledge base can be integrated with literature that examines formal coping skills intervention programs to help guide professional practice.

The development of coping intervention programs to assist athletes with the management of sport related stress is not new. In many ways, intervention programs and techniques used in sport have preceded much of the empirical evidence regarding coping in sport. Programs such as Meichenbaum's (1985) stress inoculation training (SIT) and Smith's (1980) stress management training (SMT) are two such examples. More recently, other intervention programs have been developed such as Anshel's (1990) COPE intervention. Each of these programs emphasizes the development of a variety of cognitive and behavioral coping skills that athletes can use to manage sport-related stress which is consistent with literature showing that competitive athletes utilize a wide variety of coping strategies to manage stressful situations (e.g., Crocker and Graham, 1995; Crocker and Isaak, 1997; Gould, Finch, et al., 1993; Gould et al., 1996). Each of these programs is described below.

Stress Inoculation Training

Stress inoculation training (SIT) is based largely on the principle that the needs of the athletes determine the coping skills intervention strategies being taught. SIT is founded on cognitive-behavioral principles and is designed to teach athletes a range of coping strategies to both enhance emotional control and actively change the stressful situation (Meichenbaum, 1985, 1993). The SIT program is designed so that athletes learn coping skills through multiple phases of conceptualization, skill acquisition and rehearsal, and application and follow-through. In these phases, athletes learn about the stress and coping process, develop a wide range of coping skills, and are given opportunities to practice their coping skills. In their description of a case study of "Jill" who is attempting to manage the multiple demands of performance, her role as captain, and a troubled athlete-coach relationship, Crocker et al. (2002) provided an example of how a SIT intervention could assist an athlete cope with a complex emotional experience involving multiple, and often competing, goals. Although the empirical results are somewhat mixed, there is general support for SIT in studies that have tested its effectiveness as a coping skills intervention in sport (Kerr and Leith, 1993; Kress, Schroeder, Potteiger, and Haub, 1999; Larsson, Cook, and Starrin, 1988; Mace and Carroll, 1986, 1989; Mace, Eastman, and Carroll, 1986; Ross and Berger, 1996; Whitmarsh and Alderman, 1993). Recently developed interventions, such as Botterill and Brown's (2002) emotional inoculation training program, are similar to SIT, thus demonstrating the potential of this type of coping intervention.

Stress Management Training

In stress management training (SMT), athletes develop a coping response that can be used to manage stressful sport situations (Smith, 1980). This program is carried out in four general steps. First, athletes' cognitive and behavioral coping skills are assessed. Athletes also describe typical stressful situations and coping responses used in sport. Next, an "integrated coping response" (consisting of muscular relaxation and self-statements) is developed with the athlete. Athletes then practice the newly created coping response to induced affective experience. Finally, a post-treatment evaluation is made to assess the effects of the training program. Similar to SIT, there is general support for SMT as an effective coping skills intervention in sport (Crocker, 1989a, 1989b; Crocker et al., 1988; Ziegler, Klinzing, and Williamson, 1982).

COPE Training

COPE training was developed to assist athletes in managing acute stress in sport. Similar to SMT, the COPE program involves the acquisition of strategies in a planned sequence that fosters mastery over the coping skills (Anshel, 1990). COPE training includes the four processes of "controlling emotions, organizing input into meaningful and non-meaningful categories, planning the next response, and executing skilled performance" (p. 63).

An important concept in Anshel's COPE intervention is the development of a variety of cognitive and behavioral strategies as a result of different strategies being more or less effective in managing certain specific stressors. Anshel and colleagues have shown support for COPE training as effective in helping athletes manage acute stress in sport (Anshel, 1990; Anshel, Brown, and Brown, 1993; Anshel, Gregory, and Kaczmarek, 1990).

FUTURE RESEARCH DIRECTIONS

The expansion of the coping literature over the past two decades attests to the recognition of the central role of coping in the emotion process of sport participants. Sport researchers have spent considerable attention in (1) clarifying conceptual core of the coping construct including issues surrounding its measurement, (2) identifying antecedents and outcomes of coping, and (3) developing intervention programs to develop coping skills of sport performers. In the presentation of this body of literature, we have highlighted areas where further research is required to clarify empirical and theoretical inconsistencies. This discussion is continued with the presentation of selected conceptual and measurement issues that will advance understanding, but have received limited attention from sport researchers.

Conceptual Issues

Coping is a multidimensional construct entailing a variety of strategies through which athletes attempt to manage the demands of a particular situation. Qualitative investigations of coping (e.g., Gould, Eklund, et al., 1993; Gould, Finch, et al., 1993; Gould et al., 1997a; Holt and Hogg, 2002; Park, 2000) have elegantly demonstrated that a single athlete can use a variety of coping strategies while involved in a specific situation (i.e., sport competition, training, rehabilitation). Yet, these studies have failed to account for the multivariate nature of coping by examining the relations between coping strategies and antecedent and outcome variables. The combination of coping strategies used by a sport participant during a specific encounter is likely to result from the complex interaction between person and environment antecedents and the outcome that is desired (i.e., to change the situation and/or manage emotional response; Lazarus, 1991, 1999). These types of interactions could likely best be examined by a wide variety of creative quantitative, qualitative, and/or mixed-methods designs in order to develop a more complete understanding of the coping process.

Research in the coping field also needs to more adequately address basic antecedents and outcomes of the coping responses. In general, in the sport coping literature, there is a need for experimental designs that will more adequately identify antecedents and outcomes of coping. Most of the recent sport research has involved passive observations rather than the experimental or quasi-experimental designs formally used in research assessing the effectiveness of coping skills interventions. Researchers need to be more creative in designing studies that manipulate key variables (e.g., task demands, appraisal of threat) to assess changes in coping and emotion. In addition, more research should investigate the mediating and moderating mechanisms whereby coping influences and is influenced by a variety of socio-environmental, person-related, and affective variables.

Clearly more research needs to be conducted to provide further insight into the role of state- and trait-like conceptualizations of coping. Research seems to suggest that there are both general coping "styles" that influence coping efforts and a great deal of flexibility in coping within a specific situation. Nonetheless, the socio-environmental conditions under which coping styles play a more or less prominent role in coping needs further scrutiny. As an example, the complex relation between the coping strategies used during specific encounters and related antecedents and outcomes might be revealed by coping profiles (Smith and Wallston, 1996; Suls and David, 1996). This higher order perspective entails determining (1) the combination of coping strategies that lead to the realization of specific outcomes (e.g., performance related outcomes, emotional states, social outcomes, and psychosomatic states), and (2) the person and environment antecedents influencing the choice of different multivariate coping profiles. This line of inquiry, advocated recently by Gaudreau and Blondin (2004a), could contribute to both research examining how changes in multivariate coping profiles relates prospectively to psychological and functional adjustments and to literature on intra-individual differences in coping (i.e., idiographic differences in coping across time and contexts).

Measurement Issues

A number of unresolved coping measurement issues also need to be addressed (see Carpenter, 1992; Coyne and Gottlieb, 1996; De Ridder, 1997; Schwarzer and Schwarzer, 1996; Stone et al., 1992, for more thorough discussions on conceptual and methodological issues in coping assessment). In their review, Crocker and colleagues (1998) concluded that what is assessed with respect to coping, and the manner in which the assessment is carried out, is of concern for sport researchers. Many of those issues remain relevant today.

Coping instruments that are developmentally and culturally appropriate remain an important task for sport researchers. Although age appropriate measures have occasionally been developed in sport coping research (e.g., Kowalski and Crocker, 2001), the validity of any particular measure across the life-span needs to be established. Similarly, gender and culture need to be considered when deciding on (and developing) item content and the format of the instrument. Gender is important because not only do men and women potentially experience different types of situations, they also likely respond quite differently to similar situations. Consequently, both the situations and coping dimensions on a scale need to be appropriate for both males and females (Crocker and Graham, 1995; Crocker et al., 1998; Kowalski and Crocker, 2001; Maniar et al., 2001; Pensgaard and Roberts, 2003). A limitation of comparing groups using quantitative scaling is determining whether the individuals belonging to specific groups (e.g., female and male) interpret the language of scale items similarly and attach the same meaning to the numerical score for each scale item (Hughes and Sharrock, 1997). Similarly, these issues are relevant to culture, as shown in the work by Yoo (2000) by the inclusion of a transcendental coping dimension in the CSKA. At minimum, even if not developed with specific populations, validity evidence supporting the use of coping measures across various populations is required.

There also remains a need to distinguish between measurement of coping in specific situations and a more general coping style. Most existing measures are cognizant of this at a *conceptual* level (i.e., item instructions); however, at a *measurement* level (i.e., actual test scores) the distinction is often less clear. For situational measures of coping, evidence needs to be provided that responses reflect coping in that particular situation and not an aggregated score of coping responses used across various situations. Likewise, coping style measures need to provide evidence ensuring that their scores are representing more than the mere recall of a single event.

Sport researchers tend to rely on retrospective recall in the assessment of coping. There is empirical evidence showing the limited correspondence (correlations generally around .50) between short-term retrospective recalls of coping responses (i.e., two days or more after the situation) and the assessment made during the course of the situation (i.e., momentary recall) or at the end of the day (Ptacek, Smith, Espe, and Rafferty, 1994; Smith, Leffingwell, and Ptacek, 1999; Stone et al., 1998). Although there are inherent limitations with daily and momentary assessment, this research does suggest that we need to be cautious with the retrospective recall format that currently dominates sport coping assessment. Also, if hypothetical scenarios are to be used in sport coping research (as opposed to a retrospective recall of a specific event), evidence needs to be provided that responses reflect actual future coping behavior rather than either what athletes wish they *could* use, what they have used in the past, and strategies they think will be effective.

Likely the most difficult and challenging task for sport coping researchers is to adequately assess the dynamic process of coping. Coping shifts across contexts (e.g., sport and non-sport), situations within sport (e.g., competition and rehabilitation), stages of an event (e.g., stages of competition and stages of rehabilitation), and time (e.g., with cognitive and social maturation and with the development of expertise; Lazarus, 1999). In the non-sport literature, it has been demonstrated that individuals' reports of coping are confounded by its dynamic nature (Stone, Greenberg, Kennedy-Moore, and Newman, 1991). Stone and his colleagues revealed that study participants who recalled coping strategies to manage a stressful event from the previous week were referring to different stages of a stressful event. This creates difficulty in making inter-individual comparisons because individuals might be responding to different contextual demands. A related issue is the typical procedure of assessing sport participants' coping at the conclusion of an event. This procedure is likely to result in a time bias and response distortion in coping recall that is likely moderated by the length of the time interval and by the outcomes of the situation. Creative approaches to coping assessment, such as those that integrate components of qualitative research into typical measurement procedures might be useful in order to capture the dynamic nature of coping. However, even the claim that psychological variables, such as coping, can be quantified is a hypothesis that is rarely, if ever, tested in sport and exercise psychology (see Kline, 1998, for a discussion of this psychometric issue). Regardless, capturing the unfolding nature of the coping and emotion process remains a daunting psychometric task.

CONCLUSION

We remain convinced that the study of coping is critical in understanding inter-individual and intra-individual differences in athletes' responses to stress. In this chapter, we have reviewed many issues including conceptualization, measurement, antecedents, outcomes, and professional practice. As noted in the future research section, there are many exciting research challenges. We believe that the utilization of existing (or the development of better) conceptual frameworks, along with corresponding methodologies, will likely improve our understanding of coping in sport. Sport researchers must also be cognizant of research developments in associated fields of health, development, and social psychology. Since coping is both an antecedent and consequence variable in the dynamically unfolding stress process, research is multifaceted. Susan Folkman's observations over a decade ago still stand, "Coping is a complex phenomenon. Coping research is no less so." (1992, p. 46).

ACKNOWLEDGEMENTS

We would like to acknowledge and thank the two reviewers for their excellent contributions to this chapter.

REFERENCES

Aldwin, C. M. (2000). *Stress, coping, and development: An integrative perspective.* New York: Guildford.

Aldwin, C. M., Sutton, K. J., Chiara, G., and Spiro, A. (1996). Aging differences in stress, coping, and appraisal: Findings from the normative aging study. *The Journals of Gerontology, 51B,* 179-189.

Allison, M. T. (1991). Role conflict and the female athlete: Preoccupation with little ground. *Journal of Applied Sport Psychology, 13,* 49-60.

Amiot, C. E., Gaudreau, P., and Blanchard, C. M. (2004). Self-determination, coping, and goal attainment in sport. *Journal of Sport and Exercise Psychology, 26,* 396-411.

Amirkhan, J. H. (1990). A factor analytically derived measure of coping: The Coping Strategy Indicator. *Journal of Personality and Social Psychology, 59,* 1066-1074.

Andersen, M. B., and Williams, J. M. (1988). A model of stress and athletic injury: Prediction and prevention. *Journal of Sport and Exercise Psychology, 10,* 294-306.

Anshel, M. H. (1990). Toward validation of a model for coping with acute stress in sport. *International Journal of Sport Psychology, 21,* 58-83.

Anshel, M. H. (1996). Coping styles among adolescent competitive athletes. *Journal of Social Psychology, 136,* 311-323.

Anshel, M. H. (2001). Qualitative validation of a model for coping with acute stress in sport. *Journal of Sport Behavior, 24,* 223-246.

Anshel, M. H., and Anderson, D. I. (2002). Coping with acute stress in sport: Linking athletes' coping style, coping strategies, affect, and motor performance. *Anxiety, Stress and Coping: An International Journal, 15,* 193-209.

Anshel, M. H., Brown, D. F., and Brown, J. M. (1993). Effectiveness of an acute stress coping program on motor performance, muscle tension and affect. *Australian Journal of Science and Medicine in Sport, 25,* 7-16.

Anshel, M. H., and Delany, J. (2001). Sources of acute stress, cognitive appraisals, and coping strategies of male and female child athletes. *Journal of Sport Behavior, 24,* 329-353.

Anshel, M. H., Gregory, W. L., and Kaczmarek, M. (1990). The effectiveness of a stress training program in coping with criticism in sport: A test of the COPE model. *Journal of Sport Behavior, 13,* 194-217.

Anshel, M. H., Jamieson, J., and Raviv, S. (2001). Coping with acute stress among male and female Israeli athletes. *International Journal of Sport Psychology, 32,* 271-289.

Anshel, M. H., and Kaissidis, A. N. (1997). Coping style and situational appraisals as predictors of coping strategies following stressful events in sport as a function of gender and skill level. *The British Journal of Psychology, 88,* 263-276.

Anshel, M. H., and Weinberg, R. S. (1996). Coping with acute stress among American and Australian basketball referees. *Journal of Sport Behavior, 19,* 180-203.

Anshel, M. H., and Weinberg, R. S. (1999). Re-examining coping among basketball referees following stressful events: Implications for coping interventions. *Journal of Sport Behavior, 22,* 141-161.

Anshel, M. H., and Wells, B. (2000). Personal and situational variables that describe coping with acute stress in competitive sport. *The Journal of Social Psychology, 140,* 434-450.

Anshel, M. H., Williams, L. R. T., and Hodge, K. (1997). Cross-cultural and gender differences on coping style in sport. *International Journal of Sport Psychology, 28*, 141-156.

Anshel, M. H., Williams, L. R. T., and Williams, S. M. (2000). Coping style following acute stress in competitive sport. *Journal of Social Psychology, 140*, 751-773.

Ayers, T. S., Sandler, I. N., West, S. G., and Roosa, M. W. (1996). A dispositional and situational assessment of children's coping: Testing alternative models of coping. *Journal of Personality, 64*, 923-958.

Bäckman, L., and Molander, B. (1986a). Adult age differences in the ability to cope with situations of high arousal in a precision sport. *Psychology and Aging, 1*, 133-139.

Bäckman, L., and Molander, B. (1986b). Effects of adult age and level of skill on the ability to cope with high-stress conditions in a precision sport. *Psychology and Aging, 1*, 334-336.

Bäckman, L., and Molander, B. (1991). On the generalizability of the age-related decline in coping with high-arousal conditions in a precision sport: Replication and extension. *Journals of Gerontology, 46*, P79-P81.

Baillie, P. H. F. (1993). Understanding retirement from sports: Therapeutic ideas for helping athletes in transition. *The Counseling Psychologist, 21*, 399-410.

Baron, R. M., and Kenny, D. A. (1986). The moderator-mediator variable distinction in social psychological research: Conceptual, strategic, and statistical considerations. *Journal of Personality and Social Psychology, 51*, 1173-1182.

Boekaerts, M. (1996). Coping with stress in childhood and adolescence. In M. Zeidner and N. S. Endler (Eds.), *Handbook of coping: Theory, research, and applications* (pp. 452-484). New York: Wiley.

Botterill, C., and Brown, M. (2002). Emotion and perspective in sport. *International Journal of Sport Psychology, 33*, 38-60.

Bouffard, M., and Crocker, P. R. E. (1992). Coping by individuals with physical disabilities with perceived challenge in physical activity: Are people consistent? *Research Quarterly for Exercise and Sport, 63*, 410-417.

Bourgeois, A. E., Loss, R., Meyers, M. C., and LeUnes, A. D. (2003). The Athletic Coping Skills Inventory: Relationship with impression management and self-deception aspects of socially desirable responding. *Psychology of Sport and Exercise, 4*, 71-79.

Bresler, S.A., and Pieper, W. A. (1992). Competitive trait anxiety and coping resources for stress in high school athletes. *Applied Research Quarterly for Coaching and Athletics Annual*, 163-181.

Brustad, R. J. (1998). Developmental considerations in sport and exercise psychology measurement. In J. L. Duda (Ed.), *Advances in sport and exercise psychology measurement* (pp. 461-470). Morgantown, MV: Fitness Information Technology.

Campen, C., and Roberts, D. C. (2001). Coping strategies of runners: Perceived effectiveness and match to precompetitive anxiety. *Journal of Sport Behavior, 24*, 144-161.

Carpenter, B. N. (1992). Issues and advances in coping research. In B. N. Carpenter (Ed.), *Personal coping: Theory, research, and application* (pp. 1-13). Westport, CT: Praeger.

Carver, C. S., Scheier, M. F., and Weintraub, J. K. (1989). Assessing coping strategies: A theoretically based approach. *Journal of Personality and Social Psychology, 56*, 267-283.

Cerin, E., Szabo, A., Hunt, N., and Williams, C. (2000). Temporal patterning of competitive emotions: A critical review. *Journal of Sports Sciences, 18*, 605-626.

Cleary, T. J., and Zimmerman, B. J. (2001). Self-regulation differences during athletic practice by experts, non-experts, and novices. *Journal of Applied Sport Psychology, 13*, 185-206.

Compas, B. E. (1998). An agenda for coping research and theory: Basic and applied developmental issues. *International Journal of Behavioral Development, 22*, 231-237.

Compas, B. E., Connor-Smith, J. K., Saltzman, H., Thomsen, A. H., and Wadsworth, M. E. (2001). Coping with stress during childhood and adolescence: Problems, progress, and potential in theory and research. *Psychological Bulletin, 127*, 82-127.

Compas, B. E., and Epping, J. E. (1993). Stress and coping in children and families. In C. F. Saylor (Ed.), *Children and disasters* (pp. 11-28). New York: Plenum Press.

Connor-Smith, J. K., Compas, B. E., Wadsworth, M. E., Thomsen, A. H., and Saltzman, H. (2000). Responses to stress in adolescence: Measurement of coping and involuntary stress responses. *Journal of Consulting and Clinical Psychology, 68*, 976-992.

Cornelius, A. (2002). Psychological interventions for the injured athlete. In J. Silva and D. Stevens (Eds.), *Psychological foundations of sport* (2nd ed.) (pp. 224-246). Boston: Allyn and Bacon.

Coyne, J. C., and Gottlieb, B. H. (1996). The mismeasure of coping by checklist. *Journal of Personality, 64*, 959-991.

Cramer, P. (1998). Coping and defense mechanisms: What's the difference? *Journal of Personality, 66*, 919-946.

Crocker, P. R. E. (1989a). A follow-up of cognitive-affective stress management training. *Journal of Sport and Exercise Psychology, 11*, 236-242.

Crocker, P. R. E. (1989b). Evaluating stress management training under competition conditions. *International Journal of Sport Psychology, 20*, 191-204.

Crocker, P. R. E. (1992). Managing stress by competitive athletes: Ways of coping. *International Journal of Sport Psychology, 23*, 161-175.

Crocker, P. R. E., Alderman, R. B., and Smith, F. M. (1988). Cognitive-Affective Stress Management Training with high performance youth volleyball players: Effects on affect, cognition, and performance. *Journal of Sport and Exercise Psychology, 10*, 448-460.

Crocker, P. R. E., and Graham, T. R. (1995). Coping by competitive athletes with performance stress: Gender differences and relationships with affect. *The Sport Psychologist, 9*, 325-338.

Crocker, P. R. E., Hoar, S. D., McDonough, M. H., Kowalski, K. C., and Niefer, C. B. (2004). Emotional experience in youth sport. In M. R. Weiss (Ed.), *Developmental sport and exercise psychology: A lifespan perspective* (pp. 197-221). Morgantown, WV: Fitness Information Technology.

Crocker, P. R. E., and Isaak, K. (1997). Coping during competitions and training sessions: Are youth swimmers consistent? *International Journal of Sport Psychology, 28*, 355-369.

Crocker, P. R. E., Kowalski, K. C., and Graham, T. R. (1998). Measurement of coping strategies in sport. In J. L. Duda (Ed.), *Advances in sport and exercise psychology measurement* (pp. 149-161). Morgantown, WV: Fitness Information Technology.

Crocker, P. R. E., Kowalski, K. C., and Graham, T. R. (2002). Emotional control and intervention. In J. Silva and D. Stevens (Eds.), *Psychological foundations of sport* (2nd ed.) (pp. 155-176). Boston: Allyn and Bacon.

Crocker, P. R. E., Kowalski, K. C., Hoar, S. D., and McDonough, M. H. (2004). Emotion in sport across adulthood. In M. R. Weiss (Ed.), *Developmental sport and exercise psychology: A lifespan perspective* (pp. 333-355). Morgantown, WV: Fitness Information Technology.

Czisma, K., Wittig, A., and Schurr, K. (1988). Sport stereotypes and gender. *Journal of Sport and Exercise Psychology, 10*, 62-74.

Daly, J. M., Brewer, B. W., Van-Raalte, J. L., Petitpas, A. J., and Sklar, J. H. (1995). Cognitive appraisal, emotional adjustment, and adherence to rehabilitation following knee surgery. *Journal of Sport Rehabilitation, 3*, 23-30.

De Ridder, D. (1997). What is wrong with coping assessment? A review of conceptual and methodological issues. *Psychology and Health, 12*, 417-431.

Dugdale, J. R., Eklund, R. C., and Gordon, S. (2002). Expected and unexpected stressors in major international competition: Appraisal, coping, and performance. *The Sport Psychologist, 16*, 20-33.

Eklund, R. C., Grove, J. R., and Heard, N. P. (1998). The measurement of slump-related coping: Factorial validity of the COPE and modified-COPE inventories. *Journal of Sport and Exercise Psychology, 20*, 157-175.

Encarnacion, M. L. G., Meyers, M. C., Ryan, N. D., and Pease, D. G. (2000). Pain coping styles of ballet performers. *Journal of Sport Behavior, 23*, 20-32.

Endler, N. S., and Parker, J. D. (1990). The multidimensional assessment of coping: A critical evaluation. *Journal of Personality and Social Psychology, 58*, 844-854.

Endler, N. S., and Parker, J. D. (1994). Assessment of multidimensional coping: Task, emotion, and avoidance strategies. *Psychological Assessment, 6*, 50-60.

Eubank, M., and Collins, D. (2000). Coping with pre- and in-event fluctuations in competitive state anxiety: A longitudinal approach. *Journal of Sports Sciences, 18*, 121-131.

Fields, L., and Prinz, R. J. (1997). Coping and adjustment during childhood and adolescence. *Clinical Psychology Review, 17*, 937-976.

Folkman, S. (1991). Coping across the life span: Theoretical issues. In E. M. Cummings, A. L. Greene, and K. H. Karraker (Eds.), *Life-span developmental psychology: Perspectives on stress and coping* (pp. 3-19). Hillsdale, NJ: Lawrence Erlbaum.

Folkman, S. (1992). Making the case for coping. In B. N. Carpenter (Ed.), *Personal coping: Theory, research, and application* (pp. 31-46). Westport, CT: Praeger.

Folkman, S., and Lazarus, R. S. (1985). If it changes it must be a process: Study of emotion and coping during three stages of a college examination. *Journal of Personality and Social Psychology, 48*, 150-170.

Folkman, S., Lazarus, R. S., Dunkel-Schetter, C., Delongis, A., and Gruen, R. J. (1986). Dynamics of a stressful encounter: Cognitive appraisal, coping, and encounter outcomes. *Journal of Personality and Social Psychology, 50*, 992-1003.

Ford, I. W., Eklund, R. C., and Gordon, S. (2000). An examination of psychosocial variables moderating the relationship between life stress and injury time-loss among athletes of a high standard. *Journal of Sports Sciences, 18*, 301-312.

Ford, I. W., and Gordon, S. (1998). Perspective of sport trainers and athletic therapists on the psychological content of their practice and training. *Journal of Sport Rehabilitation, 7*, 79-94.

Fox, K. R. (1997). The physical self and processes in self-esteem development. In K. R. Fox (Ed.), *The physical self: From motivation to well-being* (pp. 111-139). Champaign, IL: Human Kinetics.

Frydenberg, E. (1997). *Adolescent coping: Theoretical and research perspectives.* London: Routledge.

Gaudreau, P., and Blondin, J. P. (2002). Development of a questionnaire for the assessment of coping strategies employed by athletes in competitive sport settings. *Psychology of Sport and Exercise, 3*, 1-34.

Gaudreau, P., and Blondin, J. P. (2004a). Different athletes cope differently: A cluster analysis of coping. *Personality and Individual Differences, 36*, 1865-1877.

Gaudreau, P., and Blondin, J. P. (2004b). The differential effect of dispositional optimism and pessimism on athletes' coping, goal attainment, and emotional adjustment during a sport competition. *International Journal of Stress Management, 11*, 245-269.

Gaudreau, P., Blondin, J. P., and Lapierre, A. M. (2002). Athletes' coping during a competition: Relationship of coping strategies with positive affect, negative affect, and performance-goal discrepancy. *Psychology of Sport and Exercise, 3*, 125-150.

Gaudreau, P., Lapierre, A. M., and Blondin, J. P. (2001). Coping at three phases of a competition: Comparison between pre-competitive, competitive, and post-competitive utilization of the same strategy. *International Journal of Sport Psychology, 32*, 369-385.

Giacobbi Jr., P. R., and Weinberg, R. S. (2000). An examination of coping in sport: Individual trait anxiety differences and situational consistency. *The Sport Psychologist, 14*, 42-62.

Gill, D. L. (2003). Gender and cultural diversity across the lifespan. In M. R. Weiss (Ed.), *Developmental sport and exercise psychology: A lifespan perspective* (pp. 475-501). Morgantown, WV: Fitness Information Technology.

Goudas, M., Theodorakis, Y., and Karamousalidis, G. (1998). Psychological skills in basketball: Preliminary study for the development of a Greek form of the Athletic Coping Skills Inventory-28. *Perceptual and Motor Skills, 86*, 59-65.

Gould, D., Eklund, R. C., and Jackson, S. A. (1993). Coping strategies used by U.S. Olympic wrestlers. *Research Quarterly for Exercise and Sport, 64*, 83-93.

Gould, D., Finch, L. M., and Jackson, S. A. (1993). Coping strategies used by national champion figure skaters. *Research Quarterly for Exercise and Sport, 64*, 453-468.

Gould, D., Udry, E., Bridges, D., and Beck, L. (1997a). Coping with season-ending injuries. *The Sport Psychologist, 11*, 379-399.

Gould, D., Udry, E., Bridges, D., and Beck, L. (1997b). Stress sources encountered when rehabilitating from season-ending ski injuries. *The Sport Psychologist, 11*, 361-378.

Gould, D., Udry, E., Tuffey, S., and Loehr, J. (1996). Burnout in competitive junior tennis players: I. A quantitative psychological assessment. *The Sport Psychologist, 10*, 322-340.

Goyen, M. J., and Anshel, M. H. (1998). Sources of acute competitive stress and use of coping strategies as a function of age and gender. *Journal of Applied Developmental Psychology, 19*, 469-486.

Grove, J., Eklund, R., and Heard, N. (1997). Coping with performance slumps: Factor analysis of the Ways of Coping in Sport scale. *Australian Journal of Science and Medicine in Sport, 29*, 99-105.

Grove, J. R., and Heard, N. P. (1997). Optimism and sport confidence as correlates of slump-related coping among athletes. *The Sport Psychologist, 11*, 400-410.

Grove, J. R., Lavallee, D., and Gordon, S. (1997). Coping with retirement from sport: The influence of athletic identity. *Journal of Applied Sport Psychology, 9*, 191-203.

Grove, J. R., Lavallee, D., Gordon, S., and Harvey, J. H. (1998). Account-making: A model for understanding and resolving distressful reactions to retirement from sport. *The Sport Psychologist, 12*, 52-67.

Hammermeister, J., and Burton, D. (2001). Stress, appraisal, and coping revisited: Examining the antecedents of competitive state anxiety with endurance athletes. *The Sport Psychologist, 15*, 66-90.

Haney, C. J., and Long, B. C. (1995). Coping effectiveness: A path analysis of self-efficacy, control, coping, and performance in sport competitions. *Journal of Applied Social Psychology, 25*, 1726-1746.

Hardy, C. J., and Crace, R. K. (1991). Social support with sport. *Sport Psychology Training Bulletin, 3*, 1-8.

Hardy, L., Jones, G., and Gould, D. (1996). *Understanding psychological preparation for sport: Theory and practice of elite performers*. Chichester, UK: John Wiley.

Hoar, S. D. (2003). *The relation between social support and coping with interpersonal sport stress during early adolescence*. Unpublished doctoral dissertation, The University of British Columbia, Vancouver, British Columbia, Canada.

Holt, N. L., and Hogg, J. M. (2002). Perceptions of stress and coping during preparations for the 1999 women's soccer World Cup finals. *The Sport Psychologist, 16*, 251-271.

Hughes, J., and Sharrock, W. (1997). *The philosophy of social research* (3rd ed.). New York: Alfred A. Knopf.

Iwanaga, M., Yokoyama, H., and Seiwa, H. (2004). Coping availability and stress reduction for optimistic and pessimistic individuals. *Personality and Individual Differences, 36*, 11-22.

Jackson, S. A., Thomas, P. R., Marsh, H. W., and Smethurst, C. J. (2001). Relationships between flow, self-concept, psychological skills, and performance. *Journal of Applied Sport Psychology, 13*, 129-153.

Jerome, G. J., and Williams, J. M. (2000). Intensity and interpretation of competitive state anxiety: Relationship to performance and repressive coping. *Journal of Applied Sport Psychology, 12*, 236-250.

Johnson, U. (1996). The multiply injured versus the first-time-injured athlete during rehabilitation: A comparison of nonphysical characteristics. *Journal of Sport Rehabilitation, 5*, 293-304.

Kaissidis-Rodanfinos, A. N., and Anshel, M. H. (2000). Psychological predictions of coping responses among Greek basketball referees. *Journal of Social Psychology, 140*, 329-344.

Kaissidis- Rodanfinos, A. N., Anshel, M. H., and Porter, A. (1997). Personal and situational factors that predict coping strategies for acute stress among basketball referees. *Journal of Sports Sciences, 15*, 427-436.

Kelley, B. C., Eklund, R. C., and Ritter, T. M. (1999). Stress and burnout among collegiate tennis coaches. *Journal of Sport and Exercise Psychology, 21*, 113-130.

Kerr, G., and Leith, L. (1993). Stress management and athletic performance. *The Sport Psychologist, 7*, 221-231.

Kim, M. S., and Duda, J. L. (2003). The coping process: Cognitive appraisals of stress, coping strategies, and coping effectiveness. *The Sport Psychologist, 17*, 406-425.

Kline, P. (1998). *The new psychometrics: Science, psychology, and measurement.* London: Rutledge.

Koestner, R., Lekes, N., Powers, T. A., and Chicoine, E. (2002). Attaining personal goals: Self-concordance plus implementation intentions equals success. *Journal of Personality and Social Psychology, 83*, 231-244.

Kolt, G., Kirkby, R. J., and Lindner, H. (1995). Coping processes in competitive gymnasts: Gender differences. *Perceptual and Motor Skills, 81*, 1139-1145.

Kowalski, K. C., and Crocker, P. R. E. (2001). Development and validation of the Coping Function Questionnaire for adolescents in sport. *Journal of Sport and Exercise Psychology, 23*, 136-155.

Kress, J., Schroeder, J., Potteiger, J. A., and Haub, M. (1999). The use of psychological skills training to increase 10 KM cycling performance: An exploratory investigation. *International Sports Journal, 3*, 44-54.

Krohne, H. W. (1996). Individual differences in coping. In M. Zeidner and N. S. Endler (Eds.), *Handbook of coping* (pp. 381-409). New York: John Wiley and Sons.

Krohne, H. W., and Hindel, C. (1988). Trait anxiety, state anxiety, and coping behavior as predictors of athletic performance. *Anxiety Research, 1*, 225-234.

Krohne, H. W., and Rogner, J. (1982). Repression-sensitization as a central construct in coping research. In H. W. Krohne and L. Laux (Eds.), *Achievement, stress, and anxiety* (pp. 167-193). New York: McGraw-Hill.

Lane, A. M., Jones, L., and Stevens, M. J. (2002). Coping with failure: The effects of self-esteem and coping on changes in self-efficacy. *Journal of Sport Behavior, 25*, 331-345.

Larsson, G., Cook, C., and Starrin, B. (1988). A time and cost efficient stress inoculation training program for athletes: A study of junior golfers. *Scandinavian Journal of Sports Sciences, 10*, 23-28.

Lazarus, R. S. (1991). *Emotion and adaptation.* New York: Oxford University Press.

Lazarus, R. S. (1999). *Stress and emotion: A new synthesis.* New York: Springer Publishing.

Lazarus, R. S. (2000). Cognitive-motivational-relational theory of emotion. In Y. L. Hanin (Ed.), *Emotions in sport* (pp. 39-63). Champaign, IL: Human Kinetics.

Lazarus, R. S., and Folkman, S. (1984). *Stress, appraisal, and coping.* New York: Springer Publishing.

Mace, R. D., and Carroll, D. (1986). Stress inoculation training to control anxiety in sport: Two case studies in squash. *British Journal of Sports Medicine, 20*, 115-117.

Mace, R. D., and Carroll, D. (1989). The effect of stress inoculation training on self-reported stress, observer's rating of stress, heart rate and gymnastics performance. *Journal of Sports Sciences, 7*, 257-266.

Mace, R. D., Eastman, C., and Carroll, D. (1986). Stress inoculation training: A case study in gymnastics. *British Journal of Sports Medicine, 20*, 139-141.

Madden, C. C., Kirkby, R. J., and McDonald, D. (1989). Coping styles of competitive middle distance runners. *International Journal of Sport Psychology, 20*, 287-296.

Madden, C. C., Summers, J. J., and Brown, D. F. (1990). The influence of perceived stress on coping with competitive basketball. *International Journal of Sport Psychology, 21*, 21-35.

Mahoney, M. J., and Avener, M. (1977). Psychology of the elite athletes: An exploratory study. *Cognitive Therapy and Research, 1*, 135-141.

Maniar, S. D., Curry, L. A., Sommers-Flanagan, J., and Walsh, J. A. (2001). Student-athlete preferences in seeking help when confronted with sport performance problems. *The Sport Psychologist, 15*, 205-223.

Manuel, J. C., Shilt, J. S., Curl, W. W., Smith, J. A., DuRant, R. H., Lester, L., et al. (2002). Coping with sports injuries: An examination of the adolescent athlete. *Journal of Adolescent Health, 31*, 391-393.

Martin, J. J., Kelley, B., and Eklund, R. C. (1999). A model of stress and burnout in male high school athletic directors. *Journal of Sport and Exercise Psychology, 21*, 280-294.

Masters, K. S., and Lambert, M. J. (1989). The relations between cognitive coping strategies, reasons for running, injury, and performance of marathon runners. *Journal of Sport and Exercise Psychology, 11*, 161-170.

Masters, K. S., Ogles, B. M., and Jolton, J. A. (1993). The development of an instrument to measure motivation for marathon running: The Motivations of Marathoners Scales (MOMS). *Research Quarterly for Exercise and Sport, 64*, 134-143.

Matthews, G., Schwean, V. L., Campbell, S. E., Saklofske, D. H., and Mohamed, A. A. (2000). Personality, self-regulation, and adaptation. In M. Boekaerts, P. R. Pintrich and M. Zeidner (Eds.), *Handbook of self-regulation* (pp. 171-207). New York: Academic Press.

McLeod, S. L., Kirkby, R. J., and Madden, C. C. (1994). Coping in basketball: Differences according to ability and gender. *European Journal for High Ability, 5*, 191-198.

Meehl, P. E. (1970). Nuisance variables and the ex post facto design. In M. Radner and S. Winokur (Eds.), *Minnesota studies in the philosophy of science, 4*, (pp. 372-402). Minniapolis, MN: University of Minnesota.

Meichenbaum, D. (1985). *Stress inoculation training*. New York: Pergamon.

Meichenbaum, D. (1993). Stress inoculation training: A 20-year update. In P. M. Lehrer and R. L. Woolfolk (Eds.), *Principles and practices of stress management* (2nd Ed.) (pp. 373-406). New York: Guildford.

Messner, M. A. (1992). *Power at play: Sports and the problem of masculinity*. Boston: Beacon Press.

Meyers, M. C., Bourgeois, A. E., and LeUnes, A. (2001). Pain coping response of collegiate athletes involved in high contact, high injury-potential sport. *International Journal of Sport Psychology, 32*, 29-42.

Meyers, M. C., Bourgeois, A. E., Stewart, S., and LeUnes, A. (1992). Predicting pain response in athletes: Development and assessment of the Sports Inventory for Pain. *Journal of Sport and Exercise Psychology, 14*, 249-261.

Miller, J. L., and Levy, G. D. (1996). Gender role conflict, gender-typed characteristics, self-concepts, and sport socialization in female athletes and nonathletes. *Sex Roles, 35*, 111-122.

Murphy, S., and Tammen, V. (1998). In search of psychological skills. In J. L. Duda (Ed.), *Advances in sport and exercise psychology measurement* (pp. 195–209). Morgantown, WV: Fitness Information Technology.

Ninedek, A., and Kolt, G. S. (2000). Sport physiotherapists' perceptions of psychological strategies in sport injury rehabilitation. *Journal of Sport Rehabilitation, 9*, 191-206.

Nixon, H. L. (1993). Accepting the risks of pain and injury in sport: Mediated cultural influences on playing hurt. *Sociology of Sport Journal, 10*, 183-196.

Ntoumanis, N., and Biddle, S. J. H. (1998). The relationship of coping and its perceived effectiveness to positive and negative affect in sport. *Personality and Individual Differences, 24*, 773-788.

Ntoumanis, N., and Biddle, S. J. H. (2000). Relationship of intensity and direction of competitive anxiety with coping strategies. *The Sport Psychologist, 14*, 360-371.

Ntoumanis, N., Biddle, S. J. H., and Haddock, G. (1999). The mediating role of coping strategies on the relationship between achievement motivation and affect in sport. *Anxiety, Stress and Coping: An International Journal, 12*, 299-327.

Park, J. K. (2000). Coping strategies used by Korean national athletes. *The Sport Psychologist, 14*, 63-80.

Parker, J. D., and Endler, N. S. (1996). Coping and defense: A historical overview. In M. Zeidner and N. S. Endler (Eds.), *Handbook of coping: Theory, research, and applications* (pp. 3-23). New York: Wiley.

Parkinson, B., and Totterdell, P. (1999). Classifying affect-regulation strategies. *Cognition and Emotion, 13*, 277-303.

Pearlin, L. I. (1989). The sociological study of stress. *Journal of Health and Social Behavior, 30*, 241-256.

Pensgaard, A. M., and Roberts, G. C. (2003). Achievement goal orientations and the use of coping strategies among Winter Olympians. *Psychology of Sport and Exercise, 4*, 101-116.

Pensgaard, A. M., and Ursin, H. (1998). Stress, control, and coping in elite athletes. *Scandinavian Journal of Medicine and Science in Sports, 8*, 183-189.

Poczwardowski, A., and Conroy, D. E. (2002). Coping responses to failure and success among elite athletes and performing artists. *Journal of Applied Sport Psychology, 14*, 313-329.

Prapavessis, H., and Grove, J. R. (1995). Ending batting slumps in baseball: A qualitative investigation. *Australian Journal of Science and Medicine in Sport, 27*, 14-19.

Prapavessis, H., Grove, J. R., Maddison, R., and Zillmann, N. (2003). Self-handicapping tendencies, coping, and anxiety responses among athletes. *Psychology of Sport and Exercise, 4*, 357-375.

Ptacek, J. T., Smith, R. E., Espe, K., and Rafferty, B. (1994). Limited correspondence between daily coping reports and retrospective coping recall. *Psychological Assessment, 6*, 41-49.

Quinn, A. M., and Fallon, B. J. (1999). The changes in psychological characteristics and reactions of elite athletes from injury onset until full recovery. *Journal of Applied Sport Psychology, 11*, 210-229.

Roderick, M., Waddington, I., and Parker, G. (2000). Playing hurt: Managing injuries in English Professional Football. *International Review for the Sociology of Sport, 35*, 165-180.

Ross, M. J., and Berger, R. S. (1996). Effects of stress inoculation training on athletes' postsurgical pain and rehabilitation after orthopedic injury. *Journal of Consulting and Clinical Psychology, 64*, 406-410.

Rudolph, K. D. (2002). Gender differences in emotion responses to interpersonal stress during adolescence. *Journal of Adolescent Health, 30 Supplement*, 3-13.

Rusting, C. L., and Nolen-Hoeksema, S. (1998). Regulating responses to anger: Effects of rumination and distraction on angry mood. *Journal of Personality and Social Psychology, 74*, 790-803.

Ryska, T. A. (1993). Coping styles and response distortion on self-report inventories among high school athletes. *Journal of Psychology, 127*, 409-418.

Scheier, M. F., and Carver, C. S. (1992). Effects of optimism on psychological and physical well-being: Theoretical overview and empirical update. *Cognitive Therapy and Research, 16*, 201-228.

Schutz, R. W. (1998). Assessing the stability of psychological traits and measures. In J. L. Duda (Ed.), *Advances in sport and exercise psychology measurement* (pp. 393-408). Morgantown, WV: Fitness Information Technology.

Schwartz, J. E., Neale, J., Marco, C., Shiffman, S. S., and Stone, A. A. (1999). Does trait coping exist? A momentary assessment approach to the evaluation of traits. *Journal of Personality and Social Psychology, 77*, 360-369.

Schwarzer, R., and Schwarzer, C. (1996). A critical survey of coping instruments. In M. Zeidner and N. S. Endler (Eds.), *Handbook of coping: Theory, research, and applications* (pp. 107-132). New York: Wiley.

Seheult, C. (1997). Freud on fencing: The role of unconscious psychological defences. In R. J. Butler (Ed.), *Sports psychology in performance* (pp. 217-247). Oxford, UK: Butterworth Heinemann.

Seiffge-Krenke, I. (1995). *Stress, coping, and relationships in adolescence*. Mahwah, NJ: Lawrence Erlbaum.

Sellers, R. M., and Peterson, C. (1993). Explanatory style and coping with controllable events by student-athletes. *Cognition and Emotion, 7*, 431-441.

Skinner, E. A. (1995). *Perceived control, motivation, and coping: Individual differences and development*. Thousand Oaks, CA: Sage.

Skinner, E. A., and Edge, K. (1998). Reflections on coping and development across the lifespan. *International Journal of Behavioral Development, 22*, 357-366.

Skinner, E. A., Edge, K., Altman, J., and Sherwood, H. (2003). Searching for the structure of coping: A review and critique of category systems for classifying ways of coping. *Psychological Bulletin, 129*, 216-269.

Smith, C. A., and Wallston, K. A. (1996). An analysis of coping profiles and adjustment in persons with rheumatoid arthritis. *Anxiety, Stress and Coping: An International Journal, 9*, 107-122.

Smith, R. E. (1980). A cognitive-affective approach to stress management training for athletes. In C. Nadeau, W. Halliwell, K. Newell, and G. Roberts (Eds.), *Psychology of motor behavior and sport – 1979* (pp. 54-73). Champaign, IL: Human Kinetics.

Smith, R. E. (1986). Toward a cognitive-affective model of athletic burnout. *Journal of Sport Psychology, 8*, 36-50.

Smith, R. E. (1999). Generalization effects in coping skills training. *Journal of Sport and Exercise Psychology, 21*, 189-204.

Smith, R. E., and Christensen, D. S. (1995). Psychological skills as predictors of performance and survival in professional baseball. *Journal of Sport and Exercise Psychology, 17*, 399-415.

Smith, R. E., Leffingwell, T. R., and Ptacek, J. T. (1999). Can people remember how they coped? Factors associated with discordance between same-day and retrospective reports. *Journal of Personality and Social Psychology, 76*, 1050-1061.

Smith, R. E., Ptacek, J. T., and Smoll, F. L. (1992). Sensation seeking, stress, and adolescent injuries: A test of stress-buffering, risk-taking, and coping skills hypotheses. *Journal of Personality and Social Psychology, 62*, 1016-1024.

Smith, R. E., Schutz, R. W., Smoll, F. L., and Ptacek, J. T. (1995). Development and validation of a multidimensional measure of sport-specific psychological skills: The Athletic Coping Skills Inventory-28. *Journal of Sport and Exercise Psychology, 17*, 379-398.

Smith, R. E., Smoll, F. L., and Ptacek, J. T. (1990). Conjunctive moderator variables in vulnerability and resiliency research: Life stress, social support and coping skills, and adolescent sport injuries. *Journal of Personality and Social Psychology, 58*, 360-370.

Somerfeld, M. R. (1997). The utility of systems models of stress and coping for applied research: The case of cancer adaptation. *Journal of Health Psychology, 2*, 133-151.

Stevens, M. J., and Lane, A. M. (2001). Mood-regulating strategies used by athletes. *Athletic Insight: Online Journal of Sport Psychology, 3*.

Stone, A. A., Greenberg, M. A., Kennedy-Moore, E., and Newman, M. G. (1991). Self-report, situation-specific coping questionnaires: What are they measuring? *Journal of Personality and Social Psychology, 61*, 648-658.

Stone, A. A., Kennedy-Moore, E., Newman, M. G., Greenberg, M., and Neale, J. M. (1992). Conceptual and methodological issues in current coping assessments. In B. N. Carpenter (Ed.), *Personal coping: Theory, research, and application* (pp. 15-29). Westport, CT: Praeger.

Stone, A. A., Schwartz, J. E., Shiffman, S., Marco, C. A., Hickcox, M., Paty, J., et al. (1998). A comparison of coping assessed by ecological momentary assessment and retrospective recall. *Journal of Personality and Social Psychology, 74*, 1670-1680.

Suls, J., and David, J. P. (1996). Coping and personality: Third time's the charm? *Journal of Personality, 64*, 993-1005.

Tamres, L. K., Janicki, D., and Helgeson, V. S. (2002). Sex differences in coping behavior: A meta-analytic review and an examination of relative coping. *Personality and Social Psychology Review, 6*, 2-30.

Taylor, A. H., and May, S. (1996). Threat and coping appraisal as determinants of compliance with sports injury rehabilitation: An application of Protection Motivation Theory. *Journal of Sports Sciences, 14*, 471-482.

Thomas, P. R., Murphy, S. M., and Hardy, L. (1999). Test of Performance Strategies: Development and preliminary validation of a comprehensive measure of athletes' psychological skills. *Journal of Sports Sciences, 17*, 697-711.

Udry, E. (1997). Coping and social support among injured athletes following surgery. *Journal of Sport and Exercise Psychology, 19*, 71-90.

Ungerleider, S. (1997). Olympic athletes' transition from sport to workplace. *Perceptual and Motor Skills, 84*, 1287-1295.

Walker, L. S., Smith, C. A., Garber, J., and Van Slyke, D. A. (1997). Development and validation of the Pain Response Inventory for children. *Psychological Assessment, 9*, 392-405.

Weiner, B. (1985). An attribution theory of achievement motivation and emotion. *Psychological Review, 92*, 548-573.

Weiner, B. (1986). *An attribution theory of motivation and emotion.* New York: Springer-Verlag.

Weiss, M. R., and Williams, L. (2004). The why of youth sport involvement: A developmental perspective on motivational processes. In M. R. Weiss (Ed.), *Developmental sport and exercise psychology: A lifespan perspective* (pp. 223-268). Morgantown, WV: Fitness Information Technology.

Williams, J. M., and Krane, V. (1992). Coping styles and self-reported measures of state anxiety and self-confidence. *Journal of Applied Sport Psychology, 4*, 134-143.

Whitmarsh, B. G., and Alderman, R. B. (1993). Role of psychological skills training in increasing athletic pain tolerance. *The Sport Psychologist, 7*, 388-399.

Yoo, J. (2000). Factorial validity of the coping scale for Korean athletes. *International Journal of Sport Psychology, 31*, 391-404.

Yoo, J. (2001). Coping profiles of Korean competitive athletes. *International Journal of Sport Psychology, 32*, 290-303.

Zeidner, M., Boekaerts, M., and Pintrich, P. R. (2000). Self-regulation: Directions and challenges for future research. In M. Boekaerts, P. R. Pintrich, and M. Zeidner (Eds.), *Handbook of self-regulation* (pp. 749-768). New York: Academic Press.

Ziegler, S. G., Klinzing, J., and Williamson, K. (1982). The effects of two stress management training programs on cardiorespiratory efficiency. *Journal of Sport Psychology, 4*, 280-289.

Zuckerman, M. (1979). *Sensation seeking: Beyond the optimal level of arousal.* Hillsdale, NJ: Erlbaum.

Zuckerman, M. (1983). *Biological bases of sensation seeking, impulsivity, and anxiety.* Hillsdale, NJ: Erlbaum.

In: Literature Reviews in Sport Psychology   ISBN 1-59454-904-4
Editors: S. Hanton and S. D. Mellalieu, pp. 91-126   © 2006 Nova Science Publishers, Inc.

Chapter 3

ATHLETE BURNOUT:
CONCEPTUAL CONFUSION, CURRENT RESEARCH
AND FUTURE RESEARCH DIRECTIONS

Scott L. Cresswell[*]
University of Western Australia, Australia
Robert C. Eklund
Florida State University

ABSTRACT

There has been considerable interest in athlete burnout. Much of the literature on athlete burnout, however, is troubled by conceptual confusion because of the variety of ways that the notion of burnout has been operationalized. As a result, current commentaries on burnout do not all address a common issue. Within this chapter we review various conceptual explanations of burnout forwarded in the extant sport psychology literature and endorse the three key characteristics of burnout (i.e., exhaustion, reduced accomplishment, sport devaluation) cited in previous research. Within our discussion we highlight conceptual and methodological issues that have hampered researchers attempting to further knowledge of athlete burnout and propose guidelines for possible future research. Specifically we elaborate on current theoretical approaches and comment upon the potential utility of stress-based approaches, commitment theory and self-determination theory as conceptual frameworks for guiding future investigations in the area.

Keywords: Depression, dropout, overtraining, commitment, self-determination

---

[*] Correspondence concerning this article should be addressed to Scott L. Cresswell, School of Human Movement and Exercise Science, The University of Western Australia, Crawley, W.A. 6009, Australia, Tel: 61-8-9380-3843, Fax: 61-8-9380-1039, Email: scott@sportpsychology.co.nz

INTRODUCTION

Sport organizations, the media and researchers have proposed that burnout is a problem in sport (e.g., Coakley, 1992; Gould, Udry, Tuffey, and Loehr, 1996; Silva, 1990). Burnout was originally conceived in human care settings to describe the inability of workers to effectively carry out their roles (Freudenberger, 1975). The experiential burnout syndrome described among human care workers has three central characteristics: emotional and physical exhaustion, feelings of reduced accomplishment and depersonalization (Maslach, 1982a). Sport scientists have suggested that negative, amotivated and exhausted states sometimes described by athletes are a sport-related manifestation of the burnout syndrome (e.g., Coakley, 1992; Gould, Tuffey, Udry, and Loehr, 1996, 1997; Gould, Udry, et al., 1996). To date researchers have yet to clearly establish the prevalence of athlete burnout. Regardless, a growing number of authors allude to "burnout" in characterizing a range of negative outcomes within sport (e.g., Gould, Tuffey, et al., 1996; Gould et al., 1997; Gould, Udry, et al., 1996; Raedeke, 1997; Raedeke and Smith, 2001).

We argue that authors propounding on athlete burnout have too often confounded the antecedents, characteristics and consequences of the burnout syndrome in their commentaries (see Figure 1). This unfortunate problem has lead to confusion and misunderstandings about the nature of the burnout syndrome and related concepts. Research conducted in other settings (e.g., general work and human care) may have some limitations in its applicability to athletes given that some demands maybe relatively unique to sport. Regardless, to enable advancements in the area, athlete burnout needs to be considered in the light of burnout's conceptual origin, its development in human care/service and general work settings as well as within the context of relevant theoretical contentions.

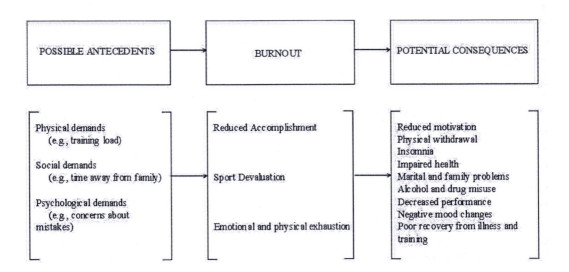

Figure 1: Schematic summary of the athlete burnout syndrome.

In this chapter we review research on burnout in general work, human care and sport settings to highlight current knowledge and future challenges in the area of athlete burnout. Specifically we review current definitional approaches along with explanations of athlete burnout presented in the extant literature. We also highlight some issues of conceptual confusion and related methodological issues evident in past research. Further the prevalence of athlete burnout and correlates observed in past research that has applied a definition consistent with the one endorsed in this chapter are summarised. In addition indepth reflections on pertinent theoretical approaches are presented along with reccomendations for future research. Finally we review the area of burnout interventions which has considerable potential to advance current theoretical and applied knowledge.

We have made a conscious decision to focus on *athlete* burnout in this chapter. While past research suggests the experiential burnout syndrome is a relatively robust phenomenon across settings, the specific demands that cause burnout (i.e., antecedents) may vary across settings. As a consequence, we have focused our comments on burnout in sport settings on athletes rather than making reference to coaches, officials, or sport administrators - even though some research on these individuals is evident in the existing literature. Further we believe that burnout as a consequence of recreational participation is not a substantial area of concern in sport. As such we have decided to focus our comments in this review upon athletes whose participation in serious sporting competition requires involvement a regular formalized training regimen (i.e., they are not "weekend warriors" or recreational sport participants).

DEFINITIONS OF BURNOUT

The concept of burnout was first introduced by Freudenberger (1975) to explain exhaustion-related ineffectiveness observed among human care workers (e.g., counselors, psychologists, nurses). He described burnout as exhaustion due to excessive demands on energy, strength or resources. Freudenberger (1975) did not regard burnout as a phenomenon exclusive to human care settings but rather proposed that it very likely existed in other environments. In fact, he specifically implicated sport as an environment with burnout-inducing potential. Despite these original contentions, there is a relative dearth of burnout research in sport compared to the extensive efforts to date in human care/service (e.g., Maslach, 1982a) and, more recently, general work settings (e.g., Schutte, Toppinen, Kalimo, and Schaufeli, 2000).

Conceptions of burnout in general psychology have been dominated by approaches based within a psychosocial framework where the burnout syndrome is proposed to be one potential consequence of chronic exposure to psychosocial stress (Maslach, 1982a). In particular, Maslach described three central characteristics of the burnout syndrome based on her work in human care settings: (a) emotional exhaustion; (b) depersonalization; and (c) reduced personal accomplishment. More recently researchers (e.g., Maslach, Jackson and Leiter, 1996; Schutte et al., 2000) in general work settings have refined this conceptualization further. Specifically Schutte et al. (2000) made the case that burnout in general work settings is most suitably characterized as a syndrome including: (a) exhaustion (both physical and emotional); (b) cynicism (indifference or a distant attitude to work in general); and (c) reduced professional efficacy (low expectations of continued effectiveness). The occurrence of burnout in these settings has been associated with negative consequences such as decreased performance, low motivation, impaired health, personal dysfunction, insomnia, increased use of alcohol and drugs as well as marital and family problems (Maslach and Goldberg, 1998; Maslach et al., 1996).

While most of this research has taken place in human care and business environments, there has also been some interest among sport scientists in the potential applicability of the burnout construct to sport. Not everyone has embraced the idea however and some have expressed skepticism about the notion that an experiential syndrome identified in human care and business environments has relevance to sport (e.g., Feigley, 1984; Garden, 1987). Specifically, it has been suggested that burnout may not translate appropriately into sport settings because athletes' motives differ significantly from those of human care professionals. Further, skeptics have argued that the emotional demands of dealing with difficult, suffering or unmotivated recipients (e.g., psychologists dealing with non-cooperative clients) are at the core of the syndrome and these demands do not correspond to those in the sporting environment.

There may be some merit to this line of reasoning but it focuses on burnout antecedents rather than the experiential syndrome itself (see Figure 1). It is reasonable to expect that the antecedents of the syndrome could vary across settings. This variation, however, does not inherently signify that the associated experiential syndrome must also differ in nature. In fact research evidence on burnout across general work situations supports the notion that a common experiential syndrome (i.e., burnout) exists even though the antecedents of that syndrome may vary (Schaufeli and Enzmann, 1998). Moreover, it is important to note that the syndrome may be manifested somewhat differently across settings, but the underlying characteristics are thought to remain constant. For example, within the human care environment, cynicism appears to be manifested as depersonalization by caregivers whereas in sport settings it may be manifested as sport devaluation by athletes.

No consistent operational definition of athlete burnout has been employed by researchers in sport (c.f. Coakley, 1992; Gould, Udry, et al., 1996; Raedeke, 1997; Silva, 1990). The lack of a precise operational definition has contributed to conceptual confusion. Raedeke, Lunney and Venables (2002) have suggested that without a precise definition, use of the term "burnout" becomes so broad and undifferentiated that it lacks meaning. Given the lack of a clear conceptualization in sport, we advocate adopting the definition and operationalisation of burnout developed within general psychology and applied to a range of different settings.

The view we advocate is that burnout is best conceptualized as an enduring experiential syndrome characterized by: (a) emotional and physical exhaustion; (b) sport devaluation; and (c) reduced accomplishment (Raedeke and Smith, 2001). Sport scientists do not universally embrace this specific conceptualization as some have described experiences including sport withdrawal (e.g., Gould, Udry, et al., 1996) or more akin to notions of overtraining (e.g., Silva, 1990) when using the term "burnout." We argue that the psychosocial approach has the most utility and we hope that our comments on this account will lead researchers toward more careful examination of the nature of athlete burnout.

The definition forwarded by Raedeke and Smith (2001) embraces research that has led to refinements that better represent the experiential syndrome in sport. For example, Raedeke (1997) proposed that sport devaluation was a more appropriate experiential manifestation of burnout among athletes than the traditional burnout characteristic of depersonalization developed in human care. Sport devaluation represents a devaluation of the perceived benefits gained from sport involvement and is arguably a sport-specific manifestation of the broader state of cynicism forwarded by Maslach, Schaufeli, and Leiter (2001). The argument for sport devaluation is similar to that forwarded for depersonalization as a manifestation of cynicism specific to human care professionals. Raedeke and Smith (2001) observed that depersonalization had not been identified as a salient characteristic of athlete burnout, but sport devaluation had. As such Raedeke and Smith's (2001) Athlete Burnout Questionnaire (ABQ) measures sport devaluation. Research has supported the efficacy of sport devaluation as a descriptor of athlete experiences (Gould, Tuffey et al., 1996; Raedeke et al., 2002).

As originally proposed by Smith (1986), a logical question "is the extent to which the nature, causes and consequences are unique and to what extent they are shared by those who suffer burnout in other domains of activity" (p. 44). In essence Smith is advocating prudence in the extrapolation of burnout syndrome as defined in human care settings to sport and the experiences of athletes. In an effort to stimulate further constructive research it is important to acknowledge the explanations of athlete burnout forwarded in the relevant sport literature to date.

EXPLANATIONS OF ATHLETE BURNOUT IN THE EXTANT LITERATURE

Several explanations for the occurrence of athlete burnout have been advanced in the sport science literature (Gould and Dieffenbach, 2002). These explanations include Silva's (1990) conceptualization of burnout as the ultimate psychophysiological maladaptation to excessive training-stress and Coakley's (1992) sociologically grounded account of burnout as a particular type of sport dropout resulting from intense sporting involvement. Perhaps the earliest effort to conceptualize burnout as a relevant matter for exploration by sport psychologists can be found in Smith's (1986) cognitive-affective model of athlete burnout. His model was conceptually grounded in social exchange theory (Thibaut and Kelley, 1959) and empirically informed by evidence implicating chronic exposure to psychosocial stress (i.e., Maslach, 1982a). More recently, Raedeke (1997) has employed commitment theory as the theoretical grounding for his research on antecedents of athlete burnout.

Athlete Burnout: The Endpoint of Excessive Physical Training

Silva (1990) proposed that maladaptive responses to physical training demands, lie on a psychophysiological continuum ranging from staleness to burnout (see Figure 2). Silva believed the plummet towards burnout starts when athletes first experience "staleness." This entry point on Silva's psychophysiological continuum results from "an initial failure of the body's adaptive mechanisms in responding to psychophysiological stress created by training stimuli" (Silva, 1990, p. 10). Staleness is posited to progress into "overtraining" when chronic training demands result in repeated failure of the body's adaptive mechanisms. "Burnout" is the ultimate consequence of the chronic experience of overtraining. It occurs when "the organism's ability to deal with the psychophysiological imposition of [training] stress is depleted and the response system is exhausted" (p. 11). Thus, in this view, burnout is an endpoint in maladaptive responses to excessive physical training that is characterized by a complete collapse of psychophysiological response systems.

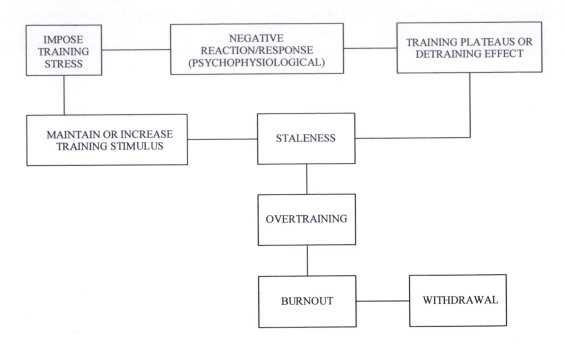

Figure 2: The training stress syndrome negative adaptation to training from Silva (1990).

Silva's description of burnout reflects some of the potential antecedents and consequences of burnout described by Maslach (1982a) rather than the experiential syndrome itself. In particular Silva's description highlights a collection of physiological symptoms (e.g., insomnia, weakened immune system) that Maslach (1982a) previously identified as possible outcomes or antecedents to stress and burnout. As such these physiological symptoms in and of themselves do not reflect the key characteristics of burnout per se but rather possible antecedents of consequences of the experience. Further Silva (1990) suggested that withdrawal from sport involvement is inevitable.

Athlete Burnout: High Accomplishment Followed by Sport Withdrawal

Coakley (1992) described athletic burnout as a physical withdrawal from sport following an intense investment of effort and high achievement—particularly when that withdrawal is not warranted (e.g., quitting while healthy and at "the top of one's game"). He contended that this pattern of involvement in highly competitive youth sport can be attributed directly to the social organization of intense sport participation. Specifically Coakley (1992) cited the development of a unidimensional identity and low autonomy as factors that lead to burnout. Coakley (1992) proposed that high achievement in sport (and the associated consuming efforts required) restricts opportunities for identity development beyond the athletic role. In effect these constraints were proposed to result in a "unidimensional identity" where an athlete's personal identity is based exclusively on his or her accomplishments/experiences in the sport domain.

After informally interviewing 15 adolescent athletes Coakley (1992) proposed that in the case of burnout, this development of a unidimensional identity was combined with a lack of autonomy or control over their own lives. Athletes become, according to Coakley (1992), "disempowered to the point of realizing sport participation has become a developmental dead-end and they no longer have meaningful control" (p. 272). In this view, athletes "burnout" of sport (i.e., terminate their sport involvement) rather than remaining in the aversive circumstance. Because Coakley (1992) defined burnout as high achievement followed by withdrawal he is describing a type of dropout, a potential consequence of burnout. Nevertheless, we feel that some of Coakley's (1992) assertions regarding possible causes of burnout are useful. Specifically he implicated perceptions of control in the burnout experience. Perceptions of control have also been included within stress and commitment approaches to burnout. We further these observations later in this chapter when discussing the potential role of autonomy in the burnout experience.

Athlete Burnout: An Experiential Consequence of Chronic Exposure to Psychosocial Stress

Smith's (1986) cognitive affective model of athletic burnout is conceptually grounded in social exchange theory (SET; Thibaut and Kelley, 1959). It is also empirically informed by evidence implicating chronic psychosocial stress as the causal agent producing the experiential syndrome afflicting health care professionals (i.e., Maslach, 1982a). As such Smith's (1986) explanation of the burnout syndrome includes a stress model and reflects components of SET. Within his approach Smith (1986) defined burnout's most notable feature as "psychological, emotional, and at times a physical withdrawal from a formerly pursued and enjoyable activity" (p. 37).

Smith's (1986) conceptual model of stress and burnout (see Figure 3) outlines four components that are influenced by personality and motivational factors. The first component represents traditional conceptions of psychosocial stress—an imbalance between demands and resources. As such Smith (1986) proposes perceptions of stress are determined by an interaction between environmental demands and personal and environmental resources. In the case of burnout this perception of stress is typified by either overload (high and conflicting demands) although underload (low demands and boredom) combined with low social support, and low rewards may also contribute to the experience.

The second component of Smith's (1986) model specifies cognitive appraisal of the situation as outlined within traditional stress appraisal research (Lazarus and Folkman, 1984). Smith (1986) proposed that in most cases of burnout a perceived imbalance in demands and resources over time leads to perceptions of low accomplishment, low perceived control and potentially a state of learned helplessness. This thought process creates a psychological reality to which the athlete responds (component three).

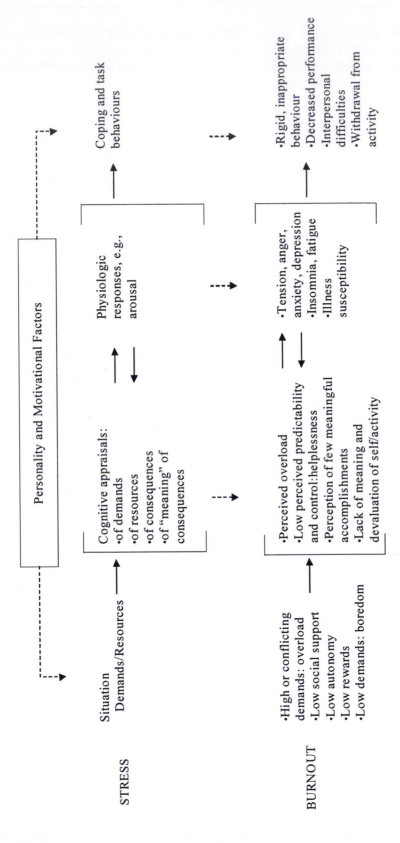

Figure 3: A conceptual model showing the parallel relationships assumed to exist among situational, cognitive, physiological and behavioral components of stress and burnout. From R.E. Smith, "Toward a Cognitive-Affective Model of Athletic Burnout," in the Journal of Sport Psychology, 8 (1): page 40, figure 1. © 1982 by Human Kinetics. Reprinted with permission from Human Kinetics (Champaign, IL).

The nature and intensity of an athlete's response is determined by the appraisal of demands, resources available, potential consequences and the meaning of these potential consequences (i.e., component two). When the appraisal process indicates a threat of harm or danger, physiological arousal occurs. These physiological responses influence future appraisal reinforcing perceptions of overload or underload. Smith (1986) proposes that in the case of burnout chronic stress produces fatigue and other negative physiological symptoms associated with burnout (e.g., sleep disorder and lethargy). The final component of the model outlines athletes' coping related behaviors. The behavioral result of burnout is proposed by Smith (1986) to involve "decreased efficiency and a psychological if not physical withdrawal from the activity" (p. 43).

The crux of Smith's (1986) explanation of burnout lies in his use of SET. SET is premised on the notion that people's behavior is heavily influenced by desires to minimize negative experience and maximize positive experience (Smith, 1986; Thibaut and Kelley, 1959). Motivated behavior, from this perspective, rests upon a rational assessment of the potential outcomes. These assessments rest not only upon the costs and benefits associated with any particular course of actions but, also, against assessments of the potential outcomes of alternative courses of action. Stress is viewed as one of the "costs" when assessing potential outcomes in sport participation. As widely advocated in social psychology (McGrath, 1970), Smith (1986) focuses his conceptualization upon "stress" as a perception or appraisal of imbalance between demands and resources rather than simply as a situational demand or imposition.

Smith (1986) suggests that athletic burnout occurs when stress-induced costs rise (without a concomitant decline in perceived sport-related benefits) to the point where an unfavorable cost-benefit ratio is perceived for engaging in a particular sporting activity. Athlete involvement in sport can be maintained despite this unfavorable perception because of: (a) the continued presence of substantially valued benefits (some perhaps especially salient from the initial motivation to become involved in the activity) and (b) a lack of recognition of an alternative perceived as providing a more attractive cost-benefit ratio. Even while maintaining physical involvement, however, burned-out athletes exhibit psychological and emotional withdrawal (e.g., persistent exhaustion, cynicism and devaluation of the activity, and a decreased sense of personal efficacy in the sport) (Smith, 1986).

A feature of Smith's (1986) cognitive affective model (and in particular his use of SET) is that it differentiates the occurrence of burnout and dropout. Within SET favorability of an activity is determined by the outcome (reward minus costs). This outcome is evaluated in relation to two standards the comparison level and the comparison level for alternatives. The comparison level is a scale of goodness to badness of outcome based on past outcomes and momentary needs. Smith (1986) proposed persistence in an activity is determined by a comparison level with alternatives, in effect the lowest outcome level an individual will accept given perceived outcomes available in alternative activities (including non-participation). Accordingly when the outcome for an activity drops below the comparison level with alternatives an individual will dropout. Ultimately the costs associated with being burned-out may result in withdrawal (if he or she is not first separated from the sport through deselection). It seems unlikely, however, that a suitably attractive alternative would be immediately evident to athletes who are deeply invested in their sport.

Stress-based explanations of burnout have not been without criticism. In particular Schmidt and Stein (1991) have outlined areas that require further attention within Smith's

(1986) cognitive affective model. Specifically, Schmidt and Stein (1991) propose that further consideration needs to be given to Smith's (1986) use of SET. First they suggest there is a need to consider how much cost can be carried before an individual drops out. It may be that in the absence of perceived viable alternatives, individuals stay involved in their sport longer and suffer burnout types of consequences as a result. Second, Schmidt and Stein (1991) noted that SET (Thibaut and Kelley, 1959) does not involve or invoke a temporal component. Without a temporal component SET cannot account for the experience of burnout through the exposure to stress across time. Research pursuing this theory clearly needs to address this lack of a temporal component. One key way future researchers could address these concerns is through longitudinal research that assesses changes in rewards, costs and alternatives relative to the occurrence of dropout and burnout.

Commitment May Augment the Risk?

Recently Raedeke and colleagues (Raedeke, 1997; Raedeke, Granzyk, and Warren, 2000) have explored the role of commitment in relation to burnout. They have built upon observations (e.g., Schmidt and Stein, 1991) that athlete burnout may be more than simply a consequence of exposure to chronic stress. Scanlan, Carpenter, Schmidt, Simons, and Keeler (1993) adapted the commitment perspective for sport based on an extension of SET and Rusbult's (1980a) investment model. Using this sport-specific adaptation of commitment theory contentions, Raedeke and colleagues have endeavored to explain why people persist in their sport involvement to the point of burning out.

Under the burnout explanation proposed by Raedeke (1997), athletes can be committed to sport for both attraction and entrapment reasons. In his view, attraction-related commitment to sport is relatively benign in terms of elevating the risk of athlete burnout because the athlete's involvement occurs because he or she *wants* to be involved. His examination of age-group swimmers supported this contention in that he found athletes reporting the lowest levels of burnout exhibited attraction-based commitment to their sport involvement.

Entrapment-based sport commitment has more sinister potential in Raedeke's (1997) opinion. In particular, he suggests that entrapped athletes may have an elevated risk of experiencing burnout. Athletes feel entrapped when they perceive they *must* maintain their sport involvement even though they are no longer intrinsically motivated to continue that participation. Determinants of entrapment-based commitment among athletes might include matters such as social constraints (e.g., participating out of a sense of obligation or because they are given/perceive no other alternatives), identity issues, investments, perceived control and alternative options. Data from his study of age group swimmers also supported this contention in that he found athletes exhibiting characteristics associated with entrapment-related sport commitment also reported elevated levels of burnout (Raedeke, 1997).

ISSUES OF CONCEPTUAL CONFUSION

Several alternative explanations of athlete burnout have been forwarded in the extant literature. Shared terminology in these explanations has resulted in definitional difficulty and conceptual ambiguity. Indeed, the explanations themselves differ in important ways that extend beyond the difficulties created by the shared terminology. These differences are too often overlooked even though they relate to fundamental matters such as the nature and attributes of burnout construct itself and extend through the causal ordering of relevant burnout-related constructs. Moreover, the term "burnout" enjoys widespread colloquial use that exacerbates problems with terminological and conceptual impreciseness. We outline our observations on these matters under the headings of: (a) are all burnout explanations addressing the same construct? (b) burnout and dropout, (c) burnout and overtraining, (d) burnout and depression and (e) burnout and performance decrements.

Are All Burnout Explanations Addressing the Same Construct?

The issues addressed in the various burnout explanations are certainly interrelated. Unfortunately, however, the notions of burnout discussed across these explanations differ in important, albeit often ignored, ways. Perhaps most fundamentally, the construct being invoked by the term "burnout" is not common across all of the commentaries. For example, Coakley's (1992) notion of "burnout" focuses upon a particular type of sport termination (i.e., unwarranted withdrawal that follows on from high accomplishment). Other commentaries (e.g., Raedeke, 1997; Silva, 1990; Smith, 1986) view dropout as a *burnout consequence rather than burnout itself*. Moreover, Coakley's conceptualization focuses upon burnout as something particular to those whose achievements are exceptional in some way. Finally, Coakley sees the experience of psychosocial stress as a *consequence* of processes leading to sport withdrawal (i.e., burnout in Coakley's terms) *rather than a cause* of sport burnout as described in other commentaries (e.g., Raedeke, 1997; Smith, 1986).

Silva's (1990) explanation has elements reminiscent of other burnout conceptualizations put forth by sport scientists in terms of likely consequences and experiential concomitants (see Figure 2). Nevertheless, it should not be assumed that the construct he advanced as burnout is the same as constructs advanced by others. Burnout, as advanced in his conceptualization, is a psychophysiological construct (i.e., the ultimate maladaptive manifestation of a negative adaptation to chronic training stress wherein there is a total collapse of psychophysiological response systems). This is a strikingly different conceptualization than notions of "burnout-as-withdrawal" (Coakley, 1992) or "burnout-as-psychosocial-syndrome" (e.g., Smith, 1996; Raedeke, 1997).

The notion advanced by Silva (1990) of "stress" being an antecedent of burnout is, superficially, common with psychosocial syndrome conceptualizations (e.g., Maslach, 1982; Raedeke, 1997; Smith, 1986). "Stress" as employed by Silva, however, is the "by-product created when an organism responds to a demand" (p. 6). He is obviously substantially (but not exclusively) concerned with the "stress" resulting from physiological impositions upon the athlete. This is substantially, and importantly, different from the social psychological process-based conceptualization employed by Smith (1986) that emphasizes the central role of cognitive appraisal of the relative balance of demands and response resources.

Finally, as previously alluded to, the constructs of athlete burnout proposed by Smith (1986) and Raedeke (1997) are closely aligned with conceptions of burnout in general psychology and hence the definition endorsed in this chapter. Smith's (1986) model is consistent with stress conceptions of the burnout syndrome that have been developed extensively in general psychology. Raedeke's (1997) explanation primarily focuses upon antecedent conditions (i.e., entrapment- versus attraction-based commitment), but explicitly embraces the idea of burnout as an experiential syndrome. Further, it is largely compatible with widely embraced psychosocial stress-based explanations of the syndrome. Within this chapter we have endorsed a psychosocial approach to burnout. As such, the notions of high stress, low perceived control, a unidimensional athletic identity and entrapment described in this review potentially contribute to the burnout experience. Overtraining is viewed as a possible antecedent to the experience whereas dropout is a potential consequence.

Burnout and Dropout

Dropout (i.e., physically withdrawing from sport) is one potential consequence of the burnout syndrome (Smith, 1986). Not all cases of burnout result in dropout. Even when individuals experience burnout to the extent that they want to discontinue their involvement, some may stay on, completing tasks with only minimal effort (Maslach and Goldberg, 1998). It is even more obvious that not all cases of dropout can be attributed to burnout (e.g., Greendorfer, 2002; Smith, 1986). There are a multitude of other reasons why individuals chose to discontinue participation and the vast majority of them are unrelated to burnout (e.g., alternative career options).

Within the athlete burnout literature some early researchers (e.g., Coakley, 1992; Smith, 1986) included physical withdrawal as an important feature of their operational definition. For example, some researchers focused upon instances where intensive sport involvement resulting in high accomplishment is followed by untimely sport withdrawal (e.g., Coakley, 1992). This is "burnout" in colloquial terms. It is an attractive perspective to take in some ways because physical withdrawal is an easily notable feature of some extreme cases of burnout. As noted within Smith's (1986) early definition a notable feature of burnout is "at times physical withdrawal" (p. 37). As such Smith indicates that physical withdrawal is only a possible feature of burnout. Dropout is a matter of salient concern to many people interested in child and adolescent welfare (e.g., parents, coaches, sport administrators, child welfare advocates) that is worthy of investigation. Researchers selecting dropouts to be participants, however, may have not been examining burnout syndrome per se - although some researchers studying burnout clearly were looking at the experience of the syndrome as a particular cause of dropout (i.e., Gould, Udry, et al., 1996). It is commonly agreed that burnout and drop out are not synonymous terms and that conceptual clarity is defeated when they are not treated as separate constructs. More recent research has not included physical withdrawal within their operational definitions (e.g., Raedeke, 1997; Raedeke and Smith, 2001).

Burnout and Overtraining

The confusion surrounding burnout and overtraining is understandable. Both terms are, independently, shrouded in some confusion. While conceptual differences exist between burnout and overtraining experientially there are several similarities. A purpose of this review is to outline some of the confusion surrounding burnout. Similar commentaries exist about the nature of overtraining (Hackney, Pearman, and Nowacki, 1990; Kreider, Fry, and O'Toole, 1998). Specifically, the term "overtraining" has been used both to refer to a process used to stimulate positive adaptive change (e.g., O'Connor, 1997) and to refer to maladaptive responses to training (e.g., Hackney et al., 1990). It is beyond the purpose of this review to dwell upon this terminological matter. Within this review we will restrict our use of the terms "overtraining" and "overtraining syndrome" to the manner that Silva (1990) employed them. Specifically, when we invoke these terms, we will be making reference to the long-term maladaptive responses that result from excessive physical training with insufficient recovery.

There are several conceptual differences between overtraining (as an endpoint) and burnout (as an experiential syndrome). First, burnout is an experiential state that results primarily from chronic exposure to psychosocial stress. Descriptive evidence suggests that burnout can occur in the absence of excessive training (e.g., Gould, Tuffey, et al., 1996). Nonetheless, it seems very likely that hard physical training (and especially the process of overtraining) has the potential to provoke psychosocial stress appraisals (Silva, 1990; Smith, 1986) that may act as antecedents to the burnout syndrome (Gould and Dieffenbach, 2002). It may also be that inadequate recovery from excessive training stress contributes to the development of the syndrome (Kellmann, 2002). The demands of training (even overtraining), however, are only a possible (but not requisite) antecedent to burnout (Fender, 1989; Gould et al., 1997). In contrast, overtraining is primarily the result of physical training, and psychosocial stress related factors are secondary. As such an athlete could experience overtraining without experiencing burnout. Nonetheless, it is likely that psychosocial stressors play a role in overtraining as they influence an athlete's ability to deal with physical training demands (Clow and Hucklebridge, 2001).

Despite these conceptual differences, burnout and the negative overtraining syndrome share a number of similar experiential characteristics. Some of the experiential characteristics of burnout and overtraining appear identical, for example exhaustion, lethargy and negative mood (e.g., O'Connor, 1997). These commonalities have lead some researchers in the past (e.g., Silva, 1990) to propose that overtraining and burnout are intimately related—in fact, so intimately related that *one (i.e., burnout) is merely the most severe manifestation possible of the other (i.e., overtraining syndrome).* As burnout and overtraining may co-exist (Gould et al., 1997), the distinction between these constructs, in practice, may be difficult to discern. Differentiating between burnout and overtraining may however be crucial in the development of preventative and intervention strategies. Specifically, there are notable differences in the causes of overtraining and burnout that would have different ramifications for prevention or intervention. For example, overtraining is primarily the result of excessive physical training. As such, a psychological intervention is unlikely to be an effective way to treat overtraining. There is no way to transform an objectively excessive training regimen into an objectively acceptable regimen through a psychological intervention.

Burnout and Depression

At first glance it does not seem unreasonable to assume that burnout and depression are, experientially speaking, one and the same thing. Similarities in symptomatologies are evident (Glass and McKnight, 1996). For example, the emotional exhaustion component of burnout has been considered similar to the sadness and fatigue experienced in depression (Leiter and Durup, 1994). The depersonalization characteristic of burnout has been considered similar to social withdrawal in depression (Leiter and Durup, 1994). In addition the reduced accomplishment within burnout has also been compared to the reduction in self-efficacy and learned helplessness within depression (Leiter and Durup, 1994). In fact, Schaufeli, Enzmann, and Girault (1993) went so far as to conclude that the similarities between these constructs are so great that it is not possible to validly distinguish between them. Nonetheless, the constructs differ in important ways—both theoretically and empirically (Glass and McKnight, 1996).

Burnout and depression experiences have long enjoyed different conceptual identities. Freudenberger (1975) took considerable pains in his seminal work conceptualizing the notion of burnout to argue that it differed from depression. He suggested, for example, that burnout is accompanied by anger and frustration while depression is accompanied by guilt. Others have noted that the initial symptoms of burnout are situation-specific (Maslach, Jackson, and Leiter, 1997) while, on the other hand, a diagnosis of depression requires pervasive symptomatology that influences "nearly all activities" (DSM-IV, 1994 p. 320; Leiter and Durup, 1994). People experiencing the initial symptoms of burnout can feel productive and happy in other areas of life. People experiencing depression attribute their depressive symptomatology to themselves and not a specific context in the way that people suffering from burnout do.

Empirical evidence supports the previously mentioned conceptual distinctions. For example Leiter and Durup (1994) evaluated health care workers' responses to the Beck Depression Inventory and the Maslach Burnout Inventory via confirmatory factor analyses. Their results indicated that burnout was a complex three-factor syndrome where each factor was more closely aligned with one another than any aspect of depression. This is not to suggest, however, that depression and burnout are empirically unrelated. Correlations between burnout constructs such as emotional/physical exhaustion and depression have consistently been reported in the moderate range (Firth, McIntee, McKeown, and Britton, 1986; Glass, McKnight, and Valdimarsdottir, 1993; Schaufeli et al., 1993).

In summary, it has become accepted that, while overlap exists between depressive symptomatology and burnout, they are independent constructs (Glass and McKnight, 1996; Leiter and Durup, 1994). In practice it is not unreasonable to assume that burnout may influence quality of personal life outside work and result in a generalized depressive state (Glass and McKnight, 1996) or that depression may impact on work performance or increase someone's vulnerability to emotional exhaustion and possibly burnout at work (Leiter and Durup, 1994). As such, an interesting empirical question may be: Are burnout and depression sequentially related? It is, nonetheless, inappropriate to assume that they are experientially one and the same thing.

Overall, major conceptual problems will continue until a consensus is reached on the nature of the burnout syndrome in athlete populations. Until this consensus is reached, researchers should be cautious when interpreting "burnout" findings because there is a reasonable likelihood that the construct under consideration will not be uniform across studies. Readers need to be sure that references to "burnout" do not actually describe other constructs (e.g., dropout) and researchers need to ensure that they are explicit about their operational definitions.

METHODOLOGICAL ISSUES

Several methodological shortcomings are evident in current athlete burnout research. Prominent shortcomings include the lack of an adequate measurement instrument and a reliance on cross-sectional research designs.

Perhaps the methodological problem posing the biggest challenge to researchers attempting to understand athlete burnout has been the lack of a sound measurement instrument. Reliable and valid measurement is a foundational requirement for investigation in any area and the absence of such a tool in the study of burnout has been a limiting factor. There is a recursive relationship between this measurement shortcoming and the conceptual confusion outlined in this chapter. Specifically, researchers have not consistently provided a precise operational definition of burnout that is conceptually linked to the method of measurement employed. This is in part due to the conceptual confusion surrounding burnout and partly due to the lack of a theoretically based and empirically sound measurement instrument.

Overtime sport scientists have employed a number of different measurement instruments with differing levels of success. Initial attempts to measure burnout in sport focused on adapting the Maslach Burnout Inventory (MBI) (e.g., Fender, 1988) originally developed by Maslach and Jackson (1986) as a measure of burnout in the human services (e.g., psychologists, nurses). Despite showing some promise, athlete adaptations of the MBI have never been employed beyond the initial unpublished validation studies. MBI adaptations have been used with more success in sport settings with coaches (Kelley, Eklund, and Ritter-Taylor, 1999) and athletic directors (Martin, Kelley, and Eklund, 1999).

Until recently the most widely used measure of athlete burnout has been the Eades (1990) Athletic Burnout Inventory (EABI) (e.g., Gould, Udry, et al., 1996). While some utility has been demonstrated in these published investigations, several difficulties with the EABI are evident. First, the instrument is not theoretically grounded. In the development of the EABI, Eades drew on a range of existing burnout descriptions and explanations (e.g., Freudenberger, 1975; Maslach and Jackson, 1986; Silva, 1990; Smith, 1986) as well as anecdotal evidence. The absence of a theoretical basis makes this eclectic instrument ungainly and data collected with it can be difficult to interpret. Moreover, rigorous empirical evaluation of the EABI has not been reported. Researchers using EABI subscales have reported moderate-to-low internal consistency (Gould, Udry, et al., 1996). As a consequence, reports employing EABI measurement of burnout have typically focused upon the global scale score (i.e., the sum of the subscales forming a single burnout score). This unidimensional measure of burnout is inherently troublesome given the multidimensional nature of the construct. In summary, the lack of a clear empirical and theoretical basis to the EABI has rendered it an ineffective measure of athlete burnout.

Stimulated by the inadequacies of previous instruments as reliable and valid measures of athlete burnout, Raedeke and Smith (2001) developed the Athlete Burnout Questionnaire

(ABQ). The ABQ has subscales measuring emotional exhaustion, reduced accomplishment and sport devaluation. As such the ABQ follows the definition endorsed within this chapter. Specifically, the term "burnout" refers to an enduring experiential syndrome characterized by three central characteristics: (a) emotional and physical exhaustion; (b) sport devaluation; and (c) reduced accomplishment. Preliminary evaluations of the ABQ have been promising (Raedeke and Smith, 2001), but further validation of this instrument is required. Prior to the work by Raedeke and Smith, Maslach and colleagues (Maslach et al., 1996) refined the MBI to measure burnout as a multidimensional construct in general work settings. The result of their efforts was the Maslach Burnout Inventory-General Survey (MBI-GS) that contains parallel modications to those evident within the development of the ABQ. Preliminary evaluation of the MBI-GS with a large sample of general workers provided promising results (Schutte et al., 2000). Overall, we would encourage researchers to outline strong links between their operational definition and the measurement instrument employed.

Another methodological shortcoming relates to the reliance on cross-sectional research designs. For some time it has been established that stress is a process where previous instances of stress and coping are likely to influence future events (Lazarus and Folkman, 1984). As such stress appraisals and the burnout syndrome should be examined in series and not isolation because previous instances of successful or unsuccessful coping are likely to influence future appraisals and experiences (Folkman and Moskwitz, 2000). Cross-sectional research designs provide information about a single moment in time and as such do not account for these previous appraisals and experiences. Examining stress appraisals and the burnout syndrome over time offers the opportunity to accurately examine conceptual explanations. In particular this approach will enable researchers to separate the antecedents, consequences and symptoms of the syndrome. Further, longitudinal research is needed to provide evidence for existing and proposed theoretical approaches to burnout. Many of the theoretical approaches to burnout specify a temporal component. As such accurate examination of these approaches requires sequential data.

PREVALENCE AND CORRELATES

Within this section it is our aim to review current research that has followed a psychosocial approach to burnout. Within this section we aim to highlight current research that provides an indication of the prevalence of athlete burnout and its association with other constructs.

The Prevalence of Athlete Burnout

Establishing the prevalence of athlete burnout should be a primary concern to researchers and practitioners. To date a small number of studies exist that contain information on the level of burnout in athlete populations. Currently, however, no research exists to indicate the level at which burnout produces undesirable consequences. As such it is only possible to review burnout in terms of the ABQ values reported in previous research. Inferences about the clinical meaningfulness of the reported values are, at present, speculative.

Raedeke's (1997) earliest study provides the most detail on the prevalence of burnout in an athletic population. In his study Raedeke (1997) employed the ABQ which measures the frequency that athletes experience burnout on a five-point Likert scale anchored by descriptors of "almost never" (1), "rarely" (2), "sometimes" (3), "frequently" (4), and "most of the time" (5). Overall age group (13 to 18 years) swimmers (N=236) reported moderately low scores on exhaustion (M=2.47, SD=0.83), reduced accomplishment (M=2.32, SD=0.74) and devaluation (M=2.02, SD=0.84) (Raedeke, 1997). One cluster of swimmers (n=26) reported what Raedeke (1997) termed high exhaustion (M=3.35, SD=0.83) as well as moderately high reduced accomplishment (M= 2.97, SD=0.64) and devaluation (M=3.40, SD=0.81). The swimmers in this cluster reported significantly higher burnout scores relative to their peers in two other clusters. This group regarded by Raedeke (1997) as reporting high burnout scores was a relatively small percentage (11%) of the total number of age group swimmers surveyed. The burnout scores of the athletes in this cluster corresponded to a score of approximately three or indicating that they "sometimes" experienced the characteristics of burnout on a five point Likert scale from one "almost never" to five "most of the time".

In subsequent studies less detail is provided about the number of athletes reporting high burnout scores. Raedeke and Smith (2001) studied a similar sample of age group (14 to 19 years) swimmers to Raedeke's (1997) first study. This second sample of swimmers (N=244) reported moderate to high scores on exhaustion (M=3.06, SD=0.82) and moderately low scores on reduced accomplishment (M=2.30, SD= 0.79) and devaluation (M=2.19, SD=0.95) (Raedeke and Smith, 2001). And in a sample of collegiate athletes (N=208) from a range of different sports athletes reported moderately low scores on exhaustion (M=2.62, SD=0.86) and reduced accomplishment (M=2.37, SD= 0.76) and devaluation (M=2.02, SD=0.88) (Raedeke and Smith, 2001).

Within their analysis Raedeke and Smith (2001) do not comment on the percentage of athletes reporting relatively high levels of burnout, but relevant deductions can be made from the descriptive statistics. The means and standard deviations for the mixed sample indicate that only a small percentage of the mixed sport collegiate sample reported experiencing the three characteristics of burnout "sometimes" (i.e., item average response of 3 or higher) on any of the individual subscales. In the second swimming sample the mean for the exhaustion subscale however, was over three suggesting that a substantial proportion of the sample "sometimes" experienced exhaustion. Reduced accomplishment and devaluation subscale scores in the second swimming sample indicate only a small percentage of players scoring above three (i.e., "sometimes"). Overall, only a small proportion of swimmers were experiencing all three characteristics of the burnout syndrome at a frequency Raedeke (1997) deemed was representative of high burnout.

In summary, preliminary evidence suggests that only a small percentage of athletes experience high levels of burnout—although it must be acknowledged that the cohorts involved in these investigations are certainly not representative of all sport participants. There may well be important differences in the incidence of the syndrome across the variety of imaginable subgroups of sport participants. For example, most research to date has been conducted in select North American sports with athlete populations thought to be at high risk of burning out (e.g., Gould, Udry, et al., 1996, tennis players; Raedeke and Smith, 2001, swimmers). Other cultures and/or sporting environments may not exhibit a similar prevalence pattern. It is certainly possible that individual differences variables such as gender, ethnicity and developmental differences may also impact on the level of burnout observed in athlete populations.

Future athlete burnout research is needed to address the key issues related to prevalence. On the whole, there is a need for a good epidemiological evaluation of incidence and patterns of occurrence of athlete burnout to provide solid answers to questions in this area. There is a strong consensus that burnout is undesirable (regardless of the particular conceptualization). There is less consensus about the point at which burnout produces manifestly undesirable consequences. Future researchers need to identify the level of burnout associated with these consequences. Past researchers have proposed that even low levels of burnout can result in negative consequences (Kelley et al., 1999; Maslach et al., 1996). Such statements should be corroborated with empirical evidence with athlete populations if they are to be used with confidence.

Athlete Burnout Correlates

An eclectic mix of burnout correlates have been identified in the extant cross-sectional research (e.g., Gould, Tuffey, et al., 1996; Gould et al., 1997; Gould, Udry, et al., 1996; Raedeke, 1997). For example, Raedeke (1997) subjected ABQ subscale score data collected from age group swimmers to cluster analyses and compared those burnout clusters on measures of enjoyment perceived benefits, swimmer identity strength, and perceived investment in the sport. Age group swimmers scoring relatively high in burnout reported relatively low enjoyment, low perceived benefits, a weak identity as a swimmer and low investments in swimming in comparison to peers in lower burnout clusters. Moreover, these athletes perceived high costs to be associated with their swimming involvements and found other activities to be more attractive. As a result Raedeke (1997) labeled this high burnout group "malcontented".

In a series of studies Gould and colleagues examined burnout in elite junior tennis players. Within these studies burnout was measured unidimensionally using the EABI total scale score (Gould, Udry, et al., 1996). Despite the limitations associated with this measure (and particularly with the global score), it appears that players scoring high in burnout reported lower levels of input into training and practiced fewer days compared to players scoring low in burnout (Gould, Tuffey, et al., 1996; Gould et al., 1997; Gould, Udry, et al., 1996). Gould and colleagues believed that perceptions of low control related to lower levels of intrinsic motivation and contributed to stress and frustration. As players in the high burnout group were purposefully sampled because they were showing signs of psychological and physical withdrawal it is not surprising they reported fewer practice days. The high burnout group also differed from the low burnout group on some psychological variables. Specifically the high burnout group reported low levels of extrinsic motivation, perfectionist tendencies and higher levels of amotivation (Gould, Udry, et al., 1996). Gould and colleagues (1997) reported the results of case studies of individual players to link the occurrence of burnout to experiences such as pressure from others, a need for a social life, perfectionistic tendencies, overtraining and inappropriate goals.

Overall the cross-sectional evaluation of burnout correlates has provided preliminary evidence that is largely consistent with what should be intuitively expected. This initial evidence suggests motivational variables (e.g., enjoyment, extrinsic motivation) commitment-related constructs (e.g., identity, investments) and stress-related constructs (i.e., control) are related to athlete burnout in unsurprising ways. For example, burnout is inversely (or negatively) associated with perceptions of control and positively associated with reliance on extrinsic sources of motivation. In addition some evidence exists that suggests perfectionist tendencies are related to athlete burnout. Further examination of burnout correlates is warranted but such efforts are likely to be most productive when grounded in theory.

REFLECTIONS ON PERTINENT THEORETICAL APPROACHES

Within this review we concentrate on three theoretical explanations of burnout compatible with our operational definition of burnout. We have presented reflections on these theoretical approaches because we believe they offer potential for further research and development. In particular, Smith's use of SET and Raedeke's notions of commitment are yet to be fully explored and consideration of their current strengths and weaknesses offers potential avenues for future research. Further, the consideration of self-determination theory (Ryan and Deci, 2000b) as a new theoretical direction also offers opportunities to extend our current understanding of burnout. We believe self-determination theory provides a possible explanation for the occurrence of burnout, either directly through the frustration of basic needs or indirectly through a stress-mediated pathway.

Smith's (1986) Cognitive Affective Model

Smith's (1986) model fits with extant descriptions of the burnout syndrome in the wider literature. Despite defining burnout's most notable feature as "psychological, emotional, and at times a physical withdrawal from a formerly pursued and enjoyable activity" (Smith, 1986, p. 37) the model is compatible with the operationalisation of burnout within this review. In fact, similar stress-based models employed in general work and human care settings have used refined versions of burnout as exhaustion, devaluation and reduced accomplishment. Smith's (1986) model has made important conceptual contributions to the understanding of burnout in sport. Nonetheless, opportunities for further research continue to exist within Smith's (1986) model. For example, Smith (1986) proposes that individual difference variables can influence situational, cognitive, affective and behavioral parts of the stress (and burnout) process (see Figure 3). Based upon Raedeke's findings (Raedeke, 1997; Raedeke et al., 2000; Raedeke and Smith, 2001), one relevant individual difference variable meriting further examination would be commitment. Smith's model may provide a useful encapsulation of notions about how commitment impacts upon burnout both directly, as suggested by Raedeke (1997), *and* indirectly via the stress process. Simultaneously modeling direct pathways from antecedents of commitment to burnout and indirect pathways through perceived stress (c.f. Kelley et al., 1999) may provide some insight into whether commitment is most influential as an individual difference variable directly impacting upon burnout or as a variable whose impact is moderated via the stress process.

Moreover, Schmidt and Stein (1991) have outlined areas that they believe require further attention within Smith's (1986) model. Their comments tend to focus on social exchange theory as the theoretical basis for Smith's model. First they highlight a need to consider how costs are evaluated and suggest that it is plausible dropout could occur solely from an unfavorable evaluation of balance between rewards and costs within the current activity. As such it may not be possible to clearly distinguish between dropout due to burnout and other types of dropout solely on the basis of rewards, costs and alternatives. It may be that, in the absence of perceived viable alternatives, individuals continue their sport participation longer than they might otherwise and, as a result, suffer burnout consequences. Empirical data are needed to explore postulated relationships among perceived rewards, costs and alternatives and how they may differentially contribute to burnout and/or dropout.

Commitment Theory

Schmidt and Stein (1991) proposed that a commitment model could explain why athletes continue participation, dropout or experience burnout. Specifically Schmidt and Stein (1991) adopted the investment parameters specified within Rusbult's (Rusbult, 1980a, 1980b, 1983; Rusbult and Farrell, 1983) approach to commitment. As such, within Schmidt and Stein's (1991) model, commitment is predicted by satisfaction (rewards minus costs), alternatives and investments. Schmidt and Stein (1991) proposed that individuals whose participation was predicted by low perceived alternatives should be at risk of burnout. Specifically these athletes may experience a sharp increase in costs with no attendant rise in rewards (i.e., low satisfaction or in Smith's (1986) terms stress-induced costs), a perception of no or low alternatives and an increase in already high investments. As such Schmidt and Stein (1991) predict that a perception of few alternatives and high investments could result in perceptions of entrapment and burnout.

Raedeke and his associates (Raedeke, 1997; Raedeke et al., 2000) have empirically demonstrated that perceptions of entrapment are associated with burnout. While this correlational evidence links the construct of commitment to burnout, it should not be interpreted as providing evidence of causation. It may be, from a self-determination perspective, that autonomy is the central need being undermined when athletes perceive entrapment in their athletic role. Further research is required to explore this possibility. For example, it may be interesting to examine whether or not perceptions of an external influence (e.g., the internalization of public opinion) and/or a perceived lack of autonomy stemming from, for example, contractual obligations or commitments are related to athlete experiences of burnout. Similarly, research is needed to establish if extrinsic rewards, such as financial payments to professional athletes, have the potential to undermine autonomy and lead to the key characteristics of athlete burnout. Simultaneous modeling of entrapment and autonomy with burnout would allow researchers to establish if autonomy contributes directly or indirectly (via entrapment) to the occurrence of burnout. Empirical evidence is then needed to support these assertions, for example longitudinal research is needed to assess changes in commitment and/or motivation relative to the occurrence burnout.

Raedeke (1997) suggests that perceptions of entrapment increase the likelihood that an athlete will experience burnout. It is likely that notions of commitment are intertwined with the stress process. Specifically when appraising possible responses to a situation it is likely that athletes also take into account relevant constraints. For example, a professional athlete may be less likely to consider certain responses, such as leaving sport, because of the associated decrease in remuneration—a decision that reflects a level of entrapment. At present, research has outlined an association between commitment and burnout (Raedeke, 1997) but this relationship requires more nuanced explanation as well as further empirical evaluation. Given current evidence, it is logical to pursue the possibility that entrapment appraisals have a direct or indirect influence on the development and experience of burnout. In order to achieve this closer examination of theory related to perceptions of entrapment is required.

Theorizing about commitment and its implications has a long and interesting history. Observations from an early commitment theorist, Becker (1960), may prove informative when considered within the context of sport. Becker (1960) was interested in (and focused upon) why people engage in "consistent lines of activity" (p. 33). The pursuit of a goal through consistent lines of activity represents an individual's commitment (i.e., investment of time and effort). Becker (1960) proposed that commitment can be impelled or developed in many ways. Now that evidence of an association between commitment and burnout has emerged, examination of the role and implications of various processes resulting in commitment vis a vis burnout merits further consideration.

Social and interpersonal processes were integral to Becker's (1960) original conceptualization of commitment and its extension in other settings (e.g., Kelley, 1983). Despite this researchers have given little consideration to how these processes may be manifested in sport settings (i.e., Scanlan et al., 1993). Social processes are integral to an individual's motivation to participate in sport (Baumeister and Leary, 1995; Buunk and Nauta, 2000; Ryan and Deci, 2002) and as such they are likely to play a central role in commitment, entrapment and athlete burnout. We feel that researchers within sport need to give greater consideration to the role of social constraints in commitment and athlete burnout.

We believe that revisiting Becker's (1960) original theorization of commitment and Kelley's (1983) extension that focused on adult relationships will help clarify and expand on the potential role of these interpersonal processes in sport proposed by Scanlan et al. (1993). In particular Becker (1960) describes interpersonal processes through which people can experience entrapment within their commitments. Becker (1960) argued that perceptions of entrapment may emerge from, or be associated with, a variety of social circumstances including: (a) cultural expectations, (b) bureaucratic arrangements, (c) individual adjustment to social position and (d) face-to-face interaction.

Cultural expectations may result in perceptions of entrapment because of the social penalties that exist within cultures to govern behavior. Athletes are not exempt from cultural expectations. In fact, for some athletes at least, the penalties can be especially exacting. In particular, high achieving athletes in western civilizations can be exposed to unwarranted or disproportionately intense criticism of (real or perceived) behavioral or personal flaws (Feather, 1994). Feather (1994) termed this propensity to scrutinize high profile individuals in order "to cut them down to size" as the "tall poppy syndrome". It is reasonably obvious that some athletes are at risk of experiencing heightened public scrutiny—and that scrutiny usually extends beyond the athletic forum in which they compete.

For example, loyalty tends to be a esteemed personal attribute in many cultures. In such cultures, an athlete who changes teams risks being perceived as being disloyal. Awareness of such risks may cause a sought-after athlete to feel entrapped (and therefore constrained) when deliberating over alternative contract offers by the potential implications of being labeled 'disloyal'. It should be noted, however, that sport transfers or trades are becoming a part of the culture of modern professional sport in the western world. As such, the risk of being perceived as disloyal may be increasingly irrelevant as a threat emanating from cultural expectations. There are many other cultural expectations that may, nonetheless, serve to provide a sense of entrapment. For example, athletes may experience cultural pressure to continue their sport participation beyond when they might otherwise want to quit just to avoid being labeled a "quitter" —something that may be seen as a personal failure in individualistic cultures or as failing the group in more group oriented cultures. At this point, no research has examined the extent to which an awareness of cultural expectations and/or the consequences of contravening these expectations can contribute to a sense of entrapment among athletes.

Bureaucratic arrangements are a necessary part of professional sport and everyday life. Contracts, for example, provide athletes with a degree of certainty as they formalize the obligations of another party. The necessary flipside of contractual arrangements is that they can be perceived as limiting and entrapping because they constrain a person to certain actions. For example, a contractual obligation (e.g., athletic scholarship) may cause an athlete to feel entrapped because of the constraints associated with his or her athletic responsibilities. Moreover, he or she may feel obligated (and entrapped) to ensure that his or her public behavior (and perhaps even private behavior!) is in keeping with the organizational priorities. Certainly the penalties associated with breeches of contractual obligations (e.g., loss of financial reward) are likely to contribute to any potential sense of entrapment. The extent to which the security such bureaucratic arrangements afford can paradoxically increase the risk of player burnout, particularly if contractual obligations invoke substantial penalties, is worth further evaluation.

Several adjustments to social position are required of athletes when coming to grips with the lifestyle demands of elite sport. Becker (1960) suggests that these sorts of adjustments to social position can produce perceptions of entrapment. For example, athletes often need to adjust their personal priorities to fit travel and time demands associated with high level or elite sports participation - not to mention the public expectations associated with occupying the role of "elite athlete." In fact, the notion of "personal priorities" itself requires considerable adjustment once an athlete arrives at elite levels of competition. Time and travel demands are the result of obligations associated with the athletic role (e.g., sponsorship appearances, training, games) that inevitably result in personal sacrifices (Gould, Tuffey, et al., 1996). An obligation for extensive travel and training leaves little time for professional development or other activities (e.g., social interaction) in areas outside sport. These concepts of priorities and adjustment to the athletic position are also highlighted within Coakley (1992) and Raedeke's (1997) discussions of athletic identity and personal investment. We agree that at the elite level an athlete may have limited or no opportunities to engage in alternative activities or occupations. Having such a one-dimensional focus does restrict opportunities for positive experiences, such as accomplishment, independent of sport involvement. It may be that related perceptions of entrapment do fuel the development of negative affectivity and burnout. Participants in Gould, Tuffey et al.'s (1996) study, for example, specifically linked perceptions of personal sacrifice (e.g., dissatisfaction with social life, time demands) to their experiences of burnout. In any event, the clinical significance of facilitating an athlete's personal and professional development beyond sport is highlighted by the integration of curricula to that end within national sport programs. For example, the Australian Institute of Sport's Athlete Career Education program is designed to provide opportunities for career development (Anderson and Morris, 2000) and has now been franchised to several different countries. Despite the value attached to these programs, no evidence presently exists regarding potential relationships among adjustments to social position variables, entrapment, and the experience of burnout (or other states of negative affectivity).

Becker (1960) also proposed an individual may perceive entrapment through interpersonal processes in *face-to-face interaction*. People are motivated to behave with some consistency. Acting in a manner that is inconsistent with a previously created image puts an individual's reputation at risk. Hence past behavior, particularly in face-to-face encounters, can effectively entrap individuals by limiting their future options to behaviors affording a sense of interpersonal consistency. For example, stating loyalty to a team or sport via face-to-face interaction will create a perception of commitment. Commitment generated via face-to-face interactions is harder for an individual to break than that created in other less personal communication channels (e.g., media reports) because of heightened personal accountability. As a result athletes may feel constrained from transferring between teams (or retiring) if they have previously publicly stated their affinity with the team (or sport). Further, failure to be consistent might result in cognitive dissonance. It has been documented that the incompatibility of two incongruent beliefs held simultaneously can result in perceptions of stress (Festinger, 1957). Further research is required to examine possible relationships between attempts to reconcile incongruent beliefs or act in a manner consistent with these beliefs and burnout.

This list of potential entrapment mechanisms is not exhaustive. While some commitments are conscious, others may be made subconsciously through related actions and decisions (e.g., signing a contract). It is not possible, however, to fully appreciate how commitment will be manifested without knowing about the individual and his/her value system (Becker, 1960). The interaction between an individual's value system and commitment could potentially explain how an athlete comes to experience key characteristics of burnout. For example dedicated athletes who aspire to represent their country at the highest level (e.g., Olympics, world championships) are likely to develop strong identities as athletes through their sports participation. This may lead to a perception of entrapment through social and cultural expectations.

In conclusion, further research is needed to empirically verify conceptual links between commitment and burnout. Raedeke's (1997) contentions about commitment theory provide a useful explanation of a potential psychosocial precipitant of burnout. Further research is needed to evaluate his contentions as well as various entrapment processes and their possible links to burnout. Recently researchers investigating commitment have employed commitment profiles (e.g., Weiss and Weiss, 2003). It may be that the accounting for the different types of commitment outlined by Schmidt and Stein (1991) provide additional information regarding the relationship between commitment and burnout. A further logical step would be to conduct research that allows the establishment of causality. Raedeke (1997) noted the correlational design of his current work does not determine the direction of the relationship between commitment and burnout. As such Raedeke suggests it is possible that commitment is an antecedent to burnout and burnout may be caused by factors other than entrapment.

Self-Determination Theory

There has been increasing interest in self-determination theory (SDT; Ryan and Deci, 2002) and notably so among researchers delving into sport psychology relevant issues (e.g., Vallerand and Rousseau, 2001; Vlachopoulas, Karageorghis, and Terry, 2000). In recent non-sport research, the utility of SDT has been demonstrated in the explanation of states of ill-being (Ryan and Deci, 2000a, 2000b). The utility of SDT to explain non-optimal states and ill-being is yet to be explored in detail within a sport context.

We believe there are several advantages to considering an SDT explanation of athlete burnout not the least of which is that SDT provides an encompassing perspective to view burnout that subsumes existing explanations. For example, an SDT explanation encompasses existing stress-based explanations for the occurrence of burnout. Specifically stress perceptions may result from frustration of fundamental psychological needs (i.e., autonomy, competence, relatedness) wherein the individual feels he/she lacks the latitude, capabilities or support to meet environmental demands. Chronic perceptions of this sort may then result in burnout as stipulated in stress-based explanations. Alternatively, burnout could also be explained from an SDT perspective as simply the direct consequence of chronic need frustration in one's sporting endeavors that produces feelings of reduced accomplishment, exhaustion and sport devaluation.

Adopting an SDT explanation of burnout also has some other advantages over existing explanations. For example, stress-based definitions propose that chronic stress leads to burnout. Yet some athletes chronically experience stress but not burnout. Within SDT it is conceivable that an athlete may appraise their circumstances as stressful yet have his/her basic psychological needs fulfilled and as a result not experience burnout-related exhaustion, devaluation and reduced accomplishment. Indeed, the idea that the satisfaction of basic psychological needs comes with a brighter side fits nicely with evidence that SDT is a useful theoretical framework for studies of positive psychology and optimal functioning (Ryan and Deci, 2000).

As such an SDT framework may guide a recent move away from exclusively focusing upon burnout as a "malfunction" toward including a "positive psychology" perspective (Schaufeli, Salanova, Gonzalez-Roma, and Bakker, 2002). For example, the experience of engagement, which is characterized by vigor, dedication and absorption (Schaufeli et al., 2002), has been proposed to directly oppose the experience of burnout (Maslach and Leiter, 1997). It is conceptually possible that the fulfillment of basic needs may result in the experience of engagement while, conversely, the chronic frustration of these needs may result in burnout. Currently there is little research on the engagement construct but it has enjoyed some popularity in clinical settings. Overall, there are interesting possibilities from a SDT perspective to explore on this account. The consideration of each of the fundamental needs is a useful way to further explore SDT's potential for explaining burnout. Subsequent subsections are dedicated to that end.

Competence

In nonsport settings, negative mood, alienation and ill-being have been linked to a failure to meet competency needs (Ryan and Deci, 2000a, 2000b). Feelings of competence relate not only to external rewards, but internal standards and goals as well. An athlete who perceives him/herself as failing to meet self imposed performance expectations and/or the standards set by significant others (for other high ranking sources of stress in elite sport see Gould, Horn, and Spreeman, 1983) is unlikely to feel competent. Researchers have specifically linked fear of failure and athletes' high, and sometimes unrealistic, expectations of their own performance to burnout (Gould, Tuffey, et al., 1996). Athletes holding these beliefs will not perceive themselves as competent or successful unless their virtually unattainable self-imposed standards are reached. The resultant perception of failure can thwart or frustrate athletes' need to feel effective and competent. In some cases it is likely that chronic frustration of competence needs will result in reduced accomplishment and burnout. While failure to meet competency needs may result in feelings of reduced accomplishment they are not one and the same thing. Competence is a need and reduced accomplishment is a resultant feeling. In some instances competence and reduced accomplishment may not be related. Specifically, it is possible that a person may not feel competent, but feel that they are accomplishing, for example in the early phases of learning a new task. While a plausible explanation of the genesis of these states, sport-specific research has yet to establish if the failure to meet this need results in states of amotivation, cynicism and/or reduced professional efficacy as observed among athletes suffering from burnout.

Relatedness

The need for relatedness amounts to an essential desire to feel connected and secure within one's environment (Deci and Ryan, 2002). Perceiving adequate social support illustrates how satisfying the need for relatedness can benefit an individual's well-being. For example, perceiving adequate social support has been found to moderate the impact of stress and burnout in some instances (Etzion, 1984; Meichenbaum, 1976; Van Dierendonck, Schaufeli, and Buunk, 1998) and aid recovery from athletic injury (Bianco, 2001; Bianco and Eklund, 2001). Conversely, an athlete who lacks social support may be at greater risk of experiencing stress and possible negative outcomes (Bianco and Eklund, 2001; Etzion, 1984). It is also possible that the frustration of relatedness needs may also lead to burnout.

Sport is rife with opportunities for frustration of the need for relatedness including isolation due to injury or non-selection and the variety of sacrifices necessary to compete at the elite level (e.g., time away from family and nonsport friends due to the logistical demands of travel and competition). Participants in Gould, Tuffey and colleagues (1996) investigation believed that feelings of social isolation due to their sport involvement was linked to their burnout experience. While evidence suggests the frustration of relatedness needs may result in less self-determined behavior the underlying mechanism is currently unclear (Ryan and Deci, 2002). Regardless, athletes who experience a sense that their behavior is low in self-determination are at risk of placing undue importance on external rewards and attainments. While this emphasis may provide a socially acceptable (even lauded) explanation of a pattern of nonsocialization with others, an emphasis upon such external aspirations has been associated with indicators of ill-being (see Ryan and Deci, 2000b for a review). Researchers using the SDT framework should also pay attention to the social context and social nature of human behavior beyond the need for relatedness (Buunk, 1995; Buunk and Nauta, 2000). Further research is required to examine possible links between relatedness needs and the key characteristics of burnout.

Autonomy

SDT proposes that the need for autonomy can be undermined through the presence of extrinsic rewards perceived as controlling an individual's behavior. Perceptions of control have been previously linked to burnout by Coakley (1992). It may be of some interest to explore the extent to which motivation low in self-determination is related to an elevated risk of burnout. Moreover, the importance of a shift from internal to external motivation in elevating the risk of burnout is also interesting. It could be that a heightened focus on less self-determined forms of motivation may result in lower levels of perceived autonomy and a heightened risk of burnout.

Sport participation previously regarded as enjoyable could also become an adverse source of stress when athletes start to regard their participation as being externally controlled (Deci and Ryan, 1985). The continued presence of perceived benefits (e.g., financial rewards) may, nonetheless, result in an athlete maintaining involvement. Moreover, alternative options may not be immediately evident until the athlete encounters a new opportunity perceived to provide a more attractive cost-benefit ratio. For example, it would take time for an athlete who perceived he/she is only participating in sport for financial incentives (i.e., experiencing a lack of autonomy) to identify a career path that will offset a financial loss with other benefits such as personal fulfillment or reduced personal sacrifices.

Overall, the consistent frustration of or failure to meet an individual's central needs as proposed by SDT may result in the key characteristics of burnout – reduced accomplishment or professional efficacy, emotional exhaustion and cynicism or devaluation. Of course an individual's perception of competence, relatedness or autonomy is likely to be relative to social norms. In addition, the relationship between burnout and motivation is almost certainly recursive in nature. While motivational regulation (e.g., struggling to "soldier on" when feeling exhausted, alienated, or out of a sense of obligation) may very well have a causal influence on the emergence of burnout, burnout is well known to have motivational implications (e.g., feelings of amotivation). As such there is likely to be a persistent and on-going interaction between athlete motivation and the key characteristics of burnout.

SDT has been extensively employed and has withstood rigorous and widespread evaluation. The SDT framework implies that ill-being can be reduced and well-being promoted through the fulfillment of basic needs. In particular several practical strategies based on SDT designed to reduce characteristics of ill-being have already been proposed and tested, albeit in nonsport settings (e.g., Deci, Eghrari, Patrick, and Leone, 1994; Ryan and Deci, 2000b). For example, providing acknowledgement of feelings and conveying choice proven to be effective in other contexts (Deci et al., 1994) may be effective in the case of burnout. Further research is needed to extend current findings on SDT to the occurrence of burnout. For example, support for a SDT explanation of burnout could be found in the associations between burnout and motivational types differing in self determination (i.e., external, intrinsic, amotivation).

Cognitive evaluation theory (CET), a subtheory of SDT, may have particular utility for exploring the motivational implications of external contingencies and the experience of burnout. According to CET, when external contingencies are interpreted as controlling a behavior (i.e., diminishing perceptions of self-determination), intrinsic motivation is undermined by that contingency. While behavioral contingencies can impact upon intrinsic motivation through perceptions of self-determination, they can also be influential by conveying information affecting an individual's sense of competence. External rewards interpreted to be positively informative about competence can enhance intrinsic motivation. Conversely, external contingencies offering information that detracts from the person's feelings of competence undermine intrinsic motivation (Deci and Ryan, 1985). CET may provide a good investigative framework from which researchers can explore the relationship between needs for autonomy or competence and negative states such as burnout.

BURNOUT INTERVENTIONS

Despite the potential importance of theoretically-based interventions aimed at the prevention and management of athlete burnout none have been empirically evaluated. Burnout is viewed as preventable as many athletes have competed until their skills diminished with age rather than through burnout experiences (Feigley, 1984). Even prior to formally empirically investigating athlete burnout researchers had proposed several intervention strategies and frameworks to assist players suffering from burnout (e.g., Fender, 1989; Murphy, 1984). These athlete burnout intervention strategies are yet to be formally implemented or evaluated. Research in human care and general work settings has also resulted in the proposal of several interventions, but few have been comprehensively tested (Schaufeli and Enzmann, 1998). The lack of formal research on burnout interventions across settings is probably indicative of a gap between researchers and practitioners (Maslach and Goldberg, 1998). Nonetheless, this research void probably also reflects the challenges of conducting intervention-based research. Difficulties associated with participant identification and recruitment as well as participant attrition can make intervention research daunting and difficult (Pines and Aronson, 1983).

The consideration of intervention research with athletes is warranted because of the potential theoretical and conceptual contribution to the literature. Intervention research offers the opportunity to implement experimental designs to establish cause and effect, a much needed strategy to advance the theoretical propositions outlined in this review. Given the paucity of empirically assessed athlete burnout interventions we will focus on: (a) burnout interventions carried out in other settings and their applicability to sport as well as (b) interventions conducted for stress and burnout-related issues in sport.

A number of different intervention frameworks have been proposed within the stress mediated approach to burnout research. While some researchers distinguish between interventions based on their phase of intervention (primary, secondary or tertiary) others distinguish programs on the level they are directed at (i.e., person-centered or situation-centered). In practice the same strategy often acts in a preventative and ameliorative manner. As such we will not attempt to separate strategies based on their phase, rather the level they are implemented at, as advocated by Maslach and Goldberg (1998).

Person- and Situation- Centered Interventions

Person-centered Interventions

Person-centered interventions are more widely implemented and researched in comparison to situation-centered interventions. The relative popularity of person-centered approaches is probably due to logistical advantages, such as lower cost and a perceived inability to modify situational factors (Maslach and Goldberg, 1998; McCann, 1995). Person-centered interventions assume the individual plays a central role in burnout and its prevention regardless of the source.

The majority of person-centered interventions have focused on cognitive appraisal and coping skills. Cognitive appraisal and coping skills are viewed as crucial within the transactional process model of stress and coping (Lazarus and Folkman, 1984). Within this cognitive approach there are two main models (often used simultaneously), cognitive mediation and coping skills. The cognitive mediation model is based on the assumption that in most cases emotional arousal is mediated by cognition (Smith, 1980). Based on this assumption a powerful means of reducing maladaptive emotional responses is to modify a person's cognitions. Within the coping skills model the participant assumes personal responsibility for developing and applying new ways of viewing and dealing with problems (e.g., Lowenstein, 1991). The majority of these coping strategies relate to changing the individual's response to the situation through cognitive restructuring (indicating significant overlap with the cognitive mediation model), sharing feelings, conflict resolution or time management strategies.

The most recognized coping skills programs that have been developed within the sport setting are cognitive-affective stress management training (SMT) (Smith, 1980) and stress inoculation training (SIT) (Meichenbaum, 1985). Both programs aim to provide a prospective defense designed to provide participants with a range of cognitive-behavioral coping skills that can be applied as needed to future stressful situations (Meichenbaum, 1985; Smith, 1980).

Both SIT and SMT have received some empirical support, however, the most detailed studies have been conducted in non-sport settings. In addition few studies, regardless of their setting have focused on chronic stress or burnout, instead these studies have been focused on acute stress or other outcomes potentially related to burnout such as absenteeism. Overall the variations of SIT and SMT programs implemented in general work and health care settings have had mixed results in reducing burnout. In general work settings researchers have demonstrated decreases in emotional exhaustion component of burnout, but not absenteeism (Higgins, 1986). West, Horan, and Games (1984) examined the effectiveness of the SIT paradigm in reducing burnout reported by registered nurses in an acute hospital department. The results of a four month follow up indicated significant decreases in burnout, anxiety and systolic blood pressure. SIT has also been effective in reducing depression and physiological indicators of stress (Ganster, Mayes, Sime, and Tharp, 1982). Within sport settings SMT and SIT programs have been demonstrated to enhance athletic performance and or reduce some acute consequences of the stress process (Crocker, Alderman, and Smith, 1988; Smith, 1980; Smith and Smoll, 1978; Ziegler, Klinzing, and Williamson, 1982) but have yet to be assessed relative to burnout.

A variety of other approaches have also been adopted that could come under the umbrella of coping skills. For example adaptations of rational emotive therapy significantly reduced emotional exhaustion and some reported symptoms (e.g., tedium, psychological strain, and somatic complaints) in nurses. However no changes in depersonalization and personal accomplishment, were reported (Schaufeli, 1995). Pines and Aronson (1983) advocated an approach consisting of education, self-awareness as well as four coping strategies. However in the assessment of a one-day workshop for social services employees based on these principles the authors reported only non-statistically significant decreases in measures of burnout. While changes in burnout did not reach significance reported satisfaction with co-workers increased significantly. The study also recorded an increase in satisfaction from supervisors, from the department, from the public, from their clients, and mainly from co-workers that remained for six months.

In addition to these approaches sport researchers have advocated adopting traditional psychological skills training (PST) methods such as relaxation, self-talk and imagery within burnout interventions (Henschen, 1998). However, no theoretical background or specific rationale is given for the inclusion of these methods. Recent research within sport suggests that those interested in preventing burnout should broaden their focus beyond traditional performance based PST directing attention towards social psychological concerns, such as expectations, pressure and a lack of enjoyment (Gould, Tuffey, et al., 1996).

In summary, to date researchers employing person-centered approaches have focused on stress management and not burnout interventions directly. Current results are inconclusive and as such these interventions may not reduce stress or burnout. These mixed results may be because interventions have been based solely within a stress approach. Future researchers are encouraged to consider alternative approaches to the prevention and management of burnout.

Situation-centered Interventions

In contrast to person-centered approaches situation-centered approaches have received little attention, possibly due to the assumption, rightly or wrongly, that organization change is not possible (Maslach and Goldberg, 1998). Proposed strategies focus on enhancing job experience and enhancing a sense of control. For example, enhancing subordinates' input in policy decisions and providing training in interpersonal skills (Maslach, 1982b). No strategies that eliminate stressors are proposed, it appears that an underlying assumption is that work is stressful and it should be acknowledged that stress will encourage people to work harder. As long as the perception that stress will enhance productivity exists there will be little motivation for organizations to reduce this effect.

Combined Approaches

Within this review we have advocated a multidimensional conception of burnout that emphasizes the individual, the situation and the interaction between individual and situational factors. As burnout encompasses personal, situational and organization domains, combined intervention programs that address all these areas are likely to be the most successful (Maslach and Goldberg, 1998).

Despite this endorsement and proposed guidelines for such interventions (e.g., Leiter and Maslach, 2000; Maslach and Goldberg, 1998; Maslach and Leiter, 1997) little published research exists to support the efficacy of a combined approach in any setting. The logistical challenges of coordinating an intervention that addresses both personal and situational factors are formidable. The absence of such investigations may merely reflect the difficulties involved in such an enterprise. Among the few published studies to date Golembiewski et al. (1987) evaluated an intervention focused on a wide range of factors including personal values, interpersonal interactions, and company culture/policy change with a small number (N=31) of human resource workers. The researchers concluded that the intervention was successful in reducing the level of burnout reported by participants who had reported adaptive perceptions of work (i.e., high perceived support and high task cohesion) prior to the intervention. In contrast participants who reported maladaptive perceptions of work (i.e., low perceived support and low task cohesion) at the commencement of the intervention did not report the same decreases in burnout, but did not appear adversely affected by the intervention. Despite the lack of evaluative research this combined approach appears to have considerable potential. Certainly in sport settings situational and personal factors have been implicated in the burnout experience (i.e., Gould, Tuffey, et al., 1996; Gould et al., 1997; Gould, Udry, et al., 1996) and hence interventions that address both these areas are likely to be effective.

In summary the evaluative data on burnout interventions overall is "suggestive but not compelling" (Maslach and Goldberg, 1998). The current lack of evaluative research on burnout interventions in general is in part due to the gap between practitioners and researchers and the difficulty associated with conducting intervention based research designs. To date no athlete burnout interventions have been empirically evaluated. Despite this research in related areas in sport, such as stress and anxiety, and research in general psychology suggest a combination of person and situation centered interventions are likely to be effective in the management or prevention of burnout. Future research that adopts experimental intervention designs has potential to offer significant theoretical and conceptual contributions to the literature.

Future Intervention Research

Current interventions reviewed above have adopted a stress based approach to burnout. An underlying assumption of this approach is that burnout is stress mediated. To date other possible causal influences (e.g., entrapment, basic needs) have been ignored. As such we propose that future researchers should consider alternative intervention approaches. Specifically within this review we have also highlighted the possible role of SDT and the commitment perspective.

Past research on athlete burnout suggests that perceptions of entrapment should also be considered within future intervention efforts (Raedeke, 1997). Information on entrapment could potentially contribute to situational interventions that address contractual and cultural aspects of the environment. For example enhancing flexibility within contracts to facilitate ease of trades/transfers between teams and/or developing team cultures that acknowledge transfers are a necessary part of professional sport. It is possible that these could be incorporated within current stress-based interventions or as a separate entity.

Within SDT research extensive knowledge has been developed regarding the brighter side of basic needs (i.e., need satisfaction). A wealth of evidence indicates that satisfaction of these needs leads to a self-determined perception of behavior, health and well-being (Ryan and Deci, 2000a). As such interventions that enhance the satisfaction of the basic needs of autonomy, relatedness and competence are likely to prevent or mange negative experiences such as burnout. For example adopting practical strategies based on SDT designed to reduce characteristics of ill-being in nonsport settings (e.g., Deci et al., 1994; Ryan and Deci, 2000b) may assist in preventing and managing burnout. Despite the potential for interventions based within SDT further research is needed to extend current findings on SDT to the occurrence of burnout in order to guide specific intervention efforts. Research assessing the comparative efficacy of entrapment, motivational and stress based intervention approaches has the potential to significantly contribute to the theoretical advancement of athlete burnout.

SUMMARY/CONCLUSION

Given the possible negative consequences associated with burnout it is an area of potential significance to athlete performance and welfare. To date research on athlete burnout has been hampered due to conceptual confusion. Within this chapter we have endorsed conceptualising burnout as a psychosocial syndrome. The majority of our review has focused on three possible theoretical explanations of the burnout syndrome. These explanations provide several opportunities for future research. Specifically further research is needed to refine stress-based (e.g., Smith, 1986) and commitment-based (e.g., Raedeke, 1997) explanations for the occurrence of burnout. Future researchers are also encouraged to examine the potential utility of self-determination theory as a conceptual framework for athlete burnout. Research is also needed to evaluate the relative utility of stress, motivation and commitment-based explanations of burnout. These different perspectives may provide complementary explanations of this experiential syndrome. This possibility (and others) requires further investigation.

REFERENCES

Anderson, D., and Morris, T. (2000). Athlete lifestyle programs. In D. Lavallee and P. Wylleman (Eds.), *Career transitions in sport: International perspectives* (pp. 59-80). Morgantown: Fitness Information Technology.

Baumeister, R. E., and Leary, M. R. (1995). The need to belong: Desire for interpersonal attachments as a fundamental human motivation. *Psychological Bulletin, 117*, 497-529.

Becker, H. S. (1960). Notes on the concept of commitment. *American Journal of Sociology, 66*, 32-40.

Bianco, T. (2001). Social support and recovery from sport injury: Elite skiers share their experiences. *Research Quarterly for Exercise and Sport, 72*, 376-388.

Bianco, T., and Eklund, R. C. (2001). Conceptual considerations for social support research in sport and exercise settings: The case of sport injury. *Journal of Sport and Exercise Psychology, 23*, 85-107.

Buunk, B. P. (1995). Comparing direction and comparing dimension among disabled individuals: Toward a refined conceptualization of social comparison under stress. *Personality and Social Psychology Bulletin, 21*, 316-330.

Buunk, B. P., and Nauta, A. (2000). Why intraindividual needs are not enough: Human motivation is primarily social. *Psychological Inquiry, 11*, 279-283.

Clow, A., and Hucklebridge, F. (2001). The impact of psychological stress on immune function in the athletic population. *Exercise Immunology Review, 7*, 5-17.

Coakley, J. (1992). Burnout among adolescent athletes: A personal failure or social problem? *Sociology of Sport Journal, 9*, 271-285.

Crocker, P. R. E., Alderman, R. B., and Smith, M. R. (1988). Cognitive-affective stress management training with high performance youth volleyball players: Effects on affect, cognition and performance. *Journal of Sport and Exercise Psychology, 10*, 448-460.

Deci, E. L., Eghrari, H., Patrick, B. C., and Leone, D. R. (1994). Facilitating internalization: The self-determination theory perspective. *Journal of Personality, 62*, 119-142.

Deci, E. L., and Ryan, R. M. (1985). *Intrinsic motivation and self-determination in human behavior*. New York: Plenum Press.

Deci, E. L., and Ryan, R. M. (2002). *Handbook of self-determination theory*. NY: University of Rochester Press.

DSM-IV. (1994). *Diagnostic and statistical manual of mental disorders fourth edition: DSM-IV*. Washington, DC: American Psychiatric Association.

Eades, A. M. (1990). *An investigation of burnout of intercollegiate athletes: The development of the Eades Athletic Burnout Inventory*. Unpublished Masters thesis, University of California, Berkeley.

Etzion, D. (1984). Moderating effect of social support on the stress-burnout relationship. *Journal of Applied Psychology, 69*, 615-622.

Feather, N. T. (1994). Attitudes towards high achievers and reactions to their fall: Theory and research concerning tall poppies. *Advances in Experimental Social Psychology, 26*, 1-73.

Feigley, D. A. (1984). Psychological burnout in high-level athletics. *The Physician and Sportsmedicine, 12*, 109-119.

Fender, L. K. (1988). Athlete burnout: A sport adaptation of the Maslach Burnout Inventory. College of Human Development and Performance, University of Oregon: Microform Publications.

Fender, L. K. (1989). Athlete burnout: Potential for research and intervention strategies. *The Sport Psychologist, 3*, 63-71.

Festinger, L. (1957). *A theory of cognitive dissonance*. California: Stanford University Press.

Firth, H., McIntee, J., McKeown, P., and Britton, P. G. (1986). Interpersonal support and nurses at work. *Journal of Advanced Nursing, 11*, 273-282.

Folkman, S., and Moskwitz, J. (2000). Positive affect and the other side of coping. *American Psychologist, 55*, 647-654.

Freudenberger, H. J. (1975). The staff burn-out syndrome in alternative institutions. *Psychotherapy: Theory, Research and Practice, 12*, 73-82.

Ganster, D. C., Mayes, B. T., Sime, W. E., and Tharp, G. D. (1982). Managing organizational stress: A field experiment. *Journal of Applied Psychology, 67*, 533-542.

Garden, A. M. (1987). Depersonalization: A valid dimension of burnout? *Human Relations, 40*, 545-560.

Glass, D. C., and McKnight, J. D. (1996). Perceived control, depressive symptomatology, and professional burnout: A review of evidence. *Psychology and Health, 11*, 23-48.

Glass, D. C., McKnight, J. D., and Valdimarsdottir, H. (1993). Depression, burnout, and perceptions of control in hospital nurses. *Journal of Consulting and Clinical Psychology, 61*, 147-155.

Golembiewski, R. T., Hilles, R., and Daly, R. (1987). Some effects of multiple OD interventions on burnout and work site features. *The Journal of Applied Behavioral Science, 23*, 295-313.

Gould, D., and Dieffenbach, K. (2002). Overtraining, underrecovery, and burnout in sport. In M. Kellmann (Ed.), *Enhancing recovery: Preventing underperformance in athletes* (pp. 25-35). Champaign, IL: Human Kinetics.

Gould, D., Horn, T., and Spreeman, J. (1983). Sources of stress in junior elite wrestlers. *Journal of Sport and Exercise Psychology, 5*, 159-171.

Gould, D., Tuffey, S., Udry, E., and Loehr, J. (1996). Burnout in competitive junior tennis players: II. Qualitative Analysis. *The Sport Psychologist, 10*, 341-366.

Gould, D., Tuffey, S., Udry, E., and Loehr, J. (1997). Burnout in competitive junior tennis players: III. Individual differences in the burnout experience. *The Sport Psychologist, 11*, 257-276.

Gould, D., Udry, E., Tuffey, S., and Loehr, J. (1996). Burnout in competitive junior tennis players: I. A quantitative psychological assessment. *The Sport Psychologist, 10*, 322-340.

Greendorfer, S. L. (2002). Socialization processes and sport behavior. In T. S. Horn (Ed.), *Advances in sport psychology* (2nd ed., pp. 377-401). Champaign IL: Human Kinetics.

Hackney, A. C., Pearman, S. N., and Nowacki, J. M. (1990). Physiological profiles of overtrained and stale athletes: A review. *Applied Sport Psychology, 2*, 21-33.

Henschen, K. P. (1998). Athletic staleness and burnout: Diagnosis, prevention, and treatment. In J. M. Williams (Ed.), *Applied sport psychology: Personal growth to peak performance* (3rd ed., pp. 398-408). California: Mayfield.

Higgins, N. C. (1986). Occupational stress and working women: the effectiveness of two stress reduction programs. *Journal of Vocational Behavior, 29*, 66-79.

Kelley, B. C., Eklund, R. C., and Ritter-Taylor, M. (1999). Stress and burnout among collegiate tennis coaches. *Journal of Sport and Exercise Psychology, 21*, 113-130.

Kelley, H. H. (1983). Love and commitment. In H. H. Kelley, E. Berscheid, A. Christensen, J. H. Harvey, T. L. Huston, G. Levinger, E. McClintock, L. A. Peplau and D. R. Petersen (Eds.), *Close relationships* (pp. 265-314). New York: W.H. Freeman and Company.

Kellmann, M. (2002). Underrecovery and overtraining: different concepts - similar impact? In M. Kellmann (Ed.), *Enhancing recovery: Preventing underperformance in athletes* (pp. 3-24). Champaign, IL: Human Kinetics.

Kreider, R. B., Fry, A. C., and O'Toole, M. L. (1998). Overtraining in sport: Terms, definitions, and prevalence. In R. B. Kreider, A. C. Fry and M. L. O'Toole (Eds.), *Overtraining in sport* (pp. vii-ix). Champaign, IL: Human Kinetics.

Lazarus, R. S., and Folkman, S. (1984). *Stress, appraisal and coping*. NY: Springer.

Leiter, M. P., and Durup, J. (1994). The discriminant validity of burnout and depression: A confirmatory factor analytic study. *Anxiety, Stress and Coping, 7*, 357-373.

Leiter, M. P., and Maslach, C. (2000). *Preventing burnout and building engagement: A Complete program for organizational renewal*. San Francisco, CA: Josey-Bass.

Lowenstein, L. (1991). Teacher stress leading to burnout - its prevention and cure. *Education Today, 41*, 12-16.

Martin, J. J., Kelley, B., and Eklund, R. C. (1999). A model of stress and burnout in male high school athletic directors. *Journal of Sport and Exercise Psychology, 21*, 280-294.

Maslach, C. (1982a). *Burnout: The cost of caring*. London: Prentice Hall.

Maslach, C. (1982b). Understanding burnout: Definitional issues in analyzing a complex phenomenon. In W. S. Paine (Ed.), *Job stress and burnout: Research, theory and intervention perspectives* (pp. 29-41). London: Sage.

Maslach, C., and Goldberg, J. (1998). Prevention of burnout: New perspectives. *Applied and Preventative Psychology, 7*, 63-74.

Maslach, C., and Jackson, S. E. (1986). *Maslach Burnout Inventory manual* (2nd ed.). Palo Alto, CA: Consulting Psychologists Press.

Maslach, C., Jackson, S. E. and Leiter, M.P. (1996). *Maslach Burnout Inventory manual* (3rd ed.). Palo Alto, CA: Consulting Psychologists Press.

Maslach, C., Jackson, S. E., and Leiter, M. P. (1997). Maslach Burnout Inventory, 3rd Edition. In C. P. Zalaquett and R. J. Wood (Eds.), *Evaluating Stress: A book of resources* (pp. 191-218). London: The Scarecrow Press.

Maslach, C., and Leiter, M. P. (1997). *The truth about burnout: How organizations cause personal stress and what to do about it.* San Francisco, CA: Jossey-Bass.

Maslach, C., Schaufeli, W. B., and Leiter, M. P. (2001). Job Burnout. *Annual Review of Psychology, 52*, 397-422.

McCann, S. (1995). Overtraining and burnout. In S. Murphy (Ed.), *Sport psychology interventions* (pp. 347-368). Champaign IL: Human Kinetics.

McGrath, J. E. (1970). *Social and psychological factors in stress.* NY: Holt, Rinehart and Winston inc.

Meichenbaum, D. (1976). Toward a cognitive theory of self control. In G. E. Schwartz and D. Shapiro (Eds.), *Consciousness and self-regulation: Advances in research* (Vol. 1, pp. 223-260). New York: Plenum.

Meichenbaum, D. (Ed.). (1985). *Stress inoculation training.* New York: Pergamon.

Murphy, L. R. (1984). Occupational stress management: A review and appraisal. *Journal of Occupational Psychology, 57*, 1-15.

O'Connor, P. J. (1997). Overtraining and staleness. In W. P. Morgan (Ed.), *Physical activity and mental health* (pp. 145-160). Washington: Taylor and Francis.

Pines, A., and Aronson, E. (1983). Combating burnout. *Children and Youth Services Review, 5*, 263-275.

Raedeke, T. D. (1997). Is athlete burnout more than just stress? A sport commitment perspective. *Journal of Sport and Exercise Psychology, 19*, 396-417.

Raedeke, T. D., Granzyk, T. L., and Warren, A. (2000). Why coaches experience burnout: A commitment perspective. *Journal of Sport and Exercise Psychology, 22*, 85-105.

Raedeke, T. D., Lunney, K., and Venables, K. (2002). Understanding athlete burnout: Coach perspectives. *Journal of Sport Behavior, 25*, 181-206.

Raedeke, T. D., and Smith, A. L. (2001). Development and preliminary validation of an athlete burnout measure. *Journal of Sport and Exercise Psychology, 23*, 281-306.

Rusbult, C. E. (1980a). Commitment and satisfaction in romantic associations: A test of the investment model. *Journal of Experimental Social Psychology, 16*, 172-186.

Rusbult, C. E. (1980b). Satisfaction and commitment in friendships. *Representative Research in Social Psychology, 11*, 96-105.

Rusbult, C. E. (1983). A longitudinal test of the investment model: The development (and deterioration) of satisfaction and commitment in heterosexual involvements. *Journal of Personality and Social Psychology, 45*, 101-117.

Rusbult, C. E., and Farrell, D. (1983). A longitudinal test of the investment model: The impact on job satisfaction, job commitment, and turnover of variations in rewards, costs, alternatives, and investments. *Journal of Applied Psychology, 68*, 429-438.

Ryan, R. M., and Deci, E. L. (2000a). The darker and brighter sides of human existence: Basic psychological needs as a unifying concept. *Psychological Inquiry, 11*, 319-338.

Ryan, R. M., and Deci, E. L. (2000b). Self-determination theory and the facilitation of intrinsic motivation, social development, and well-being. *American Psychologist, 55*, 68-78.

Ryan, R. M., and Deci, E. L. (2002). Overview of self-determination theory. In E. L. Deci and R. M. Ryan (Eds.), *Handbook of self-determination theory* (pp. 3-36). NY: University of Rochester Press.

Scanlan, T. K., Carpenter, P. J., Schmidt, G. W., Simons, J. P., and Keeler, B. (1993). An introduction to the sport commitment model. *Journal of Sport and Exercise Psychology, 15*, 1-15.

Schaufeli, W. B. (1995). The evaluation of a burnout workshop for community nurses. *Journal Health and Human Resources Administration, 18*, 11-30.

Schaufeli, W. B., and Enzmann, D. (1998). *The burnout companion to study and practice: A critical analysis*. Washington: Taylor and Francis.

Schaufeli, W. B., Enzmann, D., and Girault, N. (1993). Measurement of burnout. In W. B. Schaufeli, C. Maslach and T. Marek (Eds.), *Professional burnout: Recent developments in theory and research* (pp. 199-215). Washington, D.C: Taylor and Francis.

Schaufeli, W. B., Salanova, M., Gonzalez-Roma, V., and Bakker, A. B. (2002). The measurement of engagement and burnout: A two sample confirmatory factor analytic approach. *Journal of Happiness Studies, 3*, 71-92.

Schmidt, G. W., and Stein, G. L. (1991). Sport commitment: A model integrating enjoyment, dropout, and burnout. *Journal of Sport and Exercise Psychology, 8*, 254-265.

Schutte, N., Toppinen, S., Kalimo, R., and Schaufeli, W. (2000). The factorial validity of the Maslach Burnout Inventory-General Survey (MBI-GS) across occupational groups and nations. *Journal of Occupational and Organizational Psychology, 73*, 53-65.

Silva, J. M. (1990). An analysis of the training stress syndrome in competitive athletics. *Applied Sport Psychology, 2*, 5-20.

Smith, R. E. (1980). Theoretical and treatment approaches to anxiety reduction. In J. M. Silva and R. S. Weinberg (Eds.), *Psychological foundations of sport* (pp. 157-170). Champaign, IL: Human Kinetics.

Smith, R. E. (1986). Toward a cognitive-affective model of athletic burnout. *Journal of Sport Psychology, 8*, 36-50.

Smith, R. E., and Smoll, F. L. (1978). Psychological intervention and sport medicine: Stress management and coach effectiveness training. *University of Washington Medicine, 5*, 20-24.

Thibaut, J. W., and Kelley, H. H. (1959). *The social psychology of groups*. New York: Wiley.

Vallerand, R. J., and Rousseau, F. L. (2001). Intrinsic and extrinsic motivation in sport and exercise: A review using the hierarchical model of intrinsic and extrinsic motivation. In R. N. Singer, H. A. Hausenblas and C. M. Janelle (Eds.), *Handbook of sport psychology* (2nd ed., pp. 389-416). New York: John Wiley and Sons.

Van Dierendonck, D., Schaufeli, W. B., and Buunk, B. P. (1998). The evaluation of an individual burnout intervention program: The role of inequity and social support. *Journal of Applied Psychology, 83*, 392-407.

Vlachopoulas, S. P., Karageorghis, C. I., and Terry, P. C. (2000). Motivation profiles in sport: A self-determination theory perspective. *Research Quarterly for Exercise and Sport, 71*, 387-397.

Weiss, W. M., and Weiss, M. R. (2003). Attraction- and entrapment-based commitment among competitive female gymnasts. *Journal of Sport and Exercise Psychology, 25*, 229-247.

West, D. J., Horan, J. J., and Games, P. A. (1984). Component analysis of occupational stress inoculation applied to registered nurses in an acute care hospital setting. *Journal of Counseling Psychology, 31*, 209-218.

Ziegler, S. G., Klinzing, J., and Williamson, K. (1982). The effects of two stress management training programs on cardiorespiratory efficiency. *Journal of Sport Psychology, 4*, 280-289.

In: Literature Reviews in Sport Psychology
Editors: S. Hanton and S. D. Mellalieu, pp. 127-158

ISBN 1-59454-904-4
© 2006 Nova Science Publishers, Inc.

Chapter 4

EMOTION IN SPORT: AN IZOF PERSPECTIVE

*Claudio Robazza**

University of Padova, Italy

ABSTRACT

The renewed interest in sport psychology with reference to the antecedents and consequences of emotional responses is reflected in several conceptual views and emerging paradigms. This chapter is intended to provide a review of the emotion-performance research and applications through the comprehensive perspective of the individual zones of optimal functioning (IZOF) model as applied to emotions and psychobiosocial states. The review initially addresses several issues including defining emotion and related terms, a description of the basic emotion characteristics, an explanation for the emotion-performance relationship, and emotion dynamics. Attention is then directed towards to the IZOF model, and its ability to describe, predict, explain, and enable control of individual optimal and dysfunctional performance states. Implications for professional practice are also presented to help athletes raise self-awareness of optimal states and maximize performance. Finally, research directions are provided concerning the IZOF model and the potential links with other selected theoretical approaches.

Key words: emotions, performance, the IZOF model, psychobiosocial states, self-regulation

INTRODUCTION

Contemporary views of emotion in general psychology emphasize the role of emotion in adaptation (e.g., Izard, 1992). Emotions are thought to accustom cognitive style to situational requirements, improve decision-making, prepare motor responses, promote learning, provide

---

* Correspondence concerning this chapter should be addressed to Claudio Robazza, Dipartimento di Scienze Mediche e Chirurgiche, Polo 40 Semeiotica Medica, Via Ospedale Civile, 105, 35128 Padova, Italy. Telephone and Fax 390-49-8901139, E-mail: claudio.robazza@unipd.it

information about intentions, and regulate social behavior (Gross, 1999). In the sport domain, emotions are acknowledged by coaches, athletes, researchers, practitioners, and even spectators as an inherent part of the competitive experience (Botterill and Brown, 2002). Competition can engender opposite toned emotions such as the elation and satisfaction of victory, or despair and disappointment of defeat (Mellalieu, 2003); in turn, emotions can benefit or impair performance during practice and competition (Hanin, 2000). For many years, sport psychologists have been concerned with the study of the deleterious effects of stress and anxiety purported to be main factors in the failure of performers to fully and effectively use their skills. Consequently, several theoretical approaches borrowed mainly from mainstream psychology together with various mental preparation strategies have been proposed to help athletes cope, thus achieving optimal conditions for the task at hand. Recently, however, sport psychologists have begun adopting more sports-specific approaches and expanding their attention beyond the study of anxiety toward a range of performance-related emotions.

The broader focus of interest, encompassing stress, anxiety, and emotions, has resulted in a debate surrounding the meaning and the distinctive characteristics of emotion and related concepts, such as mood, affect, and feeling states. Moreover, several conceptual models have been proposed in an attempt to explain the emotion-performance relationship, and provide scholars and practitioners with theoretical foundations for research and applications. Leading approaches dealing with mood or emotions include the mental health model (Morgan, 1985), reversal theory (Apter, 1989, 2001), the directional approach (Mellalieu, Hanton, and Fletcher, this volume), and the individual zones of optimal functioning (IZOF) model (Hanin, 1997). As a comprehensive review of all models is beyond the scope of this chapter the aim is to provide an overview of the emotion-performance relationship through the standpoint of the IZOF model. This is purported to describe, predict, explain, and enable control of individual optimal and dysfunctional states coupled with successful and unsuccessful performances (Hanin, 2003, 2004).

Before introducing the IZOF model, emotion and related terms are defined in an attempt to disentangle the meaning of emotion from other constructs. The subjective experience, physiological responses, and action tendencies are then considered as intrinsic characteristics of emotion. Thereafter, some explanations for the emotion-performance relationship are provided and the issue of emotion dynamics in sport is discussed. The subsequent sections present the main features of the IZOF model taking into account its earlier applications to anxiety and, in greater detail, the recent developments toward the study of emotion and psychobiosocial states. Implications for professional practice are also presented with reference to the idiographic assessments of emotions and emotion control. Future IZOF-based research directions are then provided regarding the issues of emotion effects on performance, emotion regulation, assessment of psychobiosocial states, and emotion antecedents. Finally, the possible links of the IZOF model with the mental health model (Morgan, 1985) and the directional approach (Mellalieu et al., this volume) are discussed.

DEFINING EMOTION AND RELATED TERMS

The terms of emotion, mood, affect, and feeling states are often used interchangeably and treated as synonymous despite the evidence they are relatively distinct concepts (Lane and Terry, 2000; Mellalieu, 2003). Although researchers are still debating on the exact definition of the terms that seem particularly elusive, and universal consensus has not been reached, there are some emerging convergences in opinion. According to Ekkekakis and Petruzzello (2000), emotions should be referred to as "states elicited following an appraisal process during which a specific object is recognized as having the potential to either promote or endanger the survival or the well-being of the individual" (p. 76). The evolutionary standpoint is also apparent in the opinion of Lazarus (2000) who highlighted the adaptational struggle of emotion for survival and flourishing purposes. Emotions are prompted quickly following specific stimuli, are relatively short in duration and high in intensity, and convey action tendencies. On the other hand, moods often are not attributable to a specific cause or event (Lane and Terry, 2000). Clore (1994) argued an emotion arises when there is an object to the feeling, otherwise it is a mood. In addition, moods are considered relatively long lasting and low in intensity, and are associated with low or no action tendencies (Watson and Clark, 1994). Affect is a broader, more general and primitive construct than emotion or mood and refers to the experiential component of all valenced responses (i.e., hedonic tone and intensity), including emotion and mood (Gross, 1999). Affect can be understood as comprising emotion and even mood (Oatley and Jenkins, 1996). Thus, emotions and moods are more specific than affect, although comprising both hedonic tone (pleasure – displeasure) and activation (intensity) dimensions of affect.

If clarifying the constructs of emotion, mood and affect may appear to most as problematic, defining feeling states seems even more difficult. Gauvin and Spence (1998) suggested that the expression 'feeling states' accounts for a broad range of human experiences encompassing "bodily reactions, cognitive appraisal, actual or potential instrumental responses, or some combination thereof" (p. 326). Indeed, according to Averill (1994) the term feeling is inherently ambiguous because people use this word interchangeably to refer to at least three categories of enmeshed experiences, namely, *feelings of* something, *feelings about* something, or *feelings like* doing something. For example, an athlete may feel exhausted after training (feeling of bodily response), have a positive feeling about strength training (cognitive appraisal), and feel like working hard (actual or potential instrumental response).

In discussing characteristics of emotion and their role in sport, several authors (Botterill and Brown, 2002; Jones, 2003; Vallerand and Blanchard, 2000) employed the definition of Deci (1980) who proposed:

> An emotion is a reaction to a stimulus event (either actual or imagined). It involves change in the viscera and musculature of the person, is experienced subjectively in characteristic ways, is expressed through such means as facial changes and action tendencies, and may mediate and energize subsequent behaviors. (p. 85)

Three main elements are apparent in this working conceptualization of emotion: subjective experience, physiological response, and action tendencies. As Jones (2003) pointed out, according to Deci's definition, the emotional reaction is engendered by a stimulus that can be real or imagined. Indeed, there is a broad range of real or imagined stimuli that may derive from the environment (such as visual or auditory stimuli) as well as from the individual (e.g., self-talk and muscular tension). For example, an athlete may feel upset or guilty, having noticed glances and expressions of disappointment from teammates and coaches after being outperformed by an opponent, or may undermine their self-concept with cognitions regarding the potential negative consequences of an anticipated defeat.

The subjective experience refers to what an individual perceives in a particular emotional episode. Researchers in mainstream psychology (e.g., Clore, 1994) as well as in sport psychology (e.g., Botterill and Brown, 2002; Jones, 2003; Kerr, 1997) acknowledged the role of cognition in emotional responses. Lazarus (1991, 2000), in his Cognitive-motivational-relational Theory, provided a detailed description of the cognitive processes involved in generating specific emotions in ordinary life and in the sporting realm. Emotions are part of a changing person-environment relationship and arise when the individual appraises a situation as positive or negative for well-being (relational meaning). A bidirectional functional relationship is suggested between cognition and emotion. In Lazarus' view, the causal role of cognition in emotion is a necessary and sufficient condition: emotions cannot occur without some kind of thought, and thoughts are capable of producing emotions. This process of emotion arousal may mainly happen automatically, at subconscious level of information processing, without volitional control. A deliberate and volitionally controlled process of emotion production is also possible and, perhaps, most appraisals imply a mixture of either modes of cognitive activity (i.e., automatic and deliberate).

Within the cognitive-motivational-relational theory, the appraisal of significance of the environmental stimuli contains motivational components, besides cognitive ones, which include individual's goals, hierarchical relevance of goals, goal congruence or incongruence (beneficial or detrimental effects of stimuli), and beliefs about self, world, and personal resources. Thus, the term motivation comprises a person's goals and mobilization of mental and physical energies in attaining goals. Relational meaning, assumed at the heart of the process arousing emotion (Lazarus, 2000), is distinctive for each emotion. It derives from appraisal of the significance of an encounter with another person and physical environment in terms of personal harms and benefits. Two levels of appraisal are involved in an encounter. Primary appraisal concerns the individual's evaluation of a personal stake in a situation; it is primary because without a personal investment there is no potential for an emotion to arise (Lazarus, 1991). Secondary appraisal relates to one's resources to cope with the situation. Coping is a process related to cognitive and behavioral efforts to manage or regulate emotions, "by suppressing their expression, addressing and changing the environment or personality conditions that provoked it, or reappraising the personal significance of what has happened or is happening without changing the actual person-environment relationship" (Lazarus, 2000; p. 235). Coping can be problem-focused when intended to change the reality of the troubled person-environment relationship (e.g., an athlete trying to improve personal skills to prevent defeat), or emotion-focused when centered on regulating emotions without changing the reality of a stressful situation (e.g., an athlete applying self-regulation or reappraising the importance of a competition). Coping is viewed as integral part of the emotion process coming into play at the onset of emotion generation and operating throughout an emotional encounter. Therefore, people can appraise the same situation in different ways and perceive different emotions when the meaning of a situation changes. For example, a match or competition may be considered habitual and routine by an expert player who possesses effective coping strategies or challenging by a less experienced teammate who perceives the situation to be ego-threatening. Consequently, the two players would feel dissimilar states in a similar situation, perhaps boredom or lack of interest in the former and threat in the latter. However, if the opposition within the match begins dominating, even the experienced player may find their coping strategies ineffective and experience some distress.

Physiological responses are also contained in Deci's (1980) definition of emotion. The pattern of physiological change might be emotion specific (Lacey and Lacey, 1970), and can involve the autonomic nervous system, provoking changes in heart rate, blood pressure, galvanic skin response, and visceral functioning. Physiological changes in the face (e.g., blushing or paling) and facial expressions (e.g., scowling or smiling) can also occur and may amplify the emotional experience (Ekman, Levenson, and Friesen, 1983). Self-perception of visceral activity is a key component of the emotional experience. For instance, Robazza, Bortoli, and Nougier (1999, 2000) investigated female archers' perceptions of emotional arousal while competing. Heart rate, idiosyncratic emotion, and behavior assessments during practice and top-level events revealed an optimal condition to perform in one of the archers. Specifically, the archer interpreted a large enhancement of heart rate from practice to competition as facilitative, and her performance was satisfactory. A nonoptimal state was found in the other archer who experienced an enhanced heart rate as debilitative and, accordingly, performed below expectations.

Action tendencies (in Deci's definition) are a further relevant aspect of emotion. Action tendencies, often resulting in approach and avoidance (or withdrawal) behavior, are conceptualized as states of readiness to execute a given kind of action (Frijda, 1986), and sometimes are discussed in terms of appetitive and aversive motivations in the interest of survival (Lang, 2000). Emotions usually engage different modes of action readiness. For instance, anger may energize an attacking behavior in order to regain freedom of action and control, whereas fear may in some instances energize avoidance, attack behaviors, or even paralysis of action (fight, flight, or freeze responses). The physical energy of activation, that is intrinsic to emotions, is of particular importance to the athlete. This energy acts to enhance performance when properly harnessed, detrimental effects are likely when the energy is out of control.

An alternative line of inquiry is to conceptualize emotion in a holistic perspective as a specific component of the experience of a performer's psychobiosocial state. Hanin (1997, 2000) has identified seven basic modalities of a psychobiosocial state: cognitive, emotional, motivational, bodily, motor-behavioral, operational, and communicative. These seven interrelated modalities provide a relatively complete description of a performance state including experiences and their displays (expression or suppression). More recently, Hanin (2003, 2004) has distinguished three aspects of subjective emotional experiences, namely, situational experience (emotional states), relatively stable emotion patterns (emotionality), and meta-emotion. The notion of meta-emotion, or meta-experience, is used to account for knowledge, attitudes, beliefs, and preferences for an emotion that an individual can attain over the course of successful and less than successful performances. For instance, an athlete who notices that feeling worried is sometimes useful to focus attention can develop a positive attitude toward this state and interpret it as an indicator of readiness to accomplish a task. Hanin's approach is discussed in detail after explanation of the emotion-performance relationship and emotion dynamics in sport.

EMOTION-PERFORMANCE RELATIONSHIP

In a summary of the opinions of several researchers, Jones (2003) identified common mechanisms that mediate the impact of emotions on performance. These mechanisms involve motivation, physical functioning, and cognitive functioning. The motivational consequences of the adaptational functions of emotions are reflected in action tendencies (Frijda, 1986). Emotions can energize behaviors by directing individual's resources toward (e.g., enjoyment) or away (e.g., apprehension) from an object or a task (Vallerand and Blanchard, 2000). Emotions can also influence physical functioning because of the related changes that may occur in the arousal level as well as in cognitions. Enhanced physiological arousal can benefit the execution of gross motor skills requiring great effort and muscle energy expenditure (Landers and Arent, 2001). Conversely, high physiological arousal can impair the execution of fine motor skills that involve steadiness or control of unwanted muscle activity because of too much muscular tension and coordination difficulties. It should be pointed out, however, that arousal level can vary independently from emotions and that emotions can be experienced with different levels of arousal. Easterbrook's (1959) Cue Utilization Theory has been used to explain the effect of arousal elevation on attention. Enhanced emotional arousal tends to reduce the field of attention, resulting in improved or impaired performance depending on the task and the individual. Positive effects occur when the narrowing of attention blocks out external distractions, so that the performer may focus on task-relevant cues. Further arousal increases, however, lead to a too narrow focus of attention that may undermine the ability of the athlete to attend to important cues, process information properly, and make suitable decisions. Attention is also affected by the meaning and importance an individual ascribes to a situation. For example, the anger generated in a basketball player due to unfair contact on the part of an opponent may raise arousal in the offended player, thus narrowing his or her attention. As a result, the angry player may concentrate more in the game and allocate physical and mental resources to specific tasks, especially if the unfairness is perceived accidental. Alternatively, the player may divert the focus from the task in a search of the offender for purposes of retaliation, particularly if the act of the opponent is believed to be intentional.

Attentional narrowing that occurs as result of elevated emotional arousal is also accompanied by variability in visual search patterns. Increases in arousal may compromise one's ability to identify cues from the peripheral visual field. The individual tends to be more distracted by irrelevant cues and misidentify peripheral stimuli. In these circumstances, the performer typically tries to compensate the reduced availability of information with an increase of gaze fixations to peripheral locations. However, scan paths become highly variable and inefficient, thereby leading to increased probability of performance errors (Murray and Janelle, 2003; for a review, see Janelle, 2002).

The processing efficiency theory explains the effects of anxiety on cognitive functions and performance (Eysenck and Calvo, 1992). According to this theory, cognitive anxiety in the form of self-preoccupation, concern about evaluation and level of performance, occupies a portion of the total processing capacity of the working memory system devoted to executive functions. Thus, a state of high cognitive anxiety reduces resources available for task-related processing. Debilitative consequences can subsequently occur, especially for high trait-anxious individuals who are expected to allow anxiety to consume processing resources, allocate more attention to anxiety, and set unrealistically high performance goals. In some cases, a state of cognitive anxiety could increase motivation and subsequent effort toward succeeding in a task, which may compensate for the reduction of processing efficiency.

The bidirectional link between emotion and performance is better understood when emotion dynamics are examined across time. In a critical review of the temporal patterning of competitive emotions, Cerin, Szabo, Hunt, and Williams (2000) noted that the study of affective responses to competition has been so far focused on precompetition. However, emotions can fluctuate largely across the competition period, especially in long duration sports. Jones, Mace, and Williams (2000) retrospectively assessed feeling states of field hockey players during international matches. Players showed more annoyance and less tension during the game than before. Moreover, those players who performed well reported feeling nervous, quick, alert, and active before the game, and confident and relaxed during the game. Similarly, Mellalieu, Hanton, and Jones (2003) found that some collegiate performers' interpretation of feelings changed across preparation and performance. For example, feeling nervous was viewed as facilitative for preparation and debilitative for actual performance, while feeling worried was viewed as debilitative for preparation and more facilitative for actual performance.

In an attempt to integrate research on competitive emotions, Cerin et al. (2000) forwarded an interactional model of stress that underscores the temporal dimensions (such as frequency and duration) of the stress process. The model encompasses the relationship among athletic competition (demands, constraints, and opportunities), individual's appraisal of importance of situation and personal coping resources, coping strategies (problem-focused or emotion-focused), emotional response (content, intensity, hedonic tone, functionality, duration, and frequency), and ensuing performance. Emotional reactions to competition modify over time and are moderated by personal factors (i.e., gender, competitive experience, skill level, personality traits, and motivation) and situational factors (i.e., type of sport, level of competition, and interpersonal relationships). Mellalieu (2003) proposed broadening Cerin et al.'s model to incorporate moods (McNair, Lorr, and Droppleman, 1971) and Janelle's (2002) suggestions for the effects of stress on attentional processing and performance. Precompetition mood state is thought to influence the appraisal of the forthcoming event together with coping resources and personal and situational factors. Hence, an athlete's underlying mood response will influence emotions and the precompetitive experience. The stress response is then considered to modify psychological and physiological activation that, in turn, alters the width of the attentional field, the level of distractibility, the amount of investment in controlled processing, the efficiency of attentional processing, and subsequently the behavior and performance.

The interactional model predicts that an emotional state typified by mild to moderate intensity levels of threat-related emotions, such as fear and apprehension, and emotions related to approach behavior and task-focused attention, such as interest, excitement, and enjoyment, will be individually perceived as facilitating performance. In contrast, emotional states characterized by moderate to high intensity levels of threat-related emotions and the presence of emotions associated with self-focused attention, rumination, and avoidance behavior, such as sadness, shame, guilt, and self-hostility, will be experienced as debilitating performance. Threat reaction is thus construed as a pattern of emotions rather than a unitary emotion (Cerin, 2003). The emotional response can be described in terms of a limited number of discrete basic, primary or fundamental emotions, such as anger, fear, sadness, disgust, joy, surprise, and interest. Indeed, Cerin et al. (2000) suggested that basic emotions have distinctive universal expressions, antecedent events, coherence among response systems, and distinctive relational action tendencies. Because of these features, words expressing basic emotions are likely to be understood across people and cultures. Consequently, the assessment of fundamental emotions may facilitate inter-individual comparison in sport. On the other hand, the idiosyncratic emotional experience, emphasized in the IZOF model (Hanin, 2000), is better described using the vocabulary of the athlete that encompasses a vast constellation of complex emotional states, beyond fundamental emotions. Therefore, Cerin et al. (2002) recommended investigating the temporal dynamics and moderators of emotions, as conceptualized in their interactional model of stress, through the integration of basic emotions and idiosyncratic emotional descriptors.

The IZOF model actually allows for the incorporation of both basic and idiosyncratic approaches. Individual emotion descriptors are accommodated within four global emotion categories deriving from the interaction of hedonic tone (pleasant and unpleasant) and functionality (optimal and nonoptimal). The content of idiosyncratic descriptors can also be compared with the existing discrete basic emotions, as demonstrated by Ruiz and Hanin (2004) who found that the self-generated emotion descriptors of high-level Spanish karate athletes were similar to eight basic emotions (happiness, pride, relief, anger, anxiety, fright, sadness, and shame) from the 15 proposed by Lazarus (2000). The study of time dynamics showed that emotion descriptors differed prior to, during, and after performance.

Current research on temporal dynamics of emotions revolves mainly around the description of states pre-, mid-, and post-event. However, Hanin (2000, 2004) has also recommended the study of both short and long-term emotion dynamics across a competitive season, an Olympic cycle, or an athlete's career. Hanin's theoretical position regarding anxiety and emotion is presented next.

THE IZOF-ANXIETY MODEL

A great deal of research has been conducted over the years to examine anxiety-performance relationships in sport, and provide applied sport psychologist, athletes, and coaches with skills to prevent or combat the debilitative effects of anxiety. As a result of this impetus, several theoretical explanations have being forwarded (for a review, see Mellalieu et al., this volume). The inverted-U hypothesis (Yerkes and Dodson, 1908) has been dominant for many years in describing the anxiety and athletic performance relationship. This notion maintains an inverted-U shaped arousal-performance relationship in a given task, whereby an optimal performance would be attained at an intermediate arousal level. High or low arousal levels exceeding the moderate intensity would lead to decreased performance (Landers and Arent, 2001). In this view, changes in state anxiety are associated with corresponding changes in arousal and subsequent performance in a given task. Many scholars have raised serious concerns over the inverted-U hypothesis for a number of reasons, such as the unitary construct of anxiety and arousal, the shape of the curve, and the use of anxiety and arousal terms as synonymous. Neiss (1988), for example, recommended abandoning the unitary concept of arousal because it was too broad, and suggested drawing attention to cognitive, affective, and physiological components of arousal and their interaction. In a similar vein, other authors (e.g., Hardy, 1990; Jones, 1995) considered the inverted-U hypothesis simplistic and unlikely to explain adequately the anxiety, arousal, and performance interaction. A further concern is the confusion of the constructs of stress, anxiety, and arousal often used as synonymous although they are clearly distinct concepts (Gould, Greenleaf, and Krane, 2002).

The IZOF-anxiety model, often referred to as zones of optimal functioning (ZOF) model, was proposed by Hanin (1978, 1986, 1989, 1995) to account for the large variability that was shown in precompetition assessments of thousands competitors across many sports. A central tenet in the model is that each athlete possesses an individually optimal preperformance bandwidth (zone/range) of anxiety intensity within which best performance most likely occurs. If, however, the performer's anxiety level lies outside the optimal zone, performance will probably be impaired. Therefore, optimal or dysfunctional anxiety intensity–facilitating or debilitating performance–may be low, medium or high depending on the individual. In contrast to the inverted-U hypothesis, optimal anxiety is not assumed to be altered systematically by the type of task or performer's skill level. Figure 1 portrays lower and higher intensities of the feeling of worry perceived by six athletes to be facilitative of performance, showing that both the level of intensity and range are different across performers. For optimal performance to occur, athlete A tolerates modest levels of intensity (from .5 to 2) of feeling worried, whereas athlete F needs higher levels of intensity (from 5 to 10).

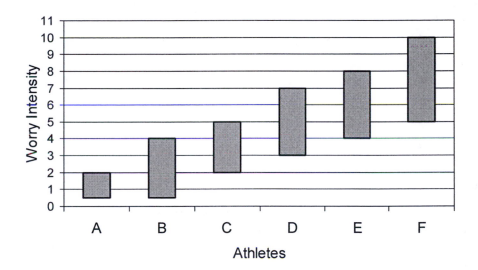

Figure 1. Zones of optimal worry in six elite athletes.

The optimal zone was initially operationally defined on a group basis, as an individual's preferred level of state anxiety for a task plus or minus four points (half of a standard deviation) on the State-Trait Anxiety Inventory (STAI; Spielberger, Gorsuch, and Lushene, 1970). This method was later abandoned, in that just as the optimal level of intensity differs across performers so does the width of the zone, with some individuals tolerating a wide range while others a narrow one (Hanin, 1995). Some researchers expressed concerns over the use of unidimensional and non sport-specific measures of anxiety, and adopted the Competitive State Anxiety Inventory-2 (CSAI-2; Martens, Burton, Vealey, Bump, and Smith,

1990) as a multidimensional measure of sport-specific anxiety in IZOF studies (e.g., Davis and Cox, 2002; see Gould and Tuffey, 1996, for a discussion).

The interindividual variability in optimal anxiety has been demonstrated within and across sports, gender, and ages (see Raglin and Hanin, 2000, for a review). Empirical evidence has also been provided for the validity of the in/out-of-zone notion applied to anxiety in the prediction of individual athletic performance. In a meta-analysis of 19 studies published from 1978 to 1997 (146 effect sizes based on 6387 participants) Jokela and Hanin (1999) examined the predictive power of the in/out of the anxiety zone construct and found an overall effect size of .44, demonstrating that those performers who were within their optimal zones were almost one-half a standard deviation unit better than those outside their zones. However, despite the findings researchers have made calls to expand the traditional arousal/anxiety performance relationship to include emotions beyond anxiety (e.g., Gould et al., 2002). Concurrently, Hanin has conceptualized emotion as a main component of psychobiosocial states.

THE IZOF-PSYCHOBIOSOCIAL MODEL

Hanin (1997, 2000, 2002) has broadened his IZOF model to take account of a vast array of idiosyncratic emotions beyond anxiety. The ZOF acronym previously used in studies of anxiety has been changed into IZOF (sometimes referred to as the IZOF-emotion model). Given the recent advancements in the IZOF conceptualization, however, it would be more appropriate to make reference to the IZOF-psychobiosocial model (or more simply to the IZOF model). The model, indeed, has been further expanded in an attempt to incorporate, in a holistic approach, performance-related psychobiosocial states in which the emotional experience is conceived as a crucial component. The IZOF model provides a comprehensive conceptual framework to describe, predict, explain, and enable control of subjective optimal and dysfunctional experiences related to successful and poor individual performances. The main features of the model are presented here.

Description of Performance-Related Psychobiosocial States

Psychobiosocial states are defined as situational, multimodal, and dynamic manifestations of the total human functioning. These states are described in terms of the five interrelated dimensions of form, content, intensity, context, and time (Hanin, 1997, 2000, 2003). Form, content, and intensity dimensions describe the structure of individual's experiences and meta-experiences (i.e., beliefs about expected effects of emotions or other psychobiosocial states), while context and time dimensions are associated with the dynamics of individual's experiences (Figure 2). The form dimension includes cognitive, emotional, motivational, bodily, kinesthetic (motor), performance (operational), and communicative (interactive) components. These interactive modalities constitute a performance-related psychobiosocial state of a person, in which psychological (cognition, emotion, and motivation), biological (body and movement), and social (performance and interaction) aspects are all represented. This multiple-form notion has received empirical support (Hanin and Stambulova, 2002; Ruiz and Hanin, 2004), although most research has focused mainly on emotional, bodily, and motivational modalities (Hanin, 1999, 2001; Hanin and Syrjä, 1995a, 1995b, 1996; Robazza and Bortoli, 2003).

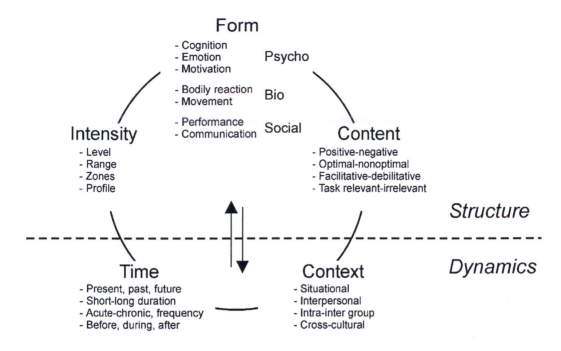

Figure 2. Dimensions of performance-related psychobiosocial states (modified from Hanin, 2000).

The content dimension has been mainly used to portray emotions, combining and extending idiosyncratic and discrete emotion approaches. The emotion content is conceptualized within two interacting independent factors, which are the hedonic tone (pleasant or unpleasant) and the functional impact upon performance (optimal or dysfunctional). From the interaction of these two factors derive four global emotion content categories: (a) pleasant-functional (P+), (b) unpleasant-functional (N+), (c) unpleasant-dysfunctional (N-), and (d) pleasant-dysfunctional (P-). Pleasant and unpleasant emotions of different intensity may exert beneficial, detrimental, or both effects on performance, depending on their idiosyncratic meaning and intensity. This four-dimension structure incorporates a constellation of idiosyncratic and task-specific emotions that the athlete may feel prior to, during, and after successful and less than successful performances.

The same two factors (hedonic tone and functionality) were used for bodily symptoms occurring in response to emotional activation (Bortoli and Robazza, 2002; Robazza and Bortoli, 2003). Hanin (1999) also suggested a four-dimensional structure to categorize the situational content of idiosyncratic motivations. The two interacting factors in this case are functional impact upon performance, and task-related tendencies of approach or avoidance. The interaction of the two factors results in four global motivation content categories including optimal-approach (effective involvement in the task), optimal-avoidance (effective withdrawal), dysfunctional-approach (ineffective involvement), and dysfunctional-avoidance (ineffective withdrawal).

The intensity dimension is a quantitative characteristic of individual experience that can be expressed in objective measures or subjective evaluations on a selected component of the performance state. Objective measures assess observable behaviors, such as performance and interactions, and psychophysical reactions; subjective evaluations are suitable for the assessment of mental states. The intensity level of emotions is linked to functional effect and hedonic tone, so that an emotion varying in magnitude can be individually interpreted as exerting functional or dysfunctional effects, and pleasant or unpleasant. The context dimension comprise situational (e.g., practice or competition), interpersonal, intragroup, and organizational factors inducing specific content and intensity of emotions. Emotional reactions in a situation are triggered by athletes' anticipated or real interactions with the coach, teammates, partners, and opponents. They depend upon culturally coded and determined beliefs of participants concerning the expected effects of specific emotions on performance and the rules of emotion displayed in a group (Hanin, 2003).

The time dimension involves topological (phases, cycles, sequencing, periodicity, timing) and metric (duration, frequency) temporal dynamics of performance-related experiences. Study findings of short-term dynamics pre-, mid-, and postperformance indicated that the athlete's emotional content and intensity vary from practice to competition and after success or failure (Hanin and Stambulova, 2002; Hanin and Syrjä, 1996; Lukkarila and Hanin, 2000). In particular, the content of emotional responses pre-, mid-, and postperformance appears somewhat balanced in practice situations, and more variable in competition. Furthermore, a spontaneous shift in the hedonic valence from pleasant to unpleasant commonly parallels the dynamics of change in appraisal pattern from gain to loss, respectively.

Prediction of Emotion-Performance Relationships

The conception that unpleasant emotions are always bad for performance and pleasant emotions are always good has been challenged by the IZOF model from the very beginning, when it was shown that anxiety can be not only detrimental but also beneficial (Hanin, 1978, 1986). Pleasant and unpleasant emotions can be helpful, harmful, or both, depending on the individual's appraisal (Hanin and Syrjä, 1995a, 1995b). Hence, an emotion can be beneficial for one athlete but detrimental for another. Moreover, an athlete may experience different intensities of an emotion as functional or dysfunctional. In both cases, reversal effects in the functional impact of emotion are apparent. The same principle applies to the individual's appraisal of pleasant or unpleasant characteristics of emotions (Robazza, Bortoli, and Nougier, 1998). Therefore, a reversal in functional impact occurs when same emotions are perceived as helpful or harmful, and a reversal in hedonic preference comes about when the same emotions are perceived as pleasant or unpleasant. Both types of reversals depend on the performer's interpretation of emotion content and intensity referred to as meta-experience, that is, the athletes' knowledge, beliefs, and attitudes about emotions (Hanin, 2004). The functional effect is likely to be a key factor in the individual's appraisal of hedonic tone. For example, a competitor who experiences rage as helpful may also perceive it to be pleasant in contrast to a teammate who perceives rage as detrimental and thus unpleasant.

With regard to the intensity dimension, the total impact of emotions on the task can be derived from the interaction of enhancing and impairing emotion effects. Successful performance is expected when functional (pleasant and unpleasant) emotion intensities lie inside an individual's optimal zone and, at the same time, dysfunctional (pleasant and unpleasant) emotion intensities lie outside the nonoptimal zone. This way, maximum enhancing and minimum impairing effects (in zone condition) are combined. In contrast, poor performance is predicted with dysfunctional emotion intensities inside an individual's nonoptimal zone, together with functional emotion intensities outside the optimal zone. In this case, high inhibitory and low enhancing effects (out of zone condition) occur (Hanin, 1997, 2000; Kamata, Tenenbaum, and Hanin, 2002). Finally, intermediate outcomes are likely to occur when both functional and dysfunctional emotion intensities are either outside optimal and nonoptimal zones, or inside optimal and nonoptimal zones. Low enhancing and low impairing effects, or high enhancing and high impairing effects are respectively observed. Research findings have provided evidence for the in/out-of-zone concept as applied to emotions (e.g., Hanin, 1997, 2000; Prapavessis and Grove, 1991; Robazza, Bortoli, and Nougier, 2002; Robazza, Bortoli, Zadro, and Nougier, 1998), and bodily symptoms concomitant with emotions (Robazza, Bortoli, and Hanin, 2004; Robazza, Pellizzari, and Hanin, 2004).

The link between emotions and performance is dynamic and bidirectional, that is, emotions influence performance and, in turn, on-going performance affects content and intensity of mid-event and post-event emotions (Hanin, 2004). Lukkarila and Hanin (2000) studied the emotion dynamics of a winning team during world junior ice hockey championship. Repeated success triggered pleasant but dysfunctional emotional states (such as complacency) in the players, which caused underestimation of the opponent's strength, insufficient energy mobilization for the game, and deterioration of subsequent performance. Hanin and Stambulova (2002) examined feeling states experienced throughout best ever and worst ever competition in skilled Russian athletes using a metaphor-generation method. Findings showed that idiosyncratic metaphors describing the content of feeling states differed across time periods (pre, mid, post). The authors suggested that differences were triggered by situational appraisals of anticipated and occurred outcomes in terms of gains and harm (Lazarus, 2000). Taken together, these findings reveal the dynamic and bidirectional characteristics of the emotion-performance relationship.

Explanation of Emotion-Performance Relationships

Adopting a psychobiosocial perspective, emotions are viewed as an unfolding process involving person-environment interactions (Hanin, 2000, 2004; Lazarus and Folkman, 1991). The individual's appraisal of these interactions causes changes in the meaning of a situation and corresponding shifts in the content and intensity of emotional experiences. The appraisal of challenge or threat before and during activity usually triggers functionally optimal emotions (P+ and N+, respectively), whereas the appraisal of gain or loss before the task is completed usually triggers dysfunctional emotions (P- and N-, respectively). The continual reappraisal of a performance process or final outcome may lead the athlete to shift from optimal to dysfunctional emotions and vice versa.

The impact of emotion on performance is explained using the two constructs of energy mobilization–demobilization and energy utilization–misuse (Hanin, 1997, 2000). Functional or dysfunctional effects of emotions would depend on the amount of energy originated (effort, intensity) and the utilization of such energy (efficiency, optimal information processing). The term energy is adopted to embrace psychological and physical factors such as vigor, vitality, intensity in mental functioning, effort persistency, and resolution in attaining goals (Hanin, 1997; Martens, 1987). Based on the resources matching hypothesis (Hanin and Stambulova, 2002), it is assumed that functional-pleasant and functional-unpleasant emotions would reflect availability of resources and their effective recruitment and utilization. Functional-pleasant emotions (e.g., feeling energetic and motivated) would help the performer to produce and utilize the energy to sustain effort and coordination for task initiation, maintenance, and completion. Functional-unpleasant emotions (e.g., feeling tense and nervous) would be more instrumental in energy production than in energy utilization. Dysfunctional-pleasant emotions (e.g., feeling tranquil and relaxed) would reflect a lack or loss of energy (decreased effort) or ineffective resource recruitment and utilization (decreased movement coordination), causing low alertness or inefficient information processing. Finally, dysfunctional-unpleasant emotions (e.g., feeling uncertain and sluggish) would determine energy misuse by diverting resources to task-irrelevant cues. In this conceptualization, the total impact of emotions upon performance (optimal, less than optimal, and dysfunctional) is better predicted by interactive effects rather than separate effects of emotion content categories. Maximum enhancing and minimum impairing effects are expected with functional (pleasant and unpleasant) emotions operative and dysfunctional (pleasant and unpleasant) emotions inoperative (in-zone condition). Conversely, maximum debilitating effects are predicted when dysfunctional emotions alone are operative (out of zone condition). Mixed effects are likely to occur when the athlete experiences a mixture of both functional and dysfunctional emotions.

Optimal effects are supposed to imply both mechanisms of energy production and energy utilization for effort and skills, whereas less than optimal effects would entail one mechanism. The constructs of energy mobilization-utilization may explain the predominance in some athletes of unpleasant emotions. For example, anger or anxiety individually considered as harmful and unpleasant emotions can impair performance because too much energy causes a narrowing in the athlete's attentional focus, and overloads the information processing mechanisms implied in the task. Many athletes, however, experience these emotions as helpful because they are able to channel the energizing effects for task execution. Given that the quality of athletic performance is related to the effective access to available energy and its efficient use, it is assumed that a same level of performance can be achieved by means of increased total effort, skillful utilization of available resources, or both processes (Hanin, 2000, 2004). It is therefore crucial for the performer to gain control over personal psychophysical states. The following section offers several professional practice suggestions as to how the IZOF model can enable athletes to achieve such an outcome.

IZOF-BASED IMPLICATIONS FOR PROFESSIONAL PRACTICE

One of the primary goals in an applied setting is to help the performer identify the content and intensity of optimal and dysfunctional emotions occurring before, during, and after successful and less than successful (poor, average, or customary) performances. These serve as individualized criteria in the evaluation of current and anticipated emotional states and also permit practitioners to comprehend the athlete's knowledge, beliefs, and attitudes about the effect of emotions on performance. Idiosyncratic assessments of such situational experiences can be effective in enhancing the athlete's awareness of functional effects of emotions. Emotion self-regulation procedures can then be employed to assist the performer to enter and stay in his or her optimal zones.

Individualized Assessments of Emotions

Idiosyncratic emotions and within-individual dynamics of performance-related states are assessed and monitored through a variety of techniques, including emotion profiling, self-generated metaphors, interviews, and narratives.

Emotion Profiling

Comparison studies showed that psychometrically sound group-oriented normative scales, such as the STAI (Spielberger et al., 1970), the Positive and Negative Affect Schedule (PANAS; Watson, Clark, and Tellegen, 1988), and the Profile of Mood States (POMS; McNair et al., 1971), do not include the approximate 80% of emotion content relevant to individual performers (Syrjä and Hanin, 1997). Individual-oriented procedures are deemed to more adequately tap the athletes' competitive experiences than group-oriented measures. An idiographic emotion profile contains meaningful descriptors evoked by the athlete, rather than items of standardized scales generated by the researcher. An emotion profile can be developed using either a direct (empirical) method or a recall (retrospective) method (see Hanin, 2000). Direct measurements of optimal and nonoptimal conditions can be accomplished by longitudinal assessment of the intensity of psychological states immediately before or after several competitions, and then contrasting them with emotion levels corresponding to best and worst performances. Since direct assessments are often impractical or intrusive, the recall procedure offers a feasible alternative. With this method, the athlete is required to recall past performances and mental states associated with best and worst accomplishments, and afterward establish emotion contents and intensities. The athlete is asked to identify pleasant and unpleasant emotions, linked to success and failure, with the help of stimulus lists of emotion words. The lists are primarily derived from positive and negative affect scales described by Watson and Tellegen (1985; see Hanin, 2000). Common functional-pleasant emotion descriptors are energetic, charged, motivated, certain, and confident, while functional-unpleasant words include tense, charged, dissatisfied, attacking, and vehement. Common dysfunctional-unpleasant labels are tired, unwilling, uncertain, sluggish, and depressed, while dysfunctional-pleasant adjectives include easy-going, excited, composed, relaxed, and overjoyed (Hanin, 1997). The athlete is encouraged to select items from the list, or generate new descriptors, that are perceived as representing their own personal experience. Afterwards, the performer is required to establish the zone values (upper and lower boundaries of intensity) for each emotion on a Borg Category Ratio scale (CR-10; see Borg, 2001, and Hanin, 2000, p. 306). Performers are consequently guided step-by-step to identify the most personally relevant descriptors of their sporting experiences, and assign intensity values to them. Recalled experiences and zones are individualized tentative criteria that need to be refined over time. Both empirical and retrospective methods permit the evaluation of current states and allow for the prediction of performance by contrasting current emotions with individual optimal and nonoptimal emotions. In an applied setting, collection of actual ratings immediately before an event may be intrusive in that they may disturb the athlete's preparation routine. Away from the competition venue, an anticipatory assessment of expected precompetition emotional states is a feasible alternative.

Reliability of emotion recall and anticipatory self-ratings has been assessed in several studies. For example, in a sample of high-level soccer players, correspondence between recalled and actual scores and between predicted and actual scores was found in 76.5% and in 70.6% of the players respectively (Hanin and Syrjä, 1996). Athletes were thus able to recall and predict their emotional states relatively accurately. Acceptable reliability has also shown in a large sample of athletes drawn from a number of individual and team sports (Robazza and Bortoli, 2003). Cronbach alphas ranged from .78 to .86 for emotional descriptors, and from .74 to .85 for bodily symptom descriptors concomitant with emotion. Finally, high congruence between actual precompetition emotions and retrospective report after a 3- to 14-day delay has been obtained in equestrians (Tenenbaum, Lloyd, Pretty, and Hanin, 2002).

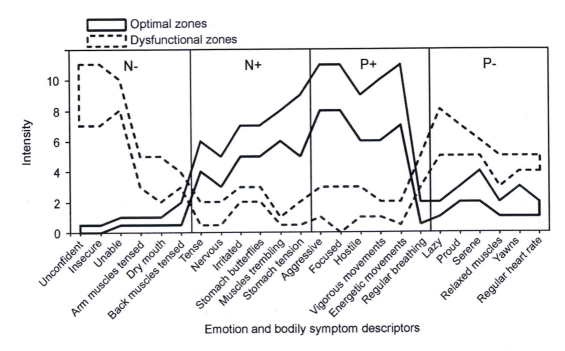

Figure 3. Emotion profile of an elite karate athlete.

Figure 3 portrays an athletes' emotion profile showing the optimal and dysfunctional zones of intensity derived for idiosyncratic labels of emotions and bodily symptoms. Optimal conditions are typified by high intensity of functional (P+, N+) descriptors combined with low intensity of dysfunctional descriptors (N-, P-) (high enhancing and low impairing effects). In contrast, dysfunctional states are characterized by low intensity of functional (P+, N+) descriptors and high intensity of dysfunctional descriptors (N-, P-) (low enhancing and high impairing effects). This pattern of emotional intensities is typically observed in athletes. When graphically plotted, with P+ and N+ in the middle, it takes a shape of an iceberg for optimal states, and a cavity for dysfunctional states (Hanin, 2000). A condition of high or low intensity of both functional and dysfunctional descriptors is also possible (high enhancing and high impairing effects, or low enhancing and low impairing effects), which would result in average performance. The athlete, therefore, should achieve a high level of P+ and N+

emotions, and a low level of N- and P- emotions in order for optimal performance to occur. In the example provided, it is interesting to note that some descriptors are not pure emotions. For instance, "focused" has cognitive connotations, whereas "unconfident" reflects motivational components. In addition, "vigorous movements" and "energetic movements" are associated more with action tendencies rather than with emotional arousal. Nevertheless, all descriptors are components of the IZOF form dimension. It is also worth noting that "aggressive" and "hostile" are subjectively perceived as pleasant emotions, likely because of the facilitative effects attributed to these states within the sport of Karate.

Idiographic assessment is also advocated by Butler and colleagues (Butler and Hardy, 1992; Jones, 1993) who developed a performance profiling procedure derived from Kelly's (1955) personal construct theory. The athlete's active participation is sought to unveil and discuss, in their own meaningful terms, the qualities typically displayed by elite competitors to succeed in a particular sport. Having identified individually perceived physical, technical, and psychological characteristics important for best achievements, ratings are assigned to each area referring first to an ideal performance and then to the athlete's current state. Ideal performance and self-ratings are then graphically portrayed to highlight the athlete's perceived strengths and weaknesses. The profile facilitates self-awareness of those areas in need of improvement and fosters commitment in attaining performance goals. Hanin (2000) has also argued that performance profile methodology focuses more on stable trait-like factors (i.e., abilities or constructs) related to ideal performance (the outcome) compared to the IZOF model that is more concerned with situational state-like factors and on the process of achieving goals. Sport-specific, trait-like characteristics would reflect developmental potential of athletes and availability of resources. On the other hand, emotions would have to do more on how this potential is used via the processes of energy production (enhancing effort) and energy utilization (organizing behavior). Despite their diversity, performance profiling and the IZOF profiling approaches can be combined for applied purposes, so to account for trait- and state-like factors affecting performance (see D'Urso, Petrosso, and Robazza, 2002; Robazza et al., 2004). A mixed trait-state profile can therefore be constructed as an effective measure to assess both performance outcome and performance process.

Self-generated Metaphors

Although emotion profiling techniques enable the capture of personally relevant emotion content, Hanin and associates (Hanin, 2000; Hanin and Stambulova, 2002; Ruiz and Hanin, 2004) have proposed a metaphor self-generation method to account for the meaning of a performance situation. This approach is based on the assumption that symbolizing, as a fundamental human capability, allows people to transmit thoughts and give structure, meaning, and continuity to their lives. A metaphor is a figure of speech that usually stands for something else and that renders understandable something difficult to describe through similarities to something already described. As symbolic representations, metaphors are related to certain holistic images that are meaningful for a person (e.g., "I feel strong as a rock"). As Ruiz and Hanin (2004) noted, metaphors allow the communication of a great deal of information, of what is difficult or impossible to express, in a succinct manner, and capture the vividness of phenomenal experience.

The metaphor-generation method allows individuals to symbolically represent feeling states prior to, during, and after best and worst performances. Athletes are introduced to the concept of a metaphor and provided with examples of metaphors describing feelings and emotions in non-sport settings. Examples such as, "When I am on a beach on a bright sunny day, I feel like..." generates a symbolic representation of a feeling state. This state can be then interpreted by completing a paraphrased sentence, "In other words, I feel myself..." When participants have grasped the idea of a metaphoric description of psychological states they are requested to recall their best ever competition (and then their worst ever competition) and to describe how they felt by completing open-ended sentences and related paraphrases: "Prior to (during or after) my best (worst) ever competition I felt like..." ("In other words, I felt myself...").

Findings by Hanin and colleagues (see Hanin, 2003, 2004) suggested that performers from several sports, across different ages and skill levels, use metaphors to describe their thoughts, emotions, bodily sensations, and behaviors. Highly idiosyncratic images symbolically represent high or low action readiness in successful and unsuccessful situations. Metaphors related to best ever competition reflect available resources ("a boat with an engine"), ability to recruit resources ("a horse in a light cart"), and efficient use of resources ("Batman in flight"). Conversely, metaphors related to worst ever competition reveal lack of resources ("an empty bottle"), inability to recruit resources ("a bird unable to fly"), and inefficient use of resources ("a bear after hibernation"). Therefore, idiosyncratic content and meaning of metaphors is usually self-empowering when related to best competition, and self-defeating when associated with worst competition. In addition, the dissimilar content of idiosyncratic metaphors across pre-, mid-, and postcompetition situations supports the contention that performing a task usually involves the three interrelated but functionally and qualitatively different stages of performance preparation, execution, and evaluation.

Interviews and Narratives

In-depth structured and semi-structured interviews with probing and open-ended questionnaires can provide the researcher with and extensive amount of information when experienced and verbally adept athletes are involved. Less adept or less aware performers may find difficulties in analyzing introspectively their thoughts and feelings, and require assistance in structuring and focusing their recall. To facilitate introspection, Hanin (2003) has recommended the adoption of Spradley's (1979) three types of open-ended questions. These consist of descriptive questions to examine emotional responses in a particular performance situation (e.g., "How did you feel when your opponent scored?"), structural questions addressing the perception of situation and coping skills ("What did you do when you felt this way?"), and contrast questions to examine experiences in various conditions ("What is the difference in what you feel when well prepared and poorly prepared for the game?"). In-depth interviews allow the athletes to display personal knowledge and experience, and awareness of optimal, customary, and dysfunctional states. Adoption of self-regulation strategies, effectiveness of self-regulation, disturbing factors, and coping processes can also be scrutinized.

Narrative practice is another promising area of qualitative inquiry. As Sparkes and Partington (2003) have noted, scholars in psychology and social sciences have begun to pay attention to the way people structure their experiences and construct personal and cultural realities through narratives and storytelling. Narratives, as self-stories, are often spontaneously related by athletes when asked to share their accounts of personal experiences and feelings or while taking part in in-depth interviews. Self-stories can describe performance situations, bring to light automatic thoughts and emotional responses, identify ways to cope with adversity, and even introduce permanent change (Hanin, 2003). Story telling has the potential to provide a holistic and dynamic representation of athletic performance as unfolding process in real-life situations. Emotion descriptors of concrete idiosyncratic experiences, individual's interpretations of experiences, and culturally determined beliefs within a specific context are all embedded in personal accounts. Such a comprehensive and dynamic picture of the individual's experience offers insight into emotional states and emotional displays (i.e., expression and suppression of feelings).

Control of Emotions

Idiosyncratic techniques of emotion assessment tend to stimulate awareness in the athlete of the effects of emotions and related states toward performance. Following this stage, emotion management procedures can be employed. Earlier attempts to apply principles stemming from the IZOF model were conducted for the optimization of precompetition anxiety of elite rowers and weightlifters (Hanin, 1978, 1986). Competitors were involved in several steps that included (a) identification of optimal anxiety zones through a retrospective method, (b) assessment of anxiety 5-7 days prior to competition, (c) assessment of expected prestart anxiety and attitudes toward competition, (d) comparison of expected prestart anxiety with optimal anxiety zones, and (e) reduction or augmentation of anxiety levels to enter and stay in the optimal zones. More recently, Annesi (1998) conducted an anxiety treatment study with three elite adolescent tennis players. The CSAI-2 (Martens et al., 1990) was administered repeatedly 45 min before tournament matches, and individual anxiety zones were derived. Two players then underwent psychological skills training and were taught to enter their optimal zones when they perceived too high or too low levels of anxiety and self-confidence. In particular, the players were trained to assess themselves just prior to a match, and either lower or raise their cognitive anxiety, somatic anxiety, and self-confidence levels when above or below optimal zones. Psychological self-regulatory skills comprised a range of cognitive and somatic procedures such as cognitive restructuring, self-talk, focus control, imagery, goal setting, breathing control, and muscular tension-relaxation. The anxiety treatment prescription was based on the matching or specific effect hypothesis (Davidson and Schwartz, 1976; see Hardy, Jones, and Gould, 1996), in that anxiety-management techniques were matched to dimensional (cognitive, somatic, self-confidence) and intensity (increase, decreased) indications. The treatment was successful and yielded post-intervention performance values higher than pre-intervention.

The recent advancements of the IZOF model toward a psychobiosocial perspective has led Hanin (2000, 2004) to formulate seven working principles for the development of self-regulation strategies. For an effective treatment one should:

a) target idiosyncratic psychobiosocial states manifested in the seven modalities (cognition, emotion, etc.) of the form dimension (multimodality principle);

b) consider individually optimal and dysfunctional emotion contents and intensity zones (multizone principle);

c) increase or decrease emotion (or other modalities) intensity levels to reduce discrepancy between current and optimal state intensity (multidirection principle);

d) evaluate the change of intensity of selected emotions (or other target modalities) as well as total emotion impact upon athletic performance (multifunction principle);

e) focus on emotion dynamics prior to, during, and postperformance (multistage principle);

f) focus on the emotion patterns associated with different tasks, settings (practice and competitions), conditions, skill level, and individual states (multitask principle);

g) include several combined and most appropriate methods of self-regulation fitting the above principles (multimethod principle).

In an attempt to apply the IZOF principles for self-regulation, Robazza et al. (2004) implemented a staggered single-subject design with expert athletes. Four roller hockey players and four gymnasts took part in the study from which six (three hockey players and three gymnasts) underwent emotion self-regulation training (Williams, 2001). The intervention comprised three phases. In the first phase, athletes were provided with information on the effects of idiosyncratic emotions on performance and asked to identify contents and intensities of emotional states associated with recalled best and worst performances. Recalled optimal-dysfunctional emotional states were thus identified to serve as individualized criteria and guidelines for athletes' self-regulation. Participants were then instructed to pay attention to their mental states in competition, and to contrast current conditions with recalled optimal-dysfunctional states. The purpose of this phase was to improve individual awareness of content and intensity of competitive emotions and their functional effects. In the second phase, attention was placed on idiosyncratic and mental preparation strategies the athletes spontaneously adopted to deal with competition demands and difficulties. Participants were required to describe in detail their precompetition routines, competition behaviors, and mental procedures to control arousal, imagery, self-talk, concentration, and emotion. The goal of this stage was to enable performers apply their effective self-regulation procedures and dismiss ineffective habits. In the third phase, athletes were provided with suggestions to improve, refine, and expand spontaneous self-regulation strategies. Participants were instructed about the benefits and the procedures of setting goals, using imagery, focusing attention, controlling internal dialogue, and applying relaxing and energizing somatic and cognitive techniques (Hardy et al., 1996; Williams, 2001).

Emphasis was always placed on the adoption of procedures matching individual needs. For example, an athlete might mentally rehearse successful performance to recover an optimal content of emotions, and then use realistic goals, task specific imagery, somatic relaxation, and de-energizing metaphors to maintain an intermediate level of emotion intensity. On the other hand, an athlete who seeks a high level of optimal emotion might focus on challenging goals, mastery imagery, positive self-talk and energizing metaphors. The treatment enabled athletes to (a) contrast current performance states with recalled optimal-dysfunctional states, (b) recover functional (P+, N+) emotional states, and remove dysfunctional (P-, N-) emotional states, (c) increase or decrease the intensity of emotional states to achieve optimal conditions, (d) monitor and handle emotional fluctuations over time, (e) verify the impact of emotions on the task, and (f) improve performance.

While the preliminary results on emotion control are encouraging, in that they are grounded in a sound theoretical position, further research is necessary to substantiate findings and test the IZOF principles of emotion self-regulation. Investigation should also focus on the effects of emotions on performance, the extension of assessment procedures to all components of a psychobiosocial state, the identification of personal factors as moderators of emotion, and the links between the IZOF model with other theoretical approaches. These issues are outlined in detail in the next section.

FUTURE RESEARCH DIRECTIONS

This section presents recommendations for directions for future research regarding the IZOF model in relation to emotion effects on performance, emotion regulation, assessment of psychobiosocial states, and emotion antecedents. In addition, while notable attempts have been made to test assumptions stemming from IZOF and other approaches, research in this area is sparse. The tentative links between the model and certain theoretical perspectives that are intuitively connected to the IZOF model including the mental health model (Morgan, 1985) and the directional approach (see Mellalieu et al., this volume) are therefore discussed with the hope of challenging investigators to determine where models and theories may differ, overlap, or integrate in order to advance understanding of the complex relationship between emotion and performance.

IZOF-based Research Directions

Emotion Effects on Performance
The constructs of energy production and utilization assume that functional-pleasant, functional-unpleasant, dysfunctional-unpleasant, and dysfunctional-pleasant emotions exert differential effects on performance. However, the mechanisms by which emotions act differently on energy production and utilization have to be examined more thoroughly and contrasted with theories often used to explain the effects of emotion on performance, such as the cue utilization theory (Easterbrook, 1959) and processing efficiency theory (Eysenck and Calvo, 1992). Instructional sets and a competitive atmosphere, video clips of performance situations, mental imagery, recall, or self-regulation techniques can be employed singularly or in combination to study the impact of emotion content and intensity manipulations on processing efficiency (reaction times, visual search pattern, working-memory function, etc.) and on performance effectiveness.

Emotion Regulation
A test of the constructs of energy production and utilization also holds significance for the study of emotion regulation. If functional-pleasant emotions serve both energy production and utilization functions, as they are supposed to, then they should form the core objective of psychological interventions. Although this issue has not been directly addressed, preliminary support has been found for the effectiveness of anxiety and emotion regulation strategies based on the IZOF model indications (Annesi, 1998; Robazza et al., 2004). Moreover, the IZOF model suggests targeting the whole range of cognitive, emotional, motivational, bodily, motor-behavioral, performance-operational, and communicative components of a performance state. The benefits of such a holistic approach for treatment selection need to be demonstrated.

Psychobiosocial Assessment

Emotion profiling research showed that athletes' descriptors usually have connotations with non-emotional concomitants of psychobiosocial state (e.g., Hanin and Syrjä, 1995a, 1995b, 1996; Robazza, Bortoli, Nocini, Moser, and Arslan, 2000). Adjectives reported often unveil components concerning cognition (e.g., alert and focused), motivation (e.g., determined and motivated), body reactions (e.g., relaxed and tense), and motor reactions (e.g., smooth movements and sharp movements). However, there is a need to extend the focus of individualized profiling to systematically encompass all modalities of an athlete's state. Initial steps in this direction have been taken in the assessment of idiosyncratic motivation (Hanin, 1999, 2001) and bodily symptoms concomitant with emotions (Bortoli and Robazza, 2002; Robazza and Bortoli, 2003). Physiological and behavioral aspects have also been considered in a few investigations (e.g., Davis, 1991; Robazza, Bortoli, and Nougier, 1999, 2000; Zaichkowsky, Hamill, and Dallis, reported by Zaichkowsky and Baltzell, 2001). Psychobiosocial states can be best understood by implementing a variety of techniques for subjective assessment (psychobiosocial profiling, self-generated metaphors, etc.), and objective assessment (physiological, behavioral, and performance measures).

Emotion Working-range

A further measurement issue is the emotion-performance link across the whole range of intensity (working range) of emotions. Taking into account the fact that working range may help overcome a limitation of the in/out-of-zone notion, Hanin (2000) argued that the zone notion entails a categorical conceptualization of emotion intensity effects, in which optimal (or nonoptimal) performance is predicted to occur when emotion intensity is within (or outside) previously established optimal intensity zones. This categorical perspective does not consider the entire range of emotion intensity associated with all performance results. In favor of a continuous rather than categorical interpretation, Kamata et al. (2002) proposed a probabilistic conceptualization based on recurrent assessments of emotion intensities and actual performance. With this methodology, however, the whole range of intensity is not necessarily covered and the athlete's meta-experiences (i.e., knowledge, attitudes, and preferences regarding emotional states) are ignored. An alternative method was adopted by Hanin (2000) who assessed the perceived effects of emotion along the working range of intensity in elite cross-country skiers. The skiers recalled their emotional contents in races and then rated emotion intensities effects on performance across all ratings of a Borg scale. The interactive effects of functional-dysfunctional, pleasant-unpleasant emotions along the intensity range were suggested to help develop individualized interventions for performance enhancement. Although intuitively appealing, the application of this methodology requires further research.

Personal Factors as Moderators of Emotion

Critics have argued that the IZOF is essentially an individual difference 'theory' without any difference variable (Gould and Tuffey, 1996; Hardy et al., 1996; Woodman and Hardy, 2001). However, one should consider that the IZOF model from the very beginning emphasized a need to first examine individual differences in emotions before investigating the impact of personality and environmental factors. Future research should identify possible personality variables or enduring factors that determine an athlete's predisposition to experience a specific content and intensity pattern of functional-dysfunctional and pleasant-unpleasant emotions. For example, in a study of collegiate athletes, Wilson, Raglin, and Pritchard (2002) showed that while a wide degree of variability in individual levels of precompetition anxiety was revealed (according to the IZOF predictions) those who displayed an optimist cognitive orientation style exhibited lower levels of anxiety compared to those who displayed a pessimist orientation. In a further study of personality traits of neuroticism and extraversion as predictors of anxiety direction, Cerin (2004) noted that neuroticism is typified by the tendency to experience negative affect, while extraversion is related to the predisposition to experience positive affect. Pessimism, intolerance to frustration, inability to cope with stress, and avoidant behaviors are features of neurotic individuals. In contrast, determination, optimism, self-confidence, tolerance to stress and frustration, and action tendencies characterize extraverts. Consequently, Cerin hypothesized that those individuals high in neuroticism should be prone to debilitative states of anxiety, while those high in extraversion should be predisposed to facilitative states of anxiety. It is here suggested that Cerin's argument may also apply to emotions within the IZOF framework. One may expect neurotics to be prone to experience dysfunctional or unpleasant emotions, and extraverts to be inclined to display functional or pleasant emotions. Other potential predictors of emotions may include coping skills, self-confidence, performance expectations, goal orientation, helplessness, self-handicapping, and hardiness.

A diverse view was offered by Zizzi, Deaner, and Hirschhorn (2003) who recommended the study of the potential link between the IZOF model and Emotional Intelligence Theory. The authors maintained that recognizing personal ideal performance states and developing emotion management skills involve both energy control and emotional intelligence (Goleman, 1998). They also hypothesized that athletes with high emotional intelligence may be more skilled at recognizing and utilizing their IZOF in specific situations than athletes with low emotional intelligence. However, while intuitively appealing and of potential interest to the study of emotion-performance relationship, these contentions require empirical verification.

The IZOF Model and other Theoretical Approaches

Few attempts have been made to compare the IZOF model with other influential perspectives on emotion in sport. These attempts include the mental health model and the directional approach. The mental health model (MHM) in sport was introduced by Morgan (1980, 1985), and purports that an inverse relationship exists between psychopathology and performance. Specifically, the model predicts that athletes scoring high on measures of undesirable psychological constructs, such as neuroticism, anxiety, depression, confusion, and fatigue, will be less successful than performers reporting lower scores on these measures. Similarly, positive and desirable aspects of mental health, such as emotional stability, low trait anxiety, and high psychic vigor, are supposed to be related to greater success in sport. Therefore, successful athletes are expected to possess desirable and healthy psychological traits. An impressive amount of research on the MHM model, to examine mood and performance relationships in sport and exercise, has typically employed the POMS (McNair et al., 1971) measurement tool. In the POMS, mood is conceptualized through six dimensions termed tension, depression, anger, vigor, fatigue, and confusion (for review, see LeUnes and Burger, 2000; for a meta-analysis see Beedie, Terry, and Lane, 2000). Five of these moods are negative and one is positive (vigor). Research has reported that successful athletes usually score lower in negative moods and higher in vigor than a normative sample. When the standardized POMS scores of successful athletes are plotted, negative moods fall below the population norms and the vigor score falls above the norms (Terry and Lane, 2000). Morgan (1985) referred to this typical mood pattern as the 'iceberg profile' and proposed it as indicator of positive mental health.

In addition to these trait-like characteristics, Raglin (2001) has called attention to the dynamic features of the MHM contending that the accuracy in predicting performance can be enhanced beyond the level attained with trait measures by incorporating regular assessments of selected psychological variables (i.e., states and mood), particularly during training. The stable feature of the MHM is concerned with the association of trait-like measures of mood with performance in groups of athletes, and therefore is nomothetic in nature. The dynamic aspect of the MHM has both nomothetic and idiosyncratic characteristics: intensive training has been found to be associated with mood disturbances and impaired performance at a group level and variability across athletes has been observed in tolerance of hard training (see Raglin, 2001). Idiosyncratic factors are also stressed within the IZOF model perspective. A comparison of the two approaches was conducted by Morgan, O'Connor, Ellickson, and Bradley (1988) in a study of elite distance runners. Positive mood state profiles in the sample were in accordance with the MHM, while interindividual variability of optimal precompetition anxiety conformed to the IZOF model predictions. Future research should take a more holistic perspective to involve the whole range of idiosyncratic emotions, beyond anxiety, so as to provide a complementary trait-state conceptual framework in the study of relationship between psychological variables and performance in training and competition. According to Raglin (2001), "Whether the MHM and IZOF model can be melded into a truly interactional framework remains to be determined from future studies; however, it is clear that employing these models conjointly can provide a greater understanding of how psychological traits and states independently influence athletic performance." (p. 883).

Similarly to the IZOF model, the directional approach endorses individual differences in functional interpretation of emotion (see Mellalieu et al., in this volume for a detailed discussion). The directional component of multidimensional competitive anxiety is typically assessed using a modified form of the CSAI-2 (Martens et al., 1990). The notion of "direction" of anxiety refers to the perceived functional effects of symptom intensity. Hence, a directional scale added to the questionnaire measures whether the intensity of symptoms is individually perceived as facilitative or debilitative. Therefore, two performers may experience a same level of precompetitive cognitive or somatic anxiety on the CSAI-2, but one of them may interpret symptoms as facilitative and the other as debilitative.

Findings of the directional approach studies suggest that a functional shift of anxiety symptoms from debilitative to facilitative followed by hedonic valence reversals of symptoms from unpleasant to pleasant occurs, as have been reported for other emotional states (e.g., Bortoli and Robazza, 2002; Robazza, Bortoli, and Nougier 1998; Robazza, Bortoli, Nocini et al., 2000). To further examine this notion and the possible link between directional and IZOF approaches, Robazza and Bortoli (2003) administered the trait version of the CSAI-2 to a sample of elite and nonelite Italian athletes representing several individual and team sports. The customary intensity scale was supplemented with a direction scale, ranging from -3 (very debilitative) to +3 (very facilitative), and a hedonic tone scale, ranging from -3 (very unpleasant) to +3 (very pleasant). IZOF-based idiographic scaling was also implemented to assess the content and intensity of emotional and body symptom descriptors. Athletes high in intensity or high in hedonic tone of self-confidence reported higher scores for functional-pleasant emotion and bodily symptoms than those low in intensity or hedonic tone of self-confidence. In addition, performers high in both cognitive and somatic anxiety intensity reported higher levels of dysfunctional-unpleasant emotions than those high on just one anxiety subcomponent. These preliminary results warrant further research to ascertain whether enduring predispositions to respond to competitive situations with different intensity and interpretation of functional effects (facilitative and debilitative) and hedonic effects (pleasant and unpleasant) of anxiety and self-confidence will predict the content and intensity of situational emotions.

The intuitive relationship between the two theoretical positions was also noted by Davis and Cox (2002). Specifically, the IZOF model predicts best performance when the athlete's anxiety is within the optimal zone and the directional approach predicts best performance when precompetition anxiety is perceived as facilitative. If both perspectives are valid, then best performance would occur when an athlete is within his or her optimal anxiety zone and perceives anxiety as facilitative. The authors hypothesized that directional scores associated with cognitive and somatic anxiety scores falling within a participant's IZOF would be significantly more facilitative than directional scores falling outside of a participant's IZOF. To test this hypothesis, Davis and Cox assessed intensity and direction of precompetitive state anxiety in high school swimmers across several meets. The results did not support the hypothesized relationship between the IZOF model and the directional approach, although some evidence was found for the concept of zone. The non-elite level of athletes involved in the investigation and the use of the CSAI-2, which was recently called into question as a valid measure of competitive anxiety (Cerin, 2003), may have been contributing causes of these findings. Despite the non significant results, this line of research is warranted to explore the intuitive link between the two theoretical approaches. Furthermore, as Cox (2002) pointed out, important applied implications derive from the IZOF notion of zone and the directionality approach. The notion of zone implies that once the individual optimal bandwidth of anxiety or emotion intensity is established, the athlete has to maintain anxiety or emotion levels within that zone. Behavioral, cognitive or somatic strategies can be adopted to raise or lower anxiety or emotion when intensity levels are below or above the optimal range (Annesi, 1998; Robazza et al., 2004). In contrast, according to the directional perspective, Hanton and Jones (1999) applied cognitive restructuring techniques to modify the individual's interpretation of anxiety intensity levels. Three elite swimmers debilitated by anxiety reported a more facilitative interpretation of precompetition symptoms posttreatment, although anxiety intensity remained stable. These theoretically grounded findings within either the IZOF or directional frameworks deserve further investigation to assess the impact of mental preparation procedures designed to modify intensities of competitive anxiety or emotion and/or reinterpret symptoms.

CONCLUSION

The renewed interest in sport psychology of the study of the antecedents and consequences of emotional responses is reflected in growing research within several conceptual views and a variety of emerging paradigms. The material presented on emotion in this chapter, far from being exhaustive, was intended to provide an overview of emotion-performance research and application primarily through Hanin's IZOF framework. Although a great deal of research has been conducted surrounding the IZOF anxiety proposals, scholars have just begun to investigate the new advancements of the IZOF psychobiosocial model. Core themes for future research involve both improvements in the IZOF methodology and the possible link between the model and other theoretical approaches. Most relevant are issues related to the IZOF model concerning the differential effects of emotion on performance, emotion regulation, psychobiosocial assessment, and personality factors as moderators of emotion. In addition, few attempts have been made to contrast the IZOF with other views. Among the main perspectives, the Mental Health Model and the directional approach seem particularly promising, in that they have similarities to the IZOF model. Comparing and combining these views can contribute to advancing the knowledge of those psychological trait and state factors that interact with performance.

ACKNOWLEDGEMENTS

The author would like to acknowledge the Reviewers Dr Yuri Hanin and Dr Arnold LeUnes for their constructive and insightful comments on earlier drafts of this chapter.

REFERENCES

Annesi, J. J. (1998). Applications of the Individual Zones of Optimal Functioning model for the multimodal treatment of precompetitive anxiety. *The Sport Psychologist, 12*, 300-316.

Apter, M. J. (1989). *Reversal theory: Motivation, emotion and personality*. London: Routledge.

Apter, M. J. (Ed.) (2001). *Motivational styles in everyday life: A guide to Reversal Theory*. Washington, D.C.: American Psychological Association.

Averill, J. R. (1994). I feel, therefore I am–I think. In P. Ekman and R. J. Davidson (Eds.), *The nature of emotion: Fundamental questions* (pp. 379-385). New York: Oxford University Press.

Beedie, C. J., Terry, P. C., and Lane, A. M. (2000). The Profile of Mood States and athletic performance: Two meta-analyses. *Journal of Applied Sport Psychology, 12*, 49–68.

Borg, G. (2001). Borg's range model and scales. *International Journal of Sport Psychology, 32*, 110-126.

Bortoli, L., and Robazza, C. (2002). Idiosyncratic performance affect in volleyball referees: An extension of the IZOF-emotion model profiling. *Journal of Sport Behavior, 25*, 115-133.

Botterill, C., and Brown, M. (2002). Emotion and perspective in sport. *International Journal of Sport Psychology, 33*, 38-60.

Butler, R. J., and Hardy, L. (1992). The performance profile: Theory and application. *The Sport Psychologist, 6*, 253-264.

Cerin, E. (2003). Anxiety versus fundamental emotions as predictors of perceived functionality of pre-competitive emotional states, threat, and challenge in individual sports. *Journal of Applied Sport Psychology, 15*, 223-238.

Cerin, E. (2004). Predictors of competitive anxiety direction in male Tae Kwon Do practitioners: A multilevel mixed idiographic/nomothetic interactional approach. *Psychology of Sport and Exercise, 5*, 497-516.

Cerin, E., Szabo, A., Hunt, N., and Williams, C. (2000). Temporal patterning of competitive emotions: A critical review. *Journal of Sports Sciences, 18*, 605-626.

Clore, G. L. (1994). Why emotions require cognition. In K. R. Scherer and P. Ekman (Eds.), *Approaches to emotions* (pp. 181-191) Hillsdale, NJ: Erlbaum.

Cox, R. H. (2002). *Sport psychology: Concepts and applications* (5th ed.). Dubuque, IA: McGraw-Hill.

Davidson, R. J., and Schwartz, G. E. (1976). The psychobiology of relaxation and relaxed states: A multi-process theory. In D. I. Mostofsky (Ed.), *Behavior control and modification of physiological activity* (pp. 399-442). Englewood Cliffs, NJ: Prentice-Hall.

Davis, H. (1991). Passive recovery and optimal arousal in ice hockey. *Perceptual and Motor Skills, 72*, 513-514.

Davis, J. E., and Cox, R. H. (2002). Interpreting direction of anxiety within Hanin's Individual Zone of Optimal Functioning. *Journal of Applied Sport Psychology, 14*, 43-52.

Deci, E. L. (1980). *The psychology of self-determination.* Lexington, MA: Heath.

D'Urso, V., Petrosso, A., and Robazza, C. (2002). Emotions, perceived qualities, and performance of rugby players. *The Sport Psychologist, 16*, 173-199.

Easterbrook, J. A. (1959). The effect of emotion on cue utilization and the organization of behavior. *Psychological Review, 66*, 183-201.

Ekkekakis, P., and Petruzzello, S. J. (2000). Analysis of the affect measurement conundrum in exercise psychology. I. Fundamental issues. *Psychology of Sport and Exercise, 1*, 71-88.

Ekman, P., Levenson, R. W., and Friesen, W. V. (1983). Autonomic nervous system activity distinguished among emotions. *Science, 221*, 1208-1210.

Eysenk, M. W., and Calvo, M. G. (1992). Anxiety and performance: The processing efficiency theory. *Cognition and emotion, 6*, 409-434.

Frijda, N. H. (1986). *The emotions.* Cambridge: Cambridge University Press.

Gauvin, L., and Spence, J. C. (1998). Measurement of exercise induced changes in feeling states, affect, mood, and emotions. In J. L. Duda (Ed.), *Advances in sport and exercise psychology measurement* (pp. 325-336). Morgantown, WV: Fitness Information Technology.

Goleman, D. (1998). *Working with emotional intelligence.* New York: Bantam Books.

Gould, D., Greenleaf, C., and Krane, V. (2002). Arousal-anxiety and sport behavior. In T. S. Horn (Ed.), *Advances in sport psychology* (2nd ed., pp. 207-241). Champaign, IL: Human Kinetics.

Gould, D., and Tuffey, S. (1996). Zones of Optimal Functioning research: A review and critique. *Anxiety, Stress, and Coping, 9*, 53-68.

Gross, J. J. (1999). Emotion regulation: Past, present, future. *Cognition and Emotion, 13*, 551-573.

Hanin, Y. L. (1978). A study of anxiety in sports. In W. F. Straub (Ed.), *Sport psychology: An analysis of athlete behavior* (pp. 236-249). Ithaca, NY: Mouvement.

Hanin, Y. L. (1986). State-trait anxiety research on sports in the USSR. In C. D. Spielberger and R. Diaz-Guerrero (Eds.), *Cross cultural anxiety* (Vol. 3, pp. 45-64). Washington, DC: Hemisphere.

Hanin, Y. L. (1989). Interpersonal and intragroup anxiety in sports. In D. Hackfort and C. D. Spielberger (Eds.), *Anxiety in sports: An international perspective* (pp. 19-28). Washington, DC: Hemisphere.

Hanin, Y. L. (1995). Individual Zones of Optimal Functioning (IZOF) model: An idiographic approach to performance anxiety. In K. P. Henschen and W. F. Straub (Eds.), *Sport psychology: An analysis of athlete behavior* (pp. 103-119). Longmeadow, MA: Mouvement.

Hanin, Y.L. (1997). Emotions and athletic performance: Individual Zones of Optimal Functioning model. *European Yearbook of Sport Psychology*, *1*, 29-72.

Hanin, Y. (1999). Sports-specific emotion-motivational profiling: An individualized assessment programme. In V. Hošek, P. Tilinger, and L. Bílek (Eds.), *Psychology of sport and exercise: Enhancing the quality of life*. Proceedings of the 10th European Congress of Sport Psychology (Part 1, pp. 238-240). Prague, Czech Republic: Charles University.

Hanin, Y. L. (Ed.). (2000). *Emotions in sport*. Champaign, IL: Human Kinetics.

Hanin, Y. L. (2001). Emotion-motivational profiling in skiing: An individualized assessment program. In E. Müller, H. Schwameder, C. Raschner, S. Lindinger, and E. Kornexl (Eds.), *Science and Skiing II*, Schriften zur Sportwissenschaft, Band 26 (pp. 688-705). Hamburg, Germany: Verlag Dr. Kovac.

Hanin, Y. L. (2002). Individually optimal recovery in sports: An application of the IZOF model. In M. Kellmann (Ed.), *Enhancing recovery: Preventing underperformance in athletes* (pp. 199-217). Champaign, IL: Human Kinetics.

Hanin, Y. L. (2003, February). Performance related emotional states in sport: A qualitative analysis. *Forum Qualitative Sozialforschung / Forum: Qualitative Social Research* [On-line Journal], *4*. Retrieved March 19, 2003, from http://www.qualitative-research.net/fqs-texte/1-03/1-03hanin-e.htm.

Hanin, Y. L. (2004). Emotion in sports. In C. D. Spielberger (Ed.). *Encyclopedia of Applied Psychology* (Vol. 1, pp. 739-750). Oxford, UK: Elsevier Academic Press.

Hanin, Y. L., and Stambulova, N. B. (2002). Metaphoric description of performance states: An application of the IZOF model. *The Sport Psychologist*, *16*, 396-415.

Hanin, Y., and Syrjä, P. (1995a). Performance affect in junior ice hockey players: An application of the Individual Zones of Optimal Functioning model. *The Sport Psychologist*, *9*, 169-187.

Hanin, Y., and Syrjä, P. (1995b). Performance affect in soccer players: An application of the IZOF model. *International Journal of Sports Medicine*, *16*, 260-265.

Hanin, Y., and Syrjä, P. (1996). Predicted, actual, and recalled affect in Olympic-level soccer players: Idiographic assessments on individualized scales. *Journal of Sport and Exercise Psychology*, *18*, 325-335.

Hanton, S., and Jones, G. (1999). The effects of a multimodal intervention program on performers: II. Training the butterflies to fly in formation. *The Sport Psychologist*, *13*, 22-41.

Hardy, L. (1990). A catastrophe model of performance in sport. In J. G. Jones and L. Hardy (Eds.), *Stress and performance in sport* (pp. 81-106). New York: John Wiley and Sons.

Hardy, L., Jones, G., and Gould, D. (1996). *Understanding psychological preparation for sport: Theory and practice of elite performers*. Chichester: Wiley and Sons.

Izard, C. E. (1992). Basic emotions, relations among emotions, and emotion-cognition relations. *Psychological Review, 99*, 561-565.

Janelle, C. M. (2002). Anxiety, arousal and visual attention: A mechanistic account of performance variability. *Journal of Sports Sciences, 20*, 237-251.

Jokela, M., and Hanin, Y. L. (1999). Does the Individual Zones of Optimal Functioning model discriminate between successful and less successful athletes? A meta-analysis. *Journal of Sports Sciences, 17*, 873-887.

Jones, G. (1993). The role of performance profiling in cognitive behavioral interventions in sport. *The Sport Psychologist, 7*, 160-172.

Jones, G. (1995). More than just a game: Research developments and issues in competitive anxiety in sport. *British Journal of Psychology, 86*, 449-478.

Jones, M. (2003). Controlling emotions in sport. *The Sport Psychologist, 17*, 471-486.

Jones, M. V., Mace, R. D., and Williams, S. (2000). Relationships between emotional state and performance during international field hockey matches. *Perceptual and Motor Skills, 90*, 691-701.

Kamata, A., Tenenbaum, G., and Hanin, Y. L. (2002). Individual Zone of Optimal Functioning (IZOF): A probabilistic estimation. *Journal of Sport and Exercise Psychology, 24*, 189-208.

Kelly, G. A. (1955). *The psychology of personal constructs*. New York: Norton.

Kerr, J. H. (1997). *Motivation and emotion in sport: Reversal theory*. East Sussex, UK: Psychology Press, Taylor and Francis.

Lacey, J. I., and Lacey, B. C. (1970). Some autonomic-central nervous system interrelationships. In P. Black (Ed.), *Physiological correlates of emotion* (pp. 205-227). New York: Academic Press.

Landers, D. M., and Arent, S. M. (2001). Arousal-performance relationships. In J. M. Williams (Ed.), *Applied sport psychology: Personal growth to peak performance* (4th ed., pp. 206-228). Mountain View, CA: Mayfield.

Lane, A. M., and Terry, P. C. (2000). The nature of mood: Development of a conceptual model with a focus on depression. *Journal of Applied Sport Psychology, 12*, 16-33.

Lang, P. J. (2000). Emotion and motivation: Attention, perception, and action. *Journal of Sport and Exercise Psychology, 20*, S122-S140.

Lazarus, R. S. (1991). Progress on a cognitive-motivational-relational theory of emotion. *American Psychologist, 46*, 819-834.

Lazarus, R. S. (2000). How emotions influence performance in competitive sports. *The Sport Psychologist, 14*, 229-252.

Lazarus, R. S., and Folkman, S. (1991). The concept of coping. In A. Monat and R. S. Lazarus (Eds.), *Stress and coping* (pp. 189-206). New York: Columbia University Press.

LeUnes, A., and Burger, J. (2000). Profile of mood states research in sport and exercise psychology: Past, present, and future. *Journal of Applied Sport Psychology, 12*, 5-15.

Lukkarila, J., and Hanin, Y. (2000). Emotion dynamics in the winning team during the 1999 world junior ice hockey championship. In J. Avela, P. V. Komi, and J. Komulainen (Eds.), *Proceedings of the 5th Annual Congress of the European College of Sport Science* (p. 456). Jyväskylä, Finland: University of Jyväskylä.

Martens, R. (1987). *Coaches guide to sport psychology*. Champaign, IL: Human Kinetics.

Martens, R., Burton, D., Vealey, R. S., Bump, L. A., and Smith, D. E. (1990). Development and validation of the Competitive State Anxiety Inventory-2. In R. Martens, R. S. Vealey, and D. Burton, *Competitive anxiety in sport* (Part III, pp. 117-190). Champaign, IL: Human Kinetics.

McNair, D. M., Lorr, M., and Droppleman, L. F. (1971). *Manual for the Profile of Mood States*. San Diego: Educational and Industrial Testing Services.

Mellalieu, S. D. (2003). Mood matters: But how much? A comment on Lane and Terry (2000). *Journal of Applied Sport Psychology, 15*, 99-114.

Mellalieu, S. D., Hanton, S., and Fletcher, D. (this volume). An anxiety review. In S. Hanton and S. D. Mellalieu (Eds.), *Literature reviews in sport psychology*. Hauppauge, NY: Nova Science

Mellalieu, S. D., Hanton, S., and Jones, G. (2003). Emotional labeling and competitive anxiety in preparation and competition. *The Sport Psychologist, 17*, 157-174.

Morgan, W. P. (1980). The trait psychology controversy. *Research Quarterly for Exercise and Sport, 51*, 50-76.

Morgan, W. P. (1985). Selected psychological factors limiting performance: A mental health model. In D. H. Clarke and H. M. Eckert (Eds.), *Limits of human performance* (pp. 70-80). Champaign, IL: Human Kinetics.

Morgan, W. P., O'Connor, P. J., Ellickson, K. A., and Bradley, P. W. (1988). Personality structure, mood states, and performance in elite male distance runners. *International Journal of Sport Psychology, 19*, 247-263.

Murray, N. P., and Janelle, C. M. (2003). Anxiety and performance: A visual search examination of the processing efficiency theory. *Journal of Sport and Exercise Psychology, 25*, 171-187.

Neiss, R. (1988). Reconceptualizing arousal: Psychobiological states in motor performance. *Psychological Bulletin, 103*, 345-366.

Oatley, K., and Jenkins, J. M. (1996). *Understanding emotions*. Cambridge, MA: Blackwell Scientific.

Prapavessis, H., and Grove, J. R. (1991). Precompetitive emotions and shooting performance: The Mental Health and Zone of Optimal Function models. *The Sport Psychologist, 5*, 223-234.

Raglin, J. S. (2001). Psychological factors in sport performance: The Mental Health Model revisited. *Sports Medicine, 31*, 875-890.

Raglin, J. S., and Hanin, Y. L. (2000). Competitive anxiety. In Y. L. Hanin (Ed.), *Emotions in sport* (pp. 93-111). Champaign, IL: Human Kinetics.

Robazza, C., and Bortoli, L. (2003). Intensity, idiosyncratic content and functional impact of performance-related emotions in athletes. *Journal of Sports Sciences, 21*, 171-189.

Robazza, C., Bortoli, L., and Hanin (2004). Precompetition emotions, bodily symptoms, and task-specific qualities as predictors of performance in high-level karate athletes. *Journal of Applied Sport Psychology, 16*, 151-165.

Robazza, C., Bortoli, L., Nocini, F., Moser, G., and Arslan, C. (2000). Normative and idiosyncratic measures of positive and negative affect in sport. *Psychology of Sport and Exercise, 1*, 103-116.

Robazza, C., Bortoli, L., and Nougier, V. (1998). Performance-related emotions in skilled athletes: Hedonic tone and functional impact. *Perceptual and Motor Skills, 87*, 547-564.

Robazza, C., Bortoli, L., and Nougier, V. (1999). Emotions, heart rate, and performance in archery: A case study. *Journal of Sports Medicine and Physical Fitness, 39*, 169-176.

Robazza, C., Bortoli, L., and Nougier, V. (2000). Performance emotions in an elite archer: A case study. *Journal of Sport Behavior, 23*, 144-163.

Robazza, C., Bortoli, L., and Nougier, V. (2002). Monitoring of precompetition affect in elite Italian archers during the world championships. *International Journal of Sport Psychology, 33*, 72-97.

Robazza, C., Bortoli, L., Zadro, I., and Nougier, V. (1998). Emotions in track and field athletes: A test of the Individual Zones of Optimal Functioning model. *European Yearbook of Sport Psychology, 2*, 94-123.

Robazza, C., Pellizzari, M., and Hanin, Y. L. (2004). Emotion self-regulation and athletic performance: An application of the IZOF model. *Psychology of Sport and Exercise, 5*, 379-404.

Ruiz, M. C., and Hanin, Y. L. (2004). Metaphoric description and individualized emotion profiling of performance related states in high-level karate athletes. *Journal of Applied Sport Psychology, 16*, 258–273.

Sparkes, A., and Partington, S. (2003). Narrative practice and its potential contribution to sport psychology: The example of flow. *The Sport Psychologist, 17*, 292-317.

Spielberger, C. D., Gorsuch, R. L., and Lushene, R. E. (1970). *Manual for the State-Trait Anxiety Inventory*. Palo Alto, CA: Consulting Psychologists Press.

Spradley, J. P. (1979). *The ethnographic interview*. New York: Holt, Rinehart and Winston.

Syrjä, P., and Hanin, Y. (1997). Measurement of emotions in sport: A comparison of individualized and normative scales. In R. Lidor and M. Bar-Eli (Eds.), *Innovations in sport psychology: Linking theory and practice. Proceedings of the IX World Congress of Sport Psychology (ISSP)*, (Part II, pp. 682-684). Israel: International Society of Sport Psychology.

Tenenbaum, G., Lloyd, M., Pretty, G., and Hanin, Y. L. (2002). Congruence of actual and retrospective reports of precompetition emotions in equestrians. *Journal of Sport and Exercise Psychology, 24*, 271-288.

Terry, P. C., and Lane, A. M. (2000). Normative values for the Profile of Mood States for use with athletic samples. *Journal of Applied Sport Psychology, 12*, 93-109.

Vallerand, R. J., and Blanchard, C. M. (2000). The study of emotion in sport and exercise: Historical, definitional, and conceptual perspectives. In Y. L. Hanin (Ed.), *Emotions in sport* (pp. 3-37). Champaign, IL: Human Kinetics.

Watson, D., and Clark, L. A. (1994). Emotions, moods, traits, and temperaments: Conceptual distinctions and empirical findings. In P. Ekman and R. J. Davidson (Eds.), *The nature of emotion: Fundamental questions* (pp. 89–93). New York: Oxford University Press.

Watson, D., Clark, L. A., and Tellegen, A. (1988). Development and validation of brief measures of positive and negative affect: The PANAS scales. *Journal of Personality and Social Psychology, 54*, 1063-1070.

Watson, D., and Tellegen, A. (1985). Toward a consensual structure of mood. *Psychological Bulletin, 98*, 219-235.

Williams, J. M. (Ed.). (2001). *Applied sport psychology: Personal growth to peak performance* (4th ed.). Mountain View, CA: Mayfield.

Wilson, G. S., Raglin, J. S., and Pritchard, M. E. (2002). Optimism, pessimism, and precompetition anxiety in college athletes. *Personality and Individual Differences*, *32*, 893-902.

Woodman, T., and Hardy, L. (2001). Stress and anxiety. In R. N. Singer, H. A. Hausenblas, and C. M. Janelle (Eds.), *Handbook of sport psychology* (2nd ed., pp. 290-318). New York, NY: John Wiley and Sons.

Yerkes, R. M., and Dodson, J. D. (1908). The relation of strength of stimulus to rapidity of habit formation. *Journal of Comparative and Neurological Psychology*, *18*, 459-482.

Zaichkowsky, L. D., and Baltzell, A. (2001). Arousal and performance. In R. N. Singer, H. A. Hausenblas, and C. M. Janelle (Eds.), *Handbook of sport psychology* (2nd ed., pp. 319-339). New York, NY: John Wiley and Sons.

Zizzi, S. J., Deaner, H. R., and Hirschhorn, D. K. (2003). The relationship between emotional intelligence and performance among college basketball players. *Journal of Applied Sport Psychology*, *15*, 262-269.

In: Literature Reviews in Sport Psychology ISBN 1-59454-904-4
Editors: S. Hanton and S. D. Mellalieu, pp. 159-197 © 2006 Nova Science Publishers, Inc.

Chapter 5

CONTEMPORARY APPROACHES TO MOTIVATION IN SPORT

Kieran M. Kingston [*]
University of Wales Institute, Cardiff (UWIC), United Kingdom
Chris G. Harwood and Christopher M. Spray
Loughborough University, United Kingdom

ABSTRACT

Motivation is widely regarded as one of the central theoretical constructs within sport psychology. Its value extends beyond academia because of its consequences and the implications that motivation has for participation, performance and persistence in sport. The purpose of this chapter is to consider three (of the possible thirty plus) motivational theories that are applicable to sport. The three areas discussed are: a) self-determination theory; b) achievement goal theory; and c) approach-avoidance motivation. These theories have been selected because of their pre-eminence in contemporary motivation research in sport. For each area, the broad theoretical underpinnings are considered, current literature is reviewed, and finally directions for future research are discussed. It is our intention that these reviews will both inform, and provide impetus to further develop the field of motivation within sport psychology.

Keywords: Motivation, self-determination, achievement goals, approach-avoidance motivation.

[*] Correspondence concerning this article should be addressed to Kieran Kingston, Cardiff School of Sport, University of Wales Institute, Cardiff (UWIC), Cyncoed Road, Cardiff, CF23 6XD, United Kingdom. Tel: 00-44-2920-417-067. Fax: 00-44-2920-416-768. E-mail: kkingston@uwic.ac.uk

INTRODUCTION

Motivation is a central and perennial issue in the field of psychology, it is at the core of biological, cognitive and social regulation, and is a pre-eminent concern to those in roles that involve mobilizing others to act (Ryan and Deci, 2000). So, what is motivation? We all know what motivation is don't we? - It's the desire, that inner fire that compels one to act and persist. Definitions often, however, describe motivation according to some behavioral indices or the effects of changes in behavior purported to reflect high levels of motivation. This has led us to conclude that, perhaps more than any other concept in sport psychology, motivation suffers simply because it is such a widely used term to which we can all attach personal meaning. The simplistic view that motivation is a stable entity synonymous with arousal does not begin to capture the complexity and the richness of the process of motivation (Roberts, 2001). Furthermore, the frequently cited definition of motivation as the direction and intensity of one's effort (Sage, 1977) does little to encapsulate the multifaceted nature of motivation. The quest for a parsimonious definition of motivation that satisfies the broad spectrum of theoretical perspectives and the personal views of sport practitioners is unfortunately destined to be ultimately frustrating. The issue is that no simple definition can effectively describe or eclipse the interactional and multidimensional aspects of the volitional drive that we associate with this ubiquitous concept.

In spite of the difficulties described above, Roberts proposed that, "in the research literature motivation refers to those personality factors, social variables and/or cognitions that come into play when a person undertakes a task at which he or she is evaluated, enters into competition with others, or attempts to attain some standard of excellence." (Roberts, 1992, p. 5). While perhaps lacking succinctness, this definition does at least accommodate trait and situation-centered views of motivation and allows one to consider multiple motives for engagement. Nevertheless, despite the difficulties in locating a widely satisfactory yet simplistic definition, understanding the dynamic and complex psychological process of motivation is critical to understanding human behavior, especially in sport (Roberts, 2001). At any given moment, there may be a number of reasons or combination of reasons for an individual starting, participating and discontinuing in sport or physical activity (e.g., to have fun, to learn, to improve performance, to outperform the competition, to feel part of a group, to protect esteem). Insight into the underlying processes that underpin these reasons can help practitioners at all levels to provide a more supportive environment for initial engagement, continued participation and sporting excellence.

THE CONCEPT OF MOTIVATION

The concept of motivation broadly refers to the personal drive that leads individuals to initiate, direct and sustain human behavior. Motivation theories are based on a set of assumptions about individuals and the factors that give volition to behavior. According to Glyn Roberts, whose work has done much to illuminate the area of motivation for students and teachers, theories describing this concept refer to the why of behavior. Further, motivation is a social cognitive 'process' in which an individual becomes motivated or demotivated through evaluation of their competencies within the achievement context and the meaning of that context (Roberts, 2001).

Motivational research has tended to dominate psychology in recent times, with one-third of all studies in psychology dealing with motivation in one form or another and, according to Roberts (1992), the majority of these are either directly or indirectly applicable to the context of sport. Moreover, when one considers the past twenty years, research into motivation in sport settings has been largely dominated by social-cognitive theories emerging from the domain of educational psychology (Dweck, 1986; Maehr and Nicholls, 1980; Nicholls, 1984, 1989). These theories and models have led to significant advancements in the study of motivation, in moving from description (what, where, who and how) to deeper interpretation and inference (Lavalee et al., 2004). Whilst each social-cognitive theory may vary in their perceptions of the determinants, the level of contribution of the context, and the methods proposed to elicit change in the motivated state, there is a consensus that variations in thought patterns (cognitions) are the principle determinants of motivation in achievement contexts (Roberts, 2001). It should be noted however, that motivational theories are not limited to explaining achievement behaviors, rather they can encapsulate wider non-achievement motives, for example, Deci and Ryan's (1985, 2000) self-determination theory, Maehr and Braskamp's (1986) personal investment theory and Allen's (2003) social goal model.

Although there are at least thirty-two distinguishable theories of motivation (Roberts, 2001), the purpose of this chapter is to highlight three of the more popular and contemporary theoretical frameworks that have been used to examine motivational processes in the field of sport psychology in recent years. Taking each theory in turn, we will describe the assumptions and central tenets of each of the theoretical frameworks, highlight recent research that has utilized the theory, and identify potential areas for attention to further develop the particular areas from a research perspective. Finally, the chapter will conclude with a general discussion that considers a number of broader issues associated with the three theories as well as highlighting research that has adopted a multi-theoretical approach considering the theories simultaneously.

MULTIDIMENSIONAL INTRINSIC AND EXTRINSIC MOTIVATION: A SELF-DETERMINED PERSPECTIVE

Self-determination theory (SDT) is one of the major theoretical frameworks concerned with motivational processes (Weiss and Ferrer-Caja, 2002). Formulated by Deci (1975) and subsequently extended by Deci and Ryan (1985), SDT is a macro-theory of human motivation concerned with the development and functioning of personality within social contexts, and specifically the causes and consequences of intrinsically motivated behavior. The frequently cited cognitive evaluation theory (Deci and Ryan, 1985) is a sub-theory of the broader SDT which is concerned with the effects of factors (e.g., rewards, goals, feedback, and communication) on intrinsic motivation and the independent mediating effects of perceived competence and control. This review, however, will not examine cognitive evaluation theory specifically.

According to SDT, there are three fundamental psychological needs that are important in energizing volitional or self-determined human behavior: the needs for competence, autonomy and relatedness. These 'needs' are essential for realizing our natural propensity for growth and integration, as well as for constructive social development and personal well-being (Ryan and Deci, 2000). They might be regarded as the nutrients that permit or restrict personal social-cognitive growth.

The need for competence implies that individuals strive to interact effectively with their environment (Harter, 1978) and seek to control outcomes and experience mastery. The need for autonomy refers to the desire to be self-initiating in the regulation of one's actions (Vallerand and Losier, 1999). Finally, the need for relatedness pertains to the desire to feel connected (through relating or caring, for example) with significant others (Ryan and Deci, 2000). According to SDT, the individual's perceptions of competence, autonomy and relatedness represent psychological mediators of the impact of social events on motivation (Vallerand and Losier, 1999). Thus, the social milieu can support the feelings of integration and coherence with the environment, and promote self-determination when the three fundamental psychological needs are satisfied. Similarly, integration, coherence and in turn self-determination may be undermined when the social context fails to support the three needs. For example, negative consequences for personal growth might be expected within a context that is: excessively controlling, over-challenging or rejecting of personal integration. To summarize, contextual variables (e.g., material, social, or verbal information) that promote or are supportive of one's feeling of autonomy, competence and relatedness will have a positive impact on one's intrinsic motivation, whereas those that undermine these needs will undermine intrinsic motivation. Furthermore, because social conditions vary greatly and individuals perceive them differently, motives for engagement in an activity will vary accordingly. Consequently, Deci and Ryan (1985) proposed that different types of motivation (motivational styles) may emerge from an individual's experiences within a given activity and its social context.

Although much of the research on intrinsic and extrinsic motivation has tended to emphasize the dichotomy between these two concepts (Petherwick and Weigand, 2002), SDT considers that this dichotomy is insufficient to adequately depict human motivation (Deci and Ryan, 1985). Rather, proponents of self-determination theory view motives for engaging in activities as existing and being ordered on a continuum of self-determination.

Defining Intrinsic and Extrinsic Motivation

Intrinsic motivation refers to the impetus of an individual to engage in an activity purely for its own sake as well as the pleasure and satisfaction derived from participation in that activity (Deci and Ryan, 1985). When a person is intrinsically motivated he or she will perform the behavior voluntarily, in the absence of material rewards or external constraints (Deci and Ryan, 1985). The roots of intrinsic motivation are in the work of White (1959), who described a concept called effectance motivation, reflecting an individual's inherent motivation to achieve competence over their environment, and resulting in feelings of self-efficacy (cf. Martens and Webber, 2002). Athletes who go out to practice because they find the activity interesting and satisfying to learn more about their sport, or athletes who practice their sport for the pleasure associated with constantly striving to surpass themselves are considered intrinsically motivated toward their sport (Pelletier et al., 1995). The highest level of self-determination is postulated to be inherent in intrinsic motivation.

In contrast to intrinsic motivation, extrinsic motivation refers to engaging in an activity as a means to an end and not for its own sake (Vallerand and Fortier, 1998). When extrinsically motivated, individuals do not participate in an activity for the inherent pleasure they may experience while performing it, but rather in order to receive something positive or avoid something negative. An athlete who competes in order to win trophies and medals does so for extrinsically motivated reasons.

Deci and Ryan (1985) also proposed a third broad motivational style, amotivation. Similar to the concept of learned helplessness (Abramson et al., 1978), amotivation refers to complete lack of motivation, and thus an absence of self-determination. Behaviors are carried out for neither intrinsic, nor extrinsic reasons; there is a lack of purpose or expectation in participation (Alexandris et al., 2002). When amotivated, an athlete does not perceive contingencies between their actions and the outcomes of their actions, and no longer identify any good reasons to continue doing the sport (Vallerand, 2001).

Multidimensional Extrinsic Motivation

In contrast to the view that extrinsic motivation is invariantly controlling and antagonistic to intrinsic motivation (e.g., deCharms, 1968), self-determination theory proposes that extrinsically motivated behaviors can vary greatly in the degree to which they are volitional versus controlled (Ryan and Deci, 2000). Within their central theory, Deci and Ryan (1985), proposed a sub-theory (organismic integration theory) which, based on the process of internalization and integration, detailed different forms of extrinsic motivation and their corresponding degree of self-determination. Internalization is an active natural process in which socially sanctioned norms become personally endorsed or internalized (Deci and Ryan, 2000), and in its simplest form, the more internalized an extrinsically motivated behavior, the more volitional (self-determined) it becomes. Consequently, they identified four different types of extrinsic motivation that can be ordered along the self-determination continuum from low to high levels of autonomy respectively - external regulation, introjected regulation, identified regulation and integrated regulation.

External regulation refers to behavior that is controlled by external sources or contingencies, such as material rewards or constraints imposed by others (Deci and Ryan, 1985). Athletes who participate in sport in order to receive financial gain or to receive praise are motivated by external regulation. Introjected regulation involves taking in a regulation but not accepting it as one's own. It is a relatively controlled form of regulation in which behaviors are performed to avoid guilt or anxiety or to attain ego enhancements such as pride (Ryan and Deci, 2000). Athletes who participate in sports because they feel pressure to be in good shape for aesthetic reasons, or feel embarrassed or ashamed when they are not performing effectively, do so for motives subsumed within introjected regulation (Pelletier et al., 1995). Identified regulation is operant when the individual comes to value and judge the behavior as important and, therefore, performs it out of choice. Athletes who participate in sport because they feel their involvement contributes to a part of their growth and development, despite the fact that it may not be inherently enjoyable, display a form of identified regulation. Finally, integrated regulation is the most internalized form of extrinsic motivation in that, as well as identifying the importance of the behaviors, individuals displaying this form of regulation also engage in an activity out of choice (Vallerand and

Fortier, 1998). This choice however is not limited solely to the activity level, but rather is a consequence of the activity now being considered a harmonious part of the organization of one's self (Vallerand, 2001). For instance, the integrated athlete may decide to stay at home (rather than go out with friends) to be ready for the next day's game (Pelletier et al., 1995).

Multidimensional Intrinsic Motivation

Developing from the original work of Deci and Ryan (1985, 2000) which considered only extrinsic motivation from a multidimensional perspective, Vallerand and his colleagues (e.g., Vallerand et al., 1992, 1993) differentiated between three types of intrinsic motivation that represented qualitatively different (yet potentially reciprocal) motives for engaging in an activity. This tripartite taxonomy is based on research studies that have revealed the presence of three clearly distinguishable types of intrinsic motivation and these have subsequently been studied on an independent basis (Pelletier et al., 1995). Each equal in their levels of self-determination, the three types of intrinsic motivation identified are: intrinsic motivation to know, intrinsic motivation towards accomplishments, and intrinsic motivation to experience stimulation.

Intrinsic motivation to know relates to several constructs such as exploration, curiosity, learning goals, and the innate need to know and understand (Pelletier et al., 1995, Vallerand and Fortier, 1998). It can be defined as performing an activity for the pleasure and the satisfaction derived from learning, exploring or trying to understand something (Vallerand, 2001). Intrinsic motivation towards accomplishments can be defined as engaging in an activity for the pleasure and satisfaction experienced when one attempts to accomplish or create something (Weiss and Ferrer-Caja, 2002). According to Vallerand (2001), intrinsic motivation towards accomplishments has been studied in other fields of psychology under such terms as mastery motivation (Kagan, 1972) and task orientation (Nicholls, 1992). Finally, intrinsic motivation to experience stimulation occurs when someone engages in an activity in order to experience stimulating sensations derived from one's engagement in the activity. Athletes who participate in their sport in order to live exciting experiences are intrinsically motivated to experience stimulation (Pelletier et al., 1995).

Towards Research from a Multidimensional Perspective

From the early work of Ryan (1977, 1980) examining the impact of sport scholarships on intrinsic motivation, there have been a plethora of studies that have examined the effects of personal and environmental variables upon intrinsic and extrinsic motivation in this context (see Vallerand, 2001, for a review). In terms of contextual factors (e.g., motivational climate, scholarships, leadership styles, parents, coaches), it is generally considered that those that are perceived as controlling (directing of individual behavior) undermine intrinsic motivation and identified regulation (one of the more self-determined forms of extrinsic motivation) towards sport and exercise, whereas those which encourage initiative and autonomy facilitate these aspects (cf. Vallerand, 2001). With regards to the consequences of various types of motivation, in their review of the self-determination paradigm, Vallerand and Losier (1999), argued that the most positive outcomes (e.g., positive affect, sportspersonship and persistence) should result from more self-determined motivational styles (intrinsic motivation and identified regulation), while negative outcomes should be a consequence of the least or non self-determined styles (external regulation, and especially amotivation).

While much of the research described has helped to further our understanding of intrinsic and extrinsic motivation in sport, it could be argued that a more precise picture of the relationship between motivation and cognitive, affective and behavioral factors can best be acquired through considering, simultaneously, intrinsic and extrinsic motivation from a multi, rather than a uni-dimensional perspective. Consequently, only studies that have utilized this approach will be considered within this brief review of contemporary research.

Research into contextual sports motivation adopting a multidimensional perspective has focused on the cognitive, affective and/or behavioral consequences of the different types of intrinsic and extrinsic motivation, as well as differences based on various categories of athletes' (e.g., gender, success level, competitive structure). According to Vallerand and Fortier (1998), there are four contextual measures of intrinsic and extrinsic motivation that have been developed in the sport and exercise domain. Only one, the Sport Motivation Scale (SMS; Pelletier et al., 1995), however, is applicable to a 'normal' population and is both multidimensional and largely congruent with the framework of self-determination theory.

The SMS is theoretically consistent with the self-determination continuum implicit in Deci and Ryan's theory (Martens and Webber, 2002) and comprises seven subscales (each of four items) assessing three forms of extrinsic motivation (identified, introjected, and external regulation), and amotivation, and the three types of intrinsic motivation congruent with Vallerand's tripartite taxonomy (to know, to accomplish things, and to experience stimulation). Although Deci and Ryan (1985) also included integrated regulation as one type of extrinsic motivation within self-determination theory, it was not included in the SMS as pilot data attempting to validate the scale revealed that integrated regulation was not a distinguishable reason for participating in sport (Brière, Vallerand, Blais, and Pelletier, 1995).

One of the first studies utilizing a multidimensional perspective (Fortier et al., 1995) examined sport structures (competitive versus recreational) with a sample of 399 mixed gender Canadian athletes (mean age 19.0 years). Their data indicated that athletes involved within a competitive structure had lower levels of intrinsic motivation (for stimulation and toward accomplishments), and higher levels of identified regulation and amotivation, than those involved within a recreational structure. Although the finding that athletes within the competitive structure had higher levels of self-determined extrinsic motivation (identified regulation), was somewhat counterintuitive, the authors reasoned that this may be due to competitive athletes' being highly committed to their sport and therefore, coming to identify themselves with, and accepting of their choice to be involved and invest heavily in this 'competitive' structure.

Vlachopoulos et al. (2000) looking at participant motivation in a sample (n=557) of mixed ability and mixed gender (55% male, 45% female) sport participants, assessed the effect of motivational styles (measured using the SMS), on cognitive, affective and behavioral outcomes using a profile approach to cluster sport participants into statistically distinguishable groups. It emerged that those sport participants who held a combination of high self-determined (exceeding the median score for all three types of intrinsic motivation and identified regulation) *and* high less or non self-determined (exceeding the median for introjected regulation, external regulation and amotivation) motives for participation scored higher on outcome variables (e.g., enjoyment, effort, positive affect, positive attitude towards participation) than those individuals who had high self-determined motives (intrinsic motivation to accomplish and to experience stimulation), yet lower levels of less or non self-determined motives (i.e., introjected regulation, external regulation and amotivation). These findings support the view that at a contextual level there may be an additive relationship between intrinsic and extrinsic motivation (Vallerand and Fortier, 1998).

Recently, Kingston et al. (2006) compared the motivational profiles of a mixed gender (n=82 male, n=90 female) sample of scholarship and non-scholarship collegiate athletes (n=172) from a variety of US colleges (n=7). Utilizing discriminant function analysis, the results indicated that the motivational style profiles (formed using the SMS) could effectively discriminate between scholarship and non-scholarship athletes (73% correctly classified on the basis of their responses to the SMS). Specifically, those athletes receiving greater than half-scholarships had lower levels of intrinsic motivation (for stimulation, and accomplishment), and higher levels of extrinsic motivation (introjected and external regulation) than non-scholarship athletes. These findings suggest that rewards such as scholarships may foster less self-determined forms of sport motivation.

Specifically regarding gender, Fortier and associates found that females in their sample of competitive and recreational athletes had higher levels of intrinsic motivation towards accomplishments and self-determined extrinsic motivation (identified regulation) than males, but lower levels of external regulation (least self-determined extrinsic motivation) and amotivation (Fortier et al., 1995). Similarly, Petherick and Weigand (2002), found in their sample of 11-19 year old swimmers (n=177), that males had higher levels of non self-determined extrinsic motivation (introjected regulation and external regulation) than females. Finally, in their study of scholarship athletes, Kingston et al. (2006), found females to have higher levels of intrinsic motivation for stimulation and lower levels of the least self-determined forms of extrinsic motivation (introjected regulation and external regulation) than their male counterparts. Although the SMS has become the measurement scale of choice to examine contextual sport motivation, it should be recognized that a number of authors have had cause to question the psychometric integrity of at least one of the subscales (see for example, Martens and Webber, 2002). This has led to the development of possible alternative measures of motivational style, for example the Behavioural Regulation in Sport Questionnaire (BRSQ; Lonsdale, 2005).

To summarize, preliminary research in sport adopting a multidimensional perspective to studying intrinsic and extrinsic motivation at a contextual level suggests that: competitive athletes engage in sport for both more self-determined *and* less or non self-determined reasons; secondly, athletes with these combined motivational style profiles appear to be more motivationally adaptive (e.g., in terms of positive responses for enjoyment, effort, positive affect, positive attitude towards participation); and thirdly, certain competitive structures and rewards may foster less self-determined motivational styles. With respect to gender, there is some evidence to suggest that the motivational styles of females are more self-determined than those of males. Specifically, they have less of a tendency to perceive that their behavior related to sport activities is controlled by external contingencies such as rewards (e.g., to receive financial gain or praise).

Discussion of Multidimensional Approaches

This section sought to review material that has examined multidimensional sport motivation at a contextual level of generality. In congruence with the suggestions of Deci and Ryan (1985), it is apparent that moving beyond a simple dichotomy between intrinsic and extrinsic motivation furthers our understanding of motivation in sport settings. The initial work of Deci and Ryan (1985) conceptualized the self-determination continuum and identified (in their organismic integration theory) the four distinct forms of extrinsic motivation. This multidimensional approach has been has been extended by Vallerand and associates to encapsulate the various types of intrinsic motivation. Pelletier et al.'s (1995) initial work and that of Li and Harmer (1996) in particular, provide compelling evidence that the conceptualization of more and less self-determined motives for participation can be supported empirically.

In line with many of the early studies into intrinsic and extrinsic motivation, there is a consensus within the research body that social factors which inhibit feelings of autonomy, competence and relatedness undermine intrinsic motivation and lead to maladaptive motivation patterns, whereas those social factors that facilitate these needs enhance intrinsic motivation and lead to a more adaptive motivation pattern. The research using a multidimensional conceptualization of intrinsic and extrinsic motivation generally supports these predictions, however, it is becoming apparent that positive versus negative motivational affect may be less to do with about absolute levels of intrinsic and extrinsic motivation, and more associated with the degree to which contextual factors create a perception that behaviors are autonomous versus controlled (i.e., the extent to which they support or undermine self-determination and effect the three basic needs of autonomy, competence and relatedness). The work of Vlachopoulos et al. (2000) appears to illuminate this issue, in suggesting that combinations of high levels of both self-determined and non self-determined motives are the most adaptive in terms of cognitive, affective and behavioral outcomes. Nevertheless, it may seem somewhat paradoxical to advocate a coaching climate that fosters greater self-determination (via competence, autonomy, and relatedness), and at the same time supports the facilitation of less self-determined motives via the same mechanisms. This issue, however, becomes less contentious when we consider that the motivational styles are orthogonal and therefore it is meaningful for performers to engage for multiple reasons that can vary in their degree of self-determination. For example, one may consider the prospect of playing in a big game with one eye on the external rewards that accompany successful performance (external regulation), yet equally spend a greater amount of time practicing alone on a specific, perhaps mundane skill because it is judged important for the good of the team (identified regulation). Indeed, it might be logical to consider that motivational styles associated with higher levels of self-determination have a buffering effect against the potential negative influence of less self-determined motivational styles, paralleling some of the suggestions from achievement goals research with regards to the buffering effects of task orientation (e.g., Roberts et al., 1996), clearly research is required to confirm this contention.

The competitive environment of sport is often associated with external rewards which encourage normative comparisons of ability. This primary concern towards obtaining favorable judgments regarding ability rather than learning or personal improvement may lead to less self-determined motives and diminish intrinsic motivation. Environments therefore, may need to provide informational feedback rather than potentially controlling feedback (i.e., informational feedback concerning ability; cf. Petherick and Weigand, 2002). To this end and in line with the suggestions of Fortier et al. (1995), cognitive evaluation theory (Deci and Ryan, 1985) could be extended to encompass other types of motivation besides intrinsic motivation (namely less self-determined forms of extrinsic motivation and amotivation). This would help to determine the extent to which social 'events' have the potential to undermine or increase intrinsic motivation as well as less self-determined extrinsic motivation and amotivation. Finally, it is important, that amotivation is further studied, possibly in accordance with a multidimensional viewpoint.

Vallerand (2001) has recently argued that the hierarchical model of intrinsic and extrinsic motivation (Vallerand, 1997) provides both an integrative framework and permits the adoption of new perspectives in the study of intrinsic and extrinsic motivation in sport settings. Clearly, this approach represents a major conceptual development in the study of motivation within the context of physical activities. However, while we acknowledge that intrinsic and extrinsic motivation need to be considered within the individual beyond the contextual level that we have taken here (i.e., at a situational and global level also), we have made the decision not to review or explicitly examine these aspects of Vallerand's model for the simple reason that we could not do it justice within the remit of this section (for an excellent review on the proposed hierarchical model, see Vallerand, 2001). This given, it is important to acknowledge that consideration for the issue of generality is central for understanding the impact of social factors on motivation within sport and exercise settings.

Future Research Directions Related to Multidimensional Approaches

To draw to a close this section on multidimensional sport motivation from a self determination perspective, a number of potential research directions might be considered as the mechanism through which our further understanding of multidimensional intrinsic and extrinsic motivation can be facilitated.

Recent research has highlighted the potential predictive ability of perceived competence to the more self-determined forms of sport motivation (Standage et al., 2003). Consequently, specific research is required which examines the motivational impact of more and less or non self-determined motives for engagement in sport, and to consider the role of perceived competence in this research. This research can be expanded to determine whether clusters or combinations of more and less self-determined motives for engagement can delineate between groups and/or predict adaptive and maladaptive cognitions.

Secondly, but related to the above, and similar to the suggestions of Roberts et al. (1996) with respect to goal orientations, it is important to examine the potential buffering effects of high levels of more self-determined motives for engagement against the potentially debilitating effects of high levels of non or less self-determined reasons for engagement in sports. Furthermore, research should consider the potential for temporal variations in motives. For example, initial engagement in an activity for predominantly less self-determined motives may, as a consequence of the process of internalization result in engagement for more self-determined reasons. The potential exists therefore, for motives to become more adaptive with the passage of time.

Thirdly, although, the psychometric integrity of the SMS appears generally robust, there are consistent concerns with the identified regulation subscale in particular. Further refinement of this, or the development of alternative measurement tools (e.g., Lonsdale's BRSQ) may therefore be required to ensure effective assessment of motivational styles. Additionally research needs to be carried out on the integrated regulation subscale, to determine if this aspect of self determined extrinsic motivation can indeed, and contrary to Briere et al.'s initial development work, be identified as an empirically distinguishable motive for participating in sport.

Fourthly, the three forms of extrinsic motivation lie, according to self-determination theory, on a continuum of self-determination which is anchored at either end by intrinsic motivation and amotivation (at the higher and lower ends of self-determination respectively). Consequently it is conceptually meaningful for researchers to weight the different types of extrinsic motivation according to their placement on the self-determination continuum and combine the different subscales into a relative autonomy (or self-determination) index (see Vallerand, 2001). Further research is required to identify the actual weightings of the multidimensional extrinsic (and perhaps intrinsic) constructs within the index of self-determination (relative autonomy index). This would illuminate the predictive qualities of motivational types on motivational consequences.

Finally, it is important to consider the effects on participants experience and motivation of the environment and social context. For example, are motivational styles amenable to change through interventions with performers directly or indirectly through the environment (for example, coaching styles, and motivational climate)? Secondly, since sport is both an achievement and social domain (Allen, 2003), it may be important to consider further the salience of social relations to the motivational styles of participants. Clearly these types of questions require more longitudinal type studies with controlled interventions in externally valid sport environments to be addressed effectively. Certainly this represents a challenge for researchers, but the potential contribution to the coaching and participation motivation literature would be significant.

ACHIEVEMENT GOAL THEORY

Achievement goals represent the meaning that individuals assign to achievement situations, providing a cognitive structure that organizes an individual's definitions of success and failure, their attributions, affective reactions and subsequent behavior. The central objectives for researchers interested in achievement goal approaches have been to understand more precisely what achievement goals exist, the mechanisms by which they are developed and adopted, and the subsequent influence that they have on psychological factors associated with participation and performance.

In the late 1970's and early 1980's, the work in classroom settings of John Nicholls, Carol Dweck and Martin Maehr provided the early foundation for our understanding of achievement goals in sport, and readers are encouraged to access these original papers (Dweck, 1986; Maehr and Nicholls, 1980; Nicholls, 1984, 1989). Within the educational context both Nicholls and Dweck developed similar, but 'competing' theories with their own conceptual nuances. In sport settings, through the original works of Glyn Roberts (1984, 1992) and Joan Duda (1987), it has been Nicholls' theoretical approach to achievement goals that has acted as the conduit for the vast majority of our research.

Nicholls' Achievement Goal Theory

Achievement goals, according to Nicholls, represent how people define success when they engage in achievement tasks for the purposes of demonstrating favorable perceptions of physical ability (often used interchangeably with the term 'competence'). He maintained that the demonstration of physical ability was a central achievement motive but also proposed that ability could be construed by individuals in two different manners. First, ability can be judged high or low with reference to the individual's own past performance or knowledge, and in this context, gains in mastery indicate competence. Second, ability can be judged as capacity relative to that of others, where a gain in mastery alone does not indicate high ability. To demonstrate high capacity, one must achieve more with equal effort or use less effort than do others for an equal performance (Nicholls, 1984).

These two conceptions of ability identified by Nicholls underpin two contrasting achievement goals. When gains in personal mastery of a skill or task offer a sense of competence to the individual, they are said to be task involved. In other words, when perceived self-improvement is sufficient to generate a sense of personal achievement, this is indicative of an individual pursuing a task involved goal. In contrast, an individual is said to be ego involved when they derive a sense of physical competence by either demonstrating superior performance to others, or via an equal performance to others but with less effort exhibited. Clearly, both achievement goals revolve around the nature of the self-concept. When an individual is in a state of task involvement, his/her main focus is on the development of the self irrespective of others. When in a state of ego involvement, the perceived ability of the self compared to others is the primary concern.

The Development of Achievement Goals

Nicholls' initial work focused upon the developmental processes through which young children from 6 to 11 years of age differentiated the concepts of ability, effort, task difficulty and luck (Nicholls and Miller, 1984). This research revealed how young children move through a temporal process whereby, within a given achievement situation, they can conceptualize ability in the two different manners. In the early stages from 5 to 7 years of age, children conceptualize ability as effort. This reflects an undifferentiated state, often referred to as an undifferentiated conception of ability. In this state, demonstrations of ability are simply equated with trying hard, learning and understanding something more fully (Nicholls, 1989). This undifferentiated state is associated with task involvement. They move through a series of cognitive-developmental stages and around the age of 12 years are able to conceptualize ability as a capacity. This conceptualization is reflected in their understanding of normative task difficulty and their ability to fully differentiate the concepts of ability, effort and luck. When children achieve this mature understanding of ability, they are capable for the first time of being ego-involved. Nicholls emphasizes that the key to maintaining optimal motivation comes from fostering task involvement even after children become capable of being ego involved. Children who employ an ego orientation perceive that ability now sets the limit on what effort can accomplish, and exerting high effort is simply not enough for them to feel successful (see Fry, 2001, for a detailed discussion of this process in the sport domain).

Achievement Goal Orientations

Nicholls supported the existence of two orthogonal goal orientations that reflected "individual differences in proneness to different types of involvement" (1989, p. 95). As a result of socialization experiences in childhood and adolescence, he suggested that individuals develop a tendency to become task and/or ego involved in any particular achievement situation. This meant that individuals could vary in their levels of each goal orientation. For example, they could possess a high level of task orientation and a low level of ego orientation, or perhaps any of the other three most basic combinations (i.e., hi-task/hi-ego; lo-task/hi-ego; lo-task/lo-ego). Nicholls never studied these in his own research, however, the dispositional combinations, popularly termed 'goal profiles' (Fox, Goudas, Biddle, Duda, and Armstrong, 1994) have since been studied more closely in sport (see later section). It is these dispositional goal orientations that have become the main focus of research in sport.

When the differentiation process is complete, Nicholls (1989) proposed that the adoption of task and ego involved goals for a specific activity would rest upon an individual's dispositional goal orientations and the nature of the achievement environment (i.e., motivational climate; Ames, 1992b) in which the individual found him or herself. For example, an individual may have a stronger tendency for ego involvement than task involvement (i.e., a higher ego orientation, lower task orientation profile) in how s/he generally approaches achievement situations. However, if placed in an environment where working on improving skills is highly valued and recognition is given purely for personal improvement and effort exerted (i.e., a mastery [task] involving motivational climate), the individual's conception of ability for that particular situation may be duly influenced. What achievement means to the achiever for that specific context reflects the importance of mastering skills and trying hard – hence a state of task involvement and pursuit of a task involved goal. What, therefore, does the pursuit of task and ego involved goals mean for the individual?

The Meaning of Achievement Goals

The principal message from Nicholls' body of research in education is that when an individual experiences a state of task involvement, a positive and adaptive pattern of cognitive, emotional and behavioral responses is likely to emerge. The individual will engage in positive achievement striving through effort, persistence, challenging task choices, and intrinsic motivation (Nicholls, 1984). At a general level, individuals high in task orientation would also have a positive belief and value structure about sport as a whole, including the causes of success in sport, its role and purpose in society, and the moral behaviors associated with such pursuits (Duda, 1993, 2001).

Nicholls suggested that a similar pattern of responses could be expected by the individual in a state of ego involvement, but only on the proviso that the individual maintained a high perception of ability. In simple terms, an athlete whose perception of himself is dependent upon winning and is confident of doing so, he is likely to approach the task and try at least hard enough to win. His sense of self in achievement terms is perceived to be less under threat. However, when perceptions of ability are lower, Nicholls suggested a more negative pattern of psychological responses including lesser motivated behaviors, external attributions, greater stress, and a less than adaptive stance on the role and purpose of sport, including morally unacceptable behaviors within such a domain (e.g., cheating, intention to injure, legitimacy of injurious acts)

Nicholls' predictions have been tested vigorously in the achievement context of sport over the past 15 years led largely by the research teams of Glyn Roberts and Joan Duda (see Duda, 2001; Roberts, 1992; 2001, for specific reviews). It is these various avenues of research to which we now turn.

Achievement Goal Research in the Sport Domain

Of the immense amount of research conducted on Nicholls' achievement goal theory, the vast majority has focused on understanding both the psychological *antecedents* and *implications* of task and ego orientations *or* of being task and/or ego-involved in specific sport or physical task situations. The measurement of task and ego goals in sport has largely comprised assessments of task and ego goal orientations, using two principle scales: The Task and Ego Orientation in Sport Questionnaire (TEOSQ; Duda and Nicholls, 1992); and the Perceptions of Success Questionnaire (POSQ; Roberts et al., 1998). Both of these scales have demonstrated a reliable internal structure over a large number of studies investigating both the determinants and consequences of goal orientations (see Duda, 2001; Duda and Whitehead, 1998; Roberts, 2001).

Participation and performance-related factors in sport such as effort exerted, achievement beliefs, attributional style, learning and achievement strategies, enjoyment and intrinsic interest, anxiety and coping, moral behaviors and psychological skills have all been significantly associated with task and ego goals. This body of literature essentially forms an attempt by researchers to explain both the positive and negative roles that certain achievement goals may play in human functioning in the context of sport. In addition, as researchers have become knowledgeable and reflective of the application of the theory to sport, there has been an increased focus on the measurement of achievement goals and the interventions to effect positive motivational change in athletes. The following section presents a review of what we consider to be the most interesting and more contemporary topics from this menu of research.

Beliefs, Cognitive States and Affective Responses

Studies focused on identifying relationships between goal orientations and belief systems, cognitive content, enjoyment/interest and emotional responses in athletes have been plentiful. Task orientation is consistently linked to the belief that hard work is a cause of success in sport (Duda and Nicholls, 1992; Duda and White, 1992; Lochbaum and Roberts, 1993; Roberts and Ommundsen, 1996), and that the purposes of sport are to foster mastery, co-operation and social responsibility. Further, a high task orientation has been associated with greater enjoyment, reported satisfaction and intrinsic interest in sport (Duda, Chi, Newton, Walling, and Catley, 1995; Ntoumanis and Biddle, 1999), as well as experiencing a flow state in sport (Jackson and Roberts, 1992). In contrast, an ego orientation has been associated with the belief that high ability and deceptive strategies (e.g., cheating) lead to success (Duda and Nicholls, 1992; Roberts, Treasure, and Kavussanu, 1996) and that the purposes of sport revolve around enhancing popularity, wealth and social status (Duda, 1989; Roberts and Ommundsen, 1996). When combined with a high task orientation, researchers found a positive relationship between ego orientation and levels of enjoyment (Biddle, Akande, Vlachopoulos, and Fox, 1996), however, much of the remaining research has found either negative relationships or no relationships between an ego orientation and enjoyment, intrinsic interest and satisfaction (see Biddle, Wang, Kavusannu, and Spray, 2003).

Of interest to coaches and practitioners in competitive settings is an awareness of the links between achievement goals and anxiety responses in athletes (see Hall and Kerr, 1997; Newton and Duda, 1995). Hall and Kerr found ego orientation to be a significant predictor of pre-competitive cognitive anxiety in young fencers. Correlations between ego orientation and cognitive anxiety for fencers with low perceived ability were positive and very high two days, one day and 30 minutes prior to competition. Task orientation scores were negatively associated, indicating that increasing levels of task orientation were associated with *lower* cognitive anxiety. Similar findings for ego orientation have emerged for concentration disruption (White and Zellner, 1996) and cognitive interference (Hatzigeorgiardis and Biddle, 1999) where "thoughts of escape" during a competition were less likely to be reported by highly task oriented snooker and tennis players, but more likely for ego oriented players with low perceived competence.

Recent research has also studied how athletes cope with stress and anxiety. Ntoumanis, Biddle, and Haddock (1999) found that task orientation was associated with the use of problem-solving coping strategies, such as trying hard, seeking social support and curtailing competing activities. Those athletes with a high ego orientation were more likely to use the emotion-focused strategy of "venting emotions", including getting upset, losing ones cool and letting out negative feelings.

Information Processing, Learning and Achievement Strategies

An innovative avenue of research has begun to establish how task and ego goals impact upon skill development and performance via examining how practice strategies, use of feedback and information processing differ according to levels of task and ego orientation. High levels of task orientation have been associated with valuing practice and committing to it for skill development reasons, whereas high levels of ego orientation have been linked to endorsements of avoiding practice and preferring simply to compete (Lochbaum and Roberts, 1993; Roberts and Ommundsen, 1996). Cury, Famose, and Sarrazin (1997) investigated how athletes high in task and ego orientation used the opportunities for feedback in different manners on a basketball dribbling task. When offered the opportunity to receive personal feedback to aid their skill development and performance, athletes high in ego orientation who doubted their ability refused to take-up the opportunity. Those high in ego orientation who were confident of their ability preferred only normative information (i.e., did I win?), and refused the opportunity of receiving self-referenced feedback and information on strategies to help them improve. Athletes high in task orientation sought out both self-referent feedback on levels of personal progress as well as information tips on how to improve their dribbling score. This prompted Cury and his colleagues (1997) to suggest that a highly ego-involved participant is not interested in learning even if he/she has tools on hand allowing him/her to progress and perform better. Moreover, if difficulties arise in this situation the participant rejects all information (most notably task information) which may be important, and thus exhibiting a learned helpless psychological state.

In a similar line of research, Thill and Brunel (1995) found that highly task involved soccer players engaged in more spontaneous and deeper processing of information when they received either positive or negative feedback on their performance than highly ego involved players. They concluded that highly ego involved athletes allocate mental resources to 'how they compare' and 'the consequences', leaving little capacity to be allocated to focusing on how to improve the task and learn – which is exactly the manner in which task involved players use the information.

Finally, recent studies by Berlant and Weiss (1997), Cumming, Hall, Harwood, and Gammage (2002), Harwood, Cumming, and Hall (2003) and Harwood, Cumming, and Fletcher (2004) have explored how goal orientations relate to the use of psychological strategies such as imagery in sport. Cumming and colleagues showed how young athletes who ranged from moderate-to-high in both task and ego orientation reported using more imagery and mental rehearsal than athletes with lower levels of both goal orientations. Athletes with this profile reported engaging in imagery associated with both skill mastery and winning in preparation for competition; these imagery functions being closely associated to the nature and level of their task and ego goal orientations. Harwood et al.'s (2004) study revealed how elite young athletes high in both goal orientations reported using goal setting, imagery, and self-talk strategies in practice and competition significantly more than other goal orientation profiles. Whilst continued research on understanding the exact cognitive-behavioral functioning of high task/high ego orientation athletes is required, these studies support certain proactive qualities of an ego orientation provided it is counterbalanced by a high task orientation (see later section).

Achievement Goals and Moral Behaviors

Duda (2001) refers to research linking task goals and task-involving climates to healthful sport including; physically active lifestyles, the prevention of eating disorders, to group processes such as effective leadership and team cohesion. However, one area of research that has received more consistent attention has been the link between achievement goals and moral behaviors. A number of studies have examined whether goal orientations relate to indices of fair play and sportspersonship such as, intentions to; take illegal advantage, break the rules, promote aggression, endorse intentionally injurious acts, and cheating per se (Carpenter and Yates, 1997; Duda, Olson, and Templin, 1991; Dunn and Dunn, 1999; Kavussanu and Roberts, 2001). The majority of studies in this area support Nicholls' (1989) predictions that those athletes with a high ego orientation and low task orientation are more likely to engage in unsportspersonlike behaviors, and take any advantage to ensure that they achieve their normative goal.

The Case for Ego Orientations: Goal Profiling Research

A key limitation of exploratory research throughout the 1990's was that studies tended to focus on investigating the correlates of each goal orientation separately as opposed to examining the athlete as an individual who possessed certain levels of each goal orientation . For example, to say that task orientation is positively correlated with 'good behavior' and ego orientation is positively correlated with 'bad behavior' oversimplifies reality a great deal. As task and ego goal orientations are largely independent of each other, the question arises, what behavioral pattern would an athlete exhibit if s/he was high or low in both goal orientations?

Whilst early correlational research failed to closely examine this interaction of the two goal orientations, recent studies have examined the athlete's achievement motivation as a two-part whole and considered both goal orientations in combination. This trend or method in data analysis is commonly referred to as goal profiling and it has emerged as popular feature of the research process in the last decade (see Cumming et al., 2002; Fox, Goudas, Biddle, Duda, and Armstrong, 1994; Harwood et al., 2003; Hodge and Petlichkoff, 2000; Roberts et al., 1996; White, 1998). As a collective body of evidence, the findings from these studies attest to the potential benefits of moderate-to-high task orientations combined with similar or corresponding levels of ego orientation. For example, Hodge and Petlichkoff (2000) found that athletes reporting this 'complementary balance' of both the desire to demonstrate superior abilities over others and to develop through personal mastery appeared to have the edge in terms of self-concept and perceived ability compared to other profiles. Ultimately, the cluster of studies that have investigated athlete goal profiles tend to endorse the beneficial role of a task orientation, but also show that a high ego orientation is not necessarily detrimental (rather the opposite in fact) provided that it is 'buffered' by a high task orientation.

Investigations of Achievement Goals at the Situational Level

The majority of studies presented thus far have explored the psychological implications of achievement goals at a dispositional level (i.e., goal orientations). Nevertheless, perhaps the most challenging research remains with the antecedents and assessment of achievement goals at the situational level. As motivational researchers, we need to understand more fully how the achievement goal states of task and/or ego involvement are activated, and what cognitive, affective and behavioral effects are associated with the performer in a specific achievement situation.

One research method has been to experimentally manipulate achievement goal states by providing task or ego involving feedback and information about a particular achievement task to a participant for the purpose of inducing an actual state of task or ego involvement (e.g., Hall, 1990). However, this technique does not account for the potential power of a participant's goal orientation, and actual states of task and ego involvement were neither reported nor checked. Attempts to measure achievement goal states have also been made in pre-competition circumstances by altering the stem of the TEOSQ to read with relevance to that context (see Harwood, 2002; Williams, 1998), or by using more crude but practical single item measures of achievement goals just prior to performance (see Harwood and Swain, 1998; Swain and Harwood, 1996).

For example, work with elite swimmers and tennis players (Harwood and Swain, 1998; Swain and Harwood, 1996) have demonstrated that reported pre-competition levels of task and ego-involvement were predicted not only by dispositional goal orientation, but also by situational factors. In tennis, these included expectancy of winning the match, the perceived importance and value of the match, and players' perceptions of the achievement goal most preferred and recognized by parents, coaches and the national governing body in the context of that match. These studies represent the few that have attempted to investigate the determinants of achievement goal states reported within one hour of actual competition. The findings of these studies do complement dispositional research where athletes perceptions of significant others' goal orientations (i.e., parents; coach) have been associated with their own levels of task and ego orientation (see Duda and Hom, 1993; Ebbeck and Becker, 1994; Escarti, Roberts, Cervello, and Guzman, 1999). Qualitative research into the antecedents of task and ego involvement has also provided a very thorough range of sources through in-depth interviews and case histories (see Harwood and Swain, 2001; Krane, Greenleaf, and Snow, 1997).

Finally, an idiographic method of accessing states of task and ego involvement 'in performance' has been to use retrospective recall of achievement goal states immediately after performance using video. Smith and Harwood (2001) tracked a professional tennis player over four tournament matches. One hour after the match, the player was taken through his videotaped performance point by point, responding to single item questions that accessed his achievement goals, cognitions and levels of performance satisfaction. The study across each match found that levels of task and ego involvement fluctuated during specific games according to point importance and value in terms of outcome. For example, higher levels of ego involvement and lower task involvement were reported on game and break points, and during the latter stages of a set compared to points early in games. This in-depth analysis provided a detailed insight into the dynamics of the player's goal states in specific match situations compared with the information gathered from merely dispositional or pre-match assessments of achievement goals.

Overall, the literature on achievement goal states is far less prominent than achievement goal orientations, yet it remains a domain in great need of sophisticated field-based research that explores the transience of goal states and their associated implications. Such research would help further sell the practical relevance of the theory to coaches and practitioners.

Intervention Studies within Achievement Goal Theory

With the plethora of research supporting the development of a task orientation, researchers have been encouraged towards intervention projects that essentially 'put achievement goal theory into practice' (Duda, 1993). However, when reviewing the amount of empirical and theoretically-based intervention programs that have applied insights from achievement goal studies, the body of published research remains surprisingly limited. Studies by Goudas, Biddle, Fox, and Underwood (1995), Lloyd and Fox (1992), and Theeboom, DeKnop, and Weiss (1995) have investigated the motivational responses of sport participants to task or ego involving teaching styles or learning conditions, with task involving styles found to be most adaptive. Nonetheless, individual field-based interventions that have attempted to specifically enhance the achievement goals of athletes remain sparse.

Most recently, a study by Harwood and Swain (2002) incorporated three one to one interventions with junior national tennis players targeted not only at enhancing their task involvement for competitive matches, but also at encouraging a complementary balance between their task and ego goals. Resourced by their qualitative findings (Harwood and Swain, 2001), the multimodal intervention program actively involved coaches and parents in educational and behavior change activities, alongside individual tasks for the players. Following the three-month intervention, results showed increases in pre-competition task involvement, self-regulation and lower perceptions of threat/higher perceptions of challenge in response to a series of matches with highly ego-involving 'stimuli'. Furthermore, although players reported states of ego involvement, the goal of winning in order to approve themselves and maintain face to others (i.e., social approval ego involvement) was heavily reduced post-intervention.

Recent Commentaries on Achievement Goal Research

A recent systematic review of merely the correlates of achievement goal orientations in sport and physical activity contexts uncovered 98 studies of an accumulated 21,076 participants (see Biddle, Wang, Kavussanu, and Spray, 2003). The sheer density of published research in achievement goal theory inevitably causes researchers to reflect upon the state of the field as far as the theory operates in sport settings. As achievement goal research begins to plateau, comprehensive reviews of theory and research have been afforded most recently by Duda (2001), Duda and Hall (2001), and Roberts (2001) and these are important reference sources for achievement goal enthusiast. In addition, Harwood (2002) presented some important caveats for both researchers and practitioners when employing the TEOSQ and POSQ to assess the achievement goals of athletes in competitive sport. He presented arguments against using these measures for diagnostic purposes by showing how elevations and decreases in reported dispositional goal orientations occur merely as a function of context (e.g., sport, competition, practice settings). He addressed the need for sport psychologists to consider more sensitive, contextual methods of measurement, as well as to include qualitative techniques in order to gain a comprehensive understanding of the athlete's motivational profile.

The application of achievement goal theory to sport has not progressed without a fair share of critique. Harwood, Hardy, and Swain (2000) and Harwood and Hardy (2001) raised a number of conceptual and measurement issues associated with the continued progress of the theory within competitive sports. A number of these issues focused upon clearer definitions and corrections in terminology, as well as questioning the two-dimensional view of achievement goals. Specifically, Harwood and colleagues proposed that task involvement could comprise two distinctly different achievement states. They offered the term 'task involvement-product' to reflect a state where a subjective sense of achievement rests upon adequate mastery, improvement and favorable perceptions of intraindividual performance as an end product. In contrast, they forwarded the term 'task involvement-process' to represent the more traditional notion of a task goal where a sense of achievement is derived merely from perceptions of effort exerted, task understanding and learning without necessarily any objective improvements in task performance. Harwood et al. (2000) proposed that failing to experience a sense of definite intraindividual improvement or mastery (i.e., task-product), particularly at higher levels of sport, can be as motivationally crippling over the long haul as failing to outperform others (i.e., ego involvement). Only with a high level of task involvement-process, where the source of achievement stems purely from task investment (e.g., consistent effort) and perceived learning (e.g., improved strategic decision making), would an individual athlete be able to deal with the non-achievement of task-product or ego involved goals. A key point to Harwood and associates argument was that traditional measurement of achievement goals does not yet allow for such a tripartite approach where, along with an ego goal, the task goal 'construct' is distinctly represented by two different means of gaining a sense of intraindividual task competence.

Treasure and colleagues (Treasure, Duda, Hall, Roberts, Ames, and Maehr, 2001) responded to these issues by arguing for misinterpretations of the theory and reinforcing the traditional principles upon which the theory was founded. In both countering and integrating their points, Harwood and Hardy (2001) closed the healthy debate with a number of avenues for future research, including the importance of continued testing in the field, and greater attention to the study of achievement goal states.

Future Research Directions in Achievement Goal Theory

In closing this particular section of the motivation chapter, several research directions for enhancing our understanding of achievement goals in sport exist.

Firstly, a clearer understanding of the formation of goal orientations needs to be developed. At what points do socialization processes start and finish with respect to shaping goal orientations to certain levels and when are goal orientations most susceptible to development, and least susceptible to change? Also, precisely how important is the role that goal orientations play within their interaction with situational cues (i.e., motivational climate) when influencing states of goal involvement?

Secondly, the working relationship between, and consequences of, a high task and high ego orientation profile needs further in-depth investigation. Are there any negatives to this profile in competitive sport (or other sport domains), and where does perception of ability fit into the equation?

Thirdly, the possible existence of further achievement goals in sport that may explain greater variance in behavior needs to be considered and explored. Is task involvement more appropriately represented by two lower order goals? Further, do behavioral differences exist between those athletes who pursue task and ego involved goals whilst being driven by the need for social approval as opposed to by intrinsic self-fulfillment?

Fourthly, achievement goal states at the situational level need to be investigated in more sophisticated manners. Researchers need a better understanding of the transience or dynamic properties of achievement goal states, their orthogonality, and the mechanisms via which they may flip on a moment to moment basis.

Finally, the actual application of achievement goal theory in training and competition settings is limited. Greater attention should be afforded to both experimental and field-based intervention programs designed to effect motivational change in athletes, coaches and/or parents within these settings.

APPROACH AND AVOIDANCE MOTIVATION AND ACHIEVEMENT GOALS

Trichotomous Achievement Goal Framework

The preceding section highlights the dominant focus of researchers in sport and physical education on the ego (performance) versus task (mastery) dichotomy to explain and predict competence-based striving. Within this body of literature, ego and task goals have been conceptualized as approach forms of motivation; that is, individuals are assumed to possess a tendency to want to demonstrate (ego) or develop (task) competence using norm-referenced or self/task-referenced criteria respectively. Thus, task and ego goals are implicitly assumed to vary only as a function of whether competence is defined relative to others or the self/task.

Educational psychologists have criticized this overly narrow focus on approach forms of achievement striving and suggest that researchers need to take account of avoidance forms of motivation (Elliot, 1997, 1999; Elliot and Church, 1997; Elliot and Covington, 2001; Elliot and McGregor, 2001; Elliot and Thrash, 2001). Elliot and colleagues argue that, in addition to considerations of how competence is defined, theorists and researchers must consider how competence is valenced. In approach motivation, behavior is instigated by a positive, desirable possibility (demonstration of competence), whereas in avoidance motivation, behavior is instigated by a negative, aversive event or possibility (demonstration of incompetence). Thus, athletes may well be concerned about performing poorly in comparison to others, or poorly in relation to their own previous standards. Striving not to finish last in a tournament or not to run a slower time compared with one's last competition are examples of performance and mastery goals respectively, but each is negatively valenced (i.e., viewed as undesirable and aversive). Any comprehensive account of motivated achievement behavior in sport should arguably attend to this approach-avoidance distinction (Elliot, 1999; Elliot and Covington, 2001).

Consideration of the integration of the approach-avoidance and performance-mastery distinctions led Elliot and co-workers to propose a trichotomous achievement goal framework (Elliot, 1997, 1999; Elliot and Church, 1997; Elliot and Harackiewicz, 1996). Important distinctions between the conceptualization of goals within this framework and the definitions of goals proffered by Nicholls (1989) and Dweck (1986, 1990) have been articulated in the literature. Specifically, Elliot and Thrash (2001) argue that the performance (ego) goal construct has typically encompassed self-presentational aspects (e.g., the desire to demonstrate competence to others), whereas the mastery (task) goal construct has encompassed general self-improvement aspects (e.g., the desire to develop competence). Both goals have also been viewed as inclusive of various interrelated beliefs, feelings and evaluative standards (e.g., feeling successful having *demonstrated* normative competence or having *developed* competence). Combining such elements within the definition of achievement goals has led to a lack of clarity regarding their precise nature. Instead, Elliot and Thrash construe goals as "concrete cognitive representations that serve a directional function in motivation by guiding the individual toward or away from specific possible outcomes" (p. 143). In achievement settings, the focus is on competence, and thus an achievement goal is "a cognitive representation of a competence-based possibility that an individual seeks to attain" (p. 144). A goal represents the aim (direction) of behavior (e.g., to perform better than others) and, when measured empirically, should be separated from its underpinning reasons (energization factors) (e.g., need for achievement) and the various processes associated with the aim itself (e.g., beliefs about effort).

In the trichotomous framework proposed by Elliot and colleagues, performance goals are partitioned into separate approach and avoidance orientations such that three independent goals are proffered: a mastery goal focused on developing competence or achieving task mastery; a performance-approach goal focused on demonstrating normative competence; and a performance-avoidance goal focused on avoiding demonstrating normative incompetence. Thus, mastery and performance-approach goals differ in the definition of competence; performance-approach and performance-avoidance goals differ in valence; and mastery and performance-avoidance goals differ in both dimensions (Elliot, 1999).

The trichotomous goal framework is a central part of the hierarchical model of achievement motivation (Elliot and Church, 1997). This model posits key reasons for the adoption of achievement goals. These reasons (antecedents) intertwine with achievement goals to form 'goal complexes' and serve to establish the broader meaning of the achievement setting for an individual (Elliot, 1999; Elliot and Thrash, 2001). Antecedents of goals include need for achievement, fear of failure, competence expectancies, and implicit theories of ability, as well as self- and relationally-based variables such as self-esteem, need for approval and fear of rejection. Moreover, Elliot and colleagues refer to the influence of gender, neurophysiological predispositions and environmental factors on the pursuit of particular achievement goals. Goals serve as the channels for these underlying motivational foundations and directly predict cognition, affect and behavior. The variety of antecedent variables, combined with possible interactive effects, highlights the complexity of achievement goal adoption and regulation. For example, goals which are adopted in response to perceived environmental cues are argued to be weaker and less stable than those which are underpinned by dispositional factors. In short, the pursuit of the same goal may lead to different processes and outcomes depending on its accompanying reason (Elliot, 1999; Elliot and Thrash, 2001).

One distinction between the hierarchical model described above and the more commonly investigated frameworks proposed by Nicholls (1989) and Dweck (1986, 1990) deals with the influence of competence perceptions on motivational processes and outcomes. According to Dweck and Nicholls, competence perceptions moderate the influence of performance (ego) goals. If perceptions are high, then performance goals are predicted to lead to adaptive striving in achievement settings, whereas if individuals doubt their competence, performance goals will lead to a host of negative processes and outcomes such as reduced effort, boredom and anxiety. In physical settings, support for the moderator hypothesis has been mixed (Biddle, Wang, Chatzisarantis, and Spray, 2003; Vlachopoulos and Biddle, 1997; Whitehead, Andree, and Lee, 2004). In Elliot's hierarchical model, however, perceptions of competence are seen as a distinct antecedent of achievement goal adoption (Elliot, 1999). The influence of competence expectancy on the regulation of achievement behavior is via its effect on achievement goal adoption. High competence perceptions are posited to lead to approach goals (both mastery and performance), whereas low competence perceptions are thought to lead to performance avoidance goals. Within this approach, it is argued that perceptions of competence may interact with other antecedents, such as entity beliefs (athletic ability is innate and immutable), to determine goal adoption and regulation.

The array of individual and environmental factors is likely to impact on the effect of goals on achievement-related processes and outcomes in diverse ways. Nevertheless, Elliot and co-workers provide broad-based predictions as to the consequences of pursuing the different types of goals (Elliot, 1999; Elliot and McGregor, 2001). Mastery goals, which are predicted to lead to positive outcomes focus on the development of personal competence or task mastery and the underlying foundations such as need for achievement, guide the individual toward a positive event. On the other hand, performance-avoidance goals are not predicted to result in positive outcomes. Antecedents such as fear of failure and low competence expectancies orient the individual toward an aversive event producing a host of negative processes and outcomes. In both cases there is congruence between the focus of the goal and its underlying source.

Predicting the cognitive, affective, and behavioral consequences for individuals pursuing performance-approach goals is more complex than it is for individuals pursuing mastery or performance-avoidance goals. This is because of the potential variability in motivational foundations of performance-approach goals. For example, if underpinned by need for achievement, positive processes and consequences are thought to ensue, similar to those resulting from mastery goal pursuit. Congruence therefore exists between the goal and its underlying motives. If, on the other hand, a performance situation is viewed as both challenging and threatening (i.e., there is both the possibility of success and failure), the athlete may exhibit approach behavior (physical effort, persistence) in order to avoid a negative possibility (e.g., finishing last). In this case, the desire to avoid something aversive results in approach forms of achievement striving. Individuals engaged in achievement behavior under this set of 'motivational conditions' are likely to give effort in order to demonstrate normative competence, but are less likely to experience positive affect and a sense of self-determination, and more likely to possess high anxiety levels because the situation is perceived as threatening (Elliot, 1997, 1999).

2 x 2 Achievement Goal Framework

Further recent theorizing and research by Elliot and colleagues (Elliot, 1999, Elliot and McGregor, 2001) has highlighted the utility of separating mastery goals into approach and avoidance orientations in order to provide a fuller account of motivation for achievement-relevant pursuits. Consequently, the trichotomous framework has been developed into a full 2 x 2 crossing of the performance-mastery and approach-avoidance distinctions. Mastery-avoidance goals are focused on avoiding self- or task-referential incompetence (Elliot, 1999). For example, athletes may become concerned about (and strive to avoid) losing their abilities or failing to master new skills as they grow older or as a result of injury. In terms of their motivational foundation, Elliot suggests mastery-avoidance goals are likely to be underpinned by fear of failure, incremental beliefs (athletic ability is malleable and can be improved through learning), low perceptions of competence, and environmental cues which highlight self and task improvement but also the possibility of failure rather than success.

As with performance-approach goals, predicting the motivational processes and outcomes arising from the adoption and regulation of mastery-avoidance goals is complex due to the variability in their antecedent profile. More negative consequences are thought to arise if the salient underpinning profile consists of fear of failure, whereas when incremental beliefs underpin mastery-avoidance goals, the outlook should be more positive. In general, mastery-avoidance goals are hypothesized to be related to a more positive set of processes and outcomes than performance-avoidance goals, but less positive than mastery-approach goals (Elliot, 1999; Elliot and McGregor, 2001).

Finally, within this theoretical overview, it is worth considering the distinction between mastery goals that focus on the task and mastery goals that focus on the self. The pursuit of completing and mastering a task may be underpinned by an antecedent profile, and lead to motivational processes and outcomes, that are separate from those antecedents and consequences linked with the pursuit of self-improvement. As a result, the 2 x 2 framework may be expanded into a 3 x 2 conceptualization whereby mastery-task, mastery-self and performance goals are crossed with approach and avoidance forms of motivation. Arguably, achievement situations exist where an individual is concerned with either task completion/mastery or personal development, but not both. To this end, it may prove insightful to examine the separate relational network of these two types of mastery-based striving (Elliot, 1999).

Empirical Support

Researchers have only recently begun to provide empirical tests of the trichotomous framework and the 2 x 2 conceptualization of achievement goals. In the educational domain, Elliot and Harackiewicz (1996) provided initial evidence that performance-approach and performance-avoidance goals could be manipulated separately. Further work on the development of measures and the examination of the antecedent and consequence profiles for each goal has attested to the notion of distinct performance-approach and performance-avoidance goals within educational settings (see, for example, Al-Emadi, 2001; Barker, McInerney and Dowson, 2002; Church, Elliot and Gable, 2001; Elliot and Church, 1997, 2003; Elliot and McGregor, 1999; Elliot and Sheldon, 1997; Middleton and Midgley, 1997; Midgley and Urdan, 2001; Skaalvik, 1997). With respect to the 2 x 2 framework, initial work has added credence to the proposition that the network of relationships for mastery-avoidance goals is more positive than that of performance-avoidance goals but less positive than that of mastery-approach goals (Elliot, 1999; Elliot and McGregor, 2001).

In the physical domain, investigation of the trichotomous conceptualization of goals has utilized both correlational and experimental approaches to delineate antecedents and consequences associated with mastery (approach) goals and the two types of performance goals (Cury, Da Fonseca, Rufo, and Sarrazin, 2002; Cury, Da Fonseca, Rufo, Peres, and Sarrazin, 2003; Cury, Elliot, Sarrazin, Da Fonseca, and Rufo, 2002; Halvari and Kjormo, 1999), although mastery-avoidance goals have yet to receive empirical attention. In a physical education (PE) setting, Cury, Da Fonseca, et al. (2002) identified entity and incremental beliefs about athletic ability to be positively and negatively related with performance-approach and performance-avoidance goals respectively, whereas perceptions of competence were positively linked with performance-approach goals but negatively correlated with performance-avoidance goals. In terms of environmental factors, the perception of a prevailing performance climate in PE was positively associated with both performance-approach and avoidance goals, while mastery goal utility was positively linked with incremental beliefs, competence perceptions and perceived mastery climate. In a study with Olympic level athletes, Halvari and Kjormo (1999) found that performance-avoidance goals were linked with the motive to avoid failure and were negatively associated with performance.

Experimental work involving physical tasks has replicated the procedures adopted by Elliot and Harackiewicz (1996) in the academic domain. Cury, Elliot, et al. (2002) identified competence valuation, state anxiety and task absorption as mediators of the goals – intrinsic motivation relationship. Specifically, using a basketball dribbling task, it was found that performance-avoidance goals undermined intrinsic motivation relative to performance-approach and mastery (approach) goals. Participants in the performance-avoidance condition reported lower competence valuation, higher state anxiety and reduced task absorption than participants in either of the other two conditions. A subsequent study provided support for these initial findings with respect to investment in learning to prepare for a sport test (Cury et al., 2003).

Future Research Directions Adopting the Approach-Avoidance Distinction

Over the past two decades, the achievement goal approach has provided a wealth of information regarding how individuals approach, experience and respond to competence-relevant pursuits. We know a great deal about the effects of goals in terms of how they influence the interpretation and meaning of achievement settings. Arguably, the recent introduction of the approach-avoidance distinction to the performance-mastery dichotomy will allow theorists and researchers to undertake a more fine-grained analysis of achievement behavior. However, research is in its infancy and there is much work to be done. A number of directions can be suggested to further our knowledge of approach and avoidance achievement goals in sport.

First, the independence of the four achievement goals in sport should be determined through factor analytic studies. In particular, we need to examine empirically the bifurcation of mastery-approach and mastery-avoidance goals. Conroy, Elliot, and Hofer (2003) recently introduced the 2 x 2 Achievement Goals Questionnaire for Sport (AGQ-S) using a university-based sample of recreational athletes. Although the psychometric properties of the AGQ-S appeared promising, because this measure could facilitate a good deal of fundamental and applied research, further psychometric work is necessary to ensure its applicability with different population groups.

Second, we should direct attention to the motivational ramifications of various antecedent-goal links or goal complexes. For example, in what ways do performance-approach goals influence the sport experience when underpinned by fear of failure versus when underpinned by need for approval? This approach will necessitate the development of measurement items that combine both goal and reason e.g., "It's important for me to perform better than others to please my friends".

Third, researchers should ascertain the salience of mastery-avoidance goals in the competence-based striving of children and young people in sport. It would be useful to determine whether, and under which conditions, young people become concerned about, and strive to avoid, self- and task-referenced incompetence.

Fourth, we need to understand more fully the socialization of the antecedents of approach and avoidance goals in sport. For example, what role do parents play in the transmission of motive dispositions (e.g., fear of failure) that lead to the adoption of performance-avoidance goals in young sport performers (see Elliot and Thrash, 2004)?

Finally, we should address the empirical utility of splitting mastery-approach and mastery-avoidance goals in sport into task- and self-referenced components. Does each component possess a (relatively) distinct antecedent and consequence profile?

GENERAL DISCUSSION

Motivation continues to be a central theme underpinning a high proportion of research within sport psychology. The applicability of motivational theory to applied practice and the plethora of approaches adopted under the umbrella of motivation ensure it's longevity as a transcending concept across sport psychology. The purpose of this motivation chapter has been to provide the informed reader with contemporary reviews of work within three of the central motivational theories studied within sport at the current time: Deci and Ryan's self-determination theory; Nicholl's achievement goal theory; and Elliot and associates approach-avoidance motivation framework. In addition to describing contemporary research and the issues surrounding this work, within each sub-section we have highlighted a number of potential research issues that may facilitate expansion of the knowledge base and provide further clarification within those areas.

This brief final section will firstly review and consider the notion of goals within each of the three theories examined, because they are often considered a key psychological mediator, especially within social cognitive theories of motivation. Secondly, we will consider recent research that has simultaneously examined motivational styles and achievement goals, and within this consider potential avenues for research that might further illuminate the motivation literature as it pertains to the theories considered, and within the context of sport. Finally, we will briefly consider broad practical implications that arise from the theoretical overviews presented.

Goal-Directed Intention

The notion of goals as the central mediator between sport and motivation reflects Roberts' view of motivation as; 'a dynamic and complex cognitive process based on subjective assessments of the outcome by the participant depending on the goal of action and the meaning of the context to the participant.' (Roberts, 2001 p. 7) We will now consider, briefly, the notion of goals within each of the theories.

Self-determination Theory

Although Deci and Ryan argue that the shift towards cognitive based theories of motivation has led to the concept of needs being largely ignored in favor of the concept of goals, they argue that a full understanding of goal directed behavior cannot be achieved without addressing the needs that give goals their psychological potency and the regulatory processes which direct goal pursuits (Deci and Ryan, 2000). Indeed they would suggest that if goals were not related to fundamental needs directly, the impact of their achievement or otherwise would be negligible – clearly, the research on goal-achievement would suggest that this is not the case.

Unlike much of the work on goal-directed behavior that simply distinguishes among types of goals or outcomes, self-determination theory also considers the regulatory processes through which goals are pursued. Specifically Deci and Ryan suggest that the psychological impact of goals reflects the extent to which the attainment of different types of goals and the process of goal pursuit satisfy the basic needs for autonomy, competence and relatedness. For example, largely independent of the specific goal content, when goal–directed behavior is autonomous rather than controlled (key aspects of self-determination theory), the consequences are more positive in terms of performance and affect (Deci and Ryan, 2000).

Achievement Goal Theory

The basic principle behind the achievement goal approach is that the individual will pursue those goals that most closely reflect his/her cognitive belief about what is required to maximize favorable perceptions of competence in that particular social context. Specifically, these beliefs are manifested through the way in which individuals in achievement settings subjectively construe achievement and define success and failure. For an individual with a high level of task orientation, these criteria for success may be based on learning, enjoyment and personal performance, whereas, for the highly ego oriented individual the criteria for success will be based on normative comparisons of ability. These goals define the meaning that individuals assign to achievement settings.

Approach-avoidance Framework

According to Elliot and associates, within achievement settings, goals can be construed as cognitive representations that serve a directional function by guiding the performer towards (approach) or away from (avoidance) possible specific competence-based outcomes. In their proposed framework (Elliot, 1997, 1999; Elliot and Church, 1997; Elliot and McGregor, 2001), there are four independent goals: mastery-approach; mastery-avoidance; performance-approach; and performance-avoidance goals). Elliot (1999), suggests that collapsing approach and avoidance goals into a unitary construct nullifies the effects of two conceptually independent types of goals, and this might explain many of the inconsistencies in results regarding performance (ego) oriented achievement goals.

To summarize, self-determination theory views goals as a mechanism through which to achieve basic psychological needs via the content of goals and process of goal pursuits. Achievement goal theory views goals as individual criteria through which individuals construe success and judge ability, and Elliot's approach-avoidance goal framework extends this conceptualization in suggesting that achievement goals have a directional aspect where individuals implicitly seek to avoid or approach the two representations of competence identified within achievement goal theory.

Link between the Theories

The avenue for potential links between self-determination theory and achievement goal theory is certainly not a recent conceptual proposal. Indeed Nicholls (1989) suggested that the quest for task mastery is intimately linked to intrinsic motivation. More recently, Ntoumanis (2001) argued that variations in achievement goals are linked to differences in self-determination.

Generally speaking, a high level of task orientation is positively associated with intrinsic motivation, while a high level of ego orientation has been associated with decrements in intrinsic motivation (Duda et al., 1995). Furthermore, adopting Elliott's framework, Cury et al. (2002) found that performance avoidance goals (negatively valenced ego-involved goals) undermined intrinsic motivation in comparison to performance approach and mastery approach goals. This is not surprising since a high level of task orientation (or task involvement at a state level) equates to self-referenced perceptions of ability which are under the performer's control, i.e., self-determination will be high. Similarly, for individuals with a high level of ego orientation (or ego involvement at a state level), self-determination is more likely to be low due to a relative lack of control regarding the outcome. It should be noted however, that much of this research has been criticized for either, adopting a unidimensional approach, or assessing the antecedents of intrinsic motivation rather than intrinsic motivation itself.

Recent research that has taken a multidimensional perspective to looking at motivational styles (multidimensional extrinsic motivation reflecting self-determination theory, and intrinsic motivation reflecting Pelletier's proposed multidimensional conceptualization) has extended the multi-theoretical approach to examining motivation in sport. For example, research using moderated hierarchical regression (Ntoumanis, 2001) advocates the adaptive role of task orientation in promoting self-determination in sport, yet more specifically, indicates that a task orientation positively predicted all three types of intrinsic motivation (to know; to accomplish; and for stimulation) and identified regulation (the most self-determined form of extrinsic motivation measured using the SMS). Conversely, ego orientation positively predicts introjected regulation and external regulation (less self-determined extrinsic motivation) and amotivation.

In congruence with this work, recent studies which examined the relationships between goal orientations and the subcomponents of the SMS (Kingston et al., 2006; Petherick and Weigand, 2002), revealed that task orientation was significantly and positively related to all aspects of intrinsic motivation and negatively related to the least self-determined forms of extrinsic motivation (introjected and external regulation). Furthermore, ego orientation was significantly (negatively) related to aspects of intrinsic motivation, and positively related to the least self-determined forms of extrinsic motivation (introjected regulation and external regulation). Similarly, in their sample of UK school children (n=328) Standage et al. (2003), looked at, amongst other motivational variables, the effects of task and ego orientations on motivational styles advanced by Deci and Ryan and Pelletier et al. The principle finding was that task orientation was positively correlated with intrinsic motivation per se, and the most self-determined forms of extrinsic motivation, however, the results for ego orientation were less conclusive. Nevertheless, collectively these studies provide further support for the link between goal orientations and motivational styles.

It is interesting to note that, although early research confirmed that ego involvement undermined intrinsic motivation (e.g., Ryan, 1982), the relationship between ego involvement (or ego orientations) and extrinsic motivation is less straightforward. Deci and Ryan (2000) likened a state of ego involvement to the motivational style of introjected regulation (where a behavior is performed to gain ego enhancements such as pride). However, social comparison objectives can also be enacted out for the purpose of gaining rewards (external regulation) or they may be governed by a desire for growth and development (identified regulation). This highlights the difference between the conceptualization of goals within achievement goal approaches and self-determination theory – the antecedents of ego involvement may vary considerably in their degree of self-determination, and hence one might consider the efficacy of considering ego involvement from a multidimensional perspective.

Although the results must be considered with some caution due to the psychometric concerns with SMS (outlined previously), recent research strongly supports the view that goal orientations and intrinsic and extrinsic motivation in sport are related. However, it is important for research to clarify the nature of this relationship especially considering multidimensional components of intrinsic and extrinsic motivation. Furthermore, research in these areas might also consider the potential moderating role of perceived competence in the effects of achievement goals and more or less self-determined aspects of motivation on cognitions, behaviors and affect, as well as the extent to which goal perspectives impact on autonomy and relatedness (as well as competence) (cf. Ntoumanis, 2001).

To date, links between approach/avoidance goals and self-determination in sport have received little attention in relation to both competence-based and other outcomes, such as persistence, effort, moral behavior, and peer relationships. Nevertheless, one might expect that behaviors engaged in for less self-determined reasons might have more of an association with avoidance characteristics since the less self-determined aspects of extrinsic motivation could be elicited through conditions of negative consequences (e.g., to avoid guilt or anxiety). Based on their control theory of regulation (Carver and Scheier, 1998), and using a similar approach-avoidance distinction to Elliot and associates, Carver and Scheier (1999) proposed that self-determination theory's distinction between controlled and autonomous regulation can be understood in approach-avoidance terms. In essence they proposed that the more self-determined (autonomous) regulations represented an approach mode of behavior, whereas less self-determined (controlled) regulations represented an avoidance mode (cf. Deci and Ryan, 2000). While this distinction may be over-simplistic because, for example, behavior focused on attaining rewards may be approach oriented yet less self-determined, and the more self-determined aspects of extrinsic motivation such as identified regulation, may be associated with approach or avoidance motives, it does provide an interesting avenue for future research. Furthermore, it would be interesting to identify how the motivational foundation underpinning performance approach or avoidance goals (e.g., fear of failure or need for achievement) impacts upon feelings of self-determination.

Although the emphasis of this chapter is unashamedly theoretical, it is perhaps salient to acknowledge briefly two of the main practical implications that arise from the theories examined. At a general level, individuals' should perceive high levels of control in the initiation of behaviors, and in effecting the outcome of events (high levels of self-determination). Autonomy should be encouraged through environmental structures that permit opportunities for decision making, and performers' perceptions of ability and criteria for success should be broadly based on gains in personal mastery of a skill or task. Feedback to performers should be informational rather than evaluative, and coaching/teaching situations should be set up to encourage development of individual perceptions of ability, and individual objectives should be challenging yet non-threatening.

From a practical perspective, these 'suggestions' can be influenced through two mechanisms; firstly, modification of the achievement environment (motivational climate and coaching styles), and secondly, by helping the performer to develop a more appropriate representation of what is regarded as a successful performance in achievement settings (i.e., develop an adaptive goal focus).

Motivational climate is defined as a situationally induced psychological environment directing goals of an action (Ames, 1992b). According to Ames, in situations where an emphasis is placed on effort, improvement, cooperation, and self-referenced goals, a task-involving climate develops. In such a climate, individuals typically adopt adaptive achievement strategies such as working hard, selecting challenging tasks, and task persistence. In contrast, when the emphasis is placed on social comparison and winning or outperforming others, then an ego-involving climate develops. In this case, individuals often adopt maladaptive achievement strategies, particularly when perceptions of competence are low (Ames, 1992b).

Correlational research in PE (e.g., Carpenter and Morgan, 1999; Treasure, 1997) has revealed that perceptions of a mastery climate relate to a higher task orientation, greater feelings of satisfaction and less boredom, higher perceived ability and intrinsic motivation, the belief that effort and ability are causes of success, and a more positive attitude toward PE. In contrast, a perceived performance climate has been related to higher levels of ego orientation, less enjoyment, greater boredom, the belief that ability leads to success and negatively related to the belief that success was due to effort and a positive attitude toward PE. Petherick and Weigand (2002) examined the impact of dispositional goals and perceived motivational climate on participant motivation (assessed using the SMS) and found that climates emphasizing personal improvements and progress through effort and mastery are more likely to foster intrinsic motivation and permit experience of satisfaction than those that emphasize interpersonal competition and normative feedback (a performance climate).

With regards to coaching structures, coaches high in autocratic behavior would be expected to undermine athletes' intrinsic motivation primarily because such a coaching style is not conductive to facilitating athletes' perception of self-determination (Amorose and Horn, 2000). Similarly, coaches high in democratic behavior should be successful in facilitating athletes' intrinsic motivation, because such behaviors enhance both athletes' perceptions of competence and their sense of self-determination (Weiss and Ferrer-Caja, 2002). These interpretations are consistent with Black and Weiss's (1992) and Amorose and Horn's (2000) findings which highlighted that an autocratic style is associated with increases in self-determined reason for engaging in activities (intrinsic motivation). Moreover, according to Petherick and Weigand (2002), if coaches wish to encourage positive achievement striving and foster intrinsic motivation, promotion of a mastery climate is advisable.

In terms of adopting an appropriate goal focus, different types of goals have been shown to differentially impact on motivational dimensions (Duda, 2001). Within the sports domain, three different types of goals are known to exist and affect motivation (Hardy et al., 1996). These have been identified as: outcome goals, performance goals, and process goals (Kingston and Hardy, 1997). Outcome goals are based on competitive outcomes and thus typically entail social comparison. An example of an outcome goal would be to aim to come first in a race. Performance goals are those specifying absolute or self-referenced standards. These are end products of a performance and usually involve a numerical value (Duda, 2001). An example of a performance goal would be a number of putts to take over the course of a round of golf. Process goals centre on the demonstration of behaviors, skills, and strategies that are part of the task performance (Kingston and Hardy, 1997). An example of a process goal would be to have a high follow-through phase on a basketball shot.

Both achievement goal theory and self-determination theory advocate a high degree of task or mastery focus (specifically in the case of Elliott's framework these should be oriented towards a positive event). Also to facilitate perceptions of control, the nature of the goals and the process of setting and pursuing those goals should be as autonomous as practicable. To most easily achieve these objectives, performers should be encouraged to set self-referenced process goals, which may refer to, for example, improvement of technique, form, thought processes and/or strategy. Process goals are completely self-referenced, controllable and achievable (Burton and Naylor, 2002), and can serve to maximize competence information and perceptions of control. It should, however, be noted that while goals based on social comparison are often discouraged within the literature, there is increasing evidence that they may not be as motivationally compromising as previously suggested (Kingston and Hardy,

1997). Further intervention research, particularly of a longitudinal nature is required to examine the effects on motivational variables through manipulating the motivational climate and/or educating performers to adopt an adaptive framework for goal-setting.

ACKNOWLEDGEMENTS

The authors would like to extend their thanks firstly to Dr. Ken Hodge and Dr. Mary Fry for their insightful and informative reviews; we hope we have done justice to your efforts. We would also like to thank Mr. Christopher Horrocks who made contributions to parts of this chapter.

REFERENCES

Abramson, L. Y., Seligman, M. E. P., and Teasdale, J. D. (1978). Learned helplessness in humans: Critique and reformulation. *Journal of Abnormal Psychology*, *87*, 49-74.

Al-Emadi, A. A. (2001). The relationships among achievement, goal orientation, and study strategies. *Social Behavior and Personality, 29,* 823-832.

Alexandris, K., Tsorbatzoudis, C., and Grouios, G. (2002). Perceived constraints on recreational sport participation: Investigating their relationship with intrinsic motivation, extrinsic motivation and amotivation. *Journal of Leisure Research, 34,* 233-252.

Allen, J. B. (2003). Social motivation in youth sport. *Journal of Sport and Exercise Psychology, 25,* 551-567.

Ames, C. (1992a). Classrooms: Goals, structures, and student motivation. *Journal of Educational Psychology, 84,* 261-271.

Ames, C. (1992b). Achievement goals, motivational climate, and motivational processes. In G. C. Roberts (Ed.), *Motivation in sport and exercise* (pp. 161-176). Champaign, IL: Human Kinetics.

Amorose, A. J., and Horn, T. S. (2000). Intrinsic motivation: Relationships with collegiate athlete's gender, scholarship status and perceptions of their coaches behavior. *Journal of Sport and Exercise Psychology, 22*, 63-84.

Barker, K. L., McInerney, D. M., and Dowson, M. (2002). Performance approach, performance avoidance and depth of information processing: A fresh look at relations between students' academic motivation and cognition. *Educational Psychology, 22,* 571-589.

Berlant, A. R., and Weiss, M. R. (1997). Goal orientation and the orientation process: An individual's focus on form and outcome. *Research Quarterly for Exercise and Sport, 86,* 317-330.

Biddle, S. J. H. (2001). Enhancing motivation in physical education. In G. C. Roberts (Ed.), *Advances in motivation in sport and exercise* (pp. 101-128). Champaign, IL: Human Kinetics.

Biddle, S. J. H., Wang, C. K. J., Chatzisarantis, N. L. D., and Spray, C. M. (2003). Motivation for physical activity in young people: Entity and incremental beliefs about athletic ability. *Journal of Sports Sciences, 21,* 973-989.

Biddle, S. J. H., Akande, A., Vlachopoulos, S., and Fox, K. (1996). Towards an understanding of children's motivation for physical activity: Achievement goal orientations, beliefs about sport success and sport emotion in Zimbabwean children. *Psychology and Health, 12*, 49-55.

Biddle, S. J. H., Wang, C. K., Kavussanu, M., and Spray, C. (2003). Correlates of achievement goal orientations in physical activity: A systematic review of research. *European Journal of Sport Sciences, 3,* 1-20.

Black, S. J., and Weiss, M. R. (1992). The relationship among perceived coaching behaviors, perceptions of ability, and motivation in competitive age-group swimmers. *Journal of Sport and Exercise Psychology, 14,* 309-325.

Brière, N. M., Vallerand, R. J., Blais, M. R., and Pelletier, L. G. (1995). On the development and validation of the French form of the sport motivation scale. *International Journal of Sport Psychology, 26,* 465-489.

Burton, D., and Naylor, S. (2002). The Jekyll/Hyde nature of goals: Revisiting and updating goal-setting research. In T. Horn (Ed.), *Advances in Sport Psychology* (pp. 459-499). Champaign, IL: Human Kinetics.

Carpenter, P. J., and Morgan, K. (1999). Motivational climate, personal goal perspectives, and cognitive and affective responses in physical education classes. *European Journal of Physical Education, 4,* 31-41.

Carpenter, P. J., and Yates, B. (1997). Relationship between achievement goals and the perceived purpose of soccer for semiprofessional and amateur players. *Journal of Sport and Exercise Psychology, 19*, 302-312.

Carver, C. S., and Scheier, M. F. (1998). *On the self-regulation of behavior.* New York: Cambridge University Press.

Carver, C. S., and Scheier, M. F. (1999). Themes and issues in the self-regulation of behavior. In R. S. Wyer, Jr. (Ed.), *Perspectives on behavioral self-regulation: Advances in social cognition* (Vol. 12, pp. 1-105). Mahwah, NJ: Lawrence Erlbaum Associates.

Church, M. A., Elliot, A. J., and Gable, S. L. (2001). Perceptions of classroom environment, achievement goals, and achievement outcomes. *Journal of Educational Psychology, 93,* 43-54.

Conroy, D. E., Elliot, A. J., and Hofer, S. M. (2003). A 2 X 2 achievement goals questionnaire for sport: Evidence for factorial invariance, temporal stability, and external validity. *Journal of Sport and Exercise Psychology, 25,* 456-476.

Cumming, J., Hall, C., Harwood, C., and Gammage, K. (2002). Motivational orientations and imagery use: A goal profiling analysis. *Journal of Sports Sciences, 20*, 127-136.

Cury, F., Da Fonseca, D., Rufo, M., and Sarrazin, P. (2002). Perceptions of competence, implicit theory of ability, perception of motivational climate, and achievement goals: A test of the trichotomous conceptualization of endorsement of achievement motivation in the physical education setting. *Perceptual and Motor Skills, 95,* 233-244.

Cury, F., Da Fonseca, D., Rufo, M., Peres, C., and Sarrazin, P. (2003). The trichotomous model and investment in learning to prepare for a sport test: A mediational analysis. *British Journal of Educational Psychology, 73,* 529-543.

Cury, F., Elliot, A., Sarrazin, P., Da Fonseca, D., and Rufo, M. (2002). The trichotomous achievement goal model and intrinsic motivation: A sequential mediational analysis. *Journal of Experimental Social Psychology, 38,* 473-481.

Cury, F., Famose, J. P., and Sarrazin, P. (1997). Achievement goal theory and active search for information in a sport task. In R. Lidor and M. Bar-Eli (Eds.), *Innovations in sport psychology: Linking theory and practice*. Proceedings of the IX World Congress in Sport Psychology: Part I (pp. 218-220). Netanya, Israel: Ministry of Education, Culture and Sport.

deCharms, R. (1968). *Personal causation*. New York: Academic.

Deci, E. L. (1975). *Intrinsic motivation*. New York: Plenum.

Deci, E. L., and Ryan, R. M. (1985). *Intrinsic motivation and self-determination in human behavior*. New York: Plenum Press.

Deci, E. L., and Ryan, R. M. (2000). The "what" and "why" of goal pursuits: Human needs and the self-determination of behavior. *Psychological Inquiry, 11*, 227-268.

Duda, J. L. (1987). Toward a developmental theory of children's motivation in sport. *Journal of Sport Psychology, 9*, 130-145.

Duda, J. L. (1989). Relationship between task and ego orientation and the perceived purpose of sport among high school athletes. *Journal of Sport and Exercise Psychology, 11*, 318-335.

Duda, J. L. (1993). Goals: A social-cognitive approach to the study of achievement motivation in sport. In R. Singer, M. Murphey, and L. K. Tennant (Eds.), *Handbook of research in sport psychology* (pp. 421-436). New York: Macmillan.

Duda, J. L. (2001). Achievement goal research in sport: Pushing the boundaries and clarifying some misunderstandings. In G. C. Roberts (Ed.), *Advances in motivation in sport and exercise* (pp. 129-182). Champaign, IL: Human Kinetics.

Duda, J. L., Chi, L., Newton, M. L., Walling, M. D., and Catley, D. (1995). Task and ego orientation and intrinsic motivation in sport. *International Journal of Sport Psychology, 26*, 40-63.

Duda, J. L., and Hall, H. K. (2001). Achievement goal theory in sport: Recent extensions and future directions. In R. Singer, H. Hausenblas, and C. Janelle (Eds.), *Handbook of sport psychology* (pp. 417-443). New York: Wiley.

Duda, J. L., and Hom, M. (1993). Interdependencies between the perceived and self-reported goal orientations of young athletes and their parents. *Pediatric Exercise Science, 5*, 234-241.

Duda, J. L., and Nicholls, J. G. (1992). Dimensions of achievement motivation in schoolwork and sport. *Journal of Educational Psychology, 84*, 290-299.

Duda, J. L., Olson, L., and Templin, T. (1991). The relationship of task and ego orientation to sportsmanship attitudes and the perceived legitimacy of injurious acts. *Research Quarterly for Exercise and Sport, 62*, 79-87.

Duda, J. L., and White, S. A. (1992). Goal orientations and beliefs about the causes of success among elite athletes. *The Sport Psychologist, 6*, 334-343.

Duda, J. L., and Whitehead, J. (1998). Measurement of goal perspectives in the physical domain. In J. L Duda (Ed.), *Advances in sport and exercise psychology measurement* (pp. 21-48). Morgantown, WV: Fitness Information Technology.

Dunn, J. G. H., and Dunn, J. C. (1999). Goal orientations, perceptions of aggression, and sportspersonship in elite youth male ice hockey players. *The Sport Psychologist, 13*, 183-200.

Dweck, C. (1990). Self-theories and goals: Their role in motivation, personality, and development. In R. Dienstbier (Ed.), *Nebraska symposium on motivation* (Vol. 38, pp. 199-235). Lincoln, NE: University of Nebraska Press.

Dweck, C. S. (1986). Motivational processes affecting learning. *American Psychologist, 41,* 1040-1048.

Ebbeck, V., and Becker, S. L. (1994). Psychosocial predictors of goal orientations in youth soccer. *Research Quarterly for Exercise and Sport, 65,* 355-362.

Elliot, A. J. (1997). Integrating the "classic" and "contemporary" approaches to achievement motivation: A hierarchical model of approach and avoidance achievement motivation. In M. L. Maehr, and P. R. Pintrich (Eds.), *Advances in motivation and achievement* (Vol. 10, pp. 143-179). Greenwich, CT: JAI Press.

Elliot, A. J. (1999). Approach and avoidance motivation and achievement goals. *Educational Psychologist, 34,* 169-189.

Elliot, A. J., and Church, M. A. (1997). A hierarchical model of approach and avoidance achievement motivation. *Journal of Personality and Social Psychology, 72,* 218-232.

Elliot, A. J., and Church, M. A. (2003). A motivational analysis of defensive pessimism and self-handicapping. *Journal of Personality, 71,* 369-396.

Elliot, A. J., and Covington, M. V. (2001). Approach and avoidance motivation. *Educational Psychology Review, 13,* 73-92.

Elliot, A. J., and Harackiewicz, J. M. (1996). Approach and avoidance achievement goals and intrinsic motivation: A mediational analysis. *Journal of Personality and Social Psychology, 70,* 461-475.

Elliot, A. J., and McGregor, H. A. (1999). Test anxiety and the hierarchical model of approach and avoidance achievement motivation. *Journal of Personality and Social Psychology, 76,* 628-644.

Elliot, A. J., and McGregor, H. A. (2001). A 2 X 2 achievement goal framework. *Journal of Personality and Social Psychology, 80,* 501-519.

Elliot, A. J., and Sheldon, K. M. (1997). Avoidance achievement motivation: A personal goals analysis. *Journal of Personality and Social Psychology, 73,* 171-185.

Elliot, A. J., and Thrash, T. M. (2001). Achievement goals and the hierarchical model of achievement motivation. *Educational Psychology Review, 13,* 139-156.

Elliot, A. J., and Thrash, T. M. (2004). The intergenerational transmission of fear of failure. *Personality and Social Psychology Bulletin, 30,* 957-971.

Escarti, A., Roberts, G. C., Cervello, E. M., and Guzman, J. F. (1999). Adolescent goal orientations and the perception of criteria of success used by significant others. *International Journal of Sport Psychology, 30,* 309-324.

Fortier, M. S., Vallerand, R. J., Brière, N. M., and Provencher, P. J. (1995). Competitive and recreational sport structures and gender: A test of their relationship with sport motivation. *International Journal of Sport Psychology, 26,* 24-39.

Fox, K. R., Goudas, M., Biddle, S., Duda, J., and Armstrong, N. (1994). Children's task and ego goal profiles in sport. *British Journal of Educational Psychology, 64,* 253-261.

Fry, M. D. (2001). The development of motivation in children. In G. C. Roberts (Ed.), *Advances in motivation in sport and exercise* (2nd ed., pp. 51-78). Champaign, IL; Human Kinetics.

Goudas, M., Biddle, S., Fox, K., and Underwood, M. (1995). It ain't what you do, it's the way that you do it! Teaching style affects children's motivation in track and field lessons. *The Sport Psychologist, 9*, 254-264.

Hall, H. K. (1990). *A social cognitive approach to goal setting: The mediating effects of achievement goals and perceived ability.* Unpublished doctoral dissertation, University of Illinois at Urbana-Champaign.

Hall, H. K., and Kerr, A. W. (1997). Motivational antecedents of precompetitive anxiety in youth sport. *The Sport Psychologist, 11*, 24-42.

Halvari, H., and Kjormo, O. (1999). A structural model of achievement motives, performance approach and avoidance goals, and performance among Norwegian Olympic athletes. *Perceptual and Motor Skills, 89*, 997-1022.

Hardy, L., Jones, G., and Gould, D. (1996). *Understanding psychological preparation for sport: Theory and practice of elite performers.* Chichester: John Wiley and Sons.

Harter, S. (1978). Effectance motivation reconsidered: Toward a developmental model. *Human Development, 1*, 34-64.

Harwood, C. G. (2002). Assessing achievement goals in sport: Caveats for consultants and a case for contextualization. *Journal of Applied Sport Psychology, 14*, 380-393.

Harwood, C. G., and Hardy, L. (2001). Persistence and effort in moving achievement goal research forward: A response to Treasure and colleagues. *Journal of Sport and Exercise Psychology, 23*, 330-345.

Harwood, C. G., and Swain, A. B. (2001). The development and activation of achievement goals in tennis: I. Understanding the underlying factors. *The Sports Psychologist, 15*, 319-341.

Harwood, C. G., and Swain, A. B. (2002). The development and activation of achievement goals in tennis: II. *The Sport Psychologist, 16*, 111-138.

Harwood, C. G., Cumming, J., and Fletcher, D. (2004). Motivational profiles and psychological skill use in elite youth sport. *Journal of Applied Sport Psychology, 16*, 318-332.

Harwood, C. G., Cumming, J., and Hall, C, (2003). Imagery use in elite youth sport participants: Reinforcing the applied significance of achievement goal theory. *Research Quarterly for Exercise and Sport, 3*, 292-300.

Harwood, C. G., Hardy, L., and Swain, A. (2000). Achievement goals in competitive sport: A critique of conceptual and measurement issues. *Journal of Sport and Exercise Psychology, 22*, 235-255.

Hatzigeorgiadis, A., and Biddle, S. J. H. (1999). The effects of goal orientation and perceived competence on cognitive interference during tennis and snooker performance. *Journal of Sport Behavior, 22*, 479-501.

Hodge, K., and Petlichkoff, L. (2000). Goal profiles in sport motivation: A cluster analysis. *Journal of Sport and Exercise Psychology, 22*, 256-272.

Jackson, S. A., and Roberts, G. C. (1992). Positive performance states of athletes: Toward a conceptual understanding of peak performance. *The Sport Psychologist, 6*, 156-171.

Kagan, J. (1972). Motives and development. *Journal of Personality and Social Psychology, 22*, 51-66.

Kavussanu, M., and Roberts, G. C. (2001). Moral functioning in sport: An achievement goal perspective. *Journal of Sport and Exercise Psychology, 23*, 37-54.

Kingston, K. M., and Hardy, L. (1997). Effects of different types of goals on processes that support performance. *The Sport Psychologist, 11,* 277-293.

Kingston, K. M., Horrocks, C., and Hanton, S. (2006). Do multidimensional intrinsic and extrinsic motivational profiles discriminate between athlete scholarship status? *European Journal of Sport Sciences* (in press).

Krane, V., Greenleaf, C. A., and Snow, J. (1997). Reaching for gold and the price of glory: A motivational case study of an elite gymnast. *The Sport Psychologist, 11,* 53-71.

Lavalle, D., Kremer, J., Moran, A. P., and Williams, M. (2004). *Sport psychology: Contemporary themes.* New York: Palgrave Macmillan.

Li, F., and Harmer, P. (1996). Testing the simplex assumption underlying the sport motivation scale: A structural equation modeling analysis. *Research Quarterly for Exercise and Sport, 67,* 396-405.

Lloyd, J., and Fox, K. (1992). Achievement goals and motivation to exercise in adolescent girls: A preliminary intervention study. *British Journal of Physical Education: Research Supplement, 11,* 12-16.

Lochbaum, M. R., and Roberts, G. C. (1993). Goal Orientations and perceptions of the sport experience. *Journal of Sport and Exercise Psychology, 15,* 160-171.

Lonsdale, C. (2005). Examining the psychometric properties of the behavioural regulation in sport questionnaire. Paper presented at the SCAPPS conference, Niagara Falls, ON, Canada. November.

Maehr, M.L., and Braskamp, L.A. (1986). *The motivation factor: A theory of personal investment.* Lexington, MA: Lexington Books/Health.

Maehr, M. L., and Nicholls, J. G. (1980). Culture and achievement motivation: A second look. In N. Warren (Ed.), *Studies in cross-cultural psychology:* (Vol. 3, pp. 221-267). New York: Academic Press.

Martens, M. P., and Webber, S. N. (2002). Psychometric properties of the Sport Motivation Scale: An evaluation with college varsity athletes from the U.S. *Journal of Sport and Exercise Psychology, 24,* 254-270.

Middleton, M. J., and Midgley, C. (1997). Avoiding the demonstration of lack of ability: An underexplored aspect of goal theory. *Journal of Educational Psychology, 89,* 710-718.

Midgley, C., and Urdan, T. (2001). Academic self-handicapping and achievement goals: A further examination. *Contemporary Educational Psychology, 26,* 61-75.

Newton, M., and Duda, J. L. (1995). Relations of goal orientations and expectations on multidimensional state anxiety. *Perceptual and Motor Skills, 81,* 1107-1112.

Nicholls, J. G. (1984). Achievement motivation: Conceptions of ability, subjective experience, task choice, and performance. *Psychological Review, 91,* 328-346.

Nicholls, J. G. (1989). *The competitive ethos and democratic education.* Cambridge, MA: Harvard University Press.

Nicholls, J. G. (1992). The general and the specific in the development and expression of achievement motivation. In G. C. Roberts (Ed.), *Motivation in sport and exercise* (pp. 31-56). Champaign, IL: Human Kinetics.

Nicholls, J. G., and Miller, A. T. (1984). Development and its discontents: The differentiation of the concept of ability. In J. G. Nicholls (Ed.), *Advances in motivation and achievement: The development of achievement motivation* (Vol. 3, pp. 185-218). Greenwich, CT: JAI Press.

Ntoumanis, N. (2001). Empirical links between achievement goal theory and self-determination theory in sport. *Journal of Sports Sciences, 19,* 397-409.

Ntoumanis, N., and Biddle, S. (1999). A review of motivational climate in physical activity. *Journal of Sports Sciences, 17,* 643-665.

Ntoumanis, N., Biddle, S. J. H., and Haddock, G. (1999). The mediating role of coping strategies on the relationship between achievement motivation and affect in sport. *Anxiety, Stress, and Coping, 12,* 299-327.

Pelletier, L. G., Fortier, M. S., Vallerand, R. J., Tuson, K. M., Brière, N. M., and Blais, M. R. (1995). Toward a new measure of intrinsic motivation, extrinsic motivation, and amotivation in sports: The Sports Motivation Scale. *Journal of Sport and Exercise Psychology, 17,* 35-53.

Petherick, C. M., and Weigand, D. A. (2002). The relationship of dispositional goal orientations and perceived motivational climates on indices of motivation in male and female swimmers. *International Journal of Sport Psychology, 33,* 218-237.

Roberts, G. C., Treasure, D. C., and Balague, G. (1998). Achievement goals in sport: The development and validation of the Perception of Success Questionnaire. *Journal of Sports Sciences, 16,* 337-347.

Roberts, G. C., and Ommundsen, Y. (1996). Effect of goal orientations on achievement beliefs, cognitions, and strategies in team sport. *Scandinavian Journal of Medicine and Science in Sport, 6,* 46-56.

Roberts, G. C. (1984). Achievement motivation in children's sport. In J. G. Nicholls (Ed.), *Advances in motivation and achievement: The development of achievement motivation* (Vol. 3, pp. 251-281). Greenwich, CT: JAI Press.

Roberts, G. C. (2001). Understanding the dynamics of motivation in physical activity: The influence of achievement goals on motivational processes. In G. C. Roberts (Ed.), *Advances in motivation in sport and exercise* (2nd ed., pp. 1-50). Champaign, IL; Human Kinetics.

Roberts, G. C. (Ed.). (1992). *Motivation in sport and exercise.* Champaign, IL: Human Kinetics.

Roberts, G. C., Treasure, D. C., and Kavussanu, M. (1996). Orthogonality of achievement goals and its relationship to beliefs about success and satisfaction in sport. *The Sport Psychologist, 10,* 398-408.

Ryan, E. D. (1977). Attribution, intrinsic motivation, and athletics. In L.I. Gedvillas, and M.E. Kneer (Eds.), *Proceedings of the National Association for Physical Education of College Men National Conference Association for Physical Education of College Women National Conference* (pp. 346-353). Chicago, IL: University of Illinois at Chicago Circle.

Ryan, E. D. (1980). Attribution, intrinsic motivation, and athletics: A replication and extension. In C. H. Nadeau, W. R. Halliwell, W. R. Newell and G. C. Roberts (Eds.), *Psychology of motor behavior and sport – 1979* (pp. 19-24). Champaign, IL: Human Kinetics.

Ryan, R. M. (1982). Control and information in the intrapersonal sphere: An extension of cognitive evaluation theory. *Journal of Personality and Social Psychology, 43,* 450-461.

Ryan, R. M., and Deci, E. L. (2000). Self-determination theory and the facilitation of intrinsic motivation, social development, and well-being. *American Psychologist, 55,* 68-78.

Sage, G. (1977). *Introduction to motor behavior: A neuropsychological approach (2nd Edition).* Reading, MA: Addison-Wesley.

Skaalvik, E. M. (1997). Self-enhancing and self-defeating ego orientation: Relations with task and avoidance orientation, achievement, self-perceptions, and anxiety. *Journal of Educational Psychology, 89,* 71-81.

Smith, J. M. J., and Harwood, C. G. (2001). *The transciency of goal involvement states in matchplay: An elite player case study.* Paper presented at the BASES conference, Newport, UK. September.

Standage, M., Duda, J. L., and Ntoumanis, N. (2003). Predicting motivational regulations in physical education: The interplay between dispositional goal orientations, motivational climate and perceived competence. *Journal of Sports Sciences, 21,* 631-647.

Swain, A. B., and Harwood, C. G. (1996). Antecedents of state goals in age-group swimmers: An interactionist perspective. *Journal of Sports Sciences, 14,* 111-124.

Theeboom, M., DeKnop, P., and Weiss, M. R. (1995). Motivational climate, psychological responses, and motor skill development in children's sport: A field-based intervention study. *Journal of Sport and Exercise Psychology, 17,* 294-311.

Thill, E. E., and Brunel, P. C. (1995). Ego-involvement and task-involvement: Related conceptions of ability, effort, and learning strategies among soccer players. *International Journal of Sport Psychology, 26,* 81-97.

Treasure, D. C. (1997). Perceptions of motivational climate and elementary schools children's cognitive and affective response. *Journal of Sport and Exercise Psychology, 19,* 278-290.

Treasure, D. C., Duda, J. L., Hall, H. K, Roberts, G. C., Ames, C., and Maehr, M .L. (2001). Clarifying misconceptions and misrepresentations in achievement goal research in sport: A response to Harwood, Hardy and Swain. *Journal of Sport and Exercise Psychology, 23,* 317-329.

Vallerand, R. J. (1997). Toward a hierarchical model of intrinsic and extrinsic motivation. In M. P. Zanna (Ed.), *Advances in experimental social psychology* (Vol. 29, pp. 271-360). New York, San Diego: Academic Press.

Vallerand, R. J. (2001). A hierarchical model of intrinsic and extrinsic motivation in sport and exercise. In G. C. Roberts (Ed.), *Advances in motivation in sport and exercise* (2nd ed., pp. 263-319). Champaign, IL: Human Kinetics.

Vallerand, R. J., and Fortier, M. S. (1998). Measures of intrinsic and extrinsic motivation in sport and physical activity: A review and critique. In J. Duda (Ed.) *Advances in sport and exercise psychology measurement* (pp. 81-101). Morgantown, WV: Fitness Information Technology.

Vallerand, R. J., and Losier, G. F. (1999). An integrative analysis of intrinsic and extrinsic motivation in sport. *Journal of Applied Sport Psychology, 11,* 142-169.

Vallerand, R. J., Pelletier, L. G., Blais, M. R., Brière, N. M., Senégal, C., and Vallières, E. F. (1992). The Academic Motivation Scale: A measure of intrinsic, extrinsic, and amotivation in education. *Educational and Psychological Measurement, 52,* 1003-1019.

Vallerand, R. J., Pelletier, L. G., Blais, M. R., Brière, N. M., Senégal, C., and Vallières, E. F. (1993). On the assessment of intrinsic, extrinsic, and amotivation in education: Evidence on the concurrent and construct validity of the Academic Motivation Scale. *Educational and Psychological Measurement, 53,* 159-172.

Vlachopoulos, S., and Biddle, S. J. H. (1997). Modeling the relation of goal orientations to achievement-related affect in physical education: Does perceived ability matter? *Journal of Sport and Exercise Psychology, 19,* 169-187.

Vlachopoulos, S. P., Karageorghis, C. I., and Terry, P. C. (2000). Motivation profiles in sport: A self-determination perspective. *Research Quarterly for Exercise and Sport, 71,* 387-397.

Weiss, M. R., and Ferrer-Caja, E. (2002). Motivational orientations and sport behavior. In T. Horn (Ed.), *Advances in sport psychology* (2nd ed., pp. 101-183). Champaign, IL: Human Kinetics.

White, S. A., and Zellner, S. (1996). The relationship between goal orientation, beliefs about the causes of sport success, and trait anxiety among high school, intercollegiate, and recreational sport participants. *The Sport Psychologist, 10,* 58-72.

White, R. W. (1959). Motivation reconsidered: The concept of competence. *Psychological Review, 66,* 297-333.

White, S. A. (1998). Adolescent goal profiles, perceptions of the parent initiated motivational climate and competitive trait anxiety. *The Sport Psychologist, 12,* 16-28.

Whitehead, J., Andree, K. V., and Lee, M. J. (2004). Achievement perspectives and perceived ability: How far do interactions generalize in youth sport? *Psychology of Sport and Exercise, 5,* 291-317.

Williams, L. (1998). Contextual influences and goal perspectives among female youth sport participants. *Research Quarterly for Exercise and Sport, 69,* 47-57.

In: Literature Reviews in Sport Psychology   ISBN 1-59454-904-4
Editors: S. Hanton and S. D. Mellalieu, pp. 199-225   © 2006 Nova Science Publishers, Inc.

Chapter 6

THE MULTIDIMENSIONAL CONSTRUCT OF SOCIAL SUPPORT

Nicholas L. Holt[*]

University of Alberta, Canada

Sharleen D. Hoar

University of Lethbridge, Canada

ABSTRACT

The purpose of this chapter is to review the construct of social support and evaluate associated sport psychology research. Social support is conceptualized as a three dimensional construct that can be distinguished by its: (a) Structural dimension (represented by social support networks), (b) functional dimension (represented by received social support exchanges), and (c) perceptual dimension (represented by appraisals of perceived social support). Based on this conceptualization, a model of the social support process in sport (Figure 1) is presented to serve as the framework for this chapter. Mechanisms, moderators, and outcomes of the social support process are examined. Finally, future directions for sport psychology research are suggested.

Keywords: Social support process, main effect, buffering effect, injury, youth sport, sport performance

---

[*] Correspondence concerning this article should be addressed to Nick Holt, Faculty of Physical Education and Recreation, University of Alberta, Edmonton, Alberta, T6G 2H9, Canada. Tel: 1-780-492-7386. Fax: 1-780-492-1008. E-mail: nholt@ualberta.ca

INTRODUCTION

Social support is one of the most important constructs in health psychology (Veiel and Baumann, 1992). Research in this area can be traced back to Émile Durkheim (1951), who argued that the underlying reason for suicide was a person's lack of social integration within her/his community. More recent evidence shows that healthy people who are connected to their social networks are at lower risk from mortality than their more isolated counterparts (Cohen and Syme, 1985). Social support has also been implicated in morbidity studies as a key intervening variable for illness (Thoits, 1995). From a psychological perspective, social support is an important factor influencing ways in which people cope with daily hassles and major life events (Aldwin, 2000).

In sport, the availability of social support can reduce uncertainty, aid physical and mental recovery, and provide reassurance for athletes (Rosenfeld, Richman, and Hardy, 1989). Social support can protect athletes under high life stress from injury (e.g., Petrie, 1993; Smith, Smoll, and Ptacek, 1990) and assist injured athletes' during their rehabilitation and recovery (e.g., Johnston and Carroll, 1998, 2000). Social support has been associated with enhancing children's affective experiences in youth sport (e.g., Babkes and Weiss, 1999; Woolger and Power, 2000). Beneficial effects of social support for athletic performance have also been observed (e.g., Rees and Hardy, 2000; Rees, Ingledew, and Hardy, 1999). Clearly, social support has immense scope and potential applications across a range of health and sport contexts.

A number of definitions of social support have been offered within the health psychology literature. Procidano and Heller (1983) described social support as the perceived availability of assistance that can be used to cope with stressors. Social support has also been defined as an exchange of resources between at least two individuals, which is perceived by the provider or the recipient to enhance the well-being of the recipient (Shumaker and Brownell, 1984). Alternatively, Sarason, Sarason, and Pierce (1990) suggested that knowing "one is loved and cared for may be the essence of social support" (p. 119). Although these broad definitions are suitable for describing the essence of social support, such vagueness has caused confusion among researchers when it comes to conceptualizing and measuring the construct (Vaux, 1992). In fact, many scholars now agree that *social support is a multidimensional construct* that involves structural, functional, and perceptual dimensions (Bianco and Eklund, 2001; Cauce, Manson, Gonzales, Hiaga, and Lui, 1994; Cohen, 1988; Vaux, 1992).

In sum, social support is an important construct in both health and sport psychology. Given the potential value of social support, the objective of this chapter is to provide a conceptualization of the social support process and assess relevant sport psychology research that has been conducted to date. Arising from this review and critique we propose several future research directions and consider applied implications for sport psychologists.

A CONCEPTUALIZATION OF SOCIAL SUPPORT

Figure 1 portrays our conceptualization of social support. It is based on various sources (e.g., Bianco and Eklund, 2001; Caspi, 1987; Cohen and Syme, 1985; Cohen and Wills, 1985; Vaux, 1992) and our own interpretations of the health and sport psychology literatures. We provide Figure 1 as a depiction of the process of social support which is intended to serve as a parsimonious framework for the organization of this chapter.

To briefly explain Figure 1, social support arises as a result of interactions between people and their social environment (Vaux, 1992). As shown in box (1), social support is conceptualized as a multidimensional construct represented by structural, functional, and perceptual dimensions (which are explained later in this chapter). We propose that social support influences health and well-being outcomes via two mechanisms (box 2). The buffering effect is based on the assumption that social support acts as a coping resource which helps people manage (or 'buffer') the negative effect of stress. The main effect is based on the assumption that social resources have a beneficial influence for health and well-being irrespective of whether people are under stress or not (Cohen, 1988; Cohen and Syme, 1985; Cohen and Wills, 1985).

The mechanisms by which social support influences health and well-being outcomes are moderated by social environmental factors (box 3a) along with sender and recipient individual factors (box 3b). Instrumental outcomes associated with social support (see box 4) refer to relieving distress (e.g., during injury rehabilitation). Relational outcomes refer to the development and strengthening of relationships (e.g., enhanced team cohesion). In the following sections we wish to lead the reader through each stage of the model in more detail, following the sequential order by which the boxes are numbered in Figure 1.

Social Support Dimensions

Social support is a construct which involves three dimensions. The structural dimension represents a person's social support networks. The functional dimension reflects exchanges of social support resources. The perceptual dimension involves an individual's appraisal of the amount and quality of support available to her/him. These three dimensions can be considered as conceptually distinct yet interrelated aspects of the social support process.

The Structural Dimension: Social Support Networks

The structural dimension of social support relates to the existence of, and interconnections between, social ties (Cohen, 1988). The structural dimension is assessed by examining social support networks. Social support networks include all social relationships that are potential sources of supportive behavior (Cauce et al., 1994). Indicators of social support networks include marital status, network size, intensity, frequency, and, homogeneity of relationships (House and Kahn, 1985; Vaux, 1985).

Milardo (1992) proposed four levels of social support networks. *Significant other networks* consist of approximately five individuals with whom the support recipient is intimate (e.g., family and close friends). *Exchange networks* include approximately 20 people (e.g., friends, neighbors, teammates, coaching staff and medical specialists) who routinely provide support. *Interactive networks* are people with whom one typically interacts on a day-to-day basis. *Global networks* consist of all those living people who are known to an individual by name and who would also recognize the person. Interactive and global networks are large, respondents are unable to guess their size accurately, and the size of these networks does not predict the size of any other kind of network.

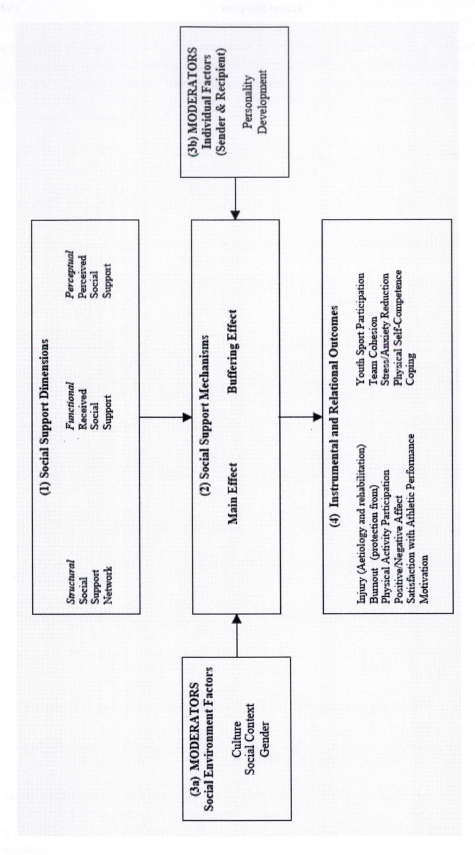

Figure 1. A conceptual model of the social support process in sport.

It is important to realize that the *mere presence* of another individual does not necessarily constitute a supportive exchange (Berndt and Hestenes, 1996). Thus, the presence of a social support network is not a guarantee that social support will be forthcoming (Bianco and Eklund, 2001). The type and quality of support obtained from a social support network is assumed to be beneficial for health outcomes (Sarason, Sarason, and Pierce, 1994).

The Functional Dimension: Received Social Support

The functional dimension of social support represents particular functions served by interpersonal relations (Cohen, 1988). The function dimension is assessed by examining received social support. Received social support refers to the *actual functions* of support (e.g., affection, belonging, or material aid) that people receive through their social interactions (Vaux, 1985). These support functions are also referred to as support exchanges (i.e., the functional exchange of support in a specific encounter). Cutrona and Russell (1990) summarized five basic social resources that are received during supportive interpersonal transactions: Emotional support, social integration or network support, esteem support, tangible aid, and information support.

Emotional support is the ability to turn to others for comfort and security during times of stress leading the person to feel that he/she is cared for by others. Social integration or network support represents a person feeling part of a group whose members have common interests and concerns. Esteem support involves the bolstering of a person's sense of competence. Tangible aid refers to concrete instrumental assistance. Finally, information support involves advice or guidance concerning possible solutions to a problem. These social resources can be measured as independent and distinct sub-constructs or combined to form a single second-order factor reflecting a global construct of received social support (Cutrona and Russell, 1990).

Cutrona and Russell (1990) developed their typology of five basic social resources in order to suggest a theory of 'optimal matching' between type of received social support and specific stress. They proposed that controllable events would require information support and emotional support that expresses confidence in the support recipient's abilities. For example, if an athlete experienced stress from making mistakes, she/he would require information support (e.g., corrective feedback from the coach) plus emotional support that expresses confidence in the athlete's abilities (e.g., the coach saying "I know that you are good enough to perform this skill"). Uncontrollable events would require emotional support plus the support component predicted by the domain in which the event occurred. For example, an elite amateur athlete who was struggling to adjust to the financial strain associated with high costs of competition would require emotional support plus tangible support (i.e., financial assistance). The implication here is that certain types of social support exchanges may influence health and well-being outcomes differently, so specificity is required in assessing components of received social support.

The Perceptual Dimension: Perceived Social Support

The perceptual dimension of social support is concerned with an individual's perception or appraisal of the amount and quality of support available to her/him (Vaux, 1985). Accordingly, the perceptual dimension is assessed by examining perceived social support. Perceived social support involves the recipient's appraisal of the availability *and the meaning* of supportive behaviors (Cohen and Syme, 1985; Cohen and Wills, 1985). Meaning is not an inherent part of supportive exchanges. Rather, meaning is constructed by via the perceptual processes of the support provider and receiver (Barnes and Duck, 1994).

One of the most robust findings in the social support literature is that the recipient's perception of being supported (whether this be accurate or not), rather than actual support behaviors, is more consistently associated with health and well-being outcomes (Sarason et al., 1990; Schwarzer and Leppin, 1991; Thoits, 1995). Another consistent finding is that support exchanges are often interpreted differently by the support provider and the recipient (Coriell and Cohen, 1995). Finally, the same social support activity is likely to be perceived differently across different contexts (Bianco and Eklund, 2001).

How can these differences in perceived social support be accounted for? Several theorists (Cohen and Syme, 1985; Pierce, Baldwin, and Lydon, 1997; Sarason et al., 1990) believe that what is actually supportive about social support is not the functional exchange of resources per se, but what is communicated about the recipient-sender relationship. From this symbolic interactionist perspective the recipient's appraisal of the implicit message or meaning of a supportive exchange is more important than the explicit message conveyed. For example, support messages that implicitly communicate interest, liking, love, empathy, concern, and willingness to help are likely to have a positive influence on the relationship between recipient and sender, thereby increasing the recipient's perceptions of social support (Barnes and Duck, 1994).

Relations Between the Dimensions

It is important to establish that the structural, functional, and perceptual dimensions of support are independent and should be considered conceptually distinct. However, in reality these three dimensions do not operate independently (Dunkel-Schetter and Bennett, 1990; Pierce, Sarason, Sarason, Joseph, and Henderson, 1996; Sarason, Shearin, Pierce, and Sarason, 1987; Vaux and Harrison, 1985). From a measurement perspective it is useful to differentiate between the dimensions of social support to better understand how each might contribute to health and well-being. But, Pierce et al. (1996) warned that only examining isolated dimensions of social support is insufficient to acquire an adequate understanding of the role of social support. A full understanding of the mechanisms by which social support influences health and well-being requires comprehensive and simultaneous examination of all three dimensions (Bianco and Eklund, 2001; Sarason et al., 1990; Winemiller, Mitchell, Sutcliff, and Cline, 1993). We were unable to locate any published studies in sport psychology which examined all three dimensions of social support.

Social Support Mechanisms

Although there are still many unanswered questions about the specific manner in which social support influences health outcomes (Thoits, 1995), two main mechanisms have been proposed: the buffering effect and the main effect (see box 2 on Figure 1).

Buffering Effect

The buffering effect refers to the notion that social support acts as a coping resource which helps people manage the negative effect of stress (Cohen, 1988; Cohen and Syme, 1985; Cohen and Wills, 1985). According to Lazarus (1999), an individual appraises the potential physical and/or psychological influence of a situation for his/her well-being in terms of threat, harm/loss, or challenge. The person deploys coping responses, which are cognitive, affective, and behavioral efforts to manage specific internal and external demands. Social support can facilitate the coping process by providing resources to 'buffer' specific demands evoked by a stressor. Thus, the buffering effect is important once an individual has appraised a situation as being stressful, and it can be considered as a protective or palliative mechanism (Bianco and Eklund, 2001).

Main Effect

The main effect (also referred to as the direct effect) proposes that social resources have a beneficial effect on health and well-being outcomes irrespective of whether people are under stress (Cohen, 1988; Cohen and Syme, 1985; Cohen and Wills, 1985). This mechanism is termed the main effect because supportive evidence is derived from the demonstration of a statistical main effect (with no Stress x Support interaction). The assumption here is that when adequate social support can be obtained people believe that they posses the resources to manage challenging situations. Therefore, social support has a direct function on health and well-being because persons who experience adequate social support appraise fewer stressors than their low-supported counterparts. The main effect can be considered as a preventative mechanism (Bianco and Eklund, 2001).

Buffering Effect or Main Effect?

The buffering and main effect mechanisms can be considered as complementary rather than antagonistic explanations of the social support process. There is evidence in favor of both the main and buffering effects of social support on health and well-being outcomes (Ryan and Solky, 1996). The buffering effect is conceptually connected to received social support (Cohen, 1988; Cohen and Syme, 1985). That is, the actual social support exchanges people receive during times of stress will help them cope with the demands they face, thus buffering the effect of stress (Cohen and Wills, 1985). The main effect is conceptually linked to perceived social support. In this case individuals who are high in perceived support (and therefore believe that they have the resources to cope with difficult situations) are less likely to view events as stressful compared with people who have low perceived social support (Sarason et al., 1990).

Despite received social support being more intimately connected with the buffering effect and perceived social support with the main effect, attempts to address the received/perceived support distinction have been marred by conceptual confusion over the meaning of the terms. As noted by Bianco and Eklund (2001), perceived support has been used to describe perceptions of social support available (the correct usage) and perceptions of satisfaction with social support received (the incorrect usage). Labelling perceptions of received support as a type of perceived social support have been so extensive that perceived support has become a construct associated with both the main effect and buffering effect (Sarason et al., 1990).

Few studies have tested the main and buffer effects within the sport context. Typically, sport psychology researchers have examined a single dimension of social support in relation to components of the stress process (i.e., goals and motives, self-concept beliefs, stress appraisal, and coping) (e.g., Smith et al., 1990; Van Yperen, 1995, 1998). These research findings do not provide a full understanding of basic mechanisms by which social support operates. Some evidence in support of a main effect and/or buffer effect function of social support comes from qualitative studies examining the application of athletes' social resources on recovery from sport injury (e.g., Bianco, 2001; Johnston and Carroll, 1998, 2000). Although main and buffering effects may be complementary, these mechanisms have yet to be adequately observed in sport psychology research.

Moderators of Social Support

Social support results from an interaction between an individual and his/her social environment. Social environment factors (box 3a on Figure 1) that moderate the social support process include culture, social structures, and gender. Sender and recipient individual factors (box 3b on Figure 1) that moderate the social support process include personality and development (Caspi, 1987).

Social Environment Factors
Factors like culture, context, and gender interact in complex ways to influence behaviors within the social environment (Marable, 2000). The social environment can be organized into two broad categories; culture and contextual social structures (Caspi, 1987). In the broadest sense, culture refers to a relatively stable pattern of beliefs, values, commitments, expected behaviors, and resources that are internalized by members of a society. Contextual social structures represent more unstable social influences that change across situational interactions (Aldwin, 2000).

Culture
Although culture is assumed to influence social behaviors, these influences have rarely been studied in psychology because it is difficult to operationally define the term 'culture' (Matsumoto, 1996). Results of the few cultural studies conducted in sport demonstrated that Japanese athletes reported greater desire for social support from coaches than Canadian athletes (Chelladurai, Malloy, Imamura, and Yamaguchi, 1987). Korean athletes utilized social support in a similar manner to US athletes (Park, 2000). No differences were observed between social support preferences of Canadian, American, and British collegiate athletes (Terry, 1984). These limited findings may be related to the fundamental difficulty of defining and conceptualizing culture. Indeed, Gill (2004) observed that in sport psychology "we have almost nothing on any cultural diversity issues" (p. 475).

Social Context
Norms of social behavior influence the types of social relationships that occur within certain contexts (Procidano and Smith, 1997). In the context of sport, people assume roles of athlete, teammate, coach, judge, or referee; and experience role-relationships such as coach-athlete and teammate-teammate. These social structures elicit a powerful influence on personal meanings derived from interpersonal encounters.

Although not a direct study of social support, Holt and Sparkes (2001) employed an ethnographic approach to observe how the social context and its associated roles and relationships influenced behaviors among players on a university soccer team. They noted that some players were unwilling to accept the roles which had been ascribed to them. Players with values that differed to the team philosophy clashed with the team sub-culture and the beliefs of other team members. Thus, contextual social structures created tensions that detracted from team task and social cohesion (see Lougheed and Hardy, this volume). Clearly not all social interactions are perceived as being positive for well-being (Rook, 1992). Further analyses of contextual social structures and their influence on social support in sport are required to understand positive and negative aspects of social relationships.

Gender

Another feature of the social environment is gender. Gender differences have been observed with respect to social support networks, amount of social support received, and perceptions of available social support (Shumaker and Hill, 1991). In sport contexts, there is some evidence that female athletes receive more emotional support exchanges than male athletes (Rock and Jones, 2002), and perceive more emotional support available from social network members (Hardy, Richman, and Rosenfeld, 1991; Rosenfeld et al., 1989). It is unclear, however, whether male and females athletes differ in the number of social support network relationships (e.g., Martin and Mushett, 1996) and perceptions held about social support exchanges (Rosenfeld et al., 1989).

Role intensification and socialization are the major contributors to these observed gender differences in social support (Blyth and Foster-Clark, 1987). A traditional female gender role emphasizes nurturance and emotional expressiveness. Alternatively, achievement, autonomy, and emotional control are emphasized within the traditional male gender role (Barbee et al., 1993). It has been suggested that competitive sport socializes people to concern themselves with achievement and autonomy, which supports more of the male gender role (Hargreaves, 1994). Sport represents a unique context in which to examine the influence of gender on a range of social support outcomes.

Sender and Recipient Individual Factors

Cultural and contextual social structures are important for understanding between-group differences. However, individuals within a cultural or social context should not be treated as a homogenous group because not all people in the same cultural or social context perceive interpersonal encounters in the same way. To some extent every individual's social reality is unique and never completely shared by others (Lazarus, 1999). Therefore, it is important to consider individual factors (of both the social support provider and recipient) that may moderate the social support process.

Personality

Rather than explore the myriad of personality research, we present one example of how personality features may moderate the social support process. It is theorized that across childhood and adolescence changing cognitive capacities and social experiences give rise to stable (i.e., dispositional) motivational achievement orientations (Duda and Hall, 2001). Nadler (1998) argued that individuals who hold high ego goal orientations are unlikely to seek out help from others because they believe that needs for help render negative social evaluation of their skills. On the other hand, individuals who hold high task goal orientations do not believe that their skills are being evaluated and are more likely to seek out help because they view others' help as a means for learning and improvement. In sport, Magyar and Feltz (2003) found evidence which partially supported the suggestion that goal orientations influence social support among 180 female high school volleyball athletes. Results demonstrated no relation between ego orientation and coach support ($r = -.09$) but a positive relation between task goal orientation and coach social support ($r = .29$).

Development

Development refers to personal resources arising from ontogenetic changes in cognitive, social, emotional, and physical abilities (Muir and Slater, 2003). As Muir and Slater explained, maturation and experience intervene between stages of childhood, adolescence, and adulthood. Therefore, development is age-related but not age-dependent. Several theorists have observed shifts in social support with development, with the most pronounced effects occurring during childhood and adolescence (Bruhn and Philips, 1987; Newcomb, 1990; Pierce et al., 1996; Vaux, 1985).

Social transitions during adolescence provide one example of how development may influence social support. During adolescence the peer group increases in importance as adolescents become more independent from the family (Coleman and Roker, 1998). As adolescents mature they often seek support from peers rather than parents when confronted with threatening situations. In sport, Côté (1999) demonstrated that parents assumed a leadership role in the initial period of childhood sport involvement (aged 6-12 years), a facilitative role in the years from 13-15, and a more distant supportive role in the latter stages of adolescence (aged 16+ years). Parents provided emotional and esteem support during children's initial sporting involvement, but during the later years they fulfilled more tangible supportive functions.

There is extensive scope for more research examining social support from a developmental perspective in sport. It should be noted that children with immature social-cognitive abilities may not be able to differentiate between the potential and actual quality of social support that is exchanged during social interactions (Clark-Lempers, Lempers, and Ho, 1991). Therefore, research that includes parents' and coaches' perspectives may be important for providing a complete picture of developmental aspects of social support among youth.

Outcomes of Social Support in Sport

Outcomes arising from social support (see box 4 on Figure 1) can be considered as instrumental or relational in nature. Instrumental outcomes refer to relieving distress and enhancing coping skills, whereas relational outcomes refer to the development and strengthening of relationships (Shumaker and Brownell, 1984). Bianco and Eklund (2001) observed that social support research in sport and exercise psychology has tended to focus on instrumental variables like adherence to athletic injury treatment (Udry, 1997). Improved social support may also have implications for relational outcomes (such as team cohesion or peer relationships). Thus, we included both instrumental and relational outcomes in our depiction of the social support process in sport.

Although social support has been linked with a broad range of outcomes, we have selected four areas that we think characterize social support research in sport: aetiology of injury, recovery from injury, youth sport participation, and sport performance.[1] We selected studies that represent the type of research that has been conducted in each area. Following our evaluation and critique of the available studies, we chose to pay particular attention to ways in which social support has been conceptualized and measured within each of these four areas of inquiry.

The Aetiology of Injury

The stress-injury model, which was introduced by Andersen and Williams (1988) and more recently revised (Williams and Andersen, 1998) predicts that three main classes of psychosocial variables influence stress reactivity and injury risk among athletes: (a) The individual's personal history of stressors (major life event stress, daily hassles, and past injury history), (b) personality characteristics (hardiness, locus of control, sense of coherence, competitive trait anxiety, achievement motivation, and sensation seeking), and (c) coping resources (general coping behaviors, social support, medication, stress management, and mental skills). Within the revised stress-injury model, social support is considered as a resource which reduces the influence of life stress on injury vulnerability. Though not explicitly stated in their model, it appears that social support is assumed to operate via a main effect mechanism because people who perceive social support to be readily available are hypothesized to have lower stress reactivity and reduced risk of injury than those with low perceived support.

Research conducted by Smith et al. (1990) provided evidence for the prediction that social support influences the effect of life stress on injury vulnerability. They examined the conjunctive (additive) and disjunctive (separate) effect of social support and coping skills on injury and life stress. Perceived social support was assessed via a measure that required athletes to rate emotional and informational support available from 20 different individuals (e.g., mother, father) and groups (e.g., teammates). Athletes rated the extent to which each individual and group provided (a) emotional support and caring, and (b) help and guidance on a five-point Likert scale ranging from *not at all helpful* (1) to *very helpful* (5). Summed scores provided overall measures of social support for two components (i.e., individual and group). Results showed that coping skills and social support exhibited a significant life stress-injury relation only for athletes with high stress. Results also indicated that social support and coping skills were statistically independent, suggesting they can operate in a conjunctive manner to reduce injury risk.

In the Smith et al. (1990) study, respondents were asked to indicate the extent to which individuals and groups provided two types of received social support (emotional and information support). These two social support measures correlated .88 with one another, which led Smith et al. to assume that the measures "can be considered to be tapping the same construct" (p. 364). The difficulty here is establishing exactly which support dimension was being assessed (social support network, received social support, or both). Similarly, a lack of conceptual clarity concerning the dimension of social support under scrutiny has been a

---

[1] We conducted a search of the social support literature using iterative techniques and other sources (e.g., SportDiscus, PsychInfo). We were able to compile and review 74 published studies which examined social support in sport. Due to space limitations we are unable to report extensively on all these studies in the present chapter. As such, we selected studies that we thought were representative of key issues in the literature. Readers are invited to contact either of the authors for a list of the studies we obtained.

recurring problem in the measurement of social support in the health psychology literature (Vaux, 1992).

In a test of the stress-injury model (Andersen and Williams, 1988; Williams and Andersen, 1998), Petrie (1993) found that playing status modified the social support-life stress injury relation for American football players. Petrie used the Social Support Inventory (SSI; Brown, Brady, Lent, Wolfert, and Hall, 1987), a 39-item measure of perceived social support. Findings indicated that more severe injuries, greater time loss, and more games missed occurred for starting players with low levels of support and high life stress. Andersen and Williams (1999) provided further evidence for their model using the Social Support Questionnaire (SSQ; Sarason, Levine, Basham, and Sarason, 1983). The SSQ is a 27-item measure which assesses perceived social support and satisfaction. Each item presents a specific scenario and asks participants to list the people who would be available for support in that situation and indicate the extent to which they are satisfied with the support. Assessing perceived social support is conceptually coherent with the main effect hypothesis and the presumed role of social support in the stress-injury model.

Rehabilitation From Injury

Social support has been implicated in athletes' rehabilitation from injury. Sport psychology researchers (e.g., Brewer, 1994; Wiese-Bjornstal, Smith, and LaMott, 1995) proposed that the role of social support in athletic injury rehabilitation is best understood from a stress-process perspective (similar to the transactional approach; Lazarus, 1999). In contrast to the stress-injury model (Andersen and Williams, 1988; Williams and Andersen, 1998), injury rehabilitation models are more closely aligned with a buffering mechanism of social support. In other words, social support helps athletes cope with the stressors they experience during the injury-rehabilitation process (e.g., Ievleva and Orlick, 1991).

Green and Weinberg (2001) examined athletic identity, coping skills, and social support as moderators of mood disturbance and physical self-esteem among 30 people who had experienced injury which prohibited physical activity for at least six weeks. They used the SSQ (Sarason et al., 1983) to measure perceived social support. Findings indicated that increased satisfaction with social support was significantly related to lower levels of mood disturbance during injury rehabilitation. Using the SSI (Brown et al., 1987) to measure perceived support, Udry (1997) examined rehabilitation adherence, coping, and social support over a 12-week period among 25 patients who had suffered Anterior Cruciate Ligament (ACL) damage. Social support was not a significant predictor of adherence at any stage during the rehabilitation period and social support remained stable over time. This study was limited in that the small sample size reduced statistical power and prohibited the examination of sub-groups, and patients were only assessed for 12 weeks rather than for the full period of their rehabilitation (Johnston and Carroll, 2000).

Johnston and Carroll (2000) examined coping and social support among 93 "high" (>3 hrs per week) and "low" (≤ 3 hrs per week) sport involvement patients at three time points over the entire period of their injury rehabilitation. Social support was assessed using a novel visual analog scale to assess participants' "perceptions of the availability of and satisfaction with informational, emotional, and practical support" (p. 293). No differences were observed between high and low involvement groups for any support variables, but women were more satisfied with practical and emotional support than men.

The larger sample and extended timeframe in Johnston and Carroll's (2000) study helped overcome some of the limitations of previous injury rehabilitation research (i.e., Green and Weinberg, 2001; Udry, 1997). There were notable differences in how social support was measured across these studies. Green and Weinberg and Udry all measured perceived support, whereas Johnston and Carroll used an unvalidated novel measure which appeared to examine both appraisal of available social support and the social support received (i.e., satisfaction with support exchanges). Such diversity in the manner in which social support is measured creates difficulties in establishing firm conclusions about the influence of social support on athletes' well-being during injury rehabilitation.

Researchers have also employed qualitative approaches to examine the role of social support in sport injury rehabilitation. For example, Bianco, Malo, and Orlick (1999) interviewed 12 elite Canadian skiers and content analyzed the data into three different phases of injury or illness recovery. The first 'injury-illness phase' represented the occurrence of the injury. The 'rehabilitation-recovery' phase lasted 1-24 months. Finally, the 'return to full activity' phase reflected the period from when the athletes returned to training until they were fully recovered. Bianco et al. reported that they used a phenomenological interviewing approach, but it was notable that the data were not subjected to a phenomenological analysis (e.g., Giorgi and Giorgi, 2003), and the results were not presented in the phenomenological tradition as a synopsis of the *meanings* associated with participants' experiences (Smith and Osbourne, 2003).

Bianco et al.'s (1999) findings were extended through what appears to be a secondary analysis of the data collected through the original interviews (Bianco, 2001). In this latter paper, data were deductively matched with Hardy et al.'s (1991) categories of support received from members of the skiers' social networks. Findings showed that members of the treatment team, ski team, and home support networks provided social support which served to reduce skiers' distress during the three phases of recovery. These data provided some support for received social support acting as a buffer to the stress associated with injury rehabilitation.

In another qualitative study, Johnston and Carroll (1998) interviewed 12 athletes with ACL injuries about the types of social support they received during rehabilitation. Participants were asked to comment on pre-determined types of received social support, and data were matched with these support types over three time periods (the beginning, middle, and end of rehabilitation). Findings suggested that emotional and practical support decreased with time, while informational support increased (and was preferred by the injured athletes). Medical professionals were cited as the primary providers of informational support requiring medical knowledge, whereas friends and family were the main sources of emotional and practical support.

Combined, these qualitative studies (Bianco, 2001; Bianco et al., 1999; Johnston and Carroll, 1998) have provided descriptive evidence about the changing nature of social support during injury rehabilitation. Similar to the quantitative literature, one difficulty comparing the findings of these qualitative studies is firmly establishing which dimensions of support were assessed. For example, consider the following question and follow-up probe: "Who supports you? How do they support you?" These questions could produce specific examples of support exchanges (i.e., received support). If a question was posed in the present tense (e.g., "who can you turn to for support?") or future tense ("if you experienced a stressful situation, who would you turn to for support?") it is likely that responses would reflect the dimension of perceived social support. Bianco et al. (1999) provided some examples of their interview questions, whereas Johnston and Carroll (1998) did not. Without this specific information the dimension of social support under scrutiny is open to interpretation.

No matter which types of data collection methods are used (i.e., qualitative or quantitative), it remains important to distinguish between the dimensions of support that are being studied. In the case of injury rehabilitation it is important to consider the entire period of rehabilitation in order to establish a complete picture of this process (Johnston and Carroll, 2000; Udry, 1997). It might be that individuals experience changes relative to each of the dimensions of social support as rehabilitation progresses. Studies that examine all three dimensions of social support longitudinally would make a valuable contribution to the literature.

Youth Sport Participation

The combined and independent influence of social support from parents, coaches, and peers for youth sport participation has received considerable attention. For example, children who experience higher levels of precompetitive anxiety do so, at least in part, because of concerns about how their performance outcomes may affect interactions with peers, parents, and coaches (Gould, Eklund, Petlichkoff, Peterson, and Bump, 1991; Smoll, Smith, Barnett, and Everett, 1993). Parental support has been positively correlated with children's enjoyment and enthusiasm (Babkes and Weiss, 1999; Stein, Raedeke, and Glenn, 1999; Woolger and Power, 2000), self-esteem (Leff and Hoyle, 1995), and subjective well-being (Van Yperen, 1995, 1998). Coaches have also been identified as an important influence on the psychological development of children (e.g., Brustad, Babkes, and Smith, 2001).

There are vast differences in the manner in which social support has been conceptualized and measured in the youth sport literature. Leff and Hoyle (1995) used an unvalidated six-item measure of general parental support, which appeared to assess perceived support (but the specific support dimension was not identified). Stein et al. (1999) created 7-point Likert scales to obtain ratings of mothers and fathers "level" and "degree" of sport involvement. Weiss and Weiss (2003) employed Harter's (1985) Social Support Scale to assess youth gymnasts' perceptions of social support. This measure comprises six-items which assess social approval from each of the following people: close friend, peer group, parents, and teachers (typically modified to coaches for sport studies). This measure gives an indication of the providers of perceived overall support, rather than (for example) the types of support significant others may be able to provide.

Although the use of different types of measures of social support is not a criticism of any one study per se, we cannot establish with certainty that researchers are all measuring the same social support construct. This is problematic when social support is treated as a single variable which is correlated with other psychological constructs. Another issue is that using measures with only a couple of items to assess social support limits reliability, potentially under representing the construct they are intended to measure, and attenuating observed empirical relationships (Vaux, 1992). Reflecting on the health psychology social support literature, House and Kahn (1985) stated that "measurement in this area is still in a fairly primitive state" (p. 102). Vaux reiterated this suggestion seven years later, observing that few measures have been subjected to thorough psychometric analysis. Similarly, measurement of social support in sport psychology is in a fairly primitive state, particularly with respect to measures appropriate for youth. The creation of developmentally-appropriate and sport-specific measures for social support networks, received support, and perceived support represent important future research directions.

Adapting a qualitative approach, Wolfenden and Holt (2005) examined the talent development experiences of elite English tennis players (aged 14-15 years). Children were asked open-ended questions like "How do your parents support you? How do your coaches support you?" Parents and coaches were asked "How do you support your child/the player?" These questions may tap into support exchanges that have occurred (i.e., received social support). Results indicated that parents fulfilled the most significant roles by providing emotional and tangible support (with the mother being more involved than the father), whereas coaches predominantly provided technical advice. In another study, interviews with 34 elite (international and professional) adolescent male soccer players revealed that fathers were an important source of soccer-specific informational support (Holt and Dunn, 2004). The authors concluded that fathers could provide informational support because many had previous soccer playing experiences themselves.

These findings (Holt and Dunn, 2004; Wolfenden and Holt, 2005) suggest that the type of support provided by parents and coaches is differentiated according to the perceived expertise of the support-provider (Rosenfeld et al., 1989). The tennis players in Wolfenden and Holt's study negatively evaluated their parents' attempts to provide informational support in competitive settings. There may be negative aspects of support activities that are presumably intended to be helpful (i.e., parents giving advice during tennis competitions). Negative aspects of support exchanges have not been extensively studied (Rook, 1992).

In addition to parents and coaches, peers appear to be an important social resource associated with the youth sport context. Friendship is a peer-relationship construct that describes a mutual, reciprocal relationship between two individuals (Weiss and Stuntz, 2004). Adolescent athletes identify intimacy, attractive qualities, similar interests/beliefs, and conflict as features of friendships (Weiss and Smith, 2002). Evidence suggests that peer relationships have a positive effect on adolescents' motivation for physical activity (Smith, 1999). The body of work on peer relationships in sport is compatible to the social support literature, but direct studies of the supportive influence of peers are limited. One reason for this may be the absence of measures which adequately assess dimensions of social support that children and adolescents experience from their peers.

Another limitation of youth sport research examining social support is that whereas the support recipient (i.e., the child) has been examined, support providers' (i.e., parents, coaches, and peers) thoughts and feelings about the support they offer have yet to be assessed. One exception to this was provided by Wolfenden and Holt (2005) because they interviewed parents and coaches (i.e., support providers) as well as junior players (i.e., support recipients). However, they did not assess the content and nature of specific instances of support exchanges from the provider's and recipient's perspectives. Although it is likely that people with perceived expertise in the particular area of concern may be the most appropriate support-providers for athletes, we know little about the actual content of these support exchanges. More information about support exchanges that occur in competitive settings would provide important applied information for practitioners and coaches who work in youth sport.

Sport Performance

Social support research in sport performance contexts has been approached from a variety of perspectives. Qualitative studies with elite athletes show that parents, team-mates, and coaches are typically considered by sport participants to be members of significant-other support networks. Extended family members, medical specialists (e.g., physiotherapist, athletic therapist), and mental training coaches can be considered as exchange network members (Gould, Guinan, Greenleaf, Medbery, and Peterson, 1999; Robbins and Rosenfeld, 2001). Interactive and global networks in sport have not been studied, but given that these networks do not appear to have a major influence on well-being (Milardo, 1992), the lack of research here is not a future priority for sport psychology researchers.

Rosenfeld et al. (1989) presented 171 college student-athletes' descriptions of their social support networks. Findings showed that coaches and teammates were the primary providers of support that required sport expertise and knowledge. Friends and parents were the primary providers of complementary types of support that did not require such knowledge (i.e., listening, emotional support, and emotional challenge). Other studies have also shown that specific social relationships (i.e., with parents versus coaches) provide specific types of social resources (e.g., Hardy et al., 1991).

Teammates can be included as a feature of social support networks unique to the sport context. Compared to athletes who compete at individual sports, athletes in sport teams may have a greater *potential* to acquire advice, emotional resources, and instrumental aid from teammates. But a large team can also negatively influence the exchange of social resources by reducing communication between group members and their feelings of task and social cohesion (Widmeyer, Brawley, and Carron, 1990). Weak correlations have been reported within the health literature linking social support network size and received functional support (Cohen and Wills, 1985). At a certain point the size of the group may become unmanageable and have a negative impact upon the individual. This highlights the importance of considering functional and perceptual dimensions of support in addition to the structure of social support networks.

The Social Support Survey (SSS; Richman, Rosenfeld, and Hardy, 1993) has been used in sport performance studies to assess social support network structure and perceptions of social support. This questionnaire comprises eight subscales of social support resources (i.e., listening support, emotional support, emotional challenge, reality confirmation, task appreciation support, task challenge support, tangible assistance, and personal assistance), but no total support score. Respondents are required to indicate their appraisals of each type of social resource in terms of (a) the number of support providers, (b) satisfaction with their support, (c) difficulties in obtaining more support, and (d) the importance to one's overall well-being. Although Richman et al. provided some support for the dimension and appraisal factors of the SSS, confirmatory factor analyses has since revealed poor goodness-of-fit for the eight dimensions and the four appraisal factors (Rees, Hardy, Ingledew, and Evans, 2000). Rees et al. suggested that researchers exercise caution using the SSS in both research and applied settings. Alternative measures to the SSS have been used to assess relations between social support and sport performance. Rees et al. (1999) examined the relation between social support and performance variables among British tournament tennis players. Social support was measured using the Interpersonal Support Evaluation List (ISEL; Cohen, Mermelstein, Kamarack, and Hoberman, 1985). Results showed that perceived social support was positively related to certain process-oriented dimensions of performance, but not outcome measures (i.e., winning or losing) of performance. This study provided interesting descriptive evidence, but was limited by a correlational research design.

In a qualitative follow up study, Rees and Hardy (2000) interviewed 10 high level sport performers about their general perceptions of social support. The authors used some principles of grounded theory data analysis (Glaser and Strauss, 1967) but deductively matched the raw data with Cutrona and Russell's (1990) four types of support resources (i.e., information, esteem, emotion, and tangible). Although the qualitative comments appeared to provide evidence for all four types of support, the authors did not distinguish between structural, functional, and/or perceptual dimensions in their analysis.

Rees et al. (1999) speculated that the sport performance literature would benefit from the creation of sport-specific measures of social support which may serve as a better indicator of the types of support used by athletes. They also noted that a less contextually specific measure of support can provide more generalizable results (cf. Gauvin and Russell, 1993). Although the strengths and weaknesses of sport-specific measures must be considered, we anticipate that the creation of sport-specific measures will increase measurement sophistication concerning social support in sport psychology (cf. Vaux, 1992). Of course, any measure should be conceptually coherent with the multidimensional nature of social support.

SUMMARY, FUTURE DIRECTIONS, AND APPLIED IMPLICATIONS

It is quite clear that a major obstacle to progress in social support has been the sheer scope and complexity of the construct (Vaux, 1992). Measurement issues for sport psychology researchers interested in social support follow similar arguments advanced in the health psychology literature. Perhaps the most important task facing social support researchers is clearly conceptualizing, defining, and then measuring the dimension of social support in which they are interested. As we have explained (see Figure 1), social support is a multidimensional construct that involves structural, functional, and perceptual dimensions. Although theoretically independent, these dimensions are interrelated in real world settings. We suggest that future studies of social support will conceptualize and measure these distinct but interrelated dimensions.

Most likely the fullest understanding of social support will be obtained by examining all three support dimensions. However, this may be beyond the scope of some studies because of logistical and time concerns arising from data collection and/or methodological demands. In cases where one or two dimensions of support are assessed, there must be coherence between the dimension of social support examined and other variables or theoretical models under scrutiny. For example, given that the stress-injury model (Andersen and Williams, 1988; Williams and Andersen, 1998) implies that social support functions as a main effect, it is conceptually coherent to assess perceived social support and perhaps social support networks.

Figure 1 may provide researchers with a way of organizing future research programs. For example, moderators of social support have received relatively limited attention in sport psychology research. There is scope for research which advances our understanding of how contextual factors such as culture, social context, and gender influence the social support process. Similarly, studies which examine developmental and/or personality influences on the support process would be a valuable contribution to the literature. Researchers have tended to focus on the support recipient's perspective, but it may also be useful to examine the support provider's viewpoint, especially in youth sport settings where parents, coaches, and peers fulfil important roles.

Unvalidated novel measures and scales with few items create difficulties in comparing findings across studies because it is open to interpretation which dimension of social support is being examined. To advance understanding of social support within the sport context theoretically based measures are required. Social support instruments that distinguish between the three support dimensions will be useful for helping to illuminate the effects of social support on health and well-being outcomes in sport. The creation of developmentally appropriate measures is another important future research direction for advancing paediatric social support research in sport.

One 'solution' to some of the measurement difficulties associated with social support has been the adoption of certain qualitative research techniques. These qualitative studies have typically engaged athletes in single interviews during which a range of issues associated with social support have been discussed (e.g., Bianco, 2001; Bianco et al., 1999; Johnston and Carroll, 1998; Rees and Hardy, 2000). Although these interviews have revealed a breadth of information about athletes' perceptions of social support in their immediate sporting context and beyond, reliance on single interviews has been criticized in the sport psychology literature (Culver, Gilbert, and Trudel, 2003). Culver et al. observed that there has been a tendency to employ "qualitative interviews as oral questionnaires, [this] combined with an overwhelming reliance on one-shot interviews, is indicative of the positivistic influence on qualitative research" (p. 7).

By embracing certain qualitative methodologies (as opposed to only employing qualitative data collection and analysis techniques), sport psychology researchers may be able to come to a more holistic understanding of social support processes operating within particular settings. For example, ethnographic approaches (involving techniques like participant-observation and interviews) could be used to examine social support exchanges within a sporting sub-culture (cf. Holt and Sparkes, 2001). This information would help researchers to identify ways in which the social environment influences the social support process in sport over time.

Phenomenological methodologies, which are concerned with the meaning of lived experiences (Giorgi and Giorgi, 2003; Smith and Osbourne, 2003), could be employed to assess the perceptual dimension of social support. Researchers could engage participants in a series of in-depth interviews to establish the meaning of lived experiences of social support exchanges through stressful sporting episodes. Such research may reveal information consistent with the symbolic interactionist view of perceived social support (Barnes and Duck, 1994). The point here is that qualitative methodologies (i.e., overall strategies and frameworks for data collection and analysis) may provide researchers with more guidance in terms of their research designs rather than relying on qualitative techniques (i.e., interviews, content analysis etc).

As we have stated, there are some problems in comparing findings from diverse studies. Advocating the adoption of qualitative methodologies may be viewed by some as adding more confusion to the situation. However, as long as researchers are clear about the dimensions of social support in which they are interested, qualitative research can add to the social support literature. Presenting vague themes simply labelled 'social support' will not represent significant contributions. Clarity concerning the specific nature of questions asked and experiences obtained during interviews will also assist in comparing findings across studies.

We believe that the growth of qualitative and quantitative research can be viewed as complementary. Some researchers have initially used qualitative interviews to provide descriptive evidence for the nature of social support within a particular setting (e.g., injury; Johnston and Carroll, 1998), before going on to quantitatively examine changes in social support over time (Johnston and Carroll, 2000). Similar mixed methods approaches have been adopted by other researchers in sport psychology (e.g., Rees and Hardy, 2000; Rees et al., 1999, 2000). Perhaps the next stage of some of these research programs will be the creation of theoretically and empirically grounded sport-specific measures of social support.

As measurement challenges are overcome researchers may turn their attention to how social support influences health and well-being outcomes in sport. Herein fundamental questions about the mechanisms and processes by which social support operates remain (Rees and Hardy, 2000). Research which compares both buffering and main effects would make an important contribution to the literature (Bianco and Eklund, 2001). Given that social support is assumed to impact psychological and physical health symptoms via both buffering and main effects (Cohen and Wills, 1985), it will be interesting to see how these combined effects influence instrumental and relational outcomes in sport settings. In the health psychology literature it has been shown that perception of support is a better predictor of health outcomes than the actual receipt of support (Sarason et al., 1990). In sport, we wonder if perceived support will be proven as a better predictor of positive adaptation to the demands of competition than received support? Again, studies which distinguish between structural, functional, and perceptual dimensions of support will advance the literature in this area.

In terms of applied implications, the most important issue for practitioners to consider is that social support is a multidimensional construct. It may be useful to identify the different dimensions of support athletes appraise. One challenge facing practitioners is connecting certain dimensions of support with specific outcomes. There is not much evidence to guide practitioners in making such connections. Given that athletes who are high in perceived support should be able to buffer the effects of stress, 'protective' support interventions may be useful for athletes with low perceived support (even if they are not experiencing stress at that specific time). For athletes who are actually experiencing stress, improving their support exchanges (received support) may help to alleviate any negative consequences.

We realize that these are somewhat vague suggestions, but the main point is that it is important to understand the social support process in order to deliver effective interventions. Gottlieb (1992) observed that because the controlled nature of interventions differs so strongly from the natural ecology in which supportive transactions take place, theoretical propositions derived from one context provide weak guidance for action in the other. Given the inherently applied nature of sport psychology, applied research leading to the creation and evaluation of interventions represents an important avenue of study.

Despite the acknowledged limitations of existing research findings, from an applied perspective social support has enormous scope. Richman, Hardy, Rosenfeld and Callahan (1989) provided several practical suggestions for promoting social support arising from a brainstorming activity they conducted with 36 practitioners at the third annual Association for the Advancement of Applied Sport Psychology conference. For example, practitioners suggested that listening support could be enhanced by providing communication training, social events, and structuring a warm, friendly, and accepting environment. They also proposed that athletes should be trained to recognize the importance of emotional support, and encouraged to provide this to others. Similarly the importance of emotional support should be emphasized among athletes' family members, coaches, and teammates. Richman et al. concluded that social support does not automatically occur with the sport setting; rather, quality social support needs to be incorporated into the working context of sport as part of an ongoing prevention program.

Accepting the premise that social support does not automatically occur in sport, there are many ways in which practitioners may influence its provision. For example, practitioners who work in youth sport may wish to ask children to identify the types of support they would like to experience from different adults, before asking them about the support they perceive right now. This exercise may reveal discrepancies between 'ideal' and 'experienced' social support. Skillful practitioners could then work with the child *and* the support providers to create a social environment which optimizes the child's development. From the research evidence available, it is likely that practitioners should encourage coaches to focus on information support whereas parents should focus on providing emotional and tangible support. In other words, provide support in the area where the person has the most (perceived) expertise.

At the group level social support can be considered as part of a team-building intervention. Rosenfeld and Richman (1997) argued that teams which employ social support as part of team-building are likely to have effective communication, shared commitment, and a team vision of success. Before creating a social support team-building intervention the existing level of social support within a team should be assessed (for example, using the SSS; Richman et al., 1993). Rosenfeld and Richman went on to propose a range of specific strategies based on those suggested provided by the practitioners in the Richman et al. (1989) study.

Unfortunately few examples of how social support influences team-building have been reported in the literature. One exception was provided by Dunn and Holt (2004). They delivered and evaluated a personal-disclosure mutual-sharing team-building intervention which involved college ice-hockey players sharing their reasons for playing the sport. This intervention provided opportunities for mutual-sharing between team-mates. Outcomes associated with the intervention were enhanced understanding (of self and others), increased cohesion (closeness and playing for each other), and improved confidence (confidence in teammates and feelings of invincibility). The authors speculated that socio-emotional bonds among group members were strengthened as the athletes understood each other better. The findings of this study show that socially-oriented interventions may positively influence team interactions.

Another important applied issue to consider is that the sport psychology practitioner will most likely become a member of an athlete's social support network. The importance of the relationship between practitioner and athlete in the creation of productive working alliances has been highlighted in the literature (e.g., Holt and Strean, 2001). As a practitioner develops trust and rapport with clients she or he may be regarded as more than the 'sport psych consultant.' Results of a recent study by Dunn and Holt (2003) showed that college ice-hockey players thought their sport psychology consultant fulfilled multiple roles (e.g., team-mate, co-coach, and liaison between coaches and players). Players also thought that the consultant was socially and emotionally involved with the team. Fulfilling multiple roles may place the practitioner in a unique situation in terms of his/her potential to provide social support. Professional training along with an understanding the process of social support should assist in managing these multiple roles.

In conclusion, we hope that the conceptual model (Figure 1) that served as the framework for this chapter is useful for organizing the process of social support in sport. The main point that has arisen from this review is that social support is a multidimensional construct, but it has not been consistently conceptualized nor assessed in this manner within the sport literature. Social support research that adheres to sound theoretical principles using appropriate methodologies will ultimately advance a more complete understanding about both the processes and the outcomes associated with social support in sport. To paraphrase Vaux (1992), it is imperative that sport psychology researchers ask themselves 'Exactly what aspect of social support do I wish to measure?'

ACKNOWLEDGEMENTS

Both authors made an equal contribution to this chapter. We would like to thank Dr. Sheldon Hanton and our reviewers who provided thoughtful commentaries that improved the quality of our work. Thanks also to Bethan Kingsley of Leeds Metropolitan University, England (who assisted with the literature search), and Michael Wall of the University of Alberta, Canada (who provided feedback on previous drafts). Although all these people helped us in the production of this chapter, any errors are purely our own.

REFERENCES

Aldwin, C. (2000). *Stress, coping, and development: An integrative perspective.* New York: Guildford Press.

Andersen, M. B., and Williams, J. M. (1988). A model of stress and athletic injury: Prediction and prevention. *Journal of Sport and Exercise Psychology, 10*, 294-306.

Andersen, M. B., and Williams, J. M. (1999). Athletic injury, psychosocial factors and perceptual changes during stress. *Journal of Sports Sciences, 17*, 735-741.

Babkes, M. L., and Weiss, M. R. (1999). Parental influence on children's cognitive and affective responses to competitive soccer participation. *Pediatric Exercise Science, 11*, 44-62.

Barbee, A. P., Cunningham, M. R., Winstead, B. A., Derlega, V. J., Gulley, M. R., Yankeelov, P. A., and Druen, P. B. (1993). Effects of gender role expectations on the social support process. *Journal of Social Issues, 49*, 175-190.

Barnes, M. K., and Duck, S. (1994). Everyday communicative contexts for social support. In B. R. Burleson, T. L. Albrecht, and I. G. Sarason (Eds.), *Communication of social support: Messages, interactions, relationships, and community* (pp. 175-194). Thousand Oaks, CA: Sage.

Berndt, T. J., and Hestenes, S. L. (1996). The developmental course of social support: Family and peers. In L. Sinclair and M. E. A. Levine (Eds.), *The developmental psychopathology of eating disorders: Implications for research, prevention, and treatment* (pp. 77-106). Mahwah, NJ: Lawrence Erlbaum.

Bianco, T. (2001). Social support and recovery from sport injury: Elite skiers share their experiences. *Research Quarterly for Exercise and Sport, 72*, 376-388.

Bianco, T., and Eklund, R. C. (2001). Conceptual considerations for social support research in sport and exercise settings: The case of sport injury. *Journal of Sport and Exercise Psychology, 23*, 85-107.

Bianco, T., Malo, S., and Orlick, T. (1999). Sport injury and illness: Elite skiers describe their experiences. *Research Quarterly for Exercise and Sport, 70,* 157-169.

Blyth, D. A., and Foster-Clark, F. S. (1987). Gender differences in perceived intimacy with different members of adolescents: Social networks. *Sex Roles, 17*, 689-718.

Brewer, B. W. (1994). Review and critique of models of psychological adjustment to athletic injury. *Journal of Applied Sport Psychology, 6*, 87-100.

Brown, S. D., Brady, T., Lent, R. W. Wolfert, J., and Hall, S. (1987). Perceived social support among college students: Three studies of the psychometric characteristics and counselling uses of the Social Support Inventory. *Journal of Counseling Psychology, 34*, 337-354.

Bruhn, J. G., and Philips, B. U. (1987). A developmental basis for social support. *Journal of Behavioral Medicine, 10*, 213-229.

Brustad, R. J., Babkes, M. L., and Smith, A. L. (2001). Youth in sport: Psychological considerations. In R. N. Singer, H. A. Hausenblas, and C. M. Janelle (Eds.), *Handbook of sport psychology* (2nd ed., pp. 604-635). New York: Wiley.

Caspi, A. (1987). Personality in the life course. *Journal of Personality and Social Psychology, 53*, 1203-1213.

Cauce, A. M., Manson, C., Gonzales, N., Hiaga, Y., and Lui, G. (1994). Social support during adolescence: Methodological and theoretical considerations. In F. Nestmann and K. Hurrelman (Eds.), *Social networks and social support in childhood and adolescence* (pp. 89-108). Berlin, Germany: Walter de Gruyter.

Chelladurai, P., Malloy, D., Imamura, H., and Yamaguchi, Y. (1987). A cross-cultural study of preferred leadership in sports. *Canadian Journal of Sports Sciences, 12*, 106-110.

Clark-Lempers, D. S., Lempers, J. D., and Ho, C. (1991). Early, middle, and late adolescents' perceptions of their relationships with significant others. *Journal of Adolescent Research, 6*, 296-315.

Cohen, S. (1988). Psychosocial models of the role of social support in the etiology of physical disease. *Health Psychology, 7*, 3, 269-297.

Cohen, S., Mermelstein, R., Kamarack, T., and Hoberman, H. M. (1985). Measuring the functional components of social support. In I. G. Sarason, and B. R. Sarason (Eds.), *Social support: Theory, research, and applications* (pp. 73-94). Hague: Martinus Nijhoff.

Cohen, S., and Syme, S. L. (1985). Issues in the study and application of social support. In S. Cohen and S. L. Syme (Eds.), *Social support and health* (pp. 3-22). Orlando, FL: Academic Press.

Cohen, S., and Wills, T. A. (1985). Stress, social support, and the buffering hypothesis. *Psychological Bulletin, 98*, 2, 310-357.

Coleman, J., and Roker, D. (1998). Adolescence. *The Psychologist, 11*, 593-596.

Coriell, M., and Cohen, S. (1995). Concordance in the face of a stressful event: When do members of a dyad agree that one person supported the other? *Journal of Personality and Social Psychology, 69*, 289-299.

Côtè, J. (1999). The influence of the family in the development of talent in sport. *The Sport Psychologist, 13*, 395-417.

Culver, D. M., Gilbert, W. D., and Trudel, P. (2003). A decade of qualitative research in sport psychology journals: 1990-1999. *The Sport Psychologist, 17*, 1-15.

Cutrona, C. E., and Russell, D. W. (1990). Type of social support and specific stress: Toward a theory of optimal matching. In B. R. Sarason, I. G. Sarason, and G. R. Pierce (Eds.), *Social support: An interactional view* (pp. 319-336). New York: Wiley.

Duda, J. L., and Hall, H. K. (2001). Achievement goal theory in sport. In R. N. Singer, H. A. Hausenblas, and C. M. Janelle (Eds.), *Handbook of sport psychology* (2nd ed., pp. 417-443). New York: Wiley.

Dunkel-Schetter, C., and Bennett, T. L. (1990). Differentiating the cognitive and social aspects of social support. In B. R. Sarason, I. G. Sarason, and G. R. Pierce, (Eds.), *Social support: An interactional view* (pp. 267-296). New York: Wiley.

Dunn, J. G. H., and Holt, N. L. (2003). Collegiate ice hockey players' perceptions of the delivery of an applied sport psychology program. *The Sport Psychologist, 17,* 351-368.

Dunn, J. G. H., and Holt, N. L. (2004). A qualitative investigation of a personal-disclosure mutual-sharing team building activity. *The Sport Psychologist, 18,* 363-380.

Durkheim, É. (1951). *Suicide.* New York: Free Press.

Gauvin, L., and Russell, S. J. (1993). Sport-specific and culturally adapted measures in sport and exercise psychology: Issues and strategies. In R. N. Singer, M. Murphey, and L. K. Tennant (Eds.), *Handbook of sport psychology* (pp. 891-900). New York: Macmillan.

Gill, D. L. (2004). Gender and cultural diversity across the lifespan. In M. R. Weiss (Ed.), *Developmental sport and exercise psychology: A lifespan perspective* (pp. 475-501). Morgantown, WV: Fitness Information Technology.

Giorgi, A., and Giorgi, B. (2003). Phenomenology. In J. A. Smith (Ed.), *Qualitative psychology: A practical guide to research methods* (pp. 25-50). Thousand Oaks, CA: Sage.

Glaser, B., and Strauss, A. (1967). *The discovery of grounded theory.* Chicago: Aldine.

Gottlieb, B. H. (1992). Quandaries in translating support concepts to intervention. In H. O. F. Veiel, and U. Baumann (Eds.), *The meaning and measurement of social support.* (pp. 293-309). New York: Hemisphere.

Gould, D., Guinan, D., Greenleaf, C., Medbery, R., and Peterson, K. (1999). Factors affecting Olympic performance: Perceptions of athletes and coaches from more and less successful teams. *The Sport Psychologist, 13*, 371-394.

Gould, D., Eklund, R.C., Petlichkoff, L., Peterson, K., and Bump, L. (1991). Psychological predictors of state anxiety and performance in age-group wrestlers. *Pediatric Exercise Science, 3*, 198-208.

Green, S. L., and Weinberg, R. S. (2001). Relationships among athletic identity, coping skills, social support, and the psychological impact of injury in recreational participants. *Journal of Applied Sport Psychology, 13*, 1, 40-59.

Hardy, C. J., Richman, J. M., and Rosenfeld, L. B. (1991). The role of social support in the life stress/injury relationship. *The Sport Psychologist, 5*, 128-139.

Hargreaves, J. (1994). *Sporting females: Critical issues in the history and sociology of women's sport.* London: Routledge.

Harter, S. (1985). *Manual for the Social Support Scale for children.* Denver, CO: University of Denver.

Holt, N. L., and Dunn, J. G. H. (2004). Toward a grounded theory of the psychosocial competencies and environmental conditions associated with soccer success. *Journal of Applied Sport Psychology, 16*, 199-219.

Holt, N. L., and Sparkes, A. C. (2001). An ethnographic study of cohesiveness on a college soccer team over a season. *The Sport Psychologist, 15*, 237-259.

Holt, N. L., and Strean, W. B. (2001). Reflecting on the initial intake meeting in sport psychology: A self-narrative of neophyte practice. *The Sport Psychologist, 15,* 188-204.

House, J. S., and Kahn, R. L. (1985). Measures and concepts of social support. In S. Cohen and S. L. Syme (Eds.), *Social support and health* (pp. 83-108). Orlando, FL: Academic Press.

Ievleva, L., and Orlick, T. (1991). Mental links to enhanced healing: An exploratory study. *The Sport Psychologist, 5*, 25-40.

Johnston, L. H., and Carroll, D. (1998). The provision of social support to injured athletes: A qualitative analysis. *Journal of Sport Rehabilitation, 7*, 267-284.

Johnston, L. H., and Carroll, D. (2000). Coping, social support, and injury: Changes over time and the effects of level of sports involvement. *Journal of Sport Rehabilitation, 9*, 290-303.

Lazarus, R. S. (1999). *Stress and emotion: A new synthesis*. New York: Springer.

Leff, S. S., and Hoyle, R. H. (1995). Young athletes' perceptions of parental support and pressure. *Journal of Youth and Adolescence, 24*, 2, 187-203.

Lougheed, T., and Hardy, J. (this volume). A cohesion review. In S. Hanton and S. D. Mellalieu (Eds.), *Literature reviews in sport psychology*. Hauppauge, NY: Nova Science.

Magyar, T. M., and Feltz, D. L. (2003). The influence of dispositional and situational tendencies on adolescent girls' sport confidence sources. *Psychology of Sport and Exercise, 4*, 175-190.

Marable, M. (2000). We need new and critical study of race and ethnicity. *The Chronicle of Higher Education*, B4-B7.

Martin, J. J., and Mushett, C. A. (1996). Social support mechanisms among athletes with disabilities. *Adapted Physical Activity Quarterly, 13*, 74-83.

Matsumoto, D. (1996). *Culture and psychology*. Pacific Grove, CA: Brooks/Cole.

Milardo, R. M. (1992). Comparative methods for delineating social networks. *Journal of Social and Personal Relationships, 9*, 447-461.

Muir, D., and Slater, A. (2003). The scope and methods of developmental psychology. In A. Slater and G. Bremner (Eds.), *An introduction to developmental psychology* (pp. 3-33). Malden, MA: Blackwell.

Nadler, A. (1998). Relationship, esteem, and achievement perspectives on autonomous and dependent help seeking. In S. A. Karabenick (Ed.), *Strategic help-seeking: Implementations for learning and teaching* (pp. 61-93). Mahwah, NJ: Lawrence Erlbaum.

Newcomb, M. D. (1990). Social support by many other names: Toward a unified conceptualization. *Journal of Social and Personal Relationships, 7*, 479-494.

Park, J. K. (2000). Coping strategies used by Korean National athletes. *The Sport Psychologist, 14*, 63-80.

Petrie, T. (1993). The moderating effects of social support and playing status on the life stress-injury relationship. *Journal of Applied Sport Psychology, 6*, 1-16.

Pierce, G. R., Sarason, B. R., Sarason, I. G., Joseph, H. J., and Henderson, C. A. (1996). Conceptualizing and assessing social support in the context of family. In G. R. Pierce, B.

R. Sarason, and I. G. Sarason, (Eds.), *Conceptualizing and assessing social support in the context of family* (pp. 3-23). New York: Plenum Press.

Pierce, T., Baldwin, M. W., and Lydon, J. E. (1997). A relational schema approach to social support. In G. R. Pierce, B. Lakey, I. G. Sarason, and B. R. Sarason (Eds.), *Sourcebook of social support and personality* (pp. 19-47). New York: Plenum Press.

Procidano, M. E., and Heller, K. (1983). Measure of perceived social support from friends and family: Three validation studies. *American Journal of Community Psychology, 11*, 1-24.

Procidano, M. E., and Smith, W. W. (1997). Assessing perceived social support: The importance of context. In G. R. Pierce, B. Lakey, I. G. Sarason, and B. R. Sarason (Eds.), *Sourcebook of social support and personality* (pp. 93-106). New York: Plenum Press.

Rees, T., and Hardy, L. (2000). An investigation of the social support experiences of high-level sports performers. *The Sport Psychologist, 14*, 327-347.

Rees, T., Hardy, L., Ingledew, D. K., and Evans, L. (2000). Examination of the validity of the social support survey using confirmatory factor analysis. *Research Quarterly for Exercise and Sport, 71*, 4, 322-330.

Rees, T., Ingledew, D. K., and Hardy, L. (1999). Social support dimensions and components of performance in tennis. *Journal of Sports Sciences, 17*, 41, 421-429.

Richman, J. M., Hardy, C. J., Rosenfeld, L. B., and Callanan, R. A. E. (1989). Strategies for enhancing social support networks in sport: A brainstorming experience. *Journal of Applied Sport Psychology, 1*, 150-159.

Richman, J. M., Rosenfeld, L. B., and Hardy, C. J. (1993). The Social Support Survey: A validation study of a clinical measure of the social support process. *Research on Social Work Practice, 3*, 288-311.

Robbins, J. E., and Rosenfeld, L. B. (2001). Athletes' perceptions of social support provided by their head coach, assistant coach, and athletic trainer, pre-injury and during rehabilitation. *Journal of Sport Behavior, 24*, 277-297.

Rock, J. A., and Jones, M. V. (2002). A preliminary investigation into the use of counselling skills in support rehabilitation from sport injury. *Journal of Sport Rehabilitation, 11*, 284-304.

Rook, K. S. (1992). Detrimental aspects of social relationships: Taking stock of an emerging literature. In H. Veiel and U. Baumann (Eds.), *The meaning and measurement of social support* (pp. 157-169). New York: Hemisphere.

Rosenfeld, L. B., and Richman, J. M. (1997). Developing effective social support: Team building and the social support process. *Journal of Applied Sport Psychology, 9*, 133-153.

Rosenfeld, L. B., Richman, J. M., and Hardy, C. J. (1989). Examining social support networks among athletes: Description and relationship to stress. *The Sport Psychologist, 3*, 23-33.

Ryan, R. M., and Solky, J. A. (1996). What is supportive about social support? On the psychological needs for autonomy and relatedness. In G. R. Pierce, B. R. Sarason, and I. G. Sarason (Eds.), *Handbook of social support and the family* (pp. 249-267). New York: Plenum Press.

Sarason, B. R., Shearin, E. N., Pierce, G. R., and Sarason, I. G. (1987). Interrelations of social support measures: Theoretical and practical implications. *Journal of Personality and Social Psychology, 52*, 4, 813-832.

Sarason, I. G., Levine, H. M., Basham, R. B., and Sarason, B. R. (1983). Assessing social support: The social support questionnaire. *Journal of Personality and Social Psychology, 44*, 1, 127-139.

Sarason, I. G., Sarason, B. R., and Pierce, G. R. (1990). Social support, personality, and performance. *Journal of Applied Sport Psychology, 2*, 117-127.

Sarason, I. G., Sarason, B. R., and Pierce, G. R. (1994). Social support: Global and relationship-based levels of analysis. *Journal of Social and Personal Relationships, 11*, 295-312.

Schwarzer, R., and Leppin, A. (1991). Social support and health: A theoretical and empirical overview. *Journal of Social and Personal Relationships, 8*, 99-127.

Shumaker, S. A., and Brownell, A. (1984). Toward a theory of social support: Closing conceptual gaps. *Journal of Social Issues, 40*, 11-36.

Shumaker, S. A., and Hill, R. D. (1991). Gender differences in social support and physical health. *Health Psychology. Special Issues: Gender and Health, 10*, 102-111.

Smith, A. L. (1999). Perceptions of peer relationships and physical activity participation in early adolescence. *Journal of Sport and Exercise Psychology, 21*, 329-350.

Smith, J. A., and Osbourne, M. (2003). Interpretative phenomenological analysis. In J. A. Smith (Ed.), *Qualitative psychology: A practical guide to research methods* (pp. 51-80). Thousand Oaks, CA: Sage.

Smith, R. E., Smoll, F. L., and Ptacek, J. T. (1990). Conjunctive moderator variables in vulnerability and resiliency research: Life stress, social support and coping skills, and adolescent sport injuries. *Journal of Personality and Social Psychology, 58*, 2, 360-370.

Smoll, F. L., Smith, R. E., Barnett, N. P., and Everett, J. J. (1993). Enhancement of coach's self-esteem through social support training for youth sport coaches. *Journal of Applied Psychology, 78*, 602-610.

Stein, G. L., Raedeke, T. D., and Glenn, S. D. (1999). Children's perceptions of parent sport involvement: It's not how much, but to what degree that's important. *Journal of Sport Behavior, 22*, 591-601.

Thoits, P. A. (1995). Stress, coping, and social support processes: Where are we? What next? *Journal of Health and Social Behavior, 35*, 53-79.

Terry, P. C. (1984). The coaching preferences of elite athletes competing at Universiade '83. *Canadian Journal of Sport Sciences, 9*, 201-208.

Udry, E. (1997). Coping and social support among injured athletes following surgery. *Journal of Sport and Exercise Psychology, 19*, 71-90.

Van Yperen, N. W. (1995). Interpersonal stress, performance level, and parental support: A longitudinal study among highly skilled young soccer players. *The Sport Psychologist, 9*, 225-241.

Van Yperen, N. W. (1998). Being a sportparent: Buffering the effect of your talented child's poor performance on his or her subjective well-being. *International Journal of Sport Psychology, 29*, 45-56.

Vaux, A. (1985). Variations in social support associated with gender, ethnicity, and age. *Journal of Social Issues, 41*, 89-110.

Vaux, A. (1992). Assessment of social support. In H. O. F. Veiel, and U. Baumann (Eds.), *The meaning and measurement of social support* (pp. 193-216). New York: Hemisphere.

Vaux, A., and Harrison, D. (1985). Support network characteristics associated with support satisfaction and perceived support. *American Journal of Community Psychology, 13*, 245-268.

Veiel, H. O. F., and Baumann, U. (1992). *The meaning and measurement of social support.* New York: Hemisphere.

Winemiller, D. R., Mitchell, M. E., Sutcliff, J., and Cline, D. J. (1993). Measurement strategies in social support: A descriptive view of the literature. *Journal of Clinical Psychology, 49*, 638-648.

Weiss, M. R., and Smith, A. L. (2002). Friendship quality in youth sport: Relationship to age, gender, and motivation variables. *Journal of Sport and Exercise Psychology, 24*, 420-437.

Weiss, M. R., and Stuntz, C. P. (2004). A little friendly competition: Peer relationships and psychosocial development in youth sport and physical activity contexts. In M. R. Weiss (Ed.), *Developmental sport and exercise psychology: A lifespan perspective* (pp. 165-196). Morgantown, VA: Fitness Information Technology.

Weiss, W. M., and Weiss, M. R. (2003). Attraction- and entrapment-based commitment among competitive female gymnasts. *Journal of Sport and Exercise Psychology, 25*, 229-247.

Widmeyer, W. N., Brawley, L. R., and Carron, A. V. (1990). The effects of group size in sport. *Journal of Sport and Exercise Psychology, 12*, 177-190.

Wiese-Bjornstal, D. M., Smith, A. M., and LaMott, E. E. (1995). A model of psychological response to athletic injury and rehabilitation. *Athletic Training, 1*, 17-30.

Williams, J. M., and Andersen, M. B. (1998). Psychosocial antecedents of sport injury: Review and critique of the stress and injury model. *Journal of Applied Sport Psychology, 10*, 5-25.

Wolfenden, L. E., and Holt, N. L. (2005). Talent development in elite junior tennis: Perceptions of players, parents, and coaches. *Journal of Applied Sport Psychology, 17*, 1-19.

Woolger, C., and Power, T. G. (2000). Parenting and children's intrinsic motivation in age group swimming. *Journal of Applied Developmental Psychology, 21*, 595-607.

In: Literature Reviews in Sport Psychology   ISBN 1-59454-904-4
Editors: S. Hanton and S. D. Mellalieu, pp. 227-255   © 2006 Nova Science Publishers, Inc.

Chapter 7

A REVIEW OF TEAM ROLES IN SPORT

Mark A. Eys[*]
Laurentian University, Canada
Mark R. Beauchamp
University of British Columbia, Canada
Steven R. Bray
McMaster University, Canada

ABSTRACT

Team members' successful execution of role responsibilities is critical to sport teams striving towards successful performance. The general purpose of this chapter is to review the literature on roles in sport. More specifically, a historical overview of the roles literature is first presented. This is followed by an outline of the structure of roles in sport teams and includes a conceptual model for the process of communicating and receiving role-related expectations. In addition, specific elements of role involvement (e.g., role ambiguity) are defined and discussed in terms of relevant research conducted in sport. Finally, implications and future directions for each role element are suggested, which highlight the importance and need for future research in this area.

Key words: Role ambiguity, role efficacy, role conflict, role acceptance, role satisfaction, role overload, role performance

INTRODUCTION

Roles have been defined as a set of expectations about behaviors for a position in a particular social context (e.g., Biddle and Thomas, 1966; Katz and Kahn, 1978; McGrath,

---

[*] Correspondence concerning this chapter should be addressed to Mark Eys, School of Human Kinetics, Laurentian University, Sudbury, OntarioP3E 2C6, Canada. Tel: 705-675-1151 ext. 1203. Fax: 705-675-4845. e-mail: meys@laurentian.ca

1984; Shaw, 1971). Roles are an integral component contributing to the structure of all groups whose purpose is to strive towards effective performance (Carron, Hausenblas, and Eys, 2005). However, the empirical study of roles has traditionally been confined to the organizational and business/industrial literature. Until recently, the importance of roles in sport has generally been communicated anecdotally in mainstream publications. For example, in reference to two athletes on a professional basketball team, Taylor (2000, June 12) observed "Their roles-the marksman and the muscle, respectively-could not be more different, nor in the same ways, more alike. They are both stone-faced specialists who, when they do their jobs well, complement perfectly their team's main attractions" (p. 34).

The research that has been conducted in sport within the last five years has empirically supported the contention that individual roles are important considerations within the team sport environment. The general purpose of this chapter is to summarize this research on roles in sport as well as provide a review of role-related research from other domains that may be useful in an athletic context. In the first section of this chapter a historical overview of the literature regarding roles will be presented along with a general conceptualization of the area as it pertains to sport. This conceptualization will include discussion on the types of roles that are present in a sport environment as well as introduce various elements related to role involvement (e.g., role ambiguity).

The chapter will then review each element of role involvement in greater depth. These include cognitive elements such as role ambiguity, role efficacy, role conflict, role overload, and role acceptance as well as affective (i.e., role satisfaction) and behavioral (i.e., role performance) elements. It will become clear that these areas differ greatly in the amount of research that has been conducted and the stage of development regarding their conceptualizations. However, each section will include an initial definition and/or current conceptualization, a review of existing empirical research conducted to date, as well as suggestions for future research and necessary areas for development. It will be equally clear that the topic of roles in sport provides enormous opportunities for future research and intervention.

HISTORICAL OVERVIEW OF ROLES WITHIN GROUP DYNAMICS

"When roles march in step the music is called team spirit: all for one and one for all". (Adair, 1986, p. 194).

Throughout the history of human existence men, women, and children have lived, worked, and performed in groups. Some authors have suggested that groups are a microcosm of the society in which we live (Hare, 1994), while others have gone even further to say that from the perspective of the individual, the group *is* society because so much of one's life is spent within them (Palazzolo, 1981). It was Kurt Lewin and his associates (Lewin, 1947, 1948; Lewin, Lippitt, and White, 1939) who first made popular the psychological term *group dynamics*. Since then, the study of groups has received considerable research attention. This is quite understandable, especially in light of Cartwright and Zander's (1960) assertion over forty years ago, that "the functioning or malfunctioning of groups is recognized increasingly as one of society's major problems...Whether one wishes to understand or to improve human behaviour, it is necessary to know a great deal about the nature of groups" (pp. 3-4). While this interest in groups has permeated several areas of psychology, it has been particularly prevalent within the field of sport psychology. This is perhaps not surprising given that so much sporting behavior is located within groups and teams[1] (cf. Carron, Hausenblas, and Eys, 2005).

In recent years a number of prominent sport psychology texts and book chapters (e.g., Carron, Hausenblas, and Eys, 2005; Lavallee, Kremer, Moran, and Williams, 2004; Paskevich, Estabrooks, Brawley, and Carron, 2001) have emerged, providing excellent summaries of the extant group dynamics literature, covering topics as varied as team cohesion, leadership, communication, goal setting, and group development. It is not the intention of this chapter to present another generic summary describing group dynamics research. Rather, our aim is to provide a comprehensive review of one particular area of group dynamics research in sport; namely roles. Within Carron, Hausenblas, and Eys' (2005) conceptual framework of group dynamics, roles contribute to the overall *structure* of the group and the study of this construct holds particular promise for understanding intra-group behavior.

From a historical perspective the word "role" can be traced as far back as the ancient Greco-Roman world of theatre, during which time actors' parts were written upon "rotula" or roles of parchment (Moreno, 1960). It was not until the 1930's, however, that the language of roles became commonplace in academic study, embraced in particular by the fields of sociology, philosophy, anthropology, and psychology. Some theorists such as Moreno (1934, 1960) and Goffman (1959) drew heavily from its dramaturgical origins, developing such innovative methods as psychodrama and dramaturgical analysis. Indeed, it was Moreno (1934, 1960) who pioneered the use of "role-playing" as a learning tool to enable individuals to perform more effectively in their occupied roles. He was also among the first writers to refer to the relationship between role-perception and role-enactment.

Others who made significant contributions to the early study of roles include Mead (1934), Newcomb (1943) and Cottrell (1933, 1942). Mead (1934) described the process of role-taking in relation to the role-appropriate behaviors of individuals required for functional interaction. Interestingly, Mead was among the first scholars to write about roles within the context of sport, in which he described the interdependent nature of role enactment in the game of baseball. Newcomb (1943) was another scholar who engaged the language of roles and was extremely influential in the genesis of the group dynamics movement. In his classic study of students at Bennington College, Newcomb examined how subjective roles and attitudes were shaped by the social norms of the groups to which the students belonged. Finally, it is worth noting the contribution of Cottrell (1933, 1942) who wrote extensively about roles and brought to the fore the potential of marital role conflict effecting marital well-being.

The study of roles soon came to be studied under the general rubric of role theory (cf. Biddle and Thomas, 1966; Biddle, 1979). However, despite the label of "theory" as Biddle and Thomas (1966) pointed out, role-theory is more of a body of knowledge and language than any one grand theory. Shaw and Costanzo (1982) perhaps described role theory best when they referred to it as a theoretical system that incorporates numerous theories with roles as the central subject matter.

---

[1] Consistent with Chan (1998) and Moritz and Watson (1998) no distinction is made between the terms 'group' and 'team'. They are used interchangeably throughout this chapter.

From the perspective of research into team roles, Bales and his colleagues (1950, 1953, 1958; Bales and Slater, 1955; Parsons and Bales, 1955) were perhaps among the most influential thinkers of their time. Bales theorized that within interdependent groups two types of roles predominate; those related to task performance and those related to socio-emotional support. The legacy of Bales work remains to this day, whereby a number of prominent psychologists have drawn from his early thinking to explain the differential contributions of specific roles for group functioning. For example, the British psychologist Meredith Belbin (1981, 1993) engaged in an extensive program of research involving hundreds of business teams, and identified nine 'key' roles (e.g., co-ordinator, implementer, specialist, resource investigator, monitor evaluator) that were believed to be necessary for effective team management and performance. Belbin (1981) suggested that in order for business teams to succeed, a necessary balance of team roles must exist and that members should be chosen carefully based upon their potential (role) contributions to the team. Belbin (1993) also described the dynamic interface between members' preferred role behaviors and those prescribed by their job demands, suggesting that when the two are inconsistent a team member's potential is unlikely to be realized.

While Bales can rightly be acknowledged as the foremost contributor to our current understanding of team roles, another group of researchers should be recognized for their substantial contribution to the role stress literature. In 1964, Kahn, Wolfe, Quinn, Snoek, and Rosenthal published their seminal work 'Organizational Stress: Studies in Role Conflict and Ambiguity' in which they presented a key conceptual model referred to as the 'role episode model'. This model was designed to identify potential antecedents and consequences of role ambiguity and role conflict (key elements within the role stress process) as well as intervening mediators and salient moderators. Despite the fact that this work was published some forty years ago, it is as relevant now as it was then. We will return to this model later in the chapter.

STRUCTURE AND PROCESS OF ROLE DEVELOPMENT IN SPORT TEAMS

As noted previously, only recently has any systematic investigation of roles in sport teams been attempted. Much of the initial conceptualization in sport has been based on research conducted in the organizational domain, which is not surprising given the similarities between the two contexts. For example, successful team performance is desired in both sport (i.e., winning) and business (i.e., gaining market share or selling a product and/or service). Also, in the majority of cases, a similar hierarchical structure exists in both contexts that consists of leaders (e.g., coaches or supervisors) and subordinate members (e.g., athletes or employees) who perform functions and responsibilities under the leaders' direction. Therefore, definitions of the types of roles as well as conceptual models regarding the processes of role development have either been adopted or closely adapted for utilization in a sport setting.

Types of Sport Roles

Two distinct categorizations of roles have been utilized to define the types of roles in sport. One major categorization relates to the degree of formalization of the role. Mabry and Barnes (1980) noted that a role can either be formal or informal. *Formal roles* are those that are directly prescribed to the individual by the group or organization. In sport, for example, these could include positional (e.g., setter in volleyball) and leadership roles (e.g., captain). *Informal roles,* also termed interaction roles, are ones that "evolve through association and interaction between members of a group or organization" (Mabry and Barnes, 1980, p. 125). Positive informal sport roles may include the team's social coordinator, team clown, or the enthusiastic bench player. However, negative informal roles can also arise that work to the detriment of the team. These may include the social outcast or the disgruntled bench player.

A second categorization that has been utilized to distinguish between types of roles in sport relates to the role's primary objective. Utilizing terminology from the work of Bales and Slater (1955; Slater, 1955; Bales, 1958), roles can either be (a) task oriented (instrumental) in that they focus on performing responsibilities related to the accomplishment of the group's objectives or (b) socio-emotional in orientation (expressive) whereby they promote harmony and integration within the group. Previous research by Rees and Segal (1984) used this categorization when they explored leadership role differentiation in two college level football teams. More specifically, Rees and Segal found that several members of each team fulfilled *both* task and social leadership roles (all were starting players) while some of the remaining members specialized in either performing task (all were starting players) *or* social (typically were high seniority/veteran players) leadership functions. Overall, it should be noted that the two categorizations discussed above (formal vs. informal roles and task vs. social roles) are not mutually exclusive. For example, it is possible to have any combination of formal and informal task roles as well as formal and informal social roles.

Attempts have been made in sport to identify more *specific* types of roles and role responsibilities that are present in teams that encompass the varying categorizations outlined above (i.e., formal and informal as well as task and social roles). In some cases, the researchers identified roles that were specific to one particular sport. For instance, Shoenfelt (2003) identified the formal task roles associated with the sport of volleyball (e.g., setter, blocker, etc.) in an intervention study designed to increase role clarity. In addition, Bray, Widmeyer, and Brawley (1998) identified offensive and defensive role responsibilities that were pertinent to the sport of basketball (e.g., offensive rebounding, one on one defending, etc.) as initial steps to gauge role efficacy. Finally, from a more general standpoint, Eys (2000) conducted focus groups with members of both independent (e.g., squash) and interdependent (e.g., rugby) sport teams in an effort to determine potential roles on those teams. Eight different general categories of roles emerged that included positional, formal leadership, informal leadership, social, communication, motivational, organizational, and guidance roles.

Overall, the examination of formal task-oriented roles (as opposed to informal and/or social roles) has dominated the literature to date. However, the lack of research into informal as well as social roles should not be viewed as an indication of lesser importance. In fact, socially established roles are likely contributors to cognitive, affective and behavioral outcomes as well. The potential value of the successful execution of social responsibilities within sport teams was recently highlighted by meta-analytic findings indicating a moderate to strong association between the social dimensions of team cohesion and performance (Carron, Colman, Wheeler, and Stevens, 2002).

A final major typology that has been examined with regards to roles in sport is gender. A gender role represents "the pattern of beliefs, attitudes, behaviors, skills, and interests which are culturally identified as reflecting femininity or masculinity" (Duda, 1991, p. 1). This construct represents an important area of study within sport psychology and has generated a large amount of discussion as well as at least one special journal issue devoted to the topic (Journal of Applied Sport Psychology, March 1991). However, it is outside the purview of this chapter to discuss roles socialized as being masculine or feminine.

Communicating Role Expectations

Regardless of whether roles are formally communicated or result from interaction with group members, the process of communicating role expectations can be examined in a similar fashion. The role episode model, originally proposed in industrial/organizational research by Kahn et al. (1964) and adapted for use in sport by Eys, Carron, Beauchamp, and Bray (2005; see Figure 1) highlights the interaction between two central actors. The first actor, termed the *role sender*, is an individual who develops and communicates expectations for a second individual who is the *focal person*. Generally, in the sporting context, the focal person (the individual who performs the role) is the athlete whereas the role sender is typically the head coach. However, there are additional potential role senders who could include assistant coaches, fellow teammates, trainers, or even the athlete's parents.

These two actors (i.e., role sender and focal person) participate in a cycle of five events during the communication, reception, and execution of a role and its associated responsibilities (see Figure 1). During the first event, the role sender develops expectations for the focal person. For example, a coach could decide what the responsibilities will be for his/her team captain (a formal role) or an athlete expects his or her teammate to make the social arrangements for a team party (an informal role in most cases). This leads to the second event whereby the role sender communicates (or sends), either formally or informally, these expectations to the focal person. Continuing the above examples, the coach may hold an individual meeting with the captain to attempt to explain his/her responsibilities or the athlete may hound his/her teammate for the details regarding the gathering. Event three occurs when the focal person experiences the pressures of the role expectation that has been sent. In this instance, the captain would interpret that there are certain responsibilities that are being conveyed to him/her or the social coordinator becomes aware that the other athlete depends on him/her for social details. Depending on a number of factors, including the clarity of the communication and the willingness to accept the responsibilities, the focal person could respond (event four) in a variety of different ways. This response could manifest itself in a positive (e.g., as the successful execution of the role responsibilities related to being a captain or social coordinator) or negative manner (e.g., anxiety over a perceived inability to perform the captain role or avoidance of informal social arrangement duties). The fifth and final event in this model highlights that the role sender will interpret the response of the focal person, which should influence current and future role expectations for that individual.

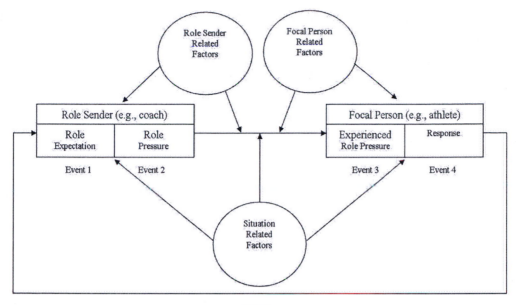

Figure 1. A theoretical framework of factors influencing the transmission and reception of role responsibilities. Adapted from Organizational Stress: Studies in Role Conflict and Ambiguity (p. 30), by R.L. Kahn, D. M. Wolfe, R. P. Quinn, J. D. Snoek, and R. A. Rosenthal, 1964, New York: Wiley.

In addition to the above events, the model also proposes that additional factors influence this cycle of events. These include factors related to (a) the role sender (e.g., ability to effectively communicate), (b) the focal person (e.g., degree to which he/she pays attention to instruction), and (c) the situation (e.g., complexity of the sport). This model can be an effective tool to assist in examining roles in sport. However, as will be shown, the majority of research has focused on the cognitive, affective, and behavioral elements that comprise the possible experiences and responses of the focal person to role pressures (events three and four of the role episode model).

Elements of Role Involvement

Figure 2 highlights the critical elements of role involvement. Prior to examining each one in more depth, two points should be raised. First, it must be conceded that there is potential overlap between certain role elements. For example, individuals may experience a lack of clarity about their role responsibilities as a result of increased role conflict (cf. Beauchamp and Bray, 2001). Likewise, some researchers have considered role overload as a form of role conflict (a case for examining role overload independently is presented in this chapter). However, each element is included separately because of its actual and/or potential significance within sport and to provide definitional clarity for the area as a whole.

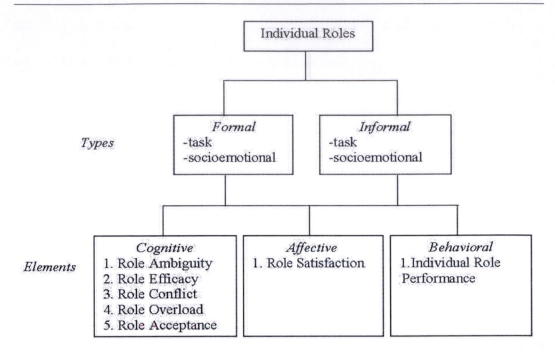

Figure 2. Components of the role dimension

The second point, as noted previously, is that there is a significant difference in the amount of research conducted among the various elements. We are hoping that the following sections will provide not only a review of literature but also guidance as to what critical 'next steps' in the investigation of roles in sport should be pursued.

COGNITIVE ELEMENTS OF ROLE INVOLVEMENT

Role Ambiguity

Role ambiguity has been defined as the lack of clear, consistent information regarding one's position (Kahn et al., 1964). As an example, an athlete who is a new member to an existing sport team and initially is unsure about how he or she fits within the group's structure might exhibit role ambiguity. Within the context of sport, role ambiguity has been the most extensively investigated element of role involvement and has undergone a conceptual and operational evolution from a unidimensional to multidimensional construct based on theorizing in the industrial/organizational literature.

Early research by Kahn and colleagues (1964) and Rizzo, House, and Lirtzman (1970) provided the basis, directly or indirectly, for the majority of sport role ambiguity research. For example, Grand and Carron (1982) adapted questions developed by Rizzo et al. (1970) to form a unidimensional measure of role ambiguity for use in their Team Climate Questionnaire. Grand and Carron subsequently found that role ambiguity was negatively related to both task and social cohesion. In addition, Dawe (1990) utilized the unidimensional role ambiguity sub-scale from Grand and Carron's Team Climate Questionnaire to show that enhanced cohesion and group performance were associated with less role ambiguity.

While the above studies were an encouraging start to examining role ambiguity in sport and demonstrated its importance in relation to other constructs, recent conceptualizations have demonstrated a more comprehensive, sport-oriented, multidimensional approach. Two studies conducted concurrently formed the basis for the most recent model. The first study, by Beauchamp and Bray (2001), sought to examine the relationship between role ambiguity and role conflict in interactive sport teams (e.g., rugby, soccer, water polo, field hockey, etc.) and utilized a conceptualization of role ambiguity that was bi-dimensional based on context. Their approach drew from earlier work by Rhoads et al. (1994) and Singh (1993) that had investigated functional dimensions of roles in organizational psychology. Specifically, Beauchamp and Bray examined beliefs regarding role understanding in both the *offensive* and *defensive* context of interactive sports. Results supported their contextual conceptualization of role ambiguity and also demonstrated that perceptions of role ambiguity were negatively related to role-efficacy, or the belief that one has the capabilities to successfully execute his or her role.

Additionally, Beauchamp and Bray (2001) noted the importance of two distinctions that should be considered when examining role perceptions. The first relates to the distinction between subjective and objective ambiguity. Subjective ambiguity refers to perceptions of ambiguity as held by the individual (e.g., an athlete may feel that she does not understand her role responsibilities despite repeated attempts to communicate them by her coach) whereas objective ambiguity is actual ambiguity or a lack of information that exists within the environment (e.g., the coach is unavailable to the athletes). It follows that if objective ambiguity exists, it is likely that subjective ambiguity will as well. However, subjective ambiguity can persist despite the absence of objective ambiguity. The second consideration relates to the fact that athletes may have perceptions of ambiguity concerning either (or both of) their formal or informal role responsibilities. Overall, sport research to date has typically focused on *subjective* ambiguity (i.e., perceptions of the role incumbent) regarding athletes' *formal* role responsibilities.

The second study was conducted by Eys and Carron (2001) and examined the relationship between role ambiguity and both task cohesion and task self-efficacy. In this case, the researchers developed a multidimensional conceptual model that drew closely from suggestions by Kahn et al. (1964). This sport model proposed that an individual athlete needs to obtain information regarding his or her role in four ways. First, the athlete needs to understand his or her *scope of role responsibilities* or generally what the role encompasses. Second, it is necessary for the athlete to understand what *behaviors are necessary to fulfill* his or her role. Third, the athlete needs to understand how he or she will be *evaluated with regards to role performance* and the fourth dimension outlines that the athlete should understand the *consequences should he or she fail to successfully fulfill role responsibilities*. The results of the Eys and Carron (2001) study found support for this conceptualization of role ambiguity as well as demonstrating that different role ambiguity dimensions were successful in predicting both task cohesion and task self-efficacy.

In an effort to construct a more comprehensive model of role ambiguity for interactive sport teams, Beauchamp, Bray, Eys, and Carron (2002) merged the above conceptualizations to form the role ambiguity model for interactive sport teams which highlights that athletes could perceive ambiguity in formal roles (subjectively) to arise with regard to four dimensions (i.e., scope of responsibilities, role behaviors, role evaluation, and role consequences) within two major contexts (i.e., offense and defense). An illustration

(Beauchamp, 2002) of this model is presented in Figure 3. In addition to the discussed subjective ambiguity components, this model also highlights that *objective* ambiguity can exist for both formal and informal roles. However, this type of role ambiguity has not yet been investigated to allow for a more comprehensive overall model to be developed.

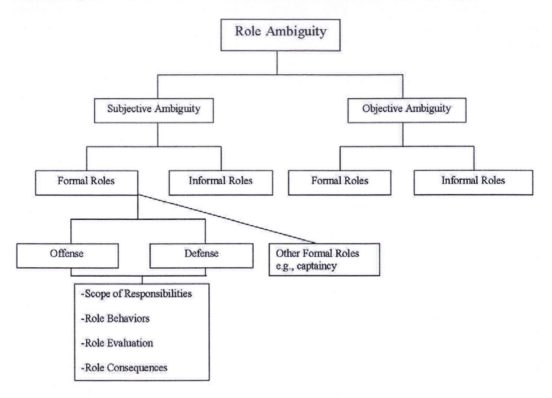

Figure 3. Conceptual model for role ambiguity.

Research on Role Ambiguity

Using this conceptualization, Beauchamp and colleagues (2002) developed the Role Ambiguity Scale, to operationalize role ambiguity in sport. The Role Ambiguity Scale is a 40-item measure that taps each of the four dimensions in both offensive and defensive contexts. Research conducted to date supports the reliability and validity of the measure. For example, Beauchamp et al. (2002) provided evidence of content validity, strong internal consistencies of the various dimensions, as well as initial support for the factorial validity of the measure through confirmatory factor analysis.

In addition to the statistical support of the Role Ambiguity Scale noted above, a number of studies have contributed to providing evidence of its construct validity and the overall importance of examining role ambiguity in sport. Beauchamp et al. (2003) examined role ambiguity in relation to competitive state anxiety (CSAI-2; Martens, Burton, Vealey, Bump, and Smith, 1990) and found that ambiguity regarding the scope of responsibilities on offense predicted cognitive state anxiety while ambiguity regarding the consequences of not fulfilling role responsibilities on offense predicted somatic state anxiety. Another study by Eys, Carron, Bray, and Beauchamp (2003) found that satisfaction with leadership aspects of the team (measured by the Athlete Satisfaction Questionnaire; Riemer, and Chelladurai, 1998) was negatively related to ambiguity regarding the scope of responsibilities on offense at both the beginning and end of a competitive season. Finally, athletes' perceptions of their intention to return to their respective teams was found to be negatively related to ambiguity regarding the scope of role responsibilities (Eys, Carron, Bray, and Beauchamp, 2005).

Additional research in this area has highlighted the need to consider other factors influencing the important relationships of role ambiguity. More specifically, there are a number of potential mediating and moderating variables involved with this construct. An extremely potent moderator that has been examined in both industry/organizational (O'Driscoll and Beehr, 2000) and sport (Bray, Beauchamp, Eys, and Carron, 2005) research is the individual's *need for clarity*. Need for clarity represents how important it is for the individual to avoid ambiguity. For example, if it does not matter to the athlete whether or not his/her role is specifically outlined then it is unlikely that any subsequent ambiguity will be related to his/her perceptions of other role-related outcomes (e.g., satisfaction). Bray and colleagues (2005) examined this question and found that the negative relationship between role ambiguity and satisfaction was significantly more prevalent for those athletes with a higher need for clarity. Other potential moderators that should be considered based on results from previous research include gender (e.g., the role ambiguity dimensions related to task self-efficacy differed between males and females; Eys and Carron, 2001), starting status (e.g., the relationship between role ambiguity and perceived leader behaviors was present for non-starters but not starters; Beauchamp et al., 2005), tenure on team (e.g., first year players exhibited greater role ambiguity than veterans; Eys, Carron, Beauchamp, and Bray, 2003), and time of season (e.g., greater role ambiguity exhibited early in competitive season as compared with late season; Eys, Carron, Beauchamp, and Bray, 2003).

Role performance is another variable that has been theorized to be related to role ambiguity—athletes who have a clearer understanding of their roles should perform better than those who lack clarity. Recent research has demonstrated this relationship but has also shown the importance of potential mediating variables (e.g., Beauchamp et al., 2002). A mediator is defined as "the generative mechanism through which the focal independent variable is able to influence the dependent variable of interest" (Baron and Kenny, 1986, p. 1173). One such mediator of the role ambiguity-role performance relationship is role efficacy. Beauchamp and colleagues (2002) demonstrated for both contexts (i.e., offense and defense) that athletes' beliefs about their ability to execute their role responsibilities (i.e., role efficacy) were influenced by how well they felt they understood their role. Role efficacy, in turn, predicted how well they actually performed their role requirements. Overall, future research needs to be cognizant of possible influential variables (in the form of both moderators and mediators) when examining the construct of role ambiguity.

Implications and Future Directions

The area of role ambiguity is the most developed element of role involvement in sport from both a theoretical and research perspective. However, in comparison to other areas of sport psychology (e.g., anxiety, cohesion, etc.) it is relatively underdeveloped. Thus, there is great opportunity and need for future research in this area. In relation to the current status of research, there are at least five pressing areas that need to be addressed. First, it is necessary to continue to examine the relationship of role ambiguity with other important constructs. Organizational commitment, coping ability and techniques, as well as empirically testing the effect of individual role understanding on group performance are all areas that need to be investigated within the sport context.

Second, related to the suggestion above, future research should employ more complex designs that can account for possible moderator and mediator variables. Potential moderator variables of role ambiguity relationships that need to be considered include gender, tenure on the sport team, starting status, and the athletes' need for clarity, whereas role efficacy has been shown in past research to be a strong mediating variable between role ambiguity and role performance (Beauchamp et al., 2002). Additionally, statistical procedures such as Multilevel Modeling or Hierarchical Linear Modeling allow for a more complex (and simultaneous) examination of both individual and group variance within nested study designs. Eys, Carron, Beauchamp, and Bray (2003) suggested that researchers examining role ambiguity should be cognizant of the potential for statistical non-independence of responses due to the athletes' affiliations with the team as well as common stimuli (i.e., the coach) that influence role perceptions. Using the role ambiguity-role efficacy relationship, Beauchamp, Bray, Fielding, and Eys (2005) provide an example of simultaneous individual and group level modeling, which may be useful for future research.

Extending the generalizability of role ambiguity research provides a third future research direction. For example, recent research has examined only formal roles within an interactive team environment. The investigation of informal role understanding as well as the degree to which athletes in independent (e.g., wrestling) and co-acting (i.e., rowing) sports understand their role responsibilities could provide extremely useful information for enhancing the structure of sport teams of all types.

A fourth area of research that needs to be examined in greater depth is the unearthing of antecedents of role ambiguity or, more specifically, the causes of decreased role understanding. Eys, Carron, Beauchamp, and Carron (2005) asked athletes to identify reasons why they may not be completely clear regarding their role responsibilities. Generally, their responses indicated that a number of different elements potentially influence the proper reception and understanding of roles. These included aspects related to (a) the role-sender or coach (e.g., lack of communication, communication that was unclear, and conflicting communication), (b) the situation (e.g., complexity of sport, prior experience levels, being new to a team), and (c) the athletes themselves (e.g., not paying attention, not attending practice). However, future research needs to determine the extent to which these factors are present on different teams and how they relate to the four manifestations of role ambiguity proposed by Beauchamp and colleagues (2002).

The provision and examination of methods by which to improve role communication and, consequently, decrease role ambiguity constitutes our final suggestion for future research. A structured intervention to enhance role understanding has been suggested (Eys, 2001) that consists of three methods to open communication channels between the focal person (i.e., the athlete) and potential role senders (i.e., coach and teammates). However, no empirical testing of these methods has been conducted.

Role Efficacy

Self-efficacy refers to "beliefs in one's capabilities to organize and execute the course of action required to produce given attainments" (Bandura, 1997, p. 3). Results of numerous reviews and meta-analyses have documented positive associations between self-efficacy and effort, persistence, and performance in sport settings (Bandura, 1997; Feltz and Chase, 1998; Feltz and Lirgg, 2001; Moritz, Feltz, Fahrbach, and Mack, 2000). Although extensive, research on the relationship between self-efficacy and behaviors such as performance has been limited to participants' beliefs regarding tasks they perform independently. Consequently, the bulk of sport efficacy research provides only a limited representation of the types of behaviors in which athletes are often engaged.

In many sport team contexts (e.g., basketball, rugby, soccer), individuals seldom act *independently* but more frequently function *interdependently* with one or several teammates as dictated by their role(s) within the team. It is this aspect that distinguishes members' role-related behaviors from those that can be carried out on one's own. Thus, within an interdependent sport team, members can develop efficacy perceptions with regards to (a) behaviors they carry out on their own (i.e., self-efficacy), (b) the capabilities of the team as a whole—a concept defined as collective efficacy, and (c) those behaviors carried out with one or more teammates in the performance of team-related roles. This latter form of efficacy is referred to as *role efficacy*, defined as: team members' beliefs about their capabilities to successfully carry out interdependent formal role functions (Bray, Brawley, and Carron, 2002).

Research on Role Efficacy

A major goal of the initial work by Bray and his colleagues (Beauchamp and Bray, 2001; Bray, 1998; Bray, Balaguer, and Duda, 2001; Bray and Brawley, 2000; Bray, Widmeyer, and Brawley, 1998) was to examine the construct validity and empirical distinctiveness of role efficacy. Collectively, results of those studies showed that role efficacy was positively related to task self-efficacy, but consistent evidence of unique variance was also obtained. Furthermore, the results were demonstrated for males and females, across sports including basketball, soccer, field hockey and rugby, and among athletes ranging in age from 13 to 28 years old.

Although preliminary in nature, the role efficacy research conducted thus far has also shown correlations with important behavioral indices – namely mastery experiences and performance. Mastery experiences are theorized to be the most important determinants of efficacy beliefs (Bandura, 1986; 1997). Bray et al. (2002) found evidence to support this hypothesis with regards to role efficacy. In their study, the authors surmised that because starting players have more experiential opportunities during practices and games, they should have stronger role efficacy than non-starters. In other words, as a result of the "back-up" nature of their roles, non-starters gain less experience in executing their role functions in games and, often, less experience than starters in the systematic practice of their game-relevant roles in training. Results showed that starters did indeed have higher scores on role efficacy than non-starters. In addition, role efficacy was positively correlated with playing time during games. In concert, the findings supported the theoretical proposition that role efficacy is determined by players' direct mastery experiences within their roles.

Evidence indicating mastery experience as a determinant lends weight to the construct validity of role efficacy and, as will be discussed later on, may have implications for coaches and practitioners. However, other findings consistently show that role efficacy is also, in turn, related to role performance. In one study, Bray and colleagues (Bray et al., 2004) found a positive relationship between role efficacy and role performance effectiveness in two samples of youth Spanish soccer players. Role efficacy – role performance correlations ranged from $r = .18$ for defense to $r = .22$ for offense when performance was rated by athletes' coaches and were substantially higher when athletes self-rated their role performance ($r = .37$ for defense to $r = .51$ for offense). Beauchamp et al. (2002) also found positive relationships between role efficacy and role performance in a sample of British male youth rugby players. In that study, the role efficacy—role performance relationship was found to be $r = .39$ and $r = .37$ for offense and defense, respectively.

In both the aforementioned studies, the researchers examined concurrent relationships between role efficacy and role performance in the separate contexts of offensive and defensive play. However, in a study of Canadian university varsity basketball players, Bray and Brawley (2002) extended these findings through prospective examination of the relationship between role efficacy, assessed during the early stages of the season and coaches' ratings of performance, which were made throughout the season. Bray and Brawley found a positive association ($r = .24$) between players' role efficacy and their role performances. Specifically, players with stronger beliefs in their abilities to successfully carry out their interdependent offensive roles during competition scored higher on coaches' ratings of their performances.

Another aim of Bray and Brawley's (2002) study was to examine role clarity (i.e., the opposite of role ambiguity) as a moderator of the role efficacy—role performance relationship. Findings revealed a moderately strong positive role efficacy—role performance relationship when role clarity was high ($R^2 = .33$), but under conditions of lower role clarity, there was no relationship between role efficacy and role performance effectiveness. To make sense of these findings, consider how athletes would be able to accurately gauge their role-related capabilities without high role clarity? For example, if they were unsure about the extent of the behaviors involved in the functions they had been assigned by the coach, they could easily overestimate or underestimate how capable they were at performing those functions. On the contrary, under conditions of higher role clarity, as the results showed, athletes' judgments of their capabilities corresponded closely to their performance of those functions.

Implications and Future Directions

Although still in its infancy, research on role efficacy indicates it is a role perception that may have important performance-related implications. The fact that role efficacy represents a social cognition, and as a consequence should be amenable to change (Bandura, 1986, 1997), implicate it as a target for future applied research on roles within sport teams. According to Bandura (1997), all forms of efficacy beliefs "have similar sources, serve similar functions, and operate through similar processes" (p. 478). With this in mind, researchers and practitioners should look to Bandura's (1997) self-efficacy theory to explore avenues for increasing role efficacy. Bandura hypothesizes there are four determinants of efficacy beliefs: mastery experiences, vicarious experiences, verbal persuasion, and emotional/physiological states. Research should begin systematic examination of these factors as potential contributors to role efficacy in laboratory and team field settings.

At the current state of the research on role efficacy in sport teams, recommendations for practice are offered conservatively. As noted earlier, research has shown findings consistent with an interpretation that mastery experiences contribute to the strength of athletes' role efficacy beliefs. With this prospective correlational evidence in mind, coaches and practitioners might consider the structure of practice (e.g., allowing team sport athletes additional exposure to game-related situations in conjunction with skill development) as well as the types of experiential opportunities they give players during games (e.g., allowing bench players or rookies playing time at appropriate intervals during the season) in order to afford them sufficient exposure to the role behaviors required of them. Purposeful attempts may be required on the coaches' part to help build players' confidence to step onto the court or pitch and carry out their roles effectively. However, such efforts should be monitored empirically to help build a sufficient knowledge base upon which to design effective interventions that will benefit athletes and their teams.

Role Conflict

Another cognitive element of role involvement described in Figure 2 relates to role conflict. Role conflict refers to the presence of incongruent or conflicting expectations placed on a role incumbent (Kahn et al., 1964), and has often been studied alongside role ambiguity (e.g., Bedeian, Mossholder, Kemmery, and Armenakis, 1990; Klenke-Hamel and Mathieu, 1990; Schaubroeck, Cotton, and Jennings, 1989; Terry, Nielsen, and Perchard, 1993). While role conflict and ambiguity have consistently been found to be correlated, it is important to point out that the two constructs are conceptually distinct and discernible by factor analysis (e.g., Beauchamp and Bray, 2001; González-Romá and Lloret, 1998; Kelloway and Barling, 1990; Rizzo, House, and Lirtzman, 1970). Role conflict research in sport has not been as extensive as it has in other areas of psychology (cf. Jackson and Schuler, 1985; Kossek and Ozeki, 1998; Tubre and Collins, 2000). Nevertheless, the importance of studying this potentially dysfunctional role perception has recently received increased attention, in contexts as varied as university teams (e.g., Beauchamp and Bray, 2001, Settles, Sellers, and Damas, 2002), athletic training (e.g., Capel, 1986), coaching (e.g., Capel, Sisley, and Desertrain, 1987; Dunn, 1997), and sports management and support teams (e.g., Collins, Moore, Mitchell, and Alpress, 1999; Moore and Collins, 1996).

From a conceptual perspective role conflict has been theorized to be multidimensional in nature (cf. Kahn et al., 1964; King and King, 1990). It was Kahn et al. (1964) who in their role episode model, first differentiated between intra-sender (i.e., conflicting expectations from a single member of a role set), inter-sender (i.e., conflicting expectations from two or more members of a single role set), and person-role conflict (i.e., incompatibility between the needs and values of a member and the demands of his or her role set). All three describe conflicting expectations associated with a single position, or what Biddle (1979) was later to describe as intra-role conflict. Kahn et al. also recognized that when people are members of more than one role set (e.g., sport team, family, social, work) and experience inconsistent or conflicting expectations from members of separate role sets they will encounter inter-role conflict.

In spite of theorizing by Kahn et al. (1964), researchers have often failed to operationalize role conflict as a multidimensional construct (e.g., Rizzo et al., 1970). The implications of failing to consider different manifestations of role conflict when they arise has been highlighted by writers such as Ilgen and Hollenbeck (1991) and King and King (1990) who commented that the nature of the conflict, as well as the strategies required to alleviate them, will vary depending on the prevalent source of that role conflict. As it relates to sport, the type of conflict experienced by an athlete receiving conflicting instructions from his/her team's two coaches (i.e., inter-sender) will differ markedly from the experience of another athlete who receives a set of expectations from his/her spouse that clash with the demands of the coach (i.e., inter-role conflict). Although both situations describe role conflict per se, the emotions, thoughts, and behaviors that arise from the two types of conflict will likely differ. Furthermore, from an interventionist perspective the strategies required to address each situation will vary considerably.

Research on Role Conflict

Despite a general failure of researchers to clearly distinguish between different types of role conflict that may exist within sport (e.g., Capel, 1986; Capel et al., 1987; Dunn and Dunn, 1997), a few studies have sought to examine the consequences for both athlete and team functioning, related to specific manifestations of role conflict. For example, Beauchamp and Bray (2001) recently set out to examine the relationships between intra-role conflict, role ambiguity, and role-related efficacy beliefs within a sample of university-level interdependent sport team athletes. Beauchamp and Bray found that intra-role conflict was negatively related to role efficacy, and that role ambiguity mediated the relationship between intra-role conflict and role efficacy perceptions. This finding is consistent with Kahn et al.'s (1964) suggestion that conflicting role expectations can affect psychological outcomes (i.e., members' competence beliefs) through an associated lack of understanding. Beauchamp and Bray did not operationalize *inter-role* conflict because they were interested in assessing athletes' beliefs about their roles within their sport team (i.e., a single role set) and not their roles outside of that specific context. However, their measure was also limited in that it did not differentially measure the three types of intra-role conflict described by Kahn et al. (1964). In their study, items measuring intra-sender, inter-sender, and person-role conflict were employed, but were combined to form a generic intra-role conflict scale (cf. Biddle, 1979).

Taking a very different approach, Settles et al. (2002) recently investigated the degree to which student athletes viewed their athletic and academic role identities as separate from and interfering with each other (i.e., inter-role conflict). For those participants that viewed being a student and an athlete as distinct roles (i.e., role separation) they also reported higher levels of well-being in comparison to those who viewed these responsibilities as part of a larger meta-role. Settles et al. argued that cognitively separating these roles may allow the student athlete to better focus on the demands of each role, and that if a 'role experience' in one context is negative at any moment in time, well-being may be bolstered by more positive experiences in the person's second role. Interestingly, Settles et al. also found that when student athletes reported high levels of role separation, but believed that their two roles interfered with each other (i.e., inter-role conflict), they tended to experience significantly higher levels of stress in comparison to those who had low role separation.

Both of the studies by Beauchamp and Bray (2001) and Settles et al. (2002) focused on different aspects of role conflict experienced by athletes. In a unique program of research, Moore and Collins (1996) set out to investigate the implications for athlete and team functioning when members of the management team (e.g., coaches, managers) are expected to perform incongruent role responsibilities. By employing a case-study methodology with a national team's management staff, Moore and Collins found that the coach and manager were each expected to provide socially supportive behaviors to the athletes as well as assume roles related to executive decision-making. The players in this study remarked that "the coach should carry out executive responsibilities and that the manager should provide administrative and social support in a non-executive way" (p. 44). Moore and Collins concluded that when members of a management team experience this type of (intra-sender) conflict (i.e., conflicting expectations emanating from any given athlete within the team), their ability to perform either role responsibility may be compromised.

Collins et al. (1999) recently extended this line of enquiry to athletic support teams (e.g., doctor, physiotherapist, sports scientist), that provide medical and scientific support to elite performers and their coaches. Again, drawing from the experiences of participants through an interview-based methodology, Collins et al. concluded that in order to prevent members of support teams receiving expectations from those in "power" (i.e., coaches, managers) that might conflict with the best interests of the client (i.e., the athlete), an 'athlete charter' should be implemented. Such a framework enables the provision of effective and ethical support to athletes on the basis of clear boundaries for professional practice. From an applied perspective, such an approach may avert the incidence of any inter-sender conflict (i.e., conflicting information from different sources within a team environment) from arising in the first place, and may be more effective than seeking to deal with the conflict once it has happened.

Implications and Future Directions

Despite the relative paucity of published role conflict research in sport, investigations conducted within other domains of psychology do present potentially interesting directions for future role conflict research in sport. For example, a number of researchers (Frone, Russell, and Cooper, 1997; Kossek and Ozeki, 1998; O'Driscoll, Ilgen, and Hildreth, 1992) have consistently found that when work-related role responsibilities conflict with family-related role responsibilities, people tend to experience significantly lower levels of work satisfaction, organizational commitment, and increased psychological strain and depressive symptoms. In the context of sport teams, it stands to reason that if athletes are subjected to role-related expectations that interfere with the expectations emanating from other role sets (e.g., family, friends, employers), such inter-role conflict might also have considerable implications for athlete well-being and functioning.

Interestingly, in a study of high school basketball coaches, Capel et al. (1987) found that role conflict was related to higher levels of coach burnout. Unfortunately, Capel et al. employed the unidimensional role conflict measure developed by Rizzo et al. (1970) and so there is no way of knowing which elements of role conflict were primarily responsible for the reported burnout. We would echo the suggestion by Cooper, Dewe, and O'Driscoll (2001) that role conflict may be a salient antecedent of emotional exhaustion. However, from both an empirical and applied perspective, it would be advantageous to know what elements of role conflict might be predictive of (athlete and coach) burnout in sport.

Role Overload

Another important role stressor that has received considerable attention within the organizational and health literature refers to role overload (e.g., Barling and MacIntyre, 1993; Coverman, 1989; Peiro, González-Romá, Tordera, and Manas, 2001). Unfortunately, research involving this role construct has not been as forthcoming in the context of sport. In addition, within the role overload literature that does exist, this construct has been inconsistently defined. For example, Kahn et al. (1964) suggested that role overload may occur when a person is presented with a set of requests from various sources, which may be impossible to complete within a given time frame. In this case, it is implied that role overload is a type of inter-sender conflict. However, Kahn et al. also theorized that role overload may also be a form of person-role conflict, when the focal person is unable to prioritize which pressures or expectations to comply with. In contrast, Cooper et al. (2001) suggested that role overload is distinct from role conflict and "refers to the number of different roles a person is expected to fulfil" (p. 39). From this perspective, role overload is viewed more as a quantitative stressor based on the amount of role-related expectations emanating from the role sender. Finally, taking a different perspective, Settles et al. (2002) argued that role overload is conceptually distinct from role conflict, and that the two constructs can be distinguished from each other on the basis of role separation. Specifically, Settles et al. suggested that role conflict involves high role interference and high role separation, whereas role overload involves high role interference but low role separation.

Although each of these writers present very different views of what constitutes role overload, one must consider the possibility that different types of role overload may exist in sport (i.e., multidimensional role overload). Indeed, within sport, it seems plausible to suggest that an athlete may be expected to perform (a) a single role responsibility that is beyond his or her capabilities (i.e., qualitative overload), (b) an excessive number of role responsibilities expected by different people (e.g., head coach, captain, assistant coach) within a given period of time (i.e., quantitative overload), or (c) a complex and demanding role that is difficult to break down into constituent components or responsibilities. Nevertheless, the truth remains that role overload represents a potentially meaningful role construct that is distinct from role conflict and, to date, has received scant attention within the sport psychology literature. Understanding what effect role overload may have for athlete cognition, emotion, and behavior, remains a major challenge for future researchers interested in sport.

Role Acceptance

Of the various role elements discussed up until this point in the chapter, few have suffered from as much definitional ambiguity and lack of conceptualization as role acceptance. For example, role acceptance has been confused with *compliance* to expectations, which constitutes an overt, behavioral response to role pressures (Biddle, 1979). Also, satisfaction with one's role (an affective element of role involvement discussed below) has been used as a description of role acceptance. In fact, Carron and Hausenblas (1998) defined role acceptance as "the degree to which the individual is satisfied with his/her role responsibilities" (p. 163).

In contrast, Biddle (1979) clarified that acceptance is a covert, cognitive process that involves the comparison between two expectations. In the sport domain, this would generally involve the athlete conducting a comparison between his or her perceived role expectations from the coach and the athlete's own expectations regarding his or her role responsibilities. Biddle also noted that acceptance occurs if the focal person (i.e., the athlete) views expectations as *similar* and *determined* by another person. Given that this comparison could lead to an incongruence in expectations (i.e., between coach and athlete), it could be suggested that a lack of role acceptance might be another form of role conflict (i.e., conflict between competing expectations for a particular role).

Based on Biddle's theorizing, a definition of role acceptance for a sport setting is offered: a dynamic, covert process that reflects the degree to which an athlete perceives his or her own expectations for role responsibilities as similar to, and agreeable with, the expectations for role responsibilities determined by his or her role senders. This definition highlights two important features of role acceptance. First, it is dynamic and, thus, open to change and intervention. A number of authors have speculated on how acceptance can be developed. For example, Biddle (1979) noted that characteristics of the role sender could influence the acceptance of roles. Drawn from literature on persuasion and conformity, role acceptance could be influenced by the degree of role sender credibility, attractiveness, and/or power. As another example, pragmatic role acceptance theory suggests that athletes might accept roles because of the accrued benefits of accepting them (e.g., remaining a member of a desirable team) and that they are conditioned to abiding the demands of authority figures (Sage, 1998).

The second feature of the proposed role acceptance definition is that the comparison of expectations is covert or, more specifically, an internal process. Biddle (1979) noted that the overt or external response to role expectations reflects different constructs such as compliance or performance. While behavioral compliance should typically imitate the degree to which the athlete accepts his or her role, there can be situations in which behavior may not reflect cognition. For example, situational constraints (e.g., time), ability, or perhaps the ability of the opponent may prevent the athlete from performing his or her role even though he or she has the full intention to do so.

Research on Role Acceptance

Given the lack of conceptual and definitional clarity of the role acceptance construct, it is not surprising that there has been a dearth of research on the subject. The Team Climate Questionnaire developed and utilized by Grand and Carron (1982), and subsequently employed by Dawe (1990), incorporated a scale measuring perceptions of role acceptance. However, this operationalization was based on role acceptance defined as the *satisfaction* of the athlete with his or her role. As discussed above, acceptance and satisfaction represent different role perceptions.

Bray (1998) distinguished between role acceptance and role satisfaction as part of a larger examination aimed at establishing the conceptual and empirical uniqueness of role efficacy. A three item scale was utilized that asked athletes of interactive sport teams to indicate the degree to which they accepted their various role responsibilities and how well they thought their role responsibilities matched their abilities on both offense and defense. Although not the main purpose of the study, strong bivariate correlations were present between perceptions of role acceptance and the other constructs such as role efficacy, role ambiguity, role satisfaction, perceived importance of role functions, as well as perceptions of task cohesion. However, Bray conceded that "It should be noted that because there are no standardized measures of role acceptance and role satisfaction that these constructs could be measured more precisely in future research" (p. 76).

While it is important to be conceptually clear regarding the differences between role acceptance and role satisfaction, it is also essential that the actors who participate in the sport domain (i.e., the athletes and coaches) are also able to distinguish between the two constructs if intervention is to be an objective. Eys and Carron (2003) conducted a preliminary study to determine coaches' perceptions of their athletes' acceptance and satisfaction of role responsibilities. More specifically, ten coaches of interactive sport teams were asked to indicate the percentage of their athletes who (a) accept and are satisfied with their role (65%), (b) accept but are dissatisfied with their role (21%), (c) do not accept but are satisfied with their role (8%), and (d) do not accept and are dissatisfied with their role (5%). The average responses of the coaches are in brackets beside each option and indicate that the two constructs seem to be viewed by practitioners in sport as different.

Implications and Future Directions

Role acceptance has been recognized both anecdotally and in a number of texts as an important aspect of developing effective groups and satisfying the needs of individual members. For example, Stevens (2002) highlighted developing role acceptance as being critical to the team-building process and suggested strategies for enhancing acceptance of roles. However, as has been discussed, basic level research has yet to properly conceptualize the construct and empirical evidence of the effectiveness of interventions has not been displayed. While the present chapter offers a more suitable definition of role acceptance for sport, future research in this area should begin by developing a valid and reliable operationalization/measure of role acceptance for the sport domain.

Once a potentially effective measure of role acceptance has been developed, an examination of correlates such as those discussed in this section (e.g., role efficacy, role ambiguity, cohesion) would be a logical next step to both support the hypothesized importance of role acceptance in sport as well as demonstrate the construct and predictive validity of the new measure. Additional variables that could be examined at this stage include those proposed by Biddle (1979) that potentially influence the degree of acceptance, such as perceptions of role sender credibility, attractiveness, and power.

AFFECTIVE ELEMENT OF ROLE INVOLVEMENT

Role Satisfaction

Role satisfaction, to date, represents the only affective element of role involvement that has been identified in previous literature. Without belaboring the point discussed in the previous section, role satisfaction has often been used as an indication of role acceptance. However, a definition that has been utilized in industrial/organization literature to describe job satisfaction can be easily adapted to the sport role domain. Locke (1976) defined job satisfaction as "a pleasurable emotional state resulting from the perception of one's job [role] as fulfilling or allowing the fulfillment of one's important job [role] values" (p. 1342).

Research on Role Satisfaction

As with role acceptance, a limited amount of research has been conducted in the area of role satisfaction in sport but the existing literature demonstrates support for its examination in future research. A study conducted by Rail (1987) with sport executives provided interesting insights into the factors that can lead to an individual deriving enjoyment or satisfaction from his or her role. Using semi-structured interviews, Rail found that four perceptions led to the role satisfaction of her participants. These included (a) the degree to which their abilities were used, (b) how significant they viewed their roles, (c) the extent to which they received feedback and recognition, and (d) the level of autonomy they were permitted in the performance of their responsibilities. It is likely that these relationships would apply in the interactive sport setting. For example, the degree to which athletes perceive that their role is significant, utilizes their abilities effectively, and is nurtured through the provision of feedback and recognition, will potentially influence their perceptions of role satisfaction.

More specifically with sport teams, Bray (1998) examined perceptions of role satisfaction of intercollegiate basketball players as part of a larger study incorporating a number of other role related variables. The role satisfaction measure utilized in this study was adapted from job satisfaction scales in organizational psychology (Brayfield and Rothe, 1951; Seigall and Cummings, 1986; Vroom, 1963). Similar to role acceptance, role satisfaction was positively associated with task cohesion, role efficacy, and role importance (perhaps an indicator of the perceived significance of the role alluded to by Rail, 1987) and negatively related to role ambiguity.

Another study conducted by Beauchamp and colleagues (2005) drew from similar literature as Bray (1998) to develop a role satisfaction measure. In this case, Beauchamp et al. examined the prospective relationships between role ambiguity and role satisfaction with rugby and field hockey players. The findings supported their hypothesis that role ambiguity experienced in the middle of a competitive season would predict the amount of role satisfaction perceived in the latter stages of that season. Interestingly, this relationship still remained evident after controlling for prior satisfaction as well as the athletes' tendency to experience negative emotions (i.e., negative affectivity).

Implications and Future Directions

The importance of role satisfaction in sport cannot be understated. In fact, it has been suggested that an athlete's satisfaction (of which role satisfaction is a part) is important because (a) satisfaction and performance are inextricably linked, (b) maintaining athlete involvement is central to athletic programs, (c) it is an antecedent or consequence within the framework of numerous other constructs (e.g., cohesion and leadership), and (d) it has been shown to be a major consequence of the behavior of coaches (Riemer and Chelladurai, 1998).

Given the importance of role satisfaction in a sport environment, there is a need for future research in this area. Initial steps will need to determine whether role satisfaction should be conceptualized and measured as a one or multidimensional construct. The research outlined above has examined it from a unidimensional perspective but little research has examined the issue in-depth. Consequently, the measurement or operationalization of role satisfaction has followed this conceptualization. For example, Bray (1998) used three general items rated on a semantic differential scale to gauge perceptions of athlete role satisfaction (e.g., "I enjoy performing my role functions tremendously....I do not enjoy performing my role functions at all") while Rail (1987) utilized one interview question to determine the satisfaction of volunteer sport executives with their various roles. Finally, Riemer and Chelladurai (1998) incorporated a dimension of overall athlete satisfaction termed 'ability utilization', which in part assesses perceptions of athlete satisfaction with their role responsibilities.

As a final suggestion for future research, an examination of the factors leading to role satisfaction as suggested by Rail (1987; use of competence, role significance, recognition/feedback, autonomy) could be conducted with athletes to determine if these factors have relevance outside of the sport organization domain.

Behavioral Element of Role Involvement

Role Performance

Role performance constitutes the behavioral element of role involvement and is likely the outcome variable from role expectations that is most often evaluated by coaches and teammates (as compared to the affective and cognitive outcomes as experienced by the individual athlete). The nature of interdependent team sports, where a number of individuals must fulfill a variety of different roles, requires a level of role performance from these individuals that is consistent with expectations from role senders for the team to perform effectively as a collective.

It is not the intention of this section to reiterate at length the literature that has been discussed previously relating role performance with other constructs. To summarize briefly, it has been shown that role performance is related to the degree to which athletes understand their role responsibilities (role ambiguity; Beauchamp et al., 2002) and believe that they have the ability to execute their roles effectively (role efficacy; Bray et al., 2004; Bray and Brawley, 2002). However, two issues need to be addressed with regard to how role performance is examined in a sport context. First, while the previous paragraph intimated that role performance is predominately an outcome variable, researchers need to recognize the potential for role performance to play the part of antecedent to other role dimensions. For instance, as discussed previously, it has been shown that successful role performance could lead to an increase in role efficacy (Bray and Brawley, 2000). Likewise, it may be possible that a poor performance of role responsibilities could lead to an athlete experiencing a lower perception of satisfaction with his or her role. Caution needs to be taken in the interpretation of results using cross-sectional data especially in those instances where role performance is measured through the self-evaluation of the athlete.

The method by which role performance is measured constitutes the second issue. Previous researchers have utilized a number of approaches to measure role performance. One approach has been to ask coaches to subjectively rate how well each athlete has performed what the coaches consider to be the athletes' role responsibilities. Both Bray and Brawley (2002) and Beauchamp and colleagues (2002) utilized this approach in studies examining role performance, role ambiguity, and role efficacy. One potential limitation, as noted by Beauchamp et al., is that coach ratings could be subject to bias. A second approach has been to ask the athletes directly how well they feel they have performed their role responsibilities. This approach was utilized in studies conducted by Bray et al. (2004) and Bray and Brawley (2000) but, while useful, may be subject to other personal biases as well as social desirability. Ideally, an objective measure for assessing role performance would be most useful. However, this presents a challenge for future researchers to develop.

Summary

The successful execution of roles within a sport team is essential to achieve that group's objectives. The purpose of this chapter was to review the research on roles in sport. To that end, a historical overview of roles literature and an outline of the structure of roles in team sports were provided. In addition, this chapter defined, reviewed in-depth, and provided implications and future directions for the various elements of role involvement (i.e., role ambiguity, efficacy, conflict, overload, acceptance, satisfaction, and performance) that constitute important considerations for sport psychology. It is only recently that empirical examinations of roles in sport have been conducted, but the significance of team roles from a practical standpoint has been longstanding. As the legendary college basketball coach John Wooden recounted,

I told players at UCLA that we, as a team, are like a powerful car. Maybe a Bill Walton or Kareem Abdul-Jabbar or Michael Jordan is the big engine, but if one wheel is flat, we're going no place. And if we have brand new tires but the lug nuts are missing, the wheels come off. What good is the powerful engine now? It's no good at all. A lug nut may seem like a little thing, but it's not. There's a role that each and every one of us must play. (Wooden and Jamison, 1997, p. 75)

ACKNOWLEDGEMENTS

This project was funded by a Social Sciences and Humanities Research Council of Canada grant to the first author. The authors are grateful for their support.

REFERENCES

Adair, J. (1986). *Effective team building.* Aldershot: Gower.

Bales, R. F. (1950). *Interaction process analysis: A method for the study of small groups.* Cambridge, MA: Addison-Wesley.

Bales, R. F. (1953). The equilibrium problem in small groups. In T. Parsons, R. F. Bales and E. A. Shils, (Eds), *Working papers in the theory of action* (pp. 111-161). New York: The Free Press.

Bales, R. F. (1958). Task roles and social roles in problem solving groups. In E. E. Maccoby, T. M. Newcomb, and E. L. Hartley (Eds.), *Readings in social psychology* (3rd ed., pp. 437-447). New York: Holt.

Bales, R. F., and Slater, P. E. (1955). Role differentiation in small decision making groups. In T. Parsons and R. F. Bales (Eds), *Family socialization and interaction process* (pp. 259-306). Glencoe, IL.: The Free Press.

Bandura, A. (1986). *Social foundations of thought and action: A social cognitive theory.* Englewood Cliffs, NJ: Prentice-Hall.

Bandura, A. (1997). *Self-efficacy: The exercise of control.* New York: W. H. Freeman and Co.

Barling, J., and McIntyre, A.T. (1993). Daily work role stressors, mood and emotional exhaustion. *Work and Stress, 7,* 315-325.

Baron, R. M., and Kenny, D. A. (1986). The moderator-mediator variable distinction in social psychological research: Conceptual, strategic, and statistical considerations. *Journal of Personality and Social Psychology, 51,* 1173-1182.

Beauchamp, M.R. (2002). *Role ambiguity: Multidimensional and multilevel investigations in sport.* Unpublished doctoral dissertation. University of Birmingham, Birmingham, U.K.

Beauchamp, M. R., and Bray, S. R. (2001). Role ambiguity and role conflict within interdependent teams. *Small Group Research, 32,* 133-157.

Beauchamp, M. R., Bray, S. R., Eys, M. A., and Carron, A. V. (2002). Role ambiguity, role efficacy, and role performance: Multidimensional and mediational relationships within interdependent sport teams. *Group Dynamics: Theory, Research, and Practice, 6,* 229-242.

Beauchamp, M. R., Bray, S. R., Eys, M. A., and Carron, A. V. (2003). The effect of role ambiguity on competitive state anxiety. *Journal of Sport and Exercise Psychology, 25,* 77-92.

Beauchamp, M. R., Bray, S. R., Eys, M. A., and Carron, A. V. (2005). Leadership behaviors and multidimensional role ambiguity perceptions in team sports. *Small Group Research, 36,* 5-20.

Beauchamp, M. R., Bray, S. R., Eys, M. A., and Carron, A. V. (2005). Multidimensional role ambiguity and role satisfaction: A prospective examination using interdependent sport teams. *Journal of Applied Social Psychology, 35,* 2560-2576.

Beauchamp, M. R., Bray, S. R., Fielding, A., and Eys, M. A. (2005). A multilevel investigation of the relationship between role ambiguity and role efficacy in sport. *Psychology of Sport and Exercise, 6,* 289-302

Bedeian, A. G., Mossholder, K. W., Kemmery, E. R., and Armenakis, A, A. (1990). Replication requisites: A second look at Klenke-Hamel and Mathieu (1990), *Human Relations, 45,* 1093-1105.

Belbin, M. R. (1981). *Management teams: Why they succeed and why they fail.* Oxford: Butterworth-Heinemann.

Belbin, M. R. (1993). *Team roles at work.* Oxford: Butterworth-Heinemann.

Biddle, B. J. (1979). *Role theory: Expectations, identities, and behaviors.* New York: Academic Press, Inc.

Biddle, B. J., and Thomas, E. J. (1966). *Role theory: Concepts and research.* New York: John Wiley and Sons, Inc.

Bray, S. R. (1998). *Role efficacy within interdependent teams: Measurement development and tests of theory.* Unpublished doctoral thesis. University of Waterloo, Waterloo, Canada.

Bray, S. R., Balaguer, I, and Duda, J. L. (2001). An examination of interdependent role efficacy beliefs among Spanish youth soccer players. In A. Papaioannou, M. Goudas, and Y. Theodorakis (Eds.), *Proceedings of the 10th World Congress of Sport Psychology,* Skiathos, Greece. Vol. 1, 11-13.

Bray, S. R., Balaguer, I., and Duda, J. L. (2004). The relationship of task self-efficacy and role efficacy beliefs to role performance in Spanish youth soccer. *Journal of Sports Sciences, 22,* 429-437.

Bray, S. R., Beauchamp, M. R., Eys, M. A., and Carron, A. V. (2005). Does need for role clarity moderate the relationship between role ambiguity and athlete satisfaction? *Journal of Applied Sport Psychology, 17,* 306-318.

Bray, S. R., and Brawley, L. R. (2000). Role efficacy and perceived role performance relationships: Longitudinal evidence for reciprocality [abstract]. *Journal of Sport and Exercise Psychology, 22,* S22.

Bray, S. R., and Brawley, L. R. (2002). Role efficacy, role clarity, and role performance effectiveness. *Small Group Research, 33,* 233-253.

Bray, S. R., Brawley, L. R. and Carron, A. V. (2002). Efficacy for interdependent role functions: Evidence from the sport domain. *Small Group Research, 33,* 644-666.

Bray, S. R., Widmeyer, W. N., and Brawley, L. R. (1998). Collective efficacy and role efficacy in sport teams [abstract]. *Journal of Sport and Exercise Psychology, 20,* S62.

Brayfield, A. H., and Rothe, H. F. (1951). An index of job satisfaction. *Journal of Applied Psychology, 35,* 307-311.

Capel, S. A. (1986). Psychological and organizational factors related to burnout in athletic trainers. *Athletic Training, 21,* 322-327.

Capel, S. A., Sisley, B. L., and Desertrain, G. S. (1987). The relationship between role conflict and role ambiguity to burnout in high school coaches. *Journal of Sport Psychology, 9,* 106-117.

Carron, A. V., Colman, M. M., Wheeler, J., and Stevens, D. (2002). Cohesion and performance in sport: A meta-analysis. *Journal of Sport and Exercise Psychology, 24,* 168-188.

Carron, A. V., and Hausenblas, H. (1998). *Group dynamics in sport* (2nd ed). Morgantown, WV: Fitness Information Technology Inc.

Carron, A. V., Hausenblas, H, and Eys, M. A. (2005). *Group dynamics in sport* (3rd ed). Morgantown, WV: Fitness Information Technology Inc.

Cartwright D., and Zander A. (1960). *Group dynamics: Research and theory* (2nd ed.). New York: Harper and Row.

Chan, D. (1998). Functional relations among constructs in the same content domain at different levels of analysis: A typology of composition models. *Journal of Applied Psychology, 83,* 234-246.

Collins, D., Moore, P., Mitchell, D., and Alpress, F. (1999). Role conflict and confidentiality in multidisciplinary athlete support programmes. *British Journal of Sports Medicine, 33,* 208-211.

Cooper, C. L., Dewe, P. J., and O'Driscoll, M. P. (2001). *Organizational stress: A review and critique of theory, research, and applications.* Thousand Oaks, CA: Sage.

Cottrell, L. S. (1933). Roles and marital adjustment. *Publications of the American Sociological Society, 27,* 107-115.

Cottrell, L. S. (1942). The adjustment of the individual to his age and sex roles. *American Sociological Review, 7,* 617-620.

Coverman, S. (1989). Role overload, role conflict, and stress: Addressing consequences of multiple role demands. *Social Forces, 67,* 965-982.

Dawe, S. L. (1990). *Cohesion, performance, role clarity, and role acceptance.* Unpublished master's thesis, University of Western Ontario, London, Ontario, Canada.

Duda, J. L. (1991). Perspectives on gender roles in physical activity. *Journal of Applied Sport Psychology, 3,* 1-6.

Dunn, T. P., and Dunn, S. L. (1997). The graduate assistant coach: Role conflicts in the making. *Journal of Sport Behavior, 20,* 260-271.

Eys, M. A. (2000). *Development of a measure of role ambiguity in sport.* Unpublished master's thesis, The University of Western Ontario, London, Ontario, Canada.

Eys, M.A. (2001, October). Role ambiguity: Research to practice. In A.V. Carron (Chair), *Group dynamics: Research to practice.* Symposium conducted at the meeting of the Association for the Advancement of Applied Sport Psychology, Orlando, Fl.

Eys, M. A., and Carron, A. V. (2001). Role ambiguity, task cohesion, and task self-efficacy. *Small Group Research, 32,* 356-373.

Eys, M. A. and Carron, A. V. (2003, March). *Athlete role acceptance: Clarifying its place in group dynamics* [abstract]. Paper presented at the annual Eastern Canada Sport and Exercise Psychology Symposium, Montreal, QC.

Eys, M. A., Carron, A. V., Beauchamp, M. R., and Bray, S. R. (2003). Role ambiguity in sport teams. *Journal of Sport and Exercise Psychology, 25,* 534-550.

Eys, M. A., Carron, A. V., Beauchamp, M. R., and Bray, S. R. (2005). Athletes' perceptions of the sources of role ambiguity. *Small Group Research, 36,* 383-403

Eys, M. A., Carron, A. V., Bray, S. R., and Beauchamp, M. R. (2003). Role ambiguity and athlete satisfaction. *Journal of Sports Sciences, 21,* 391-401.

Eys, M. A., Carron, A. V., Bray, S. R., and Beauchamp, M. R. (2005). The relationship between role ambiguity and intention to return. *Journal of Applied Sport Psychology, 17,* 255-261.

Feltz, D. L. and Chase, M. A. (1998). The measurement of self-efficacy and confidence in sport. In J. L. Duda (Ed.), *Advances in sport and exercise psychology measurement* (pp. 65-80). Morgantown, WV: Fitness Information Technology Inc.

Feltz, D. L. and Lirgg, C. D. (2001). Self-efficacy beliefs of athletes, teams, and coaches. In R. N. Singer, H. A. Hausenblas, and C. M. Janelle (Eds.), *Handbook of Sport Psychology* (pp. 340-361). New York: Wiley.

Frone, M. R., Russell, M., and Cooper, M. L. (1997). Relation of work-family conflict to health outcomes: A four-year longitudinal study of employed parents. *Journal of Occupational and Organizational Psychology, 70,* 325-335.

Goffman, E. (1959). *The presentation of self in everyday life.* New York: Doubleday.

González-Romá, V., and Lloret, S. (1998). Construct validity of Rizzo et al.'s (1970) role conflict and ambiguity scales: A multisample study. *Applied Psychology: An International Review, 47,* 535-545.

Grand, R. R., and Carron, A. V. (1982). Development of a team climate questionnaire. In *Proceedings of the Annual Conference of the Canadian Society for Psychomotor Learning and Sport Psychology, Edmonton, Alberta* (pp. 217-229).

Hare, A. P. (1994). Roles and relationships. In A. P. Hare, H. H. Blumberg, M. F. Davies, and M. V. Kent (Eds.), *Small group research: A handbook* (pp. 141-154). NJ: Ablex.

Ilgen, D., and Hollenbeck, J. (1991). Job design and roles. In M. Dunnette and L. Hough (Eds.), *Handbook of industrial and organizational psychology* (2nd ed., Vol. 2, pp. 165-208). Palo Alto, CA: Consulting Psychologists Press.

Jackson, S. E., and Schuler, R. S. (1985). A meta-analysis and conceptual critique of research on role ambiguity and role conflict in work settings. *Organizational Behavior and Human Decision Processes, 36,* 16-78.

Kahn, R. L., Wolfe, D. M., Quinn, R. P., Snoek, J. D., and Rosenthal, R. A. (1964). *Organizational stress: Studies in role conflict and ambiguity.* New York: Wiley.

Katz, D., and Kahn, R. L. (1978). *The social psychology of organizations* (2nd ed.). New York: Wiley.

Kelloway, E., and Barling, J. (1990). Item content versus item wording: Disentangling role conflict and role ambiguity. *Journal of Applied Psychology, 75,* 738-742.

King, L. A., and King, D. W. (1990). Role conflict and role ambiguity: A critical assessment of construct validity. *Psychological Bulletin, 107,* 48-64.

Klenke-Hamel, K. E., and Mathieu, J. E. (1990). Role strains, tensions, and job satisfaction influences on employees' propensity to leave: A multi-sample replication and extension. *Human Relations, 43,* 791-807.

Kossek, E. E., and Ozeki, C. (1998). Work-family conflict, policies, and the job-life satisfaction relationship: A review and directions for organizational behaviour-human resources research. *Journal of Applied Psychology, 83,* 139-149.

Lavalee, D., Kremer, J., Moran, A. P., and Williams, M. (2004). *Sport psychology: Contemporary themes.* NY: Palgrave Macmillan.

Lewin, K. (1947). Frontiers in group dynamics. *Human Relations, 1,* 143-153.

Lewin, K. (1948). *Resolving social conflicts: Selected papers on group dynamics.* New York: Harper.

Lewin, K., Lippitt, R., and White, R. (1939). Patterns of aggressive behavior in experimentally created "social climes". *Journal of Social Psychology, 10,* 271-299.

Locke, E. A. (1976). The nature and causes of job satisfaction. In M. D. Dunnette (Ed.), *Handbook of industrial and organizational psychology.* Chicago: Rand McNally.

Mabry, E. A., and Barnes, R. E. (1980). *The dynamics of small group communication.* Englewood Cliffs, NJ: Prentice-Hall.

Martens, R., Burton, D., Vealey, R. S., Bump, L. A., and Smith, D. E. (1990). Development and validation of the Competitive State Anxiety Inventory-2. In R. Martens, R. S. Vealey, and D. Burton (Eds.), *Competitive state anxiety in sport* (pp. 117-190). Champaign, IL: Human Kinetics.

McGrath, J. E. (1984). *Groups: Interaction and performance.* Englewood Cliffs, NJ: Prentice Hall.

Mead. G. H. (1934). *Mind, self and society (from the standpoint of a social behaviorist).* Chicago: University of Chicago Press.

Moore, P., and Collins, D. (1996). Role conflicts in sports team management. In J. Annett and H. Steinberg (Eds.), *How teams work is sport and exercise psychology* (pp. 40-48). Leicester, UK: British Psychological Society.

Moreno, J. L. (1934). *Who shall survive?* Washington, D. C.: Nervous and Mental Disease Publication. (Rev ed. New York: Beacon House, 1953).

Moreno, J. L. (1960). *The sociometry reader.* Glencoe, IL: The Free Press.

Moritz, S. E., Feltz, D. L., Fahrbach, K. R. and Mack, D. E. (2000). The relation of self-efficacy measures to sport performance: A meta-analytic review. *Research Quarterly for Exercise and Sport, 71,* 280-294.

Moritz, S. E., and Watson, C. B. (1998). Levels of analysis issues in group psychology: Using efficacy as an example of a multilevel model. *Group Dynamics: Theory, Research, and Practice, 2,* 285-298.

Newcomb, T. M. (1943). *Personality and social change.* New York: Dryden Press.

O'Driscoll, M. P., and Beehr, T. A. (2000). Moderating effects of perceived control and need for clarity on the relationship between role stressors and employee affective reactions. *The Journal of Social Psychology, 140,* 151-159.

O'Driscoll, M. P., Ilgen, D. R., Hildreth, K. (1992). Time devoted to job and off-job activities, interrole conflict, and affective experiences. *Journal of Applied Psychology, 77,* 272-279.

Palazzolo, C. S. (1981). *Small groups: An introduction.* New York: D. Van Nostrand Co.

Parsons, T., and Bales, R. F. (1955). *Family, socialization, and interaction process.* Glencoe, IL: The Free Press.

Paskevich, D. M., Estabrooks, P. A., Brawley, L. R., and Carron, A. V. (2001). Group cohesion in sport and exercise. In R. N. Singer, H. A. Hausenblas, and C. M. Janelle (Eds.), *Handbook of sport psychology* (2nd ed., pp. 472-494). New York: Wiley.

Peiro, J. M, González-Romá, V., Tordera, N., Manas, M. A. (2001). Does role stress predict burnout over time among health care professionals? *Psychology and Health, 16,* 511-525.

Rail, G. (1987). Perceived role characteristics and executive satisfaction in voluntary sport associations. *Journal of Sport Psychology, 9,* 376-384.

Rees, C. R., and Segal, M. W. (1984). Role differentiation in groups: The relationship between instrumental and expressive leadership. *Small Group Behavior, 15,* 109-123.

Rhoads, G. K., Singh, J., and Goodell, P. W. (1994). The multiple dimensions of role ambiguity and their impact upon psychological and behavioral outcomes of industrial salespeople. *Journal of Personal Selling and Sales Management, 14,* 1-24.

Riemer, H. A., and Chelladurai, P. (1998). Development of the Athlete Satisfaction Questionnaire (ASQ). *Journal of Sport and Exercise Psychology, 20,* 127-156.

Rizzo, J. R., House, R. J., and Lirtzman, S. I. (1970). Role conflict and ambiguity in complex organizations. *Administrative Science Quarterly, 15,* 150-163.

Sage, G. H. (1998). *Power and ideology in American sport: A critical perspective* (2nd ed.). Champaign, IL: Human Kinetics.

Schaubroeck, J., Cotton, J. L., and Jennings, K. R. (1989). Antecedents and consequences of role stress: A covariance structure analysis. *Journal of Organizational Behavior, 10,* 35-58.

Seigall, M., and Cummings, L. L. (1986). Task role ambiguity, satisfaction, and the moderating effect of task instruction source. *Human Relations, 39,* 1017-1032.

Settles, I. H., Sellers, R. M., and Damas, A. (2002). One role or two? The function of psychological separation in role conflict. *Journal of Applied Psychology, 87,* 574-582.

Shaw, M. E. (1971). *Group dynamics: The psychology of small group behavior.* New York: McGraw-Hill.

Shaw, M. E., and Costanzo, P.R. (1982). *Theories of social psychology* (2nd ed.). New York: McGraw-Hill.

Shoenfelt, E. L. (2003). A structured approach to increasing role clarity with intercollegiate volleyball players [abstract]. *Association for the Advancement of Applied Sport Psychology 2003 Conference Proceedings,* 90.

Singh, J. (1993). Boundary role ambiguity: Facets, determinants, and impacts. *Journal of Marketing, 57,* 11-31.

Slater, P. E. (1955). Role differentiation in small groups. *American Sociological Review, 20,* 300-310.

Stevens, D. E. (2002). Building the effective team. In J. M. Silva III and D. E. Stevens (Eds.), *Psychological foundations of sport* (pp. 306-327). Boston, MA: Allyn and Bacon.

Taylor, P. (2000, June 12). On a role. *Sports Illustrated, 92,* 34-39.

Terry, D. J., Nielsen, M., and Perchard, L. (1993). Effects of work stress on psychological well-being and job satisfaction: The stress buffering role of social support. *Australian Journal of Psychology, 45,* 168-175.

Tubre, T. C., and Collins, J. M. (2000). Jackson and Schuler (1985) revisited: A meta-analysis of the relationships between role ambiguity, role conflict, and job performance. *Journal of Management, 26,* 155-169.

Vroom, V. H. (1963). *Some personality determinants of the effect of participation.* Englewood Cliffs, N.J.: Prentice-Hall.

Wooden, J. R., and Jamison, S. (1997). *Wooden: A lifetime of observations and reflections on and off the court.* Chicago: Contemporary Books.

In: Literature Reviews in Sport Psychology
Editors: S. Hanton and S. D.Mellalieu, pp. 257-287

ISBN 1-59454-904-4
© 2006 Nova Science Publishers, Inc.

Chapter 8

TEAM COHESION:
FROM THEORY TO RESEARCH TO TEAM BUILDING

*Todd M. Loughead**
University of Windsor, Canada
James Hardy
University of Wales, Bangor, United Kingdom

ABSTRACT

Historically, cohesion has been identified as *the most* important small-group variable (Golembiewski, 1962; Lott and Lott, 1965). Not surprisingly, a considerable amount of research has examined the construct of cohesion over the last five decades. Therefore, the purpose of this chapter is to provide an overview of the research examining cohesion. The chapter begins by reviewing the various definitions that have been used to measure cohesion and suggests based on group theory that cohesion is best defined by the definition proposed by Carron, Brawley, and Widmeyer (1998). Using the Carron et al. definition as a basis, the characteristics of cohesion are presented along with the conceptualization and operationalization of cohesion as reflected by the Group Environment Questionnaire (GEQ; Carron, Widmeyer, and Brawley, 1985). Following this, a conceptual framework highlighting the antecedents and the consequences of cohesion—namely the cohesion-performance relationship—are examined. Finally, research is reviewed and suggestions are made for researchers and practitioners interested in building cohesive teams.

Keywords: cohesion, team building, group environment questionnaire, cohesion-performance relationship

---

* Correspondence concerning this article should be addressed to Todd Loughead, Department of Kinesiology, University of Windsor, Windsor, Ontario, Canada, N9B 3P4, Tel: 519-253-3000 x. 2450, Fax: 519-973-7056, Email: loughead@uwindsor.ca
Both authors contributed equally to this chapter and consider its authorship as joint.

INTRODUCTION

A long-standing tenet in psychology is that human behavior is a product of two factors: personal (i.e., dispositions that originate within the individual) and situational (i.e., characteristics present in the individual's environment) factors. That is, while human behavior can be described solely as an individual construct, the importance of groups in regard to behavior cannot be underestimated (McGrath, 1984). According to McGrath, groups are the "instruments for influencing, shaping, [and] changing individuals who are their members" (p. 5). In fact, Baumeister and Leary (1995) have argued that individuals have a need to belong to groups and that groups satisfy a fundamental human motive.

One perspective of group functioning has posited cohesion as being central to group success (Carron, 1982). Cohesion, historically, has been identified as *the most* important small-group variable (Golembiewski, 1962; Lott and Lott, 1965). Given its importance, it is not surprising that several definitions of cohesion have been advanced over the last five decades.

DEFINING COHESION

Festinger, Schachter, and Back (1950) proposed one of the earliest definitions of cohesion. These researchers defined cohesion as "the total field of forces that act on members to remain in the group" (p. 164). Furthermore, the authors suggested that two sources contribute to cohesion: (a) the attractiveness of the group, and (b) the ability of the group to assist individual members achieve their goals. However, later that same year, Festinger (1950) proposed another definition, which created some uncertainty as to the meaning of this construct by suggesting that cohesion was "the resultant of all the forces acting on members to remain in the group" (p. 274). According to Mudrack (1989) the distinction between the two definitions is subtle yet important. In the Festinger et al. (1950) definition the "total field of forces" implied that researchers needed to identify and subsequently measure all "forces" that influence a member to either remain or to leave a group. On the other hand, the Festinger (1950) "resultant of all the forces" definition insinuated that only those "forces" relevant to the group required attention on the part of the researcher. Gross and Martin (1952) criticized the Festinger et al. (1950) definition and subsequently forwarded cohesion as "the resistance of a group to disruptive forces" (p. 553). Gross and Martin argued that their definition was superior to the Festinger et al. (1950) definition since it addressed the construct from the perspective of what keeps groups together. Gross and Martin contended that in a crisis situation, a group would stay united depending on the bonds among its members.

Although there were various definitions of cohesion (e.g., Festinger, 1950; Festinger et al., 1950; Gross and Martin, 1952), difficulties in the operationalization of the construct existed. As Cota, Evans, Dion, Kilik, and Longman (1995) indicated that it was difficult to operationalize Festinger et al.'s "field of forces". In addition, Brawley, Carron, and Widmeyer (1988) discussed one of the difficulties of operationalizing the Gross and Martin definition. They noted that important ethical issues prevented researchers from exposing groups to disruptive events or external threats. Given the troubles in operationalizing the construct, cohesion was subsequently measured as the attraction of the group to its members

(Libo, 1953). However, it is important to note that cohesion is more than just members' attraction to the group. As a result, it was noted that unidimensional models of cohesion are problematic since they have limited generalizability to other types of groups (Cota et al., 1995). Furthermore, narrow conceptualizations of cohesion hindered the integration of empirical findings. Therefore, a conceptualization and definition that reflected the multidimensional nature of cohesion was required. In fact, several theoreticians in group dynamics (e.g., Cota et al., 1995; Mudrack, 1989) suggested that cohesion was best defined as "a dynamic process that is reflected in the tendency for a group to stick together and remain united in the pursuit of its instrumental objectives and/or for the satisfaction of member affective needs" (Carron, Brawley, and Widmeyer, 1998, p. 213). It is important to note that the Carron et al. definition evolved from a similar and earlier definition advanced by Carron in 1982. In the revised definition, however, the authors included an affective component.

THE CHARACTERISTICS OF COHESION

The advantage of Carron et al.'s (1998) definition was that it highlighted four important characteristics in understanding the nature of cohesion. The first characteristic was that cohesion be viewed as a *multidimensional* construct. That is to say, there are numerous factors that caused a group to stick together and remain united. In addition, what caused one particular group to stick together may not be present in another similar type of group. Therefore, the multidimensional nature of cohesion did not imply that all dimensions will be equally present across groups (Carron and Brawley, 2000). For example, a football team may be high in social unity (e.g., team members like each other) however may not be united about how to achieve its task objectives (e.g., some team members may be more concerned about achieving individual goals instead of team goals). On the other hand, another football team may be very cohesive on task objectives yet lack social unity.

A second characteristic of the Carron et al. (1998) definition reflected the *dynamic* nature of cohesion. Cohesion can change over time so that factors contributing to cohesion at one stage of the group's development may not be salient at another stage of the group's life. For instance, when a team initially comes together, task unity may play a fundamental role (e.g., having similar team goals), however as the group develops over time, social unity may be of primary importance (e.g., socializing with team members during the off-season).

A third characteristic reflected the *instrumental* nature of cohesion. That is, all groups come together for a purpose. Intuitively, many groups, including sport teams, form for task-oriented reasons. Moreover, even groups that appear to form for "social" reasons (e.g., social club) have an instrumental foundation for their formation. That is, individuals come together because the group fulfills the need to belong on a social level.

A fourth characteristic was the *affective* dimension of cohesion. Carron and Brawley (2000) noted that bonding whether it is for task or social reasons is satisfying to members. Baumeister and Leary (1995) pointed out that bonding is related to positive affect (e.g., enjoyment), whereas, a feeling of exclusion may lead to negative feelings (e.g., depression, anxiety, loneliness).

THE CONCEPTUALIZATION AND
OPERATIONALIZATION OF COHESION

Mudrack (1989) pointed out that defining cohesion appears to be a straightforward task since the construct seems to be intuitively easy to describe and understand. However, as Carron and Brawley (2000) noted the challenge is taking the definition and translating it into an operational measure. In fact, Mudrack argued that confusion, inconsistency, and sloppiness, historically dominated the measurement of cohesion. Furthermore, Carron, Widmeyer, and Brawley (1985) pointed out three measurement issues that characterized earlier studies of cohesion, which may have lead to the previously discussed problems. First, these early studies treated cohesion as a unidimensional construct, thus most early researchers treated only one factor of cohesion—namely attraction to other group members. As noted by its multidimensional nature, cohesion is more than interpersonal attraction (Escovar and Sim, 1974). Second and somewhat related to the first point, studies not measuring interpersonal attraction directly, measured aspects related to interpersonal attraction by examining factors such as group members' desire to stay in their current group (e.g., Schachter, Ellertson, McBride, and Gregory, 1951), group members' affinity to their group (e.g., Converse and Campbell, 1968), and the importance group members placed on group membership (e.g., Arnold and Straub, 1973). Consequently, by measuring cohesion in a variety of ways, the findings could not be compared (Carron et al., 1985). Third, the psychometric properties of these earlier measures were suspect. The use of various and inappropriate measures of cohesion made it nearly impossible to determine the reliability and/or validity of these measures (Carron et al., 1985).

In order to overcome some of the shortcomings in regard to the measurement of cohesion, Carron et al. (1985) advocated the development of a new conceptual framework. They reasoned that instead of using patchwork methods to repair existing measures, such as the Sport Cohesiveness Questionnaire (Martens, Landers, and Loy, 1972) and Multidimensional Sport Cohesion Inventory (Yukelson, Weinberg, and Jackson, 1984), or develop new measures with similar problems, it was essential to go to the root of the measurement problem—the lack of a clear conceptualization.

Given that cohesion is a group property, it was necessary to develop a conceptual model that was grounded in group dynamics theory. Carron et al.'s (1985) conceptual model was based on three fundamental assumptions from group dynamics theory. The first assumption was based on research from social cognition theory suggesting that cohesion can be evaluated through perceptions of individual group members (Carron et al., 1998). Given that groups have observable properties, such as roles and status of group members, individuals within groups experience various social situations, and develop certain beliefs about the group, which they then integrate into perceptions concerning the group.

The second assumption based on the group dynamics literature recommended the need to distinguish between the group and the individual. As a result, the Carron et al. (1985) framework assumed that each group member held cognitions concerning the cohesiveness of the group which were related to the group as a totality and the degree to which the group satisfied personal needs and objectives. Carron et al. have labeled these two types of cognitions as: (a) *group integration* "which reflects the individual's perceptions about the closeness, similarity, and bonding within the group as a whole, as well as the degree of unification of the group field" (Carron et al., 1998, p. 217) and (b) *individual attractions to the group* "which reflects the individual's perceptions about personal motivations acting to retain him or her in the group, as well as his or her personal feelings about the group" (Carron et al., 1998, p. 217).

The third assumption based on the group dynamics literature distinguished between task- and social-oriented concerns of the group and its members (cf. Cota et al., 1995). Therefore, the Carron et al. (1985) framework incorporated a task and social distinction in its conceptualization of cohesion. The *task orientation* represented the general orientation or motivation towards achieving the group's goals (Carron et al., 1998). On the other hand, the *social orientation* represented the general orientation or motivation towards maintaining and developing social relationships within the group (Carron et al., 1985).

The combination of the individual-group and task-social components resulted in a four dimension conceptual model (see Figure 1). As Figure 1 shows, the four dimensions of cohesion as represented by the conceptual model are: *Individual attractions to the group-task* (ATG-T), *Individual attractions to the group-social* (ATG-S), *Group integration-task* (GI-T), and *Group integration-social* (GI-S). Carron et al. (1998) provided a constitutive definition for each of these four dimensions. Individual attractions to the group-task (ATG-T) is viewed as the attractiveness of the group's task, productivity, and goals for the individual personally. Individual attractions to the group-social (ATG-S), on the other hand, is defined as the attractiveness of the group as a social unit and social interaction and friendship opportunities available for the individual personally. Group integration-task (GI-T) is the individual's perceptions of task unity within the group as a whole. Finally, group integration-social (GI-S) is the individual's perceptions of the social unity within the group as a whole.

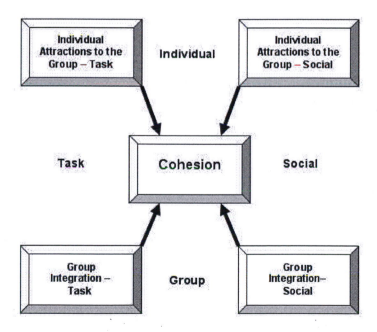

Figure 1. A conceptual framework for the study of cohesion in sport. From A.V. Carron, W.N. Widmeyer, and L.R. Brawley, "Development of an Instrument to Assess Cohesion in Sport Teams: the Group Environment Questionnaire," in the *Journal of Sport Psychology,* 7 (1): page 248, figure 1. © 1985 by Human Kinetics. Reprinted with permission from Human Kinetics (Champaign, IL).

With a theoretically driven conceptual framework established, the next step in overcoming the shortcomings of previous measures was the development of a measure that incorporated the four dimensions of cohesion as represented in the Carron et al. (1985) conceptual model. The result was the development, from 1982 to 1984, of the *Group Environment Questionnaire* (GEQ; Carron et al., 1985). The GEQ is an 18-item inventory that assesses four dimensions of cohesion and items are measured on a 9-point Likert scale anchored at the extremes by 1 (strongly disagree) and 9 (strongly agree). Out of the 18 items, 12 items need to be reversed coded; thus higher scores represent stronger perceptions of cohesiveness. The ATG-T scale contains 4 items and an example item is: "This team does not give me enough opportunities to improve my personal performance". The ATG-S scale contains 5 items and an example item is: "For me, this team is one of the most important social groups to which I belong". The GI-T scale contains 5 items and an example item is: "Our team is united in trying to reach its goals for performance". Finally, the GI-S scale contains 4 items and an example item is: "Members of our team would rather go out on their own than get together as a team".

Since the development of the GEQ (Carron et al., 1985), several studies have been undertaken to examine its psychometric properties. More specifically, research has shown that the GEQ is internally consistent (e.g., Carron et al., 1985) and demonstrates content (e.g., Carron et al., 1985), concurrent (e.g., Brawley, Carron, and Widmeyer, 1987), predictive (e.g., Carron, Widmeyer, and Brawley, 1988; Eys and Carron, 2001; Westre and Weiss, 1991; Widmeyer, Brawley, and Carron, 1990; Williams and Widmeyer, 1991), and factorial validity (e.g., Carron et al., 1985; Li and Harmer, 1996). It is worth noting that the cornerstone of any instrument is its validity (Carron et al., 1998). To date, research has shown that the GEQ is reliable and valid; however, it is important for researchers to keep in mind that validation is an on-going process and not an endpoint (Carron et al., 1998). This point is highlighted by the fact that the GEQ's factor structure has yet to be confirmed utilizing an appropriate heterogeneous sample of athletes.

One concern regarding the GEQ has been the low internal consistency values for certain GEQ subscales. This has led researchers to omit the offending subscale(s) from analyses (e.g., Bloom and Stevens, 2002). In addition, this issue has been investigated from both design and conceptual perspectives. From a design perspective, Eys, Carron, Bray, and Brawley (2003) examined the influence of negatively worded items. More specifically, Eys et al. compared the original version of the GEQ containing negatively worded items with a version of the GEQ consisting of all positively worded items. Three of the four subscales using the original GEQ had significantly lower Cronbach's alpha levels or internal consistency, as compared to the same subscales comprised of solely positively worded items. From a conceptual perspective, Carron, Brawley, and Widmeyer (2002) argued that sports teams vary in their degree of group development at any one time. Given this and cohesion's dynamic and multidimensional nature, it should be no surprise that team members have sometimes answered items assessing the same manifestation of cohesion inconsistently, leading to poor internal consistency. Moreover, negatively worded items were purposely included in the GEQ in order to counter response bias due to social desirability. Nonetheless, the GEQ represents the best measure of cohesion for sport.

The conceptually driven development of the GEQ has offered several advantages some of which were noted earlier in this chapter. For instance, cohesion has been measured as a multidimensional construct—that is, more than a single factor binds group members together.

As well, the GEQ considers the task and social dimensions of cohesion from both an individual and group perspective. Finally, the antecedents and consequences of cohesion are not incorporated into the GEQ (Carron et al., 1985). Therefore, researchers are better able to examine the factors that contribute to cohesion and the consequences of cohesion.

CONCEPTUAL FRAMEWORK FOR THE STUDY OF COHESION

Carron (1982) advanced a conceptual framework for the examination of cohesiveness in sport teams. The Carron framework is a linear model consisting of inputs, throughputs, and outputs (see Figure 2). According to Carron, the inputs are the antecedents of cohesion, the throughputs are the different manifestations of cohesion, and the outputs are viewed as the consequences of cohesion (e.g., performance). The antecedents contributing to cohesion are classified into four categories: environmental, personal, leadership, and group. The *environmental factors* represent the organizational system of the group and are viewed as the most general category contributing to cohesion. The next component influencing the cohesiveness of a group is *personal factors*. Carron noted it is difficult to outline an all-inclusive list of personal factors but these may include, although not limited to the following: task motivation (i.e., completion of group's task), affiliation motivation (i.e., establishing and maintaining happy, harmonious relationships), and self-motivation (i.e., achievement of direct, personal satisfactions from the group). The third component of factors influencing cohesion can be categorized as the *leadership factor*. According to Schriesheim (1980) there are two leadership factors that have influenced group cohesiveness: leader behavior and leadership style. The fourth component of factors influencing group cohesiveness is the *group factor* which includes aspects such as group task, group success, group orientation, group productivity norm, group ability, and group stability. In summary, the four factors (i.e., environmental, personal, leadership, and group) highlighted above will influence the throughput of cohesion.

As for the consequences or outputs of cohesion are concerned, the conceptual framework classified them into individual and group outcomes. In addition, both of these outcomes can be further classified in terms of actual and relative perceptions of performance (Carron, 1982).

Antecedents and Consequences of Cohesion

Since the development of the conceptual model of cohesion and the GEQ, research examining the antecedents and consequences of cohesion has been extensive. As a result, the following section will summarize a portion of the subsequent literature. That is, the following section will summarize some of the recent research that has examined the antecedents of cohesion within the following categories: environmental, personal, leadership, and group factors and the consequences of cohesion—that is, the cohesion-performance relationship.

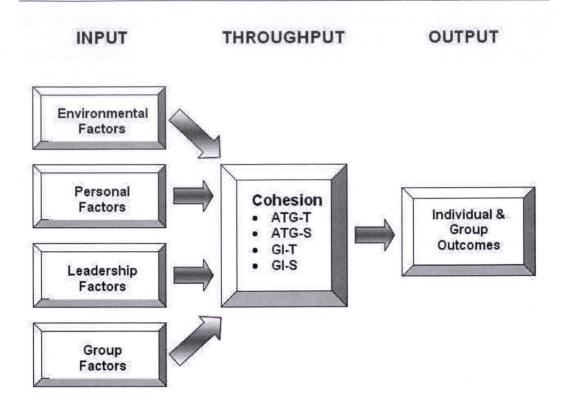

Figure 2. A conceptual model of cohesion. From A.V. Carron, "Cohesiveness in Sports Groups: Interpretations and Considerations," in the *Journal of Sport Psychology*, 4 (2): page 131, figure 1. © 1982 by Human Kinetics. Reprinted with permission from Human Kinetics (Champaign, IL).

Environmental

Group Resistance to Disruption

In examining the group resistance to disruption-cohesion relationship, Brawley et al. (1988) conducted two studies. In the first study, only elite male and female teams ($n = 7$) were sampled from a variety of sports (e.g., field hockey, ice hockey, soccer, basketball, wrestling, and volleyball). The athletes ($n = 89$) from these teams were asked to identify events that they thought would be disruptive to their team and were subsequently asked to rate the degree to which these events would be disruptive. In addition, the athletes also completed the GEQ to assess team cohesion. The results showed athletes who perceived high team cohesion (GI-T, GI-S, ATG-T) viewed their team as more resistant to disruptive events than athletes on teams with perceived low cohesiveness. In addition, the majority of disruptive events pertained to incidents involving specific individuals on the team (e.g., individual group members leaving the team). The authors argued that what was now required were disruptive events that affected the team as a whole. Using a similar protocol, Brawley et al. (Study 2) asked elite sport team athletes ($n = 102$) and intramural sport team athletes ($n = 107$) to identify events their entire team believed to be disruptive and to rate the degree of disruptiveness (e.g., the whole team not getting along). Similar to the results in the first study, both elite and intramural athletes on high cohesive teams (GI-T, GI-S, ATG-T) viewed their team as more resistant to disruptive team wide events than athletes on low cohesive teams. Taken together, these results suggested that regardless of level of competition (elite, recreational), a positive relationship was shown between group resistance to disruption and cohesion.

Group Size

Carron (1990) suggested that as groups increase in size, cohesion between group members is reduced. The author noted that the opportunity to develop strong relationships between members is more difficult in larger groups. For example, in a dyadic relationship where there are only two group members, there is only one potential relationship. On the other hand, when a group contains five members, there is a potential for 10 relationships. Therefore, it could be argued that sustaining 10 strong relationships would be more difficult than maintaining one strong relationship.

To date, research examining group size in sport has been sparse. Nonetheless, Widmeyer et al. (1990) conducted two studies examining the effects of group size on cohesion. In their first study, individuals were assigned to a team consisting of three, six, or nine member teams participating in a 3-on-3 basketball league and cohesion was measured pre-and post-season. The results indicated that the only pre-season cohesion variable able to differentiate among the three team sizes was ATG-T. Specifically, ATG-T was highest for those individuals playing on teams comprised of three members and least for teams with nine group members. On the other hand, the results showed that three post-season cohesion subscales (i.e., ATG-T, ATG-S, GI-S) were able to differentiate among the three team sizes. In particular, social cohesion was greatest in teams consisting of six members; whereas ATG-T was greater on teams of three members. In the second study, Widmeyer and colleagues examined the varying sizes of the action unit (i.e., the number of players participating during a volleyball match). Each participant competed in matches of 3 versus 3, 6 versus 6, and 12 versus 12. The findings from this second study showed that as group size increased perceptions of enjoyment decreased and cohesion decreased as group size increased. As a caveat, the type of cohesion that was affected by group size could not be discriminated since a two-item scale that assesses cohesion globally was used in the second study. Due to the rules of sports that limit the number of players/athletes competing at any one time, the applied implications of the apparent effect of group size may appear negligible. That said, it is still important for coaches to remember that carrying too many players on their roster may impact negatively on individuals' perceptions of cohesion.

Personal

Sacrifice Behavior

Sacrifice has been defined as the behavior whereby an individual voluntarily initiates an action or gives up a privilege for the sake of another individual or individuals without regard to reciprocity (Prapavessis and Carron, 1997b). Research by Prapavessis and Carron (1997b) examined the relationship between cohesion and sacrifice behavior. The researchers operationalized sacrifice behavior as a multidimensional construct consisting of four dimensions. First, *inside sacrifice* represented task-related sacrifices made by oneself and one's teammates in competitive and/or training situations. Second, *outside sacrifice* was related to sacrifices made by oneself and one's teammates at work or at home. Third, *teammates social sacrifice* represented sacrifices made by teammates in relation to their social life. Fourth, *personal social sacrifice* represented sacrifices made in one's social life. Overall, the results showed a positive relationship between cohesion and sacrifice behavior. More specifically, GI-T was related to inside sacrifice (r = .43), outside sacrifice (r = .25), and teammates' social sacrifice (r = .46). In addition, GI-S was associated with inside sacrifice (r = .34), and teammates' social sacrifice (r = .37).

In an ethnographic study of university level soccer, Holt and Sparkes (2001) examined factors that contributed to cohesion. Similar to Prapavessis and Carron (1997b), the authors found a relationship between cohesion and sacrifice behavior. According to their field notes, individual sacrifices made during game play improved group integration aspects related to the task. For instance, in explaining one of the important games during the season, the researchers noted that all the players "ran and sacrificed". When a team member could no longer compete after 60 minutes, this individual signaled to exit the game. The player had played to the point of exhaustion and had sacrificed his personal game for the benefit of the team. Another personal factor that emerged in the study was selfishness. Players who exhibited this type of behavior were viewed as a disruptive force that negatively affected the overall cohesiveness of the team. However, when the players were perceived as being less selfish and making sacrifices for the good of the team, the team climate changed from being a less cohesive to a more cohesive unit. Taken together, the sacrifice-cohesion research findings suggest that coaches and practitioners should remind team members of the sacrifices made for their teams in order to strengthen the team's task and social unity.

Anxiety

Prapavessis and Carron (1996) noted that enhancing the dynamics of the group might improve the psychological state of an individual. Prapavessis and Carron explored the relationship between cohesion and competitive state anxiety. The researchers assessed 110 high level athletes from a variety of sports (e.g., ice hockey, soccer, rugby, basketball). Athletes completed the GEQ at a midweek practice and then assessed the intensity of cognitive anxiety, somatic anxiety, and self-confidence fifteen minutes prior to competition. The results indicated that athletes who expressed higher task cohesion, manifested as ATG-T, had lower levels of precompetition cognitive anxiety.

Although the results from Prapavessis and Carron (1996) highlighted the relationship between cohesion and anxiety, state anxiety research has suggested that preexisting measures of precompetition anxiety tap only the *intensity* of symptoms and not the *direction* or *interpretation* the individual attaches to those symptoms (see Mellalieu, Hanton, and Fletcher, this voulme, for a review). Consequently, Eys, Hardy, Carron, and Beauchamp (2003) extended the work of Prapavessis and Carron by investigating the relationship between cohesion and the interpretation that athletes attach to the intensity of precompetitive cognitive and somatic symptoms associated with anxiety. Participants included 392 athletes from the sports of soccer, rugby, and field hockey. Using the same protocol as Prapavessis and Carron, athletes completed the GEQ after a practice session and completed the anxiety inventory just prior to competition. The results demonstrated that athletes who perceived their cognitive anxiety symptoms as facilitative had higher perceptions of ATG-T and GI-T than athletes who perceived their cognitive anxiety symptoms as debilitative. In addition, athletes who perceived their somatic anxiety symptoms as facilitative had higher perceptions of GI-T. Although both cohesion-anxiety studies do not permit conclusions to be made regarding causation, the findings do hint at the possibility of group level team building interventions enhancing personal level variables (e.g., state anxiety); an additional benefit to such intervention strategies.

Work Output

Prapavessis and Carron (1997a) investigated the relationship between cohesion and individual work output—operationalized as a percentage of VO_2 max using the participant's heart rate and lactic acid levels. The participants consisted of 252 elite level athletes from a wide range of interactive team sports (e.g., rugby, soccer, netball, water polo). The findings showed that task cohesion, as manifested by ATG-T, was positively related to individual work output. That is, work output was higher in participants who viewed their team as more task cohesive. Along the same line, Bray and Whaley (2001) examined the cohesion-work output relationship in 90 high school varsity basketball players. Work output was measured using an adapted version of the Expended Effort Scale from the Intrinsic Motivation Inventory (Ryan, 1982). The results revealed that work output was positively related to all four dimensions of cohesion (ATG-T, $r = .21$; ATG-S, $r = .26$; GI-T, $r = .31$; GI-S, $r = .10$). Taken together, these studies provide support for the notion that cohesion is positively related with individual work output.

Self-handicapping

The term self-handicapping represents the strategies individuals use to protect their self-esteem by adopting excuses for future events that may impede success (Carron, Prapavessis, and Grove, 1994). It is believed that sport is an ideal social context for individuals to employ self-handicapping strategies since it is a situation that is high in evaluative potential, success is uncertain, and the threat to self-esteem is present if failure occurs (Carron et al., 1994). Cohesive groups as suggested by Carron et al. could provide individuals with psychological protection by diffusing potential threats to self-esteem. Results from 221 male athletes revealed that athletes with the disposition to self-handicap, as reflected in excuse making (tendency for individuals to advance impediments that could negatively impact on performance) were more likely to perceive their team as lower in task cohesiveness as manifested by ATG-T and GI-T. In other words, a negative relationship was found between self-handicapping (excuse making) and task cohesion.

Given the previous study utilized a male only sample, Hausenblas and Carron (1996) examined both male ($n = 101$) and female athletes ($n = 144$) from a variety of sports: basketball, synchronized swimming, rowing, track and field, soccer, and volleyball. The results were similar to those found by Carron et al. (1994) whereby athletes with a higher predisposition of self-handicapping, manifested as excuse making, and who perceive their team to be highly task cohesive, as reflected by ATG-T, are more likely to set in place barriers to affect future performances. Therefore taken together, the results from these two studies showed that task cohesion was related to self-handicapping, as manifested by excuse making, in both male and female athletes across a wide variety of sports.

Mood

Cohesion has been found to be associated with an individual's mood (Terry, Carron, Pink, Lane, Jones, and Hall, 2000). Mood was measured using the Profile of Mood States-C (Terry, Keohane, and Lane, 1996), which assesses six dimensions of mood: anger, confusion, depression, fatigue, tension, and vigor. In general, the results indicated that when athletes perceive themselves to be a part of a cohesive group, they tend to experience enhanced mood. More specifically, athletes who perceived their team to be high on ATG-T were more likely to feel less tension and anger. As well, athletes perceiving their team high on GI-T were more likely to feel less depression. Insofar as social cohesion is concerned, athletes high in ATG-S were more likely to feel high in vigor and low in depression.

Leadership

Westre and Weiss (1991) were one of the first to examine the relationship between cohesion (using the GEQ) and leadership. Using male high school American football players, the researchers found that players who perceived their coaches to engage in higher levels of training and instruction, democratic behavior, social support, and positive feedback perceived higher levels of task cohesion. The testing of the relationship between social cohesion and leadership measures was not, however, possible due to inadequate internal consistency scores ($\alpha < .70$) on the social cohesion scales.

Replicating the Westre and Weiss (1991) study, Pease and Kozub (1994) examined female high school basketball players. Similar to Westre and Weiss, the results revealed that coaching behaviors were positively related to task cohesion. Specifically, the cohesion measure of GI-T was positively related to the coaching behaviors of training and instruction, and democratic behavior. As well, ATG-T was positively associated with the coaching behavior of training and instruction. In other words, athletes who perceived their coach to exhibit high levels of these coaching behaviors also perceived their team to be more task cohesive. Although, Westre and Weiss were unable to examine the relationship between social cohesion and leadership, Pease and Kozub found none of the coaching behaviors were related to the social manifestations of cohesion.

Gardner, Shields, Bredemeier, and Bostrom (1996) also examined the leader behavior-cohesion relationship in the sports of baseball and softball. The results revealed that the coaching behaviors of training and instruction, democratic behavior, social support, and positive feedback were positively related to task cohesion (a summation of ATG-T and GI-T scales). On the other hand, the coaching behavior of autocratic behavior was negatively related to task cohesion. Unlike Pease and Kozub (1994), however, the coaching behaviors of training and instruction, and social support were positively related to social cohesion (a summation of ATG-S and GI-S scales). Taken together the results revealed that a positive relationship between leadership and cohesion.

Group Factors

Norms

Gammage, Carron, and Estabrooks (2001) were among the first researchers to examine the influence of team norms on cohesion in sport. Group norms reflect what the team considers to be acceptable individual behavior (Carron and Hausenblas, 1998). The participants were 324 undergraduate university students who responded to scenarios associated with athletes training in the off-season. In the scenarios, information pertaining to both group cohesion and the norm for productivity was systematically manipulated to produce extreme conditions. In general, the results indicated that the norm for off-season productivity was a moderator in the cohesion-performance relationship. Specifically, it was found that when cohesion was high and there was a high team productivity norm led to a higher probability of off-season training.

Although the Gammage et al. study was important in establishing a norm-cohesion relationship, there were some limitations. First, there were some questions in regard to ecological validity. As Gammage et al. pointed out "the role of group norms ... should be examined using real teams involved in real competitive situations" (p. 15). Second, only one type of norm was examined: the norm for productivity in the off-season. In fact, Munroe, Estabrooks, Dennis, and Carron (1999) found, using a qualitative methodology, that norms existed within sport teams in four specific contexts: practice, competition, off-season, and team social situations.

Given the importance of studying norms using real sport teams and that several different norms exist in sport, Patterson, Carron, and Loughead (2005) examined the influence of team norms on the cohesion. The sample consisted of 298 athletes (112 males, 186 females) from 24 university and club level interactive and coactive sport teams. Four normative contexts were examined: norms for competitions, practice, the off-season, and social situations. The results showed that athletes gave greatest effort when on teams possessing stronger norms for social interactions and higher team social cohesion (i.e., GI-S).

Roles

Roles are one family of correlates of cohesion that has received increasing research attention. Roles are defined as a pattern of behavior that is expected of a person in a social situation (Carron and Hausenblas, 1998). One particular role dimension that has attracted the interest of investigators has been role ambiguity, which refers to a lack of clear, consistent information regarding the actions required in a particular position (cf. Eys and Carron, 2001). It could be expected that when role ambiguity is low, the perception of cohesion is high since all team members are not in conflict as to their function on a team. Overall, the results from a small sample ($n = 79$) of varsity basketball players demonstrated that task cohesion (ATG-T, GI-T) is related to role ambiguity (e.g., Eys and Carron, 2001). That is when role ambiguity is low; task cohesion is greater on sport teams. See Eys, Beauchamp, and Bray (this volume) for a more detailed review of roles and its relationship to team cohesion. Taken together, the group factor components of norms and roles are two factors that have recently been examined in relation to cohesion. Based on the empirical evidence to date, it appears that these two factors influence athletes' perception of cohesion. Therefore coaches and athletes should be aware of the importance in establishing standards of expectations (i.e., norms) and having clearly defined roles in attempts of fostering higher levels of cohesion.

The Relationship Between Cohesion and Performance

Researchers, practitioners, coaches, and players implicitly place great emphasis on the importance of the cohesion-performance association (e.g., Bloom, Stevens, and Wickwire, 2003), with the general belief that more cohesion is better for performance (Hardy, Eys, and Carron, 2005). Regardless of the empirical presence of a relationship between these variables, coaches prefer to work with close, cohesive teams as opposed to non-cohesive teams (Miller, 1997). Researchers from both mainstream and sport psychology have extensively investigated the presence and direction of the relation between cohesion and performance. Furthermore, research attention has also focused on whether team cohesion is the *cause* or the *result* of performance. Mullen and Copper (1994) noted "either direction is plausible. On the one hand, group cohesiveness could energize and direct group members towards successful task completion. ... On the other hand, excellence in performance should make group members feel much better about the group" (p. 215).

Although heavily criticized for their inability concerning inferences about causation (see Rogosa, 1980), the use of cross-lagged panel study designs has been frequent in cohesion research examining the direction of the cohesion-performance relationship (e.g., Carron and Ball, 1978; Martens and Peterson, 1971; Peterson and Martens, 1972; Slater and Sewell, 1994). Typically, such designs involve the measurement of cohesion and performance on (at least) two occasions (e.g., early season and late season). As a result, data examined within the same time panel (e.g., correlation between early season cohesion and early season performance) is pertinent to the presence of an association between these two variables. Moreover, information regarding the associations between early season cohesion and late season performance (i.e., cohesion as the *cause* of performance) as well as between early season performance and late season cohesion (i.e., cohesion as the *result* of performance) is generated. Simply put, a substantially stronger correlation implies the causal direction of the cohesion-performance relationship.

When individual cohesion-performance studies are inspected, a rather confusing picture emerges. The lack of conceptual and methodological clarity has been noted for this ambiguity in early cohesion research (e.g., Carron and Ball, 1978). As noted earlier, Mudrack (1989) summarized that early cohesion research was "dominated by confusion, inconsistency, and almost inexcusable sloppiness with regard to defining the construct" (p. 45). A mainstream psychology study by Bakeman and Helmreich (1975) on aquanauts offers a specific example. Bakeman and Helmreich were the first to apply the cross-lagged panel design to the examination of the cohesion-performance relationship. A moderate to strong ($r = .65$) positive correlation between the two variables was found. Although a strong positive performance-to-cohesion relationship ($r = .72$) was reported, the cohesion-to-performance association was found to be non-significant. However, it should be noted that two issues may have contributed to this finding; (a) the sample employed was small ($n = 10$), and (b) the acknowledged lack of statistical independence. Moreover, as Carron and Ball (1978) noted, the utilization of behavior-related measures of cohesion as well as the nature of the aquanauts' task limits the generalizability of the results to the sport environment.

The overall picture from the sport-specific literature is equally perplexing. Sport research has found negative (e.g., Lenk, 1969; McGrath, 1962), positive (e.g., Carron and Ball, 1978; Martens and Peterson, 1971), and no relationships (e.g., Melnick and Chemers, 1974) between cohesion and performance. To fully comprehend the relationship between cohesion and performance, it must be emphasized that early attempts to study this relationship did not distinguish between task and social cohesion. As task cohesion is directly oriented to performance a stronger positive relationship between task cohesion and performance would be expected than between social cohesion and performance. Williams and Widmeyer's (1991) golf study found some support for this prediction as task cohesion was a better predictor of performance than social cohesion. Despite the appeal of the above expectation, Slater and Sewell (1994) found limited support for a relationship between task cohesion and performance in varsity field hockey teams. However, Slater and Sewell found some support stressing the importance of social cohesion in relation to enhanced performance.

One possible explanation for the conflicting results offered by Carron and Chelladurai (1981) is that sport type (interactive and coactive team sports) might moderate the cohesion-performance relationship. Baron and Kenny (1986) defined a moderator as a variable "that affects the direction and/or strength of the relation between an independent or predictor variable and a dependent or criterion variable" (p. 1174). Within the group dynamics literature, groups involved in tasks requiring interdependence between group members and complex interactions in order to succeed are termed *interactive groups* (e.g., soccer and rugby teams). Conversely, tasks where group success is typically determined by the summation of individual group members' efforts requiring little interdependence are termed *coactive* (e.g., teams competing in athletics and swimming). Carron and Chelladurai proposed that cohesion is of critical importance for interactive team sports since it assists in the coordination of group resources. Furthermore, it was suggested that a *lack* of cohesion within coactive teams would foster increased competition between team members, thus leading to performance improvements. Although these hypotheses may have intuitive appeal, ambiguity concerning research findings remained.

With regard to the causal direction of the cohesion-performance relationship, a range of results has been reported. As noted earlier, arguments for either direction can be made. In fact, Cartwright (1968) proposed a circular or reciprocal relation between cohesion and performance. From the sport literature, Carron and Ball (1978) generated supportive evidence that increased ice hockey performance resulted in strengthened individual perceptions of cohesion. Landers, Wilkinson, Hatfield, and Barber (1982) as well as Williams and Hacker (1982) have made a similar claim. However, reinterpretation of these latter two results would actually suggest a circular relation (Slater and Sewell, 1994). As Slater and Sewell (1994) warned, "reviewers should guard against claiming that a performance-to-cohesion causal relationship is now largely established—it is not" (p. 429). In support of their argument, Slater and Sewell's field hockey data provided evidence of a circular association (i.e., no difference between the relevant cross-lagged correlations) with a slight dominance from cohesion to performance. In other words, the cohesion-to-performance correlation was of a stronger positive magnitude than the performance-to-cohesion correlation.

In order to gain a better understanding of the cohesion-performance relationship, a more systematic and objective technique has been advocated to summarize research findings. The meta-analysis technique is an excellent method for summarizing large bodies of contradictory results, as it employs effect sizes (a standardized score) to allow comparison across studies.

Consequently, Mullen and Copper (1994) reviewed experimental and correlational findings from a diverse sample of studies taken from the business, military, occupational, and sport domains to examine the cohesion-performance relationship. A small positive significant effect size was found for the cohesion-to-performance relationship. On the other hand, a significant and larger positive effect size was reported for the performance-to-cohesion relationship. Thus, while more cohesion may cause enhanced performance, performance has a larger impact on a team's resultant cohesion. Interestingly, no support was found for Carron and Chelladurai's (1981) proposed sport type moderation of the cohesion-performance relationship. Of particular relevance was the finding that commitment to the task or task cohesion as opposed to social cohesion led to increased performance. Moreover, the cohesion-to-performance relationship was strongest with sport teams compared to any other type of group (e.g., military, business, organizational).

It should be noted that Mullen and Copper (1994) did not include all the sport-related studies including unpublished studies (e.g., Ph.D. and Master's theses) available to them in their review. Furthermore, as their meta-analysis was not specific to the domain of sport, it is possible that their conclusions may not generalize to this setting. As a result, Carron, Colman, Wheeler, and Stevens (2002) conducted a thorough meta-analytic review of 55 sport-specific studies including both published and unpublished results. Carron et al.'s sport-specific effect size for the cohesion-to-performance relationship was larger than Mullen and Copper's overall effect size. Medium positive effect sizes were found for both the cohesion-to-performance (ES = .57), and performance-to-cohesion relationships (ES = .69). Although the effect size for the latter was larger than the former, a significant difference between the two directions was not found. Similar to Mullen and Copper's study, Carron and colleagues did not find support for a sport type moderation of the cohesion-performance relationship. Of practical importance and contrary to Mullen and Copper, Carron et al. found medium positive effect sizes for both task *and* social cohesion. If one were to base attempts to increase team performance via increased team cohesion, solely on Mullen and Copper's findings, methods for enhancing perceptions of social cohesion would be overlooked. Carron et al.'s sport-specific findings suggested that regardless of the type of cohesion, increased perceptions of team cohesion can lead to improved performance. However, detailed information about the underpinning mechanisms of the cohesion-to-performance relationship (e.g., communication, collective efficacy) are as yet, not well understood. As such, future research focusing on why and how this relationship functions seems warranted. Once an understanding of the mediators of the cohesion-to-performance relationship has been obtained, this information can be utilized to enhance performance since it is believed that interventions function through mediating variables (Baranowski, Anderson, and Carmack, 1998).

DEVELOPING COHESIVE TEAMS

Drawing from Lewin's (1935) perspective of group dynamics, Widmeyer and DuCharme (1997) described team building as the process of attempting to enhance a team's locomotion as well as its maintenance. Locomotion is related to productivity or performance whereas maintenance is reflective of a team's ability to stay together or be cohesive. Brawley and Paskevich (1997) offered a more precise definition of the team building process. They noted multiple purposes to team building; (a) to increase a team effectiveness, (b) to improve working conditions, (c) to satisfy the needs of its members, and (d) to enhance cohesion. There is obvious overlap between these two definitions; both place an emphasis on enhanced performance and increased perceptions of team cohesion. Given the previous discussion of the cohesion-to-performance relationship, this section focuses on methods to enhance cohesion.

Taken together, the sport-related team building literature is in its infancy (Hardy and Crace, 1997). Moreover, given the importance placed on optimally functioning sport teams by coaches and practitioners (e.g., Munroe, Terry, and Carron, 2002), there is a dearth of empirical research examining the effectiveness of team building interventions. Nevertheless, a meta-analysis of 126 studies from the business and industry setting suggested that team building interventions were the most effective technique to enhance satisfaction and work–related attitudes (e.g., positive attitudes towards others and the organization) (Neuman, Edwards, and Raju, 1989). One reason for the lack of research on team building in sport may be related to the large amount of time and effort inherently involved in field-based longitudinal study designs.

Within the team building literature, two general approaches relating to the implementation of strategies have been forwarded. The first approach involves the consultant working with the team's coaches, whereby the coaches are responsible for implementing the team-building strategies suggested to them by the sport psychologist. In essence, the consultant works via the coach. As a result, this has been termed the *indirect* approach to team building (Carron, Spink, and Prapavessis, 1997). The second approach involves the consultant working closely with the team and its players in a "hands on" fashion. Team members, coaches, and consultant form a partnership, working together to build a more cohesive team. This has been labeled the *direct* approach to team building where the consultant is a direct participant in the team building process (Carron et al., 1997). In addition to the consultant working directly with the team members, another difference between the two approaches is that the direct method actively includes team members in the team building process, thus empowering the athletes, which in turn fosters a sense of ownership in the team building program. Carron and Spink (1993) developed a protocol and conceptual framework for an indirect approach to team building for the exercise domain, which has since been adapted for the sport environment (see Carron et al., 1997; Prapavessis, Carron, and Spink, 1996). Their indirect approach to team building consists of four stages. The sport psychologist typically covers the first three stages in a workshop with the coaches. First, the *introductory stage* presents the rationale for the team building program, and the benefits of high team cohesion are outlined. Second, the *conceptual stage* presents the coaches with a conceptual framework from which they gain greater understanding of the team building process (Figure 3). As shown in the figure, aspects of a team's environment and structure are hypothesized to impact on group processes, which in turn enhance team members' perceptions of team cohesion. Third, the *practical stage* allows coaches to brainstorm with the consultant to identify strategies that impact on the factors included in the conceptual framework. Fourth, the *intervention stage* is when the coaches with their respective teams implement the team building strategies previously developed. Advantages to utilizing an indirect approach to team building include reduced time commitment for the consultant as well as the application of the program when there is a geographical barrier between consultant and coach.

The empirical-based evidence for the indirect approach to team building has been found to be positive in the exercise setting (e.g., Carron and Spink, 1993; Estabrooks and Carron, 1999). However, research within the sport setting has been mixed. Prapavessis et al. (1996) investigated the effectiveness of Carron and Spink's indirect approach to team building with soccer teams. Participants in the treatment condition (i.e., team building condition) did not significantly differ than those in the attention (placebo) control and control conditions. Nonetheless, post-hoc analyses found that respective components of the team building program uniquely predicted between 4% and 26% of the pooled sample's post-intervention cohesion variance (after controlling for pre-intervention cohesion and performance satisfaction). Moreover, Prapavessis et al.'s post-manipulation check allowed insight into the lack of hypothesized differences across the treatment groups. Specifically, the investigators examined whether there were any differences in regard to the components of the team building program. The results showed that participants in the team building condition perceived greater leadership ability of their coach following the intervention compared to the attention control group. It was suggested that because of the nature of sport teams, all coaches probably addressed at least to some extent the team building components highlighted in the Carron and Spink framework. The lack of a matched assignment to the respective conditions, based on each team's level of group development may be an additional explanation for the lack of differences found between the three treatment conditions (Brawley and Paskevich, 1997).

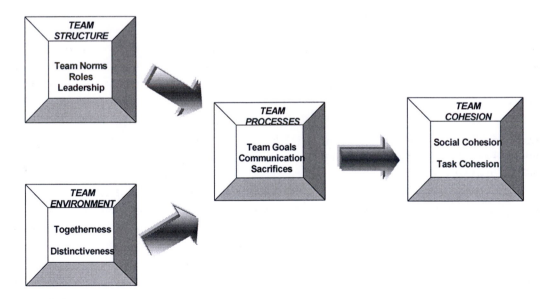

Figure 3. A conceptual framework for team building. From A.V. Carron and K.S. Spink, "Team Building in an Exercise Setting," in the *Sports Psychologist,* 7 (1): page 11, figure 1. © 1993 by Human Kinetics. Reprinted with permission from Human Kinetics (Champaign, IL).

With regard to the direct approach to team building, Yukelson (1997) reported his experiences working with Penn State University sport teams. Yukelson's direct approach to team building consists of four stages. First, the *assessment stage* allows the consultant to gain an understanding of the existing team dynamics. Observation and discussion with team members, coaches, and support staff helps to achieve this end. Second, the *education stage* presents an overview of the nature of groups. This could include discussion of Tuckman's (1965) model of group development (i.e., forming, storming, norming, and performing). Third, the *brainstorming stage* involves the identification of areas for improvement. And fourth, the *implementation stage* consists of applying tailored team building strategies that were generated in the previous stage. Advantages of the direct approach to team building include the active attempt to empower team members throughout the process, the ability to purposely shape the team building program to the needs of the team as well as allowing the consultant to lead team sessions.

Although empirical research using direct approaches to team building within the sport literature is scant, applied sport psychology researchers have adopted and reported the use of this approach. For example, Voight and Callaghan (2001) employed Yukelson's direct approach to team building with two Division 1 NCAA female soccer teams. Although cohesion was not measured (via the GEQ), team members reported that the team building program was effective in increasing individual and team performance, in addition to enhancing each team's sense of togetherness. Bloom and Stevens (2002) employed an expanded version of Yukelson's approach, adapted from the organizational literature (Beckhard, 1972; Beer, 1980), with an equestrian team. The season long program included six team building sessions focusing on the development of peer leadership, norms, communication, dealing with team selection, and competition preparation. Although pre- to post-program perceptions of team cohesion (measured via the GEQ) were strengthened, a significant increase in team cohesiveness was not found. The study's relatively small sample size (*n* = 45) may have contributed to the lack of statistical significance. Supplemental information from focus groups, however, revealed "an improvement in team harmony and closeness over the course of the season. In particular, the athletes felt more support from teammates at competitions and that the cliques were disappearing" (Bloom and Stevens, 2002, p. 6).

In the remainder of this section, a combined approach is forwarded. Specifically, although there is no "hard and fast" formula to improving team cohesion (Yukelson, 1997), practitioners are encouraged to incorporate elements of both Carron and Spink's (1993) indirect framework and Yukelson's direct approach to team building. As noted by Prapavessis et al. (1996), the absence of an assessment stage in the indirect team building method is a limitation. Yukelson (1997) stressed its importance, suggesting that assessing the situation is "the most important part of any good team building intervention" (p.86). Thus, it is recommended that the consultant assess the team's dynamics in general paying particular attention to the components contained in Carron and Spink's conceptual framework. Consequently, this combined approach has the advantage of applying sound theory, in the case of Carron and Spink's framework, with the thorough assessment of actual team dynamics, along with the active involvement of team members throughout the team building program as suggested by Yukelson. Assessing the team's dynamics prior to implementing a team building program allows the consultant to pinpoint areas for improvement specific to the team's needs. As a result, more efficient use of team building strategies is achieved. Once specific strategies are developed, the involvement of team leaders (i.e., athlete leaders) in implementing the team building program is critical to the success of program. That is to say, if the leaders of the team "buy into" the program, other teammates may realize the importance of team building and, in turn, are more likely to commit to the program (Carron et al., 1997).

Stevens and Bloom (2003) adopted a similar combined approach in their examination of the effect of a team building program in softball. Although only one team containing 16 players underwent the tailored multimodal team building sessions, when their perceptions of cohesion (measured using the GEQ) were compared against a single control team ($n = 17$ players) significant GI-T and GI-S increases were detected. Interestingly, focus group discussions revealed that although overall coach–athlete communication had improved (one area targeted for improvement), the communication tended to break down in tight game situations or games against difficult opponents.

Theory and research support Carron and Spink's (1993) conceptualization of the importance of roles (e.g., Eys and Carron, 2001), norms (e.g., Kim, 1992), peer leadership (e.g., Neubert, 1999), group goals (e.g., Widmeyer and DuCharme, 1997), and sacrifice (e.g., Prapavessis and Carron, 1997b) in relation to increased cohesion. Although specific strategies relevant to the exercise domain have been implemented (e.g., Carron and Spink, 1993), the transfer of such strategies from the minimal group setting (e.g., exercise classes) to the more dynamic sport team domain is limited. For example, Carron and Spink (1993) targeted exercise groups' *environment* (e.g., distinctiveness) by creating names, T-shirts, and slogans for each of the team building exercise groups. It is probable that such strategies are redundant in the sport environment, as they may already exist. As a result, sport-specific strategies pertinent to optimizing teams' dynamics are now presented. Emphasis should be placed on the integral involvement of individual team members in each strategy in order to promote ownership and intrinsic motivation regarding the respective intervention.

One strategy that facilitates the empowerment of team members is "team performance profiling". This technique can also aid the consultant's understanding of team members' perceptions of their team as well as what the athletes feel is important for team success. Although we propose that this technique be employed as part of an assessment phase for a team building program, others (e.g., Munroe, Terry, and Carron, 2002) have suggested that conducting team performance profiling also improves the cohesiveness of a team through the interaction and communication necessary to complete the profiling process. The team is divided into smaller (4-5 players) heterogeneous (e.g., veteran, rookie, attacker, defender) groups. Each subgroup then identifies and records the 10-12 most important aspects in their sport for success. All aspects of team play should be considered (i.e., mental, physical, technical and tactical). Assigned leaders for each of the subgroups then present their group's critical aspects to the team as a whole. Team consensus on the critical aspects for success is then obtained. Each member of each subgroup then rates how the best or most successful team at their standard of competition would score from 1 to 10 on the identified aspects (1 = could not be any worse, 10 = could not be any better). Ratings to one decimal place have been found to be useful in this process (Doyle and Parfitt, 1997) and scores close to 10 should be expected. Assigned subgroup leaders average and report to the team the ratings for the respective critical aspects. A team rating is ultimately recorded. The ideal ratings are then followed by an assessment of the actual team's current state for each of the identified aspects using the same response scale. Again individual responses are averaged to represent the subgroup and a team rating is established. Once these two team ratings have been obtained, a discrepancy score between ideal and current scores can be calculated for each aspect. Large discrepancy scores are indicative of areas for improvement as identified by the team itself. Such areas can be targeted for team building interventions. In particular, the team performance profiling procedure can be incorporated into the initial stages of a team goal setting program.

Once a thorough assessment of a team's dynamics has been completed (facilitated by the use of the performance profiling technique) tailored interventions can be implemented. With regard to the possible targeting of the *team's structure* (specifically team norms and individuals' roles within the team), two strategies are forwarded. One method to help develop appropriate team norms is to implement team discussions and obtain consensus about the behaviors of the ideal player. Team members are asked to generate a profile of how an ideal player would react to particular situations (e.g., practice, competition) (Miller, 1997). The team is divided into small heterogeneous groups. Each group is presented with the same list of hypothetical but *realistic* situations for which they generate ideas on how the "perfect player" would react. After a 20-30 minute period, spokespersons from each group present the ideas to the whole team. The team then discusses and more importantly forms a consensus as to what is acceptable and unacceptable behavior for the situations. Upon consensus, it is agreed that this is the standard by which teammates should judge one another. Miller reported the successful use of a similar discussion session with female Olympic field hockey teams. Norm-related research supports the link between task cohesion and team norms (Prapavessis and Carron, 1997b). Furthermore, from a group dynamics perspective, the presence of good team norms was identified as one of the three most important aspects of successful sport teams (Carron, 2003).

Although one-on-one meetings between the coach and individual players or small groups of players can help eliminate problems revolving around team members' roles, this can be a time consuming approach and denies the entire team understanding and acceptance how everyone's roles fit together. An alternative method that can be used under certain circumstances is the "hot seat" (Eys, Colman, Loughead, and Carron, 2004). In this procedure, individual team members present to the team (i.e., players and coaching staff) what they perceive to be their own responsibilities on the team. Following this, the coaching staff and teammates can amend, dispute, or expand the responsibilities listed by each individual. The head coach has responsibility for the final decision on matters. Use of the hot seat procedure should be avoided if the team is not comprised of mature athletes offering a supportive environment. The hot seat approach to enhancing athletes' roles has the advantage that team members' responsibilities are explicitly stated to everyone involved within the team. As a result, role clarity and acceptance for all team members should be enhanced.

With regard to the potential need to impact *team processes* (e.g., communication, team goals, and sacrifices), channels of communication can be opened via the previously discussed team performance profiling procedure. Sullivan and Feltz (2003) recently found all four aspects of team cohesion to be related to communication within sports teams. Team performance profiling also lends itself to the establishment of appropriate team goals (via the identified areas of improvement), essential for the effective functioning and cohesiveness of any sport team (see Widmeyer and DuCharme, 1997 for a detailed discussion of how team goals impact on team performance and team cohesion). According to Carron and Colman's (2000) research-based team goal setting protocol, such programs should consist of 3 stages: (a) provision of rationale for and establishment of 5-6 team performance goals; (b) game-by-game monitoring; and (c) an evaluation of the goals set. The monitoring stage should last at least 4 to 6 games (depending on the length of the season). Modifications can be made following the evaluation process whereby goals are fine-tuned and the 3-stage cycle is repeated. As with all the team building strategies presented, the involvement and support of the coaching staff is essential to the success of any goal setting program (Locke, Shaw, Saari, and Latham, 1981; Hanson and Lubin, 1988).

Specifically, in Stage 1, the team (in open forum) chooses short-term and long-term outcome-based goals that are *realistic* (e.g., 3 wins out of the next 5 games, or to finish in the top 3 in league standings at the end of the season). The setting of performance goals then follows in answer to the question; "What do you have to do especially well as a team on a game-to-game basis to maximize your chances of reaching your short-term and long-term goals?" Each team member is provided a list of specific and measurable performance indices (e.g., 50-50 tackles won, number of corner kicks awarded, number of fouls against) from which to choose 5 to 6 behaviors. The assistance of coaching staff in compiling the list may be warranted. Team members are then assigned to small heterogeneous groups in order to discuss and agree upon the most relevant indices for their team. Finally, the team as a whole forms a consensus on the goals that they are going to achieve as a team. Once the required behaviors have been agreed upon, the process is repeated with regard to generating a specific standard for each of the indices (e.g., 75% of 50-50 tackles won, 6 corners per half).

The coaching staff plays a particularly critical role in Stage 2. Without their monitoring and provision of feedback to the team, the intervention will not be effective. Similarly, coaches play an integral role in the evaluation process (i.e., Stage 3) towards progress made in achieving team goals. At this juncture in the team goal setting program, it is possible that any non-essential team goal be disregarded and replaced. This should be viewed as a positive step, as the team has now recognized the importance of selecting the most pertinent team goals (Carron and Colman, 2000), which is evidence of the team "buying into" the goal setting program, and essential for any successful intervention.

As adherence to any long-term intervention may be a potential problem, team members' intrinsic motivation to the team building program should be enhanced whenever possible. To this end, once the consultant has selected team building strategies appropriate for the needs of the team, he/she should include coaching staff and team members into the decision making process regarding which strategies to utilize. The consultant will need to explain the pros and cons of each applicable strategy. It must be noted that although the aforementioned team building strategies have either intuitive or theoretical appeal, limited research has empirically addressed the effectiveness of such interventions. Consequently, future research should examine the effects of the previously described interventions.

Caveat

Before summarizing the contents of this chapter a word of caution is warranted. In line with most coaches, practitioners, and group dynamics researchers, the present chapter has forwarded a "cohesion is good" perspective. However, Buys (1978) suggested, half jokingly, "humans would do better without groups" (p.123). Based on Prapavessis and Carron's (1996) study of cohesion and state anxiety, Paskevich, Estabrooks, Brawley, and Carron (2001) queried whether athletes in highly cohesive teams feel pressure not to letdown fellow teammates. In other words, are there any negative consequences of being a part of a highly cohesive group? Hardy et al. (2005) generated some preliminary qualitative findings focusing on this issue. Although more athletes perceived the potential for disadvantages of high task cohesion (approximately 55% of athletes surveyed), potential disadvantages of high social cohesion were also reported (approximately 30%). Furthermore, both individual and group level negative consequences to high task and social cohesion were generated. As a result, there is preliminary evidence to suggest the potential for disadvantages for some athletes on teams that are highly cohesive.

FUTURE DIRECTIONS IN COHESION RESEARCH

Although team cohesion has been the focus of sport-related research for decades, many avenues for future research remain. Presented below are three areas of future research attention we believe to be of importance.

Unit of Analysis: Individual Versus Group Level

Given that cohesion is a group property, an important consideration when conducting cohesion research is determining an appropriate unit of analysis. Historically, three approaches have been used in group dynamics research (Carron et al., 1998; Cota et al., 1995). The first approach has been to use the individual group member as the unit of analysis. For example, an investigation of how individual attractions to a group are related to the individual's adherence to that group's activities would be at this conceptual level. The second approach has been to aggregate the data, that is, simply using group averages (e.g., Carron and Ball, 1978). The third approach has been to use the intact team as the unit of analysis. The total amount of communication within a single team would be such an example. If the research question focuses on the group level, an underlying assumption is that team members' responses exhibit a group level effect. That is, there is a certain degree of shared beliefs. The combined use of intraclass correlations and the index of agreement has been employed to demonstrate such similarity in perceptions. Carron et al. (2003) recently proposed index of agreement values of .5, .6, and .7 as representative of weak, moderate, and strong agreement for variables conceptualized at the group level (e.g., GI-T, GI-S). Whereas, .4, .5, and .6 represent weak, moderate, and strong agreement for variables conceptualized at the individual level (e.g., ATG-T, ATG-S). James, Demaree, and Wolf (1984) have proposed that index of agreement values greater than .5 are adequate for research purposes. Once it has been established that members of teams respond with some similarity, intraclass correlation analyses can ascertain if members of teams respond more similarly within their teams than between teams. Following the demonstration of shared beliefs, the researcher can be confident in their decision to pool individual team members' data.

Carron et al. (1998) suggested that determining which of the aforementioned approaches is most appropriate is dependent on three factors. The first factor to consider is the nature of the research question. If the researcher is interested in examining the influence of cohesion on individual perceptions or behavior, such as personal satisfaction, then the individual level can be used as the unit of analysis. If, however, team performance was the variable under investigation, then the group level would be the appropriate unit of analysis. The second factor is the theory being tested (Carron et al., 1998; Cota et al., 1995). As Carron et al. noted a theory such as social comparison theory is based on the assumption that individuals will compare themselves to others; therefore, the aggregate value can be used as the unit of analysis. The third factor is empirical in nature (Carron et al., 1998). In some circumstances, researchers may be interested in examining either the group level or the individual level or both levels. As a result, the use of multilevel analyses would be most appropriate. The advantage of this approach is that it allows researchers the opportunity to examine the influence of individuals on groups and the influence of groups on individuals. In other words, multilevel analysis is an approach that (a) allows for the simultaneous examination of the effects of group-level and individual-level predictors, (b) accounts for the nonindependence, and (c) both between-group and within-group variation can be examined (Diez-Roux, 2000). Fully understanding team cohesion's associations at both group and individual levels presents a challenge. Nevertheless, the adoption of software programs such as HLM (Bryk, Raudenbush, and Congdon, 1994) and VARCL (Longford, 1990) by sport psychologists might allow for the systematic examination of this issue.

Underpinning Mechanisms

Although evidence of numerous correlates of cohesion has been presented, little understanding of the relationships' underlying mechanisms currently exists. Thus, our knowledge is somewhat limited. As a result, the examination of potential mediating variables—variables that explain relationships—is warranted. For example, it could be expected that collective efficacy or commitment to team goals would mediate the cohesion—performance relationship. In addition, cohesion is viewed as a mediating variable in Carron's (1982) framework. However, no research to our knowledge has been undertaken to examine cohesion as a mediator in sport. Although recent research by Loughead and colleagues (Loughead and Carron, 2004; Loughead, Colman, and Carron, 2001; Loughead, Patterson, and Carron, 2006) in the exercise domain has shown that cohesion is a mediator between leadership and exercise-related outcomes (e.g., adherence, perceived exertion, mood, satisfaction). Similar mechanisms involving cohesion may be found in sport. From an applied standpoint, understanding the role of cohesion within more complex relationships would allow practitioners to develop more effective (team building) interventions.

Complementary Methodologies

Group dynamics research in sport has focused primarily on cohesion. As a result, substantial cohesion data has been collected, analyzed, and subsequently reported. Sport cohesion research has almost exclusively been grounded in the quantitative nomothetic scientific philosophy; one notable exception is Holt and Sparkes' (2001) ethnographic soccer study. Due to the heavy reliance on a single scientific philosophy, the sport cohesion literature may be somewhat narrow and underdeveloped. It is likely that research stemming from a qualitative perspective would reveal novel insights that supplements and expands the current literature. It should be noted that the authors do not believe that one type of research (quantitative vs. qualitative) is more effective than another as each has its own strengths and limitations. Perhaps the use of combined research methodologies gives the researcher the luxury of the "best of both worlds". Recent team building research has employed qualitative methods—focus group discussions—to better understand the team building process from the coach (Bloom et al., 2003) and athlete perspectives (Stevens and Bloom, 2003). It is suggested that because of the large time and labor demands of conducting team building research, applied researchers should—when suitable—employ complementary methods to better understand various cohesion relationships. For example, Stevens and Bloom found that their team goal setting program was perceived by members of the team building group to be the most effective aspect of the team building process. This finding is divergent to the findings of a meta-analysis conducted on business and industry research that proposed that role based team building interventions were the most effective form of team building strategy (Salas, Rozell, Mullen, and Driskell, 1999). In addition, due to the pre-packaged nature of many team building interventions, it is unclear which aspects of the package (e.g., team goal setting, developing role clarity, etc.) are critical to enhanced perceptions of team cohesion; future research should address this issue.

SUMMARY

The purpose of this chapter was to present an overview of the area of cohesion in sport. In order to achieve this purpose, we highlighted some of the shortcomings of earlier definitions of cohesion and forwarded the Carron et al. (1998) definition that best describes cohesion. Based on the Carron et al. definition, we outlined the multidimensional nature of cohesion, highlighted its characteristics, and advanced a conceptual model of cohesion that was used for the development of the Group Environment Questionnaire (GEQ). Following this, we reviewed some of the current literature relating to the factors associated with cohesion (e.g., environmental, personal, leadership, and group) including a discussion on the cohesion-performance relationship. As well, we reviewed the literature pertaining to the development of cohesion using team building. Finally, three areas for future research consideration were advanced. It is our hope that the present chapter will assist scholars in formulating their own exciting research questions. In addition, to those interested in developing team cohesion, we hope that the literature and ideas forwarded will be helpful in designing the most effective team building environment.

REFERENCES

Arnold, G., and Straub, W. (1973). Personality and group cohesiveness as determinants of success among interscholastic basketball teams. In I. Williams and L. Wankel (Eds.), *Proceedings of the Fourth Canadian Psycho-Motor Learning and Sport Psychology Symposium* (pp. 346-353). Ottawa, ON: Department of National Health and Welfare.

Bakeman, R., and Helmreich, R. (1975). Cohesiveness and performance: Covariation and causality in an undersea environment. *Journal of Experimental Social Psychology, 11,* 478-489.

Baranowski, T., Anderson, C., and Carmack, C. (1998). Mediating variable framework in physical activity interventions: How are we doing? How might we do better? *American Journal of Preventive Medicine, 15,* 266-297.

Baron, R. M., and Kenny, D. A. (1986). The moderator-mediator relationship variable distinction in social psychological research: Conceptual, strategic, and statistical considerations. *Journal of Personality and Social Psychology, 51,* 1173-1182.

Baumeister, R. F., and Leary, M. R. (1995). The need to belong: Desire for interpersonal attachments as a fundamental human motivation. *Psychological Bulletin, 117,* 497-529.

Beckhard, R. (1972). *Organizational development.* Reading, MA: Addison-Wesley.

Beer, M. (1980). *Organizational change and development: A systems review.* Glenview, IL: Scott, Foresman.

Bloom, G. A., and Stevens, D. E. (2002). A team-building mental skills training program with an intercollegiate equestrian team. *Athletic Insight, 4,* http://www.athleticinsight.com/Vol4Iss1/Applied_Issue.htm

Bloom, G. A., Stevens, D. E., and Wickwire, T. L. (2003). Expert coaches' perceptions of team building. *Journal of Applied Sport Psychology, 15,* 129-143.

Brawley, L. R., Carron, A. V., and Widmeyer, W. N. (1987). Assessing the cohesion of teams: Validity of the Group Environment Questionnaire. *Journal of Sport Psychology, 9,* 275-294.

Brawley, L. R., Carron, A. V., and Widmeyer, W. N. (1988). Exploring the relationship between cohesion and group resistance to disruption. *Journal of Sport and Exercise Psychology, 10,* 199-213.

Brawley, L. R., and Paskevich, D. M. (1997). Conducting team building research in the context of sport and exercise. *Journal of Applied Sport Psychology, 9,* 11-40.

Bray, C. D., and Whaley, D. E. (2001). Team cohesion, effort, and objective individual performance of high school basketball players. *The Sport Psychologist, 15,* 260-275.

Bryk, A. S., Raudenbush, S. W., and Congdon, R. T. (1994). HLM 2/3. *Hierarchical linear modeling with the HLM/2L and HLM/3L programs.* Scientific Software International: Chicago, IL.

Buys, C. J. (1978). Humans would do better with out groups. *Personality and Social Psychology Bulletin, 4,* 123-125.

Carron, A. V. (1982). Cohesiveness in sport groups: Interpretations and considerations. *Journal of Sport Psychology, 4,* 123-138.

Carron, A. V. (1990). Group size in sport and physical activity: Social psychological and performance consequences. *International Journal of Sport Psychology, 21,* 286-304.

Carron, A. V. (2003, June). *What I've come to believe (So far).* Senior Scholar Address, North American Society for the Psychology of Sport and Physical Activity, Savannah, GA.

Carron, A. V., and Ball, J. R. (1978). Cause-effect characteristics of cohesiveness and participant motivation in intercollegiate hockey. *International Review of Sport Sociology, 12,* 49-60.

Carron, A.V., and Brawley, L. R. (2000). Cohesion: Conceptual and measurement issues. *Small Group Research, 31,* 89-106.

Carron, A. V., Brawley, L. R., Eys, M. A., Bray, S. R., Dorsch, K., Estabrooks, P., Hall, C. R., Hardy, J., Hausenblas, H., Madison, R., Paskevich, D., Patterson, M. M., Prapavessis, H., Spink, K. S., and Terry, P. C. (2003). Do individual perceptions of group cohesion reflect shared beliefs? An empirical analysis. *Small Group Research, 34,* 468-496.

Carron, A.V., Brawley, L. R., and Widmeyer, W. N. (1998). Measurement of cohesion in sport and exercise. In J. L. Duda (Ed.), *Advances in sport and exercise psychology measurement* (pp. 213-226). Morgantown, WV: Fitness Information Technology.

Carron, A. V., Brawley, L. R., and Widmeyer, W. N. (2002). *The group environment questionnaire: Test manual.* Morgantown, WV: Fitness Information Technology.

Carron, A. V., and Chelladurai, P. (1981). Cohesion as a factor in sport performance. *International Review of Sport Sociology, 16,* 2-41.

Carron, A. V., and Colman, M. M. (2000). A team goal-setting program for elite sport: From research to practice. In B. A. Carlsson, U. Johnson, and F. Wetterstrand (Eds.), *Proceedings of the sport psychology in the new millennium conference* (pp. 20-29). Center for Sport Science, Halmstead University, Sweden.

Carron, A. V., Colman, M. M., Wheeler, J., and Stevens, D. (2002). Cohesion and performance in sport: A meta analysis. *Journal of Sport and Exercise Psychology, 24,* 168-188.

Carron, A.V., and Hausenblas, H. A. (1998). *Group dynamics in sport* (2nd ed.). Morgantown, WV: Fitness Information Technology.

Carron, A. V., Prapavessis, H., and Grove, J. R. (1994). Group effects and self-handicapping. *Journal of Sport and Exercise Psychology, 16,* 246-257.

Carron, A. V., and Spink, K. S. (1993). Team building in an exercise setting. *The Sport Psychologist, 7,* 8-18.

Carron, A. V., Spink, K. S., and Prapavessis, H. (1997). Team building and cohesiveness in the sport and exercise setting: Use of indirect interventions. *Journal of Applied Sport Psychology, 9,* 61-72.

Carron, A. V., Widmeyer, W. N., and Brawley, L. R. (1985). The development of an instrument to assess cohesion in sport teams: The Group Environment Questionnaire. *Journal of Sport Psychology, 7,* 244-266.

Carron, A. V., Widmeyer, W. N., and Brawley, L. R. (1988). Group cohesion and individual adherence to physical activity. *Journal of Sport Psychology, 10,* 119-126.

Cartwright, D. (1968). The nature of group cohesiveness. In D. Cartwright and A. Zander (Eds.), *Group dynamics: Research and theory* (3rd ed., pp. 91-109). New York: Harper and Row.

Converse, P., and Campbell, A. (1968). Political standards in secondary groups. In D. Cartwright and A. Zander (Eds.), *Group dynamics* (pp. 199-211). New York: Harper and Row.

Cota, A. A., Evans, C. R., Dion, K. L., Kilik, L., and Longman, R. S. (1995). The structure of group cohesion. *Personality and Social Psychology Bulletin, 21,* 572-580.

Diez-Roux, A. V. (2000). Multilevel analysis in public health research. *Annual Review of Public Health, 21,* 171-192.

Doyle, J., and Parfitt, G. (1997). Performance profiling and construct validity. *The Sport Psychologist, 11,* 411-425.

Escovar, L. A., and Sim, F. M. (1974). *The cohesion of groups: Alternative conceptions.* Paper presented at the meeting of the Canadian Sociology and Anthropology Association, Toronto, Ontario, Canada.

Estabrooks, P. A., and Carron, A. V. (1999). Group cohesion in older adult exercisers: Prediction and intervention effects. *Journal of Behavioral Medicine, 22,* 575-588.

Eys, M. A., Beauchamp, M. R., and Bray, S. R. (this volume). A review of team roles in sport. In S. Hanton and S. D. Mellalieu (Eds.), *Literature reviews in sport psychology.* Hauppauge, NY: Nova Science.

Eys, M. A., and Carron, A. V. (2001). Role ambiguity, task cohesion, and task self-efficacy. *Small Group Research, 32,* 356-373.

Eys, M. A., Carron, A. V., Bray, S. R., and Brawley, L. R. (2003). Effect of item wording on the reliability of the Group Environment Questionnaire. *Journal of Sport and Exercise Psychology, 25,* S55.

Eys, M. A., Colman, M. M., Loughead, T. M., and Carron, A. V. (2004). Team building and cohesiveness in sport. *Manuscript submitted for publication.*

Eys, M. A., Hardy, J., Carron, A. V., and Beauchamp, M. R. (2003). The relationship between task cohesion and competitive state anxiety. *Journal of Sport and Exercise Psychology, 25,* 66-76.

Festinger, L. (1950). Informal social communication. *Psychological Review, 57,* 271-282.

Festinger, L., Schachter, S., and Back, K. (1950). *Social pressure in informal groups.* New York: Harper and Row.

Gammage, K. L., Carron, A.V., and Estabrooks, P. A. (2001). Team cohesion and individual productivity: The influence of the norm for productivity and the identifiability of individual effort. *Small Group Research, 32,* 3-18.

Gardner, D. E., Shields, D. L., Bredemeier, B. J., and Bostrom, A. (1996). The relationship between perceived coaching behaviors and team cohesion among baseball and softball players. *The Sport Psychologist, 10,* 367-381.

Golembiewski, R. (1962). *The small group.* Chicago: University of Chicago Press.

Gross, N., and Martin, W. E. (1952). On group cohesiveness. *American Journal of Sociology, 52,* 546-554.

Hanson, P. G., and Lubin, B. (1988). Team building as group development. In W. B. Reddy and K. Jamison (Eds.), *Team building: Blue prints for productivity and satisfaction* (pp. 76-78). Alexandria, VA: National Institute for Applied Behavioral Science.

Hardy, C. J., and Crace, R. K. (1997). Foundations of team building: Introduction to the team building primer. *Journal of Applied Sport Psychology, 9,* 1-10.

Hardy, J., Eys, M. A., and Carron, A. V. (2005). Exploring the negative consequences of high cohesion in sports teams. *Small Group Research, 36,*166-187.

Hausenblas, H. A., and Carron, A. V. (1996). Group cohesion and self-handicapping in female and male athletes. *Journal of Sport and Exercise Psychology, 18,* 132-143.

Holt, N. L., and Sparkes, A. C. (2001). An ethnographic study of cohesiveness in a college soccer team over a season. *The Sport Psychologist, 15,* 237-259.

James, L. R., Demaree, R. G., and Wolf, G. (1984). Estimating within-group interrater reliability with and without response bias. *Journal of Applied Psychology, 69,* 85-98.

Kim, M. (1992). The relation of performance norms and cohesiveness for Japanese school athletic teams. *Perceptual and Motor Skills, 74,* 1096-1098.

Landers, D. M., Wilkinson, M. O., Hatfield, B. D., and Barber, H. (1982). Causality and the cohesion-performance relationship. *Journal of Sport Psychology, 4,* 170-183.

Lenk, H. (1969). Top performance despite internal conflict. In J. W. Loy and G. S. Kenyon (Eds.), *Sport, culture and society* (pp. 393-397). Toronto, Ontario, Canada: MacMillan.

Lewin, K. (1935). *A dynamic theory of personality.* New York: McGraw-Hill.

Li, F., and Harmer, P. (1996). Confirmatory factor analysis of the Group Environment Questionnaire with an intercollegiate sample. *Journal of Sport and Exercise Psychology, 18,* 49-63.

Libo, L. (1953). *Measuring group cohesiveness.* Ann Arbor: University of Michigan Press.

Locke, E. A., Shaw, K. N., Saari, L. M., and Latham, G. P. (1981). Goal setting and task performance: 1969-1980. *Psychological Bulletin, 90,* 125-152.

Longford, N. T. (1990). *Software for variance component analysis of data with nested random effects (Maximum likelihood).* Educational Testing Service, Princeton, NJ.

Lott, A. J., and Lott, B. E. (1965). Group cohesiveness as interpersonal attraction: A review of relationships with antecedent and consequent variables. *Psychological Bulletin, 64,* 259-309.

Loughead, T. M., and Carron, A. V. (2004). The mediating role of cohesion in the leader behavior-satisfaction relationship. *Psychology of Sport and Exercise, 5,* 355-371.

Loughead, T. M., Colman, M. M., and Carron, A. V. (2001). The effects of leadership and class cohesion on the adherence of older adult exercisers. *Small Group Research, 32,* 558-575.

Loughead, T. M., Patterson, M. M., and Carron, A. V. (2006). The impact of group factors on mood. *Manuscript submitted for publication.*

Martens, R., Landers, D. M., and Loy, J. W. (1972). *Sport cohesiveness questionnaire.* Unpublished manuscript, University of Illinois: Champaign, IL.

Martens, R., and Peterson, J. A. (1971). Group cohesiveness as a determinant of success and member satisfaction in team performance. *International Review of Sport Sociology, 6,* 49-61.

McGrath, J. E. (1962). The influence of interpersonal relations on adjustment and effectiveness in rifle teams. *Journal of Abnormal and Social Psychology, 65,* 365-375.

McGrath, J. E. (1984). *Groups: Interaction and performance.* Englewood, NJ: Prentice-Hall.

Mellalieu, S. D., Hanton, S., and Fletcher, D. (this volume). A competitive anxiety review: Recent directions in sport psychology research. In S. Hanton and S. D. Mellalieu (Eds.), *Literature reviews in sport psychology.* Hauppauge, NY: Nova Science.

Melnick, M. J., and Chemers, M. M. (1974). Effects of group social structure on the success of basketball teams. *Research Quarterly, 45,* 1-8.

Miller, B. P. (1997). Developing team cohesion and empowering individuals. In R. J. Butler (Ed.), *Sports psychology in performance* (pp. 105-125). Oxford, UK: Butterworth Heinemann.

Mudrack, P. E. (1989). Defining group cohesiveness: A legacy of confusion? *Small Group Behavior, 20,* 37-49.

Mullen, B., and Copper, C. (1994). The relation between group cohesiveness and performance: An integration. *Psychological Bulletin, 115,* 210-227.

Munroe, K., Estabrooks, P., Dennis, P., and Carron, A. V. (1999). A phenomenological analysis of group norms in sport teams. *The Sport Psychologist, 13,* 171-182.

Munroe, K., Terry, P., and Carron, A. (2002). Cohesion and teamwork. In B. D. Hale and D. J. Collins (Eds.), *Rugby tough* (pp.137-153). Champaign, IL: Human Kinetics.

Neubert, M. J. (1999). Too much of a good thing or the more the merrier? Exploring the dispersion and gender composition of informal leadership in manufacturing teams. *Small Group Research, 30,* 635-646.

Neuman, G. A., Edwards, J. E., and Raju, N. S. (1989). Organizational development interventions: A meta-analysis of their effects on satisfaction and other attitudes. *Personnel Psychology, 42,* 416-489.

Paskevich, D. M., Estabrooks, P. A., Brawley, L. R., and Carron, A. V. (2001). Group cohesion in sport and exercise. In R. N. Singer, H. A. Hausenblas, and C. M. Janelle (Eds.), *Handbook of sport psychology* (2nd ed., pp. 472-494). New York: John Wiley.

Patterson, M. M., Carron, A. V., and Loughead, T. M. (2005). The influence of group norms on the cohesion-performance relationship: A multi-level analysis. *Psychology of Sport and Exercise, 6,* 479-493.

Pease, D. G., and Kozub, S. A. (1994). Perceived coaching behaviors and team cohesion in high school girls basketball teams. *Journal of Sport and Exercise Psychology, 16,* S93.

Peterson, J. A., and Martens, R. (1972). Success and residential affiliation as determinants of team cohesiveness. *Research Quarterly, 43,* 62-76.

Prapavessis, H., and Carron, A. V. (1996). The effect of group cohesion on competitive state anxiety. *Journal of Sport and Exercise Psychology, 18,* 64-74.

Prapavessis, H., and Carron, A. V. (1997a). Cohesion and work output. *Small Group Research, 28,* 294-301.

Prapavessis, H., and Carron, A. V. (1997b). Sacrifice, cohesion, and conformity to norms in sport teams. *Group dynamics: Theory, Research, and Practice, 1,* 231-240.

Prapavessis, H., Carron, A. V., and Spink, K. S. (1996). Team building in sport. *International Journal of Sport Psychology, 27,* 269-285.

Rogosa, D. (1980). A critique of cross-lagged correlation. *Psychological Bulletin, 88,* 245-258.

Ryan, R. M. (1982). Control and information in the interpersonal sphere: An extension of cognitive evaluation theory. *Journal of Personality and Social Psychology, 43,* 736-750.

Salas, E., Rozell, D., Mullen, B., and Driskell, J. E. (1999). The effect of team building on performance: An integration. *Small Group Research, 30,* 309-331.

Schachter, S., Ellertson, N., McBride, D., and Gregory, D. (1951). An experimental study of cohesiveness and productivity. *Human Relations, 4,* 229-238.

Schriesheim, J. F. (1980). The social context of leader-subordinate relations: An investigation of the effects of group cohesiveness. *Journal of Applied Psychology, 65,* 183-194.

Slater, M. R., and Sewell, D. F. (1994). An examination of the cohesion-performance relationship in university hockey teams. *Journal of Sports Sciences, 12,* 423-431.

Stevens, D. E., and Bloom, G. A. (2003). The effects of team building on cohesion. *Avante, 9,* 43-54.

Sullivan, P., and Feltz, D. L. (2003). The preliminary development of the scale for effective communication in team sports (SECTS). *Journal of Applied Social Psychology, 33,* 1693-1715.

Terry, P. C., Carron, A. V., Pink, M. J., Lane, A. M., Jones, G. J. W., and Hall, M. P. (2000). Perceptions of group cohesion and mood in sport teams. *Group Dynamics: Theory, Research, and Practice, 4,* 244-253.

Terry, P. C., Keohane, L., and Lane, H. J. (1996). Development and validation of a shortened version of the Profile of Mood States suitable for use with young athletes. *Journal of Sports Sciences, 14,* 49.

Tuckman, B. W. (1965). Development sequences in small groups. *Psychological Bulletin, 63,* 384-399.

Voight, M., and Callaghan, J. (2001). A team building intervention program: Application and evaluation with two university soccer teams. *Journal of Sport Behavior, 24,* 420-431.

Westre, K. R., and Weiss, M. R. (1991). The relationship between perceived coaching behaviours and group cohesion in high school football teams. *The Sport Psychologist, 5,* 41-54.

Widmeyer, W. N., Brawley, L. R., and Carron, A. V. (1990). The effects of group size in sport. *Journal of Sport and Exercise Psychology, 12,* 177-190.

Widmeyer, W. N. and DuCharme, K. (1997). Team building through team goal setting. *Journal of Applied Sport Psychology, 9,* 97-113.

Williams, J. M., and Hacker, C. M. (1982). Causal relationships among cohesion, satisfaction, and performance in women's intercollegiate field hockey teams. *Journal of Sport Psychology, 4,* 324-337

Williams, J. M., and Widmeyer, W. N. (1991). The cohesion-performance relationship in a coacting sport. *Journal of Sport and Exercise Psychology, 13,* 364-371.

Yukelson, D. (1997). Principles of effective team building interventions in sport: A direct services approach at Penn State University. *Journal of Applied Sport Psychology, 9,* 73-96.

Yukelson, D., Weinberg, R., and Jackson, A. (1984). A multidimensional group cohesion instrument for intercollegiate basketball teams. *Journal of Sport Psychology, 6,* 103-117.

In: Literature Reviews in Sport Psychology   ISBN 1-59454-904-4
Editors: S. Hanton and S. D. Mellalieu, pp. 289-319   © 2006 Nova Science Publishers, Inc.

Chapter 9

PSYCHOLOGICAL RESPONSES TO SPORT INJURY: A REVIEW OF CURRENT RESEARCH

Lynne Evans, * *Ian Mitchell and Stuart Jones*

University of Wales Institute, Cardiff (UWIC), United Kingdom

Lynne Evans, Ian Mitchell, and Stuart Jones, Cardiff School of Sport, University of
Wales Institute, Cardiff (UWIC), United Kingdom.

ABSTRACT

Research has acknowledged that sports injury can be a significant source of stress and
may have differential cognitive, emotional, and behavioral implications for the athlete.
Indeed over the last 10 years, there has been increased research interest in the role of a
number of psychological variables within the sport injury process. The purpose of the
present chapter is to provide an updated review of the psychological response and
rehabilitation adherence literature. In providing an overview of the current empirical
research, the review examines current conceptual models of injury rehabilitation and
developments in intervention research, and explores some of the methodological issues
that have been inherent within the research to date. Finally, we outline a number of
evidence-based implications for researchers and practitioners.

Keywords: Emotional, rehabilitation, adherence

INTRODUCTION

Over the last 10 years there has been an increase in the amount of research investigating
athletes' psychological responses to and rehabilitation from sports injury (e.g., Bianco, 2001;
Brewer, 1994; Duda, Smart, and Tappe, 1989). Junge (2000) suggested that regular updates,

---

* Correspondence concerning this article should be addressed to Lynne Evans, Cardiff School of Sport, University
of Wales Institute, Cardiff, Cyncoed Campus, Cardiff (UWIC), Wales, CF23 6XD, United Kingdom. E-mail:
levans@uwic.ac.uk. Telephone: 44 29-2041-6516. Fax.: 4429-2041-6768.

via literature reviews, were warranted to signify the current trends of injury-based research and to assist researchers in exploring avenues that require further research attention.

The last review paper to examine the psychology of sport injury rehabilitation was compiled by Brewer (2001). Whilst this review was extensive and many of its conclusions still hold significance, the continued developments in the literature suggest that an updated review is now required. The present review will focus primarily on the empirical research carried out since Brewer (2001). However, there remains a need to refer to some studies, which are outlined in prior reviews such as Brewer's to enable readers to contextualize and conceptualize the current state of knowledge and understanding.

This chapter will only focus on research that relates to injured athletes' psychological responses (incorporating emotional response and coping strategies) and adherence to rehabilitation programs. While other related areas of research (e.g., such as predictors of injury occurrence) are undoubtedly of interest to injury researchers it is not possible to incorporate them in to the present review. The review is divided into five major sections; the first section examines the research that has explored athletes' psychological responses following injury; the second section considers rehabilitation adherence; and subsequent sections focus on intervention studies, methodological issues (including recommendations for future research), and the practical implications of the research. Finally, because of the difficulty in assessing the integrity of the research it is not our intention to include the findings that have been reported in conference proceedings within this review.

PSYCHOLOGICAL RESPONSES TO INJURY

Athletes' emotional responses following injury have been documented within the research literature for some years (e.g., Chan and Grossman, 1988; Gordon and Lindgren, 1990; Ievleva and Orlick, 1991). Although a number of conceptual models have been proposed within the literature, this section of the review examines the theoretical model that has provided the basis for much of the recent research.

Conceptual Model of Injury Response

Based upon mainstream psychology theory, several models have been proposed within the literature to explain the processes that underpin athletes' emotional responses to injury. However, the most comprehensive model and the one that has received the most empirical support is Wiese-Bjornstal, Smith, Shaffer, and Morrey's (1998) integrated model of response (A modified version of Wiese-Bjornstal et al.'s model is presented in Figure 1). This stress-based cognitive appraisal model suggests that both preinjury and postinjury factors influence emotional responses. The salience of these factors is mediated by an athlete's appraisal processes which are thought to influence cognitions, emotions and behavior. As a stress-process model it embraces the concept of change (Evans and Hardy, 1999; Wiese-Bjornstal et al., 1998). As a result, the recovery process is viewed as a dynamic, interactive process in which cognitions, emotions, and behavior, are explained within a cyclical cognitive framework; a framework that reflects and is consistent with the general assumptions held within the appraisal literature (cf. Lazarus and Folkman, 1984). Wiese-Bjornstal et al. (1998) posited that both personal (e.g., injury variables such as injury history, individual difference variables such as motivation, demographic variables such as age, and physical variables such as health status), and situational factors (e.g., sport, social, and environmental) can impact upon the injured athlete's responses whereas the process of appraisal mediates self-perception and the sense of the loss. The latter is important, given that Wiese-Bjornstal et al. suggested the model also has the potential to account for responses characteristic of grief.

Based upon the thinking of Kübler-Ross (1969) and her work with terminally ill patients, the concept of grief and its application to athletes' responses to injury received early support from a number of researchers (Gordon and Lindgren, 1990; McDonald and Hardy, 1990). Grief is hypothesized to result from the loss of a significant attachment, the significance of which is determined by an individual's own value system (Bowlby, 1991; Evans and Hardy, 1995; Simos, 1977). As such, grief can be perceived as a normal reaction to what someone considers to be a significant loss (Rodgers and Cowles, 1991). The loss may constitute various types of loss that may result from injury (e.g., loss of self-esteem, loss of functional ability; Peretz, 1970). Recently, it has been suggested that the concept of grief and the grief response could be subsumed within a stress-based appraisal model (Evans and Hardy, 1999; Wiese-Bjornstal et al., 1998).

Emotional Responses

Early research that examined athletes' emotional responses to injury suggested that injured athletes experience a range of negative emotions, including tension, depression, anger, and confusion (Gordon and Lindgren, 1990; Leddy, Lambert, and Ogles, 1994; McDonald and Hardy, 1990; Pearson and Jones, 1992; Smith, Scott, O'Fallon, and Young, 1990). Subsequent qualitative research has identified a number of other emotional responses (e.g., frustration and anxiety), and has suggested that these responses can be temporally defined (e.g., Bianco, Malo, and Orlick, 1999; Gordon and Lindgren, 1990; Granito, 2001; Johnston and Carroll, 1998; Udry, Gould, Bridges, and Beck, 1997a). For example, shock, anxiety, and depression have been found to be prevalent immediately following injury, whereas anger, depression, frustration, and apathy have been reported as characterizing the middle phase of rehabilitation. Impatience, anticipation, and increased confidence have been reported to eventually replace these emotions (Bianco, 2001; Granito, 2001; Johnston and Carroll, 1998).

Recently, Tracey (2003) examined the emotional responses of college level athletes recovering from moderate to severe injuries during three phases of injury recovery via in-depth interviews: onset, one week and three weeks post injury. In the initial phase of rehabilitation, and consistent with earlier studies, athletes' responses comprised anger, depression, feeling down, fear, confusion, frustration, worry, shock, and a decrease in self-esteem. In contrast to previous studies that have reported the prevalence of depression in the middle phase of rehabilitation (Bianco et al., 1999; Johnston and Carroll, 1998), and although negative emotions, such as frustration were still common, many athletes also experienced positive emotions (e.g., as a result of seeing a physical improvement in their injury such as a reduction in swelling). Further, it was noted that the athletes attempted to rationalize their

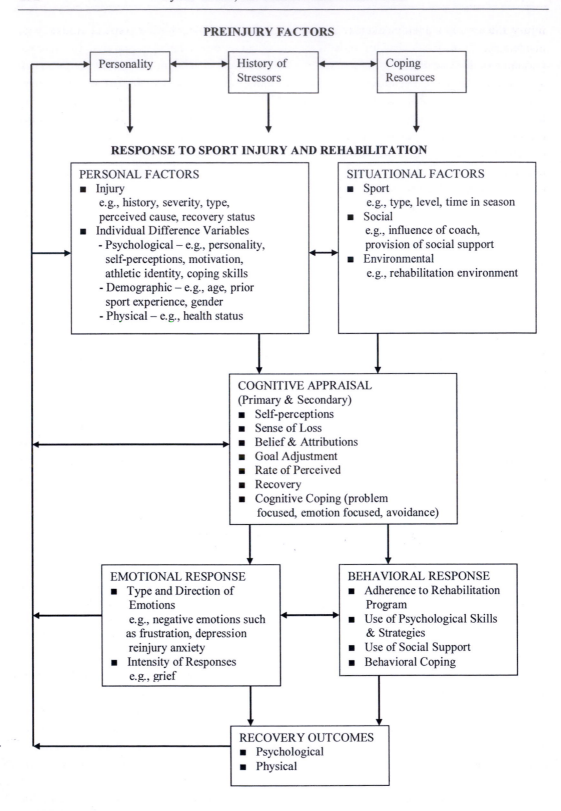

Figure 1. Modified version of the integrated model of response to sport injury (Wiese-Bjornstal et al., 1998, p.49)

injury situation in a positive manner and directed resources toward other responsibilities (e.g., academic). Toward the end of rehabilitation, positive emotions were related to athletes' perceptions of their recovery and the rehabilitation strategies used, and negative emotions, such as fear and worry, were related to the possibility of the coach discarding them. However, Tracey found that these negative thoughts would be used as a motivational tool, which in turn, would result in increases in confidence. In contrast to previous research, athletes did not report a fear of reinjury, only a fear of returning to sport. The absence of a fear of reinjury is not consistent with previous research (e.g., Evans, Hardy, and Fleming, 2000; Gould, Udry, Bridges, and Beck, 1997b), but may be explained by differences in participants' levels of injury severity in this and other studies.

A key feature of emotional responses to injury is, therefore, their transient nature (Evans and Hardy, 1999). Although the importance of this feature has been acknowledged by a number of researchers (e.g., Brewer, 2001; Evans and Hardy, 1995; Johnston and Carroll, 1998, 2000; McDonald and Hardy, 1990; Quackenbush and Crossman, 1994; Smith et al., 1990; Tracey, 2003; Udry and Anderson, 2002; Wiese-Bjornstal et al., 1998), it has still received limited research attention in the quantitative injury research. Generally, the trend in emotions reported from this research has reflected a move from negative to positive responses over time (e.g., McDonald and Hardy, 1990; Quackenbush and Crossman, 1994; Quinn and Fallon, 1999). There has been less support for an oscillation in responses between highs and lows, despite Morrey, Stuart, Smith, and Wiese-Bjornstal (1999) reporting a slight increase in negative emotions towards the end of the rehabilitation period. However, within the quantitative research there has been much variability in the frequency and timing of data collection during the rehabilitation period (relative to the onset of injury and return to sport). This has made the generalization of findings in relation to the temporal pattern of emotional responses problematic, and offers one possible explanation for the differences in responses reported in the quantitative and qualitative research. In addition, the differences between sample characteristics (particularly in relation to injury severity both within and between studies) have confounded the interpretation of the findings across both quantitative and qualitative research. The use of the Profile of Mood States (POMS; McNair, Lorr, and Droppleman, 1971) in the quantitative research as a measure of athletes' emotional responses has further hampered the development of our knowledge and understanding. POMS has been the preferred measure within much of the research in to athletes' emotional responses to injury. However, as Evans and Hardy (1999) suggested, POMS was not developed in-conjunction with any psychological model of injury or indeed for use with injured populations. As a result, the validity of POMS with regard to injured populations must be questioned. Indeed, it is perhaps not what POMS does measure that is the issue, rather what it does not measure. The latter is highlighted by the prevalence of emotions reported in the qualitative research that are not accounted for by POMS (e.g., frustration).

This discourse is not intended to suggest that the qualitative findings reported are more valid than the quantitative findings; there are similar methodological issues associated with this body of research (e.g., sampling, approaches to interviewing). Rather it is intended to highlight the need for a psychometrically derived population specific measure of athletes' psychological responses to injury.

As noted earlier, according to Wiese-Bjornstal et al.'s (1998) model, emotional responses are influenced by a number of personal and situational variables. The effect of these variables on emotional responses is mediated by cognitive appraisal. The personal or individual difference variables that have been examined in the published research and associated within athletes' emotional responses include self perceptions (e.g., self-esteem [Chan and Grossman, 1988; Leddy et al., 1994; McGowan, Pierce, Williams, and Eastman, 1994], self-concept [McGowan et al., 1994], and self-confidence [Magyar and Duda, 2000; Quinn and Fallon, 1999]), age (Brewer, Linder, and Phelps, 1995a; Smith et al., 1990), optimism and hardiness (Ford, Eklund, and Gordon, 2000; Grove and Bianco, 1999), explanatory style (Grove and Bianco, 1999), coping skills (Rotella and Heyman, 1993; Weiss and Troxel, 1986), injury severity (Smith et al., 1990; Smith et al., 1993), and athletic identity (Brewer, 1993; Young and White, 1995; Young, White, and McTeer, 1994). Links between athletic identity and emotional response to injury may be mediated by an athlete's level of participation. For example, a study by Green and Weinberg (2001) found that athletic identity did not mediate the emotional response (i.e., mood disturbance) to injury in a sample of recreational athletes.

In a recent study, Granito (2002) examined gender and sports injury in thirty-one intercollegiate athletes. Interview data suggested that females were more concerned about the effects that an injury may have on physical health in later years compared to males. Females were more inclined to be critical of the quantity and quality of social support that they were receiving from their coaches, and unlike the males, did not deem the social support received from their significant other as important.

With the exception of Tracey's (2003) study, which revealed previous injury experience influenced the emotional response particularly later on in the rehabilitation process, there has been no further focus on the aforementioned personal factors within an injury context since Brewer's (2001) review. However, injury severity warrants a little further discussion. As injury severity has been found to affect the intensity of athletes' emotional responses to injury (e.g., Brewer et al., 1995a; Smith et al., 1990) it is surprising that research that has explored the effects of a variety of personal and situational variables on athletes' responses continues to fail to adopt a definition of injury that adequately accounts for severity (Aldwin, 1994). Appraisal processes are influenced by the perceived consequences and potential outcome of any event. Clearly where the perceived significance of loss is great, or there is uncertainty about recovery the emotional reaction would potentially intensify. Since it appears that injury severity has the potential to influence the perceived consequences and outcome, and may heighten uncertainty it plays an important role in emotional response to injury research, and warrants far greater attention in study design and implementation. However, this is not to suggest that low severity injuries will not cause high levels of emotionality. Once again when considered in an appraisal framework, perceived consequences and outcome (significance) come in to play. For example, if a low-grade injury is sustained prior to a major sporting event the timing of the injury may cause heightened levels of emotional response. These examples suggest that the appraisal process is influenced by different factors that can impact upon emotional and behavioral responses. Indeed, in a recent study, Gayman and Crossman (2003) examined noninjured athletes' perceptions about how they would feel if they sustained an injury relative to the possible timing of the injury in relation to the sporting season. If the injury occurred preseason the majority of athletes suggested they would feel frustrated and disappointed because of the effect on preparation, and the potential for missing out on selection. Mid season responses were felt to be dependent on their role in the team. Frustration was felt to be the most salient response if they sustained an injury at the end of the season, particularly if they were in their final year of eligibility. However, there is no evidence to suggest that predicting how one would feel in a hypothetical situation in any way resembles the actual feelings one would experience in that situation. The complexity of emotional responses following injury is such that these findings should be interpreted with caution.

Of other situational factors that have been proposed to have an influence on emotional response following injury, the factor that has received the most attention is social support (see later section). Less support has been reported for recovery progress (McDonald and Hardy, 1990) and impairment of sport performance (Brewer et al., 1995a).

Coping Strategies

Injury has been described as a significant source of stress for athletes (Tracey, 2003). It is perhaps not surprising, therefore, that stress-related coping strategies have received an increasing amount of research attention in the injury literature. However, although there is an established body of literature that explores how coping strategies can mediate a variety of stressors (e.g., Aldwin, 1994; Lazarus and Folkman, 1984; Wheaton, 1997) empirical research in coping and sports injury is less developed.

Coping can be seen as the person's ever-changing efforts to manage circumstances that are appraised as stressful (Lazarus and Folkman, 1984). This perspective, proposes a bi-directional transaction between the person and the environment, where coping is thought to vary within individuals, depending on the circumstances, and in turn, circumstances depending upon individual differences. Cognitive appraisal or an individual's interpretation of a situation can take two forms, primary appraisal and secondary appraisal (Lazarus and Folkman, 1984). The former involves an assessment of what is at stake; the latter involves what coping options are available. The individual's appraisal determines the emotional response, which can serve a number of functions: (a) the quality and intensity of the response indicate the importance of the ongoing relationship between the person and the environment; (b) the response indicates what is important in a given situation; (c) the response provides insight into a person's belief about 'self and world'; and (d) the response reveals how a person has appraised a situation with respect to its significance for well-being (Lazarus, 1991, p. 22). Furthermore, if coping is not effective in dealing with short-term stress, it is suggested that the resultant long-term (or chronic) stress can lead to anxiety and depression (Gottlieb, 1997), and possibly burnout (Wheaton, 1997). Several dimensions of coping have been identified in the literature, which have emerged from Lazarus and Folkman's transactional model and their distinction between functional higher-order dimensions of coping: task oriented, emotion oriented, and avoidance coping. Gaudreau and Blondin (2002) conceptualized task-oriented coping as actions employed to change some aspects of a perceived stressful situation, and emotion-oriented coping as actions employed to change the meaning of a stressful situation and to control the resulting negative emotions. Avoidance-oriented coping was conceptualized as actions employed to disengage from the task and redirect attention on task-irrelevant cues. As a stress-based model Wiese-Bjornstal's model of injury response borrows heavily from Lazarus and Folkman's conceptualization of appraisal models.

Despite the research attention that coping strategies have received in dealing with non-injury related forms of athletic stress (e.g., Bjorck and Cohen, 1993; Gould, Guinan, Greenleaf, Medbury, and Peterson, 1999; Hardy et al., 1996; Orlick and Partington, 1998), a number of important issues have been identified. For example, there are concerns over whether coping is a conscious as opposed to an automatic process (Carver, Scheier, and Weintraub, 1989; Hardy et al., 1996; Krohne, 1993; Lazarus, 1990; Lazarus and Folkman, 1984), whether the concept of coping infers effectiveness in responding to stress (Aldwin and Revenson, 1987; Crocker, Kowalski, and Graham, 1998), and whether there is a difference between coping style and coping strategies (Anshel, 1996; Carver et al., 1989; Krohne, 1993; Lazarus and Folkman, 1984; McCrae, 1992; Miller, 1989; Suls and Fletcher, 1985). As a result some researchers suggest that relatively little is known about the coping processes undertaken during stressful events experienced within sporting competition (e.g., Anshel, Kim, Chang, and Eom, 2000).

Both the mainstream and sport psychology research supports the view that coping actions change across situations (e.g., Frydenberg and Lewis, 1994; Sellers, 1995), across the same situation over time (e.g., Crocker and Isaak, 1997; Stewart and Schwarzer, 1996), and across the different stages of a situation (Carver and Scheier, 1994; Folkman and Lazarus, 1985), endorsing a process-oriented approach to coping (Cerin, Szabo, Hunt, and Williams, 2000; Crocker, Kowalski, and Graham, 1998; Hardy et al., 1996). This is perhaps particularly salient in the context of injury, because the sources of stress during the injury rehabilitation period have also been found to change as a function of individual and situational changes (e.g., Evans et al., 2000; Gould et al., 1997a; Johnston and Carroll, 1998). For example, sources of stress identified in the research literature include: watching others compete, the inability to train, isolation, putting on weight, the coach, and fear of reinjury (Bianco, 2001; Johnston and Carroll, 1998). The antecedents of these sources of stress which include loss and disruption of normal functioning, physical and medical concerns, financial concerns, and reinjury and performance issues (Evans et al., 2000; Gould et al., 1997a) have been associated with different time frames during rehabilitation.

The temporal nature of coping strategies presents perhaps one of the major challenges to researchers examining the coping strategies used to deal with stress (Hardy et al., 1996). For example, Quinn and Fallon (1999) suggested that athletes' use of passive coping (reflecting a passive approach to dealing with injury) and emotion-focused/denial coping strategies remained constant across multiple assessments, but Udry (1997) found significant changes across the rehabilitation period in the use of negative emotion coping and palliative coping. Notwithstanding some findings to the contrary, it appears that the uses of coping strategies are temporally defined and vary according to individual difference and contextual variations (Brewer, 2001).

Within the sport injury literature both qualitative and quantitative research has suggested that a range of cognitive, emotional, and behavioral coping strategies have been used by athletes to deal with injury (Bianco, Malo, and Orlick, 1999; Gould et al., 1997b; Quinn and Fallon, 1999, 2000; Udry, 1997; Udry et al., 1997). Qualitative studies have suggested that coping strategies are characterized by themes such as accepting the injury, driving through (e.g., did things normally, determination/motivation, set/worked toward goals) distracting oneself, avoidance and isolation, achieving rehabilitation goals, seeking social resources, learning about their injuries, building up physical strength, and focusing on getting better (Bianco, 2001; Bianco et al., 1999; Evans et al., 2000; Gould et al., 1997b). Quantitative studies have also demonstrated that athletes use a range of strategies to cope with injury. For example, Udry (1997) found that instrumental coping (i.e., attempts to alleviate the source of stress through activities such as finding out more about the injury) was the most used coping strategy among participants in her study. This type of coping was similar to the problem-focused coping identified by Folkman and Lazarus (1985). However, as Anshel et al. (2000) pointed out, since the use of coping strategies may vary as a function of differences in what individuals bring to a given situation the same strategy may serve very different functions for different people, or different strategies may serve similar functions for different people, or indeed one person.

Corban, Snape, and Taylor (2003) recently examined the specific coping behaviors employed by injured athletes. Seeking social support emerged as a coping mechanism rugby players of varying ability frequently used. The least favored coping strategy by athletes was denial/ avoidance coping. Seeking social support can be seen as characteristic of problem-focused coping and may be particularly prevalent within the subculture of a sport that prompts reciprocal beliefs and lends itself to support from team mates (Anshel et al., 2000).

In a recent study, Albinson and Petrie (2003) examined the relationships among a number of preinjury and postinjury variables included within Wiese-Bjornstal et al.'s (1998) model of response, including postinjury stress and coping. Albinson and Petrie found that day 7 appraisals were related to greater avoidance coping, days 14 and 28 with greater behavioral coping, and day 28 less active cognitive coping. Consistent with Daly, Brewer, Van Raalte, Petitpas, and Sklar's (1995) findings regarding injured athletes' cognitive appraisals of their coping abilities, Albinson and Petrie supported the dynamic view of the cognitive appraisal process; at three data collection points during the first week post injury, primary and secondary appraisals were significantly related, and suggested that athletes' appraisal of their injuries as stressful/difficult to cope with at one time point were unchanged at the subsequent time point. Similarly, athletes who perceived coping with their injury to be difficult, later in the rehabilitation period viewed their injuries as stressful, depicting a relationship between secondary and subsequent primary appraisals. Results also supported the relationship hypothesized by Wiese-Bjornstal et al. (1998) between cognitive appraisals and emotional responses; both primary and secondary appraisals were correlated with higher levels of mood disturbance and with the choice of coping strategies used. In relation to the choice of coping strategy used, athletes demonstrated greater avoidance coping at the end of the first week post injury, greater active behavioral coping at days 14 and 28, and less active cognitive coping at the end of one month. Active behavioral coping was associated with greater mood disturbance, and active cognitive coping and avoidance coping were inversely related. Although this study embraced a number of important features of Wiese-Bjornstal et al.'s model that have not been previously addressed, as the authors acknowledged, the study has a number of limitations (viz. sample size and non-assessment through post rehabilitation). In reality, the results have to be viewed with some caution, because of the definition of injury adopted (inability to participate for 1 day) and the small number of participants injured beyond one week (cf. Udry and Anderson, 2002)

Over the last few years, research exploring the relationship between sports injury and coping strategies has been characterized by a number of limitations. These include small sample sizes, variability in terms of the definition of injury, and the homogeneity of the sample in relation to injury severity (Albinson and Petrie, 2003; Green and Weinberg, 2001). Additional research might also seek to clarify the strategies employed by athletes to cope with injury, and factors that might influence the type and the effectiveness of the strategies employed.

Social Support

Several studies within the sport injury literature (e.g., Bianco, 2001; Johnston and Carroll, 1998, 2000; Udry, 1996, 1997) have shown that social support plays an important role in the way an athlete copes with and rehabilitates from sport injury. Indeed, within the stress process model (Wiese-Bjornstal et al., 1998) social support is identified as a coping resource hypothesized to directly affect injury outcome (Wiese-Bjornstal and Shaffer, 1999).

Social support is viewed as a complex multiconstruct that consists of a number of inter-related dimensions, which include support networks, support exchanges, and support appraisals (see Holt and Hoar's chapter for a comprehensive review of social support). Social support is conveyed through a number of behaviors (Albrecht and Adelman, 1984) that have been classified as: emotional support (includes listening support, emotional comfort, and emotional challenge), informational support (includes reality confirmation, task appreciation, and task challenge), and tangible support (includes material and personal assistance; Hardy and Crace, 1993). These specific social support types have been linked with certain coping behaviors. It has generally been accepted that emotional support is intended to encourage and sustain emotion-focused forms of coping, whereas informational and tangible support are focused toward augmenting and sustaining problem-focused coping (Bianco and Eklund, 2001). Generally, injured athletes will turn to close friends and family for emotional support, and people with the relevant expertise for informational support (Hardy and Crace, 1993; Johnston and Carroll, 1998; Rosenfeld, Richman, and Hardy, 1989; Udry et al., 1997b).

In a recent qualitative study into the social support needs and provider preferences of injured athletes, Bianco (2001) found emotional support was required when there was psychological disruption and the skiers were engaged in emotion-focused coping. Informational support was needed when coping efforts were intended to manage specific aspects of the stressful situation (i.e., to overcome obstacles of a practical nature). The athletes' preferences for the providers of social support were influenced by the provider's level of expertise, level of intimacy, and the quality of the relationship (Bianco, 2001). Injured skiers turned to family and close friends for emotional support, medical personnel for specific medical information, and coaches, administrators and former team members for sport-related information. This is consistent with Lin's (1986) social resources theory that suggests relationship closeness is a consideration (not a necessary condition) in the provision of social support (i.e., close relationships facilitate emotion-focused coping and more distant relationships facilitate problem-focused coping). Indeed, injured skiers received more than one type of social support from network members that was generally well accepted. This finding highlights the need for caution in classifying social support types and suggests that a number of people can be important sources of emotional, informational, and tangible support to injured athletes (Johnston and Carroll, 1998, 2000; Rosenfeld et al., 1989; Udry et al., 1997b).

The quality of the support exchange (communication) between recipient and provider is an important feature of social support and has important implications for members of the injured athletes' network because it will increase the chance of successful exchanges (Bianco and Eklund, 2001; Hobfoll and Vaux, 1993). Bianco (2001) found that when participants perceived a positive relationship with their coach, support from that coach was desirable, perceived to be helpful, and had motivational consequences. Alternatively, when this relationship was perceived to be poor, support from the coach was not sought. This latter finding is consistent with those from a recent study of athletes' emotional responses to moderate to severe injuries (Tracey, 2003). According to Tracey, although injured athletes felt they generally benefited from the social support that they received there was some fluctuation in the extent to which it satisfied athletes' needs. The injured athletes did not request support from their coaches because they felt that they did not want to admit to the seriousness of their injuries and felt uncomfortable asking for help. Such factors linked to self-esteem and saving face (i.e., concerns about self-image) have been identified as important mediators of social support exchanges (e.g., Bianco et al., 1999). In fact, in their study of athletes' perceptions of social support provided by their head coach, assistant coach and athletic trainer, Robbins and Rosenfeld (2001) reported that injured athletes perceived their trainers' emotional and informational support as more influential to their well being than support from either of their coaches.

There are many factors that contribute to the differences in provider and recipient perceptions of social support (e.g., whether support meets the needs of the recipient, and recipient expectation for support). Injured athletes may have specific expectations of the social support they receive from network members and subsequent satisfaction may be determined by whether or not their expectations are met. Green and Weinberg (2001) in their quantitative study of recreational injured athletes (n=30) reported that an increase in satisfaction with social support was significantly correlated with lower levels of mood disturbances post injury. This supports earlier research (e.g., Bianco et al., 1999; Ford, 1999) but is an area that has received limited attention to date.

An important issue within social support research is whether activities or messages determine support effectiveness (Bianco and Eklund, 2001). Cutrona and Russell's (1990) matching hypothesis posits that specific support activities should match stressor characteristics. However, Thoits (1985) contended that the regularization of social interaction, rather than the provision of social support per se, is responsible for the maintenance of well being. Both the reception and perception of social support have been considered in attempting to explain the causal association between social support and health outcomes, and are respectively linked to the buffering hypothesis and main effect theory (Cohen and Wills, 1985; Sarason, Pierce, and Sarason, 1990). Empirical research posits that received social support endorses a palliative coping mechanism and alleviates the stress of the injury experience (e.g., Bianco, 2001; Duda et al., 1989; Fields, Murphey, Horodyski, and Stopka, 1995; Gould et al., 1997b; Ievleva and Orlick, 1991; Johnston and Carroll, 1998, 2000; Tracey, 2003; Udry et al., 1997b), whereas perceived support will encourage injured athletes to develop effective coping skills if they perceive they have the necessary resources available to deal with the stress of injury (e.g., Andersen and Williams, 1988; Ford et al., 2001; Green and Weinberg, 2001; Hardy, Richman, and Rosenfeld, 1991; Petrie, 1993; Rosenfeld et al., 1989; Smith et al., 1990). Whether received or perceived social support is the dominant influence on health outcome is a difficult question to answer because they have not been simultaneously examined in the research. Both main effect theory and the buffering hypotheses need further consideration within the sport injury literature, particularly as they may now not be seen as mutually exclusive (Cohen, Gottlieb, and Underwood, 2000).

ADHERENCE TO SPORT REHABILITATION

An important factor that contributes to recovery is adherence to the rehabilitation program prescribed by the medical practitioners. Recent research examining treatment adherence to rehabilitation has demonstrated the full extent of the challenge facing sports injury practitioners. For example, recent estimates of adherence to prescribed rehabilitation regimens have ranged from 40-91% (Alkmekinders and Alkmekinders, 1994; Daly et al., 1995; Laubach, Brewer, Van Raalte, and Petitpas, 1996; Taylor and May, 1996; Vasey, 1990; Sluijs, Kok, and van der Zee, 1993). These figures reinforce the need for empirical research that examines the factors that affect athletes' rehabilitation adherence. This section provides an overview of the theoretical approaches that have been adopted in adherence to sport injury rehabilitation research and the findings that have emerged from the research.

Conceptual Models of Adherence

The development and testing of theoretically derived models of injury response is essential to the enhancement of knowledge and understanding of factors that may impinge upon adherence behaviors. To guide their research into the role that a variety of factors may have in sport injury rehabilitation adherence researchers have adopted a number of theoretical approaches. These have included personal investment theory (Maehr and Braskamp, 1986), protection motivation theory (Maddux and Rogers, 1983; Rogers, 1975, 1983), the integrated model of psychological response (Wiese-Bjornstal et al., 1998), and the biopsychological model of sport injury rehabilitation (Brewer, 2001). Of these approaches the most tested are the integrated model of psychological response, and protection motivation theory. The central tenet of Wiese-Bjornstal et al.'s model, appraisal, is hypothesized to influence emotional responses, and importantly in the context of adherence, behavioral responses and recovery outcomes. Empirical support has been reported for a number of the personal and situational variables that the model hypothesizes to affect both adherence behaviors and recovery outcomes (e.g., Brewer et al., 2000a; Lampton, Lambert, and Yost, 1993).

Protection motivation theory suggests that adherence behavior is influenced by the perceived severity of the health threat, susceptibility to the health threat, the perceived effectiveness of the behaviors in addressing the health threat (treatment efficacy), and the expectancy of the ability to perform the desired behavior (self-efficacy). Taylor and May (1996) provided initial support for the association between the aforementioned factors and one or more indices of adherence to a home-based sport injury rehabilitation program. Brewer et al. (2003a) have recently provided additional support for the application of protection motivation theory in a sport rehabilitation adherence context; severity was the only component found not to be associated with one of three indices of adherence.

There has also been support for the application of Bandura's (1977) theory of self-efficacy in the context of rehabilitation adherence (e.g., Evans and Hardy, 2002a, 2002b). Although the purpose of Evans and Hardy's (2002a) study was not to test the application of Bandura's theory, the results of the goal setting intervention (and follow-up study; Evans and Hardy, 2002b) supported some of the central theoretical tenets of self-efficacy in relation to athletes' adherence (e.g., the results provided support for the effect of goal setting upon self-efficacy and adherence, with goals enacting performance accomplishments in a rehabilitation setting).

Some six years ago, in the first major review of adherence to sport injury rehabilitation programs Brewer (1998) suggested the need for researchers to examine the application of a variety of different theoretical frameworks in the context of sport injury adherence to advance knowledge and understanding of factors affecting adherence. Since that time progress has been slow and although there has been further support for components of both Wiese-Bjornstal et al.'s model and protection motivation theory, more research would appear necessary in relation to these and other theoretical models.

Personal and Situational Variables Associated with Rehabilitation Adherence

As a result of correlational and qualitative studies, and prospective and retrospective studies a number of variables have been reported that can be associated with one or more measures of adherence. The measures of adherence used within this research have included adherence to home-based rehabilitation activities (including cryotherapy; usually self-report), attendance at rehabilitation sessions (ratio of those attended to sessions scheduled), and estimates of athletes' clinic based rehabilitation behaviors (e.g., using the Sport Injury Rehabilitation Adherence Scale [SIRAS; Brewer, Van Raalte, Petitpas, Sklar, and Ditmar, 1995b]). The variables examined have generally been categorized according to Wiese-Bjornstal et al.'s model of response as either personal or situational. Of these, personal factors associated with adherence include self-motivation (e.g., Brewer, 2000b; Duda et al., 1989; Fields et al., 1995), pain tolerance (Byerly, Worrell, Gahimer, and Domholdt, 1994; Fields et al., 1995), tough mindedness (Wittig and Schurr, 1994), self-esteem (Lampton et al., 1993), internal locus of causality (Laubach et al., 1996; Murphy, Foreman, Simpson, Molloy, and Molloy, 1999), and perceived injury severity (Taylor and May, 1996). The findings for task involvement have been equivocal (Duda et al., 1989; Lampton et al., 1993), and an inverse relationship has been reported for ego involvement (Duda et al., 1989; Lampton et al., 1993).

Recently, additional support has been reported for the association between self-efficacy (Brewer et al., 2003a; Evans and Hardy, 2002a), self-motivation (Pizzari, McBurney, Taylor, and Feller, 2002), and perceived injury severity (Brewer et al., 2003a) and injury rehabilitation adherence. Support has also been provided for the relationship between age and adherence. Brewer et al. (2003b) examined the relationships between four psychological factors (self-motivation, social support, athletic identity, and mood disturbance) and rehabilitation adherence as a function of age. Although age did not serve as a moderator in the relationships between the four psychological factors and adherence to clinic-based rehabilitation, it did serve as a moderator in the relationships between three of the four psychological factors assessed and home-based rehabilitation adherence. Self-motivation and social support were positively associated with adherence to home-based exercises in the older participants, but not in the younger ones. Athletic identity was positively associated with adherence to the home exercise protocol in the younger participants, but not in older participants.

Wiese-Bjornstal et al.'s model hypothesized that psychological skills should also affect athletes' adherence to rehabilitation programs. Scherzer et al. (2001) assessed ACL patients' use of goal setting, healing imagery, and positive self-talk (five weeks post-surgery) and four measures of adherence. Goal setting, imagery and self-talk were assessed using a modified version of the Sports Injury Survey (SIS; Ievleva and Orlick, 1991). The findings from this correlational study suggested that goal setting was a significant predictor of both clinic (SIRAS) and home based rehabilitation protocols, but not of home cryotherapy completion or attendance. There was a significant positive correlation between the use of positive self-talk and home exercise completion but there was no relationship between the use of healing imagery and any of the measures of adherence. Scherzer et al. (2001) concluded that any potential links between healing imagery and rehabilitation outcome might occur independently of rehabilitation adherence. Not least because the SIS appears to lack adequate psychometric integrity the findings from this study should not be considered in isolation. Rather they should be considered alongside the findings that have emerged from the relatively small number of intervention studies that have been conducted, a number of which have also explored the efficacy of what could be categorized as psychological skills (discussed later in this chapter).

The other category of variables that has been examined in the adherence literature is situational variables. Using protection motivation theory as a framework, and consistent with some of the earlier findings of Taylor and May (1996), Brewer et al. (2003a) provided support for the relationship between two measures (SIRAS scores, and home exercise and cryotherapy completion) of adherence and the Sports Injury Rehabilitation Beliefs Survey (SIRBS) subscales of susceptibility, treatment efficacy, and self-efficacy. Attendance was not correlated with any of the subscales. Perhaps surprisingly, belief in the efficacy of the treatment is not identified explicitly as a situational factor in Wiese-Bjornstal et al.'s model (1998); however, it is fundamental to adherence in protection motivation theory and could be considered an implicit part of any treatment.

In a recent qualitative study, Pizzari et al. (2002) reported empirical support for the influence of a number of variables that have particular relevance to the practitioner-athlete interaction, the rehabilitation environment, and the treatment protocol. Specifically Pizzari et al. found a relationship between enjoyment and progression in rehabilitation activities, the comfort of the clinical environment, therapist support, and modeling and adherence behaviors. Perceived lack of time was considered to have an inverse relationship with adherence, with particular reference to home-based rehabilitation protocols. Pizzari et al. suggested that for some of the participants, lack of time was often used as an excuse for nonadherence. Although in an earlier qualitative study, Evans et al. (2000) found modeling and social comparison to detract from adherence, Pizzari et al.'s findings reinforce the importance of the role of the practitioner and the rehabilitation environment in optimizing athletes' levels of adherence during injury rehabilitation.

The aforementioned findings add to the existing research literature that has reported an association between a number of situational variables and measures of rehabilitation adherence: treatment efficacy (Duda et al., 1989; Noyes, Matthews, Mooar, and Grood, 1983), comfort of clinical environment (Brewer, Daly, Van Raalte, Petitpas, and Sklar, 1994; Fields et al., 1995; Fisher, Domm, and Wuest, 1988), convenience of rehabilitation scheduling (Fields et al., 1995; Fisher et al., 1988), importance or value of rehabilitation activities, perceived exertion during rehabilitation (Brewer et al., 1994; Fisher et al., 1988), treatment efficacy (Taylor and May, 1996), patient practitioner communication (Webborn, Carbon, and Miller, 1997), provision of written program instructions (Webborn et al., 1997), and social support for rehabilitation adherence (Bianco, 2001; Byerly et al., 1994; Duda et al., 1989; Fisher et al., 1988). However, there has been some inconsistency in the findings in relation to a number of these variables. For example, Brewer et al. (2000a) failed to find a relationship between self-motivation and adherence to clinic-based activities; injury severity was not associated with any of the measures of adherence used in Brewer et al.'s (2003a) study; and self-efficacy was not associated with adherence in Pizzari et al.'s (2002) study. The inconsistency observed in some of the findings can be attributed to methodological differences between studies and the measures of adherence used. However, the findings also highlight the interaction between personal and situational factors in determining adherence to rehabilitation programs.

Relationship between Rehabilitation Adherence and Rehabilitation Outcome

The basic premise that underlies much of the adherence research is that either directly or indirectly variables associated with rehabilitation adherence will have a positive or beneficial effect (or at least not a negative effect) on rehabilitation outcome. Rehabilitation outcome may reflect a number of variables. Although Gilbourne and Taylor (1998) suggested return to preinjury performance levels (given clinical factors are fine) would be an appropriate indication of outcome and particularly salient in a psychology of sport injury context, traditionally, rehabilitation outcome is equated to treatment or clinical outcome. As Meichenbaum and Turk (1987) suggested, because of the number of variables that can affect clinical outcome, the relationship between adherence and clinical outcome is far from clear (e.g., individual differences in healing rates). In addition, in a performance environment rehabilitation outcome may include psychological features such as confidence and mental readiness to return to sport. Ultimately the goal of adherence research is to demonstrate a relationship between the variables hypothesized to affect rehabilitation adherence and one or more indices of rehabilitation outcome. In effect, as Brewer et al. (2000b) hypothesized, it is thought that rehabilitation adherence mediates the relationship between psychological factors, such as self-motivation, and rehabilitation outcome. Unfortunately, existing research examining the adherence-outcome relationship in both general health psychology and sport psychology has produced inconsistent findings (Dunbar-Jacob and Schlenk, 1996; Hays et al., 1994).

A positive adherence-outcome relationship has been observed in studies examining musculoskeletal injuries and illnesses in a non-sporting population (e.g., Hawkins and Switlyk, 1993; Rejeski, Brawley, Ettinger, Morgan, and Thompson, 1997; Rives, Gelberman, Smith, and Carney, 1992;), and case study research involving sporting and non sporting injury and illness have generally been universal in their support of a positive adherence-outcome relationship (e.g., Derscheid and Feiring, 1987; Hawkins, 1989). However, a study conducted by Noyes et al. (1983) on anterior cruciate ligament (ACL) patients found no significant relationship between rehabilitation adherence and rehabilitation outcome. Indeed, Shelbourne and Wilckens's (1990) study on ACL patients demonstrated an inverse adherence-outcome relationship. Brewer et al. (2000b), in the first study of its kind in injury research, examined the relationships among psychological factors, rehabilitation adherence, and rehabilitation outcome. Self-motivation was found to predict one measure of adherence (home exercise completion), and athletic identity and psychological distress predicted one of three measures of rehabilitation outcome (knee laxity). In relation to the influence of adherence on rehabilitation outcome, attendance, and home cryotherapy completion were significant predictors of the measure of functional ability (one leg-hop index). However, no significant findings were observed regarding the mediating relationship between psychological factors, rehabilitation adherence, and rehabilitation outcome. In other words, those participants high in rehabilitation adherence did not necessarily score highly in terms of rehabilitation outcome. However, a positive relationship between rehabilitation adherence and functional ability was observed. This study contradicts some of the earlier research and further demonstrates the need to assess the relationship between adherence and outcome. The inconsistencies in the findings concerning the adherence-outcome relationship and the limited amount of empirical research suggest that research into this area of enquiry should be considered a priority for researchers. The first step in this process should be to conceptualize rehabilitation outcome in the context of psychology research and as a basis for adopting appropriate measures of outcome.

INTERVENTION STUDIES

Although a growing body of literature has demonstrated an association between a variety of factors and responses to, and consequences of sports injury, there remains a paucity of well-controlled empirical research that has examined the efficacy of intervention strategies in an injury context (Durso-Cupal, 1998). This is particularly salient because experimentally based controlled intervention studies offer researchers the strongest evidence of causal relationships. Durso-Cupal's (1998) comprehensive review of intervention research suggested that at that time there were only five published empirical studies that included a control group. These studies provided support for the effects of biofeedback and increased EMG output, strength, range of movement, and greater extensor torque and quadriceps fiber recruitment (Draper, 1990; Draper and Ballard, 1991; Krebs, 1981; Levitt, Deisinger, Wall, Ford, and Cassisi, 1995), and stress inoculation training and reduced anxiety and pain, and increased physical functioning (Ross and Berger, 1996). Perhaps not surprisingly, given the importance of methodological rigor and control required for good intervention research (see Durso-Cupal, 1998) despite some progress, developments in this area of research have been a little slow.

In an injury rehabilitation context, Gilbourne, Taylor, Downie, and Newton (1996) conducted one of the first studies to explore the effects of a psychological intervention on rehabilitation adherence. In this qualitative action research study, the practitioners (physiotherapists) delivered a goal-setting intervention to injured athletes during rehabilitation. The study provided support for the effects of a task-oriented goal setting intervention in enhancing adherence. Adopting a similar approach to Gilbourne et al. (but with a sport psychologist delivering the intervention), Evans et al. (2000) provided further support for the effect of goal-setting as well as for the effect of social support on rehabilitation adherence. According to Evans et al., outcome expectancy, financial concerns, and social comparison all emerged as important to adherence. Rock and Jones (2002) reinforced the importance of social support as a predictor of rehabilitation adherence as a result of a 12-week counseling skills intervention. However, none of these studies included a control group.

Further support for the use of goal setting as a means of enhancing rehabilitation adherence has emerged from experimentally controlled research (e.g., Evans and Hardy, 2002a; Theodorakis, Beneca, Malliou, and Goudas, 1997; Theodorakis, Malliou, Papaioannou, Beneca, and Filactakidou, 1996). Evans and Hardy (2002a) examined the effects of a 5-week goal-setting intervention on athletes' rehabilitation adherence, self-efficacy, treatment efficacy, and the psychological response variables dispirited and reorganization. The results confirmed the hypothesized effects of the goal-setting intervention; athletes in the goal-setting group demonstrated significantly higher levels of self-reported adherence than athletes in the control group and social support (control) group. The goal-setting intervention also resulted in significant group differences for self-efficacy (the goal-setting group having the highest level of self-efficacy). A follow-up qualitative study suggested the possible mechanisms for the observed effects of the goal-setting intervention on adherence included the effects of goal setting on self-efficacy, attributions, perceptions of control, and attention (Evans and Hardy, 2002b). These studies not only demonstrate the effect of a goal-setting intervention on athletes' self-report levels of adherence, but also offer some insight into the mechanisms underpinning the intervention effects; an important development in injury adherence research.

The injury research literature also provides support for the effects of goal setting on rehabilitation outcome. Theodorakis et al. (1996) reported significant increases in knee extension performance for injured athletes who were set goals as compared to noninjured athletes who were not set goals. They also reported significant correlations between goal setting and self-efficacy, self-satisfaction, and performance. In a later study, significant increases in quadriceps performance were obtained for injured athletes following a 4-week goal-setting intervention. However, no significant differences were found between the goal-setting and injured control group on self-efficacy (Theodorakis et al., 1997).

These findings are consistent with earlier research that showed a relationship between goal setting and adherence. For example, Duda et al.'s (1989) correlational study found that injured athletes who adhered more closely to their rehabilitation programs were more goal directed and put more emphasis on mastery or task involvement goals. In separate adherence-based research, Taylor and May (1996) and Brewer et al. (2003a) found greater self-efficacy regarding ability to perform prescribed rehabilitation modalities was related to adherence. Taken together, the findings from the aforementioned studies provide support for the motivational and cognitive effects of goal setting in an injury rehabilitation context (cf. Locke and Latham, 1990), for the proposed relationship between goal setting and self-efficacy (Bandura and Cervone, 1983), and the effects of self-efficacy on coping behaviors (Bandura, 1977, 1982).

In a randomized clinical trial, Perna, Antoni, Baum, Gordon, and Schneiderman (2003) assessed the efficacy of a cognitive behavioral stress management (CBSM) intervention to reduce post-intervention period illness and injury. The 4-week intervention involved athletes being trained in the use of relaxation, visuo-motor behavioral rehearsal, emotive imagery, and cognitive restructuring. Athletes who were randomly assigned to the CBSM group experienced significant reductions in the number of illness and injury days, and had half the number of health service visits compared to the control group. The effect of the intervention on illness and injury was partially mediated by treatment effects on post-intervention negative affect. Indeed, the authors concluded that intervention effects on negative affect might be one mechanism for explaining subsequent health (Perna et al., 2003). Although the study had a number of limitations specifically in relation to the monitoring and documentation of post intervention injury and illness, the results suggest that a time-limited CBSM intervention may reduce the incidence of injury and illness among competitive athletes.

In an earlier longitudinal study over a 6-month recovery period, Cupal and Brewer (2001) examined the effects of a relaxation and guided imagery intervention on knee strength, reinjury anxiety, and pain following anterior cruciate ligament reconstruction. The results showed significantly greater knee strength and significantly less reinjury anxiety and pain for the treatment group at 24 weeks post surgery than for the placebo and control group participants. Knee strength was correlated with both a reduction in reinjury anxiety and pain reduction. Cupal and Brewer suggested that possible mechanisms underlying the intervention effects included participants' enhanced perception of control, greater engagement in the rehabilitation program (because reductions in reinjury and anxiety and pain helped them to relax), and enhanced motivation. Although the authors suggest that it was possible physiological processes may have mediated the results, this study makes a significant contribution to the research literature and highlights the need for further controlled psychological interventions. To date, the intervention studies conducted have predominantly focused on behavioral and clinical outcomes. In addition to intervention studies that examine behavioral and clinical outcomes, researchers are encouraged to implement intervention studies that examine a variety of emotional outcomes, the relationship between behavioral, clinical and emotional outcomes, and importantly the mechanisms through which the interventions exert their effects.

METHODOLOGICAL CONSIDERATIONS AND RECOMMENDATIONS FOR FUTURE RESEARCH

A number of methodological issues have been posited to be key to the development of research in the areas of emotional response and adherence (e.g., Brewer, 1994). These encompass the conceptualization and measurement of key variables (e.g., adherence, coping, emotional responses, and behavioral outcomes); methodological control in terms of sample characteristics (including injury severity); the types of research design (including the use of prospective as opposed to retrospective research designs); and, the frequency of assessment.

In adherence research the measurement of adherence has proven to be particularly salient to the integrity of the research. Measures of adherence have tended to include attendance at scheduled rehabilitation sessions and the use of the Rehabilitation Adherence Questionnaire (RAQ) (e.g., Fisher et al., 1988). However, the RAQ has subsequently been shown to lack psychometric integrity, and the assessment of attendance at rehabilitation sessions also lacks validity as a measure of adherence (Brewer, 1998). The term adherence denotes the importance of the active, volitional involvement of the patient in both clinic-based and home-based rehabilitation activities, and should be assessed accordingly (Duda et al., 1989). As such it reflects multiple factors that might provide for indices of specific types of adherence behaviors that (collectively) reflect adherence per se (Meichenbaum and Turk, 1987). The use of multiple measures of adherence in recent studies, including patient and practitioner ratings of adherence to both home-based and clinic-based activities (including home cryotherapy), practitioner behavioral observations / judgments during clinic-based sessions, and the Sport Injury Rehabilitation Adherence Scale (SIRAS; Brewer et al., 2000c) have addressed many of the limitations of some of the earlier research (Brewer, 1998; Brewer, 1999; Meichenbaum and Turk, 1987). However, research that has employed multiple measures of adherence suggests differential effects for the variables assessed. Attempting to account for these differential effects presents a new challenge to researchers and is an important consideration for future research into sport injury rehabilitation adherence in relation to the measures of adherence adopted.

The progress in identifying and employing valid and reliable measures of rehabilitation adherence has not been mirrored by similar developments in measuring rehabilitation outcome. This is perhaps not surprising, given the challenges associated with access to clinical environments and the type of collaborative relationship that is required with medical practitioners to both identify and employ appropriate measures. However, as we identified earlier, much injury adherence research is based on the premise that there is a relationship (either directly or indirectly) between adherence and indices of rehabilitation outcome. At present, researchers have rarely proposed measures that reflect specific indices of outcome. Clinical measures of functional ability will vary according to the site of the injury and injury prognosis; however, there may be additional indices that can compliment clinical measures. Researchers are encouraged to explore the efficacy of different measures of outcome, particularly in the context of adherence research.

A variety of measures have been adopted to assess the psychological response variables of interest in injury research. However, measures adopted to assess for example, emotional response and social support have varied in their psychometric integrity for use with injured (and sporting) populations (Brewer, 2001; Evans and Hardy, 1999). As previously suggested, although POMS has been the preferred measure of athletes' emotional responses to injury, it was not developed for use with injured populations, or derived from any model of injury response. Along similar lines, measures of social support fail to take in to account current conceptualizations of social support (i.e., models of stress buffering and main effect). This has important implications for the conceptual currency of the findings and their generalizability. Researchers are strongly encouraged wherever possible to ensure that populations specific measures are utilized that are shown to possess appropriate levels of content validity. Along with greater consistency in the measures adopted, this would ensure that more meaningful comparisons could be made between studies (Evans and Hardy, 1999). This approach should lead to greater gains in our knowledge and understanding of the role that psychological variables play in the injury process.

Sample size and composition is an issue that has pervaded the integrity of much of the early research (e.g., definitions of injury and homogeneity of sample in relation to severity). However, much of the more recent research has controlled for, or at least tested for the effects of a variety of potential moderating and confounding variables (e.g., Cupal and Brewer, 2001; Evans and Hardy, 2002a, 2002b; Theodorakis et al., 1997). This has certainly enhanced the integrity and interpretability of the findings. Sampling in quantitative research invites a pay-off between size and composition. In pursuit of large sample sizes, researchers have tended to conduct interindividual research using cross sectional data. However intraindividual approaches also have much to merit them, and importantly lend themselves to assessing the process of change (to be discussed next). Sampling is clearly less troublesome in relation to the qualitative research process, particularly in relation to sample size, and as a result it is perhaps not surprising that sampling has been more meaningful in many of these studies. However, for qualitative research to continue to make a contribution to our knowledge and understanding it is important that sampling is conceptually meaningful. Future quantitative research should attempt to continue to control for (or at the very least test) the moderating and confounding effects of sample characteristics such as severity, age, level of participation (e.g., elite versus non elite, professional versus amateur), and possibly gender. This will be challenging, given the importance of statistical power, but is important conceptually.

Regardless of the methodological approach, it is essential that researchers take account of, and examine the temporal changes implicit within models of injury. Repeated measure prospective and retrospective designs should embrace the full recovery period including athletes' reentry in to competitive sport (Brewer, 2001; Evans and Hardy, 1999; Wiese-Bjornstal et al., 1998). This is essential if we are to understand the antecedents of specific cognitions, emotions, and behaviors, the potential mechanisms through which effects are exerted, and as a result employ appropriate intervention strategies to expedite athletes' recovery. Indeed, consistency between research in the frequency / regularity of assessment in order to capture the process of change would undoubtedly help to speed up progress.

Finally a number of studies have examined psychological variables in conjunction with physiological variables of occurrence, response, and rehabilitation (e.g., Cupal and Brewer, 2001; Noyes et al., 1983; Ross and Berger, 1996). These studies have enhanced our understanding of the interaction between physical and psychological indices related to injury research. Future research needs to examine the interaction between physical, psychological, medical, sociological, and possibly biomechanical variables in a heuristic approach to injury research.

Qualitative or interpretative approaches have served to enhance our understanding of athletes' emotional responses to injury and factors affecting adherence to rehabilitation programs (e.g., Bianco, 2001; Gilbourne et al., 1996; Gould et al., 1997a). The research has also evidenced a variety of approaches (e.g., case studies, action research). In addition to providing descriptive accounts of athletes' experiences, this body of research has importantly provided an insight into the mechanisms affecting behavioral and cognitive outcomes (e.g., Evans and Hardy, 2002b). Researchers are encouraged to explore a greater range of interpretive approaches than have traditionally been adopted to pursue specific areas of response and adherence research. Prospective designs such as ethnography may provide particularly interesting insights in to the injury experience as will a variety of other approaches (e.g., autobiographies) that provide an in-depth examination of some of the variables that have been proposed to impact upon the injury process.

Researchers have employed a variety of research designs in their pursuit of greater knowledge and understanding of the relationship between, and effect of, a number of factors that may affect the recovery process. Complimenting the early correlational research, a number of experimental intervention studies have recently been conducted. Experimental studies, by their very nature adopt a prospective design, whereas the correlational studies have embraced both prospective and retrospective methodologies. In a similar vein, qualitative studies have also embraced both prospective and retrospective type designs. To date there have been fewer case studies. All research designs have inherent limitations in terms of depth, generalizability, and the ability to infer cause and effect, but there is undoubtedly a place for a variety of approaches in future response and adherence research (assuming the quality of the research question).

Implications for Professional Practice

Strategies to minimize adverse psychological responses to injury and enhance rehabilitation adherence have been widely identified within the research literature. Many of these strategies are theoretically underpinned having emerged from empirical research, but some lack this same theoretical underpinning and are based on intuition and experience. The implications for practice suggested here are based on empirical research.

When considered together the empirical findings for the association between motivation and task focus and adherence (e.g., Duda et al., 1989) and goal-setting and adherence and rehabilitation performance (e.g., Evans and Hardy, 2002a; Theodorakis et al., 1996, 1997) provide strong support for the use of goal setting in a rehabilitation context. A task-focused coping strategy, goals direct attention, regulate and prolong the effort a person puts in to a given task, and motivate people to develop alternative strategies in their attempts to reach the goal (Locke and Latham, 1990). Although athletes will invariably want to focus on the date they can return to full activity, focusing on the process of achieving that goal makes a successful outcome more likely to occur.

In addition to enhancing motivation, there is support in the adherence research literature for the relationship between goal setting and the development of self-efficacy (Theodorakis et al., 1996, 1997). In view of the growing body of research that has shown a relationship between self-efficacy and adherence (e.g., Taylor and May, 1996), this is an important finding, and reinforces the benefits of using goal setting to enhance self-efficacy in addition to motivation, adherence, and rehabilitation outcome. However, despite a lack of research at the present time, it also provides some support for the use of other self-efficacy enhancing strategies (e.g., self-talk).

Researchers such as Byerly et al. (1994), Duda et al. (1989), Evans and Hardy (2002a), and Evans et al. (2000) have all provided support for the effect of social support on adherence. Despite some findings to the contrary (e.g., Brewer et al., 2000b), it appears that individuals involved in the rehabilitation environment should be receptive to providing social support as and when it is deemed appropriate. For example, Pizzari et al. (2002) found that social support offered by the rehabilitation professional had a profound positive effect on rehabilitation adherence, particularly to clinical based activities. The support from fellow patients was also considered a motivating factor, as the participants were then able to compare their progress. Social support helps individuals cope with a variety of life stressors, including physical injury. Social support can enhance athletes self esteem and self-confidence, reduce feelings of isolation, and influence their emotional state and feeling of well-being. By providing support for a task-focused approach to rehabilitation (e.g., goal setting), it may also enhance motivation and adherence. Therapists can provide emotional support by listening to athletes' concerns and doubts, task support by encouraging and helping them to set appropriate goals (or reinforcing goals that they may have already set), and esteem support by providing positive feedback which may help increase injured athletes' levels of self esteem and self confidence. However, it is important that network members are educated to ensure that they become effective support providers, both in terms of the quantity and quality of the support they make available to the injured athlete. This support will potentially help athletes feel less isolated; particularly if as a result of injury they have lost contact with their normal network of support providers. In addition to task support, informational support will help the athlete to regain a sense of control (over their injury), and enable them to attribute their recovery internally (to themselves and their own efforts as opposed to those of the therapist). An important feature of effective therapy is for the therapist to enhance the patient's sense of control over both the therapeutic process and outcome. Informational and task support may also enhance the athlete's belief in the effectiveness of the treatment and the rehabilitation program. Given that there is empirical support for the relationship between treatment efficacy and athlete perception of severity and adherence (e.g., Taylor and May, 1996; Brewer, Cornelius, et al., 2003a), and locus of causality and adherence (Laubach et al., 1996; Murphy et al., 1999) the role of social support in injury rehabilitation may be all the more vital. The provision of effective social support requires good communication skills, but in particular good listening skills; listen to the athlete and respond to their needs, as opposed to what you think their needs should be.

Although there is extensive support for the use of imagery and self-talk in the sport psychology literature there is less support for the use of these strategies in the injury rehabilitation literature. Scherzer et al. (2001) and Evans et al. (2000) have provided support for the use of self-talk in enhancing adherence. The findings in relation to imagery are equivocal (e.g., Iveleva and Orlick, 1991; Scherzer et al., 2001). In the absence of additional research, psychologists are advised to examine the sport psychology literature for guidance in the use of these strategies (e.g., Hardy, Gammage, and Hall, 2001; Hardy et al., 1996; Martin, Moritz, and Hall, 1999; Munroe, Hall, Weinberg, and Giacobbi, 2000), specifically, to explore the use of self-talk to increase self-efficacy and treatment efficacy, control attention and effort, and relearn movement and skills (Zinsser, Bunker, and Williams, 1998). The aforementioned are particularly salient given their reported relationship with adherence. In a similar vein, and in addition to using motivational, mastery, and skill based imagery to enhance adherence, there is some support for the use of healing imagery in the injury and health literature which provides support for its use in achieving rehabilitation outcomes (e.g., Sordoni, Hall, and Forwell, 2001).

REFERENCES

Albinson, C. B., and Petrie, T. A. (2003). Cognitive appraisals, stress and coping: Preinjury and post injury factors influence psychological adjustment to sport injury. *Journal of Sport Rehabilitation, 12,* 306-322.

Albrecht, T. L., and Adelman, M. B. (1984). Social support and life stress: New directions for communication research. *Human Communication Research, 11,* 3-22.

Aldwin, C. M. (1994). *Stress, coping and development: An integrative perspective.* New York: Guilford Press.

Aldwin, C. M., and Revenson, T. A. (1987). Does coping help? A reexamination of the relationship between coping and mental health. *Journal of Personality and Social Psychology, 53,* 337-348.

Alkmekinders, L. C., and Alkmekinders, S. V. (1994). Outcome in the treatment of chronic overuse sports injuries: A retrospective study. *Journal of Orthopaedic and Sports Physical Therapy, 19,* 157-161.

Andersen, M. B., and Williams, J. M. (1988). A model of stress and athletic injury: Prediction and prevention. *Journal of Sport and Exercise Psychology, 10,* 294-306.

Anshel, M. H. (1996). Coping styles among adolescent competitive athletes. *Journal of Social Psychology, 136,* 311-324.

Anshel, M. H., Kim, K. W., Chang, K. J., and Eom, H. J. (2000). A model for coping and stressful events in sport, theory, application and future directions. *Medicine and Science in Sports and Exercise, 30,* 43-75.

Bandura, A. (1982). Self-efficacy mechanism in human agency. *American Psychologist, 37,* 122-147.

Bandura, A. (1997). *Self-efficacy: The exercise of control.* New York: Freeman.

Bandura, A., and Cervone, D. (1983). Self-evaluative and self-efficacy mechanisms governing the motivational effects of goal systems. *Journal of Personality and Social Psychology, 45,* 1017-1028.

Bianco, T. (2001). Social support and recovery from sport injury: Elite skiers share their experiences. *Research Quarterly for Exercise and Sport, 72,* 376-388.

Bianco, T., and Eklund. R. C. (2001). Conceptual consideration for social support research in sport and exercise settings: The case of sport injury. *Journal of Sport and Exercise Psychology, 23,* 85-107.

Bianco, T., Malo, S., and Orlick, T. (1999). Sport injury and illness: Elite skiers describe their experiences. *Research Quarterly for Exercise and Sport, 70,* 157-169.

Bjorck, J., and Cohen, L. (1993). Coping with threats, losses, and challenges. *Journal of Social and Clinical Psychology, 12,* 56-72

Bowlby, J. (1991). *Attachment and loss: Loss, sadness and depression.* Middlesex, England: Penguin.

Brewer, B. W. (1993). Self-identity and specific vulnerability to depressed mood. *Journal of Personality, 61,* 343-364.

Brewer, B. W. (1994). Review and critique of models of psychological adjustment to injury. *Journal of Applied Sport Psychology, 6,* 87-100.

Brewer, B. W. (1998). Adherence to sport injury rehabilitation programs. *Journal of Applied Sport Psychology, 10,* 70-82.

Brewer, B. W. (1999). Adherence to sport injury rehabilitation regimens. In S. Bull (Ed.), *Adherence issues in sport and exercise* (pp. 145-168). Chichester, England: Wiley.

Brewer, B. W. (2001). Psychology of sport injury rehabilitation. In R. N. Singer, H. A. Hausenblas, and C. M. Janelle (Eds.), *Handbook of sport psychology* (2nd ed.) (pp. 787-809). New York: Wiley.

Brewer, B. W., Cornelius, A. E., Van Raalte, J. L., Petitpas, A. J., Sklar, J. H., Pohlman, M. H., and Ditmar, T. D. (2000a). Attributions for recovery and adherence to rehabilitation following anterior cruciate ligament reconstruction: A prospective analysis. *Psychology and Health, 15,* 283-291.

Brewer, B. W., Cornelius, A. E., Van Raalte, J. L., Petitpas, A. J., Sklar, J. H., Pohlman, M. H., Krushell, R. J., and Ditmar, T. D. (2003a). Protection motivation theory and adherence to sport injury rehabilitation revisited. *The Sport Psychologist, 17,* 95-103.

Brewer, B. W., Cornelius, A. E., Van Raalte, J. L., Petitpas, A. J., Sklar, J. H., Pohlman, M. H., Krushell, R. J., and Ditmar, T. D. (2003b). Age-related differences in predictors of adherence to rehabilitation after anterior cruciate ligament reconstruction. *Journal of Athletic Training, 38*, 158-162.

Brewer, B. W., Daly, J. M., Van Raatle, J. L., Petitpas, A. J., and Sklar, J. H. (1994). A psychometric evaluation of the Rehabilitation Adherence Questionnaire. *Journal of Sport and Exercise Psychology, 16(Suppl.)*, S34.

Brewer, B. W., Linder, D. E., and Phelps, C. M. (1995a). Situational correlates of emotional adjustment to athletic injury. *Clinical Journal of Sport Medicine, 5*, 241-245.

Brewer, B. W., Van Raalte, J. L., Cornelius, A. E., Petitpas, A. J., Sklar, J. H, Pohlman, M. H., Krushell, R. J., and Ditmar, T. D. (2000b). Psychological factors rehabilitation adherence and rehabilitation outcome after anterior cruciate ligament reconstruction. *Rehabilitation Psychology, 45*, 20-37.

Brewer, B. W., Van Raalte, J. L., Petitpas, A. J., Sklar, J. H., and Ditmar, T. D. (1995b). A brief measurement of adherence during sport injury rehabilitation sessions [Abstract]. *Journal of Applied Sport Psychology, 7*, S44.

Brewer, B. W, Van Raalte, J. L, Petitpas, A. J. Sklar, J. H., Pohlman, M. H., Krushell, R. J, Ditmar, T. D., Daly, J. M., and Weinstock, J. (2000c). Preliminary psychometric evaluation of a measure of adherence to clinic-based sport injury rehabilitation. *Physical Therapy in Sport, 1*, 68-74.

Byerly, P. N., Worrell, T., Gahimer, J., and Domholdt, E. (1994). Rehabilitation compliance in an athletic training environment. *Journal of Athletic Training, 29*, 352-355.

Carver, C. S., and Scheier, M. F. (1994). Situational coping and coping dispositions in a stressful transaction. *Journal of Personality and Social Psychology, 66,* 267-283.

Carver, C. S., Scheier, M. F, and Weintraub, J. K. (1989). Assessing coping strategies: A theoretically based approach. *Journal of Personality and Social Psychology*, *56*, 267-283.

Cerin, E., Szabo, A., Hunt, N., and Williams, C. (2000). Temporal patterning of competitive anxiety and emotions: A critical review. *Journal of Sports Sciences, 18*, 605-626.

Chan, C. S., and Grossman, H. Y. (1988). Psychological effects of running loss on consistent runners. *Perceptual and Motor Skills, 66,* 875-993.

Cohen, S., Gottlieb, B. H., and Underwood, L. G. (2000). Social relationships and Health. In S. Cohen, L. G. Underwood and B. J. Gottlieb (Eds.), *Social support measurement and intervention: A guide for health and social scientists* (pp. 3-25). New York: Oxford University Press.

Cohen, S., and Wills, T. A. (1985). Stress, social support and the buffering hypothesis. *Psychological Bulletin, 98,* 310-357.

Corban, R. M., Snape, R., and Taylor, J. (2003). Investigation of differences in coping styles of professional and amateur rugby players. *Journal of Sports Sciences, 21,* 345.

Crocker, P. R. E., and Isaak, K. (1997). Coping during competitions and training sessions: Are youth swimmers consistent? *International Journal of Sport Psychology*, *28*, 355-369.

Crocker, P. R. E., Kowalski, K. C., and Graham, T. R. (1998). Measurement of coping strategies in sport. In J. L. Duda (Ed.), *Advances in measurement of sport and exercise psychology* (pp. 149-161). Morgantown, WV: Fitness Information Technology.

Cupal, D. D., and Brewer, B. W. (2001). Effects of relaxation and guided imagery on knee strength, reinjury anxiety, and pain following anterior cruciate ligament reconstruction. *Rehabilitation Psychology, 46,* 28-43.

Cutrona, C. E., and Russell, D. W. (1990). Type of social support and specific stress: Toward a theory of optimal matching. In B. R. Sarason, I. G. Sarason, and G. R. Pierce (Eds.), *Social support: An interactional view* (pp. 319-336). New York: Wiley.

Daly, J. M., Brewer, B. W., Van Raalte, J. L., Petitpas, A. J., and Sklar, J. H. (1995). Cognitive appraisal, emotional adjustment, and adherence to rehabilitation following knee surgery. *Journal of Sport Rehabilitation, 4*, 23-30.

Derscheid, G. L., and Feiring, D. C. (1987). A statistical analysis to characterize treatment adherence of the 18 most common diagnoses seen at a sports medicine clinic. *Journal of Orthopedic and Sports Physical Therapy, 9*, 40-46.

Draper, V. (1990). Electromyographic biofeedback and recovery of quadriceps femoris muscle function following anterior cruciate ligament reconstruction. *Physical Therapy, 70*, 11-17.

Draper, V., and Ballard, L. (1991). Electrical stimulation versus electromyographic biofeedback in the recovery of quadriceps femoris muscle function following anterior cruciate ligament surgery. *Physical Therapy, 71*, 455-464.

Duda, J. L., Smart, A. E., and Tappe, M. K. (1989). Predictors of adherence in rehabilitation of athletic injuries. *Journal of Sport and Exercise Psychology, 11*, 367-381.

Dunbar-Jacob, J., and Schlenk, E. (1996). Treatment adherence and clinical outcome: Can we make a difference. In R. J. Resnick and R. H. Rozensky (Eds.), *Health psychology through the life span: Practice and research opportunities* (pp. 323-343). Washington, DC: American Psychological Association.

Durso-Cupal, D. (1998). Psychological interventions in sport injury prevention and rehabilitation. *Journal of Applied Sport Psychology, 10*, 103-123.

Evans, L., and Hardy, L. (1995). Sport injury and grief responses: *A review. Journal of Sport and Exercise Psychology, 17*, 227-245.

Evans, L., and Hardy, L. (1999). Psychological and emotional response to athletic injury: Measurement issues. In D. Pargman (Ed.), *Psychological bases of sport injuries* (pp. 49-66). Morgantown, WV: Fitness Information Technology.

Evans, L., and Hardy, L. (2002a). Injury rehabilitation: A goal-setting intervention study. *Research Quarterly for Exercise and Sport, 73*, 310-319.

Evans, L., and Hardy, L. (2002b). Injury rehabilitation: A qualitative follow-up study. *Research Quarterly for Exercise and Sport, 73*, 320-329.

Evans, L., Hardy, L., and Fleming, S. (2000). Intervention strategies with injured athletes: An action research study. *The Sport Psychologist, 14*, 188-206.

Fields, J., Murphey, M., Horodyski, M., and Stopka, C. (1995). Factors associated with adherence to sport injury rehabilitation in college-age recreational athletes. *Journal of Sport Rehabilitation, 4*, 172-180.

Fisher, A. C., Domm, M. A., and Wuest, D. A. (1988). Adherence to sports-injury rehabilitation programmes. *The Physician and Sports Medicine, 16*, 47-52.

Folkman, S., and Lazarus, R. (1985). If it changes it must be a process: Study of emotion and coping during three stages of a college examination. *Journal of Personality and Social Psychology, 48*, 150-170.

Ford, I. W. (1999). *Psychosocial processes in sport injury occurrence and rehabilitation.* Unpublished doctoral thesis, The University of Western Australia.

Ford, I. W., Eklund, R. C., and Gordon, S. (2000). An examination of psychosocial variables moderating the relationship between life stress and injury time-loss among athletes of high standard. *Journal of Sports Sciences, 18,* 301-312.

Frydenberg, E., and Lewis, R. (1994). Coping with different concerns: Consistency and variation in coping strategies used by adolescents. *Australian Psychologist, 29,* 45-48.

Gaudreau, P., and Blondin, J. P. (2002). Development of a questionnaire for the assessment of coping strategies employed by athletes in competitive sport setting. *Psychology of Sport and Exercise, 3,* 1-34.

Gayman, A. M., and Crossman, J. (2003) A qualitative analysis of how the timing of the onset of sports injuries influences athlete reactions. *Journal of Sport Behavior, 26,* 255-271.

Gilbourne, D., and Taylor, A. H. (1998). From theory to practice: The integration of Goal Perspective Theory and life development approaches within an injury-specific goal setting programme. *Journal of Applied Sport Psychology, 10,* 124-139.

Gilbourne, D., Taylor, A. H., Downie, G., and Newton, P. (1996). Goal-setting during sports injury rehabilitation: A presentation underlying theory, administration procedure, and an athlete case study. *Sports Exercise and Injury, 2,* 192-201.

Gordon, S., and Lindgren, S. (1990). Psycho-physical rehabilitation from a serious sport injury: Case study of an elite fast bowler. *Australian Journal of Science and Medicine in Sport, 22,* 71-76.

Gottlieb, B. H. (1997). Conceptual and measurement issues in the study of coping with chronic stress. In B. H. Gottlieb (Ed.), *Coping with chronic stress* (pp. 3-42). New York: Plenum.

Gould, D., Guinan, D., Greenleaf, C., Medbury, R., and Peterson, K. (1999). Factors affecting Olympic performance: Perceptions of athletes and coaches for more and less successful teams. *The Sport Psychologist, 13,* 371-394.

Gould, D., Udry, E., Bridges, D., and Beck, L. (1997a). Coping with season ending injuries. *The Sport Psychologist, 11,* 379-399.

Gould, D., Udry, E., Bridges, D., and Beck, L. (1997b). Stress sources encountered when rehabilitating from season-ending ski injuries. *The Sport Psychologist, 11,* 361-378.

Granito Jr., V. J. (2001). Athletic injury experience: A qualitative focus group approach. *Journal of Sport Behavior, 24,* 63-82.

Granito, Jr., V. J. (2002). Psychological response to athletic injury: Gender differences. *Journal of Sport Behavior, 25,* 243-260.

Green, S. L., and Weinberg, R. S. (2001). Relationships among athletic identity, coping skills, social support, and the psychological impact of injury in recreational participants. *Journal of Applied Sport Psychology, 13, 40-59.*

Grove, J. R., and Bianco, T. (1999). Personality correlates of psychological processes during injury rehabilitation. In D. Pargman (Ed.), *Psychological bases of sport injuries* (pp. 89-110). Morgantown, WV: Fitness Information Technology.

Hardy, C. J., and Crace, R. K. (1993). The dimensions of social support when dealing with sport injuries. In D. Pargman (Ed.), *Psychological bases of sport injury* (pp. 121-144). Morgantown, WV: Fitness Information Technology.

Hardy, C. J., Gammage, K., and Hall, C. (2001). A descriptive study of athlete self-talk. *The Sport Psychologist, 15,* 306-318.

Hardy, C. J., Richman, J. M., and Rosenfeld, L. B. (1991). The role of social support in the life stress/injury relationship. *The Sport Psychologist, 5,* 128-139.

Hardy, L., Jones, G., and Gould, D. (1996). *Understanding psychological preparation for sport: Theory and practice of elite performers.* Chichester, England: Wiley.

Hawkins, R. B. (1989). Arthroscopic stapling repair for shoulder instability. A retrospective study of 50 cases. *Arthroscopy: The Journal of Arthroscopic and Related Surgery, 2,* 122-128.

Hawkins, R. J., and Switlyk, P. (1993). Acute prosthetic replacement for stress fractures of the proximal humerus. *Clinical Orthopaedics and Related Research, 289,* 156-160.

Hays, R. D., Kravitz, R. L., Mazel, R. M., Sherbourne, C. D., DiMatteo, M. R., Rogers, W. H., and Greenfield, S. (1994). The impact of patient adherence on health outcomes for patients with chronic disease in the medical outcomes study. *Journal of Behavioural Medicine, 17,* 347-360.

Hobfoll, S. E., and Vaux, A. (1993). Social support: Social resources and social context. In L. Goldberger and S. Breznitz (Eds.), *Handbook of stress* (2nd ed.) (pp. 685-705). New York: Free Press.

Ievleva, L., and Orlick, T. (1991). Mental links to enhanced healing: An exploratory study. *The Sports Psychologist, 5,* 25-40.

Johnston, L. H., and Carroll, D. (1998). The provision of social support to injured athletes: A qualitative analysis. *Journal of Sport Rehabilitation, 7,* 267-284.

Johnston, L. H., and Carroll, D. (2000). Coping, social support, and injury: changes over time and the effects of level of sports involvement. *Journal of Sport Rehabilitation, 9,* 290-303.

Junge, A. (2000). The influence of psychological factors in sport injury: Review of literature. *American Journal of Sports Medicine, 28,* S10-S15

Krebs, D. E. (1981). Clinical EMG feedback following meniscectomy: A multiple regression experimental analysis. *Physical Therapy, 61,* 1017-1021.

Krohne, H. W. (1993). Vigilance and cognitive avoidance as concepts in coping research. In H.W. Krohne (Ed.), *Attention and avoidance* (pp. 19-50). Seattle, WA: Hogrefe and Huber.

Kübler-Ross, E. (1969). *On death and dying.* New York: Macmillan.

Lampton, C. C., Lambert, M. E., and Yost, R. (1993). The effects of psychological factors in sports medicine rehabilitation adherence. *Journal of Sports Medicine and Physical Fitness, 33,* 292-299.

Laubach, W. J., Brewer, B. W., Van Raalte, J. L., and Petitpas, A. J. (1996). Attributions for recovery and adherence to sport injury rehabilitation. *Australian Journal of Science and Medicine in Sport, 28,* 30-34.

Lazarus, R. S. (1990). Theory-based stress measurement. *Psychological Inquiry, 1,* 3-13.

Lazarus, R. S. (1991). *Emotion and adaptation.* New York: Oxford Press.

Lazarus, R. S., and Folkman, S. (1984). *Stress, appraisal, and coping.* New York: Springer.

Leddy, M. H., Lambert, M. J., and Ogles, B. M. (1994). Psychological consequences of athletic injury among high-level competitors. *Research Quarterly for Exercise and Sport, 65,* 347-354.

Levitt, R., Deisinger, J. A., Wall, J. R., Ford, L., and Cassisi, J. E. (1995). EMG feedback-assisted postoperative rehabilitation of minor arthroscopic knee surgeries. *The Journal of Sports Medicine and Physical Fitness, 35,* 1-4.

Lin, N. (1986). Conceptualizing social support. In N. Lin, A. Dean, and W. M. Ensel (Eds.), *Social support, life events and depression* (pp. 17-30). Orlando, FL: Academic Press.

Locke, E. A., and Latham, G. P. (1990). A *theory of goal setting and task performance.* Englewood Cliffs, NJ: Prentice-Hall.

Maddux, J. E., and Rogers, R. W. (1983). Protection motivation and self-efficacy: A revised theory of fear appeals and attitude change. *Journal of Experimental Social Psychology, 19,* 469–479.

Maehr, M. L., and Braskamp, L. A. (1986). *The motivation factor: A theory of personal investment.* Lexington, MA: D.C. Heath and Company.

Magyar, T. M., and Duda, J. L. (2000). Confidence restoration following athletic injury. *The Sport Psychologist, 14,* 372-390.

Martin, K. A., Moritz, S. E., and Hall, C. R. (1999). Imagery use in sport: A literature review and applied model. *The Sport Psychologist, 13,* 245-268.

McCrae, R. R. (1992). Situational determinants of coping. In B. N. Carpenter (Ed.), *Personal coping: Theory research and application* (pp. 65-76). Westport, CT: Praeger.

McDonald, S. A., and Hardy, C. J. (1990). Affective response patterns of the injured athlete: An exploratory analysis. *The Sport Psychologist, 4,* 261-274.

McGowan, R., Pierce, E., Williams, M., and Eastman, N. (1994). Athletic injury and self diminution. *Journal of Sports Medicine and Physical Fitness, 34,* 299-304.

McNair, D. M., Lorr, M., and Droppleman, L. F. (1971). *Manual for the Profile of Mood States.* San Diego, CA: Educational and Industrial Testing Service.

Meichenbaum, D., and Turk, D. C. (1987). *Facilitating treatment adherence: A practitioner's guidebook.* New York: Plenum.

Miller, S. M. (1989). Cognitive informational styles in the process of coping with threat and frustration. *Advances in Behavior Research and Therapy, 11,* 223-234.

Morrey, M. A., Stuart, M. J., Smith, A. M., and Wiese-Bjornstal, D. M. (1999). A longitudinal examination of athletes' emotional and cognitive responses to anterior cruciate ligament injury. *Clinical Journal of Sport Medicine, 9,* 63-69.

Munroe, K., Hall, C., Weinberg, R., and Giacobbi, P. (2000). The four W's of imagery use: Where, when, what and how. *The Sport Psychologist, 14,* 119-137.

Murphy, G. C., Foreman, P. E., Simpson, C. A., Molloy, G. N., and Molloy, E. K. (1999). The development of a locus of control measure predictive of injured athletes' adherence to treatment. *Journal of Occupational and Organisational Psychology, 72,* 83-99.

Noyes, F. R., Matthews, D. S., Mooar, P. A., and Grood, E. S. (1983). The symptomatic anterior cruciate-deficient knee. Part II: The results of rehabilitation, activity modification, and counseling on functional disability. *Journal of Bone and Joint Surgery, 65-A,* 163-174.

Orlick, T., and Partington, J. (1988). Mental links to excellence. *The Sport Psychologist, 2,* 105-130.

Pearson, L., and Jones, G. (1992). Emotional effects of sports injuries: Implications for physiotherapists. *Physiotherapy, 78,* 762-770.

Peretz, D. (1970). Development, object-relationships, and loss. In B. Schoenberg, A. C. Carr, D. Peretz, and A. H. Kutscher (Eds.). *Loss and grief: Psychological management in medical practice* (pp. 3-19). New York: Columbia University Press.

Perna, F. M., Antoni, M. H., Baum, A., Gordon, P., and Schneiderman, N. (2003). Cognitive behavioral stress management effects on injury and illness among competitive athletes: A randomized clinical trial. *Annals of Behavioral Medicine, 25,* 66-73.

Petrie, T. A. (1993). Coping resources, competitive trait anxiety, and playing status: Moderating effects on the life stress-injury relationship. *Journal of Sport and Exercise Psychology, 15,* 261-274.

Pizzari, T., McBurney, H., Taylor, N. F., and Feller, J. A. (2002). Adherence to anterior cruciate ligament rehabilitation: A qualitative analysis. *Journal of Sport Rehabilitation, 11,* 90-102.

Quackenbush, N., and Crossman, J. (1994). Injured athletes: A study of emotional responses. *Journal of Sport Behavior, 17,* 178-187.

Quinn, A. M., and Fallon, B. J. (1999). The changes in psychological characteristics and reactions of elite athletes from injury onset until full recovery. *Journal of Applied Sport Psychology, 11,* 210-229.

Quinn, A. M., and Fallon, B. J. (2000). Predictors of recovery time. *Journal of Sport Rehabilitation, 9,* 62-76.

Rejeski, W. J., Brawley, L. R., Ettinger, W., Morgan, T., and Thompson, C. (1997). Compliance to exercise therapy in older participants with knee osteoarthritis: Implication for treating disability. *Medicine and Science in Sports and Exercise, 29,* 977-985.

Rives, K., Gelberman, R., Smith, B., and Carney, K. (1992). Severe contractures of the proximal interphalangeal joint in Dupuytren's disease: Results of a prospective trial of operative correction and dynamic extension splinting. *The Journal of Hand Surgery, 17,* 1153-1159.

Robbins, J. E., and Rosenfeld, L. B. (2001). Athletes' perceptions of social support provided by their head coach, assistant coach, and athletic trainer, pre-injury and during Rehabilitation. *Journal of Sport Behavior, 3,* 277-297.

Rock, J. A., and Jones, M. V. (2002). A preliminary investigation into the use of counseling skills in support of rehabilitation from sport injury. *Journal of Sport Rehabilitation, 11,* 284-304.

Rodgers, B. L., and Cowles, K. V. (1991). The concept of grief: An analysis of classical and contemporary thought. *Death Studies, 15,* 443-458.

Rogers, R. W. (1975). A protection motivation theory of feat appeals and attitude change. *Journal of Psychology, 91,* 93-114.

Rogers, R. W. (1983). Cognitive and physiological processes in fear appeals and attitude change: A revised theory of protection motivation. In J. R. Cacioppo and R. E. Petty (Eds.), *Social psychology: A sourcebook* (pp. 153-176). New York: Guilford.

Rosenfeld, L. B., Richman, J. M., and Hardy, C. J. (1989). Examining social support networks among athletes: Description and relationship to stress. *The Sport Psychologist, 3,* 23-33.

Ross, M. J., and Berger, R. S. (1996). Effects of stress inoculation on athletes' post-surgical pain and rehabilitation after orthopedic injury. *Journal of Consulting and Clinical Psychology, 64,* 406-410.

Rotella, R., and Heyman, S. (1993). Stress, injury, and the psychological rehabilitation of athletes. In J. M. Williams (Ed.), *Applied sport psychology: Personal growth to peak performance* (pp. 338-355). Mountain View, CA: Mayfield.

Sordoni, C., Hall, C., and Forwell, L. (2000). The use of imagery by athletes during injury rehabilitation. *Journal of Sport Rehabilitation, 9*, 329-338.

Sarason, B. R., Pierce, G. R., and Sarason, I. G. (1990). Social support: The sense of acceptance and the role of relationships. In B. R. Sarason., I. G. Sarason., and G. R. Pierce (Eds.), *Social support: An interactional view* (pp. 397-426). New York: Wiley.

Scherzer, C. B., Brewer, B. W., Cornelius, A. E., Van Raalte, J. L., Petitpas, A. J., Sklar, J. H., Pohlman, M. H., Krushell, R. J., and Ditmar, T. D. (2001). Psychological skills and adherence to rehabilitation after reconstruction of the anterior cruciate ligament. *Journal of Sport Rehabilitation, 10,* 165-172.

Sellers, R. M. (1995). Situational differences in the coping processes of student-athletes. *Anxiety, Stress and Coping, 8,* 325-336.

Shelbourne, K. D., and Wilckens, J. H. (1990). Current concepts in anterior cruciate ligament rehabilitation. *Orthopedic Review, 19,* 957-964.

Simos, B. G. (1977). Grief therapy to facilitate healthy restitution. *Social Casework, 58,* 337-342.

Sluijs, E. M., Kok, G. J, and van der Zee, J. (1993). Correlates of exercise compliance and physical therapy. *Physical Therapy, 73*, 771-786.

Smith, A. M., Scott, S. G., O'Fallon, W. M., and Young, M. L. (1990). Emotional responses of athletes to injury. *Mayo Clinic Proceedings, 65,* 38-50.

Smith, A. M., Stuart, M. J., Wiese-Bjornstal, D. M., Milliner, E. K., O'Fallon, W. J., and Crowson, C. S. (1993). Competitive athletes: Pre and post injury mood state and self-esteem. *Mayo Clinic Proceedings, 68*, 939-947.

Stewart, S. M., and Schwarzer, R. (1996). Stability of coping in Hong Kong medical students: A longitudinal study. *Personality and Individual Differences, 20*, 245-255.

Suls, J., and Fletcher, B. (1985). The relative efficacy of avoidant and non-avoidant coping strategies: A meta-analysis. *Health Psychology, 4*, 249-288.

Taylor, A. H., and May, S. (1996). Threat and coping appraisal as determinants of compliance to sports injury rehabilitation: An application of protection motivation theory. *Journal of Sports Sciences, 14*, 471-482.

Theodorakis, Y., Beneca, A., Malliou, P., and Goudas, M. (1997). Examining psychological factors during injury rehabilitation. *Journal of Sport Rehabilitation, 6*, 355-363.

Theodorakis, Y., Malliou, P., Papaioannou, A., Beneca, A., and Filactakidou, A. (1996). The effect of personal goals, self-efficacy, and self-satisfaction on injury rehabilitation. *Journal of Sport Rehabilitation, 5*, 214-223.

Thoits, P. A. (1985). Social support and psychological well-being: Theoretical possibilities. In I. G. Sarason and B. R. Sarason (Eds.), *Social support: Theory, research and applications* (pp. 51-72). Dordrecht, Netherlands: Martinus Nijhoff.

Tracey, J. (2003). The emotional response to the injury and rehabilitation process. *Journal of Applied Sport Psychology, 15,* 279-293.

Udry, E. (1996). Social support: Exploring its role in the context of athletic injuries. *Journal of Sport Rehabilitation, 5,* 151-163.

Udry, E. (1997). Coping and social support among injured athletes following surgery. *Journal of Sport and Exercise Psychology, 19*, 71-90.

Udry, E., and Andersen, M. B. (2002). Athletic injury and sport behavior. In T. Horn, *Advances in sport psychology* (2nd ed.) (pp. 529-553). Champaign, IL: Human Kinetics.

Udry, E., Gould, D., Bridges, D., and Beck, L. (1997a). Down but not out: Athlete response to season-ending injuries. *Journal of Sport and Exercise Psychology, 19,* 229-248.

Udry, E., Gould, D., Bridges, D., and Tuffey, S. (1997b). People helping people? Examining the social ties of athletes coping with burnout and injury stress. *Journal of Sport and Exercise Psychology, 19,* 368-395.

Vasey, L. M. (1990). DNA's and DNCT's – Why do patients fail to begin or to complete a course of physiotherapy treatment? *Physiotherapy, 76,* 575 – 578.

Webborn, A. D. J., Carbon, R. J., and Miller, B. P. (1997). Injury rehabilitation problems: "What are we talking about?" *Journal of Sport Rehabilitation, 6,* 54-61.

Weiss, M. R., and Troxel, R. K. (1986). Psychology of the injured athlete. *Athletic training, 21,* 104-109.

Wheaton, B. (1997). The nature of chronic stress. In B. H. Gottlieb (ed.). *Coping with chronic stress* (pp. 43-73). New York: Plenum.

Wiese-Bjornstal, D. M., and Shaffer, S. (1999). Psychosocial dimensions of sport injury. In R. Ray and D. M. Wiese-Bjornstal (Eds.), *Counseling in sport medicine* (pp. 23-40). Champaign, IL: Human Kinetics.

Wiese-Bjornstal, D. M., Smith, A. M., Shaffer, S. M., and Morrey, M. A. (1998). An integrated model of response to sport injury: Psychological and sociological dynamics. *Journal of Applied Sport Psychology, 10,* 46-69.

Wittig, A. F., and Schurr, K. T. (1994). Psychological characteristics of women volleyball players: Relationships with injuries, rehabilitation, and team success. *Personality and Social Psychology Bulletin, 20,* 322-330.

Young, K., and White, P. (1995). Sport, physical danger, and injury: The experiences of elite women athletes. *Journal of Sport and Social Issues, 19,* 45-61.

Young, K., White, P., and McTeer, W. (1994). Body talk: Male athletes reflect on sport, injury, and pain. *Sociology of Sport Journal, 11,* 175-195.

Zinsser, N., Bunker, L., and Williams, J. N. (1998). Cognitive techniques for building confidence in enhancing performance. In J. M. Williams (Ed.), *Applied sport psychology: Personal growth to peak performance* (3rd ed.) (pp. 270-295). Mountain View, CA: Mayfield.

In: Literature Reviews in Sport Psychology　　　　　　　ISBN 1-59454-904-4
Editors: S. Hanton and S. D. Mellalieu, pp. 321-374　　© 2006 Nova Science Publishers, Inc.

Chapter 10

AN ORGANIZATIONAL STRESS REVIEW: CONCEPTUAL AND THEORETICAL ISSUES IN COMPETITIVE SPORT

*David Fletcher** and *Sheldon Hanton*
University of Wales Institute, Cardiff, United Kingdom
Stephen D. Mellalieu
Swansea University, United Kingdom

ABSTRACT

This chapter provides a review of current issues in organizational stress in competitive sport. Two main areas are addressed: (a) conceptual and operational considerations, culminating in definitions of stress-related constructs, and (b) theoretical relationships among stress, emotions and performance, based on a meta-model outlining key processes, moderators and consequences. As the chapter progresses, attention focuses on the practical implications and research directions emanating from the literature review.

Key words: transactional perspective, relational meaning, stressor-strain relationships, meta-model, sport performers

INTRODUCTION

Sport in the new millennium is firmly established as a global industry. Spurred on by national pride, sport has successfully traversed almost every border to influence the lives of nearly everyone on the planet (Maguire, Jarvie, Mansfield, and Bradley, 2002; Westerbeek

---

* Correspondence concerning this chapter should be addressed to David Fletcher, Cardiff School of Sport, University of Wales Institute, Cardiff (UWIC), Cyncoed, Cardiff CF23 6XD, United Kingdom. Telephone: 4429-2041-7104. Fax: 4429-2041-6768. E-mail: DFletcher@uwic.ac.uk

and Smith, 2003). Indeed, Westerbeek and Smith (2003) observed that sport as an institution has such a penetrating affect on modern life that there are few places of refuge. Through the expansion of the globalized economy, the explosion of commercialism, the progress of technology and the media, the crossover with entertainment, and the impact of Western culture, sport has become an almost universal phenomenon. It may well be that it was never intended to be such an immense business enterprise, nor anticipated that elite performers could command the emotional and financial commitment of billions of otherwise rationale people (Wann, Melnick, Russell, and Pease, 2001; Westerbeek and Smith, 2003). But the reality is, competitive sport is currently entrenched in the fabric of contemporary society and shows no sign of receding.

Allied to these developments has been the rapid evolution of sport organizations. Making up an integral part of the sport industry is a wide array of public, private and voluntary organizations. A sport organization has been conceived as "a social entity involved in the sport industry; it is goal-directed, with a consciously structured activity system and a relatively identifiable boundary" (Slack, 1997, p. 5). It is important to recognize, however, that when considered in the broadest sense, precise definition becomes elusive because of the intricate systems of historically and socially constructed hierarchies, with constantly changing frontiers. Indeed, an organization often has multiple constituents that have overlapping, sometimes ambiguous, relationships with other sport and nonsport organizations. These include, for example, national governing bodies and international federations; governmental agencies and departments; sports leagues and events; high performance and local participation sports teams, squads and clubs; athletes' agents and representatives; various business enterprises, including media, entertainment, and advertising groups; sponsorship and merchandising companies; doping control; medical personnel; lawyers; gambling; and so the list goes on.

This highly complex social and organizational environment imposes numerous demands on sport performers and other personnel that function within it. As a result, athletes frequently seek advice from psychologists on dealing with the pressures that accompany their participation in competitive sport, particularly at the higher levels. It has become apparent that, in many instances, organizations have not been sufficiently active in recognizing and addressing such issues. In fact, well-respected International Olympic Committee (IOC) member, Dr. Rubén Acosta Hernández, recently commented that:

> Athletes naturally want to win. However, they often bear the brunt of their country's poor organizational structures. They rebel against their national sport organizations for being unsupportive, neglecting their duties, eluding their responsibilities, and shying away from accountability. In developing countries, many organizations conceal their incompetence behind political influence and sometimes a hesitant media's fear of retaliation. Athletes have needs – such as a place to practice sports, an event to compete in, an instructor to improve their skills and abilities, and a performance to achieve – that most sport organizations today are not truly satisfying. If these needs continue to be forgotten, athletes will feel compelled to break the inertia of their own sport organizations and look elsewhere for... the fulfillment of their dreams... (Acosta Hernández, 2002, p. 6)

In view of these observations, it is perhaps somewhat surprising that researchers have failed to systematically investigate stress in sport organizations. This is in contrast to the considerable empirical attention focused on the demands and responses commonly associated with competitive performance. More than two decades of study have generated a substantial body of evidence on the competitive stress experience, particularly anxiety and its relationship with performance (see, for recent reviews, Burton, 1998; Mellalieu, Hanton, and Fletcher, this volume; Woodman and Hardy, 2001b). Much less is known, however, about athletes' experiences of stress related to the organizational environment within which they are operating. Despite repeated calls for research (see, e.g., Hardy and Jones, 1994; Hardy, Jones, and Gould, 1996; Jones, 1995b), psychologists' understanding of this area remains limited.

The preponderance of organizational stress knowledge has been derived from research conducted in business, medical and educational settings; thus, in the absence of systematic work in the athletic domain, this review draws heavily from this knowledge base to help guide theory and research in sport psychology. The few sport-related studies that exist have tended towards the analysis of elite or professional performers (Fletcher and Hanton, 2003a; Woodman, 2003; Woodman and Hardy, 2001b). This is, of course, not to suggest that recreational or participation-based sport is free from organizational stress, only that it may be more prevalent and pertinent at the higher levels of competitive performance.

This chapter is about organizational stress in competitive sport and concepts, theories and research relating to this area. The review of literature comprises two major sections. The first considers conceptual and operational issues and provides a contemporary definition of organizational stress based on a transactional perspective. The second section discusses a meta-model of stress, emotions and performance and the theoretical relationships among key processes, moderators and consequences of the organizational stress process.

CONCEPTUAL AND OPERATIONAL ISSUES

Almost all reviews of stress (and anxiety) in sport begin by drawing attention to the difficulties associated with, and the confusion surrounding, the way in which stress-related terms have been conceptualized and operationalized (see, e.g., Jones and Hardy, 1990; Hardy et al., 1996; Woodman and Hardy, 2001b). Stress has variously been defined as an environmental stimulus, a person's response, or the result of an interaction between the person and the environment. As the body of knowledge has developed, particularly that surrounding the appraisal of stimuli and the interpretation of responses, researchers have increasingly considered the nature of the interaction and, most importantly, the psychological processes through which it takes place (Jones, 1990; Jones and Hardy, 1989; Woodman and Hardy, 2001b).

The fact that stress has been related to a range of conditions (i.e., stimulus, response, interaction) has impeded systematic development in both sport and mainstream psychology. For this reason, some commentators have suggested that the stress concept be relegated to a secondary position behind a more general framework of "stress research" (e.g., House, 1974), or even abandoned altogether because it is too all encompassing a phenomenon to investigate (e.g., Kasl, 1983). However, we agree with Cooper, Dewe, and O'Driscoll (2001) who maintained that it is important scholars continue to pursue and debate the nature of stress for two main reasons. First, conceptualizations give a sense of time and historical perspective to research that, in turn, provide an insight into why certain approaches prevail and the explanatory potential of such work. Second, operational definitions have a key role to play in determining the nature and direction of research and provide conceptual boundaries to help guide theoretical and empirical development.

The vague rhetoric often surrounding the study of stress in sport is perhaps best exemplified by the pervasive use of the terms "competition stress" and "noncompetition stress". While at first glance these labels may seem intuitively reasonable, Fletcher and Hanton (2003a) argued that the latter term is too imprecise to adequately contribute to theory and practice and does little to capture the essence of the stress experience. To this end, they proffered the terms *competitive stress*, *organizational stress*, and *personal stress* to conceptually differentiate between major categories of stress in sport performers. Their rationale for this distinction related to three main areas: (a) the specific origins and nature of the stimuli encountered; (b) the differences in the psychological processes underlying the responses to these demands; (c) the appropriateness of interventions to manage competitive, organizational and personal strain (cf. Fletcher and Hanton, 2003b; Hanton, Fletcher, and Coughlan, 2005; Jones, 2002; Woodman and Hardy, 2001a).

Due to the definitional difficulties in this area and the relative infancy of organizational stress in the sport psychology literature, this section provides an overview of traditional views of stress, discusses their strengths and limitations, and describes the evolution of a transactional conceptualization. We conclude the section by providing definitions of relevant constructs, including a contemporary conceptualization of organizational stress based on a transactional perspective.

Stress as a Stimulus and a Response

The phrase "being under stress" is one that most sport performers can relate to. Implied in this expression are environmental stimuli exerting demands on an athlete. The origins of stimulus-based definitions of stress can be found in physics and engineering (Hinkle, 1973; Mason, 1975), where stress refers to external pressure applied to a structure and strain to the deformation of that structure. The aphorism "the straw that breaks the camel's back" has been used to illustrate the essence of this approach (see Cooper et al., 2001). The meaning being that a person who is constantly assailed by demands (i.e., stress) may encounter just one more apparently minor or innocuous event that will disrupt the delicate balance in his or her functioning (i.e., strain). In short, this perspective conceives stress as an environmental or independent variable.

In sport psychology, definitions of stress are often embedded in a stimulus-based conceptualization emphasizing external events or "some demand [which] is placed upon the individual" (Hardy et al., 1996, p. 141). These events or demands, which are commonly referred to as *stressors*, reflect an athlete's environmental conditions and potential sources of strain. Over the past fifteen years or so, qualitative research has unearthed a wide range of "sources of stress" in sport performers (e.g., Campbell and Jones, 2002b; Giacobbi, Foore, and Weinberg, 2004; Giacobbi, Lynn, Wetherington, Jenkins, Bodendorf, and Langley, 2004; Gould, Jackson, and Finch, 1993; Holt and Hogg, 2002: James and Collins, 1997; Noblet and Gifford, 2002; Park, 2004; Scanlan, Stein, and Ravizza, 1991; see also Dugdale, Eklund, and Gordon, 2002). Collectively, the stressors identified in these studies were associated with competitive performance (e.g., opponents), the sport organization within which the athlete was operating (e.g., finances), and personal "nonsporting" life events (e.g., family).

Of course, sport performers don't just talk of "being under stress"; they also speak of actually "being stressed". This phrase refers not so much to environmental stimuli but an athlete's responses to such demands. The origins of response-based definitions of stress can be found in physiology and medicine (Hinkle, 1973; Mason, 1975). In the 1930s and 1940s, Hans Selye (1936, 1946) introduced the notion of stress-related illness in terms of the general adaptation syndrome (GAS), proposing that stress is a nonspecific response of the body to a demand. The stages of response described within the GAS are: alarm, resistance, and exhaustion. The alarm stage is essentially analogous to what Cannon (1914, 1915, 1929, 1932, 1935) labeled the emergency reaction, or "fight or flight" response, involving a neuroendocrine reaction to mobilize the body physiologically for action. In short, this approach considers stress as a person or dependent variable.

Response-based conceptualizations of stress are also popular among sport psychologists (see, e.g., Franks, 1994; Kellmann and Kallus, 2001; Tenenbaum, Jones, Kitsantas, Sacks, and Berwick, 2003a, 2003b). This perspective was reflected in two independent interview studies conducted with figure skaters, which adopted the following definition of stress:

> When we discuss stress or pressure now, I am referring to the negative emotions, feelings, and thoughts that you might have had with respect to your skating experience. These would include feelings of apprehension, anxiety, muscle tension, nervousness, physical reactions (such as butterflies in the stomach, shaking, or nervous sweating), thoughts centered on worry and self-doubt, and negative statements to yourself. (Gould, Jackson, and Finch, 1993, p. 136; Scanlan et al., 1991, p. 105; see also Giacobbi et al., 2004; James and Collins, 1997)

At this juncture it is interesting to note that Selye (1950, 1956), in developing his ideas on stress, actually attempted to apply the previously mentioned analogy from physics and engineering, where stress represents the stimulus and strain the response. But Selye, who was an Austro-Hungarian, misunderstood the English terminology and labeled a person's response as "stress", thereby spoiling the analogy and – to his later regret – causing confusion as to whether stress should be conceived as a stimulus or a response (Selye, 1973, 1975, 1976a, 1976b, 1976c; see also Levi, 1996, 1998). In some instances, sport psychologists appear to have circumvented this ambiguity by essentially operationalizing stress as *both* a stimulus and a response. For example, the "sources of stress" research noted earlier typically included performers' competitive anxiety responses, such as worries and doubts, under the rubric of "sources of stress". Smith, Smoll, and Wiechman (1998) summarized this approach in their review of anxiety in sport:

> The term *stress* is used in two different but related ways. First, it is used in relation to situations (termed "stressors") that place significant demands on the organism... The second use of the term stress refers to the responses of individuals to stressors... including aversive emotional states, such as anxiety, depression, and anger. (pp. 105-106)

Regardless of whether one conceptualizes stress as a stimulus, a response, or both, there are a number of limitations associated with these approaches (Appley and Trumbull, 1986; Cooper et al., 2001; Cox, 1978, 1985, 1990; Lazarus and Folkman, 1984; Lazarus and Launier, 1978; Mason, 1975). First, they largely overlook individual differences that account for the fact that responses to stimuli do not always follow the same pattern. Much of this drawback can be summed up by the observation that two sport performers in a similar situation, such as a conflict with management, will often react in different ways. Second, by focusing on the distinct components of what is an ongoing process they tend to draw attention away from the process itself. Hence, researchers can only conclude that demands have the *potential* to result in strain or that responses *may* be a negative reaction to a stressor. A stimulus or response can only be regarded as a stressor or strain when the two components are considered in relation to one another. Third, these approaches fail to fully capture the dynamics of the overall stress process. It is the relationship between the person and the environment, and the psychological processes that underpin this relationship, which are pivotal in understanding the nature of stress.

In spite of these shortcomings, some scholars (e.g., Hobfoll, Schwarzer, and Chon, 1996) have argued that a key strength of stimulus and response-based definitions is their impact on research designs which, as a result, are able to rely on empirical observations rather than inferences of abstract processes. Indeed, studies that have adopted this paradigm have generated a substantial amount of information relating to the stressors encountered by sport performers and the nature of their responses to these demands. Such an approach is insightful and necessary; however, it is important that researchers continue to progress by exploring the complex relationship that exists between a person and the environment (Lazarus, 1999; Woodman and Hardy, 2001b). Recent efforts in sport psychology to examine this relationship have tended to focus on the notion of *interaction*.

Stress as an Interaction

The interactional approach to defining stress emphasizes the interaction between a person and the environment (Appley and Turmbull, 1967). As sport psychology researchers have recognized the limitations of stimulus and response-based conceptualizations, they have increasingly used the term "interaction" to describe their perspective of stress (see, e.g., Anshel, Kim, Kim, Chang, and Eom, 2001; Campbell and Jones, 2002b; Fletcher and Hanton, 2003b; Holt and Dunn, 2004; Jones, 1990, 1991; Jones and Hanton, 2001; Kelley, 1994; Kelley, Eklund, and Ritter-Taylor, 1999; Kelley and Gill, 1993; Martens, 1971; Martens, Vealey, and Burton, 1990; Martin, Kelley, and Dias, 1999; Martin, Kelley, and Eklund, 1999; Vealey, Udry, Zimmerman, and Soliday, 1992; Woodman and Hardy, 2001a). In statistical terms, an interaction refers to the combined effect of two (or more) independent variables on a dependent variable. Hence, interaction implies a cause and effect, whereby the person and the environment give rise to cognitive-emotional reactions but nonetheless maintain their distinctiveness (Appley and Turmbull, 1986; Lazarus, 1966; Lazarus and Folkman, 1984). The causal variables are considered detachable structural components which remain unchanged and independent of each other during their interaction. However, although interaction is certainly relevant, it is also important to recognize that during stressful encounters the person and the environment can, and often do, mutually affect one another (Lazarus, 1981; Lazarus and Launier, 1978). Furthermore, the meaning the person construes from his or her relationship with the environment occurs at a higher level of abstraction than the distinct variables themselves. Therefore, in addition to interaction, sport psychologists need to consider the dynamics of *transaction* and *relational meaning*.

Stress as a Transaction and the Notion of Relational Meaning

Transactional definitions of stress are less focused on the specific components of an interaction and more concerned with the psychological processes – such as the cognitive-motivational-relational concepts of appraisal and coping – that underpin an encounter (cf. Dewey and Bentley, 1949; Lazarus and Launier, 1978). Stress is viewed as an ongoing transaction between the environmental demands and a person's resources, with strain resulting from an imbalance between these demands and resources (Cox, 1978, 1985; McGrath, 1970; Lazarus and Folkman, 1984). Rather than implying static relationships involving statistical correlations between variables, Lazarus (1998) argued that the term transaction adds meaning to a person's interaction with his or her environment:[1]

> Transaction... is much more than interaction... [it] brings the causal variables together at a higher level of abstraction; namely, the relational meaning constructed by the individual who is confronted by (or selects) a particular environment. (p. xix)

Contemporary definitions adopting a transactional perspective emphasize that stress neither resides in the person nor the environment, but in the relationship between the two (Lazarus, 1981). It is conceived as a dynamic cognitive state reflecting a person's continuous transaction with his or her environment. Hence, in the study of organizational stress in sport, researchers should focus their attention on the critical issues surrounding, and cognitive processes underpinning, a performer's relationship with his or her sport organization. What distinguishes this approach from others is the importance it places on the ongoing process – in particular those features that link the components of the process – and its emphasis on the reciprocal and adaptive nature of the process itself (Aldwin, 2000; Cooper et al., 2001).

The transactional perspective recognizes the recursive principle that a person, the environment, and psychological reactions all mutually affect one another. Relevant here is cybernetics theory (Ashby, 1966; Weiner, 1948), which states that cognitive functioning involves the processing of information and use of feedback to control purposeful behavior. This process essentially represents a homeostatic mechanism operating to maintain a state of equilibrium where behavior is directed at reducing deviations from a specific goal-state (Carver and Scheier, 1981, 1985; Cummings and Cooper, 1979, 1998; Edwards, 1992, 1998; Kagan and Levi, 1975; Latack, Kinicki, and Prussia, 1995; Levi, 1998; McGrath, 1976; Miller, Galanter, and Pribram, 1960; Powers, 1973; Tapp, 1985). Hence, a transactional approach suggests that while environmental demands and personal characteristics combine to influence how sport performers might react to a situation; how they react will, through the processes of coping and adaptation, in turn, affect environmental conditions, personal resources, and future reactions.

Sport psychologists have recognized for some time now the concept of stress as a process (see, e.g., Craft, Magyar, Becker, and Feltz, 2003; Dugdale et al., 2002; Gill, 1994, 2000; Gould, 1987; Gould and Krane, 1992; Jones, 2002; Martens, 1977; Martens et al., 1990; Passer, 1982; Spielberger, 1989; Tenenbaum et al., 2003a, 2003b; Wrisberg, 1994). However,

---

[1] In elaborating on the difference between *interaction* and *transaction*, Lazarus (1999) made an enlightening analogy with the terms *perception* and *apperception*; to apperceive is to consider the implications of and add meaning to what is perceived.

the term *transaction*, despite making some sporadic appearances in the literature (i.e., Gill, 1994; Rotella and Lerner, 1993; Smith, 1985, 1986) and becoming well established in mainstream psychology, has generally been overlooked by our field. We suspect this has been largely due to the ascendance of interactional definitions, which is unfortunate because, as noted above, the term "interaction" fails to truly capture the essence of the stress experience (Lazarus, 1990). Nevertheless, transactional conceptualizations have made a recent resurgence (see Anshel, Jamieson, and Raviv, 2001; Campbell and Jones, 2002b; Dugdale et al., 2002; Giacobbi, Lynn et al., 2004; Gill, 2000; Hammermeister and Burton, 2001; Holt and Hogg, 2002; Jones, 2002; Kim and Duda, 2003; Tenenbaum et al., 2003a), a trend that needs to continue if significant advances are to be made in the study of stress in sport (Fletcher and Hanton, 2003a; see also Hanton et al., 2005).

Inherent in transactional definitions of stress is the notion of relational meaning, which focuses on the meaning a person construes from his or her relationship with the environment (Lazarus, 1991b, 1998; Lazarus and Launier, 1978). In his recent work, Lazarus (2000c) cited relational meaning as the "conceptual bottom line" (p. 665) of his approach and arguably the most appropriate term to describe the overall dynamics of the stress process:

> Because of confusion between what interaction and transaction are all about, it is better to use the term *relational meaning*, as it is construed by the person… Psychology needs to develop a new conceptual language. Instead of the traditional stimulus and response phraseology, which implies that the two terms are separable, we need a language of relationships. (Lazarus, 1999, p.13)

In line with the assumptions underlying the transactional paradigm, relational meaning is not found in the environment or person alone. It takes the conjoining of both environmental demands and personal characteristics to generate cognitive-evaluative reactions and ascribe meaning to an encounter. Sport psychology researchers have yet to truly espouse the notion of relational meaning (Lazarus, 2000a, 2000b). However, its overarching importance in the stress process would suggest that it offers considerable potential for furthering theory and practice in our field (Fletcher and Hanton, 2003a; see also Hanton et al., 2005).

Definitions of Stress-Related Constructs

Stress has proved to be a heuristic but vague construct in the field of sport psychology; hence, careful consideration has been given here to defining organizational stress before considering theoretical issues in this area. Whilst it is important that conceptualizing stress does not become an onerous initiation for investigators, the key message to emerge from the definitional debate is that it is not just an obligatory exercise in semantics. As Cooper et al. (2001) pointed out, operational definitions have a fundamental impact on the nature and direction of theory and research. Furthermore, researchers in this area have a moral obligation to define stress so that they capture the experiences of those whose lives they wish to investigate. In line with the transactional perspective of stress, this review adopts the following conceptual definitions (cf. Cooper et al., 2001; Fletcher and Hanton, 2003a):

- *Stress*: an ongoing process that involves individuals transacting with their environments, making appraisals of the situations they find themselves in, and endeavoring to cope with any issues that may arise (adapted from Lazarus, 1998, 1999).
- *Stressors*: environmental demands (i.e., stimuli) encountered by an individual.
- *Strain*: an individual's negative psychological, physical and behavioral responses to stressors.

Stressors, therefore, are events, situations or conditions, and *strain* is a person's negative reaction to stressors. The term *stress* should not be used to describe specific components of the transaction between the person and the environment (Lazarus, 1990), but rather to represent the overall process incorporating stressors, strains, appraisals and coping responses. Consequently, the tautology "sources of stress" should be avoided since stress already encapsulates the sources of this process (i.e., stressors); however, the term *sources of strain* may be useful when referring to those stressors that give rise to negative responses. In extending these conceptualizations, we propose the following organizational stress-related definitions (cf. Cooper et al., 2001; Fletcher and Hanton, 2003a):

- *Organizational stress:*[2] an ongoing transaction between an individual and the environmental demands associated primarily and directly with the organization within which he or she is operating (adapted from Woodman and Hardy, 2001a).
- *Organizational stressors:*[3] environmental demands (i.e., stimuli) associated primarily and directly with the organization within which an individual is operating.
- *Organizational strain*: an individual's negative psychological, physical and behavioral responses to organizational stressors.

As alluded to in the introduction of this chapter, identifying issues associated with an organization is rarely straightforward due to the complex nature of the social and organizational environment. It may, therefore, be more operationally useful to consider what is *not* deemed organizational stress. Those issues not normally directly related to the organization, such as demands associated primarily with competitive performance (e.g., opponents) and personal "nonsporting" life events (e.g., family), should not be considered aspects of the organizational stress process (cf. Fletcher and Hanton, 2003a, 2003b; Hanton et al., 2005; Woodman and Hardy, 2001a).

---

[2] In mainstream psychology, the term *organizational stress* is often used interchangeably with "occupational stress", "workplace stress", and "job stress". We suggest the later terms are perhaps best avoided in a competitive sport context because of the ambiguity often surrounding professional/amateur performers and paid/voluntary personnel that function within sport organizations.

[3] It is worth noting that some organizational psychologists have proposed the term "psychosocial hazards" in preference to *stressors* (and "sources of stress"). This is to bring stress terminology more in line with legislation which governs psychological health at work and the requirements it places on employers relating to risk assessment and the monitoring and control of hazards (see, e.g., Cox, 1993; Rick and Briner, 2000; Rick, Briner, Daniels, Perryman, and Guppy, 2001).

A META-MODEL OF STRESS, EMOTIONS AND PERFORMANCE

The preceding commentary has focused on conceptual and operational issues relating to organizational stress in competitive sport. It is important, however, that definitional debate eventually gives way to a more theoretical- or model-based discussion that provides some insight to help guide inquiry (cf. Popper, 1959). Of course, for theories to aid understanding they require a sound conceptual basis from which models can arise. To this end, scholars have urged researchers investigating stress to employ theoretical models that reflect the sequence of events in transactions (e.g., McGrath, 1970, 1976) and the meaning a person construes from his or her relationship with the environment (e.g., Lazarus, 1998, 1999). Without this conceptual grounding, it is difficult to develop a robust body of knowledge because there are no defined boundaries to be supported or refuted (Cook and Campbell, 1979).

In most instances, theories emerge from a combination of personal intuition, systematic observation, and analytical thinking (Siegrist, 1998). They are conceived to identify those critical components within complex realities that determine outcomes. Gall, Borg, and Gall (1996) defined theory as "an explanation of a certain set of observed phenomena in terms of a system of constructs and laws that relate these constructs to each other" (p. 8). Theoretical models are, therefore, instrumental in illustrating causal relationships among concepts and explaining or predicting variance in observations. They provide not only a platform upon which rational planning can occur but also stimulate systematic lines of inquiry (Levanthal, 1997).

Given the somewhat belated recognition of organizational stress in sport, it is perhaps not surprising that psychologists' understanding of the relationships among organizational stressors, emotional responses, and athletic performance remains limited (Fletcher and Hanton, 2003a). Interestingly, it is also worth noting that while competitive stress researchers have investigated the anxiety-performance relationship in some detail, most of the theoretical models in this area offer little or no explanation of *how* and/or *why* stress-related constructs might affect sport performance (Woodman and Hardy, 2001b). The juxtaposition of these points stimulated Fletcher and Fletcher (2004, 2005) to extensively review the approaches adopted by models which have provided the theoretical context for investigating stress. Following a synthesis of pertinent mainstream and sport psychology theories, they developed a meta-model outlining the relationships among stress, emotions and performance (see Figure 1). It was described as a "meta-model" for a number of reasons. First, it offered a supraordinate and integrative perspective of the stress process and its relationship with human performance. Second, it subsumed the fundamental assumptions and relationships consistent throughout existing theoretical work in this area. Third, it was designed to accommodate the psychological processes that underlie performers' responses to any conceivable situation, thereby encompassing competitive, organizational and personal stressors. Finally, it was intended that it would provide a high degree of explanatory potential for any person functioning in a demanding "performance" environment. Such persons might include athletes, business managers, performing artists, public speakers, and emergency and armed service personnel.

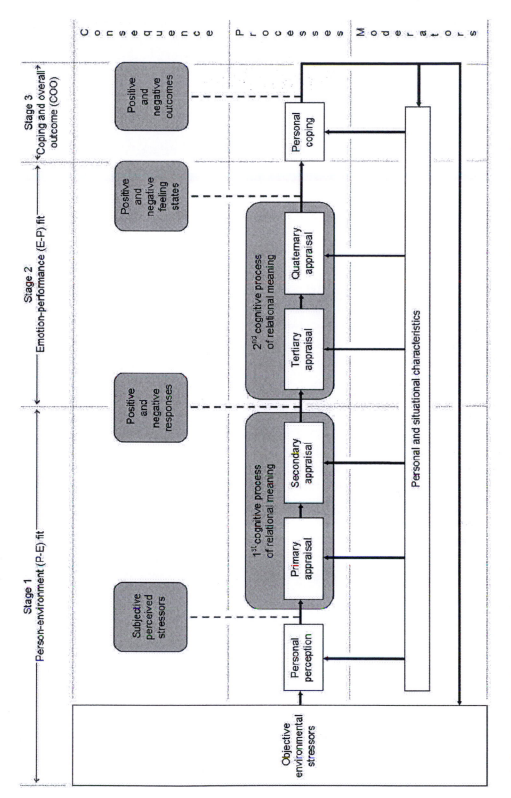

Figure 1. A meta-model of stress, emotions and performance (reproduced with permission from Fletcher and Fletcher, 2004, 2005).

To the best of our knowledge, the meta-model is the first theoretical explanation that was conceived to be readily applicable to the study of organizational stress-related constructs in sport performers. The model's conceptual foundations, theoretical framework, practical implications, and research directions have been discussed in detail elsewhere (see Fletcher and Fletcher, 2004, 2005; Fletcher and Hanton, 2004; see also Mellalieu et al., this volume). This section, therefore, provides an overview of these aspects as they relate to stress in sport organizations.

Conceptual Foundations

Prominent in the development of the meta-model was Lazarus' cognitive-mediational-relational theory of emotions (Lazarus, 1991b, 1993, 1998, 1999, 2000a). Lazarus' theory is based around the notion of relational meaning and the evaluative process of appraisal. According to the theory, relational meaning is the cognitive foundation of emotion, where emotions are the response to appraisal mechanisms. Put simply, the theory relates to how a person thinks about what is happening and how he or she reacts.

In addition to Lazarus' theory, the meta-model drew from the following models from mainstream psychology: the person-environmental (P-E) fit model of stress (Edwards, 1991; French, Rogers, and Cobb, 1974); the stress cycle model (McGrath, 1976); the facet model of occupational stress (Beehr, 1998; Beehr and Newman, 1978; Newman and Beehr, 1979); the cybernetic model of workplace stress (Cummings and Cooper, 1979, 1998; Edwards, 1992, 1998); the job demands-control model of stress (Karasek, 1979); the general systems model of stress (Cox and McKay, 1981); a model of stress and human performance (Sanders, 1983); and the control theory of the job stress process (Spector, 1998). This selection of models was by no means exhaustive, but it did serve to identify a number of common features that reflect the assumptions underpinning contemporary stress theory. Several points of convergence were highlighted, in particular the notion that stress entails a sequence of events that includes: (a) the presence of demands; (b) a set of cognitive processes through which demands are evaluated; and (c) the generation of responses to demands (cf. Cooper et al., 2001; Kahn and Byosiere, 1992). Much of this work is based on the fundamental premise that strain occurs when there is an imbalance or misfit between the environmental demands and personal resources.

The above theories were supplemented with the following models from sport psychology: the notion of directional anxiety interpretations (Jones, 1991; 1995a, 1995b); a conceptual model for integrating arousal construct terminology (Gould and Krane, 1992); a control model of debilitative and facilitative competitive state anxiety (Jones, 1995b); the application of Hanin's individual zones of optimal functioning model to emotions and athletic performance (Hanin, 1997); a model illustrating factors that affect the arousal-performance relationship (Landers and Boutcher, 1998); the application of Lazarus' cognitive-mediational-relational theory of emotions to sport (Lazarus, 2000a, 2000b); and a basic model of stress and coping (Jones, 2002). Although their terminology often differs, these models share a number of key theoretical themes which contributed to the development of the meta-model. Most of these theories are generally congruent with those from mainstream psychology in that they place an emphasis on some kind of cognitive-evaluative process. However, what often distinguishes this work from the previously mentioned models is the attention they give to the relationship between emotions – particularly anxiety – and performance.

Theoretical Framework

The meta-model itself offers a theoretical explanation of the relationships among stress, emotions and performance (see Figure 1). The basic premise being that stressors arise from the environment the performer operates in, are mediated[4] by the processes of perception, appraisal and coping, and, as a consequence, result in positive or negative responses, feeling states, and outcomes. This ongoing process is moderated by various personal and situational characteristics. The meta-model can be divided into three main theoretical stages: (a) person-environment (P-E) fit; (b) emotion-performance (E-P) fit; and (c) coping and overall outcome (COO).

Stage 1: Person-environment (P-E) Fit

This stage focuses on the notion of P-E fit, which is either explicitly or implicitly common to most contemporary theories of psychological stress. It proposes that strain arises not from the person or environment separately, but rather by their misfit or incongruence with one another (Caplan, 1983, 1987a, 1987b; Caplan and Harrison, 1993; Caplan, Cobb, French, Harrison, and Pinneau, 1975; Edwards, 1991, 1996; Edwards, Caplan, and Harrison, 1998; French, Caplan, and Harrison, 1982; French, Rogers, and Cobb, 1974; Harrison, 1978, 1985; Kulka, 1979). Hence, the main point here relates to an individual's ability to manage an encounter, which, of course, represents the essence of a transactional process. Central to this stage are personal perception and an (initial) cognitive process of relational meaning involving the appraisal of stressors resulting in emotional responses.

Before proceeding, it is important to note the distinction between the processes of personal perception and cognitive appraisal, which is a difference seldom stated in the extant literature (Lazarus, 1999). Perception refers to a person's *awareness* of the environment they are operating in and is filtered, modified and supplemented by perceptual distortions (e.g., repression, denial, illusion), construction processes (Weick, 1979), social information (Salancik and Pfeffer, 1978), information processing capabilities (March and Simon, 1958), and organizational structures with limited access to objective information (Caplan, 1987b; Harrison, 1978). Appraisal (or apperception), which will be discussed in more detail later, refers to a person's cognitive *evaluation* of the meaning and significance of a perceived demand (Lazarus, 1966).

Following on from this point, another important distinction is made between objective and subjective representations of environmental stressors (Parasuraman and Alutto, 1981; Spector, 1998, 1999). Objective stressors include competitive, organizational and personal demands as they exist independent of the person's perceptions, whereas subjective stressors refer to those demands that are perceived by the person. Environmental stressors have

---

[4] A *mediator* is defined as a variable that "accounts for the relation between the predictor and the criterion" (Baron and Kenny, 1986, p. 1176). A mediator, therefore, provides a link between one variable and another. In contrast, a *moderator* is a variable that "affects the direction and/or strength of the relation between an independent or predictor variable and a dependent or criterion variable" (Baron and Kenny, 1986, p. 1174). That is, some third factor that exerts an influence on the correlation between two variables.

commonly been conceived by scholars as major life events (see, e.g., Dohrenwend and Dohrenwend, 1974; Holmes and Rahe, 1967; Sarason, Johnson, and Siegel, 1978; Turner and Wheaton, 1995) and daily hassles (see, e.g., Eckenrode and Bolger, 1995; Kanner, Coyne, Schaefer, and Lazarus, 1981; Lazarus, 1984b; Monroe, 1983). Over the past few decades, researchers have attempted to measure and study these phenomena within a sport context (e.g., Albinson and Pearce, 1998; Bramwell, Masuda, Wagner, and Holmes, 1975; Hamilton, Hamilton, Meltzer, Marshall, and Molnar, 1989; Passer and Seese, 1983; Rushall, 1987, 1990; Williams, Tonymon, and Andersen, 1991). Regarding major life events, recent studies have identified the organizational structure and climate as a significant factor affecting elite performers' preparation for, and performance in, the Olympic Games (Gould, Guinan, Greenleaf, Mudbery, and Peterson, 1999; Pensgaard and Duda, 2002). From a slightly different perspective, the role of daily hassles in the development of overtraining syndrome in athletes has also been investigated (Kentta and Hassmen, 1998; Meehan, Bull, Wood, and James, 2004). These findings are particularly interesting in the context of this review because they suggest that both major and relatively "minor" organizational-related events can have a significant impact on athletes' well-being and performance.

The initial work investigating organizational stress in sport did not begin with a clearly defined conceptualization or theoretical model. Indeed, the research did not even begin with a focus on organizational stress at all. Rather, it emerged from the studies mentioned earlier examining "sources of stress" in sport performers (i.e., Gould, Jackson, and Finch, 1993; Scanlan et al., 1991; see also Campbell and Jones, 2002b; Dugdale et al., 2002; Giacobbi, Foore et al., 2004, Giacobbi, Lynn et al., 2004; Holt and Hogg, 2002: James and Collins, 1997; Noblet and Gifford, 2002; Park, 2004). This empirical work revealed a wide range of stressors, including a significant number associated with the sport organization within which the athlete was operating (Hardy and Jones, 1994; Hardy et al., 1996; Jones, 1995b). Stressors identified were broadly related to the following areas: preparation and performance problems; judges decisions and competition organization; coach and teammate influences; coaching, managerial, and administrative decisions; social support; accommodation, travel, nutrition, and training facilities; and financial and time pressures.

Given the likely prominence of sub-optimal group dynamics within these areas, Woodman and Hardy (1998, 2001a) developed a theoretical framework of organizational stress in sport based on Carron's (1982) model of group cohesion. This framework represented the first theoretical inroad into the study of organizational stressors in athletes and highlighted four main stress-related areas: environmental issues, personal issues, leadership issues, and team issues (cf. Carron, 1982). In developing their work, Woodman and Hardy (2001a) interviewed elite performers from a single sport with regard to the organizational stressors they encountered in preparation for major international competitions. The main environmental issues identified were: selection, the training environment, and finances. The main personal issues were: nutrition, injury, and goals and expectations. The main leadership issues were: coaches, and coaching styles. The main team issues were: team atmosphere, support network, roles, and communication. Fletcher and Hanton (Fletcher, 2001; Fletcher and Hanton, 2003b; Hanton et al., 2005) provided considerable support for these findings with samples from a wide range of sports. They also identified a number of additional environmental issues: accommodation, travel, competition environment, and safety. Interestingly, the primary focus of Hanton et al.'s study was the comparison of organizational stressors with competitive stressors in elite performers. Contrary to what the wider literary context might suggest, they found that this population appears to experience (and recall) more stressors associated primarily and directly with the sport organization than with competitive performance. Furthermore, they appear more likely to mention varied organizational stressors but similar competitive stressors, probably because the former are essentially extraneous and widely distributed whereas the latter are, by definition, inherent and endemic to elite sport.

This recent line of inquiry has highlighted organizational stress as an important research domain in contemporary sport psychology and has also provided consultants with a wide range of stressors that athletes' encounter. However, the application of Carron's (1982) model of group cohesion to organizational stress has raised some concerns relating predominately to: (a) the subsequent bias of the framework toward interpersonal dynamics, and (b) the appellation of the different categories within the structure (Fletcher and Hanton, 2003a; see also Bringer, Johnston, and Brackenridge, 2004). In an attempt to overcome these limitations and avoid premature theory building in this area, Fletcher and Hanton (2003a) proposed an alternative framework of organizational stressors in sport performers (see Figure 2). The conceptual foundations of this structure were derived from recent research developments in the fields of organizational behavior (see, for a review, Cooper et al., 2001) and sport psychology (e.g., Fletcher and Hanton, 2003b; Hanton et al., 2005). Specifically, the framework consists of a three-level hierarchical structure of organizational stressors. Based on Cooper et al.'s work, five general dimensions were identified: factors intrinsic to the sport; roles in the sport organization; sport relationships and interpersonal demands; athletic career and performance development issues; and, organizational structure and climate of the sport. Preliminary evidence for the conceptual integrity of the new framework was recently presented in an exploratory study with high-level performers (Hanton and Fletcher, 2003) and a brief report which reflected on potential stressors within each dimension (Hanton and Fletcher, 2005).

While stressors are clearly a salient feature of sport performers' lives, they only reflect one component of the stress process and say little about the evaluative mechanisms underling an encounter. The cognitive process of appraisal is pivotal here (Arnold, 1960; Grinker and Spiegel, 1945; Lazarus, 1964, 1966; Speisman, Lazarus, Mordkoff, and Davison, 1964). As mentioned earlier, appraisal relates to how a person evaluates his or her transactions with the environment. People constantly evaluate the significance of what is happening with respect to its implications for well-being and what might be done about it. In the context of organizational stress in sport, cognitive appraisal involves evaluating the relevance of a stressor, for example a conflict with management, and its personal significance for well-being. If the conflict is considered meaningful, the performer then evaluates whether he or she has the sufficient personal resources available to cope with the stressor. Situational variables that influence the appraisal process include demands, constraints, opportunities and culture. Personal variables include goals and goal hierarchies, beliefs about self and world, and personal resources (Lazarus, 1998, 1999).

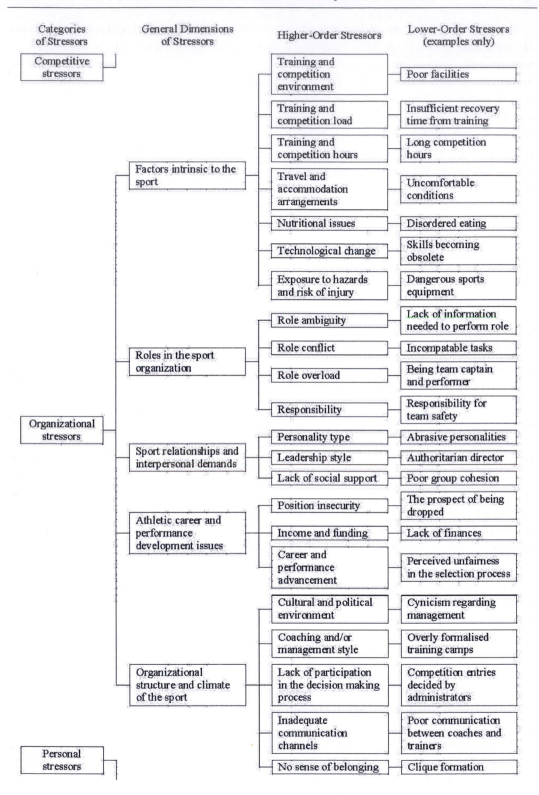

Figure 2. A conceptual framework of organizational stressors in sport performers (adapted with permission from Fletcher and Hanton, 2003a; Hanton and Fletcher, 2003, 2005).

According to Lazarus' (1966) original theory of psychological stress, there are two types of appraisal: primary and secondary. Primary appraisal involves the evaluation of an encounter with regard to whether or not it is relevant to one's values, goal commitments, beliefs about self and world, and situational intentions. During this process, a person considers the implications of what is at stake ("how does this affect me?"), thus giving meaning to an encounter. The meanings that best express a stressful encounter are those involving harm/loss, threat and challenge (Lazarus, 1966, 1981; Lazarus and Folkman, 1984; Lazarus and Launier, 1978). It is important to note that these categories can occur simultaneously in a transaction and should, therefore, only be separated for the convenience of analysis. The term "primary" is used because if the encounter is considered meaningless there is no potential for further cognitive processes. Secondary appraisal begins if meaning is ascribed to an encounter. This process is concerned with the identification and availability of coping resources to deal with the harm/loss, threat and challenge ("what can I do about this?"). Lazarus (1999) emphasized a number of points concerning this stage of the process. First, this mechanism is nothing more than an evaluation of coping options and is not actually the initiation or implementation of coping strategies. Second, the term "secondary" is not intended to connote a process of less importance, but rather an evaluative reaction to the identification of a significant encounter.

Over the past few decades a substantial amount of mainstream psychology research has supported the fundamental premise of Lazarus' appraisal-centered theory of stress and coping (see, for a list of studies, Lazarus, 1999). This literature is supplemented by a growing number of studies in sport psychology that have investigated athletes' appraisals (e.g., Anshel, Jamieson et al., 2001; Campbell and Jones, 2002a; Dugdale et al., 2002; Hammermeister and Burton, 2001; Holt and Dunn, 2004; Kim and Duda, 2003; Lewthwaite, 1990). While this line of inquiry did not specifically examine cognitive-evaluative reactions to organizational stressors, its findings do suggest that such mechanisms may play an important role in this process in sport. For example, Anshel, Jamieson et al. (2001) found that performers who were criticized or reprimanded by a coach reported high levels of threat, moderate levels of harm/loss, and low levels of challenge appraisals. Other research has shown that some anxious endurance athletes evaluate adverse environmental conditions as particularly threatening (Hammermeister and Burton, 2001). In a study of elite male wheelchair basketball players, Campbell and Jones (2002a) found that the demands or costs of the sport, negative coach style/behavior, and relationship issues were more negatively appraised (i.e., threat or harm/loss) than other sources of stress. Other elite performers evaluated unexpected stressors as more threatening than expected stressors (Dugdale et al., 2002), particularly selection-related issues (Holt and Dunn, 2004). Collectively, these findings indicate that the cognitive mechanism of appraisal is central in determining how sport performers react to the stressors they encounter (cf. Anshel, Kim et al., 2001; Burton, 1998; Burton and Naylor, 1997; Gill, 1994; Rotella and Lerner, 1993; Tenenbaum et al., 2003a; see also Anderson and Williams, 1988; Smith, 1980, 1985, 1986).

In developing his theory, Lazarus (1991b, 1993, 1995, 1999; Lazarus and Lazarus, 1994) has increasingly emphasized the role of appraisal in generating emotions, a trend which has been reflected in the sport psychology literature (Gill, 2000; Lazarus, 2000a; Vallerand and Blanchard, 2000; see also Gill, 1994; Gould and Urdy, 1994; Jones, 1995b; Vallerand, 1983). According to this perspective, how a person evaluates a stressor will determine whether or not he or she exhibits a strain reaction. It is generally accepted that there are three major categories of possible stress responses or strain: physiological, psychological and behavioral (Cooper et al., 2001; Kahn and Byosiere, 1992). For the reminder of this subsection we focus on psychological responses; not because they are necessarily the primary or most frequent reactions to organizational stressors, but because of the available space and central focus of this book.

Particularly prominent within this category of responses are the emotions and their associated cognitive and somatic symptoms. Theorists have commonly attempted to classify emotions based upon their affective tone or valence (see, e.g., Ekman, Friesen, and Ellsworth, 1982; Izard, 1977; Lazarus, 1993). Lazarus (1995), for instance, proposed 15 discrete emotions which he grouped together under three main headings: positive emotions (i.e., happiness, pride, relief, love), negative emotions (i.e., anger, anxiety, guilt, shame, sadness, envy, jealousy, disgust), and mixed emotions (i.e., hope, compassion, gratitude). Each emotion "tells a different tale" about how a person appraises the environmental demands he or she encounters (Lazarus, 1999). Factors that influence the generation of emotions include goal relevance, goal congruence, type of ego involvement, options for coping, coping potential, and future expectations. In a recent excursion into the sport psychology literature, Lazarus (2000b) selected a number of emotions (i.e., anger, anxiety, guilt, relief, happiness and pride) that he considered most important in competitive sport and discussed their influence on athletic performance.

Given that models of stress are essentially theories about emotion (Lazarus, 1993), it is perhaps somewhat surprising that the study of emotions within an organizational context is sparse. Indeed, Pekrun, and Frese (1992) began their review of emotions in work and achievement by stating that "there is little research that speaks directly to the issue of work and emotions... organizational psychology *ought* to take the issue of emotions at work more seriously" (p. 153). A number of reasons have been posited for this lack of interest (see, e.g., Briner, 1995; Cooper et al., 2001; Wright and Doherty, 1998). First, in their search for the happy and productive worker, researchers have frequently confounded emotions (e.g., happiness) with attitudes (e.g., job satisfaction). Second, a "myth of rationality" appears to persist whereby behavior is largely viewed in rational-cognitive terms and emotions are regarded as something of an inconvenience. Finally, of all the possible responses to stressors, emotions may be the most difficult to measure and study.

Within the field of sport psychology, there has been a recent surge of theoretical and empirical interest in the topic of emotions (see, e.g., Cerin 2003; Cerin, Szabo, Hunt, and Williams, 2000; Cerin, Szabo, and Williams, 2001; Gauvin and Spence, 1998; Hanin, 1993, 1997, 2000; Mellalieu, 2003; Pensgaard and Duda 2002, 2003; Robazza, this volume). This has served to establish the importance of the emotions in sport and their potential affect on athletes' well-being and performance. This attention has, however, tended to focus on competitive issues as the antecedents of emotional responses. In one of the few published examples of an organizational antecedent, Pensgaard and Duda (2002) relate an occasion when an Olympic champion reacted angrily to a coach's defensive tactics. In another example, Lazarus (2000b) uses interpersonal conflict to illustrate how anger is likely to be a principal emotion in organizational contexts:

> With respect to anger in competitive sports, actions by... [a] referee, ball handler, the spectators, coach, wife, or lover with whom an angry verbal interchange the night before may have deprived the athlete of needed relaxation and sleep, can readily get the athlete's

goat. The object of one's anger is the person whom one blames for an offense and toward whom one wants to exact revenge in order to repair a wounded self-esteem. (p. 243)

Stage 2: Emotion-performance (E-P) Fit

This stage focuses upon the notion of E-P fit which proposes that negative feeling states occur when the relationship between an emotion and performance is out of equilibrium (Fletcher and Fletcher, 2004, 2005). A negative feeling state essentially reflects those emotional responses that are interpreted as debilitative to performance. Hence, the main point here is an individual's ability to deal with his or her cognitive and somatic reactions to stressors which, of course, continues the theme of a transactional relationship. Central to this stage is a (further) cognitive process of relational meaning involving the appraisal of emotions resulting in feeling states.

Sport psychologists are increasingly considering the "orientation" of athletes' emotions in relation to their consequences for performance (cf. Hanin, 1997, 2000; see also Jones, 1991, 1995a, 1995b). In the present context, orientation refers to the nature of emotional responses: that is, will these cognitive and somatic symptoms have a positive or negative effect on performance? Fletcher and Fletcher (2004, 2005) referred to this process as the notion of facilitating and debilitating dimensions of emotional responses or "emotional orientation". This approach is, of course, either explicitly or implicitly common to many conceptualizations of the emotions in sport (see, e.g., Hanin, 1997, 2000; Cerin, 2003; Pensgaard and Duda, 2003), including anger (see, e.g., Isberg, 2000) and anxiety (see, e.g., Burton, 1990; Mahoney and Avener, 1977; Murray, 1989; Parfitt, Jones, and Hardy, 1990; Rotella and Lerner, 1993; Nordell and Sime, 1993; Jones, 1991, 1995a, 1995b). According to Hanin (1997, 2000), emotions can be categorized as positive or negative based on two dimensions: hedonic tone (i.e., pleasantness-unpleasantness) and functional impact (i.e., optimizing-dysfunctional). It is the later of these dimensions which is relevant to the second stage of the meta-model. More specifically, the cognitive mechanism underpinning this dimension involves the interpretation and labeling of an emotion with regard to its effect on performance. Jones (1995b) described such a process as:

> A further level of cognitive appraisal which has the function of interpreting the meaningfulness of the cognitive and physiological symptoms experienced following earlier appraisal of the congruence between situational demands and ability to meet those demands. (p. 463)

Fletcher and Fletcher (2004, 2005) elaborated on this second cognitive process by distinguishing between two additional types of appraisal: tertiary and quaternary. Tertiary appraisal involves the evaluation of an emotion with regard to whether or not it is relevant to one's performance. During this process, a person considers the implications of what is at stake ("how does this emotion and performance affect me?"), thus giving meaning to symptoms. It is important to note that emotions can occur simultaneously in a transaction and should, therefore, only be separated for the convenience of analysis. If an emotion is considered meaningless there is no potential for further cognitive processes. Quaternary appraisal begins if meaning is ascribed to an emotion. This process is concerned with the identification and availability of coping resources to deal with the emotion ("what can I do about this emotion?"). This mechanism is nothing more than an evaluation of coping options and is not actually the initiation or implementation of coping strategies. Furthermore, the terms "tertiary" and "quaternary" are not intended to connote processes of less importance than "primary" and "secondary" appraisal, but rather an interpretative reaction to emotional responses to stressors. Fletcher and Fletcher (2004, 2005) suggested that how a person interprets and labels an emotion with regard to its affect on performance will determine the nature of his or her feeling state. It was hypothesized that performers who have confidence in their ability to control and cope with their emotional responses will experience facilitative feeling states.

Emotional orientations, therefore, refer to how performers interpret their emotions and associated symptoms on a facilitative-debilitative continuum. In an organizational context, one performer might label their anger in response to a conflict with management as having a debilitative effect on performance and, consequently, feel frustrated and in a futile state. Another performer who is also angry due to a similar event might label such an emotional response as facilitative and spur him or her into investing more effort and being more determined, thus resulting in a motivated feeling state (cf. Lazarus, 2000b). Hence, two performers experiencing almost identical emotional responses to their initial appraisal mechanisms might interpret their symptoms at opposite ends of a facilitative-debilitative continuum. Another common organizational-related occurrence is the upheaval of managerial and coaching staff, which often results in changes to funding criteria, team selection, and training programs. Two hypothetical performers, who have the same emotional responses to these events, say, for example, a degree of anxiety about the future, could interpret their symptoms differently with regard to performance. For one individual, the anxiety they are experiencing may result in feelings of apprehension about his or her competitive career, but conversely, the other one may feel excited about his or her performance prospects (cf. Jones, 1995a). In this way, a person's emotional responses and associated symptoms – regardless of whether they are positive or negative reactions to his or her initial appraisal mechanisms – might be positively or negatively orientated with regard to performance, depending on the further level of cognitive appraisal.

It is possible, perhaps even likely, that a feeling state in which symptoms are interpreted as being facilitative to performance bears little resemblance to the initial emotional responses to stressors. The complex cocktail of emotions that a performer is experiencing can potentially be interpreted and labeled in a functional or dysfunctional way depending on the powerful influence of personal and situational characteristics. Such characteristics moderate the processes described above and help account for variance in emotions and feeling states across performers. Put another way, these factors may serve as buffers or exacerbates of P-E and E-P relationships (see Bolger and Zuckerman, 1995; Cohen and Edwards, 1989; Semmer, 1996). Specifically, such variables affect performers' resilience or vulnerability to stressors and help account for the variance in consequences by influencing whether psychological responses are positively or negatively toned.

Of the numerous modifiers identified in the mainstream psychology literature, Type A/B behavior pattern (TABP/TBBP; Ganster, 1987; George, 1992), positive/negative affect (Schaubroeck, Ganster, and Fox, 1992; Spector, Zapf, Chen, and Frese, 2000), hardiness (Orr and Westman, 1990; Kobasa, 1979), self-esteem (Ganster and Schaubroeck, 1995; Pierce, Gardner, Dunham, and Cummings, 1993), and self-confidence and self-efficacy (Jex and Gudanowski, 1992; Schaubroeck and Merritt, 1997) appear to be among the most influential individual difference variables. In addition to those outlined above, several other personality and dispositional factors have been implicated as potential moderators: optimism/pessimism (Chang, 1998); locus of control (Perrewe, 1987); neuroticism (Bolger and Zuckerman, 1995); emotional state (Watson and Clark, 1984); constructive thinking (Epstein and Meier, 1989); hope (Snyder, Harris, Anderson, Holleran, Irving, Sigmon, Yoshinobu, Gibb, Langelle, and Harney, 1991); learned resourcefulness (Rosenbaum, 1990); sense of coherence (Antonovsky, 1987); coping styles (Menaghan, 1983); self-reliance (Quick, Joplin, Nelson, Mangelsdorff, and Fiedler, 1996); alexithymia (Taylor and Bagby, 2000); and perfectionism (Frost and Marten, 1990). Among the situational moderators and other variables that might influence P-E and E-P relationships include: the degree of available autonomy or control (Jones and Fletcher, 1996); social support (Winnubst and Schabracq, 1996); individual physiological susceptibility; gender; and flexibility (see Beehr, 1998; Quick, Quick, Nelson, and Hurrell, 1997).

Interestingly, it is likely that the ubiquitous term, "mental toughness", represents a composite variable which is a conglomerate of the more manifest personal moderators (cf. Dienstbier, 1989; Garmezy and Masten, 1986; Rutter, 1987; Semmer, 1996; Wofford and Daly, 1997; Wofford, Goodwin, and Daly, 1999; Wolff, 1995). To illustrate, performers high in mental toughness might posses more TBBP, more positive affect, more hardiness, more self-esteem, and more self-confidence and self-efficacy, thus inoculating them against the risk of negative consequences. Conversely, performers low in mental toughness might posses more TABP, more negative affect, less hardiness, less self-esteem, and less self-confidence and -efficacy, thus predisposing them to greater risk of negative responses. Mental toughness can, therefore, be defined as "an individual's propensity to manage the demands of environmental stressors, ranging from an absolute resilience to extreme vulnerability" (Fletcher, 2005, p. 1246; Fletcher and Fletcher, 2005, p. 158). It is likely, of course, that the relevance of the moderators that constitute mental toughness will depend on the combination of the different personal, organizational and competitive stressors encountered by a performer in a particular situation. Unfortunately, empirical research investigating these moderators and the notion of mental toughness in relation to organizational stress in sport is virtually nonexistent.

Stage 3: Coping and Overall Outcome (COO)

This stage focuses on coping with stress-related reactions and proposes that negative outcomes occur through the inadequate or inappropriate use of coping strategies (Fletcher and Fletcher, 2004, 2005). Sub-optimal well-being and/or performance is essentially a reflection of an individual's inability to cope. Hence, the main point here relates to an individual's ability to cope with his or her environmental stimuli and personal responses which, of course, continues the theme of a transactional relationship. Central to this stage is the cognitive process of personal coping resulting in overall outcomes.

There is general agreement that coping is a major component of the overall transactional stress process (Aldwin, 2000; Folkman, Lazarus, Dunkel-Schetter, Delongis, and Gruen, 1986; Lazarus and Folkman, 1984). Following a review of the coping literature, Dewe, Cox, and Ferguson (1993) highlighted three main characteristics of coping: (a) *relational* in that it reflects the relationship between a person and the environment (Folkman, 1982); (b) a *process* in contrast to the more traditional trait-context orientated approaches (Cox, 1987, Edwards, 1988, Folkman, Lazarus, Dunkel-Schetter, De Longis, and Gruen, 1986); and (c) *integrative* in nature linking other components of the stress process (Cox and Ferguson, 1991).

Consistent with these themes, they defined coping as "the cognitions and behaviors, adopted by the individual following the recognition of a stressful encounter, that are in some way designed to deal with that encounter or its consequences" (Dewe et al., 1993, p. 7). Hence, coping involves the occurrence of an event which impinges upon the person, appraisal of that event as threatening to oneself, and the engagement of cognitive or behavioral strategies to remove or alleviate the threat (O'Driscoll and Cooper, 1994).

The most common approach to studying coping can be described as taxonomic, where researchers attempt to categorize coping strategies based upon the focus of a particular cognition or behavior. Lazarus and Folkman (1984) differentiate between two major coping strategies: (a) *problem-focused*, in which an individual attempts to deal with the environmental demands he or she encounters and (b) *emotion-focused*, in which an individual attempts to deal with his or her emotional responses to stressors. This is captured in the meta-model where coping strategies focus on eliminating or reducing the quantity, frequency and/or intensity of the demands or on modifying individuals' responses through altering personal or situational moderators resulting in a more favorable reappraisal of the stressors.

The functions of coping in the organizational stress process have been the focus of considerable interest to mainstream psychology researchers. The extant literature generally goes well beyond the mere description of coping strategies by delineating the conditions under which different strategies are employed and assessing the effectiveness of such strategies. However, because the literature on coping with organizational stress is so diverse and voluminous, the interested reader is directed to relevant reviews of this area for more information (e.g., Dewe et al., 1993; Newton, 1989; O'Driscoll and Cooper, 1994). Within the sport psychology literature, the process of coping has attracted increasing attention in recent years (see, e.g., Anshel, Kim et al., 2001; Crocker, Kowalski, and Graham, 1998; Hardy et al., 1996; Hoar, Kowalski, Gaudreau, and Crocker, this volume). This interest has tended to focus on performers' ability to cope with competitive-related demands and emotions (see, e.g., Campen and Roberts, 2001; Crocker and Graham, 1995; Hammermeister and Burton, 2001; Holt and Dunn, 2004; Kim and Duda, 2003; Krohne and Hindel, 1988; Nicholls, Holt, & Polman, 2005; Williams and Krane, 1992), although a significant number of studies have touched on coping in organizational-related contexts such as environmental conditions, training programs, travelling arrangements, injury rehabilitation, expectations and pressure, interpersonal relationships with coaches and teammates, and communication with the media and officials (see, e.g., Anshel and Delany, 2001; Anshel, Jamieson et al., 2001; Crocker, 1992; Crocker and Isaak, 1997; Dugdale et al., 2002; Gould, Eklund, and Jackson, 1993; Gould, Finch, and Jackson, 1993; Hanson, McCullagh, and Tonymon, 1992; Holt and Hogg, 2002; Madden, Kirkby, and McDonald, 1989; Madden, Summer, and Brown, 1990; Nicholls, Holt, Polman, & James, 2005). Collectively, the findings suggest that sport performers use a wide range of strategies to cope with organizational stressors and strain. These include multiple problem- and emotion-focused strategies which are often used in combination with one another. There is also some evidence to show that different strategies are used to deal with organizational stressors compared to competitive stressors. Furthermore, these strategies may be related to the specific demands encountered by the performer. Finally, coping strategies are often so well learned that some performers automatically execute them in response to particular organizational-related events.

Depending largely on the usage and effectiveness of coping strategies, a wide range of positive or negative overall outcomes may occur. For example, lack of effective stress management may lead to significant decrements in well-being, feelings of disengagement from the sport, dissatisfaction, and reduced athletic performance (Burton, 1990; Hardy et al., 1996; Schmidt and Stein, 1991). Prolonged maladaptive coping may ultimately induce a chronic, highly debilitating form of strain know as burnout (Cordes and Dougherty, 1993; Hobfoll and Shirom, 1993; Smith, 1986). Conversely, effective stress management may lead to significant increases in well-being, sport satisfaction, self-esteem, and enhanced athletic performance (Aldwin, 2000; Aldwin and Stokols, 1988; Antonovsky, 1987; Dienstbier, 1989; Eysenck and Calvo, 1992; Fay, Sonnentag, and Frese, 1998; Folkman and Moskowitz, 2000; Hardy, 1990, 1997, 1998; Hardy and Fazey, 1987; Hardy et al., 1996; Humphreys and Revelle, 1984; Ickovics and Park, 1998; Lazarus, 2000b, 2000c; Mahoney and Avener, 1977; Masters, 1992; Wegner, 1989, 1994, 1997; Woodman and Hardy, 2001b). Prolonged adaptive coping may ultimately lead to experiences of flow, resonance and self-actualization (Jackson and Csikszentmihalyi, 1999; Maslow, 1968; Newburg, Kimiecik, Durand-Bush, and Doell, 2002).

Unfortunately, there are virtually no studies investigating the psychological and performance-related outcomes of organizational stress in sport. In the first of two notable exceptions, Noblet, Rodwell, and McWilliams (2003) found that job control and work support were significant predictors of job satisfaction in professional Australian footballers and that social support has a significant impact on both job satisfaction and psychological health outcomes. In the second, Fletcher and Hanton (2003c) examined the mechanisms by which organizational stress might affect sport performance. They found that poorly managed organizational issues were generally detrimental to performance via three possible routes: concentration disruption, maladaptive emotional responses, and dysfunctional changes in activation levels. These findings add empirical support to recent theoretical advances which state that emotions can affect performance via complex changes in cognitive, motivational and attentional functioning (see Botterill and Brown, 2002; Cerin et al., 2000; Hanin, 1997, 2000; Janelle, 2002; Jones, 2003; Lazarus, 2000b; Mellalieu, 2003; Vallerand and Blanchard, 2000).

Practical Implications

Despite the growing recognition that organizational stress can potentially affect athletes' well-being and performance, the amount of attention given by sport organizations and psychologists to addressing this issue has been limited, particularly when compared to the strategies designed to deal with competitive stress (see, e.g., Anshel, in press; Burton, 1990; Hardy et al., 1996). Moreover, researchers have commented on the general lack of congruence that often exists between applied practices and theoretical and empirical work in this area of performance enhancement (see, e.g., Fletcher and Hanton, 2003a, 2004; Hanton and Fletcher, 2005; Hanton and Jones, 1999a, 1999b; Hardy et al., 1996; Jones and Hardy, 1990). They have argued for a more cogent approach to stress management in sport, one that is underpinned by a rational evidence-based philosophy.

To this end, Fletcher and Hanton (2004) further developed the meta-model by superimposing a multi-intervention framework for understanding stress management in performance environments (see Figure 3). The overlay of this structure helps bridge the gap between theory and practice and also facilitates knowledge transfer from mainstream psychology (e.g., Briner and Reynolds, 1999; Cooper et al., 2001; Murphy, 1995; Murphy, Hurrell, Sauter, and Keita, 1995; Quick and Quick, 1997; Quick, Quick, and Nelson, 1998). As a result, Fletcher and Hanton (2003a, 2004) argued that efforts to manage the stress process in performers can be differentiated by: (a) the level at which an intervention occurs (i.e., primary, secondary, tertiary); (b) the scope of the intervention activity; (c) its target; and (d) the assumptions underlying each intervention (Cooper et al., 2001; Quick and Quick, 1997; see also Last, 1988; Winett, 1995). Although the levels of intervention outlined in Figure 3 are designed to manage any of the potential stressors that performers may encounter, the remainder of this subsection will focus on their application in sport-related organizational settings.

Primary interventions are based on the assumption that the most effective way to combat strain is to eliminate or at least reduce the quantity, frequency and/or intensity of organizational stressors, hence alleviating the overall demand placed upon sport performers. This type of intervention is the most proactive and preventative approach to stress management and involves altering training and competition environments, technologies, or organizational structures. Examples include: rule changes, role restructuring, organizational restructuring, profiling the organization, and educational workshops. Secondary interventions focus on stress management training to modify sport performers' psychological responses to stressors, rather than adapting the organizational conditions. These interventions aim primarily to increase performers' awareness of their stress-related reactions and to enhance their resiliency to stressors through "mental toughness" training programs. Examples include: stress management training, communication and information sharing, "wellness" programs, contingency planning incorporating "what if?" scenarios, and simulation training. Tertiary interventions are concerned with minimizing the damaging consequences of stressors by helping athletes cope more effectively with reduced well-being or performance as a result of strain. These interventions focus on the rehabilitation and treatment of problems once they have occurred. Examples include: performer assistance programs, clinical counseling, and educational coping programs.

These levels of intervention are, of course, not mutually exclusive and to some extent there is overlap between the different strategies. For example, Cooper et al. (2001) describe how conflict resolution sessions may be useful for preventing the onset or development of interpersonal conflict (i.e., primary intervention) and/or confronting and dealing with conflict after it has already surfaced (i.e., secondary intervention). Nevertheless, this framework presents a systematic approach to stress management that can aid consultants in optimizing well-being and performance in athletes. Clearly, the choice of approach will have a significant impact on the efficacy of interventions and such strategies need to be tailored to address the specific issues manifested within a sport organization.

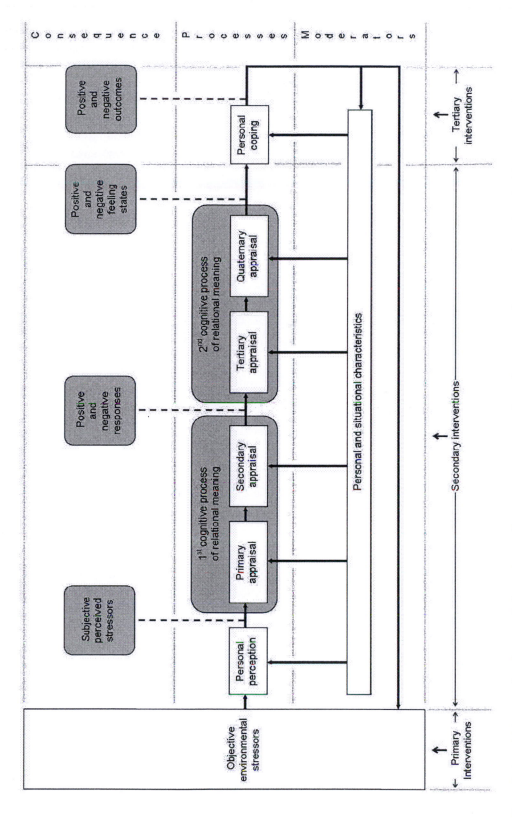

Figure 3. A multi-intervention framework for understanding stress management in performance environments (reproduced with permission from Fletcher and Hanton, 2004).

At this juncture, it is worth exploring some of the practical issues and guidelines relating to the implementation of stress management interventions. Burton's (1990) observation that "stress management is a topic that is easier to theorize about than to apply effectively" (p. 171) is particularly pertinent in the context of this discussion. The climate within sport organizations is often characterized by a skepticism of psychological support, particularly if senior management suspect that an assessment may portray an unfavorable picture of the organization. Hence, given the often sensitive nature of organizational-related issues, consultants should continually emphasize that a greater understanding of this area can provide a positive stimulus for change (Fletcher and Hanton, 2003b; Woodman and Hardy, 2001a). Despite the potential benefits, a psychologist working in a sport organization should not lose sight of the fact that this is one of the most demanding of environments:

> The psychology professional wishing to consult for a sport organization faces an often daunting and confusing task. There are few areas where psychological consultation presents the challenges that are to be found in the sport world. (Perna, Neyer, Murphy, Ogilvie, and Murphy, 1995, p. 235)

There are many reasons why difficulties may arise when attempting to implement organizational-level stress management interventions. These appear to relate predominately to a historical emphasis of placing the onus for stress management on athletes, senior management's beliefs about the impact of the organizational environment on performers, and the financial, legal and political repercussions of making organizational-level changes (Acosta Hernández, 2002; Fletcher and Hanton, 2003a; Hardy et al., 1996). On the occasions when systematic stress management has been evident in sport, the focus has tended to be on psychological skills training to tackle performers' anxiety responses associated with competitive performance (e.g., Hanton and Jones, 1999b; Mamassis and Doganis, 2004). Our intention here is not to undervalue such individual-orientated approaches but simply to highlight that these may not be sufficient in combating all aspects of stress experienced by performers. It may be that this situation has arisen due to the heavy bias that currently exists in many sport psychology certification programs toward psychological skills training and performance enhancement techniques (Hanton and Fletcher, 2005; Woodman and Hardy, 2001a). Another contributory factor may be that, from a managerial perspective, such strategies are often less costly and can be more readily implemented than longer-term organizational restructuring. Interestingly, Cooper et al. (2001) also suggested that, in the business domain, fear of litigation might have resulted in management abnegating their responsibilities in an attempt to circumvent the legal and political ramifications of excessive organizational strain. Regardless of the specific underlying reasons, a climate and culture has prevailed in sport where organizations have tended to resist change when it involved alterations to their practices and procedures.

When this observation is considered in relation to recent empirical findings (i.e., Hanton et al., 2005), it becomes evident that consultants will probably need to exercise a degree of flexibility and pragmatism to optimize the effectiveness of their work. To elaborate, as mentioned earlier, Hanton et al.'s work indicates that whereas competitive stressors are, not surprisingly, inherent and endemic to elite sport, organizational stressors are, on the other hand, essentially extraneous and widely distributed. Hence, they went on to argue that it may be judicious for consultants to focus on secondary level interventions to restructure performers' responses to competitive stressors and, in contrast, to focus on primary interventions to reduce organizational stressors. However, while it is certainly important to tailor interventions to meet the specific demands encountered by performers, it is also important to balance this need with the constraints imposed by the managerial politics that exist within sport organizations. Furthermore, organizational stress management is not solely about attempting to eliminate stressors. Consultants need to appreciate the ever-changing nature of environments and that some organizational demands are an unavoidable part of contemporary sport. Organizational stress management interventions must also enable performers to develop their own personal resources and enhance their "mental toughness" to cope with stressors and strain. Indeed, it may be that positive consequences result from such an approach:

> Some organizational stress is both inevitable and desirable. The intent of preventative stress management is to maximize eustress and performance, is to minimize distress, but not to eliminate stress. While this is an ongoing process, people at work need not be left with the problem of Sisyphus, king of Corinth in Greek mythology. Sisyphus was left in a state of perpetual, hopeless, joyless struggle after he tricked Death and was condemned to push a rock endlessly up a hill, only to have the rock always roll back down before the task was finished. (Quick et al., 1998, p. 265)

Findings from mainstream psychology indicate that organizational-level interventions are generally most effective when implemented systematically and as a result of careful monitoring of the environment (Burke, 1993; Ivancevich and Matteson, 1987; Murphy, 1988). The processes of assessment and evaluation are critical here. In terms of conducting an organizational level "stress audit", an interdisciplinary approach that utilizes techniques from psychology, physiology and medicine is likely to provide to the most complete picture of the organization and its influences. It should also be emphasized that assessment is an ongoing process involving continued analysis, rather than intermittent snapshot evaluations. Diagnostic methods could include self-monitoring, behavioral observation, self-report inventories, survey questionnaires, interviews, and organizational profiling. Turning to the process of evaluation, a wide range of surveillance indicators and research methods can be employed to assess the impact of stress management interventions on organizational stress-related consequences. These methods should, of course, not only be valid, reliable and feasible but also produce findings that are understandable and meaningful to executive boards and managerial committees (see, e.g., Woodman and Hardy, 1997). A fundamental feature of these recommendations will likely be the establishment and maintenance of communication lines and a dismantling of policies that stimulate, rather than help to alleviate, the negative consequences of organizational stress. Strategies should encourage supportive organizational norms, which recognize that the experience of stress is not a sign of performer weakness or incompetence. The importance of involving athletes and coaches in this process should not be underestimated. An active participation in the stress management process, which promotes greater individual control over the organizational environment, has been repeatedly emphasized in the mainstream psychology literature (Murphy, 1995; Schurman and Israel, 1995).

Finally, in view of the points raised here, the authors concur with Ravizza's (1988) recommendation that consultants should pay careful attention to the constantly unfolding "organizational politics" within contemporary sport. Of central importance is identifying the key decision-makers within an organization and the personnel (e.g., performance directors) whose input will likely influence any potential interventions. It is also worth noting who within the organization is receptive to psychological support (Hardy et al., 1996). The extent of commitment from all layers of the organization – the executive board, managerial committees, technical and support staff, coaches, athletes – to alleviating the negative consequences of stress is critical to the success of stress management interventions. However, as Hardy et al. (1996) pointed out, consultants should tread carefully in the milieu of organizational politics and not confuse an informed awareness with over involvement:

> Effective consultants, then, must become politically astute so they can understand and hopefully circumvent potential politically based problems. However, in the authors' experience, it is usually a grave mistake for consultants to become involved in organizational politics, so being politically astute certainly should not be interpreted as meaning being politically active. (pp. 292-293)

To summarize, the practical implications of the meta-model offer a rational evidence-based approach to understanding stress management in performance environments. Consultants' efforts to implement such interventions will be more effective if a number of steps are taken. These include: (a) identification of potential organizational stressors; (b) thorough assessment of the levels of organizational strain experienced by performers; and (c) implementation of interventions designed to resolve problems and deal with symptoms (Cooper et al., 2001). The challenge remains to convince personnel of the advantages of systematic stress management that benefits not only athletes' well-being and performance, but also the sport organization as a whole.

Research Directions

To conclude this section, we suggest some directions for future research in this area. These suggestions are not intended to be exhaustive, nor are they presented in any specific order of importance, but they do highlight what we believe are the key issues to be addressed if psychologists are to further their understanding of organizational stress in sport. In light of the foregoing discussion, the majority of these research questions can be categorized under five main areas: (a) objective and subjective stressors, (b) appraisal mechanisms relating to responses and feeling states, (c) personal and situational characteristics that moderate the process, (d) coping processes and strategies, and (e) effects on well-being and performance.

Objective and Subjective Stressors

There is considerable debate in the mainstream psychology literature about whether organizational stressors should be studied objectively or subjectively (see, e.g., Spector, 1999). From an objective standpoint, it is argued that certain stressors transcend individual cognitions and, therefore, attention should focus on establishing a consensus on which events represent significant stressors. On the other hand, the subjective position emphasizes that it is a person's perception and appraisal of a stimulus that is the critical factor in determining its potential significance. It is likely, of course, that progress will only be made in this area by examining the implications of both objective and subjective aspects of the stress process

(Cooper et al., 2001; Spector, 1999). Future researchers in sport psychology may also wish to investigate the different properties of stressors, such as the intensity (high vs. low demand; Cooper et al., 2001), duration (acute vs. chronic; Anshel, Kim et al., 2001; Elliot and Eisdorfer, 1982), prevalence (frequent vs. infrequent occurrence, Fletcher and Hanton, 2003b), quantity (many vs. few demands; Hanton et al., 2005), and other aspects such as the timing (e.g., competition vs. training settings; Fletcher and Hanton, 2003b), specificity (specific vs. global demand; Fletcher and Hanton, 2003b), closeness (proximal vs. distal to the individual; Jessor, 1981), and weighting (additive or multiplicative; Cooper et al., 2001). Finally on the topic of stressors, two other important areas of study are (a) the interface between, and (b) the interactive impact of competitive, organizational and personal stressors (Hanton et al., 2005). To elaborate briefly, it is likely that managing the interface between these categories of stressors places further demands on performers (cf. O'Driscoll, 1996), particularly for those competing at a subelite or amateur standard. Furthermore, the combined effect of all the different stressors encountered by performers needs to be considered because, as Cooper et al. (2001) pointed out, "the whole (effect) may well be more than the sum of the parts!" (p. 53).

Appraisal Mechanisms Relating to Responses and Feeling States

The meta-model points to two processes of relational meaning that link the performer to the environment. These are operationalized in terms of cognitive-evaluative appraisal mechanisms. Further research efforts are needed to explore the explanatory potential of these concepts and their role in the stress process in sport. In terms of performers' responses to organizational stressors, future research should consider adopting an interdisciplinary approach, combining information from psychometric testing (e.g., self-report measures), behavioral analysis (e.g., observational techniques), and physiological indices (e.g., blood pressure, catecholamines and cortisol levels). From a psychological perspective, it is important that researchers consider the distinction between what has been described as display rules (emotions that are expected to be expressed) and feeling rules (emotions that should be felt). Put simply, performers functioning in a sport organizations may express certain appropriate, organizationally desired emotions, which are different from the emotions actually being felt (cf. Ashforth and Humphrey, 1993; Briner, 1995; Rafaeli and Sutton, 1987). It is also worth examining in greater detail the intensity and frequency of emotional responses (cf. Brief and Weiss, 2002; Fisher, 2002; Pekrun and Frese, 1992) and how these dimensions mediate emotional orientations. Given the likely complexity of these relationships, it appears that identifying how performers' responses interact and give rise to feeling states presents a challenging, but potentially fruitful, line of work for future researchers.

Personal and Situational Characteristics that Moderate the Process

The potential influences of the organizational stress process can be considered under two broad categories: (a) personality and dispositional variables, and (b) situational and social variables. It is important that future researchers examine these areas because developing adaptive characteristics and climates will likely play an important role in helping performers deal with organizational stressors that cannot be changed and hence have to be "lived with". Findings from mainstream psychology suggest that some of the most influential individual difference variables include: Type A/B behavior pattern (TABP/TBBP; Ganster, 1987;

George, 1992); positive/negative affect (Schaubroeck, Ganster, and Fox, 1992; Spector, Zapf, Chen, and Frese, 2000); hardiness (Orr and Westman, 1990; Kobasa, 1979); self-esteem (Ganster and Schaubroeck, 1995; Pierce, Gardner, Dunham, and Cummings, 1993); self-confidence and self-efficacy (Jex and Gudanowski, 1992; Schaubroeck and Merritt, 1997); the degree of available autonomy or control (Jones and Fletcher, 1996); and social support (Winnubst and Schabracq, 1996). One important issue to consider in this area of research is the possible confounding of effects due to a lack of conceptual differentiation and measurement redundancy between such variables as optimism, self-esteem, negative affectivity, and neuroticism (Cooper et al., 2001). Researchers examining the significance of mental toughness in sport will need to demonstrate that composite constructs exert direct and interactive influences on the stress process. Hence, a complete understanding of mental toughness and moderator effects can only be obtained if they are studied within the context of a transactional conceptualization of stress.

Coping Processes and Strategies

Despite the accumulated knowledge on coping generated by mainstream and sport psychology researchers, there is still little known about the specific strategies that athletes use to cope with organizational stress. For researchers wishing to explore this area, their first priority should be to develop coping classifications systems that take into account not just the focus (problem vs. emotion) of a particular strategy but also its form (cognitive or behavioral) and the variety of different strategies used (Latack and Havlovic, 1992). Some potential research areas include: (a) the coping strategies used with specific organizational stressors, (b) the effectiveness of such strategies, (c) the personal and situational characteristics which moderate the use of strategies in organizational contexts, (d) the mediational properties of coping in the organizational stress process, and (e) the relationship between coping and performers' well-being and performance. Finally, sport psychologists should ensure that their research designs clearly reflect the conceptual distinction between coping "behaviors" and "styles". Cooper et al. (2001) hypothesized that specific behaviors function as mediators between stressor-strain relationships, with dispositional styles moderating the strength of this relationship.

Effects on Well-being and Performance

A fundamental issue pervading stress research in general is the effect of strain responses on human performance. It behooves sport psychology researchers to examine the mechanisms by which stress responses might affect sport performance (Fletcher and Hanton, 2003c) and how much performance variance might be accounted for by organizational strain (Woodman and Hardy, 2001a). Researchers working in this area should be wary of potential physiological, biomechanical and tactical confounds that may threaten the internal validity of their studies. For example, a performer may identify a lack of food or inappropriate diet as a correlate of poor performance at a competition, but the question remains as to what extent performance decrement is due to psychological mechanisms relating to dysfunctional responses, or physiological mechanisms relating to glycogen depletion (Fletcher and Hanton, 2003c). Other issues that warrant more systematic investigation relate to the impact of organizational strain on psychological health (Noblet et al., 2003), athletic burnout (cf. Smith, 1986), and overtraining syndrome (Meehan et al., 2004). Greater attention needs to be given to the specific nature of the stressor-strain relationships that are instrumental in affecting the overall outcomes of the process. For example, dissatisfaction with the sport (or aspects of the organization) may have a differential impact on performers who vary in terms of sport involvement. It may be that sport dissatisfaction is more salient for elite athletes whose performance is central to their self-esteem than for nonelite athletes whose performance is peripheral. Future research needs to clearly define the impact of organizational strain on a range of psychological and performance indices.

In addition to these main areas, scholars may wish to further examine the fundamental theoretical tenets of the meta-model. Fletcher and Fletcher (2004) acknowledged that a potential limitation of the model concerns the validity of the linear stage framework evident within its structure. Jones (1990) recognized this potential drawback in stress-performance models over a decade ago when he provocatively posed the question, "do sports performers process information in a strict serial manner, so that a stage becomes passive once it has processed information and passed it on to the next stage?" (p. 37). Indeed, while it has been argued that "the one-dimensional scheme can be used as a frame of reference for interpreting when and how a second dimension operates" (Sanders, 1980, p. 335), more recent evidence from cognitive neuroscience indicates that sequential, unitary approaches are rather simplistic and that parallel, multiple processes offer a more ecologically valid conceptualization (Gazzaniga, 1989; Ornstein and Thompson, 1984). For scholars working in this area, parallel distributive processing theory may be instructive (Hinton, 1992; McClelland, Rumelhart, and the PDP Research Group, 1987; Rogers, and McClelland, 2004; Rumelhart, McClelland, and the PDP Research Group, 1987; Scientific American, 1999). This theory is grounded in models of networked knowledge – sometimes known as "neural networks" or "connectionism" – and posits that the activation of a single brain node stimulates pathways to other nodes, and so forth. In this way, node activity spreads and can occur simultaneously in multiple parts of the brain, with ongoing *processing* occurring in *parallel* and being *distributed* via neural connections throughout the cognitive system. Aldwin's (2000) comments on hemispheric brain functioning suggest that such an approach may have utility in refining the meta-model and, therefore, enhancing psychologists' understanding of performers ongoing appraisals of demands *and* responses:

> If emotional processing is mediated more by the right hemisphere, and rational processing by the left hemisphere, then it should not be surprising that both mechanisms are involved and that one can inform the other... (p. 41)

The adaptation of the meta-model to accommodate recent developments in cognitive neuroscience would offer, in the authors' opinion, something of a middle ground in the cognition-emotion debates of stress reactions (see Ellis, 1985; Lazarus, 1981, 1982, 1984a 1991a; Parkinson, and Manstead, 1992; Zajonc, 1980, 1984). On the one hand, Lazarus (1981, 1982, 1984a 1991a) argued that the cognitive process of appraisal is primary in determining an individual's emotional responses. On the other hand, Zajonc (1980, 1984) argued that emotional responses occur before, and may be at odds with, the cognitive process of appraisal. Hence, if the two processes of relational meaning in the meta-model operate in parallel then it is likely that *both* cognitions and emotions can simultaneously occupy primary positions in the stress process. Put simply, in any instant a performer is thinking and responding, and *also* experiencing emotions and reacting to them.

Such theoretical advances are likely to open up further avenues of inquiry relating to the level and speed of cognitive processing in sport performers (cf. LeDoux, 1995; Murphy, 2001). Lazarus (1999) has argued that appraisal mechanisms can operate at a conscious or unconscious level, and over time or instantaneously:

> ...there are two main contrasting ways an appraisal can come about. First, the process of appraising can be deliberate and largely conscious. Second, it can be intuitive, automatic, and unconscious. The distinction is important because the circumstances of appraising vary greatly. Sometimes an appraisal requires a slow, deliberate search for information on which to predicate how we should react, especially about what can be done to cope with one's predicament. At other times, a very rapid appraisal is called for. (p. 82)

Interestingly, it has been argued that these two modes operate in an often simultaneous and parallel fashion, and may in fact be contradictory (Aldwin, 2000; Lazarus, 1999; Lazarus, and commentators, 1995). The proposal that there may be two conflicting appraisals at the same time appears to provide a cognitive explanation as to why an athlete may experience primarily negative emotional responses to a stressor (e.g., anger, anxiety), and yet simultaneously be able to maintain an overall positive feeling state in terms of their outlook on performance (e.g., anticipatory excitement). Indeed, this notion is well-supported by the literature addressing multiple affective systems (e.g., Cacioppo, Gardner, and Berntson, 1999; Davidson, 1992; Gray, 1994) and meta-moods (e.g., Mayer and Gaschke, 1988; Mayer, Salovey, Gomberg-Kaufman, and Blainey, 1991; Mayer and Stevens, 1994). Unraveling the complexities of parallel cognitive processing and the levels at which it may occur represents one of the major challenges for sport psychologists investigating the stress-emotion-performance relationship.

Finally, we conclude this section with a selection of research questions that are particularly worthy of further investigation if psychologists are to gain a more comprehensive understanding of organizational stress in sport:

- What are the experiences of organizational stress in "non-performing" personnel (Woodman and Hardy, 2001a), such as coaches (cf. Kelley, 1994; Kelley, Eklund, and Ritter-Taylor, 1999; Taylor, 1992), managers and directors (cf. Busser, 1990; Byers, 1987; Copeland and Kirsch, 1995; Martin, Kelley, and Eklund, 1999), support team professionals (cf. Reid, Stewart, and Thorne, 2004; Sullivan and Nashman, 1998), and officials, referees and umpires (cf. Anshel and Weinberg, 1995; Rainey, 1995, 1999; Rainey and Hardy, 1999)?
- What are the characteristics and qualities of optimally functioning organizations (Fletcher and Hanton, 2003b; Weinberg and McDermott, 2002)? What are the most effective strategies for managing organizational stress in sport settings (Woodman and Hardy, 2001a)? To what extent can consultants teach performers the necessary skills to cope with organizational stress (cf. Dewe et al., 1993)? What methodological designs are most appropriate for the evaluation of organizational stress management interventions (cf. Beehr and O'Hara, 1987; Hanton and Fletcher, 2005)?

CONCLUDING REMARKS

This chapter has reviewed literature on organizational stress from the fields of mainstream and sport psychology in order to reflect on what this work can tell us about stress in sport organizations. This discussion helps to focus attention on the important conceptual and theoretical issues relating to organizational stress in competitive sport, how such issues affect performers, and the role psychologists can play in better understanding the nature of this phenomenon. Also, this review has hopefully provided the groundwork for scholars and academics in their efforts to identify future areas of fertile research. While many issues arise from the preceding discussion, there are two questions particularly worthy of consideration:

What Methodologies Should we Employ to Investigate Organizational Stress in Sport?

A critical concern for researchers is to ensure that their work captures the complex and dynamic nature of the stress process in sport organizations. The conceptual stance adopted in this chapter has viewed stress as relational in nature, involving ongoing transactions between the performer and the environment. This theme was developed within the meta-model, in which a series of cognitive-evaluative processes were outlined to best express the relational-transactional nature of stress in performance environments. Hence, if understanding organizational stress in sport is best advanced by exploring individual appraisals and subjective meanings, then researchers must utilize methods that capture the contextual richness of such processes and the idiographic nature of the stress experience. This raises an important question of whether the prevailing research methodologies in sport psychology, based largely on cross-sectional designs, satisfactorily capture the dynamics of this process. Indeed, Spicer (1997) argued that rather than addressing the notion of a transaction, traditional research methods employed in mainstream psychology simply reflect an interactional perspective of stress where the various structural components (stressors, strain, and coping) are operationalized as static constructs.

In contrast, the transactional conceptualization suggests that research needs to explore the ongoing interplay that exists among stress-related constructs and examine the possibility of multidirectional (mutual) causality. Given the complexity of such relationships, longitudinal, prospective, and microanalytic approaches would appear to be among some of most effective research strategies because they provide an opportunity to clarify casual relationships that are otherwise indeterminable through cross-sectional analysis (see Kahn and Byosiere, 1992; Lazarus, 2000c). Cooper et al. (2001) suggested that such approaches are probably best operationalized through multivariate analysis and qualitative techniques to expand the scope of research and generate a richer understanding of the organizational stress process.

How do We Measure Organizational Stress in Sport?

Measurement is an important aspect of the scientific method and, as Fletcher and Hanton (2003b) pointed out, it will be very difficult to make significant advances in sport psychologists' understanding of this area without valid and reliable measures. While there are a number of inventories which assess organizational-related issues in a sport context (see, e.g., Albinson and Pearce, 1998; Bramwell et al., 1975; Rushall, 1987, 1990), these instruments have rarely been exposed to rigorous psychometric testing or employed in systematic research programs. Hence, it appears that researchers are now at a critical stage in building a body of knowledge; namely, that there exists an urgent need to develop a comprehensive measure of organizational stress in sport performers.

Of paramount importance in the progress toward such a measure is the establishment of validity, reliability, relevancy, sensitivity and stability criteria. While space unfortunately precludes a discussion of these issues, it is worth highlighting some key implications that researchers will need to pay careful attention to: (a) the nature and content of items, (b) the scoring of response scales, and (c) the manner in which psychometrics are established (cf. Cooper et al., 2001; Dewe, 2000). Given the conceptual ambiguity that has existed in this area, researchers must be particularly wary of measurement confounding and ensure that inventories do not purport to assess one construct (e.g., a stressor) when in reality they tap into another (e.g., a strain).

In conclusion, this chapter has discussed a wide range of issues and challenges facing sport psychologists and organizations in the early years of the twenty-first century. Consideration has been given to the ever-changing context in which performers function, in particular how sociocultural, political, economic, occupational and technological forces shape sport organizations and how they in turn can affect athletes' well-being and performance. While experiencing some organizational demands is an unavoidable aspect of contemporary sport, there is much that can be done to influence the consequences and overall outcomes of this phenomenon at both an individual and organizational level. Only a concerted effort from the sport community as whole will result in sustained improvements in the well-being and performance of athletes, sport organizations and ultimately the societies in which they live and function. However, the damaging consequences of neglecting these issues are, according to Acosta Hernández (2002), likely to only be matched by their far-reaching impact:

> The worst enemy of a sport organization today is neither another sport organization, nor another sport, nor the social environment, nor the athletes, nor even their critics or opponents; public enemy number one is the local organizational structure and the sport organization itself... Inertia, combined with a lack of organizational structure, the absence of administrative procedures, and the ineptitude of managers, will not only destroy the sport organization itself but also the sport movement as we know is today. (p. 7)

ACKNOWLEDGEMENTS

This review is part of an ongoing program of work currently being undertaken by the authors addressing conceptual and measurement issues within the context of stress and anxiety in sport. We would like to thank Mr. Jim Fletcher for his insightful comments on earlier drafts of this chapter.

REFERENCES

Acosta Hernández, R. (2002). *Managing sport organizations*. Champaign, IL: Human Kinetics.

Albinson, J. G., and Pearce, W. (1998). *The Athlete Daily Hassle Scale* (4th ed.). Ontario: Queens University.

Aldwin, C. M. (2000). *Stress, coping, and development: An integrative perspective*. New York: Guilford.

Aldwin, C. M., and Stokols, D. (1988). The effects of environmental change on individuals and groups: Some neglected issues in stress research. *Journal of Environmental Psychology, 8*, 57-75.

Anderson, C. A., and Williams, J. M. (1988). A model of stress and athletic injury: Prediction and prevention. *Journal of Sport and Exercise Psychology, 10*, 721-786.

Anshel, M. H. (in press). Strategies for preventing and managing stress and anxiety in sport. In D. Hackford, J. Duda, and R. Lidor (Eds.), *Handbook of research in applied sport psychology*. Morgantown, WV: Fitness Information Technology.

Anshel, M. H., and Delany, J. (2001). Sources of acute stress, cognitive appraisals, and coping strategies of male and female child athletes. *Journal of Sport Behavior, 24*, 329-353.

Anshel, M. H., Jamieson, J., and Raviv, S. (2001). Cognitive appraisals and coping strategies following acute stress among skilled competitive male and female athletes. *Journal of Sport Behavior, 24*, 129-143.

Anshel, M. H., Kim, K. W., Kim, B. H., Chang, K. J., and Eom, H. J. (2001). A model for coping with stressful events in sport: Theory, application, and future directions. *International Journal of Sport Psychology, 32*, 43-75.

Anshel, M. H., and Weinberg, R. S. (1995). Sources of acute stress in American and Australian basketball referees. *Journal of Applied Sport Psychology, 7*, 11-22.

Antonovsky, A. (1987). *Unraveling the mystery of health: How people manage stress and stay well*. San Francisco: Jossey-Bass.

Appley, M. H., and Trumbull, R. (1967). On the concept of psychological stress. In M. H. Appley and R. Trumbull (Eds.), *Psychological stress*. New York: Appleton-Century-Crofts.

Appley, M. H., and Trumbull, R. (1986). A conceptual model for the examination of stress dynamics. In M. H. Appley and R. Trumbull (Eds.), *Dynamics of stress: Physiological, psychological, and social perspectives* (pp. 21-45). New York: Plenum.

Arnold, M. B. (1960). *Emotion and personality. Vol I: Psychosocial aspects*. New York: Columbia University Press.

Ashby, W. R. (1966). *An introduction to cybernetics*. New York: Wiley.

Ashforth, B. E., and Humphrey, R. H. (1993). Emotional labor in service roles: The influence of identify. *Academy of Management Review, 18*, 88-115.

Baron, R., and Kenny, D. (1986). The moderator-mediator variable distinction in social psychological research: Conceptual, strategic and statistical considerations. *Journal of Personality and Social Psychology, 51*, 1173-1182.

Beehr, T. A. (1998). An organizational psychology meta-model of occupational stress. In C. L. Cooper (Ed.), *Theories of organizational stress* (pp. 6-27). Oxford, UK: Oxford University Press.

Beehr, T. A., and Newman, J. E. (1978). Job stress, employee health, and organizational effectiveness: A facet analysis model, and literature review. *Personnel Psychology, 31,* 365-399.

Beehr, T. A., and O'Hara, K. (1987). Methodological designs for the evaluation of occupational stress interventions. In S. Kasl and C. Cooper (Eds.), *Stress and health: Issues in research methodology* (pp. 79-112). New York: Wiley.

Bolger, N., and Zuckerman, A. (1995). A framework for studying personality in the stress process. *Journal of Personality and Social Psychology, 69,* 890-902.

Botterill, C., and Brown, M. (2002). Emotion and perspective in sport. *International Journal of Sport Psychology, 33,* 38-60.

Bramwell, S. T., Masuda, M., Wagner, N. N., and Holmes, T. H. (1975). Psychological factors in athletic injuries: Development and application of the Social and Athletic Readjustment Rating Scale (SARRS). *Journal of Human Stress, 1,* 6-20.

Brief, A., and Weiss, H. (2002). Organizational behavior: Affect in the workplace. *Annual Review of Psychology, 53,* 279-307.

Briner, R. B. (1995, April). *The experience and expression of emotion at work.* Paper presented at the 1995 British Psychological Society Occupational Psychology Conference, Warwick, UK.

Briner, R. B., and Reynolds, S. (1999). The costs, benefits and limitations of organizational level stress interventions. *Journal of Organizational Behavior, 20,* 647-664.

Bringer, J. D., Johnston, L. H., and Brackenridge, C. H. (2004). Maximizing transparency in a doctoral thesis: The complexities of writing about the use of QSR*NVIVO within a grounded theory study. *Qualitative Research, 4,* 247-265.

Burke, R. (1993). Organizational-level interventions to reduce occupational stressors. *Work and Stress, 7,* 77-87.

Burton, D. (1990). Multimodal stress management in sport: Current status and future directions. In G. Jones and L. Hardy (Eds.), *Stress and performance in sport* (pp. 171-201). Chichester, UK: Wiley.

Burton, D. (1998). Measuring competitive state anxiety. In J. L. Duda (Ed.), *Advances in sport and exercise psychology measurement* (pp. 129-148). Morgantown, WV: Fitness Information Technology.

Burton, D., and Naylor, S. (1997). Is anxiety really facilitative? Reaction to the myth that cognitive anxiety always impairs performance. *Journal of Applied Sport Psychology, 9,* 295-303.

Busser, J. A. (1990). The relationship between stress and wellness for public leisure service managers. *Journal of Park and Recreation Administration, 8,* 44-59.

Byers, S. K. (1987). Organizational stress: Implications for health promotion managers. *American Journal of Health Promotion, 2,* 21-27.

Cacioppo, J. T., Gardner, W. L., and Berntson, G. G. (1999). The affect system has parallel and integrative processing components: Form follows function. *Journal of Personality and Social Psychology, 76,* 839-855.

Campbell, E., and Jones, G. (2002a). Cognitive appraisal of sources of stress experienced by elite male wheelchair basketball players. *Adapted Physical Activity Quarterly*, *19*, 100-108.

Campbell, E., and Jones, G. (2002b). Sources of stress experienced by elite male wheelchair basketball players. *Adapted Physical Activity Quarterly*, *19*, 82-99.

Campen, C., and Roberts, D. C. (2001). Coping strategies of runners: Perceived effectiveness and match to precompetitive anxiety. *Journal of Sport Behavior*, *24*, 145-161.

Cannon, W. B. (1914). The emergent function of the adrenal medulla in pain and the major emotions. *American Journal of Physiology*, *33*, 356-372.

Cannon, W. B. (1915). *Bodily changes in pain, hunger, fear, and rage: An account of recent researches into the function of emotional excitement.* New York: Appleton.

Cannon, W. B. (1929). Organization for physiological homeostasis. *Physiological Review*, *9*, 339-430.

Cannon, W. B. (1932). *The wisdom of the body* (2nd ed.). New York: Norton.

Cannon, W. B. (1935). Stresses and strain of homeostasis. *American Journal of Medical Science*, *189*, 1-14.

Caplan, R. D. (1983). Person-environment fit: Past, present, and future. In C. L. Cooper (Ed.), *Stress research* (pp. 35-78). New York: Wiley.

Caplan, R. D. (1987a). Person-environment fit in organizations: Theories, facts, and values. In A. W. Riley and S. J. Zaccaro (Eds.), *Occupational stress and organizational effectiveness* (pp. 103-140). New York: Praeger.

Caplan, R. D. (1987b). Person-environment fit theory and organizations: Commensurate dimensions, time perspectives, and mechanisms. *Journal of Vocational Behavior*, *31*, 248-267.

Caplan, R. D., Cobb, S., French, J. R. P., Jr., Harrison, R. V., and Pinneau, S. R., Jr. (1975). *Job demands and worker health: Main effects and occupational differences.* Cincinnati, OH: National Institute for Occupational Safety and Health.

Caplan, R. D., and Harrison, R. V. (1993). Person-environment fit theory: Some history, recent developments, and future directions. *Journal of Social Issues*, *49*, 253-275.

Carron, A. V. (1982). Cohesiveness in sport groups: Interpretations and considerations. *Journal of Sport Psychology*, *4*, 123-138.

Carver, C. S., and Scheier, M. F. (1981). *Attention and self-regulation: A control-theory approach to human behavior.* New York: Springer-Verlag.

Carver, C. S., and Scheier, M. F. (1985). Self-consciousness, expectancies, and the coping process. In T. M. Field, P. M. McCabe, and N. Schniederman (Eds.), *Stress and coping* (pp. 305-330). Hillsdale, NJ: Erlbaum.

Cerin, E. (2003). Anxiety versus fundamental emotions as predictors of perceived functionality of pre-competitive emotional states, threat, and challenge in individual sports. *Journal of Applied Sport Psychology*, *15*, 223-238.

Cerin, E., Szabo, A., Hunt, N., and Williams, C. (2000). Temporal patterning of competitive emotions: A critical review. *Journal of Sports Sciences*, *18*, 605-626.

Cerin, E., Szabo, A., and Williams, C. (2001). Is the experience sampling method (ESM) appropriate for studying pre-competitive emotions? *Psychology of Sport and Exercise*, *2*, 27-45.

Chang, E. (1998). Dispositional optimism and primary and secondary appraisal of a stressor: Controlling for confounding influences and relations to coping and psychological and physical adjustment. *Journal of Personality and Social Psychology*, *74*, 1109-1120.

Cohen, S., and Edwards, J. R. (1989). Personality characteristics as moderators of the relationship between stress and disorder. In W. J. Neufeld (Ed.), *Advances in the investigation of psychological stress* (pp. 235-283). New York: Wiley.

Cook, T. D., and Campbell, D. T. (1979). *Quasi-experimentation: Design and analysis issues for field settings*. Boston: Houghton Mifflin.

Cooper, C. L., Dewe, P. J., and O'Driscoll, M. P. (2001). *Organizational stress: A review and critique of theory, research, and applications*. Thousand Oaks, CA: Sage.

Copeland, B. W., and Kirsch, S. (1995). Perceived occupational stress among NCAA Division I, II, and III athletic directors. *Journal of Sport Management*, *9*, 70-77.

Cordes, C., and Dougherty, T. (1993). A review and integration of research on job burnout. *Academy of Management Review*, *18*, 621-656.

Cox, T. (1978). *Stress*. New York: Macmillan.

Cox, T. (1985). *Stress* (2nd ed.). New York: Macmillan.

Cox, T. (1987). Stress, coping and problem solving. *Work and Stress*, *1*, 5-14.

Cox, T. (1990). The recognition and measurement of stress: Conceptual and methodological issues. In J. R. Wilson and N. E. Corlett (Eds.), *Evaluation of human work: A practical ergonomics methodology* (pp. 628-647). Philadelphia, PA: Taylor and Francis.

Cox, T. (1993). *Stress research and stress management: Putting theory to work*. London: HMSO.

Cox, T., and Ferguson, E. (1991). Individual differences, stress and coping. In C. L. Cooper and R. Payne (Eds.), *Personality and stress: Individual differences in the stress process* (pp. 7-30). New York: John Wiley.

Cox, T., and McKay, C. (1981). A transactional approach to occupational research. In E. N. Corlett and J. Richardson (Eds.), *Stress, work design and productivity* (pp. 91-115). New York: John Wiley.

Craft, L. L., Magyar, T. M., Becker, B. J., and Feltz, D. L. (2003). The relationship between the Competitive State Anxiety Inventory-2 and sport performance: A meta-analysis. *Journal of Sport and Exercise Psychology*, *25*, 44-65.

Crocker, P. R. E. (1992). Managing stress by competitive athletes: Ways of coping. *International Journal of Sport Psychology*, *23*, 161-175.

Crocker, P. R. E., and Graham, T. R. (1995). Coping by competitive athletes with performance stress: Gender differences and relationships with affect. *The Sport Psychologist*, *9*, 325-338.

Crocker, P. R. E., and Isaak, K. (1997). Coping during competitions and training sessions: Are youth swimmers consistent? *International Journal of Sport Psychology*, *28*, 355-369.

Crocker, P. R. E., Kowalski, K. C., and Graham, T. R. (1998). Measurement of coping strategies in sport. In J. L. Duda (Ed.), *Advances in sport and exercise psychology measurement* (pp. 149-161). Morgantown, WV: Fitness Information Technology.

Cummings, T. G., and Cooper, C. L. (1979). A cybernetic theory of occupational stress. *Human Relations*, *32*, 395-418.

Cummings, T. G., and Cooper, C. L. (1998). A cybernetic theory of organizational stress. In C. L. Cooper (Ed.), *Theories of organizational stress* (pp. 101-121). Oxford, UK: Oxford University Press.

Davidson, R. J. (1992). Emotion and affective style: Hemispheric substrates. *Psychological Science, 3,* 39-43.

Dewe, P. (2000). Measures of coping with stress at work: A review and critique. In P. Dewe, M. Leiter, and T. Cox (Eds.), *Coping, health and organizations* (pp. 3-28). New York: Taylor and Franics.

Dewe, P., Cox, T., and Ferguson, E. (1993). Individual strategies for coping with stress at work: A review. *Work and Stress, 7,* 5-15.

Dewey, J., and Bentley, A. F. (1949). *Knowing and the known.* Boston: Beacon Press.

Dienstbier, R. A. (1989). Arousal and physiological toughness: Implications for mental and physical health. *Psychological Bulletin, 96,* 84-100.

Dohrenwend, B. S., and Dohrenwend, B. P. (1974). *Stressful life events: Their nature and effects.* New York: Wiley.

Dugdale, J. R., Eklund, R. C., and Gordon, S. (2002). Expected and unexpected stressors in major international competition: Appraisal, coping, and performance. *The Sport Psychologist, 16,* 20-33.

Eckenrode, J., and Bolger, N. (1995). Daily and within-day event measurement. In S. Cohen, R. C. Kessler, and L. U. Gordon (Eds.), *Measuring stress: A guide for health and social scientists* (pp. 80-101). New York: Oxford University Press.

Edwards, J. R. (1988). The determinants and consequences of coping with stress. In C. L. Cooper and R. Payne (Eds.), *Causes, coping and consequences of stress and work* (pp. 233-263). New York: John Wiley.

Edwards, J. R. (1991). Person-job fit: A conceptual integration, literature review, and methodological critique. *International Review of Industrial and Organizational Psychology, 6,* 283-357.

Edwards, J. R. (1992). A cybernetic theory of stress, coping, and well-being in organizations. *Academy of Management Review, 17,* 238-274.

Edwards, J. R. (1996). An examination of competing versions of the person-environment fit approach to stress. *Academy of Management Journal, 39,* 292-339.

Edwards, J. R. (1998). Cybernetic theory of stress, coping, and well-being: Review and extension to work and family. In C. L. Cooper (Ed.), *Theories of organizational stress* (pp. 122-152). Oxford, UK: Oxford University Press.

Edwards, J. R., Caplan, R. D., and Harrison, R. V. (1998). Person-environment fit theory: Conceptual foundations, empirical evidence and directions for future research. In C. L. Cooper (Ed.), *Theories of organizational stress* (pp. 28-67). Oxford, UK: Oxford University Press.

Ekman, P., Friesen, W. V., and Ellsworth, P. (1982). Conceptual ambiguities. In P. Ekman (Ed.), *Emotion in the human face* (2nd ed., pp. 7-20). New York: Cambridge University Press.

Elliott, G. R., and Eisdorfer, C. (Eds.). (1982). *Stress and human health: Analysis and implications for research.* New York: Springer.

Ellis, A. (1985). Cognition and affect in emotional disturbance. *American Psychologist, 40,* 471-472.

Epstein, S., and Meier, P. (1989). Constructive thinking: A broad coping variable with specific components. *Journal of Personality and Social Psychology, 57,* 332-350.

Eysenck, M. W., and Calvo, M. G. (1992). Anxiety and performance: The processing efficiency theory. *Cognition and Emotion, 6,* 409-434.

Fay, D., Sonnentag, S., and Frese, M. (1998). Stressors, innovation, and personal initiative. In C. L. Cooper (Ed.), *Theories of organizational stress* (pp. 170-189). Oxford, UK: Oxford University Press.

Fisher, C.D. (2002). Antecedents and consequences of real-time affective reactions at work. *Motivation and Emotion, 26*, 3-30.

Fletcher, D. (2001). *Sources of organisational stress in elite sports performers.* Unpublished master's thesis, Loughborough University, Leicestershire, United Kingdom.

Fletcher, D. (2005). "Mental toughness" and human performance: Definitional, conceptual and theoretical issues [Abstract]. *Journal of Sports Sciences, 23*, 1246-1247.

Fletcher, D., and Fletcher, J. (2004, September). *A meta-model of stress, emotions and performance: Conceptual foundations, theoretical framework, and research directions.* Oral presentation presented at the annual meeting of the British Association of Sport and Exercise Sciences, Liverpool, UK.

Fletcher, D., and Fletcher, J. (2005). A meta-model of stress, emotions and performance: Conceptual foundations, theoretical framework, and research directions [Abstract]. *Journal of Sports Sciences, 23*, 157-158.

Fletcher, D., and Hanton, S. (2003a, April). Research in organisational stress and British Olympic athletes: Conceptual, theoretical and practical issues. In S. J. Bull (Chair), *Building and supporting an Olympic management team.* Symposium conducted at the meeting of the British Olympic Association Psychology Advisory and Steering Group, Milton Keynes, UK.

Fletcher, D., and Hanton, S. (2003b). Sources of organizational stress in elite sports performers. *The Sport Psychologist, 17*, 175-195.

Fletcher, D., and Hanton, S. (2003c, October). *The effects of organizational stress upon sports performance: An exploratory study.* Poster session presented at the annual meeting of the Association for the Advancement of Applied Sport Psychology, Philadelphia, PA.

Fletcher, D., and Hanton, S. (2004, October). *A meta-model of stress, emotions and performance: Practical implications for applied sport psychologists.* Poster session presented at the annual meeting of the Association for the Advancement of Applied Sport Psychology, Minneapolis, MN.

Folkman, S. K. (1982). An approach to the measurement of coping. *Journal of Occupational Behavior, 3*, 95-107.

Folkman, S. K., Lazarus, R., Dunkel-Schetter, C., De Longis, A., and Gruen, R. (1986). Dynamics of a stressful encounter: Cognitive Appraisal, coping and encounter outcomes. *Journal of Personality and Social Psychology, 50*, 992-1003.

Folkman, S. K., and Moskowitz, J. T. (2000). Positive affect and the other side of coping. *American Psychologist, 55*, 647-654.

Franks, B. D. (1994). What is stress? *Quest, 46*, 1-7.

French, J., Caplan, R., and Harrison, R. V. (1982). *The mechanisms of job stress and strain.* New York: Wiley.

French, J. R. P., Jr., Rogers, W. L., and Cobb, S. (1974). Adjustment as person-environment fit. In G. V. Coelho, D. A. Hamburg, and J. E. Adams (Eds.), *Coping and adaptation* (pp. 316-333). New York: Basic Books.

Frost, R. O., and Marten, P. A. (1990). Perfectionism and evaluative threat. *Cognitive Therapy and Research, 14*, 559-572.

Gall, M. D., Borg, W. R., and Gall, J. P. (1996). *Educational research: An introduction* (6th ed.). New York: Longman.

Ganster, D. C. (1987). Type A behavior and occupational stress. In J. M. Ivancevich and D. C. Ganster (Eds.), *Job stress: From theory to suggestion* (pp. 61-84). New York: Haworth Press.

Ganster, D. C., and Schaubroeck, J. (1995). The moderating effects of self-esteem on the work stress-employee health relationship. In R. Crandall and P. Perrewe (Eds.), *Occupational stress: A handbook* (pp. 167-177). Washington, DC: Taylor and Francis.

Garmezy, N., and Masten, A. S. (1986). Stress, competence, and resilience: Common frontiers for therapist and psychopathologist. *Behavior Therapy, 17*, 500-521.

Gauvin, L., and Spence, J. C. (1998). Measurement of exercise-induced changes in feeling states, affect, mood, and emotions. In J. L. Duda (Ed.), *Advances in sport and exercise psychology measurement* (pp. 325-336). Morgantown, WV: Fitness Information Technology.

Gazzaniga, M. S. (1989). Organization of the human brain. *Science, 245*, 947-952.

George, J. (1992). The role of personality in organizational life: Issues and evidence. *Journal of Management, 18*, 185-213.

Giacobbi, P. R., Jr., Foore, B., and Weinberg, R. S. (2004). Broken clubs and expletives: The sources of stress and coping responses of skilled and moderately skilled golfers. *Journal of Applied Sport Psychology, 16*, 166-182.

Giacobbi, P. R., Jr., Lynn, T. K., Wetherington, J. M., Jenkins, J., Bodendorf, M., and Langley, B. (2004). Stress and coping during the transition to university for first-year female athletes. *The Sport Psychologist, 18*, 1-20.

Gill, D. L. (1994). A sport and exercise psychology perspective on stress. *Quest, 46*, 20-27.

Gill, D. L. (2000). *Psychological dynamics of sport and exercise* (2nd ed.). Champaign, IL: Human Kinetics.

Gould, D. (1987). Promoting positive sport experiences for children. In J. R. May and M. J. Asken (Eds.), *Sport psychology: The psychological health of the athlete* (pp. 77-98). New York: PMA.

Gould, D., Eklund, R. C., and Jackson, S. A. (1993). Coping strategies used by U.S. Olympic wrestlers. *Research Quarterly for Exercise and Sport, 64*, 83-93.

Gould, D., Finch, L. M., and Jackson, S. A. (1993). Coping strategies used by national champion figure skaters. *Research Quarterly for Exercise and Sport, 64*, 453-468.

Gould, D., Guinan, D., Greenleaf, C., Mudbery, R., and Peterson, K. (1999). Factors affecting Olympic performance: Perceptions of athletes and coaches from more and less successful teams. *The Sport Psychologist, 13*, 371-394.

Gould, D., Jackson, S. A., and Finch, L. M. (1993). Sources of stress in national champion figure skaters. *Journal of Sport and Exercise Psychology, 15*, 134-159.

Gould, D., and Krane, V. (1992). The arousal-athletic performance relationship: Current status and future directions. In T. S. Horn (Ed.), *Advances in sport psychology* (pp. 119-142). Champaign, IL: Human Kinetics.

Gould, D., and Urdy, E. (1994). Psychological skills for enhancing performance: Arousal regulation strategies. *Medicine and Science in Sports and Exercise, 26*, 478-485.

Gray, J. A. (1994). Three fundamental emotion systems. In P. Ekman and R. J. Davidson (Eds.), *The nature of emotions: Fundamental questions* (pp. 243-247). New York: Oxford University Press.

Grinker, R. R., and Spiegel, J. P. (1945). *Men under stress*. Philadelphia, PA: Blakiston.

Hamilton, L. H., Hamilton, W. G., Meltzer, J. D., Marshall, P., and Molnar, M. (1989). Personality, stress, and injuries in professional ballet dancers. *American Journal of Sports Medicine*, *17*, 263-267.

Hammermeister, J., and Burton, D. (2001). Stress, appraisal, and coping revisited: Examining the antecedents of competitive state anxiety with endurance athletes. *The Sport Psychologist*, *15*, 66-90.

Hanin, Y. L. (1993). Optimal performance emotions in top athletes. In S. Serpa, J. Alves, V. Ferreira, and A. Paula-Brito (Eds.), *Sport psychology: An integrated approach. Proceedings from the VIII World Congress of Sport Psychology* (pp. 229-232). Lisbon, Portugal: ISSP.

Hanin, Y. L. (1997). Emotions and athletic performance: Individual zones of optimal functioning model. *European Yearbook of Sport Psychology*, *1*, 29-72.

Hanin, Y. L. (2000). Individual zones of optimal functioning (IZOF) model: Emotion-performance relationships in sport. In Y. L. Hanin (Ed.), *Emotions in sport* (pp. 65-89). Champaign, IL: Human Kinetics.

Hanson, S. J., McCullagh, P., and Tonymon, P. (1992). The relationship of personality characteristics, life stress, and coping resources to athletic injury. *Journal of Sport and Exercise Psychology*, *14*, 262-272.

Hanton, S., and Fletcher, D. (2003, October). *Toward a conceptual understanding of organizational stress in sports performers*. Poster session presented at the annual meeting of the Association for the Advancement of Applied Sport Psychology, Philadelphia, PA.

Hanton, S., and Fletcher, D. (2005). Organizational stress in competitive sport: More than we bargained for? *International Journal of Sport Psychology*, *36*, 273-283.

Hanton, S., Fletcher, D., and Coughlan, G. (2005). Stress in elite sport performers: A comparative study of competitive and organizational stressors. *Journal of Sports Sciences*, *23*, 1129-1141.

Hanton, S., and Jones, G. (1999a). The acquisition and development of cognitive skills and strategies: I. Making the butterflies fly in formation. *The Sport Psychologist*, *13*, 1-21.

Hanton, S., and Jones, G. (1999b). The effects of a multmodal intervention program on performers: II. Training the butterflies to fly in formation. *The Sport Psychologist*, *13*, 22-41.

Hardy, L. (1990). A catastrophe model of anxiety and performance. In G. Jones and L. Hardy (Eds.), *Stress and performance in sport* (pp. 81-106). Chichester, UK: Wiley.

Hardy, L. (1997). Three myths about applied consultancy work. *Journal of Applied Sport Psychology*, *9*, 277-294.

Hardy, L. (1998). Responses to the reactants on three myths in applied consultancy work. *Journal of Applied Sport Psychology*, *10*, 212-219.

Hardy, L., and Fazey, J. (1987, June). *The inverted-U hypothesis: A catastrophe for sport psychology?* Paper presented at the annual conference of the North American Society for the Psychology of Sport and Physical Activity, Vancouver, Canada.

Hardy, L., and Jones, G. (1994). Current issues and future directions for performance related research in sport psychology. *Journal of Sports Sciences*, *12*, 61-90.

Hardy, L., Jones, G., and Gould, D. (1996). *Understanding psychological preparation for sport: Theory and practice of elite performers*. Chichester, UK: Wiley.

Harrison, R. V. (1978). Person-environment fit and job stress. In C. L. Cooper and R. Payne (Eds.), *Stress and work* (pp. 175-205). New York: Wiley.

Harrison, R. V. (1985). The person-environment fit model and the study of job stress. In T. A. Beehr and R. S. Bhagat (Eds.), *Human stress and cognition in organizations* (pp. 23-55). New York: Wiley.

Hinkle, L. E., Jr. (1973). The concept of "stress" in the biological and social sciences. *Science, Medicine and Man, 1*, 31-48.

Hinton, G. E. (1992, September). How neural networks learn from experience. *Scientific American, 267*, 144-151.

Hoar, S. D., Kowalski, K. C., Gaudreau, P., and Crocker, P. R. E. (this volume). A review of coping in sport. In S. Hanton and S. D. Mellalieu (Eds.), *Literature reviews in sport psychology*. Hauppauge, NY: Nova Science.

Hobfall, S. E., Schwarzer, R., and Chon, K-K. (1996). Disentangling the stress labyrinth: Interpreting the meaning of the term stress as it is studied. *Japanese Health Psychology, 4*, 1-22.

Hobfoll, S., and Shirom, A. (1993). Stress and burnout in the workplace. In R. Golembiewski (Ed.), *Handbook of organizational behavior* (pp. 41-60). New York: Marcel Dekker.

Holmes, T. H., and Rahe, R. H. (1967). The Social Readjustment Rating Scale. *Journal of Psychosomatic Research, 11*, 213-218.

Holt, N. L., and Dunn, J. G. H. (2004). Longitudinal idiographic analyses of appraisal and coping responses in sport. *Psychology of Sport and Exercise, 5*, 213-222.

Holt, N. L., and Hogg, J. M. (2002). Perceptions of stress and coping during preparations for the 1999 women's soccer World Cup finals. *The Sport Psychologist, 16*, 251-271.

House, J. S. (1974). Occupational stress and coronary heart disease: A review and theoretical integration. *Journal of Health and Social Behavior, 15*, 12-27.

Humphreys, M. S., and Revelle, W. (1984). Personality, motivation, and performance: A theory of the relationship between individual differences and information processing. *Psychological Review, 91*, 153-184.

Ickovics, J. R., and Park, C. L. (1998). Paradigm shift: Why a focus on health is important. *Journal of Social Issues, 52*, 237-244.

Isberg, L. (2000). Anger, aggressive behavior, and athletic performance. In Y. L. Hanin (Ed.), *Emotions in sport* (pp. 113-133). Champaign, IL: Human Kinetics.

Ivancevich, J., and Matteson, M. (1987). Organizational level stress management interventions: A review and recommendations. *Journal of Organizational Behavior Management, 8*, 229-248.

Izard, C. E. (1977). *Human emotions*. New York: Plenum Press.

Jackson, S. A., and Csikszentmihalyi, M. (1999). *Flow in sports: The keys to optimal experiences and performances*. Champaign, IL: Human Kinetics.

James, B., and Collins, D. (1997). Self-presentational sources of competitive stress during performance. *Journal of Sport and Exercise Psychology, 19*, 17-35.

Janelle, C. M. (2002). Anxiety, arousal and visual attention: A mechanistic account of performance variability. *Journal of Sports Sciences, 20*, 237-251.

Jessor, R. (1981). The perceived environment in psychological theory and research. In D. Magnusson (Ed.), *Toward a psychology of situations: An interactional perspective* (pp. 297-317). Hillsdale, HJ: Erlbaum.

Jex, S., and Gudanowski, D. (1992). Efficacy beliefs and work stress: An exploratory study. *Journal of Organizational Behavior, 13*, 509-517.

Jones, F., and Fletcher, B. C. (1996). Job control and health. In M. Schabracq, J. Winnubst, and C. Cooper (Eds.), *Handbook of work and health psychology* (pp. 33-50). New York: John Wiley.

Jones, G. (1990). A cognitive perspective on the processes underlying the relationship between stress and performance in sport. In G. Jones and L. Hardy (Eds.), *Stress and performance in sport* (pp. 17-42). Chichester, UK: Wiley.

Jones, G. (1991). Recent developments and current issues in competitive state anxiety research. *The Psychologist, 4*, 152-155.

Jones, G. (1995a). Competitive anxiety in sport. In S. J. H. Biddle (Ed.), *European perspectives on exercise and sport psychology* (pp. 128-153). Champaign, IL: Human Kinetics.

Jones, G. (1995b). More than just a game: Research developments and issues in competitive anxiety in sport. *British Journal of Psychology, 86*, 449-478.

Jones, G. (2002). Performance excellence: A personal perspective on the link between sport and business. *Journal of Applied Sport Psychology, 14*, 268-281.

Jones, G., and Hanton, S. (2001). Pre-competitive feeling states and directional anxiety interpretations. *Journal of Sports Sciences, 19*, 385-395.

Jones, G., and Hardy, L. (1989). Stress and cognitive functioning in sport. *Journal of Sports Sciences, 7*, 41-63.

Jones, G., and Hardy, L. (1990). *Stress and performance in sport*. Chichester, UK: Wiley.

Jones, M. V. (2003). Controlling emotions in sport. *The Sport Psychologist, 17*, 471-486.

Kagan, A. R., and Levi, L. (1975). Health and environment – psychosocial stimuli: A review. In L. Levi (Ed.), *Society, stress and disease – childhood and adolescence* (pp. 241-260). Oxford, UK: Oxford University Press.

Kahn, R. L., and Byosiere, P. (1992). Stress in organizations. In M. D. Dunnette (Ed.), *Handbook of industrial and organizational psychology* (pp. 571-648). Chicago: Rand McNally.

Kanner, A. D., Coyne, J. C., Schaefer, C., and Lazarus, R. S. (1981). Comparison of two modes of stress management: Daily hassles and uplifts versus major life events. *Journal of Behavioral Medicine, 4*, 1-39.

Karasek, R. A. (1979). Job demands, job decision latitude, and mental strain: Implications for job redesign. *Administrative Science Quarterly, 24*, 285-308.

Kasl, S. (1983). Pursuing the link between stressful life experiences and disease: A time for reapprasisal. In C. I. Cooper (Ed.), *Stress research* (pp. 79-102). New York: Mentor Books.

Kelley, B. C. (1994). A model of stress and burnout in collegiate coaches: Effects of gender and time of season. *Research Quarterly for Exercise and Sport, 65*, 48-58.

Kelley, B. C., Eklund, R. C., and Ritter-Taylor, M. (1999). Stress and burnout among collegiate tennis coaches. *Journal of Sport and Exercise Psychology, 21*, 113-130.

Kelley, B. C., and Gill, D. L. (1993). An examination of personal/situational variables, stress appraisal, and burnout in collegiate teacher-coaches. *Research Quarterly for Exercise and Sport, 64*, 94-102.

Kellmann, M., and Kallus, K. W. (2001). *Recovery-stress questionnaire for athletes: User manual*. Champaign, IL: Human Kinetics.

Kentta, G., and Hassmen, P. (1998). Overtraining and recovery: A conceptual model. *Sports Medicine, 26*, 25-39.

Kim, M. S., and Duda, J. L. (2003). The coping process: Cognitive appraisals of stress, coping strategies, and coping effectiveness. *The Sport Psychologist, 17*, 406-425.

Kobasa, S. (1979). Stressful life events, personality and health: An inquiry into hardiness. *Journal of Personality and Social Psychology, 37*, 1-11.

Krohne, H. W., and Hindel, C. (1988). Trait anxiety, state anxiety, and coping behaviors as predictors of athletic performance. *Anxiety Research, 1*, 225-235.

Kulka, R. A. (1979). Interaction as person-environment fit. In L. R. Kahle (Ed.), *New directions for methodology of behavioral science* (pp. 55-71). San Francisco: Jossey-Bass.

Landers, D. M., and Boutcher, S. H. (1998). Arousal-performance relationships. In J. M. Williams (Ed.), *Applied sport psychology: Personal growth to peak performance* (3rd ed., pp. 170-184). Mountain View, CA: Mayfield.

Last, J. M. (1988). *A dictionary of epidemiology* (2nd ed.). New York: International Epidemiological Association.

Latack, J. C., and Havlovic, S. J. (1992). Coping with job stress: A conceptual evaluation framework for coping measures. *Journal of Organisational Behaviour, 13*, 479-508.

Latack, J. C., Kinicki, A. J., and Prussia, G. E. (1995). An integrative process model of coping with job loss. *Academy of Management Review, 20*, 311-342.

Lazarus, R. S. (1964). A laboratory approach to the dynamics of psychological stress. *American Psychologist, 19*, 400-411.

Lazarus, R. S. (1966). *Psychological stress and the coping process*. New York: McGraw-Hill.

Lazarus, R. S. (1981). The stress and coping paradigm. In C. Eisdorfer, D. Cohen, A. Kleinman, and P. Maxim (Eds.), *Models for clinical psychopathology* (pp. 177-214). New York: Spectrum.

Lazarus, R. S. (1982). Thoughts on the relations between emotion and cognition. *American Psychologist, 37*, 1019-1024.

Lazarus, R. S. (1984a). On the primacy of cognition. *American Psychologist, 39*, 124-129.

Lazarus, R. S. (1984b). Puzzles in the study of daily hassles. *Journal of Behavioral Medicine, 7*, 375-389.

Lazarus, R. S. (1990). Theory-based stress measurement. *Psychological Inquiry, 1*, 3-13.

Lazarus, R. S. (1991a). Cognition and motivation in emotion. *American Psychologist, 46*, 352-367.

Lazarus, R. S. (1991b). *Emotion and adaptation*. New York: Oxford University Press.

Lazarus, R. S. (1993). From psychological stress to the emotions: A history of changing outlooks. *Annual Review of Psychology, 44*, 1-21.

Lazarus, R. S. (1995). Vexing research problems inherent in cognitive-mediational theories of emotion – and some solutions. *Psychological Inquiry, 6*, 183-265.

Lazarus, R. S. (1998). *Fifty years of the research and theory of R. S. Lazarus: An analysis of historical and perennial issues*. Mahwah, NJ: Erlbaum.

Lazarus, R. S. (1999). *Stress and emotion: A new synthesis*. London: Free Association.

Lazarus, R. S. (2000a). Cognitive-motivational-relational theory of emotion. In Y. L. Hanin (Ed.), *Emotions in sport* (pp. 39-63). Champaign, IL: Human Kinetics.

Lazarus, R. S. (2000b). How emotions influence performance in competitive sports. *The Sport Psychologist, 14*, 229-252.

Lazarus, R. S. (2000c). Toward better research on stress on coping. *American Psychologist*, *55*, 665-673.

Lazarus, R. S., and commentators. (1995). Vexing problems inherent in cognitive-mediational theories of emotion, and some solutions. *Psychological Inquiry*, *6*, 183-265.

Lazarus, R. S., and Folkman, S. (1984). *Stress, appraisal, and coping*. New York: Springer.

Lazarus, R. S., and Launier, R. (1978). Stress-related transactions between person and environment. In L. A. Pervin and M. Lewis (Eds.), *Perspectives in interactional psychology* (pp. 287-327). New York: Plenum.

Lazarus, R. S., and Lazarus, B. N. (1994). *Passion and reason: Making sense of our emotions*. New York: Oxford University Press.

LeDoux, J. E. (1995). Emotion: Clues from the brain. *Annual Review of Psychology*, *46*, 209-235.

Levanthal, H. (1997). Systems as frameworks, theories and models: From the abstract to the concrete instance. *Journal of Health Psychology*, *2*, 160-162.

Levi, L. (1996). Introduction: Spice of life or kiss of death? In C. L. Cooper (Ed.), *Handbook of stress, medicine, and health* (pp. 1-10). Boca Raton, FL: CRC Press.

Levi, L. (1998). Preface: Stress in organizations – theoretical and empirical approaches. In C. L. Cooper (Ed.), *Theories of organizational stress* (pp. v-xii). Oxford, UK: Oxford University Press.

Lewthwaite, R. (1990). Threat perception in competitive trait anxiety: The endangerment of important goals. *Journal of Sport and Exercise Psychology*, *12*, 280-300.

Madden, C. C., Kirkby, R. J., and McDonald, D. (1989). Coping styles of competitive middle distance runners. *International Journal of Sport Psychology*, *20*, 287-296.

Madden, C. C., Summer, J. J., and Brown, D. F. (1990). The influence of perceived stress in coping with competitive basketball. *International Journal of Sport Psychology*, *21*, 21-35.

Maguire, J., Jarvie, G., Mansfield, L., and Bradley, J. (2002). *Sport worlds: A sociological perspective*. Champaign, IL: Human Kinetics.

Mahoney, M. J., and Avener, M. (1977). Psychology of the elite athlete: An exploratory study. *Cognitive Therapy and Research*, *1*, 135-141.

Mamassis, G., and Doganis, G. (2004). The effects of a mental training program on juniors pre-competitive anxiety, self-confidence, and tennis performance. *Journal of Applied Sport Psychology*, *16*, 118-137.

March, J. G., and Simon, H. A. (1958). *Organizations*. New York: Wiley.

Martens, R. (1971). Anxiety and motor behavior: A review. *Journal of Motor Behavior*, *2*, 151-179.

Martens, R. (1977). *Sport competition anxiety test*. Champaign, IL: Human Kinetics.

Martens, R., Vealey, R. S., and Burton, D. (1990). *Competitive anxiety in sport*. Champaign, IL: Human Kinetics.

Martin, J. J., Kelley, B. C., and Dias, C. (1999). Stress and burnout in female high school athletic directors. *Women in Sport and Physical Activity Journal*, *8*, 101-116.

Martin, J. J., Kelley, B. C., and Eklund, R. C. (1999). A model of stress and burnout in male high school athletic directors. *Journal of Sport and Exercise Psychology*, *21*, 280-294.

Maslow, A. (1968). *Toward a psychology of being* (2nd ed.). New York: Van Nostrand Reinhold.

Mason, J. W. (1975). A historical view of the stress field. *Journal of Human Stress*, *1*, 6-12, 22-36.

Masters, R. S. W. (1992). Knowledge, knerves, and know-how: The role of explicit versus implicit knowledge in the breakdown of a complex motor skill under pressure. *British Journal of Psychology*, *83*, 343-358.

Mayer, J. D., and Gaschke, Y. N. (1988). The experience and meta-experience of mood. *Journal of Personality and Social Psychology*, *55*, 102-111.

Mayer, J. D., Salovey, P., Gomberg-Kaufman, S., and Blainey, K. (1991). A broader conception of mood experience. *Journal of Personlity and Social Psychology*, *60*, 100-111.

Mayer, J. D., and Stevens, A. A. (1994). An emerging understanding of the reflective (meta-) experience of mood. *Journal of Research in Personlity*, *28*, 351-373.

McClelland, J. L., Rumelhart, D. E., and the PDP Research Group (1987). *Parallel distributed processing: Explorations in the microstructure of cognition. Vol. 2: Psychological and biological models*. Cambridge, MA: MIT Press.

McGrath, J. E. (1970). A conceptual formulation for research on stress. In J. E. McGrath (Ed.), *Social and psychological factors in stress* (pp. 10-21). New York: Holt, Rinehart and Winston.

McGrath, J. E. (1976). Stress and behavior in organizations. In M. D. Dunnette (Ed.), *Handbook of industrial and organizational psychology* (pp. 1351-1395). Chicago: Rand McNally.

Meehan, H. L., Bull, S. J., Wood, D. M., and James, D. V. B. (2004). The overtraining syndrome: A multicontextual assessment. *The Sport Psychologist*, *18*, 154-171.

Mellalieu, S. D. (2003). Mood matters: But how much? A comment on Lane and Terry (2000). *Journal of Applied Sport Psychology*, *15*, 99-114.

Mellalieu, S. D., Hanton, S., and Fletcher, D. (this volume). A competitive anxiety review: Recent directions in sport psychology research. In S. Hanton and S. D. Mellalieu (Eds.), *Literature reviews in sport psychology*. Hauppauge, NY: Nova Science.

Menaghan, E. G. (1983). Individual coping efforts: Moderators of the relationship between life stress and mental health outcomes. In H. B. Kaplan (Ed.), *Psychosocial stress: Trends in theory and research* (pp. 157-191). New York: Academic Press.

Miller, G. A., Galanter, E., and Pribram, K. H. (1960). *Plans and the structure of behavior*. New York: Holt, Rinehart, and Winston.

Monroe, S. M. (1983). Major and minor life events as predictors of psychological distress: Further issues and findings. *Journal of Behavioral Medicine*, *6*, 189-205.

Murphy, L. (1988). Workplace interventions for stress reduction and prevention. In C. L. Cooper and R. Payne (Eds.), *Causes, coping and consequences of stress at work* (pp. 301-339). New York: Wiley.

Murphy, L. (1995). Occupational stress management: Current status and future directions. In C. Cooper and D. Rousseau (Eds.), *Trends in organizational behavior* (Vol. 2, pp. 1-14). New York: Wiley.

Murphy, L., Hurrell, J., Sauter, S., and Keita, G. (Eds.) (1995). *Job stress interventions*. Washington, DC: American Psychological Association.

Murphy, S. T. (2001). Feeling without thinking: Affective primacy and the nonconscious processing of emotion. In J. A. Bargh and D. K. Apsley (Eds.), *Unraveling the complexities of social life: A festschrift in honor of Robert B. Zajonc* (pp. 39-53). Washington, DC: American Psychological Association.

Murray, J. M. (1989). *Competitive anxiety as positive affect.* Unpublished doctoral dissertation, University of Virginia, Charlottesville.

Newburg, D., Kimiecik, J., Durand-Bush, N., and Doell, K. (2002). The role of resonance in performance excellence and life engagement. *Journal of Applied Sport Psychology, 14,* 249-267.

Newman, J. E., and Beehr, T. A. (1979). Personal and organizational strategies for handling job stress: A review of research and opinion. *Personal Psychology, 32,* 1-43.

Newton, T. J. (1989). Occupational stress and coping with stress: A critique. *Human Relations, 42,* 441-461.

Nicholls, A. R., Holt, N. L., and Polman, R. C. J. (2005). A phenomenological analysis of coping effectiveness in golf. *The Sport Psychologist, 19,* 111-130.

Nicholls, A. R., Holt, N. L., Polman, R. C. J., and James, D. W. G. (2005). Stress and coping among international adolescent golfers. *Journal of Applied Sport Psychology, 17,* 333-340.

Noblet, A. J., and Gifford, S. M. (2002). The sources of stress experienced by professional Australian footballers. *Journal of Applied Sport Psychology, 14,* 1-13.

Noblet, A. J., Rodwell, J., and McWilliams, J. (2003). Predictors of the strain experienced by professional Australian footballers. *Journal of Applied Sport Psychology, 15,* 184-193.

Nordell, K. A., and Sime, W. (1993). Competitive trait anxiety, state anxiety, and perceptions of anxiety: Interrelationships in practice and in competition. *The Journal of Swimming Research, 9,* 19-24.

O'Driscoll, M. P. (1996). The interface between job and off-job roles: Enhancement and conflict. *International Review of Industrial and Organizational Psychology, 11,* 279-306.

O'Driscoll, M. P., and Cooper, C. L. (1994). Coping with work related stress: A critique of existing measures and proposal for an alternative methodology. *Journal of Occupational and Organizational Psychology, 67,* 343-354.

Ornstein, R., and Thompson, R. F. (1984). *The amazing brain.* Boston: Houghton Mifflin.

Orr, E., and Westman, M. (1990). Does hardiness moderate stress, and how? A review. In M. Rosenbaum (Ed.), *Learned resourcefulness: On coping skills, self-control and adaptive behavior* (pp. 64-94). New York: Springer.

Parasuraman, S., and Alutto, J. A. (1981). An examination of the organizational antecedents of stressors at work. *Academy of Management Journal, 24,* 48-67.

Parfitt, G., Jones, G., and Hardy, L. (1990). Multidimensional anxiety and performance. In G. Jones and L. Hardy (Eds.), *Stress and performance in sport* (pp. 43-80). Chichester, UK: Wiley.

Park, J. K., (2004). The perceived sources of competitive stress in Korean national athletes. *International Journal of Sport Psychology, 35,* 207-231.

Parkinson, B., and Manstead, A. S. R. (1992). Appraisal as a cause of emotion. *Review of Personality and Social Psychology, 13,* 122-149.

Passer, M. W. (1982). Children in sport: Participation motives and psychological stress. *Quest, 33,* 231-244.

Passer, M. W., and Seese, M. D. (1983). Life stress and athletic injury: Examination of positive versus negative events and three moderator variables. *Journal of Human Stress, 9,* 11-16.

Pekrun, R., and Frese, M. (1992). Emotions in work and achievement. *International Review of Industrial and Organizational Psychology, 7*, 153-200.

Pensgaard, A. M., and Duda, J. L. (2002). "If we work hard we can do it!" A tale from an Olympic (gold) medallist. *Journal of Applied Sport Psychology, 14*, 219-236.

Pensgaard, A. M., and Duda, J. L. (2003). Sydney 2000: The interplay between emotions, coping, and the performance of Olympic-level athletes. *The Sport Psychologist, 17*, 253-267.

Perna, F. P., Neyer, M., Murphy, S. M., Ogilvie, B. C., and Murphy, A. (1995). Consultations with sport organizations: A cognitive-behavioral model. In S. M. Murphy (Ed.), *Sport psychology interventions* (pp. 235-252). Champaign, IL: Human Kinetics.

Perrewe, P. (1987). The moderating effects of activity level and locus of control in the personal control-job stress relationship. *International Journal of Psychology, 22*, 179-193.

Pierce, J., Gardner, D., Dunham, R., and Cummings, L. (1993). Moderation by organization-based self-esteem of role condition-employee response relationships. *Academy of Management Journal, 36*, 271-288.

Popper, K. R. (1959). *The logic of scientific discovery.* New York: Basic Books.

Powers, W. T. (1973). *Behavior: The control of perception.* Chicago: Aldine.

Quick, J. C., Joplin, J. R., Nelson, D. L., Mangelsdorff, A. D., and Fiedler, E. (1996). Self-reliance and military service training outcomes. *Journal of Military Psychology, 8*, 279-293.

Quick, J. C., and Quick, J. D. (1997). Stress management programs. In L. H. Peters, C. R. Greer, and S. A. Youngblood (Eds.), *The Blackwell encyclopedic dictionary of human resource management.* Oxford, UK: Blackwell.

Quick, J. C., Quick, J. D., Nelson, D. L., and Hurrell, J. J., Jr. (1997). *Preventative stress management in organizations.* Washington, DC: American Psychological Association.

Quick, J. D., Quick, J. C., and Nelson, D. L. (1998). The theory of preventive stress management in organizations. In C. L. Cooper (Ed.), *Theories of organizational stress* (pp. 246-268). Oxford, UK: Oxford University Press.

Rafaeli, A., and Sutton, R. I. (1987). Expressions of emotions as part of the work role. *Academy of Management Review, 12*, 23-37.

Rainey, D. W. (1995). Sources of stress among baseball and softball umpires. *Journal of Applied Sport Psychology, 7*, 1-10.

Rainey, D. W. (1999). Sources of stress, burnout, and intention to terminate among basketball referees. *Journal of Sport Behavior, 22*, 578-588.

Rainey, D. W., and Hardy, L. (1999). Sources of stress, burnout and intention to terminate among rugby union referees. *Journal of Sports Sciences, 17*, 797-806.

Ravizza, K. (1988). Gaining entry with athletic personnel for season-long consulting. *The Sport Psychologist, 2*, 234-274.

Reid, C., Stewart, E., and Thorne, G. (2004). Multidisciplinary sport science teams in elite sport: Comprehensive servicing or conflict and confusion? *The Sport Psychologist, 18*, 204-217.

Rick, J., and Briner, R. B. (2000). Psychosocial risk assessment: Problems and prospects. *Occupational Medicine, 50*, 310-314.

Rick, J., Briner, R. B., Daniels, K., Perryman, S., and Guppy, A. (2001). *A critical review of psychosocial hazard measures.* Norwich, UK: HSE Books.

Robazza, C. (this volume). Emotion in sport: An IZOF perspective. In S. Hanton and S. D. Mellalieu (Eds.), *Literature reviews in sport psychology*. Hauppauge, NY: Nova Science.

Rogers, T. T., and McClelland, J. L. (2004). *Semantic cognition: A parallel distributed processing approach*. Cambridge, MA: MIT Press.

Rosenbaum, M. (Ed.) (1990). *Learned resourcefulness: On coping skills, self-control, and adaptive behavior*. New York: Springer.

Rotella, R. J., and Lerner, J. D. (1993). Responding to competitive pressure. In R. N. Singer, M. Murphey, and L. K. Tennant (Eds.), *Handbook of research on sport psychology* (528-541). New York: Macmillan.

Rumelhart, D. E., McClelland, J. L., and the PDP Research Group (1987). *Parallel distributed processing: Explorations in the microstructure of cognition. Vol. 1: Foundations*. Cambridge, MA: MIT Press.

Rushall, B. S. (1987). *Daily analysis of life demands for athletes*. Spring Valley, CA: Sports Science Associates.

Rushall, B. S. (1990). A tool for measuring stress tolerance in elite athletes. *Journal of Applied Sport Psychology, 2*, 51-66.

Rutter, M. (1987). Psychosocial resilience and protective mechanisms. *American Journal of Orthopsychiatry, 57*, 316-331.

Salancik, G. R., and Pfeffer, J. (1978). A social information processing approach to job attitudes and task design. *Administrative Science Quarterly, 23*, 224-253.

Sanders, A. F. (1980). Stage analysis of reaction processes. In G. E. Stelmach and J. Requin (Eds.), *Tutorials on motor behavior* (pp. 331-354). Amsterdam: North-Holland.

Sanders, A. F. (1983). Towards a model of stress and human performance. *Acta Psychologica, 53*, 64-97.

Sarason, I. G., Johnson, J. H., and Siegel, J. M. (1978). Assessing the impact of life changes: Development of the Life Experiences Survey. *Journal of Consulting and Clinical Psychology, 46*, 932-940.

Scanlan, T. K., Stein, G. L., and Ravizza, K. (1991). An in-depth study of former elite figure skaters: III. Sources of stress. *Journal of Sport and Exercise Psychology, 1*, 102-120.

Schaubroeck, J., Ganster, D., and Fox, M. (1992). Dispositional affect and work-related stress. *Journal of Applied Psychology, 77*, 322-335.

Schaubroeck, J., and Merritt, D. (1997). Divergent effects of job control on coping with work stressors: The key role of self-efficacy. *Academy of Management Journal, 40*, 738-754.

Schmidt, G. W., and Stein, G. L. (1991). Sport commitment: A model integrating enjoyment dropout and burnout. *Journal of Sport and Exercise Psychology, 8*, 254-265.

Schurman, S., and Israel, B. (1995). Redesigning work systems to reduce stress: A participatory action research approach to creating change. In L. Murphy, J. Hurrell, S. Sauter, and G. Keita (Eds.), *Job stress interventions* (pp. 235-264). Washington, DC: American Psychological Association.

Scientific American (Eds.). (1999). *The Scientific American book of the brain*. New York: The Lyons Press.

Selye, H. (1936). A syndrome produced by diverse nocuous agents. *Nature, 138*, 32.

Selye, H. (1946). The general adaptation syndrome and the distress of adaptation. *Journal of Clinical Endocrinology, 6*, 117-196.

Selye, H. (1950). *The physiology and pathology of exposure to stress*. Montreal: Acta.

Selye, H. (1956). *The stress of life*. New York: McGraw-Hill.

Selye, H. (1973). Evolution of the stress concept. *American Scientist, 61*, 692-699.

Selye, H. (1975). Confusion and controversy in the stress field. *Journal of Human Stress, 1*, 37-44.

Selye, H. (1976a). Forty years of stress research: Principle remaining problems and misconceptions. *Canadian Medical Association Journal, 115*, 53-56.

Selye, H. (1976b). *Stress in health and disease*. Oxford, UK: Butterworths.

Selye, H. (1976c). *The stress of life* (2nd ed.). New York: McGraw-Hill.

Semmer, N. (1996). Individual differences, work stress and health. In M. Schabracq, J. Winnubst, and C. Cooper (Eds.), *Handbook of work and health psychology* (pp. 51-86). New York: Wiley.

Siegrist, J. (1998). Adverse health effects of effort-reward imbalance at work. In C. L. Cooper (Ed.), *Theories of organizational stress* (pp. 190-204). New York: Oxford University Press.

Slack, T. (1997). *Understanding sport organizations: The application of organization theory*. Champaign, IL: Human Kinetics.

Smith, R. E. (1980). Development of an integrated coping response through cognitive-affective stress management training. In I. G. Sarason and C. D. Spielberger (Eds.), *Stress and anxiety* (Vol. 7, pp. 265-280). Washington, DC: Hemisphere.

Smith, R. E. (1985). A component analysis of athletic stress. In M. Weiss and D. Gould (Eds.), *Competitive sports for children and youths: Proceedings of the Olympic Scientific Congress* (pp. 107-112). Champaign, IL: Human Kinetics.

Smith, R. E. (1986). Toward a cognitive-affective model of athletic burnout. *Journal of Sport Psychology, 8*, 35-50.

Smith, R. E., Smoll, F. L., and Wiechman, S. A. (1998). Measurement of trait anxiety in sport. In J. L. Duda (Ed.), *Advances in sport and exercise psychology measurement* (pp. 105-127). Morgantown, WV: Fitness Information Technology.

Snyder, C. R., Harris, C., Anderson, J. R., Holleran, S. A., Irving, L. M., Sigmon, S. T., Yoshinobu, L., Gibb, J., Langelle, C., and Harney, P. (1991). The will and the ways: Development and validation of an individual difference measure of hope. *Journal of Personality and Social Psychology, 60*, 570-585.

Spector, P. E. (1998). A control theory of the job stress process. In C. L. Cooper (Ed.), *Theories of organizational stress* (pp. 153-169). Oxford, UK: Oxford University Press.

Spector, P. E. (1999). Objective versus subjective approaches to the study of job stress. *Journal of Organizational Behavior, 20*, 737.

Spector, P. E., Zapf, D., Chen, P., and Frese, M. (2000). Why negative affectivity should not be controlled in job stress research: Don't throw the baby out with the bath water. *Journal of Organizational Behavior, 21*, 79-95.

Speisman, J. C., Lazarus, L., Mordkoff, A. M., and Davison, L. A. (1964). The experimental reduction of stress based on ego-defense theory. *Journal of Abnormal and Social Psychology, 68*, 367-380.

Spicer, J. (1997). Systems analysis of stress and coping: A testing proposition. *Journal of Health Psychology, 2*, 167-170.

Spielberger, C. D. (1989). Stress and anxiety in sports. In D. Hackfort and C. D. Spielberger (Eds.), *Anxiety in sports: An international perspective* (pp. 3-17). New York: Hemisphere.

Sullivan, P. A., and Nashman, H. W. (1998). Self-perceptions of the role of USOC sport psychologists in working with Olympic athletes. *The Sport Psychologist*, *12*, 95-103.

Tapp, J. T. (1985). Multisystems holistic model of health, stress and coping. In T. M. Field, P. M. McCabe, and N. Schniederman (Eds.), *Stress and coping* (pp. 285-304). Hillsdale, NJ: Erlbaum.

Taylor, G. J., and Bagby, R. M. (2000). An overview of the alexithymia construct. In R. Bar-On and J. D. A. Parker (Eds.), *Handbook of emotional intelligence* (pp. 40-67). New York: Wiley.

Taylor, J. (1992). Coaches are people too: An applied model of stress management for sports coaches. *Journal of Applied Sport Psychology*, *4*, 27-50.

Tenenbaum, G., Jones, C. M., Kitsantas, A., Sacks, D. N., and Berwick, J. P. (2003a). Failure adaptation: Psychological conceptualization of the stress response process in sport. *International Journal of Sport Psychology*, *34*, 1-26.

Tenenbaum, G., Jones, C. M., Kitsantas, A., Sacks, D. N., and Berwick, J. P. (2003b). Failure adaptation: An investigation of the stress response process in sport. *International Journal of Sport Psychology*, *34*, 27-62.

Turner, R. J., and Wheaton, B. (1995). Checklist measurement of stressful life events. In S. Cohen, R. C. Kessler, and L. U. Gordon (Eds.), *Measuring stress: A guide for health and social scientists* (pp. 29-58). New York: Oxford University Press.

Vallerand, R. J. (1983). On emotion in sport: Theoretical and social psychological perspectives. *Journal of Sport Psychology*, *5*, 197-215.

Vallerand, R. J., and Blanchard, C. M. (2000). The study of emotion in sport and exercise: Historical, definitional, and conceptual perspectives. In Y. L. Hanin (Ed.), *Emotions in sport* (pp. 3-37). Champaign, IL: Human Kinetics.

Vealey, R. S., Udry, E. M., Zimmerman, V., and Soliday, J. (1992). Intrapersonal and situational predictors of coaching burnout. *Journal of Sport and Exercise Psychology*, *14*, 40-58.

Wann, D. L., Melnick, M. J., Russell, G. W., and Pease, D. G. (2001). *Sports fans: The psychological and social impact of spectators*. New York: Routledge.

Watson, D., and Clark, L. (1984). Negative affectivity: The disposition to experience negative aversive emotional states. *Psychological Bulletin*, *96*, 465-498.

Wegner, D. M. (1989). *White bears and other unwanted thoughts: Suppression, obsession, and the psychology of mental control*. New York: Viking.

Wegner, D. M. (1994). Ironic processes of mental control. *Psychological Review*, *101*, 34-52.

Wegner, D. M. (1997). Why the mind wanders. In J. D. Cohen and J. W. Schooler (Eds.), *Scientific approaches to consciousness* (pp. 295-315). Hillsdale, NJ: Erlbaum.

Weick, K. E. (1979). *The social psychology of organizing* (2nd ed.). Reading, MA: Addison-Wesley.

Weinberg, R., and McDermott, M. (2002). A comparative analysis of sport and business organizations: Factors perceived critical for organizational success. *Journal of Applied Sport Psychology*, *14*, 282-298.

Weiner, N. (1948). *Cybernetics*. Cambridge, MA: MIT Press.

Westerbeek, H., and Smith, A. (2003). *Sport business in the global marketplace*. Basingstoke, UK: MacMillan.

Williams, J. M., and Krane, V. (1992). Coping styles and self-reported measures of state anxiety and self-confidence. *Journal of Applied Sport Psychology*, *4*, 134-143.

Williams, J. M., Tonymon, P., and Anderson, M. B. (1991). Effects of stressors and coping resources on anxiety and peripheral narrowing in recreational athletes. *Journal of Applied Sport Psychology, 3*, 126-141.

Winett, R. A. (1995). A framework for health promotion and disease prevention and programs. *American Psychologist, 50*, 341-350.

Winnubst, J., and Schabracq, M. (1996). Social support, stress and organization: Toward optimal matching. In M. Schabracq, J. Winnubst, and C. Cooper (Eds.), *Handbook of work and health psychology* (pp. 87-102). New York: Wiley.

Wofford, J. C., and Daly, P. (1997). A cognitive process approach to understanding individual differences in stress response propensity. *Journal of Occupational Health Psychology, 2*, 134-147.

Wofford, J. C., Goodwin, V. L., and Daly, P. S. (1999). Cognitive-affective stress propensity: A field study. *Journal of Organizational Behavior, 20*, 687-707.

Wolff, S. (1995). The concept of resilience. *Australian and New Zealand Journal of Psychiatry, 29*, 565-574.

Woodman, T. (2003). Le stress organisationnel dans le sport de haut niveau (Organizational stress in high-level sport). In C. Le Scanff (Ed.) Le Manuel de Psychologie du Sport: L'intervention en Psychologie du Sport (The Handbook of Sport Psychology: Sport Psychology Interventions, 2nd ed., pp. 357-375). Paris: EP.S.

Woodman, T., and Hardy, L. (1997, Winter). Getting the management right. *Coaching Focus, 36*, 17-18.

Woodman, T., and Hardy, L. (1998, March). *Le stress organisationnel: une étude de cas (Organizational stress: A case study)*. Presentation made at the Journées nationales d'études de la société Française de psychologie du sport, Poitiers, France.

Woodman, T., and Hardy, L. (2001a). A case study of organizational stress in elite sport. *Journal of Applied Sport Psychology, 13*, 207-238.

Woodman, T., and Hardy, L. (2001b). Stress and anxiety. In R. N. Singer, H. A. Hausenblas, and C. M. Janelle (Eds.), *Handbook of sport psychology* (pp. 290-318). New York: Wiley.

Wright, T. A., and Doherty, E. M. (1998). Organizational behavior "rediscovers" the role of emotional well-being. *Journal of Organizational Behavior, 19*, 481-485.

Wrisberg, C. A. (1994). The arousal-performance relationship. *Quest, 6*, 60-77.

Zajonc, R. B. (1980). Feeling and thinking: Preferences need no inferences. *American Psychologist, 35*, 151-175.

Zajonc, R. B. (1984). On the primacy of affect. *American Psychologist, 39*, 117-123.

Contributor Details and Reviewer List

Contributors

Mark Beauchamp, Ph.D.

Dr. Mark R. Beauchamp is an Assistant Professor in the School of Human Kinetics at the University of British Columbia, Canada. He received his Ph.D. in 2002 from the University of Birmingham, UK. His research focuses on the social psychology of groups within sport and exercise settings, with a particular interest in communication processes, role perceptions, and motivation. Mark has published in a wide range of sport and social psychology journals including the *Journal of Sport and Exercise Psychology*, *Small Group Research*, and *Group Dynamics: Theory, Research, and Practice*. His current research is funded by the Nuffield Foundation. Mark has also worked in a consulting capacity with athletes from a range of sports including amateur, professional and international competitors.

Steven Bray, Ph.D.

Dr. Steven Bray is an Associate Professor in the Department of Kinesiology at McMaster University in Hamilton, Canada. His research focus is on social perceptions that arise in interdependent contexts such as patient-practitioner interactions and sport teams and how those perceptions relate to the thoughts, feelings, and behaviors of the participants. Steven teaches courses in Health and Exercise Psychology as well as Research Methodologies. He is on the editorial board of the journal *Avante* and is the Psychology Section Editor for the *European Journal of Sport Science*.

Scott L. Cresswell, Ph.D.

Dr. Scott Cresswell holds a research position in the School of Human Movement and Exercise Science at the University of Western Australia. He is an accredited consultant with Sport Science New Zealand and a contracted sport psychology provider to the New Zealand Academy of Sport. Following a three-year project with New Zealand rugby on player burnout funded by the New Zealand Rugby Union (NZRU) Scott's recent research has focused on player burnout in professional English rugby. The primary aims of this program of research include developing and assessing practical strategies to help prevent and manage player burnout. This research is supported by the Rugby Football Union (RFU), Premier Rugby Limited (PRL) and the Professional Rugby Players Association (PRA) through the provision of a three-year research grant.

Peter Crocker, Ph.D.

Dr. Peter Crocker received his Ph.D. from the University of Alberta after receiving a B.A. (Psychology) and a M.Sc. (Kinesiology) from Simon Fraser University. He is a Professor and the former Director of the School of Human Kinetics at the University of British Columbia. He is a two-time president of the Canadian Society of Psychomotor Learning and Sport Psychology and a former Editor of *The Sport Psychologist*. He presently is an editorial board member for the *Journal of Sport and Exercise Psychology*, the *Journal of Applied Sport Psychology*, and *The Sport Psychologist*. His research has several interrelated themes related to physical activity: stress, coping, and emotion; determinants of physical activity in children and youth; the role of the physical self in health related behaviors, and the role of peer relations in motivated physical activity behavior in adolescents. He has published over 50 peer-reviewed papers in scholarly journals and his research has been funded by Social Sciences and Humanities Research Council of Canada and the Canadian Heart and Stroke Foundation. He is married with two adolescent children, and enjoys soccer, golfing, and fishing.

Robert C. Eklund, Ph.D.

Dr. Eklund is a Professor in the Department of Educational Psychology and Learning Systems at Florida State University. He has a long-standing interest in psychological factors associated with elite athlete performance dating back to his experiences as a freestyle wrestling coach and competitor representing Canada in international competition. Bob is a widely published sport scientist who is the current Editor-in-Chief of the *Journal of Sport and Exercise Psychology*. He has been involved in a variety of research projects examining the experiences of elite athletes including the study of 1988 US Olympic wrestlers and 1998 NZ Commonwealth Games athletes. His current projects include the New Zealand Rugby Football Union funded study of burnout among NZ rugby players with Scott Cresswell and the study of elite athlete experience during the return to competition following severe athletic injury with Leslie Podlog.

Lynne Evans, Ph.D.

Dr. Lynne Evans is a Senior Lecturer in Sport Psychology and Course Director of the M.Sc. in Sport Psychology at the University of Wales Institute, Cardiff where she contributes to undergraduate and postgraduate programmes in sport psychology. The main focus of

Lynne's research, the psychology of injuries, has resulted in a number of peer-reviewed journal papers. She is also actively involved in research in the areas of imagery, anxiety, and hardiness. Lynne is a British Olympic Association Registered Sport Psychologist and a British Association Accredited Sport Psychologist. In her consultancy capacity Lynne works with a variety of elite sport team and individual coaches and performers in the area of performance enhancement.

Mark Eys, Ph.D.

Dr. Mark A. Eys is an Assistant Professor in the School of Human Kinetics at Laurentian University in Sudbury, Ontario, Canada. He received his Ph.D. in 2004 from The University of Western Ontario, Canada. His general research area is group dynamics in sport and exercise settings. Specifically, Mark has research interests in the development of roles and cohesion in sport groups as well as the social influences involved in exercise adherence. His research has been published in journals such as the *Journal of Sport and Exercise Psychology*, *Journal of Sports Sciences*, *Journal of Applied Sport Psychology*, and *Small Group Research*. Mark teaches courses in exercise psychology and group dynamics and is on the editorial board for *Athletic Insight*.

David Fletcher, M.Sc.

David Fletcher is a Lecturer and Research Scholar in Sport Psychology at the University of Wales Institute, Cardiff. In 2001, he was awarded an M.Sc. in Sports Science with Distinction (Loughborough University) while working as a Sports Scientist on British Swimming's World Class Performance Plan. Since then, David has published in and reviewed for a number of international peer-reviewed journals, including the *Journal of Applied Sport Psychology*, *The Sport Psychologist*, the *Journal of Sports Sciences,* the *Psychology of Sport & Exercise*, and the *International Journal of Sport Psychology*. Recently, he was invited to present his work to the British Olympic Association and British Swimming in support of their respective Olympic management and coaching teams, and consulted with the IMG Bollettieri Tennis and Leadbetter Golf Academies in Florida. Prior to his sport psychology career he competed at a high level in swimming, including meets such as the World Cup and Olympic Trials.

Patrick Gaudreau, Ph.D.

Dr. Patrick Gaudreau, is an Assistant Professor at the School of Psychology of the University of Ottawa. He received his Ph.D. in psychology at the Université de Montréal, where he taught courses on self-regulation, motivation, and emotion. His research focuses on the role of self-regulatory processes in goal attainment and psychological adjustment of individuals in performance-related activities. Ongoing research includes the validation of the Coping Inventory in Competitive Sport across different countries as well as the examination of personality, environmental, and motivational processes in the prediction of coping utilization in performance-related situations. He has published a series of peer-reviewed articles on coping in sport and social psychology journals and the Social Sciences and Humanities Research Council of Canada supports his research program.

James Hardy, Ph.D.

Having obtained his undergraduate degree at the University of Birmingham, Dr. James Hardy completed his graduate training (both M.A. and Ph.D.) at The University of Western Ontario, Canada, under the supervision of Dr. Craig Hall. He has published numerous peer-reviewed research articles focusing on self-talk, imagery, and group dynamics in both the sport and exercise domains. James recently returned to his nätive North Wales to accept a lecturing position within the School of Sport, Health and Exercise Sciences, at the University of Wales, Bangor.

Chris Harwood, Ph.D.

Dr. Chris Harwood is a Senior Lecturer within the School of Sport and Exercise Sciences at Loughborough University. His personal research and teaching interests lie in the area of achievement motivation, optimal performance environments and educational consulting, with a particular focus on youth sport. He has published extensively within these areas. As a practitioner, Chris is a BASES Accredited and BPS Chartered Sport Psychologist whose areas of consultancy extend to a youth and senior athletes, coaches and parents across variety of team and individual sport organizations.

Sharleen Hoar, Ph.D.

Dr. Sharleen Hoar is an Assistant Professor in the Department of Kinesiology and Physical Education at The University of Lethbridge. She received her Ph.D. in 2003 at The University of British Columbia. She has been a co-author on book chapters and peer-reviewed journal articles in the areas of coping and emotional development. Her research has several interrelated themes including: stress, coping, and emotion; the role of the sport social network in the development of coping skills in adolescence; help-seeking behavior in sport; and determinants of physical activity in the transition to post-secondary education. Sharleen applies her expertise in the area of mental skills development by working with Canadian athletes of all ages and skill abilities.

Nick Holt, Ph.D.

Dr. Nick Holt is an Assistant Professor in the Faculty of Physical Education and Recreation at the University of Alberta, Canada. Nick conducts research in the areas of talent development, motivation, and coping, and quality of children's and parents' experiences in sport. He received the "Dissertation of the Year" Award in 2002 from the Association for the Advancement of Applied Sport Psychology (AAASP) in recognition of his Ph.D. research into the talent development experiences of elite soccer players. Nick is an Accredited sport psychology consultant with the British Association of Sport and Exercise Sciences, and a Certified Consultant with AAASP. He has provided sport psychology support for professional, international, national, university, and youth athletes in Canada and England.

Stuart Jones, M.Sc.

Stuart Jones is currently undertaking a Ph.D. in the psychology of sports injury at the University of Wales Institute, Cardiff. A full graduate member of both the British Association of Sport and Exercise Sciences and the British Psychological Society, Stuart has assisted in research studies in sport psychology, sport and exercise science, and educational psychology. In addition to the psychology of sports injury, other research interests include the psychology of drugs in sport, the use of psychological skills in sport, and anxiety, stress, and coping.

Kieran Kingston, Ph.D.

Dr. Kieran Kingston is a Senior Lecturer and Discipline Director of sport psychology at the University of Wales Institute, Cardiff. He received his Ph.D. in 1999 from the University of Wales, Bangor, and currently his research interests are focussed on the motivational aspects of sport, including goals, self-determination, burnout and confidence. He also continues to pursue his work into the psychology of golf. Kieran has been a BASES accredited sport psychologist since 1997, and has acted as a consultant in a variety of individual and team sports. At present he is a consultant sport psychologist to a number of amateur and professional golfers, Olympic athletes, and a professional rugby team in Wales. He has also contributed to the Professional Golfers Association professional development programme.

Kent Kowalski, Ph.D.

Dr. Kent Kowalski is an Associate Professor of Sport and Exercise Psychology in the College of Kinesiology at the University of Saskatchewan, Canada. He has been co-author of a number of book chapters and peer-reviewed journal articles in the areas of coping and emotion in sport. His research and writing also focuses on self-presentation issues in adolescence and the measurement of physical activity. Kent has a long-term involvement in sport as an athlete and is currently an assistant coach with the University of Saskatchewan Huskie Men's Soccer Program. In addition, he has worked with many athletes and coaches from a wide variety of sports as a mental skills consultant with the Sport Medicine and Science Council of Saskatchewan and course conductor for the Canadian National Coaching Certification Program.

Todd Loughead, Ph.D.

Dr. Todd Loughead is an Assistant Professor in the Department of Kinesiology at University of Windsor in Windsor, Canada. He teaches undergrad and graduate courses in the area of sport and exercise psychology. Todd has published many peer-reviewed journal articles focusing on group dynamics issues . His research has been published in journals such as the *The Sport Psychologist, Journal of Sports Sciences, Psychology of Sport and Exercise, Journal of Sport Behavior, International Journal of Sport and Exercise Psychology,* and *Small Group Research.* His research areas of interest include the social psychology of sport, exercise, and physical activity with an emphasis on group cohesion, athlete leadership, adherence behavior, and aggression. Todd's research has been funded by Social Sciences and Humanities Research Council of Canada and Hockey Canada. He is married with one child and enjoys ice hockey, soccer, tennis, and golfing.

Ian Mitchell, M.Sc.

Ian Mitchell is a Senior Lecturer in Sport Psychology and Director of Football at the University of Wales Institute, Cardiff where he contributes to undergraduate and postgraduate programmes in Sport Psychology, Sports Medicine, Coaching Science, and Research Issues. He is currently undertaking his Ph.D. in the area of psychological responses to sport injury under the supervision of Dr. Lynne Evans. His research focuses on the psychological responses of injured athletes together with the role of social support within the rehabilitation process. As a former professional and international footballer, Ian's applied work has been mainly in performance enhancement and coaching behavior within professional football.

Claudio Robazza, Ph.D.

Dr. Claudio Robazza is an Associate Professor in the Faculty of Medicine at the University of Padova. He received his Ph.D. in Sciences and Techniques of Physical Activities and Sports from the University of Grenoble, France. As a sport psychologist, he has been working with top level athletes of different sports, including golf, archery, modern pentathlon, and rugby. He has conducted field-based studies in physical education, motor learning, and sport performance domains, and his primary research interest is in the area of performance-related emotions. Claudio has published refereed journal articles, and is the author of several book chapters and books. He is also a member of the Editorial Board of the *Psychology of Sport and Exercise.* In his leisure time he enjoy running, cycling, downhill skiing, and playing with his children.

Chris Spray, Ph.D.

Dr. Christopher Spray is a Lecturer in sport and exercise psychology at Loughborough University, UK. He received his Ph.D. in 1997 from the University of Exeter, UK and he is a

Registered Chartered Psychologist (The British Psychological Society) and Accredited sport and exercise scientist (British Association of Sport and Exercise Sciences). His research focuses on achievement motivation in young people, with particular regard to approach-avoidance achievement goals in school physical education.

REVIEWERS

The chapters contained within this edited text have progressed through a rigorous peer-reviewed process. Our sincere gratitude is therefore extended to the following individuals who acted as referees:

Marcel Bouffard, Ph.D.

Professor, Faculty of Physical Education and Recreation, University of Alberta

Paul Carpenter, Ph.D.

Professor, Chair, Department of Kinesiology and Physical Education, Northern Illinois University

Krista Munroe-Chandler, Ph.D.

Associate Professor, Faculty of Human Kinetics, The University of Windsor

Robert C. Eklund, Ph.D.

Professor, Department of Educational Psychology and Learning Systems, Florida State University

Doris Fay, Ph.D.

Lecturer, Work and Organisational Psychology Group, Aston Business School, Aston University

Mary Fry, Ph.D.

Associate Professor, Department of Health and Sport Sciences, University of Memphis

David Gilbourne, Ph.D.

Principal Lecturer and Director of Social Science Research and Postgraduate Programmes, Research Institute for Sport and Exercise Science, Liverpool John Moores University

Yuri L. Hanin, Ph.D.

Professor and Senior Researcher, KIHU-Research Institute for Olympic Sports, Jyäskylä

Ken Hodge, Ph.D.

Associate Professor, School of Physical Education, University of Otago

Lynne Johnston, Ph.D.

Principal Research Fellow, The Centre for Sport and Exercise Science, Sheffield Hallam University

Graham Jones, Ph.D.

Professor, Director of Research and Diagnostics, Lane 4 Management Group Ltd.

Steve Kozub, Ed.D.

Principal Lecturer, School of Physical Education and Sport Science, De Montfort University

Arnold D. LeUnes, Ph.D.

Professor, Department of Psychology, Texas A&M University

Jeffrey J. Martin, Ph.D.

Associate Professor, Division of Kinesiology, Health, and Sport Studies, Wayne State University

Andrew Noblet, Ph.D.

Senior Lecturer, Organisational Behavior, Deakin Business School, Deakin University

Michael O'Driscoll, Ph.D.

Professor, Department of Psychology, University of Waikato

Dave Paskevich, Ph.D.

Associate Professor, Faculty of Kinesiology, University of Calgary

Ronald E. Smith, Ph.D.

Professor of Psychology Director, Clinical Psychology Program, University of Washington

Diane E. Stevens, Ph.D.

Associate Professor, Department of Physical Education and Kinesiology, Brock University

Adrian Taylor, Ph.D.

Reader in Exercise and Health Psychology, School of Sport and Health Sciences, University of Exeter

Owen Thomas, Ph.D.

Senior Lecturer, Cardiff School of Sport, University of Wales Institute, Cardiff

EDITOR PROFILES

SHELDON HANTON, PH.D.

Dr. Sheldon Hanton is a Professor in the Cardiff School of Sport at the University of Wales Institute, Cardiff. He received his Ph.D. in 1996 from Loughborough University, UK. He is the current Professional Practice Editor of *The Sport Psychologist*, a member of the Editorial Advisory Board for the *Journal of Sports Sciences* and sits on the Editorial Board's for the *Journal of Applied Sport Psychology* and the *Journal of Imagery Research in Sport and Physical Activity*. Sheldon has published a wide range of peer-reviewed journal articles in sport performance psychology and lists his main interests as stress and anxiety, organizational issues, and mental toughness. The journals that have published his work include: *Anxiety, Stress, and Coping, European Journal of Sports Science, International Journal of Sport Psychology, International Journal of Sport and Exercise Psychology, Journal for Science and Medicine in Sport, Journal of Applied Behavior Analysis, Journal of Applied Sport Psychology, Journal of Sport and Exercise Psychology, Journal of Sports Sciences, Personality and Individual Differences, Psychology of Sport and Exercise, Reflective Practice, Research Quarterly for Exercise and Sport, Scandinavian Journal of Science and Medicine in Sport* and *The Sport Psychologist*. He is a registered consultant with the British Olympic Association and the British Association of Sport and Exercise Sciences and regularly advises elite performers on psychological preparation.

STEPHEN MELLALIEU, PH.D.

Dr. Stephen D. Mellalieu is a Lecturer in Applied Sport and Exercise Psychology in the Department of Sports Science at Swansea University where he contributes to undergraduate and postgraduate programmes in Sports Science. He received his Ph.D. in 2000 from the University of Gloucestershire, UK, and has since published over 30 research papers in a wide range of national and international sport and social psychology journals and texts. His current research interests lie in the areas of stress and performance, mental toughness, and the organizational environment of elite sport. He is currently a member of the editorial board of *The Sport Psychologist* and regularly reviews for a number of journals in the field of sport psychology. He is also a nationally accredited sport and exercise psychologist (British

Association of Sport and Exercise Sciences) with consultancy experience in a number of Olympic and Professional sports. Stephen is a former junior international rugby union player and the current Director of Rugby at Swansea University. When he is not working, Stephen enjoys spending time with his family and taking part in outdoor pursuits including surfing, fishing, and mountain biking.

INDEX

B

C

D

E

F

M

S

U

T

V

W